HANDBOOK OF ISLAMIC MARKETING

Handbook of Islamic Marketing

Edited by

Özlem Sandıkcı

Assistant Professor of Marketing, Bilkent University, Turkey

Gillian Rice

Professor Emerita, Thunderbird School of Global Management, USA

Edward Elgar
Cheltenham, UK • Northampton, MA, USA

Published by
Edward Elgar Publishing Limited
The Lypiatts
15 Lansdown Road Cheltenham
Glos GL50 2JA
UK

Edward Elgar Publishing, Inc.
William Pratt House
9 Dewey Court Northampton
Massachusetts 01060
USA

A catalogue record for this book is
available from the British Library

Library of Congress Control Number: 2011925781

ISBN 978 1 84980 013 6 (cased)
     978 1 78100 276 6 (paperback)

Typeset by Servis Filmsetting Ltd, Stockport, Cheshire
Printed and bound in Great Britain by the CPI Group (UK) Ltd

Contents

PART III   MARKETING PRACTICES

PART IV   GLOBALIZATION, POLITICS AND RESISTANCE

PART V   THE FUTURE

Contributors

Bekir Ağırdır is the Manager Partner at KONDA Research & Consultancy Company. He received his BA from the department of Business Administration at the Middle East Technical University.

Rula Al-Abdulrazak is a Senior Lecturer in International Marketing and Branding at Royal Docks Business School, University of East London. Prior to academia, Rula held consultancy and specialist positions at a European Commission Business Centre and AFPC/Shell operating company on the Mediterranean. Her research interest is in global branding, nation and destination branding, cultural diplomacy and place marketing, and ethical and Islamic branding. Her current studies are focused on the Middle East. Her PhD is on the 'Nation Brand State: a comparative review in the Middle East' (University of London).

Abbas J. Ali is Professor of Management and Director, School of International Management, Eberly College of Business, Indiana University of Pennsylvania. His current research interests include strategy and international management. He has published more than 160 scholarly journal articles and fifteen book chapters. He has authored six books, including *Islamic Perspectives on Management and Organization* (Edward Elgar, 2005) and *Business and Management Environment in Saudi Arabia* (Routledge, 2008). He serves as editor of the *International Journal of Commerce and Management*, *Advances in Competitiveness Research*, *Competitiveness Review*, and *Competition Forum*. Ali serves on the editorial board of more than 10 professional journals.

Sharifah Faridah Syed Alwi received her PhD from Manchester Business School, UK and is a Senior Lecturer of Marketing in the University of Malaya, Malaysia. She teaches MBA courses such as brand management, marketing, research methodology and statistics. Her previous research was in the area of corporate and Internet branding and her recent interests include Islamic branding and marketing in the service sector.

Yonca Aslanbay is a Professor of Marketing at İstanbul Bilgi University. She received her BA and MBA degrees from Boğaziçi University and her PhD degree from Marmara University in İstanbul. Her teaching expertise lies in Marketing, Consumer Behavior and Research Methodology. Her recent research focus is new types of networks over cyberspace.

Alexandru Balasescu holds a PhD in Anthropology at UC Irvine (2004) and an MA in Social Sciences at University Lyon II (1998). He taught at UCI, UC Critical Center in Paris, the American University in Paris, the Royal University for Women in Bahrain and the National School of Political and Administrative Studies in Bucharest. He worked for Renault Technologies with responsibility for Socio-cultural and Economic Perspective studies. His research interests include body, material culture, sexuality, development and environment. He is the author of *Paris Chic, Tehran Thrills. Aesthetic Bodies, Political Subjects* (Zeta Books, 2007), *Voioasa Expunere a Ordinii Mondiale* (*The Joyful Display of*

ix

Global Order) (Curtea Veche, Bucharest, 2010) and a number of articles in academic journals. Currently, he is Deputy Director of the Romanian Cultural Institute in Istanbul.

Russell Belk is Kraft Foods Canada Chair in Marketing at the Schulich School of Business at York University. He is past president of the International Association of Marketing and Development, and is a fellow, past president, and Film Festival co-founder in the Association for Consumer Research. He has received the Paul D. Converse Award, the Sheth Foundation/*Journal of Consumer Research* Award for Long Term Contribution to Consumer Research, two Fulbright Fellowships, and honorary professorships on four continents. He has over 475 publications and his research involves the meanings of possessions, collecting, gift-giving, materialism, and global consumer culture. His work is often cultural, visual, and interpretive.

Jennifer D. Chandler is an Assistant Professor at the University of Hawai'i at Mānoa Shidler College of Business. She holds a BA from UCLA, an MBA from the University of Hawaii, and a PhD from the University of California, Irvine. Before entering academia, Dr Chandler had a successful career in international marketing and advertising. After working with media giants Clear Channel Communications and Raycom Media, she began her own marketing agency working across various sectors including retailing, tourism, nonprofit, entertainment, and manufacturing. Dr Chandler's research interests include the resource-based view of the firm, social networks analysis, strategy, service, international marketing, organizational buying, business markets, design and collaborative innovation. She takes a multi-method research approach that combines qualitative research and predictive modeling, as based on structuration theory.

Derrick Chong is a Senior Lecturer in Management at Royal Holloway, University of London; he also holds an adjunct position in art business at Sotheby's Institute of Art in London. He read business administration and art history at various universities in Canada before completing a PhD at the University of London. Various intersections between management and the arts are a core research interest. He is author of *Arts Management, 2nd edn* (2010) and co-editor of *The Art Business* (2008), both published by Routledge.

Malcolm H. Cone is Director of the Asia Institute at the University of Otago, Dunedin, New Zealand. Since gaining his PhD in a study of neo-modernism in Islam in South East Asia, Dr Cone has retained an active research interest in Islam and the issues around the understanding of Islam as an ethical tradition that rivals western accounts of what constitutes civilizational responses to a changing world.

Mohamed El-Fatatry is the founder and CEO of Muxlim Inc., an integrated media company and the world's largest Muslim lifestyle network. Coming from a computer science background, Mohamed is the youngest business leader named among *Chief Executive* magazine's 'Leaders of Tomorrow'. Originally from Egypt and the UAE, Mohamed has been named the 'Egyptian Technology Figure of the Year'. Recently he was also among 200 business leaders recognized by President Obama at his 'Presidential Summit on Entrepreneurship' and was named by Georgetown University and the Royal Islamic Strategic Studies Center among the world's '500 Most Influential Muslims' (2009 and 2010).

Mohamed Farid ElSahn is a Professor of Marketing at the University of Bahrain. He worked as a chairperson of the Business Administration department and Vice Dean of the Faculty of Commerce, Alexandria University, Egypt. He has been a Visiting Professor in a number of universities. His major area of research interest is services marketing. He has also published a number of research papers in fields such as market orientation, service quality, internal marketing, and relationship marketing He has supervised many master's and doctoral theses and participated in many consultation and training services for different organizations in the Arab region.

André M. Everett is Associate Professor of International Management at the University of Otago, Dunedin, New Zealand, and Adjunct Professor at Huazhong University of Science and Technology in Wuhan, China. His writings on international and operations management strategy have been published or presented in over 30 countries, and he has taught MBA-level courses in Argentina, Austria, Brazil, Chile, China, France, New Zealand, and the USA. He is a member of the Academy of Management, Academy of International Business, Decision Sciences Institute, Pan-Pacific Business Association, Production and Operations Management Society, and several New Zealand societies.

Maya F. Farah is a full-time Assistant Professor of Marketing at the Olayan School of Business, American University of Beirut. Dr Farah teaches marketing at both the undergraduate and the MBA levels. She was recently a Visiting Professor at Toulouse Business School. Dr Farah holds a PhD degree in Marketing from Manchester Business School. Her dissertation discusses boycotting behavior from a cross-cultural/religious perspective, a research field that is still at the top of her research agenda. Dr Farah has bidded for a number of research grants and was granted last year the competitive British Academy and the ESRC Visiting Fellowship scheme for South Asia and the Middle East. She actively participates in leading international conferences and her work appears in top marketing journals. She is a member of a number of academic organizations and maintains strong contacts with industry in France, England, Mexico and the Middle East.

Güliz Ger is Professor of Marketing at Bilkent University, Turkey. She has a PhD (1985) in Marketing from Northwestern University (USA), MBA (1977) from Middle East Technical University (Turkey), and BS (cum Laude) (1974) in Psychology from University of Illinois at Champaign-Urbana (USA). Ger has publications in journals such as the *Journal of Consumer Research, California Management Review, Journal of Economic Psychology, Journal of Public Policy and Marketing, Journal of Material Culture*, and volumes such as *Time, Consumption and Everyday Life, Handbook of Qualitative Research Methods in Marketing, Clothing as Material Culture, The Why of Consumption,* and *Consumption in Marketizing Economies.* She is currently working on consumption among immigrants, production and consumption of cultural products, historical foundations of consumer culture, and temporality and materiality of consumption practices.

Ghofrane Ghariani is a PhD candidate at the Institut Supérieur de Gestion de Tunis, Tunis University. Her main research deals with experiential consumption, consumer behaviour and management of the arts and culture, particularly the field of cinema.

Kate Gillespie received a BA from Harvard University, an MBA from the University of Virginia, and a PhD from London Business School. She is an Associate Professor of International Business in the Marketing Department at the University of Texas at Austin. She has also served as associate director of the university's Center for Middle Eastern Studies and program co-chair for the Middle East Studies Association (MESA) Annual Meeting. Her academic research has centered on marketing and management issues of emerging markets including Egypt, Iran, Turkey and the West Bank. She is also first author of a global marketing textbook (South-Western/Cengage Learning) currently in its third edition.

Farooq Haq is a Lecturer in the School of Business and Law at the Charles Darwin University, Australia. He has completed his PhD in the area of marketing spiritual tourism. He has published in journals of marketing and tourism. His major research interests are marketing spirituality related products and services, studying the behaviour of spiritual tourists and marketing strategies for specialized and Islamic products.

Siti Hasnah Hassan is a Senior Lecturer in the School of Management, Universiti Sains Malaysia. She received her PhD from the Australian National University. Her thesis topic examined functional food consumption in multicultural society. Her research has been published in the *British Food Journal*, *Journal of Agribusiness Marketing and Journal of Asia Pacific Marketing*. She has also published book chapters and her work has been presented at the Australian and New Zealand Marketing Academy Conference. Her research interests include consumer behaviour, Islamic marketing and branding, cross-cultural marketing and health food marketing.

Özlem Hesapçı Sanaktekin is an Assistant Professor of Marketing at İstanbul Bilgi University. She received her BA in Business Administration from Marmara University, MA in Social Psychology from Boğaziçi University and her PhD degree in Marketing from Bocconi University. She teaches Marketing, Consumer Behavior and Research Methodology courses. Her main research focus is on the psychological processes that underlie consumption behaviour.

Hayiel Hino is a Lecturer in the Department of Economics and Business Management, Ariel University Center, Israel. He received his PhD in Business Administration from the Hebrew University, Israel. Primary research interests include international retailing, food retailing, and the influence of religious and cultural factors on the diffusion, adoption and use of modern food retail formats. His particular areas of teaching include Retailing, Marketing and International Marketing.

Elizabeth C. Hirschman is Professor II of Marketing, School of Business, Rutgers University, New Brunswick, USA. She is a Past President and Fellow of the Association for Consumer Research. Her research interests include ethnicity, race and religion as influences on consumption processes, semiotics, product symbolism, gender issues and self-identity. She was named in 2009 as one of the most highly cited scholars in Business and Economics by the Institute for Scientific Information.

Tariq Khan is the President of Muxlim Inc. Tariq is also the founder of Global Diversity Marketing, Inc., a New York based management-planning firm helping Fortune companies. Tariq has had a twenty-year career, working in companies including MetLife, Nationwide, and ING. Before joining Muxlim, Tariq was Senior Vice President and Head of Market Development for ING's US Wealth Management group. Tariq is also an Adjunct Professor of Marketing and Public Relations at New York University SCPS. Khan earned a bachelor's degree in international marketing and advertising from Baruch College, New York, and an MBA in marketing and management from St John's University, New York.

Mazen Kurdy has an MA degree in Political Science from the University of Central Florida, Orlando, with an emphasis on international affairs. His research interests include the fundamentalist Islamic resurgence and the Russian foreign policy goals in relation to the Caspian region, Syrian politics in Southwest Asia, and Islamic marketing and branding issues. Mazen also has an Executive MBA degree from the ESSEC & Mannheim Executive MBA Programme.

Chae Ho Lee is an Assistant Professor of Design at the University of Hawaiʻi at Mānoa. His work spans advertising, exhibition, identity, publication, and web design. He has worked for a number of prestigious advertising agencies and design studios in the Pacific Rim, New York, and Dubai. He has exhibited his design work nationally and internationally and has presented his research at international conferences in England, Japan, and Egypt. His current research has been published by the journals *Creative Quarterly* and *Visible Language*, among others. He received his MFA with honors from the Rhode Island School of Design in 1999.

Stephen Lee is the first Chief Operating Officer of Muxlim Inc. and currently acts as an advisor to the company. In the last ten years Stephen has founded and been an executive in several global Finnish startup companies in industries ranging from filmmaking to mobile software. Since 1986, his career has focused on managing people, technology and processes for companies like Bosch, Advanced Digital Information Corp. and General Motors. Stephen has a BS in Mechanical Engineering from the General Motors Institute and an MBA from the Helsinki School of Economics. He is a frequent lecturer on business strategy and social media marketing.

Vili Lehdonvirta is a Visiting Scholar at the Interfaculty Initiative in Information Studies, University of Tokyo, and a Researcher at the Helsinki Institute for Information Technology, Finland. His research interests are virtual goods, currencies and economies, digital consumption, online sociability and persuasive technology. Vili is a co-founder of the Virtual Economy Research Network and a member of the Advisory Board at Live Gamer, Inc. Vili has a PhD in Economic Sociology from Turku School of Economics and a MSc (Tech) from Helsinki University of Technology.

T.C. Melewar is a Professor of Marketing at Brunel Business School, Brunel University, United Kingdom. He has previous experience at Warwick Business School, MARA Institute of Technology in Malaysia, Loughborough University, UK and De Montfort University, UK. T.C. Melewar teaches Marketing Management, Marketing Communications and International Marketing on a range of undergraduate, MBA, and executive courses with companies such as Nestlé, Safeway, Corus and Sony. He has conducted seminars and courses in Russia, the Republic of Georgia, Moldova, Germany,

France, Denmark and Indonesia. T. C. Melewar is also the joint editor in chief of the highly acclaimed *Journal of Brand Management* (Palgrave).

Nazlida Muhamad is Assistant Professor at the College of Business Administration, Academic Campus for Girls, Jazan University, Kingdom of Saudi Arabia. She earned her PhD in Marketing from The University of Western Australia. She previously taught marketing courses at the Universiti Utara Malaysia and has served as a board member for the Malaysian Consumer and Family Economic Association. Her primary research interests include understanding the psychology of religion and spirituality and its role in consumers' marketplace behaviour.

Rusnah Muhamad received her PhD in Islamic Accounting from the University of Malaya, Malaysia and is a Senior Lecturer of Accounting in the University of Malaya, Malaysia. Her PhD research was related to financial reporting for the Islamic banking industry. Rusnah teaches Financial Accounting and Reporting, Accounting for Business Decision Making and Islamic Banking and Finance on a range of undergraduate, MBA, and executive courses at the University of Malaya. Her research interests among others are Islamic banking and finance, financial reporting from an Islamic perspective and Islamic business ethics.

Sonja Prokopec is an Assistant Professor of Marketing at ESSEC Business School, Paris. She has a PhD in Business from the University of Houston, Texas. She has an MBA in Finance and a BA degree in Marketing from the University of Central Florida, Orlando. Her primary research interests focus on self-regulation, mental accounting, and luxury branding issues. As a secondary area of research interest Sonja focuses on consumers' perceptions of brands in virtual worlds. Her research has appeared in the *Journal of Consumer Research*, the *Electronic Commerce Research Journal* and numerous conference proceedings (for example, ACR, AMA, EMAC, SCP). Sonja has been named the ESSEC LVMH Chaired Professor of Luxury Brand Management in 2010.

Gillian Rice is Professor Emerita at Thunderbird School of Global Management. Prior to joining Thunderbird, she held positions at the State University of New York in Buffalo, Concordia University (Montreal), West Virginia University and the University of Michigan-Flint. She holds a PhD from the University of Bradford. She has published widely in international business, specifically in the areas of Islamic business ethics, the environmentally responsible behavior of consumers, political risk, creativity, forecasting and trade shows. During the 1996–97 academic year, Dr Rice was a Senior Fulbright Scholar at the University of Bahrain, which enabled her to focus on her special interest of marketing in the Middle East. She serves on the editorial boards of several academic journals and is a columnist for *Global Business and Organizational Excellence: A Review of Research & Best Practices*.

Özlem Sandıkcı teaches marketing at Bilkent University, Turkey. She has an MBA from Birmingham University, UK and PhD from the Pennsylvania State University, USA. Her research addresses sociocultural dimensions of consumption and focuses on the relationship between globalization, marketing, and culture. Her current research interests include the Islamic marketplace, identity–space–consumption interaction, and branding in emerging markets. Her work is published in the *Journal of Consumer Research*,

Journal of Business Research, Fashion Theory, Place Branding and Public Diplomacy as well as in several edited books including *Handbook of Qualitative Research Methods in Marketing, Clothing as Material Culture*, and *Contemporary Consumption Rituals*. In 2003, she received the Franco Nicosia Association for Consumer Research Competitive Paper Award. She is an editorial board member of the *Journal of Islamic Marketing*.

Fatma Smaoui is Associate Professor at the Department of Marketing in the Institut Supérieur de Gestion de Tunis, Tunis University. She holds a PhD in marketing from the University of Strasbourg 2, France. Her research interests cover international marketing and country of origin, branding, practices of consumption and experiential consumption, and consumer behavior in emerging markets.

Rana Sobh earned her PhD in marketing from the University of Auckland in New Zealand in 2006. She is currently Assistant Professor in Marketing at the College of Business and Economics in Qatar University. Her research interests are in the area of consumer culture.

Paul Temporal is a leading global expert on brand creation, strategy development, and management, with over thirty years of experience in consulting and training. He has worked with many leading companies and governments, and is well known for his practical and results-oriented approach. He is director of a major research and education project focused on Islamic branding and marketing at the Saïd Business School, University of Oxford, UK, where he is an Associate Fellow. He has lectured at many of Asia's top business schools, is a Visiting Professor at Shanghai Jiao Tong University, China, an Associate Fellow at Green Templeton College, University of Oxford, and a member of the editorial boards of the *Asia Pacific Journal of Marketing and Logistics*, and the *Journal of Islamic Marketing*. Dr Temporal has published widely in many journals and global media, and is the author of 15 best-selling books on branding.

Sultan Tepe is Associate Professor of Political Science at the University of Illinois at Chicago. She received her PhD from the University of Texas at Austin in government and her BA from Boğaziçi University in Istanbul, Turkey in international relations and political science. She is the author of *Beyond Sacred and Secular: Politics of Religion in Israel and Turkey* (Stanford University Press, 2008), which received the 2009 Choice: Current Review for Academic Libraries Outstanding National Title Award. She has also published numerous articles and book chapters on the role of religion in politics, international affairs and economics.

Cameron Thibos received his bachelor's degree from Indiana University, Bloomington in journalism, economics, and Near Eastern studies, and his MA degree from the Center for Middle Eastern studies at the University of Texas at Austin. He is currently a doctoral student at the Department of International Development at the University of Oxford, UK. His research interests include transnational politics, international migration, and development in emerging markets. His current research focuses on these issues in the context of Turkey.

Mourad Touzani is an Associate Professor of Marketing at Rouen Business School, France. He also gives courses at the University of Tunis. He previously taught at the University of Aix-Marseille and at the State University of New York. He has a master's degree and a PhD in marketing from the Institut d'Administration des Entreprises d'Aix-en-Provence. Dr Touzani teaches and does research in the areas of international marketing, retailing, innovation, CCT, and consumer behavior. He is regularly in charge of missions in relationship with the Tunisian Ministry of Higher Education. He is an active consultant and has taught several executive seminars on customer satisfaction, marketing research, and qualitative data analysis.

Ho Yin Wong is a Senior Lecturer at the School of Management and Marketing, Central Queensland University, Australia. He has published in *International Marketing Review, Journal of Strategic Marketing, Journal of Product and Brand Management*, and *Journal of Global Marketing*, among others. His main research interest is international marketing, branding and marketing strategy.

Omneya Mokhtar Yacout works as an Assistant Professor of Business Administration in the Faculty of Commerce, Alexandria University, Egypt. She worked as a Visiting Professor at Vaxjo University, Sweden and a Visiting Scholar at Georgia State University, USA. She has published a number of papers on subjects including experiential marketing, segmentation and targeting strategies in touristic markets, service quality, customer relationship management, international market knowledge transfer, and customer adoption of e-banking. In 2008, she received the Best Paper Award from the Journal of Touristic Research, published by the Egyptian Ministry of Tourism.

Kenneth Beng Yap is an Assistant Professor at the University of Western Australia. Having both worked in the financial services industry and consulted for retail banking and insurance firms, he is particularly interested in the marketing of financial services. Currently, he is researching the influence of religion on consumer financial decision making, which includes a study on Islamic banking. His other research interests include macromarketing, social capital, and societal welfare issues. His work has been published in the *Journal of Services Marketing, International Journal of Bank Marketing*, and *Journal of Macromarketing*.

Raja Nerina Raja Yusof is a Senior Lecturer in the Faculty of Economics and Management, Universiti Putra Malaysia. She received her PhD from the University of Otago, Dunedin, New Zealand in 2010. She serves as an editorial board member for her faculty's *Asian Journal of Case Research* and is also a member of the Academy of International Business. Her research interest is in the area of international business management focusing on multinational corporations, cross-cultural management and Islamic business practices.

Acknowledgements

We would both like to thank Ben Booth at Edward Elgar for his vision and support in the preparation of this *Handbook*, and Tekin Türkdoğan for providing cover photographs.

Özlem Sandıkcı and Gillian Rice

Acknowledgements are due to Gül Yücel, my assistant at Bilkent University, Faculty of Business Administration, who helped considerably in the difficult task of assembling the final manuscript. I have the deepest gratitude for my parents, Süheyla and Sırrı Sandıkcı, for always supporting me in all my endeavors. And my greatest thanks are to my husband, Tekin Türkdoğan, who stood by me throughout this project and continuously offered his support and love.

Özlem Sandıkcı

I thank my husband, Essam Mahmoud, for his kindness, patience and encouragement throughout my career and especially with respect to this project. Much appreciation also to my parents, Bill and Joy Rice, who have always persuaded me to have the confidence to pursue my dreams.

Gillian Rice

Glossary

This section explains some of the Arabic words and terms that occur in the *Handbook*.

Abaya is a woman's gown or cloak.

Ahadith is the plural form of *hadith* (see below).

Akhlaq means morals and values.

Al-akhira is the hereafter.

Al-din or *din* is used to refer to the religion of Islam.

Alim is a scholar of Islam.

Allah is the Arabic word for God (used by both Muslims and Christians).

Al-muaamala means social intercourse and activities.

Al-mus'uliyya al-ijtima'iyya lil-sharikat is corporate social responsibility.

Awra is that which needs to be covered in the presence of someone to whom an individual would be eligible to be married.

Bai'al dayn means the sale of debt or a liability at a discounted or negotiated price.

Bai bi-thamin ajil is deferred payment sale by installments.

Bai'muajjal is deferred payment sale.

Bai'salam is prepaid purchase.

Burqa is a face-covering garment.

Dawa means a call, appeal, or invitation and is used to mean 'inviting someone to learn about Islam'.

Dhul-Hijja is the month (on the 9th and 10th days) in which the *hajj* pilgrimage takes place.

Din see Al-din

Eid-ul-Adha is the holiday following the rituals of the *hajj* pilgrimage when Muslims slaughter a sacrificial animal.

Eid-ul-Fitr is the holiday at the end of the fasting month of Ramadan.

Fatwa is a ruling made by religious scholars.

Gharar means the presence of uncertainty most of the time concerning economic or financial transactions.

Hadith is a saying of the Prophet Muhammad (pl. *ahadith*). *Hadith* is also a collective noun referring to all of the Prophet's sayings.

Hajj is the compulsory pilgrimage to Mecca, once in a Muslim's lifetime, as long as he/she is financially and physically able to do it.

Hajji/hajja is a Muslim (male/female) who has performed the *hajj.*

Halal means lawful, permissible.

Hanafi is one of the four major schools of thought/law in Islam.

Hanbali is one of the four major schools of thought/law in Islam.

Haram means unlawful.

Hijab means cover and is used to refer to a woman's head covering.

Hijri means the Hegira, the migration of the Prophet Muhammad from Mecca. The Muslim calendar dates from this time; for example, 1433 AH means 1433 years after the Hegira.

Iftar is the fast-breaking meal eaten nightly in Ramadan.

Ihsan is beneficence or goodness.

Ijara is a leasing contract.

Ijara wa iktina is a lease-purchase contract, whereby the client has the option of purchasing the contract.

Ijma means consensus.

Ijtihad refers to the independent or original interpretation of problems not precisely covered by the Qur'an or *hadith.*

Ijtima means a meeting.

Istisnaa refers to future delivery as in a contract to manufacture.

Jihad is a fight, battle, or struggle.

Kaaba is the cube-shaped building covered with a black cloth at the centre of the Grand Mosque in Mecca.

Kafala is a contract of guarantee or taking of responsibility for a liability provided by a guarantor.

Kasb means acquisition, earnings, gain or profit.

Mahrem means someone who is unlawful for a woman to marry because of marital or blood relationships.

Majlis means a living room, a conference room or a gathering.

Makruh is detested.

Maliki is one of the four major schools of thought/law in Islam.

Mandub means recommended.

Mu'aamalat means political, social and economic activities undertaken by Muslims.

Muakkad is a type of Islamic ruling that connotes strong recommendation of particular practices among Muslims, especially in Islamic religious rituals.

Mubah is permissible

Mudarib is the entrepreneurial partner in a *mudaraba* partnership who provides the expertise and management.

Mudaraba is a trustee financing contract, where one party, the financier, entrusts funds to the other party, the entrepreneur, for undertaking an activity.

Mufti is a professional jurist who interprets Muslim law.

Muhkam means precise.

Munafasa means competition.

Murabaha is a resale with a stated profit (using the cost plus mark-up principle).

Musharaka is an equity participation contract, where two or more partners contribute funds to undertake an investment.

Muslimah is a female Muslim.

Mutashabih means allegorical.

Nafs means soul, desire, or personal identity.

Najis is unclean.

Nas is evidence.

Nisab is the threshold of wealth in regards to the payment of *zakat* (obligatory charity).

Niyya is intention.

Qadar means destiny.

Qadi is a judge.

Qard hasan is a benevolent or interest-free loan.

Qibla is the direction towards which Muslims pray (the direction of the *kaaba*).

Qiyas is analogy.

Qur'an means the book Muslims believe was revealed by God through the Angel Gabriel to Muhammad, the Prophet of Islam.

Rahn is a security or mortgage.

Ramadan is the 9th month of the Islamic calendar, when Muslims fast daily for the entire month.

Riba means interest.

Rihla is a journey undertaken for the pursuit of knowledge.

Sadaqa is voluntary alms giving/charity.

Sahur is the last meal before daybreak during the month of Ramadan.

Salah is the obligatory prayer, performed five times daily.

Saum means fast (fasting from food, water, sex, smoking, and arguments or being angry).

Shahadah is the declaration of faith made by Muslims (to believe in no other god but God and that Muhammad is His Prophet).

Shafi'i is one of the four major schools of thought/law in Islam.

Sharia is Islamic law.

Shayla is a head covering.

Sidq is truth.

Sufi is a person who practices Sufism or mysticism in Islam.

Sukuk is a corporate bond.

Sunnah refers to the recorded sayings and living habits of Prophet Muhammad.

Tabligh is a tradition of Muslim men traveling to visit other Muslims in mosques and their houses for the revival of Islam.

Takaful is insurance.

Tawhid is used to refer to the oneness/unity of Allah (God)

Ulama (plural of *alim*) refers to the scholars of Islam.

Ummah means the community of Muslims

Umra is the 'lesser pilgrimage,' which can be made to Mecca during any time of the year.

Thoub is a gown (often white) worn by men.

Wadia means safe custody or deposit.

Wadia yad damaana means savings with guarantee.

Wakala involves a contract of agency on a fee-for-service basis.

Wajib is prescribed.

Waqf is a permanent religious endowment.

Zaka means to thrive; to grow, increase; to be pure in heart, be just, righteous, good.

Zakat is obligatory charity given by Muslims.

Ziyara is a journey made to visit holy places and tombs.

1   Islamic marketing: an introduction and overview
Özlem Sandıkcı and Gillian Rice

Islamic marketing is a field in emergence. In recent years, an interest in understanding Muslims as consumers and as marketers has become apparent across academic and managerial circles. Many social, cultural, political and economic developments underlie this interest: the emergence of a Muslim middle class attentive to the values of Islam and interested in modern consumption; the increasing visibility of a new class of Muslim entrepreneurs who innovatively and successfully blend religious principles and capitalist aspirations; the growth of the *ummah*, a supranational community of Muslim believers, connected through values and lifestyles; the increasing social, economic and political power and influence of the new Islamic social movements; and the post 9/11 forces shaping the global political economy and international relations. Given the significance of these developments, it is not difficult to predict that academic and managerial attention to understanding Muslim consumers and markets will continue to grow in the coming years.

The goal of this *Handbook* is to provide a collection of state-of-the-art scholarship on Islamic marketing and lay out an agenda for future research. Consistent with the spirit of the *Handbook* – to offer an up-to-date, critical and multidisciplinary approach to the study of the intersection of Islam, consumption and marketing – the contributors come from a variety of backgrounds. Scholars from different disciplines such as marketing, anthropology, political science and art history, as well as consultants and practitioners offer a rich array of insights into Islamic marketing. The essays cover topics ranging from fashion and food consumption practices of Muslims, to retailing, digital marketing, spiritual tourism, corporate social responsibility, and nation branding in the context of Muslim marketplaces. Several other chapters look at the relationship between morality, consumption and marketing practices, and examine the implications of politics and globalization on Islamic markets. In studying their topics, researchers utilize different methods, such as surveys, ethnographic methods and case studies, and highlight the utility of methodological diversity in understanding market dynamics. Finally, the chapters discuss consumption and marketing practices observed in a diverse range of Muslim majority and minority countries, including Australia, Bahrain, Iran, Malaysia, Tunisia, Turkey, the United Arab Emirates, and the United States. Overall, the *Handbook* aims to attend to the foundational issues as well as to emerging trends in Islamic marketing and to generate questions to be pursued in future research. Before we introduce the individual chapters, a few points need to be clarified.

The title of the *Handbook* should not mislead the readers. The purpose of this collection is not to define what Islamic marketing is or should be. On the contrary, the *Handbook* is first and foremost about sensitizing all those interested in the topic to the diversity, multiplicity and dynamism of Muslim consumers and the complexity of the relationship between Islam and marketing. Is it meaningful to speak of Islamic marketing? What is Islamic in Islamic marketing? Why do we need, if we do, Islamic marketing? These are some of the questions that underlie this project and the many chapters that comprise it. Each of the essays looks at these questions, explicitly or implicitly, and offers a particular viewpoint. They are in consensus with each other neither in how they conceptualize 'Islamic marketing' nor in what they find in regard to the practices of consumers and marketers. However in their totality the chapters clearly demonstrate that the interaction between marketing and Islam is multifaceted and complex and shaped by the historical and current cultural, political, social and economic forces. The essays also repeatedly demonstrate that Muslims are not a homogenous and static group, whose behaviors can be easily categorized and predicted. On the contrary, like any other consumer group, Muslims are characterized by diversity and dynamism. While Islam provides a set of normative ethical principles and values, how these are interpreted and negotiated in the everyday lives of consumers and marketers varies across time, contexts and communities.

Such complexity and multiplicity render Islamic marketing an exciting field. Yet complexity and multiplicity also carry with them significant liabilities for researchers and practitioners. That is, while studying Muslim marketplaces, appealing to Muslim consumers or competing with Muslim businesses, one needs to develop not only an understanding of Islamic norms, principles and values but also to attend to the interactions between Islam and other institutional and structural forces and discourses that shape people's practices. It is on these issues that we hope the chapters in this collection offer insights.

MORALITY AND THE MARKETPLACE

Abbas Ali, in Chapter 2, explores the nature and scope of marketing-related ethical principles in Islam. He shows how religion can be a strong force in ethics formation and application. Muslims worldwide reiterate their commitment to religious directives daily, and in everyday conversation, they tend to utter ethical and religious sayings. Ali acknowledges that these are sayings and might not necessarily be reflective of people's deeds. Nevertheless, by a detailed discussion of transactions according to normative Islamic ethics, he demonstrates clearly that marketers and academic researchers need to pay particular attention to this dimension of Islam. According to Islamic teachings, the concept of *ihsan* (beneficence or goodness) permeates everything in human life. Ali's historical perspective and numerous illustrations suggest that marketing was conceptualized early as a process for meeting the ever-changing needs of customers and society. In Islam there is a tight link between society and business, which has notable implications for corporate social responsibility in contemporary society.

Extending Ali's exploration of ethics, Nazlida Muhamad (Chapter 3) focuses on the *fatwa*, the religious ruling issued by scholars in Islam. When deciding whether to make or purchase or how to choose among brands, Muslims might place a priority on religious decision criteria. Some Muslim consumers prefer to obtain information from a scholar or religious committee they respect and trust. Consumers find easy access to *fatwa* rulings on the Internet. Using the Malaysian context and several contemporary *fatwa* rulings as illustrations, Muhamad details the process by which the rulings are made, how consumers learn about them, and how people decide whether or not to abide by a particular *fatwa.* She argues that the degree to which Muslims follow religious precepts about insurance services, financial products, contraception services, and entertainment choices, for example, depends on whether they are intrinsically or extrinsically motivated. Complicating the task for researchers and practitioners who want to learn more about how Muslims use and process information from *fatwa* rulings is the fact that consumers in one country do not necessarily rely only on scholars from their own nations, but seek out rulings from well-known scholars around the globe. Thus, *fatwa* rulings from overseas can have an impact on local consumers. The decentralization of religious authority in Islam as well as the varying degrees of religious orientation (and therefore compliance with *fatwa* rulings issued by an authority) combine to provide a challenge for firms that market any products or services that might be subject to religious purview.

In Chapter 4, Alexandru Balasescu offers an assessment of the underlying moral principles of advertising in Islamic places. Instead of seeing Islamic ethical principles as impositions to be followed by marketers, he proposes to conceptualize them as 'recommendations'. Through his analysis of advertising in two distinct domains, fashion and investment planning, he shows that Islamic principles generate a space of various possibilities rather than rigid rules. While fashion and finance appear unconnected, the parallel analysis of how they are promoted in Iran and the Gulf countries reveals curious threads of commonality: according to Islamic morality, for example, it is production and not 're-production' that is acceptable. This is true for fashion in the public space. For finance, it remains true both publicly and privately. The promotion of both products is not without controversy and Balasescu concludes that an understanding of cultural specificities in Islam is vital to successful marketing. Yet, as he and other contributors to the *Handbook* illustrate, these specificities vary considerably from one Muslim market to another.

MUSLIM CONSUMPTIONSCAPES

A key theme in the *Handbook* is change. Changes are occurring in the Muslim world at an ever-increasing pace. In Chapter 5, Russell Belk and Rana Sobh address this theme with respect to the issue of privacy as it relates to gender. Based on ethnographic fieldwork over a three-year period, they analyze how local cultures in Qatar and the UAE affect consumption and marketing. The context is one of dramatic changes: a significant increase in national and personal wealth, growth of financial, educational and media centers, dilution of local populations by the expatriates and guest workers who comprise more than 80 per cent of residents, as well as an influx of foreign media, brands, and retail stores. Globalization has both attenuating and stimulating effects on traditional cultural patterns. Belk and Sobh demonstrate how social and economic changes are inextricably linked with Muslims' search for, and expression of, their identities.

Belk and Sobh situate their discussion in a broad historical context of the meaning of privacy in the Western cultures that have grown more individualistic. They then compare this to privacy among the collectivist Muslim cultures in the Gulf. Results of the fieldwork reveal that such tensions are reflected in many aspects of consumption including the configuration and use of houses, and the design and uses of public or quasi-public spaces like shopping malls. Belk and Sobh pay particular attention to interpreting how both men and women manifest the tensions in their choice of clothing, a much-misunderstood aspect of Muslim consumption behavior.

Fatma Smaoui and Ghofrane Ghariani focus on fashion as they expand upon the subject of tensions between the pull of the West and the desire to maintain an Islamic or national Tunisian identity. They ask questions such as: how do Tunisian consumers experience fashion? How do cultural, social and religious factors shape their relationship with fashion? What is the place of identity in the Tunisian consumer-fashion relationship? Their goal is to investigate the consumer-fashion relationship in a Tunisian Arab-Muslim context and to emphasize the role played by the identity concept in this relationship.

In Chapter 6, they report on their research, which involved in-depth, semi-structured interviews with Tunisian consumers aged 21 to 60, of various backgrounds. The results revealed that for these Tunisians, relationships with fashion are complex, and affect the construction of their individual, social, and cultural identities. Although Smaoui and Ghariani purposely avoided asking about Islam, their informants readily raised the subject of religion. At least two interpretations exist: while some interviewees denigrate fashion, especially that originating in the West as materialistic, unIslamic, and something to be avoided, others refer to the Islamic teaching that God loves beauty and if fashion is beautiful, it can be acceptable. Despite the heterogeneous sample, the results support earlier studies, highlighting tensions in identity formation and expression. In addition, the Tunisian interviewees echo subjects in other research studies in emerging markets when they express a desire for individuals and companies from their countries to develop products that would appeal to local consumers.

Elizabeth Hirschman and Mourad Touzani, in Chapter 7, investigate the process of acculturation that occurs as the legacy of the earlier colonization of one country by another, by focusing on Tunisia's subjugation to France. The cultural influence of the French colonizer continues to linger among a particular community in Tunisia that remains Francophone – not merely in language, but in values, attitudes, and consumer behavior. Hirschman and Touzani give a historical perspective to show how first the Berbers of North Africa converted to Islam within two centuries; it took several more centuries for them to adopt the Arabic language. The French annexation of Tunisia created a cultural battlefield between Arabic and French. The in depth interview study by Hirschman and Touzani targeted highly French-acculturated individuals who had never lived in France; they are acculturated *in situ*. Through their conversations with the researchers, the subjects reveal how their acculturation affects their consumer behavior, for example, their store patronage habits, education choices, clothing, home décor and entertainment selection. What is especially important and has implications both for marketing practice and for future research is that the informants do not say they want to be French; rather they denigrate the Arabic Tunisian style. Interestingly, however, when they want to be Tunisian, and in particular, to experience their Muslim identities (as during the Muslim fasting month of Ramadan, for example) they will choose Tunisian and Arabic television channels over French-language ones. The tension remains.

What is the situation in Turkey? Yonca Aslanbay, Özlem Hesapçı Sanaktekin and Bekir Ağırdır describe the details of Turkish Muslims' lifestyles. In Chapter 8, they report on a descriptive study of 6236 Turks living across the country. Turkey has a very different history from Tunisia, yet its inhabitants face similar challenges in adapting to rapid social change and economic development. Rather than a choice between national-based cultures (such as Tunisian versus French), in Turkey, people choose between modern and traditional lifestyles. This choice is associated with religiosity and with degree of urbanization. Interestingly, in rural areas in particular, some people who describe themselves as unbelievers still undertake religious practices, and the women may cover. This shows the pervasive influence of culture must be taken into account when attempting to isolate any relationship between religiosity and consumer behavior. Aslanbay et al. discover a new identity in Turkey, a country that has been a secular democratic republic since 1923. They attribute the new identity directly to changes in society such as the liberalization and globalization of the economy, rapid and huge urbanization, and the development of the mass media. The identity is a conservative outlook based on Islam, but also bearing a relatively close proximity to a modern lifestyle and the consumption patterns of the urban dweller.

The next two chapters explore specific consumptionscapes relating to food. In Chapter 9, Hayiel Hino presents an analysis of Muslims' food retail shopping behavior. How do Muslims adapt to changing food retailing formats? Based on a literature review, he explores the theoretical and empirical understanding of the role Islam plays in shaping consumers' shopping and consumption patterns. Specifically, he investigates the meaning of *halal* and the implications for food shopping. He asks: what is the impact of religion on Muslim consumers' shopping patterns? How does Muslims' adherence to Islamic law affect the degree of use of the various food store types (one-stop supermarkets or hypermarkets versus small neighborhood stores)? He finds that Islam has a salient impact on shopping and consumption. Muslims practice selective purchasing that tends to differ from typical shopping practices found in non-Muslim communities. Many Muslim consumers tend to split their shopping basket according to product category types. This results in a reduced usage of modern supermarket/hypermarket formats. They prefer to patronize traditional formats for fresh products, even though supermarkets and hypermarkets have a broad assortment of these products. However they buy non-perishables at both modern and traditional formats. Hino's interpretation is that the Muslim shoppers have more trust in the smaller neighbourhood outlets to provide genuine *halal* products. His findings have implications for both practitioners (with respect to *halal* certification, for example) and researchers (who should undertake cross-national studies, for instance, to evaluate the validity of results that are based primarily on Middle Eastern markets).

The significance of *halal* certification to Muslim consumers is also apparent in Siti Hasnah Hassan's findings. In Chapter 10, she reports on a qualitative study of Malay Muslims that investigated how they form preferences and negotiate among their variously held values in order to select among a growing number of functional foods. The functional food market is rapidly growing and is particularly attractive to practicing Muslims, who are exhorted in the Qur'an and the *sunnah* to eat pure foods. Muslims believe that their bodies are provided to them as a trust from God, and so they are obligated to take care of them and maintain good health. Functional foods are foods that provide health benefits beyond basic nutritional requirements. From her study using ethnoconsumerist methodology and a diverse sample of Malays (different genders, ages, education levels, experience with functional foods and so on), Hassan discovers the salient role of local cultural values in addition to Islamic values and personal values when consumers choose functional foods. The role of oral tradition is also readily apparent. Like other authors (see Chapter 14, for example), Hassan sees how the Islamic market can be extended: a certified *halal* product is not only welcomed by Muslim consumers locally and worldwide but is even acceptable by non-Muslim consumers as well because *halal* certified products represent a symbol of quality.

MARKETING PRACTICES

What are the implications of the observance of *halal* practices by consumers for the multinational retailers that market to them? This question is studied by Raja Nerina Raja Yusof, André Everett and Malcolm Cone in Chapter 11. Acknowledging that multinational retailers are market-oriented because of their emphasis on serving consumers, Yusof et al. investigate through case research, the degree to which the retailers are influenced by the *halal* and *haram* practices of Islam. Specifically, the study applies the Convergence-Divergence-Crossvergence (CDC) framework and evaluates whether the retailers form different types of subsidiary cultures. The study is conducted in Malaysia, a country that is taking the lead globally with respect to *halal* certification. Case studies, based on interviews, observation, and archival material reveal that there are differences among three hypermarket chains (Carrefour, Tesco, Giant) in Malaysia in their adaptation to *halal* practices. The findings, illustrated by interviewee quotations, highlight the importance of being proactive. For example, Carrefour Malaysia exhibits a crossvergence subsidiary culture, which Yusof et al. also describe as a 'fusion' culture because of the influence of Islamic practices on the retailer's corporate culture. Crossvergence, in this study by Yusof et al. is a firm's voluntary efforts or initiatives to excel in the marketplace through compromise and utilization of local culture.

In general, when marketing to Muslims, is a standardized approach around the globe or an adaptation approach for specific markets more suitable? In Chapter 12, Sonja Prokopec and Mazen Kurdy broaden the approach of Yusof et al. from retailing and *halal* practices to consider the standardization versus adaptation debate in the context of Islamic marketing as a whole. Parallel to the notion of 'think global, act local,' they advocate managers should 'think *sharia*, act local.' In support of this idea, Prokopec and Kurdy point to what numerous contributors to this *Handbook* observe: the considerable heterogeneity within the global Muslim community, and even within Muslim communities in single nations.

Referring to Ogilvy and Mather's index of Muslim-friendly brands, Prokopec and Kurdy illustrate how the marketing mix elements of product, price, promotion, and place are best operationalized when marketing to Muslims. To illustrate, they discuss the marketing of various product categories. Some companies, such as Nestlé, have a first-mover advantage among global firms; Nestlé has had a *halal* committee since the 1980s and 18 per cent of its factories are geared for *halal* production. Prokopec and Kurdy provide evidence that is primarily anecdotal and they urge researchers to conduct additional studies on Muslim consumer behavior.

The authors of Chapters 13 to 15 are concerned with practices in the Islamic financial services industry. Kenneth Beng Yap, in Chapter 13, focuses on Islamic banking. He argues that what separates the notion of Islamic banking from conventional banking is the former's Profit-and-Loss-Sharing (PLS) arrangements. These reflect Islamic ideals regarding financial affairs, risk and equity in welfare distribution that are especially valuable in regions of income inequality and injustice. Yet Yap opines that current Islamic banking practices have diverged from Islamic ideals because most Islamic banking products cannot be easily distinguished from those of conventional banks. In these circumstances, according to Yap, it is difficult to isolate the role of religiosity in consumer behavior with respect to selection of Islamic banking services. He proposes that research should focus on the PLS arrangements, because, as these are riskier, only those individuals who have a certain level of faith, would participate in these kinds of banking services. Yap is interested in the variables that encourage Muslim consumers to give up the certainty of investment returns in order to fulfill their religious duty. What marketing factors might be relevant? Presently marketers promote many Islamic banking products for their investment returns and product features because Muslim consumers, familiar with conventional banking products, can easily compare the offerings of both banking alternatives. PLS-based products, however, could be marketed as a method of investing that helps consumers achieve their Islamic ideals. For example, if the decision to invest in PLS-based products is based on religiosity, then banks must insure that consumers perceive them as adhering to Islamic principles. Yap presents a detailed conceptual model to guide future research.

In Chapter 14, Rusnah Muhamad, T.C. Melewar and Sharifah Faridah Syed Alwi report the results of two research studies conducted to explore market segmentation in the Islamic financial services industry and to gauge Malaysian Muslim consumers' awareness of the services offered. Perhaps because, as Yap points out, on the surface, there appear to be few differences between conventional and Islamic banking products, consumers have little understanding of Islamic financial instruments. Muhamad et al., like Yap, are interested in the role played by consumer religiosity when choosing Islamic financial products. An in-depth interview study of key industry informants (*sharia* scholars, regulators, bankers, lawyers, consultants, insurance operators, and fund managers) from Malaysia and other countries reveals that four consumer segments exist in Islamic financial services. One group consists of consumers who have deep religious conviction and choose their financial services on that basis alone. Muhamad et al. quote one interviewee, a retail banker, who declares that some consumers will stay with a particular banker for one reason alone – because they trust that it is the best at following *sharia* – and no other criteria matter. Another segment comprises people who are religious, but balance their religiosity with economic rationality. A third segment is composed of ethically observant individuals and a fourth segment consists of people who make decisions on the basis of economic rationality. These latter two segments can include Muslims and non-Muslims and so might provide an opportunity for Islamic financial services to expand beyond the Muslim market, as has happened to a small extent in the US, for example. The consumer awareness study reported by Muhamad et al. reveals that the only demographic variable associated with the use of Islamic financial services in Malaysia, however, is religion. Being Muslim is the variable that determines whether someone will choose Islamic banking and insurance services.

Omneya Mokhtar Yacout and Mohamed Farid ElSahn offer an explanation for people's poor knowledge of specific Islamic banking products. In Chapter 15, they suggest that Islamic banks might not be doing so well on a strategic issue: brand equity.

As emphasized by Yap, Islamic banking services can potentially help people, especially those who live in developing countries and have limited funds but innovative business ideas. Yacout and ElSahn agree that Islamic banks should stress financial programs that promote socioeconomic development. However, although there are high levels of awareness among Muslims about the existence of Islamic banks, levels of knowledge remain low. This can hinder consumers' patronage of Islamic banks.

Yacout and ElSahn report the results of a comprehensive brand equity study of consumers in Bahrain. They investigated the sources and outcomes of brand equity in banking services and the differences between customers of Islamic and conventional banks with respect to these brand equity variables. The level of analysis is the corporate brand. The most important predictor of overall brand equity was perceived service quality, followed by brand trust. There was, however, a non-significant effect of brand equity on customers' share-of-wallet. Yacout and ElSahn posit that although Islamic banks have built brand awareness among their customers as well as among the customers of their non-Islamic rivals, these competitors retain their customers by offering superior service. Thus, although consumers are aware of Islamic banks, they continue to patronize non-Islamic banks.

In Chapter 16, Cameron Thibos and Kate Gillespie tackle the issue of how Arab firms practice Corporate Social Responsibility (CSR). Their study includes a survey of the corporate websites of major companies in the Arab world, specifically those companies which have a section designated for CSR activity, and an analysis of CSR initiatives reported in the Arab press. Their purpose is to examine the role of Islamic authorization and moralization in the legitimization discourse for CSR initiatives. Thibos and Gillespie discuss in detail how *zakat*, the Islamic faith pillar which relates to obligatory charity, is associated with CSR. Surprisingly, even when companies use Islam as a justification for their CSR – when they undertake activities during Ramadan and to help orphans, for example – there is a certain level of understatement in the discourse. An investigation of how charitable works are conducted in Islamic societies reveals that charity should be given secretly, otherwise there is a risk of vanity. Because the discourse is taking place in primarily Muslim societies, little information about Islamic authorization needs to be presented: readers understand and know from one or two cues. An additional complicating factor is that much of the Arab press is government-owned and government officials, while not hostile to Islam, usually prefer not to promote the religion, and instead may want to associate any benefits of CSR with their country's economic development. This chapter reveals an intricate relationship between culture and Islam, one that is often complicated by politics. Thibos and Gillespie raise numerous questions for further research into this area.

Farooq Haq and Ho Yin Wong offer an exploration of marketing strategies that tour operators can utilize in promoting Islamic spiritual tourism. Chapter 17 contains the results of their in-depth interview study of Australian and Pakistani Muslims' motivations for spiritual travel and their recommendations for companies. They analyze three types of spiritual travel: first, for pilgrimage to Mecca; second, for knowledge, in the tradition of Ibn Battuta; and third, for journeying to holy places, to see holy people, or the shrines of saints. The differences that are apparent between Australians and Pakistanis provide further evidence for the heterogeneity of the Muslim market. These differences include the motivations for travel, which have implications for marketing communications practice. Australians travel to explore their self-identities and to understand themselves better. The Pakistanis interviewed tended to search for self-fulfillment from spiritual tourism. There were also cross-cultural differences in information sources, purchase location and satisfaction with the travel service experience.

To conclude Part III on Marketing Practices, in Chapter 18, Mohamed El-Fatatry, Stephen Lee, Tariq Khan and Vili Lehdonvirta examine how growing internet usage and social media permit marketers to serve Muslim consumers more effectively and efficiently. Using numerous case study illustrations, El-Fatatry et al. demonstrate how well-executed digital strategies can engender functional connections, personal connections, satisfaction and trust in the brand-customer relationship, subsequently resulting in deeper customer commitment. Some of the case examples come from the research and findings of Muxlim Inc. Muxlim is an integrated media company that provides services to help companies reach the global Muslim market. Muxlim Inc. runs an online Muslim lifestyle network to deliver customer campaigns and to gather data on trends and content consumption among Muslims online.

El-Fatatry et al. emphasize the diversity in the Muslim market noted in previous chapters. Around the world, Muslim communities represent a cross-section of all socio-economic classes, age groups, nationalities and races. Although this makes the Muslim market more difficult and more expensive to target as a mass market, digital media can easily reach narrow segments. Importantly, digital media permit marketers to target Muslim consumers without overtly using their 'religious' identity to attract their attention. Rather, regardless of a customer's religiosity, marketers can use digital media to integrate brand messages within lifestyle content in subtle ways on specialized websites: sports, fashion, technology and entertainment. Marketers can use Muslim-focused or ethnic media, which are already trusted by the potential customers. Importantly, in emerging markets (many of which have Muslim-majority populations), mobile penetration is growing rapidly. Fatatry et al. point out that one unique use for digital mobile marketing in Islamic marketing is to reach emerging market consumers who have little access to any other media.

GLOBALIZATION, POLITICS AND RESISTANCE

As Muslim consumptionscapes emerge and expand, the social and political implications are of interest to both practitioners and researchers. These implications can involve consumer resistance as well as consumer demand. In order to illustrate these dynamics, Sultan Tepe, in Chapter 19, deconstructs a legal case that was brought against Tekbir, a Turkish clothing company that markets clothing to covered Muslim women. The case concerns the authentic meaning of religious symbols and ideas, as Tekbir is a word (in Arabic, *takbir*) which refers to the exclamation, *Allahu akbar*, meaning 'God is great.' Whether something can be authentically Islamic is also influenced by the role of religion in the social, political and economic system – in this case, in Turkey. According to Tepe, when religion has a different role in these three systems, it presents a complex decision making environment for customers. In particular, as the Islamic market for consumer goods develops, Tepe considers ways in which faith-based products declare their authenticity. Unexpected key players that surface are Islamic scholars. Recall Nazlida

Muhamad's analysis of how Malaysian consumers use *fatwa* rulings from scholars to guide their consumption. Tepe observes that the religious authenticity of Tekbir's products in Turkey (and in the other countries in which they are sold) appears to rest on its owner's personal authority or discretion to define what is both Islamic and acceptable. While the company has grown considerably, Tepe discusses the resistance shown by a particular group of Muslim consumers, who insist that to follow fashions is unIslamic and who accuse companies like Tekbir of capitalist exploitation.

While Tepe studies Turkish Muslims who resist buying products intended to be Muslim-oriented but which they believe to be exploiting Islam, Maya Farah examines Arabs who resist buying American products. Although Farah's research, reported in Chapter 20, uses both Muslim and Christian subjects in Lebanon, her results have particular implications for marketing to Muslims. She grounds her research in the Theory of Planned Behavior and reports on a qualitative interview study and a quantitative survey. Considerably more Muslims have participated in the Arab boycott than have Christians. The Muslims' rationales originate in their religious belief system and they often follow the lead of Muslim scholars, and abide by *fatwa* rulings, for example. Farah suggests that boycotters' behavioral beliefs might be the most suitable targets for marketers seeking to develop communication messages to reduce boycott participation. Changing the beliefs central to the attitude toward boycotting could lead to a change in behavioral intention, and ultimately, in boycotting behavior. Marketing communications to reinforce belief strength about a boycott's negative outcomes could emphasize that participating in the boycott would endanger local employees' jobs.

Marketing campaigns for Muslim markets can be difficult to develop because of the diversity within these markets. That marketers of especially global corporations need to consider likely boycott implications is an added challenge. Chae Ho Lee and Jennifer Chandler focus on a particular diverse, multicultural location: Dubai, a city-state that is primarily populated by Muslim expatriates as well as Emirati nationals. In Chapter 21, Lee and Chandler define two marketing approaches relevant to marketing professionals as they design communications campaigns. These approaches are moments of departure (when cultural elements are adapted) and moments of arrival (when cultural elements remain untouched). They discuss these in a human resources context: interpersonal communications in the workplace and team-building. For example, in Dubai, it is necessary to have Arabic designers, to have Indian staff to know how to talk to Indian audiences (a large proportion of the expatriate community in Dubai), as well as other people who can write English copy. Lee and Chandler show how each marketer's experience and identity help to connect the marketing team members, and then, in turn, help to connect the team, through cultural production, to the diverse audience in Dubai. The marketing professionals interviewed by Lee and Chandler adapt the work of marketing in different ways that include collaboration and learning with other marketers. The professionals rely on one another as sources of cultural knowledge. Deciding which cultural elements should stand on their own through moments of arrival, or which cultural elements can be adapted through moments of departure, is a cultural brokerage skill. Identifying the significance of cultural elements is especially important in Muslim markets. What are acceptable adaptations? For instance, Emirati consumers do not want to be portrayed as just Arab and Muslim; they have their own unique history, culture and future, separate from those of the other Gulf countries. The identity tensions resurface.

In Chapter 22, Rula Al-Abdulrazak and Derrick Chong also focus on the UAE. They evaluate its attempts to create a national identity and analyze how the government, along with international art organizations, is forging a center for world-class culture and art. This evaluation includes a review of discourses about Orientalism, cultural diplomacy, public diplomacy and nation branding. To nurture the brand of the UAE means to present stories and myths about it – although reality matters, it is possible, in a marketing sense, especially for those with vested interests, to help shape what is perceived as real. Not surprisingly, the UAE uses a non-traditional approach to cultural diplomacy by emphasizing the commercial culture associated with the art market trade (of buying and selling art). The UAE is developing an 'experience economy,' where a number of different experiences are possible, art being merely one. The experience matters in the minds of the visitors, tourists, and people who choose to live and work in the UAE. Like Prokopec and Kurdy in Chapter 12 and Lee and Chandler in Chapter 21, Al-Abdulrazak and Chong stress the diversity within the Muslim marketplace. While engendering common values is a key tenet of cultural diplomacy, and the UAE as a cultural hub accentuates this theme, the opportunity for adaptation and moments of departure is ever-present.

THE FUTURE

The two final chapters deal with the future of Islamic marketing. Paul Temporal in Chapter 23 focuses on what this future holds for practitioners, and in Chapter 24, Özlem Sandıkcı and Güliz Ger ponder the future of Islamic marketing for researchers. Islam, observes Temporal, is a way of life and Islamic values and principles influence the everyday lives of Muslims more so than in the case of any other faith. The growth of the Muslim middle class provides marketing opportunities at the same time as it fosters entrepreneurs from among its ranks. Temporal's emphasis is on branding and he considers both how Muslims can grow their own brands and how global companies can market to Muslims. He points to successful Muslim entrepreneurial ventures in social media, financial products, entertainment, food and clothing. Some of these ventures target only Muslims, but there are also brands that appeal more broadly. Ahiida Pty Ltd of Australia, marketer of the 'Burqini' (modest swimwear for Muslim women), has diversified into 'sunsafe swimwear'. The challenges for Muslim brands as they expand internationally and into the non-Muslim marketplace include building awareness, dealing with strong, established competitors and earning customer trust. Because Muslim firms often come from developing countries or even countries that have a poor image among Western buyers, nation branding is also imperative, according to Temporal. For global firms seeking to improve their performance among Muslim customers, Temporal emphasizes that while Muslims have similarities such as shared values, there are many differences among them: location, culture, language, religiosity and marketing sophistication. It is essential for practitioners to understand their market thoroughly, in order that they can engage in appropriate and effective emotional brand-building and communications.

Sandıkcı and Ger in Chapter 24 contemplate the reasons for the attention to Islam and marketing, now, at this particular juncture in time. Why did people ignore the Muslim market for so long? Why has it now come to the attention of researchers, consultants and managers? Political, socioeconomic and technological changes have led to the growth in a new class of Muslim entrepreneur: individuals who seek profit and success, but also want to maintain their faith. Members of the burgeoning Muslim middle class around the globe search for products and services that will help them solve problems in their lives. How can Muslim women who prefer to dress modestly still keep fit and engage in sports like swimming, for example?

Much scholarly interest in the Muslim market focuses on the differences between Muslims and non-Muslims and emphasizes the distinction between *halal* and *haram*. According to Sandıkcı and Ger, and as stressed by many other contributors to this *Handbook*, the Muslim market is heterogeneous and elements of it must be studied in context. It is too restrictive to examine the Muslim market solely through the perspective of religion. A valuable research approach is ethnoconsumerism: scholars should investigate specific Muslim groups in specific contexts and scrutinize the practices, discourses, power relationships and dynamics that typify those contexts. Such an outlook can also benefit executives, who then will discover additional business opportunities, whether these represent Muslim entrepreneurs with whom they might collaborate or new consumer market segments.

CONCLUSION

Muslims constitute around twenty per cent of the world population and actively participate in the global economy as investors, suppliers, manufacturers, bankers and traders. Muslim consumers represent one of the fastest growing consumer segments. However, despite its increasing significance, the intersection between Islam and marketing theory and practice remains still largely understudied and poorly understood. This *Handbook* addresses this gap and offers several valuable contributions to the study of Islamic marketing. Overall, the essays reveal the difficulties in describing and categorizing Islamic markets and the necessity of going beyond treating religion merely as a segmentation variable. Furthermore, the chapters point to several exciting research avenues, among which are: the socio-culturally informed analyses of consumption practices of Muslims in different locations; the aspirations, values and marketing practices of Muslim entrepreneurs; the influence of social media on the practices of Muslim consumers and marketers; and the public policy implications of Islamic marketing.

We conclude this introduction with a reemphasis on the complexity and multiplicity of the concept of 'Islamic marketing'. Rather than assuming that Islamic marketing will converge to some definitive and stable definition, we should acknowledge that there will always be multiple and even conflicting conceptualizations of the relationship between Islam, consumption, and marketing. It is our belief that through such multiplicity and diversity in research and practice, 'Islamic marketing' as a field will develop and enrich. We also believe that continuing research in this area will not only enable a deeper understanding of Muslims, both as consumers and as marketers, but will also contribute to the development of marketing theory. Understanding Muslim consumers and marketers, however, as understanding any consumer or marketer group, requires a situated understanding. Such a situated understanding goes beyond a focus on differences and instead emphasizes interactions and interrelationships. While differences culminate in a misperception of uniqueness, interactions allow generating productive and sustainable solutions. After all, we need to keep in mind that Muslim consumers are not only Muslim but *consumers* and Muslim marketers are not only Muslim but *marketers*. Hence, our goal should be not to prioritize one term over the other but to focus on their co-constitutive relationship.

PART I

MORALITY AND THE MARKETPLACE

2 Islamic ethics and marketing
Abbas J. Ali

The increasing acceptance of the multistakeholder concept in business practices constitutes a major milestone in the world of business. It highlights the significant contributions of organizations to society and gives credibility to the notion that at the end, it is society that grants legitimacy to any organization. Among business functions, marketing plays a pivotal role in the society. The marketing function is a 'social institution that is highly adaptive to its cultural and political context' (Wilkie and Moore, 2007). This reality, along with current global business developments, underscores the strategic link between cultural ethics and marketing.

Societies espouse various ethical principles which are assumed to be prioritized differently depending on cultural preferences and the importance attached to each. The evolution of business ethics in a culture is influenced by many factors including the stage of economic development, religion and openness. The interplay of these factors shapes how people in certain societies and time periods deal with business issues and emerging or pressing events. Religion, however, remains a determining force in ethics formation and application. Indeed, each religion has its own set of values and beliefs which in turn determines what is considered right and wrong and the standards upon which a behavior/ conduct is judged; in short, the application of values and beliefs to reality is ethics.

The elaboration of ethical prescriptions appears to differ across religions. Some religions, like Judaism and Islam, have detailed ethical instructions and treatises based in revelation. Others may have brief specifications of ethics or it may be left to the people to ponder relevant and necessary ethical guidelines in line with the general religious instructions. For example, Shintoism in Japan has no written scriptures, no body of religious law and each *kami* (spirit or god) presents certain social ethics and instructions. Likewise, Buddhism is not anchored on revelation and thus its philosophers have developed social ethics and spiritual precepts.

These differences in origin and nature of religion do not necessarily weaken their applications in the marketplace. Ultimately, it is the people and their respective institutions who give meaning and validity to ethical guidelines. The more attached people are to their religions, the stronger is their identification with and commitment to religiously sanctioned ethics. It is this particular point that makes Islamic ethics powerful and durable. Muslims across geography and time reiterate their commitment to their religious directives and in everyday conduct often utter ethical sayings and instructions. While this fact does not translate automatically into deeds, it does manifest the high likelihood of the continuity and renewal of religiously sanctioned ethics.

Marketing activities are an integral part of the economic system. Some of these activities are sanctioned and some not. Fisher (1988, p. 144) reiterated this when he stated, 'Despite the frequent assertion that sentimentality and the pursuit of economic interests don't mix, economic systems are in fact ethical systems. Whether by law and regulation or by custom, some economic activities are sanctioned while others are not. And what is sanctioned differs from culture to culture.' Such cultural differences make the understanding of ethical priorities a must for those who are engaged in marketing activities. This is because certain societal ethics are prioritized, often widely shared and therefore play a significant role in shaping marketing expectations and conduct.

Muslim societies are generally traditional, and their cultures have shown remarkable endurance despite rapid economic changes. This has situated the dominant ethics as a powerful standard for judging what is right and what is wrong. These ethics set the boundaries for acceptable conduct and, more importantly, are broadly utilized by members of the society in the assessment of individual character and morality. Since most of these societies are characterized by the supremacy of personal relations, the boundaries between personal and public roles are blurred. This fact alone deepens the influence of ethics in all spheres of life and helps to spread its impact to broader activities relative to societies with clearly delineated boundaries of private and public matters.

The purpose of this chapter, therefore, is to examine the nature and scope of marketing functions in light of Islamic ethics. However, this chapter not only provides insight into Islamic ethics in the marketplace, but also sheds light on ways of minimizing or preventing market abuses while having confidence in market institutions and assuring their vitality and continuity. The chapter offers a definition of Islamic ethics, reflects on the foundations of ethics, identifies pillars of Islamic ethics, outlines aspects of transactions conducted in accordance with normative Islamic ethics and provides certain implications. In constructing business or specific marketing arguments, the chapter relies heavily on the Qur'an, the sayings (*hadith*) of the Prophet Muhammad, and pre-modern and contemporary Muslim writers.

DEFINITION OF ISLAMIC ETHICS

Generally, ethics are the application of values to human actions and behaviors. In Islam, ethics deal with issues of right and wrong, morality of conduct and relationships in the marketplace. Ethics are moral standards that govern human conduct and individual relations with others. Islamic ethics are founded on four interrelated concepts: *ihsan*, relationship with others, equity and accountability. These set the framework for ethical conduct and behavior. The philosophy of *ihsan* implies goodness and generosity in interaction and conduct, be it at a personal or organizational level. *Ihsan* is a commonly held philosophy which closely shapes individual and group interaction within organizations. As a projection of goodness and generosity, *ihsan*, practically and spiritually, encompasses mercy, justice, forgiveness, tolerance and attentiveness. These aspects are related to the second element which is succinctly articulated by the Prophet Muhammad's saying: '*Al-din al-muaamala*' (religion is found in the way of dealing with other people). That is, judging whether any action or conduct is right or wrong must stem primarily from its benefit to people and society.

Stating it differently, the philosophy of *ihsan* treats relationships and interaction as primarily personal, non-discriminatory, and beneficial beyond self and immediate interests. The Qur'an (49:13) states, 'The noblest of you in the sight of God is the best of you in conduct.' The Prophet Muhammad underscored this when he defined the obligations of the faithful in terms of relationships to others and with a responsibility to: 'feed (the poor) and offer salutation to whom you know and to whom you do not know.' In the marketplace, the Prophet underscores the necessity of sincere and pleasant conduct: 'May God have mercy on the person who is generous when he buys and when he sells and in what he demands.' Human considerations, therefore, in the marketplace, take a priority in matters related to organizational conduct and exchange. According to the Qur'an (2:148), 'To each is a goal to which God turns him; then strive together towards all that is good.'

This non-discriminatory aspect, in terms of exchange, implies a fair and equal treatment of all players in the marketing process. The Qur'an (49:13) explains, 'O mankind! We created you from a single (pair) of male and female and made you into nations and tribes that you might know each other . . .' Knowing each other implies not only a quest for familiarity but also an exchange process. It is in this exchange process that neither coercion nor deception is sanctioned. This is exemplified by the saying of the Prophet, 'The buyer and the seller have the option (of cancelling the contract) as long as they have not parted, then if they are both truthful and transparent, their transaction shall be blessed, and if they conceal and tell lies, the blessing of their transaction shall be obliterated.' Furthermore, the goal of the exchange must be beneficial to all participants and to the society at large. The Prophet elevates selflessness to the level of faith in stating, 'None of you has faith unless he loves for his brother what he loves for himself' and 'Every good deed is charity.' This along with Qur'an instruction (49:13) is expected to lead to harmonious relations among players in the exchange function resulting in smooth transactions and operations.

Equity constitutes a necessary element in the workplace to ensure that social welfare is strengthened and fairness is not overlooked. It is reported that an Arab woman questioned the fourth Muslim Caliph, Ali (598–661 CE), because her food allowance was equal to that of a non-Arab female. He informed her, 'I looked in the Qur'an and did not find a preference for the sons of Ismail [Arabs] over those of Isaac [Jews]' (quoted in Glaachi, 2000, p. 39). Nevertheless, differences do exist in knowledge and capabilities. The Qur'an (46:19) states, 'And to all are degrees according to their deeds' and (39:9) 'Say: "Are those equal, those who know and those who do not know?" ' In marketing, this implies that while corporations should treat customers equally regardless of where they are residing, customers in their capacity to buy, spend and perceive marketing messages, among others, are different. These differences must be capitalized on in order to optimize service to customers and meet the demands of multistakeholders (influential actors who have an interest in the actions of a company).

The fourth foundation of Islamic ethics is responsibility. The Qur'an clarifies that what one does is solely his/her responsibility and no one should be held responsible for the mistakes of others (17:15): 'No bearer of burdens can bear the burden of another.' In the context of marketing, responsibility primarily centers on avoiding cheating and misleading others. For this reason, Islamic ethics prohibit hiding known defects. The Prophet instructs, 'A seller must not sell an item to a buyer without stating its defect' (quoted in Raghib, 1995, p. 341). Furthermore, decoy shoppers (those who bid on a product to induce a potential buyer to pay a higher price and elicit interest in the item or who intentionally lure a consumer to select a product over others) are prohibited as evidenced in the instruction of the Prophet: 'Decoying in sales is prohibited' (quoted in Raghib, 1995, p. 341).

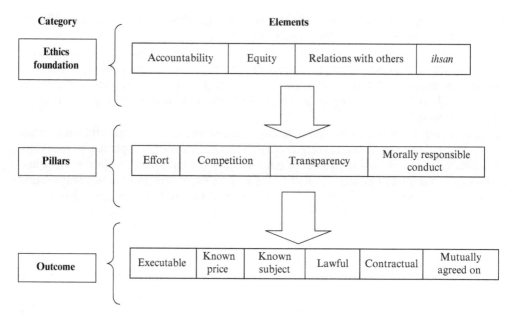

Figure 2.1   The interplay of transactional elements

Accordingly, Islamic ethics refer to specified rules that govern individuals and organizational conduct and seek to ensure generosity, openness, and accountability in behavior and actions while safeguarding societal interests. In the workplace, Islamic ethics are an orientation that shape and influence the involvement and participation of market actors to be transparent, responsible and committed to serving their interests without jeopardizing the welfare of other actors or the society (Ali, 2005). In the context of marketing, Islamic ethics seek to sustain responsible marketing conduct in accordance with religiously sanctioned instructions, from prevention of deception and fraudulent behavior to strengthening transparent operation and munificent behavior.

PILLARS OF ISLAMIC ETHICS

The preceding foundations give rise to certain pillars of ethics. In the context of Islamic normative instruction, transactions are assumed to be guided by the pillars of Islamic ethics and by the necessity to observe ethical foundations. While the foundations are general and related to all aspects of life, the pillars are equally applicable to the exchange function. Figure 2.1 depicts the relationships between ethical foundations, pillars of ethics and the expected outcome.

Islamic ethics, in their focus on exchange, relations with others and on benefiting society, establish moral boundaries for marketing functions. These boundaries constitute the sanctioned arena where interface with organizational stakeholders takes place. The latter, be they individuals or organizations, have their own aspirations, expectations and goals. In an environment of trust and responsible conduct, exchange is assumed to occur to the satisfaction of those who are involved. In contrast, where competing interests collide, the exchange function may not be optimally realized.

In the work place, Islamic ethics encompass four components: effort, competition, transparency and morally responsible conduct. Collectively, these pillars provide a practical framework for guarding the interests of those who are partners in the exchange function and those who might be affected indirectly. Indeed, the first two pillars thrive only when transparent and moral conduct is observed. The meaning and marketing implication for each component are briefly discussed.

Effort

Effort is a cornerstone of the Islamic Work Ethic (IWE). Effort is seen as the necessary ingredient for serving self and society. That is, productive involvement minimizes social and economic problems, while allowing a person to obtain reasonable living standards for self and family. What is significantly important is that effort in Islam is held in the highest regard. The Qur'an underscores this fact asserting (53:39), 'That a person can have nothing but what he strives for.' Moreover, the Qur'an links effort to productive and quality work. According to the Prophet: 'God blesses a person who perfects his craft (does the job right)' and 'God loves a person who learns precisely how to perform his work and does it right.' Perfection in marketing implies avoidance of deception, cheating, withholding of goods to manipulate prices, and so on.

Effort, too, implies purposeful conduct. The Qur'an (25:67) instructs believers to 'pursue not that of which you have no knowledge.' The fourth Muslim Caliph, Ali, states that a person 'who acts according to knowledge is like one whose road is clear' (Ali, 1989, p. 550). In this context, the Qur'an underlines that the end goal is serving people. That is, anything that an organization engages in should aim at furthering the interests of the people, meeting their ever-changing needs and satisfying them. Jasim (1986) argues that whatever serves people serves God. The Prophet Muhammad articulated this message in his sayings: 'The best work is that which results in benefit' and 'The best of people are those who benefit others' (quoted in Al-Barai, A. and Abdeen, 1987, p. 144). Consequently, the purpose of marketing in Islam should be to meet societal demands and to be in line with societal goals.

Likewise, effort implies not holding back. The Prophet instructs, 'Begin early to seek your livelihood and fulfill your aspirations because the effort ensures blessing and success' (quoted in Al Pashehi, 2004, p. 418). The fourth Muslim Caliph, Ali, asserted the same when he declared, 'Slothfulness opens the door to misery and produces scarcity leading to calamity' (quoted in Al Pashehi, 2004, p. 418). In marketing, the message is clear: companies should introduce products on a timely basis and customers should be served efficiently. Furthermore, marketing personnel should probe and anticipate market needs, offering products/services that satisfy market demands.

Competition

While Islam underscores the necessity for competition in the marketplace, it calls for responsible conduct to either prevent or minimize any harm to market participants or society. The Qur'an states (4:29), 'Eat not up your property among yourselves in vanities; but let there be amongst you trade by mutual good-will' and (2:275) 'God has permitted trade and forbidden usury.' In Islam, the whole globe is a market arena for competition and there are no limitations except on prohibited items and activities (for example alcohol, pork and gambling) and price manipulation. The Qur'an states (45:13), 'He [God] has also made subservient to you all that is in the heavens and the earth' and (62:10) 'disperse through the land and seek of the bounty of God.'

Though Hashim (2003) argues that competition in Islam is sanctioned, his view of competition focuses on the concept of racing. This is based on an event during which the Prophet organized a competition among muscular and skinny horses, and on an instruction in the Qur'an (8:60), 'Against them make ready your strength to the utmost of your power.' From these, he concluded that competition in Islam is permissible. The Qur'an encourages competition (*munafasa*) stating literally (83:26), 'let competitors compete' (Note: commonly it is translated as 'let those aspire, who have aspirations' by Qur'anic experts). Islamic instructions have certain conditions for competition. These are:

(a) It should ease market transactions rather than leading to monopolies and concentrations of power. The Prophet states, 'Whoever withholds a commodity from the market is a sinner' and, furthermore, 'He who brings goods to the market is blessed and the hoarder is cursed' (quoted in Mahmud, 2000, p. 158).

(b) There should be no manipulation of the price. The Prophet left that to market conditions. Two sayings attributed to him are commonly accepted (see Asaf, 1987; Raghib, 1995 for details). These are: 'If a buyer has an existing agreement with one seller, another seller should not ask the buyer to cancel his original agreement, so that he can sell him his commodities,' and 'Pricing belongs to God's domain. He provides and withholds sustenance. Therefore, I shall not determine pricing for fear that I would be questioned in the hereafter for possible harm done to any actor in the market.' The first saying implies that a buyer is about to buy a commodity and is approached by a rival who offers him better goods at the same or a lower price. This amounts to not only driving a competitor out of business, but it is also an unethical act that threatens confidence in market norms and operations. The second saying has far-reaching implications for market mechanisms. Not only should the state not intervene under normal conditions in setting the market price (Asaf, 1987, p. 212), but also the market is the best place, in its absence of manipulation and unrestrained access, to ensure fairness and justice. That is, the price should be left to supply and demand in order not to burden either the buyer or the seller. The fourth Muslim Caliph, Ali (1989, p. 331), instructed his governor saying, 'Buying and selling should be conducted in mutual consent . . . and fair prices for both buyer and seller. If anyone engages in monopoly after you have abolished it give him severe, but not excessive, punishment.' The state, however, may intervene in price setting in case of crisis or when prices skyrocket (Asaf, 1987).

(c) It should not be used to drive other competitors out of the market. It was reported that the second Muslim Caliph, Omar, noticed that a seller was deliberately lowering his prices and undercutting the prices of the rest. He told him 'either you bring your price up, or leave the market' (quoted in Raghib, 1995, p. 344). Dumping, therefore, is treated as an act that hurts other rivals and may lead to monopolies.

(d)   It should serve the public interest. As the Qur'an (16:90) instructs, 'God commands justice and *ihsan*' in any transaction, Muslim experts agree that competition should aim at enhancing the welfare of society and setting the foundations for just market operations (see Asaf, 1987; Glaachi, 2000). This is precisely the reason for outlawing hoarding. Hoarding is viewed as an obstruction of free market exchange and a manipulation of market function. It not only obstructs competition but also harms society and endangers its welfare. The Prophet states, 'He who brings goods to the market is blessed and the hoarder is cursed' and 'Shame on the hoarder when the price is low he is sad and when it is high he rejoices' (quoted in Glaachi, 2000, p. 16). Abu Talib al-Maki (died 996) recorded that a grain merchant sent a shipment to his agent in Basra, Iraq. He told him that the commodity must be sold on the day it arrived. The agent consulted with local merchants who told him they expected the price to go up the following Friday. The agent hoarded the shipment and sold it on the Friday, thus doubling the profit. When the agent informed his boss of his activities, the latter was angry and told his agent 'you violated our order and committed sin by hoarding . . . give all the amount of sales to the poor in Basra as I do not like to be party to hoarding'(Al-Maki, 1995, p. 508).

(e)   Competition should lead to improving the quality of products and services. That is, rivals should compete in introducing new and better quality goods or services (Asaf, 1987; Raghib, 1995). Like any other activity, competition should have an end game – serving the people.

Transparency

The need for trust and truthfulness in transaction are reiterated in the Qur'an and the Prophet's sayings. This underscores the necessity of having ethical and moral foundations. The Qur'an (22:30) instructs, 'Shun the word that is false.' The Prophet states that 'Truthfulness leads to good deeds and the latter guides to heaven' (quoted in Al-Hashimi (2001, p. 209). Truthfulness is a prerequisite for morally responsible transactions. For this reason, the Prophet asserted that 'He who cheated, is not one of us.' In the business world, truthfulness is seen as a mainstay for prosperity and success. According to the Prophet, 'The truthful, honest merchant is with the prophets.' Thus, he bestows on merchants who conduct their affairs with no duplicity a religious and economic prestige.

   In the marketplace, the transparency issue becomes essential for being a vital player. It was reported that the Prophet Muhammad once inspected a bin for dates and found that those that were not good were hidden underneath the fresh dates. The Prophet ordered the merchant to differentiate between the quality of the dates saying, 'He who cheated us is not one of us' and if buyers and sellers 'conceal and tell lies, the blessing of their transaction shall be obliterated.' His saying 'Those who declare things frankly will not lead to each other's destruction' underlies the significance of transparency in any business transaction and the necessity for enhancing trust and reducing problems in the marketplace. Transparency has a moral dimension as it manifests a commitment to the faith. It has, too, an economic dimension. This is because it is based on an understanding that faulty conduct and acts of deception obstruct justice and limit freedom of action in the marketplace. Morally based conduct is an essential precondition for sustaining a prosperous economy and a vital business community. Nasr (1984) asserts that Islam provides a climate of work within which the ethical is not separated from the economic. He argues (p. 35) that Islam bestows 'an ethical dimension on all kinds of work and in extending the ethical to include even the qualitative aspect of the work in question.'

Abu Talib al-Maki (1995, p. 509) reported a story which demonstrates that for the faithful, transparency in transaction is taken seriously. A representative to a sugar merchant informed his boss that the sugar crop that year was infected with disease. Thus, he urged the merchant to buy a large quantity of sugar and store it. The merchant bought a huge quantity from a supplier. When the time came the merchant sold the sugar making 30 000 dirham as profit. The next day, the merchant informed the supplier that he had committed a mistake in not revealing the complete information before he bought the sugar that the sugar crop for that season was infected and the price of the sugar in the market would go up. So, he requested the supplier to take the whole profit as it was lawfully his.

Morally Responsible Conduct

For the above pillars to be fruitful, they have to be based on morality. Competition, effort, and transparency may produce benefits to self and others in the short term. However, their durability without morally guided action is questionable in the long term and may lead to disastrous results. Islamic ethics sharply differ from the current prevailing philosophy on Wall Street. This philosophy states, 'If buyers and sellers can be found, we'll create and trade almost anything, no matter how dubious' (Samuelson, 2010). At least three aspects differentiate Islamic ethics from this belief. First, Islamic ethics place a priority on intention. In Islam, it is that intention rather than result that is the criterion upon which work is evaluated in terms of benefit to community. Any activity that is perceived to do harm, even though it results in significant wealth to those who undertake it, is considered unlawful. Prophet Muhammad stated, 'God does not look upon either your appearance or wealth, rather God examines your intentions and actions' and 'The value of work is derived from the accompanying intention rather than its results.' Second, Islam abhors deception and therefore it does not look favorably at the commonly uttered Western saying, 'Buyer beware.' The underlying assumption of this concept implies that deception is not only a possibility, but a normalcy of market operation. The prohibition of this saying stems primarily from the fact that it shifts the responsibility of inspection from the producer/supplier to the buyer or customer. That is, acting on this saying leads to a hidden cost and essentially it creates formidable obstacles to free and fair market practice. In fact, the concept implies that a competitive environment is inclined toward corruption and abuse. Third, dubious activities are considered obstructive for fruitful trade and legitimate business. Furthermore, certain activities are altogether prohibited (Qur'an 5:90): 'Intoxicants and gambling . . . are the devil's work, shun them' and (2:275) 'God hath permitted trade and forbidden usury.'

The ethical dimension of conduct is exemplified in the Islamic view of pricing and profit. While Islam, generally, sanctions prices that are determined freely in the marketplace, under conditions of emergency (for example, food crisis and price manipulation) when prices are rocketing, the state is permitted, as mentioned before, to intervene to place a temporary limit. There are two considerations, however, that should be kept in mind. The first is related to the quality of product, risk involved in distribution, and distance (Ibn Khaldun, 1989). If the risk is high, the sellers are permitted to charge higher prices to compensate for losses. Likewise, if the country of origin is far, the merchants may find it appropriate to charge a higher price than if it were sold in the home country or nearby cities. Ibn Khaldun states (1989, p. 310):

> It is more advantageous and more profitable for the merchant's enterprise if he brings goods from a country that is far away and there is danger on the road. In such a case, the goods transported will be few and rare . . . When goods are few and rare, their prices go up.

Similarly, the highest quality of any type of goods is demanded by wealthy people who are very few in number. Therefore, the price is normally high relative to the goods which are of 'medium quality' which suits the majority of the people.

The second consideration in pricing is related to the logic of *ihsan* and the degree of the seller's observance of the faith. In some cases, even though the competitive market may permit a higher price, a seller, guided by *ihsan,* may consider the state of customers and opt to charge them a price that they can handle. Recently, the *Washington Post* (see Bahrampour, 2010) reported on a Muslim farmer in Virginia who, in raising animals and in setting his prices, is motivated by his faith. The *Post* indicated that the market price for organic non-*halal* goat meat is anything between $12 and $14 a pound. But the Muslim farmer sells his meat for $3.75 to $4.75 a pound, just like any commercially produced nonorganic goat meat. The farmer was quoted saying, 'Philosophically speaking, the whole concept is, as social beings we have some responsibility – it's not just cutthroat I'll-make-as-much-as-I can.'

In the context of profit, there is agreement among scholars that the concept of profit maximization is inconsistent with Islamic ethics (for example, see Ali, 2005; Raghib, 1995). The fourth Caliph, Ali, stated, 'Do not discard the low profit margin, so you will not be deprived of more profit' (quoted in Ibn Al Josie (d. 1177), 1995). Likewise, a Sufi Muslim, Maruf Al Karkhi (d. 815), called for doing business transactions with little or no profit stating that 'Capital grows through transactions (like pastures)' (quoted in Jasim, 1990, p. 83). Moreover, Abu Talib al -Maki (died 996), an Islamic jurist and scholar, stated, 'God will bless your wealth though you engage in trade and commerce even without making a profit' (Al-Maki, 1995, p. 500).Islamic thinking views a moderate profit positively. Ibn Khaldun argued (1989, p. 312) that many times a little [profit] is much.' The preference for a moderate profit in Islamic ethics may stem from two reasons: Islamic precepts reflect an abhorrence of greed and a belief that maximization of profit harms society and obstructs the efficiency of the exchange system. The Qur'an (92:8–11) states, 'But he who is a greedy miser and thinks himself self-sufficient, . . . We will indeed make smooth for him the path to misery; nor will his wealth profit him when he falls headlong (into the pit).' Greed may harm society when a member of the transaction aspires to charge higher prices or withhold commodities hoping to accumulate wealth at the expense of others. It leads to injustice and adversely impacts market function. Such action, therefore, violates market trust and ethical principles. Actions inspired by greed weaken trust in business relationships and market institutions. More importantly, as Rice (1999) argued, an obsession with material wealth can obscure the ultimate objective of enriching human lives.

Therefore, morally based conduct is an essential precondition for sustaining a prosperous and functional economy. Nasr (1984) asserts that Islam provides a work environment within which the ethical is not separated from the economic. He argues (p. 35) that Islam bestows 'an ethical dimension on all kinds of work and in extending the ethical to include even the qualitative aspect of the work in question.'

ETHICAL OUTCOMES

The general foundations of ethics and their related pillars are shaped by early Islamic vision and events. It is useful, therefore, to probe first three general aspects which shaped market conduct during the formative years of the Islamic state: the focus of the early years of the Islamic state on trade and related activities, the merchants' roles in society being favorably perceived and an unwavering commitment to safeguarding human interests. To put things in perspective, it should be noted that, according to Islamic belief and tradition, God first revealed Islam to the Prophet Muhammad in Arabia in a cave on Mount Hira near Mecca around 610. Prior to the revelation, Muhammad served as a trade representative to a Meccan merchant woman, whom he later married. Mecca, before the emergence of Islam, was both a trade and spiritual center for Arabs who lived in Arabia and the surrounding area.

A few trade centers existed at the time in addition to Mecca. These were Yathrib, Aden, and Akhaz which were scattered in and around Arabia. Mecca and Yathrib were more prominent than the others, mainly because people from major tribes and from various cultural backgrounds and religious beliefs populated them. In Mecca, the trade was controlled by members of the Quraeshi tribe, especially the Umayyad clan. In Yathrib, trade was primarily in the hands of the Jews. Since there was no central government and the nearby empires never managed to control the heart of Arabia, trade routes were subjected to constant raids by various tribal groups. Powerful social classes had to provide protection to all trade centers. These classes allied themselves with the military and political forces in and around Arabia to secure trade routes and ensure their profitability. Because of the absence of law and order, trading involved high risks and traders experienced great hardships in bringing both essential and luxurious commodities to major cities. Consequently, Arabians regarded merchants with respect. Moreover, merchants were not only the primary instrument in maintaining survival and prosperity for communities, but they were also perceived to be courageous and brave – qualities that were admired by traditional Arab society.

The emergence of the new faith, Islam, added a religious dimension to engaging in trade and business activities. Work was seen as a divine duty. The Prophet Muhammad preached that hard work causes sins to be absolved and assured that 'there is no better food than that which has been gained from one's labor.' Like traders, moneylenders had assumed an important social and economic role before Islam. They facilitated the operations of merchants, farmers, and chiefs of tribes. However, due to economic uncertainty, war and changing allegiances, moneylenders tended to charge interest well above the principal. This practice, while accelerating the accumulation of wealth for moneylenders, enlarged the gulf between the rich and the rest of society. This very reason, along with the perception that high interest rates could place unbearable burdens on merchants and the general public, was why usury was prohibited by Islam. As the Qur'an states (Qur'an: 2:275), 'God has permitted trade and forbidden usury.'

Recognizing the importance of trade in the survival and the continuity of the new city-state, the Prophet Muhammad emphasized that merchants should perform tasks that were not only morally required, but essential for the survival and flourishing of a society. He declared, 'I commend the merchants to you, for they are the couriers of the horizons and God's trusted servants on earth' and 'the honest, truthful Muslim merchant will stand with the martyrs on the Day of Judgment' (see Ali, 2005 for details). Likewise, his son-in-law and the fourth caliph, Ali, in his letter to the Governor of Egypt, demonstrated his esteem for merchants as he urged the Governor to:

> Take good care of the merchants and artisans, and ensure their well-being whether they are settled or traveling, or working on their own. Those are the providers of benefits and goods, which they bring from far away by sea or by land through mountains and valleys, securing them for people who are unable to reach them. Those are the people who will assure you of durable peace and respected allegiance. Give them due care in your vicinity and in other areas of your land. (Ali, 1989, p. 329–30)

During the first six centuries of Islam's Golden Age (from the seventh century of the Common Era), trade, industry, agriculture, and construction of complex organizations flourished. Work and creativity were honored in all their forms. Subsequent dynasties that came to power committed to merchants and artisans and were guided both by their understanding of the crucial role that trade plays in maintaining stability and economic prosperity and by their faith which was articulated by Qur'anic principles and prophetic prescriptions. Even after the collapse of the Islamic state, when the Mongols captured Baghdad in 1258 CE, the essence of trade and work was present in Muslim minds. For example, Ibn Khaldun (1332–1406 CE), the medieval Arab sociologist, argued (1989, p. 238), 'civilization and its well-being, as well as business prosperity, depends on productivity and people's efforts in all aspects for their own interest and profit. When people no longer do business in order to make a living, and when they cease all gainful activity, the business of civilization slumps and everything decays.' He asserted that labor is the source of value, stating (p. 241), 'labor belongs to the things that constitute capital. Gain and sustenance represent the value realized from labor among civilized people. By their efforts and all their labors they (acquire) capital and (make a) profit.' More importantly, Ibn Khaldun considered trade to be a source for economic growth, thereby bestowing on marketing and exchange activities a significant role in maintaining affluence. He stated (p. 300), 'Commerce is a natural way to make a profit' and (p. 312) 'In the attempt to earn the increase (of capital) that constitutes profit, it is unavoidable that one's capital gets into the hands of traders, in the process of buying and selling and waiting for payment.' Ibn Khaldun argued that, once a society and civilization progressed and cities were established, the public would start thinking about luxurious items and various forms of industries would flourish. He stated (p. 315):

> When civilization flourishes and the luxuries are in demand, it includes the refinement and development of the crafts . . . When the civilization is fully developed, these different kinds are perfected and refined to the limit . . . In fact, they become the most lucrative activities, because urban luxury demands them.

The third aspect – an unwavering commitment to safeguarding human interests – conveys that everything on earth is created to serve mankind and to minimize burdens. The Qur'an (67:15) states, 'It is He Who has made the earth manageable for you, so traverse through its tracts and enjoy of the sustenance which He furnishes' (70:24–25); 'those in whose wealth is a recognized right for the (needy) who asks and him who is deprived' and (57:7) '. . . spend (in charity) out of (substance) whereof He has made you heirs.' According to the Prophet Muhammad 'The best of people are those who benefit others.' Similarly, the fourth Caliph, Ali (1989, p. 706), stated, 'Do not shy from giving only a little; deprivation is still less.' These are clear instructions with specific implications for the exchange process and marketing functions in particular. Furthermore, in Islamic teaching, human beings are considered custodians of their surrounding environment. As such, individuals and their organizations must not only be responsible for its thriving but also show an understanding of the linkage between their welfare and the protection of nature – be it earth or atmosphere. Nature is the whole of which people and corporations are a part. Therefore, protecting it is part of the process that furthers people's interests and those of their society.

Likewise, the above instructions convey that if wealth is to flourish those members of society who are in need should not be neglected. Corporations are in a position to move beyond providing monetary contributions and should embark, in their marketing activities, on innovative ways to make their products accessible to those who are less fortunate. This does not mean that corporations should offer charity, but it suggests that corporations in their distribution and marketing methods should be creative in meeting the demands of the poor and those in far places.

The aforementioned aspects, along with the pillars of Islamic ethics, set the boundaries for morally accepted transactions and result in contracts which have the following qualities:

(a)   Mutual agreement.   There should be no coercion in the transaction. The Qur'an (4:29) specifies that it must be an outcome of mutual agreement, free of any deception or coercion: 'let there be amongst you trade by mutual good-will.'

(b)   Contractual.   Contractual agreements intended so that neither party's rights or duties are overlooked and promises are fulfilled without serious misunderstandings or disagreements. The Qur'an instructs (2:282):

> To write (your contract) for a future period, whether it be small or big, it is more just in the sight of God, more suitable as evidence, and more convenient to avoid doubts among yourself. But if it be a transaction which you carry out on the spot among yourselves, there is no blame on you if you reduce it not to writing. But have witnesses whenever you make a commercial contract and let neither scribe nor witness suffer harm.

(c)   Lawful.   The subject of transaction must be lawful (for example, distributing alcohol, drugs, and gambling are prohibited). Furthermore, any contract that involves usury is prohibited. The Qur'an states (2:275), 'Those who devour usury will not stand except as one whom Satan by his touch has driven to madness. . . . God has permitted trade and forbidden usury.'

(d)   Items of the transaction are known to each partner   (Asaf, 1987; Glaachi, 2000). That is, the parties to the contract must know exactly what they are embarking on. In case of purchasing, the Prophet instructs, 'He who bought something without having seen it, has the option to reject it after seeing it' (quoted in Asaf, 1987, p. 230).

(e)   Known and agreed upon price   The amount of the transaction item should be known to each party. Though under certain conditions the price is left to experts to appraise, the party to the contract has the right to dissolve the contract (see Asaf for details).

(f)   Execution   The subject of transaction is deliverable. In the case of selling, the Prophet instructs, 'Do not sell that which you do not have' (quoted in Glaachi, p. 108).

APPLICATIONS AND IMPLICATIONS

Islamic ethics set the boundaries for acceptable conduct and behavior. Corporations and individuals who are responsible for marketing functions are judged, by the state and the society, on whether they carry out their activities in line with sanctioned ethics. Observing Islamic ethics situates corporations in a competitive position and eases market growth and expansion. However, the focus of Islamic ethics, as discussed before, places priority on meeting social demands and enhancing societal welfare. The question is, 'does this priority prevent corporations from conducting their business activities in the market-place?' To answer this question, two issues stand out: the meaning of marketing and the role of organization in the society. The American Marketing Association defines market-ing as an 'organizational function and a set of processes for creating, communicating, and delivering value to customers and for managing customer relationships in ways that benefit the organization and its stakeholders' (quoted in Ferrell, 2007, p. 860). The defini-tion highlights two important elements: benefiting stakeholders and delivering value to customers. Though the latter sounds specific in the context of customers, any benefits to customers are by necessity a benefit to the society. Their interests are broad and generally approximate that of the larger society and they come from various segments and social groups. The stakeholders, however, can be anyone who has a stake in the corporation or is influenced by or concerned with its activities. Those concerns reflect, to a larger degree, that of the society. Since the primary concern of Islamic ethics is societal welfare, their precepts provide useful guidelines for marketing functions and processes. This ranges from promotion and pricing, to packaging, distribution, storing, and delivery. For example, Islamic ethics prohibit deception in advertising and exaggerating benefits, char-acteristics, or qualities of a commodity. The sellers are held responsible for any trickery or unfounded claims. Unlike prevailing market ethics in some Western countries which endorse profit maximization and drive competitors out of business, Islamic ethics do not consent to such intentional and deliberate actions.

According to Islamic ethics, firms are primarily social and economic actors that gain their legitimacy from optimally serving societal interests and evolving needs. It is this legitimacy that allows organizations to compete, create value, and grow. In fact, adher-ing to general instructions of avoiding deception, cheating, and manipulating the public

Table 2.1   Selected ethical issues and their marketing implications

Category	Implications
Profit margin	A moderate profit benefits the company and does not inflict harm on society; excessive profit manifests greed and limits its market
Usury	Avoid issues related to imposing interest[a] in any transaction; alternatives exist and should be discussed with experts before any are selected
Consumerism	A drive to maintain balanced tendencies; maintain modesty in spending according to Qur'anic instructions (25:67): 'Those who, when they spend, are not extravagant and not niggardly, but hold a balance between those extremes'
Bribes	Prohibited religiously and prudence is required in considering them
Generosity	Should market different variations of a product to satisfy customers with varying income levels, utilize discount policy, and offer free samples, especially in areas where less fortunate subjects reside
Deception	Fraudulent activities weaken confidence in market institutions and may result in market turmoil
Transparency	Openness and truthfulness enhance customer loyalty and market reputation
Competition	Avoid destructive approaches and those which drive rivals out of business
Effort	Commitment to contractual agreements, meeting promotional promise, and reciprocating offers
Moral responsibility	Commitment to the welfare of society is not divorced from commitment to safeguarding the environment

Note: [a] Hasan (2008) indicates that Muslim scholars agree, with few dissentions, that in Islam the prohibition of *riba* is total and complete. The verdict makes no distinction between usury and interest.

situates firms as responsible players in the marketplace and the society. That is, from an Islamic perspective, firms have obligations toward the society and meeting these obligations enhances their reputation and ultimately strengthens their survival and competitive position. Indeed, as firms shun deception and are transparent, they not only minimize their overall transaction cost but also engage their suppliers, customers, and even competitors in matters that have both organizational and societal benefits.

Islamic ethics have useful implications for marketers. These ethics and their corresponding implications are provided in Table 2.1. The emphasis here is on the most relevant and essential ethics that frequently confront marketers. In particular, we cover ethical issues which have either specific marketing implications (for example usury, bribery, consumerism and profit margin) and those which are general in their meaning but have far-reaching impact on the position of the firm in the marketplace (for example transparency, competition and moral responsibility).

The listed ethical categories and their implications underscore the fact that the marketing function and process are an integral part of the organization and its goal for enhancing survival and growth, while serving societal goals and meeting emerging needs. That is, ethical conduct sends a clear message to stakeholders that societal goals and priorities are a strategic concern for the company. More importantly, commitment to ethical conduct manifests a moral stance where a company views its employees and customers

Table 2.2   Selected marketing elements and their implications

Elements	Implications
Price	Should take into consideration the risk involved, geographic distance, season, and quality. Executives should consider the welfare of the community and market conditions in setting prices
Hoarding	Avoid it as it is not looked on favorably; hoarding for personal use is permitted
Product	Avoid dealing with a prohibited product. Quality should be satisfactory to a wide range of the population
Value creation	Delivering new products, finding new applications, improving quality, etc. all serve as instruments for positioning a firm competitively.
Promotion	Avoid exaggeration or claims that are difficult to prove
Place	Transactions should take place in the market and be documented

equally as citizens and their desires and aspirations are considered in marketing planning and execution.

Table 2.2 presents the implications for specific elements of marketing and related issues. The implications of these highlight that the philosophy of *ihsan* is assumed to permeate all organizational activities. For example, pricing policies may differ due to various factors but should not hurt either the seller or the buyer. Ibn Taymiyah, (died 1328 CE) stated, 'forcing sellers, without sound reason, to sell at an unfavorable price or prohibiting them from that which God has made permissible is religiously unacceptable' (1900, p. 14). However, mutual agreement and societal well-being shape the direction of pricing deliberations. Likewise, promotion should revolve around upholding the truth while advancing the corporate goals in the marketplace. In other words, in line with Qur'anic instructions (2:83), 'Speak fair to the people'; marketers in their advertising, sales promotions and packaging activities should neither boast false claims nor should they inflate the quality or the safety standard of their products. They should, too, give buyers the opportunity to make their own minds up without undue pressure.

Other important dimensions identified in Tables 2.1 and 2.2, such as profit margins, generosity, consumerism, and competition set Islamic ethics apart from what prevails in some western countries. Profit maximization is not sought. Rather, a modest profit is thought to serve self and society better. Likewise, generosity implies that parties to a contract should go beyond what is specified in the contract to ensure *ihsan* and harmonious relations. For example, in the service contract the provider often performs additional services free of charge. The Qur'an (64:16) declares, 'And those saved from the covetousness of their own souls – they are the ones that achieve prosperity.'

Traditionally, the market place has been a designated public area where exchange functions are performed and/or sales are set up. However, modern developments in technology now make virtual markets not only a possibility but also a necessity. In fact, the flourishing of Internet marketing activities in the world, including countries with Muslim majorities, has opened new avenues for marketers. Marketers, however, should still observe the aforementioned morally accepted transaction elements. That is, whether on the Internet or in a designated open area, market transactions should be carried out according to sanctioned ethical norms.

The notion of 'I am what I buy' in consumerism is not appreciated and is perceived as extravagant behavior inconsistent with core religious beliefs of maintaining a balance between one's own interests and those of the society. That is, celebrating consumption and spending for the sake of shopping may not fare well with the concept of moderation and *ihsan*. Likewise, *ihsan* finds its full expression in the marketplace through the sanctioned meaning of competition. Competitors are not expected to engage in cutthroat activities. These are treated as aggressive attempts aimed at driving one's rivals out of the market. While Islamic ethics condone free market principles, they place limitations on behaviors which are perceived to be destructive to both market actors and society at large. Competition in the Qur'an is treated as an instrument to inspire and energize rather than frustrate and destroy. Likewise, marketers have to take note that in Muslim societies, customers react favorably to messages and advertisements that underscore societal norms and the contributions of corporations to the community. This, along with the perception that firms create value to society constitutes a social capital essential for positioning the company strategically.

CONCLUSION

In this chapter, Islamic ethics are examined as they relate to marketing functions and processes. First, the paper has explored the factors that induce Muslims to give priority to trade and commerce. Trade was essential to facilitating the survival of the new Muslim city-state and the risks and hardships that merchants experienced situated them in positions of respect and influence. Foundations of Islamic ethics have been discussed in the context of today's business world. These foundations establish the boundaries for morally accepted conduct and set the stage for performing market activities in a purposeful way. The exchange functions and market processes are viewed as instruments to create value for society without discarding the benefits to the organizations. This balanced tendency is founded in the logic of *ihsan*, which strengthens the drive to do what is good and minimizes the urge to engage in questionable behavior.

A few primary implications stand out. In a free market economy, marketers face the pressures of competition and often seek profit maximization goals. These pressures may induce marketers to overlook Islamic ethics, therefore making the application of *ihsan* impossible. However, in an Islamic setting, observing the prescriptions of *ihsan* and other ethical elements strengthens relationships with customers and communities. This eventually leads to improving a company's public image and market share, and situates the firm competitively.

Furthermore, in today's business environment, where customers are generally informed and identify with and are sensitive to their cultural identity, executives may find it rewarding to serve vibrant Muslim segments in various parts of the world. For example, the *halal* (lawful) industry has recently flourished and is worth about $2.1 trillion (Campbell, 2008). In fact, the *halal* food market is expected to reach 20 per cent of the global trade by 2025 (Watts, 2009). The *halal* industry is broad and is not confined to meat and grocery markets but includes other sectors such as tourism, financial services, and cosmetics. In recent years, Muslims have shown increasing interest in products and services that provide information about their compliance with *halal* specifications. Therefore, firms that are known for their commitment to *halal* standards, be they in tourism, retailing, banking or the food industry, are destined to gain a competitive advantage over their rivals.

More importantly, due to the recent publicity of corporate frauds and corruption, there has been an increasing demand for government regulation of corporate activities and involvement. By observing Islamic prescriptions and factoring societal demands and needs into decision making, as well as the necessity for creating value for society, marketers can minimize the risk of intrusive government regulations and reduce, if not avoid, the possibility of costly litigation and public outrage.

Researchers, too, may find it intellectually challenging to address the vitality of Islamic ethics in enhancing market functions and minimizing fraud and corruption. In particular, future research should tackle the application of Islamic ethics in marketing processes, functions and innovation. In particular, researchers should explore the rise and evolution of Islamic marketing. Furthermore, as Muslim communities across the globe become socially mobile and economically vibrant, there is a need to investigate their market needs and to determine how such needs can be optimally met through product adaptation and innovation.

This chapter underscores the linkage between cultural ethics and marketing. Indeed, marketing functions are characteristically linked and associated with prevailing cultural norms and values. The more widely and deeply held these values and norms (for example, elements of *ihsan,* prohibition of usury, and so on), the deeper they shape marketing expectations and conduct. As members of a society become more aware and sensitive to their cultural values and identity, the more they expect organizations to market goods and services that conform to their beliefs.

However, most scholars have been indoctrinated with the notion that corporations have to seek profit maximization. In most business schools, this doctrine has not been challenged and is taken for granted. Islamic teachings, as documented in this chapter, abhor profit maximization. Scholars working in Muslim countries or who serve as consultants to MNCs should revisit this doctrine and devise a paradigm which takes into consideration Islamic prescriptions without endangering the survivability of the firm.

Furthermore, the interplay between ethical foundations and the pillars of ethics in the marketplace can produce a market exchange which ensures firm integrity while guarding societal interests. Indeed, the internalization of the pillars of ethics by market actors minimizes selfish desires and tendencies to corruption, thereby guaranteeing smooth market operations, strengthening trust in market institutions and actors, and safeguarding the interests of participants in the exchange process.

It is argued in the chapter that the early Islamic conceptualization of marketing as a process for meeting the ever-changing needs of customers and societies underscores the link between society and business. The challenge is how to make organizations in societies with Muslim majorities which have been influenced by the Western conceptualization of business more in tune with Islamic prescriptions. This task requires the cooperation of business people and scholars and the building of independent foundations for furthering knowledge creation responsive to social and cultural developments.

In summary, both managers and researchers may find the discussion and the religious instructions and justifications relevant to addressing and dealing with prevailing and emerging marketing issues. The chapter presents the argument that Islamic ethics provide a practical framework for guarding the interests of those who are partners in the exchange function and those who might be affected indirectly. Only morally driven conduct inspires confidence in the market and reinforces social contracts and ethical understanding, and encourages market players to focus their priorities on meeting their organizational responsibilities while serving societal interests.

REFERENCES

Al-Barai, A. and A Abdeen (1987), *Management in Islamic culture*, Jeddah, Saudi Arabia: Modern Service Library.
Al-Hashimi, Ahmed (2001), *Selected Hadiths of the Prophet*, Beirut, Lebanon: al-Maktaba Alysyria.
Al-Maki, Abu Talib (1995), *Qut Al-Qulub, Part II*, Beirut, Lebanon: Dar Sader Publishers.
Al Pashehi, Shihabaldeen (2004), *Al Mustatrif*, Beirut, Lebanon: Al Noor Publishing Institute.
Ali, Imam (1989), *Nahjul Balagah* (translated and edited by F. Ebeid), Beirut, Lebanon: Dar Alkitab Al-Lubnani.
Ali, Abbas (2005), *Islamic Perspectives on Management and Organization*, Edward Elgar, Cheltenham, UK and Northampton, MA, USA.
Asaf, M. (1987), *The Islamic Way in Business Administration*, Cairo, Egypt: Ayen Shamis Library.
Bahrampour, T. (2010), 'Muslim immigrant fills niche raising goats on Virginia farm', *Washington Post*, 13 April, B1.
Campbell, S. (2008), 'Tapping the *halāl* market', *Arabian Business*, 15 October. available at http://www.arabianbusiness.com/534137-tapping-the-halāl-market.
Ferrell, O.C. (2007), 'Nature and scope of marketing ethics', in G. Gundlach, L. Block, and W. Wilkie (eds), *Exploration of Marketing in Society*, Mason, OH: Thompson Higher Education, pp. 858–75.
Fisher, G. (1988), *Mindsets: The Role of Culture and Perception in International Relations*, Yarmouth, ME: International Press.
Glaachi, M. (2000), *Studies in Islamic Economy*, Kuwait: Dar An-Nafaes.
Hasan, Zubair (2008), 'Theory of profit from Islamic perspective', International Islamic University, Malaysia (IIUM), Kuala Lumpur. Available at http://mpra.ub.uni-muenchen.de/8129/MPRA Paper No. 8129, posted 08. April 2008
Hashim, A. (2003), 'The concept of competition and award in Islam', *Arab Law Quarterly*, **18** (3/4), 309–25.
Holy Qur'an (1989), *English Translation of the Meanings and Commentary*, Al-Madinah Al-Munawarah King Fahd Holy Quar'an Printing Complex.
Ibn Al Josie, Abu Alfaraj (1995), *The Organized in the History of Kings and Nations*, Beirut, Lebanon: Dar Al kitob Al Alymaeha.
Ibn Khaldun, Abd al-Rahman (1989), *The Magaddimah* (trans. Franz Rosenthal, ed. N.J. Dawood), Princeton, NJ: Princeton University Press.
Ibn Taymiyah, Ahmad (1900), *al-Hisba fi al-Islam* (*Public Duties in Islam*), Cairo, Egypt: Al-Mu'ayyad Print.
Jasim, Aziz Syed (1986), *The Tormented Flower*, Baghdad, Iraq: Al-Yagdha Al Arabia Bookstore.
Jasim, Aziz Syed (1990), *Sufi of Baghdad*, Baghdad, Iraq: Shrekit AlMuarifa for Publishing and Distribution.
Mahmud, Hussein (2000), *Financial and Economic System in Islam*, Riyadh, Saudi Arabia: Dar Al Naser Al Dawely.
Muhammad Ali, M. (1977), *A Manual of Hadith*, New York: Olive Branch Press.
Nasr, S. (1984), 'Islamic work ethics', *Hamdard Islamicus*, **7** (4), 25–35.
Raghib, H. (1995), 'Islamic values and beliefs and their impact on marketing policy: comparative analysis study', in M. Al-Barai and M. Marcy (eds), *Management in Islam*, Jeddah, Saudi Arabia: Islamic Institute for Training and Research, pp. 307–55.
Rice, G. (1999), 'Islamic ethics and the implications for business', *Journal of Business Ethics*, **18**, 345–58.
Samuelson, R. (2010), 'Goldman's rendezvous with reality', *Washington Post*, 22 April, A19.
Watts, B. (2009), 'Reaping the reward,' *Arabian Business*, 28 November. Available at http://www.arabianbusiness.com/573757-reaping-the-rewards.
Wilkie, W. and E. Moore (2007), 'Marketing's contributions to society', in G. Gundlach, L. Block and W. Wilkie (eds), *Exploration of Marketing in Society*, Mason, Ohio: Thompson Higher Education, pp. 2–39.

3 *Fatwa* rulings in Islam: a Malaysian perspective on their role in Muslim consumer behaviour
Nazlida Muhamad

INTRODUCTION

For many, the word *fatwa* is synonymous with the infamous death penalty sentence declared by Ayatollah Khomeini for Salman Rushdie in 1989. For others, a *fatwa* permits Muslims to use suicide bombing in Middle East conflicts. In reality, *fatwa* rulings play a larger role than permitting the death penalty in the Muslim community. In the modern world, *fatwa* rulings guide and shape Muslim consumers' marketplace behaviours.

The Muslim market is a large and growing religious segment whose behaviour tends to be significantly influenced by Islamic rulings. Recently, there has been evidence of a religious awakening and greater conservatism in the Muslim world (Bokhari, 2007; Hague and Masuan, 2002; Pereira, 2005; Perlez, 2007). A recent survey reported that the majority of Muslims identify themselves as Muslims first, rather than as belonging to a particular nationality (for example Malay or Malaysian, British or English) (Anonymous, 2006; Yusof, 2009). Frustrated with problems of the modern world, such as materialism, many Muslims report seeing Islamic teachings as a solution to modern social problems (Aziz and Shamsul, 2004). This highlights the huge potential influence of *fatwa* rulings on Muslim consumers.

A *fatwa* declaration is a mechanism that allows new rulings to be introduced into *sharia* law. It is a product of Islamic scholars' *(ulama)* interpretation and adaptation of Qur'anic verses and *hadith* on contemporary issues, rather than explicit doctrine from the Qur'an or *hadith* (Wiechman, et al. 1996). A *fatwa* declaration is a dynamic ruling mechanism in *sharia* law that makes it relevant throughout time. A *fatwa* in Islamic law provides contemporary rulings on current issues, and evidence suggests that it has an effect on Muslim consumer behaviour. However, much about *fatwa* rulings and their impact on Muslim consumer behaviour remains unknown to marketers and businesses. Given the growing trend of Muslims turning to their religion for guidance, *fatwa* rulings are emerging as important sources for forming Muslim consumers' decision-making in the marketplace.

This chapter explains the position of *fatwa* rulings in Islam and Muslim communities, describes the mechanism of *fatwa* declarations, delineates the types and categories of *fatwa* rulings, and discusses recent issues in regards to *fatwa* rulings in the global marketplace. Also discussed are Muslim consumers' motivations in following their religion as they make choices among products and services. Lastly, the chapter offers suggestions to marketers for dealing with *fatwa* rulings. These issues are discussed in the Malaysian context.

EVIDENCE OF MUSLIM CONSUMERS' RELIANCE ON ISLAMIC TEACHINGS

To recognize the potential effects of *fatwa* on Muslim consumers, we need to be informed about religion's importance and position in these consumers' lives. We must also understand where *fatwa* fits in this picture.

According to Bailey and Sood (1993), Muslim consumers tend to be more committed to their religious beliefs and practices than those of other faiths. Comparisons between Muslims' and other believers' acceptance of several shared major religious beliefs and practices showed that more Muslims report that they still believe and practise the doctrines of their faith as compared with other believers. For example, whereas 82 per cent of Muslims reported that they believe in a Day of Judgement, fewer Christians (60 per cent of Catholics and 54 per cent of Protestants) and Jews (22 per cent) reported that they accept that belief. Muslims' higher commitment to religious beliefs and practices is also reflected in other areas, such as prohibitions on eating certain foods, and fasting. Findings from Bailey and Sood (1993) also show that more Muslims than Hindus or Jews report that they accept taboos on certain types of foods.

Muslims' commitment to Islamic rulings is also evidenced in contemporary business; many businesses today offer financial products based on Islamic financial principles, including the Dow Jones *sharia*-compliant bond and no-interest loans (El Qorchi, 2005). Financial giants such as Lloyds TSB (UK) offer Islamic business accounts, mortgages, insurance and bonds (Bokhari, 2007). Generally, we can say that Muslim consumers tend to have a greater need to live their lives based on their religious beliefs, rules and regulations as compared to other believers. Along the way, they are likely to turn to Islamic solutions that satisfy their consumer needs and wants.

Because Islam is more than 1400 years old, specific modern needs and wants are not individually addressed in the Islamic main texts – the Qur'an and the *hadith*. To fill this gap, *fatwa* rulings offer an interpretation of the verses of the Qur'an and *hadith* in light of the contemporary issues raised by Muslims. Owing to the rise in contemporary issues (such as product innovations and modern needs and wants that are not addressed directly in the original *sharia* sources), *fatwa* rulings have become a fundamental element in the life of modern Muslims.

It is imperative to know the key players in *fatwa* declarations and to understand the nature and sources of *sharia* law in order to appreciate the role of *fatwa* rulings in Muslim consumer behaviours.

THE ROLE OF THE *ULAMA* IN THE MUSLIM WORLD

In order to understand how *sharia* law influences Muslims in the form of *fatwa* rulings, it is essential to discuss the main authority in *sharia* law, the *ulama* . In Arabic, the word *ulama* (singular: *alim*) means 'knowledgeable people'; the *ulama* are considered to be the most knowledgeable people in a Muslim society (Azra, 2005). The *ulama* are scholars who specialize in Islamic law, usually with a formal *sharia* law qualification from a well-known Islamic university, such as the Al-Azhar University in Cairo (Hossain, 2002). Since the Prophet Muhammad died more than 1400 years ago, religious Muslim communities, if not all Muslims, turn to individuals who are considered knowledgeable in religious matters for guidance on how to apply Islam in their lives (Azra, 2005).

The concept of an 'established church' does not exist in the Islamic religion as it does in Christianity (Sedgwick, 2000). The *ulama* may be the only source of religious identity. Thus, they play an important role in Muslim society (Sedgwick, 2000). In Muslim states, prominent *ulama* are made the *mufti* of the state, or are involved in a committee to oversee applications of *sharia* law (Sedgwick, 2000). For example, Harussani is a *mufti* of the state of Perak in Malaysia, head of the *fatwa* Committee for the state (Anonymous, 2008c) and also a member of the Malaysian National *Fatwa* Committee (Anonymous, 2008b). Yusuf Al-Qaradawi is a renowned Egyptian Sunni *alim* (Pierret, 2005; Sachedina, 1990) who lives in Qatar (Sivan, 2003), and is well recognized and influential among Muslim communities throughout the Sunni world (Bruinessen, 2003). He is a professor with a doctoral degree in *sharia* law from Al-Azhar University in Cairo (Sivan, 2003). Quoted by scholars in various disciplines, he has published important books on *sharia* law (Al-Qaradawi, 2001). He also serves on religious committees in various countries including the United Kingdom (Bertrand, 2003) and Palestine (Sivan, 2003). Another example is Sheikh Ibn Qatada, a Palestinian-Jordanian who lives in London and serves as a *mufti* in Algeria (Sivan, 2003).

Usually *ulama* claim that their main responsibility is 'fulfilling Islam's prime ethical imperative' (Hefner, 2005, p. 7). The *ulama* are respected in Muslim societies for their knowledge and understanding of Islam, and for describing and preaching on the religion's beliefs and practices from the Qur'an and *sunnah* (Sedgwick, 2000). Most importantly, they are the figures that are responsible for declaring *fatwa* rulings in the Muslim world.

In terms of legal enforcement, the *ulama* have no direct authority over the general Muslim public. Upon acknowledging a *fatwa*, Muslims may compare related *fatwa* from various *ulama* until they are satisfied with the arguments based on Qur'an verses and *sunnah* (Sedgwick, 2000). The decision as to which *ulama* Muslims choose to recognize or follow is considered an individual choice (Roy, 2004).

A *fatwa* declaration in the Muslim world represents the *ulama's* efforts to encompass all possible human activities under *sharia* law. This practice runs parallel to *sharia* law, which claims to be comprehensive or holistic in governing the believer's life affairs. It is also aligned with the religion's claims to provide believers with 'a way of life' (that is, *ad-din*; Turner, 2006). From this perspective, a *fatwa* appears to be a dynamic source of *sharia* law that acts as the mechanism for change (Murad, 1996).

THE SOURCES OF *SHARIA* LAW

In order to understand Muslim consumer behaviour, one must gain an understanding of the framework for sources of Islamic law and its influence. Currently, the Sunni represent the majority (80 per cent) of Muslims around the world (Sedgwick, 2000). The second largest group is the Shiah (Sedgwick, 2000). There are differences in the *sharia* law framework between the Sunni and Shiah groups. This chapter focuses on the Sunni sect. For the Sunni, all Islamic teachings and rulings are derived from the four foundations of *sharia* law: the Qur'an, *sunnah* (that is, the anecdotes of life of the Prophet Muhammad), *ijma* and *ijtihad* (Table 3.1).

Table 3.1   Sharia *law and its sources*

Sources of *Sharia* law	Form of references/products	Authority	Characteristics
The Qur'an (prime source)	Verse	Allah (God)	Independent. Main reference. Final arbiter, principal guide.
Sunnah (prime source)	*Hadith*	Muhammad (The Prophet)	Dependence on the Qur'an. Detailing the principles in the Qur'an.
Ijma (consensus)	*Fatwa*	*Ulama* (*sharia* scholars)	Dependence on both Qur'an and *sunnah*, and precedents (*fatwa*)
Ijtihad (personal judgement/opinion)	Opinion	*Ulama* (*sharia* scholars)	Dependence on the Qur'an, *sunnah* and precedents (*ijma*)

Source: Reproduced with permission from Muhamad and Mizerski (2010).

The Qur'an

The main contents and structure of *sharia* law come from the Qur'an, which serves as the final arbiter on discussions of law (Wiechman et al., 1996). Muslims believe that the Qur'an is a compilation of the words of Allah (the Arabic word for God), a revelation from Allah that was sent down to the Prophet Muhammad through the Angel Gabriel (Turner, 2006). Despite differences in ideology among Muslim groups, it is the most fundamental belief of all Muslims that the Qur'an is the word of Allah (Azra, 2005; Turner, 2006).

The beginning of Islam dates to the initial revelation of the Qur'anic verses in around 610 CE in Mecca (Bailey and Sood, 1993), located in present-day Saudi Arabia. The series of revelations was completed after a period of 23 years (Turner, 2006), and was marked by the death of the Prophet Muhammad (Sachedina, 1990). The initial record of the Qur'anic verses was written on a loose collection of animal skins; they were also memorized before compilation into a book during the time of the third Muslim Caliph, Uthman (Turner, 2006). It is generally accepted by both Muslim and non-Muslim scholars that the contents of the Qur'an have stayed the same since the time of the Prophet Muhammad (Turner, 2006).

As the main reference for *sharia* law, the Qur'an contains 'injunctions' on the *tawhid* (that is, believing in the oneness of Allah as the creator and owner of the universe) (Muwazir et al. 2006). These injunctions centre on the conscious recognition of the unity of God and include beliefs regarding prophethood, divine decree, angels, the holy books (including the originally revealed versions of the Bible and the Torah) and the Day of Judgement (Choudhury, 1990). These represent the most fundamental beliefs for a Muslim. Muslims also believe that the Qur'anic contents regarding the fundamental beliefs, the *tawhid*, are not subject to investigation by *sharia* legislative bodies (Choudhury, 1990). This limitation means that new *fatwa* rulings cannot redefine the fundamentals of Islamic beliefs that have been explicitly mentioned in the Qur'an (Choudhury, 1990).

The Qur'an contains general principles (Murad, 1996), such as, 'And cast not yourselves into ruin with your own hands and do good' (2:196). It also has some specific rules for various aspects of the believer's life such as prohibitions on financial interest, pork and alcohol (Wiechman et al., 1996). The Qur'an does not comment in great detail on many human behaviours. Therefore, general Qur'anic principles must be interpreted for application in contemporary settings, which is the basic principle in declaring *fatwa* rulings.

Nonetheless, as with interpretations of other religions' scriptures such as the Bible and the Torah, there remain discrepancies in the interpretation of Qur'anic verses among Muslims (Smith, 1980). Because the Qur'an is the primary source for *sharia* law, differences in interpreting the Qur'anic verses can lead to further variations in *sharia* law rulings, including when a new *fatwa* is declared.

The Qur'anic verses are primarily contextual to events in the life of the Prophet Muhammad. These were documented in the form of anecdotes known as *sunnah*, and the interpretation and elaboration of the Qur'an verses are based on the *sunnah* (Choudhury, 1990).

The *Sunnah*

In Islamic law, the primary role of the *sunnah* is to clarify the Qur'an. The Qur'an describes the *sunnah* as the essential guide for Muslims' code of conduct in life: 'You have indeed in the Messenger of Allah a beautiful pattern (of conduct) for any one whose hope is in Allah and the Final Day, and who engages much in the Praise of Allah' (33:21).

The significance of the *sunnah* in *sharia* law is also suggested in the last *hadith* of the Prophet Muhammad: 'I leave behind me two things, the Qur'an and my example, the *sunnah*, and if you follow these you will never go astray' (Al-Bukhari, 1971).

The *sunnah* refers to the recorded sayings or traditions of the Prophet Muhammad (Wiechman et al., 1996). It contains stories and anecdotes called *hadith* (plural *ahadith*) to illustrate concepts from the Qur'an and plays an important role in explaining the principles described in the Qur'an (Wiechman et al., 1996). To use an analogy, the Qur'an is comparable to the constitution of a country, while the *sunnah* is similar to the law that enforces the constitution's principles. A firm understanding of the *sunnah* is required for describing, extracting and implementing Qur'anic principles across Muslim cultures (Wiechman et al., 1996). In that sense, the *sunnah* is an important source for justifying a *fatwa*.

Muslims widely accept that the Qur'an is the word of Allah as given to the Prophet Muhammad; however, there are controversies regarding the authenticity of a portion of the *sunnah* (Azra, 2005). Certain Muslim leaders are believed to have manipulated or even to have created some of the *hadith* (Azra, 2005). Because the *sunnah* (or the *hadith* in particular) is used to assist Muslims to understand the principles in the Qur'an, the availability of non-credible *hadith* allows variation in understanding Qur'anic texts.

To clarify, *hadith* scholars have classified them into several levels of authenticity, such as false, weak and authentic (Al-Faruqi, 1985). Bukhari and Muslim are two scholars who compiled authentic *hadith* collections, which are recognized as the main sources (Al-Faruqi, 1985). The *ulama* must quote a *hadith* from the Bukhari and/or Muslim collection to gain greater acceptance for new rulings (Al-Faruqi, 1985). When certain issues arise that are not decided in the Qur'an and *sunnah*, two other sources are available: *ijma* and *ijtihad* (Azra, 2005).

Ijma

Ijma is a consensus among *ulama* (Wiechman et al., 1996) that results in a *fatwa* (Hossain, 2002). The *ijma* is used to rule on an issue that is not explicitly discussed in the Qur'an and *sunnah* (Murad, 1996; Wiechman et al., 1996). Usually, it is used to settle dubious issues (Hossain, 2002), and to revise a previous *fatwa* in light of superior arguments regarding the issue (Murad, 1996).

The *ijma* method has long been used in Islamic history, dating from medieval times (Murad, 1996). A *fatwa* declared during the reigns of the first four Caliphs after the Prophet, and during the time of the Prophet's companions, is theoretically accepted by Muslim scholars as binding (Murad, 1996). For the majority of Muslims in the Sunni sect, *Ijma* and *ijtihad* (discussed below) are recognized sources for *sharia* law (Sachedina, 1990). A few Islamic sects, such as the Shiah, are reported to reject its practices, accepting only the Qur'an and *sunnah* as *sharia* law sources (Sachedina, 1990).

Ijtihad

Similar to *ijma*, the key players in *ijtihad* are the *ulama* (Murad, 1996). But instead of representing the consensus of several *ulama*, *ijtihad* refers to a sole *alim*'s judgements (for example, opinion, analogy) on new issues that are not found explicitly in the Qur'an, *sunnah* and *ijma* (Wiechman et al., 1996). In many cases, *ijtihad* serves as a precursor for *ijma* or a *fatwa* (Murad, 1996). For example, before the *fatwa* that banned smoking was declared, the *ulama* may have issued an *ijtihad* to prohibit the behaviour. The issue would later be investigated by other *ulama*, followed by a call for consensus. This process would result in a *fatwa* on smoking. In Malaysia, an *alim*'s declaration of certain rulings is considered *ijtihad* until it is gazetted by the *fatwa* committee (Nasohah, 2005).

THE MECHANISM AND TYPES OF *FATWA*

In recent times, *fatwa* rulings have been declared by the authorized *ulama* of Muslim states, or by a committee consisting of *ulama* (such as the Malaysian National *Fatwa* Committee; Hossain, 2002). Among new *fatwa* rulings that have been declared by the Malaysian National *Fatwa* Committee is legalization regarding the use of the *zakat* fund (Islamic taxation system) to support fellow Muslims in prison, and a decision regarding the validity of a divorce declared through a mobile phone text message. *Fatwa* rulings were necessary in the above cases because there were no direct precedents.

One may wonder why *sharia* law produces *fatwa* rulings on all aspects of life, including listening to music (Al-Faruqi, 1985). Al-Qaradawi (2001) provides a perception of how rulings on human behaviours in *sharia* law represent degrees of harm and benefit to Muslims:

If *sharia* (Islamic Law) says something concerning these mundane matters, it is in order to teach good behaviour. Accordingly, it has prohibited whatever leads to strife, has made obligatory that which is essential, has disapproved that which is frivolous, and has approved that which is beneficial. All this has been done with due consideration for the kind of activities involved, their magnitudes and properties. (Al Qaradawi, 2001, p. 17)

The *sharia* law of the four mainstream Sunni schools of thought (that is, *hanafi*, *maliki*, *hanbali* and *shafi'i*) are equivalent in most respects, with no theological or sociologically significant differences (Sedgwick, 2000). Sunni Muslims may recognize each other's rules and regulations regardless of their school of thought: 'For all their disputes, [the Sunni] have always recognized each other's orthodoxy' (Anderson, 1960, p. 547).

In each school of thought there are several prominent 'senior and respected' scholars who are in the most credible position to declare a *fatwa* (Sedgwick, 2000, p. 201) to be recognized by Sunni Muslims throughout the world. This is key for facilitating global or international *fatwa* as Muslim consumers may recognize *fatwa* rulings from other Sunni Muslim states or *ulama* in other countries. Moreover, Muslims are reported to freely choose *fatwa* from *ulama* in whom they tend to have more confidence (Sedgwick, 2000).

The basic principle in Islamic law is that products or behaviours that are beneficial to humans are permissible unless there is strong evidence (based on the Qur'an or *sunnah*) against buying or consuming them (Al-Qaradawi, 2001). For example, there may be benefits to consuming swine and wine, but these behaviours are not permissible due to the explicit prohibition in the Qur'an. Explicit rulings from the Qur'an and *sunnah* are widely accepted in the Muslim world and need no further rulings from *ulama*. An example of a Qur'anic verse that explicitly prohibits intoxicants (including alcohol), gambling and fortune telling is as follows: 'O you who believe! Intoxicants and gambling, (dedication of) stones, and (divination by) arrows, are an abomination, – of Satan's handwork: eschew such (abomination), that you may prosper' (5:90; Ali, 2004).

Fatwa rulings are based on principles derived from the Qur'an and *sunnah* (Turner, 2006). The establishment of a *fatwa* ruling in Islamic law requires strong support (generally known as *nas* or evidence) from either Qur'anic verses or authentic and clear *hadith* (such as those of Bukhari or Muslim). The *ulama* can provide support for the establishment of a ruling for a particular behaviour or towards products by quoting relevant verses from the Qur'an and relevant authentic *hadith*. Other supporting evidence, such as research findings and expert opinions are sometimes used to support a *fatwa* (Ghouri et al., 2006). For example, the *fatwa* prohibiting smoking was based on selected verses from the Qur'an and the *sunnah*, as well as on findings about the effects of smoking on human health (Ghouri et al., 2006).

The type of *fatwa* ruling on a product varies depending on the *ulama*'s judgment of the harmful effects (or benefits) of buying or consuming the product (Al-Qaradawi, 2001). Elements considered to be generally beneficial, or more beneficial than harmful, are termed *halal* (lawful) (Al-Qaradawi, 2001). There are five types of *fatwa* rulings (see Table 3.2); obligatory (prescribed or *wajib*), recommended (known as *mandub*), unlawful or prohibited (*haram*), offensive (*makruh*) and permissible (*mubah*) (Al-Nawawi, 2002).

An unlawful or prohibited behaviour is a mandatory ruling and carries a punishment

Table 3.2   The five types of sharia/fatwa rulings on Muslims' actions and examples

General ruling	Rulings of Sacred Law	Other terms	Types	Ruling	Example
Lawful	Obligatory (*wajib*)	• Prescribed • Mandatory • Required	• Personal obligatory • Societal obligatory	Performance: rewarded Non performance: punished	• Performing the five daily prayers known as *salat* (Al-Nawawi, 2002) • Contributing critical benefits to society e.g. undertaking beneficial occupations
	Recom-mended (*mandub*)	• *Sunnah* • Preferable • Desirable	• Required (*muakkad*)	Performance: rewarded Non performance: not punished	• Almost all behaviours that the Prophet Muhammad said, did, approved of in others. e.g. night (*tahajjud*) prayer (Al-Nawawi, 2002)
	Permissible (*mubah*)	Nil	Nil	Performance: not rewarded Non performance: not punished	• Taking hepatitis B injections (Anonymous, 1988)
Un-lawful	Offensive (*makruh*)	• Detested • Offensive • Disliked	Nil	Performance: not punished Non performance: rewarded	• To colour one's hair in order to be accepted by others (Anonymous, 2002)
	(Prohibited) (*haram*)	Nil	Nil	Performance: punished Non performance: rewarded	• Involved in interest-based transactions (Al-Qaradawi, 2001) • Involved in life insurance transaction (Anonymous, 1979) • Taking Botox injection (Aglionby, 2006)

Source: Unpublished dissertation, N. Muhamad (2008).

by means of *sharia* law, in this world if it is legally enforceable, or in the hereafter (Al-Nawawi, 2002; Turner, 2006). This framework is used in the declaration of conventional *fatwa* rulings on products and services across *fatwa* categories. While the 'type' of *fatwa* rulings refers to levels of strictness of *sharia* rulings on a particular behaviour (for example, consumption of certain good), the *fatwa* 'category' – in this chapter – refers to the grouping of declared *fatwa* rulings based on human activities.

CATEGORIES OF *FATWA* RULING

In Islam, human activities or behaviours fall into two categories: everyday and worshipping (Al-Qaradawi, 2001). Worshipping activities are subject to the principle of limitation: nothing can be legislated except that which has been prescribed in the Qur'an (Al-Qaradawi, 2001). Islamic worship activities are positioned in *sharia* law as an established area that does not need further regulation, such as the creation of new worship rituals (Al-Qaradawi, 2001). There are a few *fatwa* rulings in this area, but they do not involve marketplace behaviours. For example, the Malaysian National *Fatwa* Committee's *fatwa* on worshipping behaviour states that it is permissible for Muslim police or soldiers who are pursuing urgent tasks to miss obligatory Friday prayer, on the condition that they cannot miss three consecutive Friday prayers.

The other category of Muslim activities in *sharia* law includes 'everyday activities' and covers areas other than worshipping behaviours. These activities often relate to consumers' activities (Al-Qaradawi, 2001), known in Arabic as *mu'aamalat*. *Mu'aamalat* covers political, social and economic-related activities (Muwazir et al 2006). Most of the time, the Qur'an provides only general principles regulating human activities (Al-Qaradawi, 2001), which makes *fatwa* rulings particularly important in the regulation of Muslims' daily activities including those related to marketplace behaviours and products.

A recent study on a contemporary Malaysian *fatwa* compilation shows that *fatwa* rulings were issued in regards to various aspects of human life (Muhamad and Mizerski, 2010).[1] It shows that *fatwa* rulings with direct implications for marketing and businesses are listed in the *mu'aamalat* category (Muhamad and Mizerski, 2010). The study found that the Malaysian National *Fatwa* Committee listed 100 *fatwa* rulings related to non-religious activities, as compared with only 31 rulings concerning worshipping and fundamental religious beliefs (Muhamad and Mizerski, 2010). The larger number for non-religious activities implies the significant role of these rulings in guiding the consumption habits of modern Malaysian Muslims. This significant role is underscored by the fact that *fatwa* rulings are declared based upon questions or requests from Muslim communities to their *ulama* or religious authorities on matters that have no prior or clear rulings.

Among the top twenty most-viewed *fatwa* rulings,[2] five are directly related to consumers' marketplace behaviours. The top two rule on the permissibility of insurance products and the IVF method; the others show the permissibility of a premium certificate scheme (a financial product; ranked 15th), a film titled 'The Message', and money gained through financial interest (ranked 20th). Overall, the issues behind the rulings deal with Malaysian Muslim consumers' concerns ranging from adopting conventional financial products and new innovative fertility treatments. The usage of the Malaysian e-*fatwa* website – as indicated by the number of 'hits' in Muhamad and Mizerski's (2010) study – may suggest that the Malaysian Muslim consumers are interested in seeking advice on the status of conventional goods and behaviours from an Islamic perspective.

The consumers' interest in such rulings suggests meticulousness and scepticism when facing new products. Those who are concerned about *fatwa* rulings are probably those who know Islam well enough to view new products with suspicion. These individuals may tend to be keen on living according to Islamic principles and lifestyles.

Some *fatwa* declarations, however, fail to describe the criteria for prohibiting a certain product in detail. For example, the *fatwa* about the film, *The Message* is the fifth most viewed ruling; it has been ruled not permissible for viewing but no clear rationale for the ban appears on the page. Although the criteria must have been discussed by the authorities when deciding on the ruling, for some reason, the justification is not available on the website. Such information is critical for marketers and businesses to understand the Islamic stand on certain issues and business practices. The information could assist them in planning future marketing activities, such as product development and marketing communications, especially for those catering to a predominantly Muslim market.

RECENT *FATWA* RULINGS

Fatwa rulings are continuously declared on demand in every part of the Muslim world. Table 3.3 lists some of the recent rulings declared by Malaysian *fatwa* committees that potentially affect Muslim consumer behaviour in the marketplace. The *fatwa* rulings are published on the Malaysian e-*fatwa* portal (www.e-fatwa.gov.my).

Malaysian and Indonesian *fatwa* authorities have issued *fatwa* rulings that prohibit Muslims from practising yoga, claiming it erodes the Muslim faith (Brant, 2008; Tedjasukmana, 2009). Both parties claim that although physical yoga practices are permissible, those that include Hindu chants are prohibited. Using the Hindu chants is considered to be performing another religion's ritual, which in Islam is considered erosive to the Muslim faith (besides actions, any words or beliefs that run against Islamic belief are also considered erosive) (Anonymous, 2010a; Nik Anis, 2008). This *fatwa* may affect Malaysian Muslim consumers' choice of joining a health club or exercise programme.

Quizzes and contests through short messaging systems are among the recent development in interactive marketing efforts to yield immediate consumers' responses. In Malaysia, a *fatwa* rules that Malaysian Muslim consumers are not allowed to participate in such contests or quizzes.

Table 3.3   Recent fatwa *rulings*

No.	Issues and issuers	*Fatwa* verdicts
1.	Commercial quizzes and contests through short messages system – Malaysian National *Fatwa* Committee	Prohibited among others, the presence of uncertainty (*gharar*), exploitation and gambling elements.
2.	Yoga exercise regime – Malaysian National *Fatwa* Committee	Prohibited – the regime includes Hindu concepts, practices and chants. Islam prohibits its followers from performing other religions' practices.
3.	Promoting conventional insurance products – Malaysian National *Fatwa* Committee	Prohibited – Muslims are prohibited from promoting conventional products that involve or are based on financial interest or usury.
4.	Qur'anic verses as ringtones – Saudi Arabia *Fatwa* Authority	Prohibited – The verses may be misunderstood, as taken out of their original context.

A *fatwa* declared by Saudi Arabia's Board of Muftis posted on the Malaysian Muslim Consumer Association website prohibits the use of Qur'anic verses as mobile phone ring tones (Anonymous, 2008a); it is apparently an international *fatwa* that seems to be positively received by the association. The board declared that it is *haram* (prohibited) to use the verses from the Qur'an as ring tones because it would mean taking them out of their original context. They argued that such ring tones would alter the original meaning of the verses and may be misunderstood.

The purchase of conventional insurance by Malaysian Muslim consumers was ruled as not permissible in the year 1979 (Muhamad and Mizerski, 2010). In December 2009, a *fatwa* was issued that prohibits Malaysian Muslims from promoting the product. The booming Islamic insurance or *takaful* products in Malaysia (Khan and Bhatti, 2008), may be a result of the *fatwa* rulings prohibiting conventional insurance in the country. The latest *fatwa* ruling could further challenge the marketing of conventional insurance in the future in Malaysia.

FATWA IN THE MALAYSIAN CONTEXT

The Malaysian constitution of 1957 established Islam as the country's official religion (Aziz and Shamsul, 2004). In eleven states, Islamic affairs are the responsibility of the state's sultan. In the other four states without a sultan but within federal territory, Islamic affairs are governed by the *Yang di-Pertuan Agung*, the Malaysian king (Aziz and Shamsul, 2004). Malaysia is reported to be the only Islamic country to have numerous Islamic legislative councils, and there has been a call to unite the councils into one central body in order to standardize Islamic law in the country (1997).

The structure of Islamic authority in Malaysia consists of 13 formal Islamic legislative councils that have often produced inconsistencies and contradictions in regulating and implementing Islamic law among the Malaysian states (Anonymous, 1997). This criticism also applies to *fatwa* declarations in Malaysia (Nasohah, 2005).

Besides the Malaysian National *Fatwa* Committee, each Malaysian state has its own *fatwa* committee that has the authority to declare *fatwa* rulings (Nasohah, 2005). The difference with the Malaysian National *Fatwa* Committee is that a *fatwa* declared by the National Committee is put forward to the individual states' committees to be gazetted. In Malaysia, a *fatwa* is binding only after it is gazetted by the state in which a particular citizen resides.

Nonetheless, most states disregard *fatwa* rulings from the Malaysian National *Fatwa* Committee, or amend them to suit their preferences (Nasohah, 2005). For example, the prohibition on smoking declared by the Malaysian National *Fatwa* Committee was gazetted by only one of the Malaysian states; meanwhile, others changed the *fatwa* to prohibit smoking only in the mosque areas or decided not to gazette the *fatwa* at all (Nasohah, 2005). For some Malaysians, the lack of uniformity in the acknowledgement and interpretation of *fatwa* rulings may have generated a lack of confidence in their validity. Intrinsically motivated Malaysian Muslims, who are relatively more concerned about conforming to Islamic rulings in their lives, may tend to be more receptive to, and comply with, *fatwa* rulings. On the other hand, extrinsically motivated followers may see ignoring a *fatwa* as a practical option owing to the lack of enforcement of *sharia* law in Malaysia. (See next section for an account of intrinsic and extrinsic motivation.

When the British and Dutch colonized Malaysia (then known as Malaya), the role of Islam and *sharia* law declined. This trend continued with the development of a constitution upon independence (Aziz and Shamsul, 2004). Consequently, Islamic law is seen to be subordinate to the primary Malaysian civil law system; only limited aspects of *sharia* law are applied (for example marriage and divorce-related issues, collecting Islamic taxes) through the states' Islamic authorities (Aziz and Shamsul, 2004).

It appears that the Malaysian version of *sharia* law is rather limited compared to its application in a country such as Saudi Arabia, where the law's application covers wider aspects including Islamic criminal law (Souryal, 1987). The application of Islamic law in Malaysia is seen as symbolic rather than substantive (Aziz and Shamsul, 2004). Consequently, *sharia* law and *fatwa* declarations face numerous barriers to acceptance in Malaysia.

Political pressures are apparent in some issues when prominent political figures may intervene and express views that contradict those of the *ulama* on contemporary religious issues. For example, when a scholar condemned a musical concert being held to celebrate Eid – the most important Islamic celebration – some political figures openly challenged the scholar's point of view (Bernama, 2006).

The Malaysian government sometimes refuses to acknowledge *fatwa* rulings, as is the case with the ruling prohibiting smoking declared by the Malaysian National *Fatwa* Committee (Anonymous, 1995; 1997). Government support of a *fatwa* ruling is necessary for *fatwa* information dissemination and enforcement. The challenges facing *sharia* law implementation in Malaysia make it difficult for a Malaysian *fatwa* to be passed or to be accepted by Muslim consumers. This is indeed one phenomenon driving modern Muslim consumers to turn to overseas *ulama* for *fatwa* rulings.

Due to the nature and position of *fatwa* rulings in Islam and Muslim societies, Muslim consumers' motivation to follow religious teachings tends to explain their attitudes in the marketplace. The following section discusses the concept of religious orientation and its potential to affect Muslim consumers deciding to behave as prescribed by *fatwa* rulings.

RELIGIOUS ORIENTATION

Religious orientation measures people's motivation for following their religion. Based on this measure, one's approach in following a religion can be identified as either intrinsic or extrinsic (Allport and Ross, 1967). Intrinsically religious individuals are described as those who feel that religion is their purpose in life (Allport and Ross, 1967). Other life objectives are brought into concordance with their religious expectations, which they attempt to incorporate fully into daily activities (Allport and Ross, 1967). Individuals with this type of motivation tend to have a greater commitment to religious teachings and rulings (Wiebe and Fleck, 1980). Research in religious psychology has provided empirical evidence of the significant effect of religious motivation on the human cognitive function. Those who are more intrinsically motivated in following their religion tend to internalize, understand and remember religious teachings more effectively than their less intrinsically motivated counterparts (Wenger, 2004).

On the other hand, religion is not the prime motive in the lives of extrinsically motivated religious individuals (Allport and Ross, 1967). Nonetheless, they still benefit from religion in some situations, such as support in times of grief, social acceptance, status, and/or justification for times of hardship (Allport and Ross, 1967). Therefore, religious teachings are selectively adopted at various times to suit their other, more primary, life objectives (Allport and Ross, 1967).

To illustrate the concept of being intrinsically or extrinsically religious, we may consider one statement used in measuring such motivation: 'Although I am a religious person, I refuse to let religious considerations influence my everyday affairs.' An extrinsically motivated person will strongly agree with this statement while the intrinsically motivated will strongly disagree.

Allport and Ross (1967) described intrinsically and extrinsically motivated individuals and suggested that extrinsic individuals tend to adhere to religious teachings in order to achieve certain objectives, such as social recognition and solace. However, the researchers provide less explicit explanation of why intrinsic individuals tend to be more motivated to abide by more comprehensive religious teachings. Nonetheless, based on the intrinsic items used in the religious motivation construct, it is possible that intrinsically motivated individuals tend to have a greater need for spirituality than their extrinsic counterparts. They may also tend to prefer having more structure and organization in life as compared to the extrinsic individuals who tend to be more flexible in dealing with life situations, adapting as necessary. This idea is in line with previous reports that suggest that intrinsically motivated individuals are more submissive to others; such people also tend to be more conscientious and in need of greater consistency in life (Wiebe and Fleck, 1980). In contrast, the extrinsically motivated individual tends to be more flexible, self-reliant and pragmatic in nature (Wiebe and Fleck, 1980).

Personality traits may lead to intrinsic or extrinsic motivation in terms of religion. Intrinsically motivated persons may allow religious teachings and rulings to form their framework for life due to their need for structure and consistency. Extrinsically motivated individuals turn to religious teachings when necessary to suit their pragmatic approach to handling matters in life. However, Allport and Ross (1967) reject the idea that the intrinsic approach towards religion is an instrumental approach; they also suggest that the extrinsic approach towards religion is utilitarian in form. These aspects of intrinsic and extrinsic motivation are expected to affect Muslim consumers when deciding whether or not to adhere to behaviours prescribed by *fatwa* rulings.

The Religious Orientation Construct

Initial studies using the concept of religious orientation investigated the influence of religion on prejudice towards Jews and African-Americans in the United States. One of the earliest studies on extrinsic motivation is that of Wilson (1960) who found that the motivation is more important than other religious constructs, such as orthodoxy and fundamentalism in explaining ethnic prejudice.

Although Allport and Ross (1967) developed a systematic measure of the concept of religious orientation, it is criticized for being weak, particularly because of the addition of two groups (non-religious and pro-religious groups) to the original intrinsic and extrinsic religious groups. Many claim that these additional two groups do not fit in the original intrinsic and extrinsic frameworks (Kirkpatrick and Hood, 1990). Most previous studies focused on the original intrinsic and extrinsic approach in applying the concept in their studies (Donahue, 1985; Hunt and King, 1971).

Despite these criticisms, the concept and measurement of religious orientation (Allport and Ross, 1967) has been used in more than 70 studies over more than twenty years (Donahue, 1985). The concept of religious orientation is recognized as the most dominant conceptual and measurement paradigm in tapping into the influence of religion on human behaviour (Donahue, 1985; Hunt and King, 1971; Kirkpatrick and Hood, 1990). Still, the concept of religious orientation has not been widely applied in marketing studies. A study by Essoo and Dibb (2004) reported that extrinsically religious consumers tended to be trendier, putting more importance on brand names and stores with well-known brands. They also tended to be more innovative (trying new products) and more demanding (attaching more importance to product quality) than their intrinsic counterparts. The intrinsically religious consumers were reported to be more conservative (more trusting of advertising and looking for bargains), and mature (less innovative and trendy) than their extrinsic counterparts (Essoo and Dibb, 2004).

Muslim consumers in the study were found to be less informed shoppers, which may be related to Islam's fundamental belief in predestiny (Essoo and Dibb, 2004). Unfortunately, the effects found in this study offer limited insight into the influence of religion on buyer behaviour.

Motivation and Religion

The motivational element is suggested to contribute to the survival of religious teachings and rulings (Whitehouse, 2002). Religious leaders often use a motivational approach to 'mobilize' others to act in a way suggested by a religion (Ryan and Deci, 2000). For example, believers are promised positive rewards (such as eternal life) to maintain religious practices, and warned of punishments through negative rewards (such as eternal damnation) if they fail to perform the practices (Whitehouse, 2002).

Overall, motivation in general appears to be a relevant factor in driving one's adherence to religious teachings (Whitehouse, 2002). The robustness of the dual intrinsic and extrinsic motivational approach (Ryan and Deci, 2000) provides further advantage to the religious orientation construct as a credible approach in studying one's motivation towards an object or behaviour. This fact is supported by numerous reports on its efficacy in explaining religious influences over the years.

The verses from the Islamic holy book, the Qur'an, and reports of the Prophet Muhammad's traditions, suggest that Islam stresses the type of followers' motivation over their commitment to the religion. The Islamic religion believes that Muslims' performance of Islamic teachings can be motivated by intrinsic or extrinsic motivation. Some may perform religious observances out of their motive to conform to religious teachings, or to satisfy or achieve worldly needs, such as to alleviate sorrow or grief, or to be socially accepted by others. In fact, the religion suggests that the merit for Muslims' obedience to Islamic rulings eventually depends on the type of motivation that drives them to follow Islam. This concept is illustrated in the following *hadith*:

I heard the Messenger of Allah saying, 'The reward for deeds depends upon their intentions, and every person will get a reward according to what he has intended. So whoever emigrated (to Medina) for worldly benefits or for a woman to marry, his emigration was for that which he emigrated.' (Al-Bukhari, 1971)

Islam thus seems to distinguish between Muslims' commitment to their religion and their motivation in adhering to it, which is in line with the distinction found in a previous study comparing religious motivation and religious commitment factors (Himmelfarb, 1975).

Apparently, the concept of religious motivation has a significant place in the Islamic religion. It also appears to be a credible concept for understanding the influence of Islam on consumer behaviour in the marketplace, particularly in regards to behaviours subjected to *fatwa* rulings.

SEARCHING FOR *FATWA* RULINGS

Given the dynamism and volatility of *fatwa* rulings in the globalized world, finding information on *fatwa* rulings that conform to one's beliefs may not be easy. Owing to the complex nature of the *fatwa* rulings, Malaysian Muslim consumers were found to be strongly reliant on others in acquiring information on a *fatwa* (Muhamad and Mizerski, 2010).[3] It requires considerable religious knowledge to confirm the truthfulness or credibility of a particular *fatwa* ruling.

The Muslim community is becoming more globalized in the borderless digital era. Muslims can ask questions about *fatwa* rulings and access *fatwa* databases through the Internet (Roy, 2004). For those who do not have access to the Internet, the collective values within their community are the key to rapid dissemination of information regarding a particular *fatwa*. The nature of *fatwa* rulings, as discussed earlier, makes it possible to search for *fatwa* information across geographical borders. Websites such as 'Islamonline,' which is overseen by the prominent scholar Yusuf Al-Qaradawi, is one of the most visited English/Arabic Islamic web portals, offering a bank of *fatwa* rulings with interactivity (Graf, 2008). Muslim consumers rely on their religious leaders, attend religious classes, or use reading materials and web pages to learn about *fatwa* rulings (Muhamad and Mizerski, 2010).

Nevertheless, Malaysian Muslim consumers differ in their sources for information about *fatwa* rulings depending on their motivation in following Islam (Muhamad and Mizerski, 2010). Those consumers who are intrinsically motivated tend to acquire information on *fatwa* rulings through informal sources, such as religious talks and religious classes as well as from family members and friends. On the other hand, the extrinsically motivated consumers tend to depend more on mass media and online sources in getting information on *fatwa* rulings.

The differences in information sources for *fatwa* rulings amongst Malaysian Muslim consumers may rest on the nature of their religious motivation. The intrinsically motivated Muslims' reliance on informal sources is in line with their relatively greater desire to adopt Islamic values, rules and regulations in life – which guides them to venues of religious talks and casual religious classes not frequented by their extrinsic counterparts.

Information sources for *fatwa* rulings also tend to differ based on the type of behaviour (for example, smoking versus listening to music) and/or type of ruling (for example, explicit prohibition versus conditional prohibition). Even the status of the ruling (for example, controversial versus non controversial) may have an impact (Muhamad and Mizerski, 2010). Apparently, Malaysian Muslim consumers reported acquiring information for the *fatwa* on smoking mostly from the Internet, family members, friends and mass media (Muhamad and Mizerski, 2010). This fact is in contrast to their reported information sources for listening to popular music, which mostly comes from their knowledge from informal religious sources (for example religious talks, casual religious classes) and books and magazines.

The difference in the sources for *fatwa* rulings among Malaysian Muslim consumers presumably is due to the sensitivity of the behaviour in the Malaysian Muslim community, that is, the degree of controversy of the issue. It can easily be comprehended that the ruling about smoking might be controversial: more than half of Malaysian men smoke. In a culture where men generally hold higher authority in societal hierarchies (for example family and religious institutions), such a ruling may not get a warm reception. Thus, instead of seeking information about the *fatwa* ruling from public sources such as religious talks (as for the listening to music *fatwa*), they tend to acquire information about the smoking prohibition from their family members, their own Internet search and selective readings.

IMPLICATIONS FOR MARKETERS

Owing to the nature of *fatwa* declarations, those targeting predominantly Muslim markets need to be aware of any *fatwa* that might relate to their products. Accessing new *fatwa* rulings can be a challenge for marketers. It is also imperative to note that *fatwa* rulings from overseas could have an effect on local consumers, especially on those who are strongly motivated to adopt Islamic values, rules and regulations as part of their lifestyles. Muslim consumers' motivation in following Islamic teachings has the potential to affect their compliance with *fatwa* rulings on products and services in the marketplace.

Marketers need to be aware of possible disparities between political or government policies and the Islamic authorities in recognizing *fatwa* rulings throughout the Muslim world and in Malaysia particularly. Depending on the country in which marketers are operating, the religious authority and the government can be two completely different entities. Marketers could benefit from investigating the Muslim consumer's reaction towards certain *fatwa* rulings; it may help them to assess which party (religious authority or government) consumers tend to obey. This information is important in creating more consumer-friendly brand images and to avoid getting caught in political disputes or being perceived negatively by consumers.

Marketers require a deeper understanding of the segregation within a Muslim community, a fragmentation that can result from multiple religious authorities issuing *fatwa* rulings. In most cases, following the local mainstream religious authority seems to be the best option, but in this era of globalization, it is also worthwhile to crosscheck local mainstream *fatwa* with global *fatwa* within similar Islamic sects. This practice acknowledges the increasing trend of global *fatwa* searches through the Internet, as well as the flexibility for a Muslim to choose *fatwa* rulings in which they have more confidence. For example, Sunni Malaysian Muslims may choose to adopt the global *fatwa* prohibiting the purchase of brands that are alleged to support Israel, because of their belief that Sheikh Yusuf Al Qaradawi is more credible than their local religious authority or *fatwa* committee.

Marketers need to understand the reason why a product is subject to *fatwa* ruling in order to deal with the situation more effectively. For example, if a brand is prohibited for Muslim consumption because it is wrongly associated with certain Middle Eastern tensions, they could work with the *ulama* in order to clear up the misunderstanding.

Marketers could also turn prohibition rulings on certain products or behaviours into business opportunities if they had a better understanding of *fatwa* declarations and rulings. In Muslim markets with high sensitivity to religious issues, marketers could develop alternative products for Muslim consumption. For example, as a result of the consumption prohibition associated with the Coca-Cola soft drink brand, numerous new cola brands, such as Mecca Cola and Qibla Cola, managed to create market presence in predominantly Muslim communities (Shazana, 2006).

Ultimately, it is imperative for marketers to be updated constantly on new *fatwa* rulings in Muslim countries and any disputes that relate to them locally and internationally. These precautions could help prevent companies from offending religious sentiment or falling victim to negative rumours that could harm product sales and brand or company images.

CONCLUSION

This chapter provides general, yet comprehensive coverage, on the nature, scope, and mechanism of *fatwa* rulings in Muslim communities, particularly in the Malaysian context. The information offers insights into the position of *sharia* or Islamic law as well as the volatility of *fatwa* rulings. The chapter also provides a glimpse into the classification of *fatwa* rulings and delineates areas that are more likely to have an impact on Muslim marketplace behaviour.

The discussion detailed the nature of both intrinsically and extrinsically motivated religious individuals from the Islamic and religious psychology perspectives. It further elaborated the possible link between the construct and Muslim consumers' compliance with *fatwa* rulings in the marketplace. Although there is evidence on the role of Muslim consumers' religious motivation in explaining their information sources for *fatwa* rulings, the potential effect of the construct on Muslim consumers' compliance with *fatwa* rulings in the marketplace has yet to be proven.

Going back to the roots of marketing philosophy, understanding the impact of *fatwa* rulings in the marketplace comes down to recognizing the importance of religion as a key cultural factor in consumers' decision-making. Marketers once viewed religion as a taboo subject and not subject to scientific inquiry and discussion.

Although it seems that religion will always be a taboo, it is also an increasingly important factor that affects Muslim consumer behaviour in particular. The emerging conservatism and increasing religiosity among Muslim consumers underlines the importance of understanding the general effect of religion, and of *fatwa* rulings in particular, on Muslim consumers' marketplace behaviours.

The decentralized religious authority in the global Muslim community, particularly among Sunni Muslims, is probably one of the biggest challenges to multinational marketers in understanding the declarations. There have been calls to establish a central global *fatwa* institute (Salhani, 2008) to deal with independent *fatwa* issuers. In Malaysia, the World *Fatwa* Management and Research Institute was established in 2002 to assist in this situation (Anonymous, 2010b).

Muslim consumers, who make up the second largest religious segment in the world and constitute more than 50 per cent of the Malaysian population, tend to be strongly committed to their religious rules and regulations. Although understanding religious needs and demands due to *fatwa* rulings can be challenging, adapting to such consumers remains a wise marketing tactic.

NOTES

1. The study was based on content analysis of the Malaysian official online *fatwa* bank.
2. The ranking of the *fatwa* rulings was based on the number of 'hits' that are automatically recorded by the website for each ruling's page (a ruling per webpage).This represents the number of times each ruling has been viewed by webpage visitors.
3. The study explores young Malaysian Muslim consumers' information sources for *fatwa* rulings. A total of 204 respondents were surveyed in the study.

BIBLIOGRAPHY

Aglionby, J. (2006), 'Malaysian Muslims told not to use Botox', *The Guardian*, 28 July.
Al-Bukhari, M.I. (1971), Sahih Al-Bukhari, from http://www.usc.edu/dept/MSA/fundamentals/hadithsunnah/bukhari/060.sbt.html.
Al-Faruqi, L.I. (1985), 'Music, musicians and Muslim law', *Asian Music*, 17 (1), 3–35.
Al-Nawawi (2002), *Al-Maqasid* (trans. N.H.M. Kelle, second edn), Maryland: AMANA.
Al-Qaradawi, Y. (2001), *The Lawful and The Prohibited in Islam* (trans K. El-Helbawy, M.M. Siddiqui and S. Shukry), Kuala Lumpur: Percetakan Zafar Sdn. Bhd.
Ali, A.Y. (2004), *The Meaning of the Holy Qu'ran*, 11th edn, Beltsville, MD: Amana Publications.
Allport, G.W. and Ross, M. (1967), 'Personal religious orientation and prejudice', *Journal of Personality and Social Psychology*, 5 (4), 432–43.
Anderson, J.N.D. (1960), 'A law of personal status for Iraq', *The International and Comparative Law Quarterly*, 9 (4), 542–63.
Anonymous (1979), 'Keputusan Jawatankuasa Fatwā Kebangsaan berkenaan Insuran Nyawa' ('*Fatwa* on Life Insurance by Malaysian National *Fatwa* Committee'). Retrieved 5 May 2008, from http://www.e-fatwā.gov.my/jakim/keputusan_view.asp?keyID=96.
Anonymous (1988), 'Keputusan Jawatankuasa Fatwā kebangsaan berkenaan Pengambilan Suntikan Hepatitis B' ('*Fatwa* regarding taking Hepatitis B injection by Malaysian National *Fatwa* Committee'). Retrieved 5 May 2008, from http://www.e-fatwa.gov.my/jakim/keputusan_view.asp?keyID=54.
Anonymous (1995), 'Tiada Cadangan Haramkan Merokok', *Berita Harian*, 28 December.
Anonymous (1997), 'Memorandum on the Provision in the Syariah Criminal Offences Act and Fundamental Liberties', from http://www.sistersinislam.org.my/memo/080897.htm.
Anonymous (2002), 'Keputusan Jawatankuasa Fatwā Negeri Sembilan berkenaan Mewarnakan Rambut bertujuan agar diterima Masyarakat' ('Fatwa on Colouring one's Hair to be Accepted by Others, Declared by State of the 'Negeri Sembilan's' Fatwa Committee'). Retrieved 5 May, 2008, from http://www.efatwa.gov.my/mufti/fatwa _search_result.asp?keyID=676.
Anonymous (2006), 'It's ok to say happy Diwali', *The Straits Times*, 27 October.

Anonymous (2008a), 'Emel Pilihan-Fatwā Lembaga Mufti-Mufti Arab Saudi'. Retrieved 20 April 2010, from http://muslimconsumer.org.my/ppim/news.php?extend.572.

Anonymous (2008b), 'Penubuhan Majlis Agama Islam Perak', 16 June. Retrieved 17 June 2008, from http://mufti.perak.gov.my/profil/profil.htm#atas.

Anonymous (2008c), 'Senarai Ahli Muzakarah Jawatankuasa Fatwā Majlis Kebangsaan Bagi Hal Ehwal Agama Islam Malaysia' ('List of Malaysian National Fatwā Committee Members') 17 June. Retrieved 17 June 2008, from http://www.islam.gov.my/informasi/jawatankuasafatwakebangsaan.html.

Anonymous (2010a), 'Fatwā Yoga', 20 April. Retrieved 20 April 2010, from http://www.islam.gov.my/portal/yoga_Bm.php.

Anonymous (2010b), 'Latabelakang Institut Pengurusan dan Penyelidikan Fatwa Sedunia', 11 February. Retrieved 25 March 2010, from http://www.usim.edu.my/infad/my/latarbelakang.htm.

Aziz, A. and A.B. Shamsul (2004), 'The religious, the plural, the secular and the modern: a brief critical survey on Islam in Malaysia', *Inter-Asia Cultural Studies*, **5** (3), 341–56.

Azra, A. (2005), 'Islamic thought: theory, concepts, and doctrines in the context of Southeast Asian Islam', in K.S. Nathan and M.H. Kamali (eds), *Islam in Southeast Asia: Political, Social and Strategic Challenges for the 21st Century* Singapore: Institute of Southeast Asian Studies, p. 362.

Bailey, J.M. and J. Sood (1993), 'The effects of religious affiliation on consumer behavior: a preliminary investigation', *Journal of Managerial Issues*, **5** (3), 328–52.

Bernama (2006), 'Let Fatwa Council decide on Aidilfitri Concert, says Rais', *Bernama Daily Malaysian News*, 18 October.

Bertrand, R. (2003), 'Islam and politics in Europe and in Asia: comparative reflections', *Asia Europe Journal*, **1**, 323–31.

Bokhari, F. (2007), 'Lloyds TSB spots growing appetite', *Financial Times*, 11 June, p. 6.

Brant, R. (2008), 'Malaysia clerics issue yoga fatwa'. Retrieved from http://news.bbc.co.uk/2/hi/7743312.stm.

Bruinessen, M.V. (2003), 'Making and unmaking Muslim religious authority in Western Europe', in *The Production of Islamic Knowledge in Western Europe*, Florence: Robert Schuman Centre for Advanced Studies.

Choudhury, M.A. (1990), 'Syllogistic deductionism in Islamic choice theory', *International Journal of Social Economics*, **17** (11), 4–20.

Donahue, M.J. (1985), 'Intrinsic and extrinsic religiousness: review and meta analysis', *Journal of Personality and Social Psychology*, **48** (2), 400–419.

El Qorchi, M. (2005) 'Islamic finance gears up', *Finance and Development*, **42** (4).

Essoo, N. and S. Dibb (2004),'Religious influences on shopping behaviour: an exploratory study', *Journal of Marketing Management*, **20** (7–8), 683–712.

Ghouri, N., M. Atcha and A. Sheikh (2006), 'Influence of Islam on smoking among Muslims', *British Medical Journal*, **332**, 291–4.

Graf, B. (2008), 'Islamonline.net: interactive, independent, popular', *Arab Media and Society*, January.

Hague, A. and K.A. Masuan (2002), 'Religious psychology in Malaysia', *International Journal for the Psychology of Religion*, **12** (4), 277–89.

Hefner, R.W. (2005), 'Introduction: modernity and the remaking of Muslim politics', in R.W. Hefner (ed.), *Remaking Muslim Politics: Pluralism, Contestation, Democratization*, Princeton, NJ: Princeton University Press, pp. 1–36.

Himmelfarb, H.S. (1975), 'Measuring religious involvement', *Social Forces*, **53** (4), 606–18.

Hossain, M. (2002), 'The story of fatwa', *Interventions: International Journal of Postcolonial Studies*, **4** (2), 237–42.

Hunt, R.A. and M. King (1971), 'The intrinsic-extrinsic concept: a review and evaluation', *Journal for the Scientific Study of Religion*, **10** (4), 339–56.

Khan, M.M. and I.M. Bhatti (2008), 'Islamic banking and finance: on its way to globalisation', *Managerial Finance*, **34** (10).

Kirkpatrick, L.A. and R.W.J. Hood (1990), 'Intrinsic-extrinsic religious orientation: the boon and bane of contemporary psychology of religion?', *Journal for the Scientific Study of Religion*, **29** (4), 442–62.

Muhamad, N., and D. Mizerski (2010), 'Exploring Muslim consumers' information sources for fatwa ruling on products and behaviors', *Journal of Islamic Marketing*, **1** (1).

Murad, K. (1996), *Shari'a the Way to God*, Leicester: The Islamic Foundation Markfield Dawah Centre.

Muwazir, M.R., R. Muhamad and K. Noordin (2006), 'Corporate responsibility disclosure: a *tawhidic* approach', *Journal Syariah*, **14** (1), 125–42.

Nasohah, Z. (2005), 'Undang-Undang Penguatkuasaan Fatwā di Malaysia', *Islamiyyat*, **27** (1), 25–44.

Nik Anis, M. (2008), 'Fatwa Council says yoga with worshipping, chanting is prohibited'. Retrieved from http://thestar.com.my/news/story.asp?file=/2008/11/22/nation/20081122111842andsec=nation.

Pereira, A. (2005), 'Religiosity and economic development in Singapore', *Journal of Contemporary Religion*, **20** (2), 161–77.

Perlez, J. (2007), 'Muslims' veils test limits of Britain's tolerance', electronic, *The New York Times*.

Pierret, T. (2005), 'Internet in a sectarian Islamic context', ISIM, **15**, spring.

Roy, O. (2004) *Globalized Islam: The Search for a New Ummah*, New York: Columbia University Press.

Ryan, R.M. and E.L. Deci (2000), 'Intrinsic and extrinsic motivations: classic definitions and new directions', *Contemporary Educational Psychology*, **25** (1), 57–64.

Sachedina, Z. (1990), 'Islam, procreation and the law', *International Family Planning Perspectives*, **16** (3).

Salhani, C. (2008), 'Moderate Muslims urge action against extremists', *Washington Times*. Retrieved from http://www.washingtotimes.com/news/2008/oct/08/moderate-muslim-urge-action-against-extremists.

Sedgwick, M. (2000) 'Sects in the Islamic world', *Nova Religio*, **3** (2), 195–240.

Shazana, S. (2006) 'Justice and charity through business, the Mecca Cola model', *The Halal Journal*, **10** (48 and 50).

Sivan, E. (2003), 'The clash within Islam', *International Institute for Strategic Studies*, **45** (1), 25–44.

Smith, W.C. (1980), 'True meaning of scripture: an empirical nonreductionist interpretation of the Quran', *International Journal of Middle East Studies*, **11** (4), 487–505.

Souryal, S.S. (1987), 'The religionalization of society: the continuity of Shariah law in Saudi Arabia', *Journal for the Scientific Study of Religion*, **26** (4), 429–49.

Tedjasukmana, J. (2009), 'Indonesia's *fatwa* against yoga', *Time*. Retrieved from http://www.time.com/time/printout/0,8816,1874651,00.html.

Turner, C. (2006) *The Basics: Islam*, New York: Routledge.

Wenger, J.L. (2004), 'The automatic activation of religious concepts: implications for religious orientations', *International Journal for the Psychology of Religion*, **14** (2), 109.

Whitehouse, H. (2002), 'Modes of religiosity: towards a cognitive explanation of the sociopolitical dynamics of religion', *Method and Theory in the Study of Religion*, **14**, 293–315.

Wiebe, K.F., and J.R. Fleck (1980), 'Personality correlates of intrinsic, extrinsic, and nonreligious orientations', *Journal of Psychology*, **105** (2), 181–87.

Wiechman, D.J., Kendall, J.D., and Azarian, M.K. (1996), 'Islamic law: myths and realities', *Crime and Justice International Online*, **12** (3, May–June).

Wilson W.C. (1960), 'Extrinsic religious values and prejudice', *Journal of Abnormal and Social Psychology*, **60**, 286–8.

Yusof, S. (2009), 'Reflections on the Singapore Muslim identity', *Karyawan*, 2–3

4 Investment, fashion and markets in the Muslim world

*Alexandru Balasescu**

INTRODUCTION

When I first set out to write this chapter, the questions that came into my mind were: Why talk about marketing that is specifically Islamic? Can marketing – an activity that is economic by nature – be linked in any meaningful way with a religious identity? And who needs Islamic marketing anyway? Involuntarily this made me think of an experience that happened in 2001 while pursuing my PhD studies at the University of California in Irvine. The summer promised to be a long one, and I proposed to the committee of the School of Social Sciences to teach a summer course on 'Muslims in Europe'. My proposition was politely rejected, interest on that subject matter was little, if any, I was told . . . I took a summer job at the library and set out to do my preparatory fieldwork later that summer in, of all places, Paris – to study the question of the Islamic headscarf and fashion industry. I flew to Paris on 9 September 2001 and flew back three weeks later to a radically changed United States. So changed that a letter was waiting in my departmental mailbox asking me equally politely if I would like to teach my proposed class on Muslims in Europe in the spring quarter. I gladly accepted and I found, not unexpectedly, students from various backgrounds, Muslim and non-Muslim, attended the class. I even received an invitation from a Saudi-American student to take an air trip across Southern California in his small mono-engine plane that he was learning to fly. We took off from John Wayne Airport in an adventure that became one of my best memories from the graduate school. Reality beats irony. As some of the 9/11 hijackers were thought to be of Saudi origins, flying with an aspiring pilot coming from Saudi Arabia was, at that time, tantamount to being not entirely all right.

FINANCE AND FASHION

A step into the offices of a financial corporation in the Muslim world may not bring to mind anything special or 'other'. Nothing in the partition of spaces, office furniture, or people's smiles would suggest that the financial industry has any particular features just because transactions take place in an Islamic space. The dream of 'free flowing' capital looks real, borderless, ungoverned by any other rules than those of the flow. As if to reinforce this vision, one of the financial hubs of the world continues to be (despite the financial crisis and the real estate bubble burst) positioned in the heart of the Muslim world, in Dubai.

On the streets and in the commercial spaces of Dubai – and in all other major Muslim Middle East cities – one can see advertising for commodities, from cars to fashion articles. However, here the particularities are visible at the first glance. The bodily figurative representations are kept to a minimum; in some places they are absent completely. Along with the free flowing of commodities, rules of public display are present in the advertising business.

The next pages will explore the underlying principles of fashion and financial advertising in Islamic spaces. The starting point is Tehran street advertising and a major Gulf-based financial institution (anonymous for the purpose of this chapter). The accounts are based on fieldwork in 2002–03 for my PhD thesis and on work experience in the world of Gulf finance in 2006.

Taking fashion as a system of signs that precedes and sometimes replaces the body, the chapter also looks at the financial instruments that precede (and sometimes replace) money and profit: the investment propositions. While advertising for fashion and consumption commodities in general is dominated by graphic and photographic representation, the materials handed out to potential investors are dominated by text. As bodies appear in advertising following general identifiable rules (as we will see), texts about finance and flow of capital contain special passages regarding financing geared towards the Islamic investors. They both point to the same direction: a set of rules with moral undertones does govern the space of 'pure exchange'.

Text and body and the body of text in these two instances reveal both accepted and appealing practices of advertising and underlying moral rules. These in turn become principles of organization of the flow of money and commodities by creating a transactional space (visual, textual and economic) governed by them.

The analysis of fashion and commodities advertising will focus on how body is used (or not) in order to render an object appealing. Differences linked to representations of male and female bodies, movements and commodities associated with them will be presented and discussed in relation to the spatial organization and presence of these representations (the mall, the street, and so on). A general observation regarding the body and its public presence in different spaces concludes this section.

The process of production and the content of the text regarding banking and financing of investment plans will be presented in a second part of the article. While principles of the Islamic banking system have been already deeply analyzed by economists, anthropologists, and others, the way in which these principles are advertised to potential investors has received less attention. The proposition to potential investors comes by way of printed materials that I will call Investment Presentation (IP). The way in which financing through the Islamic banking system is presented in an IP will be the focus of this analysis.

The chapter proposes a general assessment of the underlying moral principles of advertising in Islamic spaces. However the argument will be that these principles do not generate a system of rigid rules. I will emphasize their character of recommendation rather than imposition, which generates a space of various possibilities, so necessary to any marketing endeavor. The chapter aims to illustrate the variety and difference necessary for consumer choice to be exercised and exactly where that variety lies. In this the chapter contributes both to the anthropological conversation on Islam and modernity, and to those who are interested in promoting capital and commodities in Islamically predominant environments or commercial niches. The conclusion will ponder on the place of culture in the 'free market' and the smokescreen effects that uncounted-for-specificities may generate.

TEXT AND CONTEXT

In the past 10 years something has changed between the Muslim and non-Muslim worlds (even if one may not really speak of any clearly distinct worlds). Despite the overt conflicts in Afghanistan and Iraq, and the Islamic terrorism threats that are diffused in many parts of the world, there is no confirmation of Huntington's doctrine of the clash of civilizations. On the contrary the economic, cultural and political exchanges have intensified and transformed the very way we think about and act in our world. It has given new meanings to the categories of culture, economy, and politics. One can only speculate about the 'whys and hows' of this phenomenon. It is known that throughout history, wars and conflicts have intensified exchanges among 'others'. More often than not, arch-enemies end up either creating strong albeit problematic coalitions (see the courtship between France and Germany today, or France and the Ottoman Empire in the seventeenth to eighteenth centuries) or resembling and imitating each other's *moeurs* or institutional reforms up to a certain point (as is the case with the Ottoman and the Persian Empires that later became Turkey and Iran).

Since the end of the 1990s and even more after the September 11 event, there has been a heightened sense of reciprocal curiosity between the Muslim and non-Muslim worlds. The story of my UCI course is one of many similar experiences. An Afghan friend from California told me how surprised she was when people she occasionally met at the gym started showing interest in knowledge about her country (albeit only related to the distinctive names of cities such as Kabul or Kandahar). People started searching for knowledge in order to make sense of what has happened post-September 11. The explanations may be valid or not, but the collateral effect of knowledge searching opens new paths. Genuine pursuit may bring people to new career paths or lead them to new travels in search of new opportunities (usually enrichment, be it economic or just experiential).

In parallel with this, in countries in the Middle East, North Africa or Asia, social, political and economic change has introduced a new type of actor: the modern, moderate middle class person from a Muslim background. In places or times of relative stability and economic reforms geared towards encouraging individual initiative, many business and trade links are created by an increasingly active and cosmopolitan population who prosper from engaging in economic activities. The causes of such a transformation are multiple. Certainly a combination of reasons and actions with psychological resort contributed to this economic and, I think, soon cultural, post-modern Renaissance of the Islamic world. It is very likely that many Muslims from the Middle East (and from elsewhere), being under constant suspicion of producing 'terrorists,' will orient towards showing a completely different picture of their world. Aspirations of well being and prosperity are doubled by the desire to put the Middle East on the map otherwise than by being on the 'axis of evil.' For example, preoccupation with the arts and cultural heritage has captured the minds, energies, and money of local artists or entrepreneurs who do not shy away from investing in cultural ventures.

Two decisive shifts have happened. One is the changing political strategy – from militant Islamism to playing on Islamic identity in order to gain a place in civil society and politics (Göle, 2002, 2003). Second is the desire to counterbalance the negative stereotypes that emerged or intensified after 9/11 at both the individual and state levels. Successful economic reforms in some states, such as Turkey, opened up a previously untapped job market and an important pool of human resources. Other countries – such as those in the Gulf – developed a strategy of seduction, attracting financial speculation and creating a market for financial products and derivatives. Political reforms are less popular there; however, in some places (such as Bahrain) precisely because of the presence of these markets, civil society is forming and pushing towards constitutional changes.

As a consequence of these strategic shifts in the Muslim world, a new middle class is emerging. It has a strong attachment to traditions (Islam) and an even stronger determination to succeed on the global economic scene. Called by some authors 'the Islamic Calvinists', they are the engine of social change and growing prosperity in regions such as Anatolia or some parts of Lebanon. In other countries, such as Iran, they are the ones who form the social fabric and oppose a political system perceived as too controlling for their ambition of both prosperity and liberalism (Nasr, 2009).

Formed initially by small and medium business men (and sometimes women), merchants and/or white collar workers (lawyers in the case of Pakistan) in the mid 1980s, this Islamic middle class has grown to have strong ties with the global business world. They display traditional values concerning families, society and relations to others *but they have a strong predilection for pluralism and social/political liberalism*, because they perceive that economic prosperity exists best in a pluralist environment.

In his analysis, Vali Nasr presents some main characteristics of this new Islamic middle class:

- Conservative/pious in relation to the family and the community
- Liberal economic and social thinking
- Globally connected/cosmopolitan
- Economically active and prosperous on international scene
- Goal oriented – not motivated by ideology (not fundamentalists)

One model of effective development is Turkey, a country that managed to liberalize its economy successfully in the late 1980s (up to then, the industry was mostly state owned, a predicament of Republican Nationalism). In central Anatolia, local entrepreneurs re-launched the dying textile industry by starting small businesses. They bought the state-owned companies and, using their tools and the new economic regulations, they opened up the local economy to the competitive international market. As an example, 6.5 per cent of the world's denim production takes place in Kayseri (a city in Anatolia), the equivalent of €2 billion of business (Nasr, 2009). The young entrepreneurs are internationally well connected and Turkey has developed its own internationally successful brands.

Politically this class is attached to the AKP (the Muslim Party in power in Turkey) – a party that is roughly equivalent to the Christian Democratic parties of Europe, or US Republicans. The AKP party has a pragmatic approach to the economy and management of resources (human or otherwise). Some Turkish entrepreneurs also have links with the Islamic modernist movement initiated by Fethullah Gulen (accused in 1998 of anti-secular activities and exiled from Turkey). One of the important financing sources of the movement is Ulker – a successful biscuit producer with international distribution. In the new political environment in Turkey, the Gulen movement gained momentum (for example a number of Gulen Schools opened recently in Turkey) (Sitaru, 2010).

In Iran, we find a more complicated predicament concerning the rise of the middle classes after the Iran-Iraq war, based on the partial liberalization during the 1990s and early 2000s. During his presidency (1989–97), Rafsanjani encouraged the return of exiled Iranian business men and women (mainly from the US). Starting with that period the Iranian business (middle) class developed strong commercial links with Dubai and continued to prosper during the Khatami regime (1997–2005). Due to the nuclear crisis and consequent economic embargo, the current political situation has put this class in difficulty but it continues to strive (Nasr, 2009).

More recently (October 2010), *Time* magazine covered the story of investment and entrepreneurship (both local and international) in the West Bank. The commentators point out that, while not being able to replace political actions with peace, these economic movements do change (for the better) the face of this territory.

Such a broad narrative as outlined above seems heartening and confirms the economic ideal of people, capital, and commodities moving unobstructed and somehow separated from local cultural characteristics or idiosyncrasies. Along with the seemingly universal value of (and desire for) prosperity, particular values with moral or religious roots shape the expectations of this new class. Big decisions for engaging in trade or small choices to buy one article or another for daily use are more likely than not determined by concerns of moral adequacy. Returning to my initial questions, the new prosperous Muslim middle classes form a large, relatively unknown and mostly untapped market that is developing an internal dynamic with global networks. The world economy is influenced by this market, and its reactions are as unpredictable as any other. However its dynamic is still linked to definitions of ethics and morality that the given economic narrative ignores. The case of the drastic fall in sales of Danish dairy products in the Middle East during the infamous 'cartoon crisis' in 2006 is just one example. But markets are globally linked (and thus less territorially defined than some like to think), and so is the Muslim population. The rise of Islamic banking products (including mortgages) in the United States shows just how the niches are unexpectedly large for specifically designed products (Maurer, 2006).

Therefore a global answer is required in response to my initial questions. Most decision makers in industry (not only marketers) need to have at least some idea about the specifics of Muslim markets, if only because many of their products end up being used by Muslims. Those products do not have to be imbued necessarily with Muslim values (there was nothing special about the Danish butter I used to buy in Bahrain), but the multiple messages the social life of the object carries may have a strong influence on its market evolution. The size of the global Muslim population should be reason enough for the necessity of a specific market understanding. Numbers tend to be a good enough argument in the economic world. Not only numbers, but also the intensity of links increased by the rapidity of communication and exchanges in our world make this knowledge all the more necessary. Arguably a bigger problem for the Danish dairy products than the cartoon itself was the speed with which it travelled. Smoothness of the economic flow may mean taking into account bumps in the road, and not ignoring them by creating ideal type market models.

The following pages aim to describe two instances of specific marketing practices in the Muslim world that reveal a major characteristic of Muslim markets. I examine the design of strategies for those markets. The two apparently separate domains are fashion

Source: Personal archive.

Figure 4.1   ECUT advertising in Iran, 2003

and finance. I hope to render visible their common marketing ground in the Muslim specific markets. At the same time I indicate the direction that the economy (as a science) is bound to take. It is already in the process of taking up these directions, introducing multidisciplinary approaches made all the more urgent now after the crisis of the 'free market' revealed its limitations. Definitions at the core of economics need to reengage with specific human realities (in) which the economy is developing.

NO-BODY IN FASHION

In the Middle East everybody loves fashion. But there is no body in it . . .

Driving or walking through Tehran, one cannot help but notice the advertisements of 'ECUT'. 'ECUT', a ready-to-wear fashion brand for men, uses 'stars' to advertise its products. The star Mohammad Reza Golzar, lead singer in the Aryan band, appears in two different poses: at the seashore, barefoot, dressed in an ECUT three-piece suit, and petting a horse (only the head of the horse is visible, and Mr Golzar from the chest up). Because women's bodies are prohibited from being shown in public, advertising of women's clothing via billboards is almost entirely absent.

Body visibility is a delicate issue and spatial segregation of the sexes is an important moral concern in Muslim contexts. Therefore practices surrounding representations of bodies are predictably sensitive to these contexts. Photography is a matter of concern in any public space, be it Muslim or not. Representing an object (body) through photography means not only invoking the specter of that object but also recreating its material presence, albeit a two-dimensional one. In the streets of Tehran representations of women's bodies are subjected to the requirement of modesty. This refers not only to photographs for billboards, but also to shop window mannequins, which lack the upper half of their heads and facial features (as opposed to male or child mannequins, realistic in their representation). As opposed to women's bodies in movement, mannequins and photographs are fixed, identifiable and thus more easily subjected to the dominant discourse. Photographic practices in Tehran's fashion world reveal a certain mode of imagining and representing (women's) bodies in relation to modern repertoires (like fashion), in the spatial regime of ideal public and private separation along the lines of gender (Figure 4.2). While body mobility and exposure is equated with Western-type modernity, in Tehran's public spaces women's bodies are ideally immobile and covered. Men appear to move more freely on the billboards. Nevertheless, no uncovered parts of the body (arms, legs) appear in the pictures. They may appear engaged in sports or 'manly' pursuits (when they are not heads of happy nuclear families), but the body is generally covered following the rules of decency present in the public space.

There is no exception to the rule of how women should be represented; all have to have their heads covered, not to mention the body. As an alternative to this, and in order to avoid certain monotony in the representations, some commodities appear on billboards accompanied by hands that hold them and give the object a human touch.

Although I met three photographers who worked with fashion designers in Tehran, I would hesitate to speak of an established field of fashion photography in Iran. A young designer, Mehran, first took me to the workshop of the photographer with whom he works. The workshop is situated downtown, not far from Baharestan. The studio was on the fourth floor of a building, in a modified apartment. I was invited to have a tea by the photographer (a young woman, very dynamic, wearing glasses, well coiffed, Laya), along with her other guests, three young women in their twenties. I later found out that one of them acted as a model for Mehran's creations. They were sitting on a low bed in the middle room of the apartment, now converted into the office of the studio. On the desk there was a telephone, a set of photography journals (*Aks*, the local photography publication), a calendar, and fiscal receipts, along with other office supplies. The room to the left of the entrance was the laboratory to which I did not have access. I was invited into the studio, the room at the right of the entrance. The studio was equipped with two projectors, some tripods and an electric heater, which the host turned on.

During our talk we mainly discussed photography as a profession in Tehran. The lack of an appropriate space for a studio bothered Laya the most. Nevertheless she showed me some of her works, most of which were portraits; her passion was portraits, especially women's portraits. Laya confessed that due to the specificity of the public spaces in Tehran, not all of her work can be shown. Her collaboration with Mehran was limited to the collection he did as a student for his BA degree. That collection was later sent to Finland for an international fashion exhibit in 2002. At first glance, her photographs disturbed me, but I was not exactly sure why. Only later, while witnessing a photographic session, did I realize that what seemed odd to me was the static position of the fashion models in the pictures. The bodies in the photographs suggested immobility in their poses. Even the photographs of fashion creations had a quality reminiscent of old-fashioned wedding pictures. The bodies have a static, albeit elegant, pose. In contrast,

Source: Personal archive journal cover.

Figure 4.2   Cover of Lotous – *an Iranian fashion magazine, 2003*

the fashion photographs in Europe are characterized by a certain mobility of the body, achieved through different techniques, from rapid shooting to image collages.

Professional photographers in Tehran resent these requirements of modesty and especially the immobility of the bodies. Being modern is associated in the first place with being mobile and, while Iranians tend to be quite mobile in their daily life, their bodies are represented in a static manner. The need to refrain from mobility has deep roots in

Source: Personal archive.

Figure 4.3   L'Oreal publicity in Istanbul, 2007

the local culture of modesty and avoidance, the averted and lateral looks being also a part of this elaborate code of conduct.

A somehow similar approach to fashion and bodies appears in the Gulf countries. Despite being seen as a shopping heaven for the fashionable, Dubai has similar rules to Iran – this may not be so surprising for anybody who remembers the trial of the 'kissing couple' in 2009–10 (two English expatriates who were caught kissing on a beach in Dubai, were tried, fined and imprisoned). Though much less restricted than in Iran, the public billboards and fashion advertising in the shopping malls do not reveal bodies. This is in contrast to Turkish public space, where publicity photographs depicting young women in bikinis lying on the beach co-exist with real women dressed according to the Islamic code with a modern touch. Turkey provides an interesting example of multilayered significations, as revealed in Figure 4.3, a L'Oreal street banner from Istanbul. The model's hair in this picture plays the role of the veil – a powerful ironic undertone to the photo, because the hair is the very body part that the headscarf is meant to conceal.

For the moment it is important to keep in mind that two aspects of the (female) body are eliminated in fashion (and product) advertising in some Middle Eastern Islamic markets (with the clear exception of Turkey): movement and the skin.[1]

How to move now from bodies and fashion to the world of finance? It was a question that I had to answer when I had to choose between studying the introduction of the euro in the Eurozone (a theme I was focusing on when still in Europe) and approaching issues of the body that started haunting as being a rather *petit* dark young man in Southern California. I found fashion to be the answer, because it creates the link between the body and the financial system: it both represents a multibillion global business with clear strategies of investment, delocalization of production, and so on, and its products are displayed on bodies to represent the actual or aspirational wealth of the people wearing them. Clothes mark identities and deconstruct them at the same time. Financial markets and strategies also mark people and bodies (ethnic, racial or otherwise) (Dymski, 2010), and offer the conditions for development or disappearance of bodies and population, and through money flows in parallel the fashion system of signs from one part of the world to another.

PIOUS VENTURES

The subtitle borrows from Bill Maurer's book, *Pious Property* (2006), which tackles the rise of the Islamic mortgage market in the United States. It's a very succinct phrase that summarizes the difference between Islamic and non-Islamic financial markets, which we can paraphrase as how Europe settled the question of usury in the Renaissance. What remains instead is the 'unsettled usury' in the Islamic world and the system of Islamic banking. The Renaissance also settled the centrality of the body in scientific and philosophical preoccupation and gave birth, not without pain, to humanism (one may think only of the regime of secrecy in which da Vinci or Michelangelo practiced dissections).

The financial products proposed to investors from the Islamic world are no different than other venture capital propositions. A fund for China Realty bears witness to this. It is real estate in all aspects possible. Firms of wealth management across the Gulf provide services for their wealthy (Muslim) clients who desire to invest their money worldwide.

The structure is common across the finance world: they receive a General Partnership proposition (GP), which allows the creation of multiple Limited Partnerships (LP) companies, incorporated offshore. The GP is entirely owned by the on-shore beneficiary, and it owns 100 per cent of the LPs. Each of the LPs is entitled to create on-shore companies – the Special Purpose Vehicles (SPV), which in turn own (entirely or with a local partner) the project to be developed – in our case real estate. The project is presented to the potential investors on a private basis, using the Investment Proposition, IP; the investors are invited to buy shares in the LP. At the end of the project, the SPV is sold, and the benefits return to the LP in the proportion of its participation in the SPV. The profits are further distributed among the investors and the on-shore beneficiary company, following the conditions set forth in the Investment Proposition. The GP and the LP are incorporated in 'fiscal paradises'.

The Investment Propositions arrive in a standardized form in the offices of the wealth management firms in order to be analyzed and further proposed to the capital owners (individual persons or other investment funds). The standardized form comprises two or three different brochures, one containing the details of the investment itself, the other

Your Logo Here
XXX CHINA REALTY XXX
XXX Contract & Application Forms

Note: The cover has been modified to hide the name of the investment scheme.

Source: Personal archive.

Figure 4.4   Cover of the investment proposition brochure

details about the procedure of the investment and the subscription materials and a third eventually explaining the SPV created (juridical personalities that move the capital from the investors to the investment ground). The costs of different products are higher than the capacity of investment, so there is a necessary bank leverage in the venture. Up to this point there was no principle that contradicted Islamic views on finance, but the bank and its interest rates do. Therefore, it is specified in the brochures that banking is done following the Islamic banking rules. I will not enter into details on Islamic banking, as many authors have dealt with various aspects of its mechansims (DiVanna, 2006; Vogel and Hayes, 1998; Sudin and Bala, 1997; El Gamal, 2008, Maurer, 2005), I only underline that Islamic morality does not accept usury (in fact, around this point my entire argument turns).

The Chinese Realty brochure (the investment period is long finished, the proposition was between 2005 and 2006) is an interesting object in itself (Figure 4.4) On the cover one can admire a picture of a necklace of (Chinese) coins tied together by a ribbon. Inside, the pages are decorated with photos of the latest developments in the Chinese real estate market and 'culturally specific' images of food and cutlery (chopsticks) used in Chinese restaurants. The local flavor is a must in order to be more explicit. No portraits of any people appear.

The subscription brochure explains the terms and conditions of the investment: minimum investment, risk, cash flows, warranties, and so on. Among them, we find the following terms defined:

> '**Religious Supervisory Board** means the religious supervisory board of the *mudarib*, constituted from time to time;
>
> *Sharia* **or Islamic Jurisprudence** means the general body of Islamic law as interpreted by the Religious Supervisory Board;'

The brochure goes on to explain what are the regulations specific to this, and the laws that prevail.

'Conformity with the *sharia*
The XXX Assets shall be invested and managed in accordance with the *sharia*. The decisions of the Religious Supervisory Board in respect of the investment of the XXX Assets shall be binding upon the XXX and the Investor.

[. . .]

Governing Law
This XXX Contract shall be governed by the laws of (a state) provided that the same do not contradict with the *sharia*, in which case the *sharia* shall prevail.

[. . .]

Arabic Text

In all circumstances the Arabic text of this [. . .] Contract shall prevail.'

In the brief of the document it is also specified that each individual investment shall be reviewed by the board in order to verify the *sharia* compliance. The leverage of this investment is naturally done through Islamic banking.

Note three things. First, it is the *sharia* law that prevails over the state law (and this includes financial matters). In the Western history of money, finance systems always wanted to escape the state-law in order to create their own autonomous governing body. Money, both as materiality and as rules for moving around capital, tried to spiral out from competing bodies of law, and remain bare – with the risk of losing its materiality. However, even immaterial money must refer back to *sharia* which regulates how money can move and produce. Islamic banking regulations are the ones that basically govern these investments.

Second, the fund creates its own religious supervisory board that meets from time to time in order to certify that this financial product complies with the requirements of *sharia* as interpreted by them. According to Maurer (2006), *ijtihad*, the process of making a legal decision by independent interpretation, opened the doors for Islamic financial experimentation in the twentieth century. This allowed for the imagining of ways in which usury could disappear from a financial product; the way this happens is rather controversial. The basic methods are those of entrusting money to managers who in return are paid and also take a part of the profit that the money may generate. The bank acts thus as a trusted manager and the returns depend on the productive (not reproductive) power of money, which in turn depends on the socio-economic and cultural contexts in which the monies are invested. The basics are outlined in the principles of *mudaraba* (profit sharing with entrusted management), *musharaka* (profit sharing with participative management), *bai'muajjal* (deferred payment sale) and *qard hasan* (interest-free benevolent loan). There exist critics who maintain that the principles form merely a smoke screen in the face of the interest of global markets, or are practices that are hardly inductive to the start-up of business and risk taking initiatives (Kuran, 2005; Wiedl, 2007). Others see the approach as a tool for interpretation in itself, and there are yet others who need Islamic banking to finance their homes and to be in compliance with their own faith. Without entering the technicalities of Islamic finance, I will retain for the sake of the argument the fact that Islamic banking does offer possibilities for money to circulate through the real world (or give that impression for that matter) in order to generate profit.

A third point to note in the brochure is that the prevalent language is Arabic, the language of Qur'anic interpretation, written from right to left (Messick, 1996). It is the *logos* of the *sharia*, and as such it rules Islamic jurisprudence.

At this point I would like to go back to the cover in the figure and use its visual metaphor in order to exemplify the argument on Islamic finance: the coins in the photo are not bare. They are dressed in the ribbon which ties them together and gives them a different legitimacy – the ribbon is passing through them and they are passing through the world. Compare this photo with the iconic popular images of wealth in the Western iconic representations of 'bare money': piles of coins hiding Uncle Scrooge from view, or a rain of dollar bills falling directly into the hands of the investor. It seems that, while in Western representations money covers (or dresses) the investor, in Islamic finance money is dressed. The coins in the photo are not naked. They do not reproduce themselves (as they are bound to do in conventional – read Western – financial markets) but they produce value which in turn can be sold for more money – this is the image which codes how Islamic financing is explained.

Money produces, not re-produces. And the representations of the bodies are likewise. Their reproductive capacity (or any detail that would allude to reproduction) must be hidden from sight. Dress is there to cover and not to dis-cover. In fact belief does influence the way in which believers of any kind (that means us, human beings) relate to the world, and organize its reality. The particular religious belief of the unity of God and its power of creation does contain in it the potential of denying that power to any-body else. Reproduction (biological and otherwise) is as close to creation as one can get. It is thus both deemed sacred – see the pro-life advocacy – and subtracted from the world – as in the examples given. Marketing in a world of hidden reproduction obliges both the changing repertoires of attraction and the re-organizing of practices (financial or otherwise) in order to match the 'worldview on the ground.' Abstract notions such as finance and fashion – ideally a free-floating world of signifiers put on paper or dress tags – stop short of the materialities of the places in which they perform. At the same time, forms of 'universal categories' (fashion and finance) find new expressions of existence that necessitate the reconsideration of the specific fields from which they originate.

CONCLUSION

Cultural specificity is as much a barrier as it is a stimulus for economic movements. If we continue to operate with an ideal image of the economic exchange as being free of cultural determinants we will periodically encounter smokescreens of specificity in the same way that the European air traffic was paralyzed by the Icelandic volcano. However, the same volcanic smokescreen created opportunities for ground transport companies, and led to a reorganization of the European air space regulations.

In order to avoid the fragility of an economy based on the ideology of free transparent flows taking place in an idealized, abstract economic space, we need an understanding of economic practices grounded on observation. It includes cultural differentiation that marketing people intuitively understand and that most of them apply in their daily work. Forced by the developments of recent years, this notion is moving to the core of economic science. It may seem slower and the road bumpier, but its long term advantages are hard to ignore: understanding and evaluating risk has a highly important cultural component. Thus, when promoting products that do not appear to have any cultural weight, businesspeople may hit specificities of the markets in different ways (and coming from unpredictable directions). Besides the already discussed Danish cartoon controversy, the case of Skoda Octavia in India is a good example (without being specifically about Muslim markets) that shows precisely the unexpected consequences of overseen cultural 'details'. The specific car model did not really 'fly' in the first round of offers, and marketers did not know why. The price range and styling of the model was suitable in India for people who usually hire a chauffeur instead of driving themselves. So, at the showroom, potential customers would sit in the back seat. When marketers realized this (local representatives revealed it to the company), the manufacturer paid more attention to the back seat, moved the central commands for the windows and air conditioning to the back, and the model started selling. This example perfectly illustrates how class, caste, markets, and bodily engagement with the object intersect and influence market performance. The same happens in the case of Muslim dominated markets. Beyond obvious moral codes that operate in these markets – there are underlying moral principles of 'covering' any bodies with reproductive capacities, be they money or women's bodies[2] – these choices are determined by a web of social practices that link global events with local dynamics. Social and bodily practices, identities (religious, ethnic or sexual), and ideologies communicate in a technologically enhanced manner. Marketers are (or should be) aware of them, and of the 'weak signals' that may topple the market dynamic. There is no magic formula. Speaking about Muslim markets, one must keep in mind that one deals with markets in 'plural'. There are markets for different objects as there are different markets in the Muslim world, each bearing the cultural specificities of the place in which religion is only one of the influencing factors.[3]

NOTES

*   Special thanks to Wendy Harcourt for her advice and the careful revision and editing of this chapter.
1. Some may argue that in Europe the body also disappears from the fashion displays. The erasure of the

body in Western fashion display is due to the trend towards the dematerialization of consumption. While this trend has also moral undertones, it is a different story than the one found in the Middle East.

2. Male bodies are viewed, traditionally, as productive and socially engaged, dominating the public sphere of work and creating value, not reproducing it. This may partially explain at this level the relative tolerance of male bodies in movement.

3. The other slope that marketing must ride is offered by the field of neuro-bio-psychology – more specifically the part which studies brain activity and decision making. As studies of the brain progress and a certain universality of brain activity is revealed, one may (and does) wonder where the decisions are made, and how. This is certainly another source of information that could be used to complement the studies on cultural specificities bound to reveal the ways in which declinations of the same object, symbol or commodity take place in different environments or on different markets.

BIBLIOGRAPHY

Al-Ali, Nadje (2000), *Secularism, Gender, and the State in the Middle East. The Egyptian Women's Movement*, Cambridge: Cambridge University Press.

Alloula, Malek (1986), 'The colonial harem', in *Theory and History of Literature*, vol. 21, Minneapolis, MN: University of Minnesota Press.

Buck-Morss, Susan (1991), *The Dialectics of Seeing: Walter Benjamin and the Arcades Project*, Cambridge, London, UK: MIT Press.

Dymsky, G.A. (2010), 'Development as social inclusion: reflections on the US subprime crisis', *Development*, **53** (3), 368–75.

DiVanna, Joseph A. (2006), *Understanding Islamic Banking. The Value Proposition that Transcends Cultures*, Cambridge, UK: Leonardo and Francis Press.

El Gamal, Mahmoud A. (2008), *Islamic Finance: Law, Economics, and Practice*, Cambridge: Cambridge University Press.

Göle, N. (2002), 'Islam in public: new visibilities and new imaginaries', *Public Culture*, **14** (1), 173–190.

Göle, N. (2003), 'The voluntary adoption of Islamic stigma symbols', *Social Research*, **70** (2), 809–27.

Haron, Sudin and Shanmugan, Bala (1997), *Islamic Banking System. Concepts and Applications*, Singapore: Pelanduk Publications.

Hayes, Samuel and Vogel, Frank (1998), *Islamic Law and Finance: Religion, Risk, and Return*, Leiden: Martinus Nijhoff Publishers.

Kuran, Timur (2005), *Islam and Mammon: The Economic Predicaments of Islamism*, Princeton, NJ: Princeton University Press.

Maurer, Bill (2005) *Mutual Life, Limited: Islamic Banking, Alternative Currencies, Lateral Reason*, Princeton, NJ: Princeton University Press.

Maurer, Bill (2006), *Pious Property: Islamic Mortgages in the United States*, New York: Russell Sage Foundation Publications.

Messick, Brinkley (1996), *The Calligraphic State: Textual Domination and History in a Muslim Society*, Berkeley, CA: University of California Press.

Moghadam, Valentine M. (2003), *Modernizing Women. Gender and Social Change in the Middle East*, Boulder, Colorado and London: Lynne Riener Publishers.

Nasr, Vali (2009), *Forces of Fortune: The Rise of the New Muslim Middle Class and What It Will Mean for Our World*, New York: Free Press Edition.

Ossman, Susan (2002), *Three Faces of Beauty, Casablanca, Paris, Cairo*, Durham, NC: Duke University Press.

Perman, S. (2010), 'A national economy – without the nation: West Bank entrepreneurs are building businesses in case peace breaks out', *Time*, October.

Sitaru, L. (2010), 'Umbra lui Gulen' ('The Shadow of Gulen'), *Foreign Policy Romania*, March/April.

Sudin, Haron and Shanmugam Bala (1997), *Islamic Banking System: Concepts and Applications*, Subang Jaya, Malaysia: Pelanduk Publications.

Tarlo, Emma (2010), *Visibly Muslim: Fashion, Politics, Faith*, Oxford: Berg Editions.

Vogel, Frank E. and Samuel L. Hayes III (1998), *Islamic Law and Finance: Religion, Risk, and Return*, The Hague: Kluwer Law International.

Wiedl, Kathrin Nina (2007), *The Islamic Banking System – Not Conducive to the Start-up of Young, Innovative Business Firms*, Munich and Ravensburg, Germany: Grin Verlag editions.

PART II

MUSLIM CONSUMPTIONSCAPES

PART II

MUSLIM
CONSCRIPTION SEPOYS

5 Gender and privacy in Arab Gulf states: implications for consumption and marketing
Russell Belk and Rana Sobh*

GENDER AND PRIVACY

Privacy and gender segregation are anchors for identity in Arab-Gulf Countries. The significant need for privacy of individuals in the region impacts different aspects of life including consumption. However, the meaning of privacy in Islam is different from that in Western culture and so the reason why it is prized in the Gulf is somewhat different from the reasons why it is valued in the West. Thus, a good understanding of this concept in the region and its implications for marketing practices is of paramount importance. In this chapter we report and analyze the findings of two qualitative studies involving gender and privacy in the Arab Gulf states of Qatar and United Arab Emirates. One involved the gendered spaces of the home and the second involved the privacy provided by 'covering' among young women. We find that privacy for females remains a key consideration in home design and use, while it is becoming less of a concern in the clothing and grooming practices of university students. Part of evolution in covering practices is generational, with young women wanting to distinguish themselves from older generations. Part is also due to their feeling greater attraction to 'modern' and 'Western' practices in response to increased wealth, openness to Western media, and the influx of foreigners in their countries. But part of the covering practices of these young women remains rooted in the same cultural traditionalism expressed in the conspicuous gender segregation found in the home. At the same time that clothing and grooming are imitating elements of Western fashion, the traditionalism of covering itself expresses a cultural resistance to the West. We discuss this tension and derive implications for understanding and marketing to those in the changing Arab Gulf cultures.

PRIVACY

If you are an academic, the chances are good that you are reading this in the privacy of a personal office with a door that can be closed and a personal computer that is perhaps connected to a personal printer, surrounded by some of your personal effects. This is likely to be the case regardless of whether you are in a workplace or a home office. However, the old model of private workplace offices, personal secretaries, closing office doors, and hierarchical spaces designating status within vertical organizations, is giving way to a new model of open cubicles, shared spaces and resources, and non-hierarchical flat organizations (Florida, 2002). This newer model has often been met with resistance, especially among those who are used to the sorts of private office space that you most likely enjoy (Lohr, 1997). Tian and Belk (2005) find that in order to counter the lack of acoustic privacy in open plan offices, many workers bring their own music systems, noise-cancelling headphones, and even white noise machines. They also observe that the size and privacy of offices continue as marks of status in organizations. In other words, privacy and space are luxuries in the contemporary business world.

The contemporary home has followed a somewhat similar evolution to the office in the past 300 years, evolving in many cultures from discrete rooms with doors between them to a more open plan with great rooms, kitchens that flow into other living spaces, and higher floors that are open onto lower ones (Attfield, 1999; Gallagher, 2006). However, going back a bit farther in time suggests that privacy is itself a rather new concept. In the sixteenth century most houses had a few large rooms that served multiple purposes (Rybczynski, 1986). People ate, slept, received guests, and worked in a space that was open to everyone who entered. But over the following centuries spaces in homes, especially those of the wealthy, grew more and more private. There were eventually rooms and areas where family members could retreat not only from public view, but from each other. Tuan (1982) attributes this privatization of the home to the rise of individualism in Europe.

As the home became more private and home sizes of average consumers grew, even children in households began to have their own rooms and spaces, which they generally regarded as being their territories (Altman, 1975; Munro and Madigan, 1999; Salinger, 1995). Rooms were no longer multi-purpose and kitchens, bedrooms, living rooms or parlors, and eventually family rooms, dens, and laundry rooms became common in middle class homes in much of the world (Allan and Crow, 1989). We now feel such a right to our private home spaces that we are offended when someone enters our room uninvited and may even feel a sense of violation or contagion (Belk, 1988).

As homes grew, their size, the number of rooms, and the degree of specialization of these rooms all became marks of status. Although work moved out of the home with the coming of the Industrial Revolution, it is coming back into the home in the Information Age (Nippert-Eng, 1996; Tian and Belk, 2005). The adoption of the Internet, e-mail, text messaging, cell phones, and other such technologies are bringing white collar work back into the home and this means that absolute home privacy is disappearing in a manner paralleling the decline of private offices in the away-from-home workplace (Jackson, 2002; Morley, 2000; Riley, 1999). And in society at large, especially with the growth of post-9/11 security measures, public surveillance means that we are losing privacy in many aspects of our lives (Nissenbaum, 2010; Wacks, 2010). Some of this we are quite aware of, as with the scans and searches at airports and other transportation portals, but other means of surveillance, from the video cameras in ATM machines to the street scenes of Google Maps and the increasingly ubiquitous security cameras, remain largely invisible. Retail shops are also increasing their use of hidden video cameras to analyze shopping behavior and increase sales (Rosenbloom, 2010). Technologies used in medicine mean that even the secrets inside our bodies are no longer entirely private (Romanyshyn, 1989). So in our bodies, homes, offices, public spaces, and commercial spaces, we may be coming closer to the panopticon surveillance envisioned by Jeremy Bentham for controlling confined prison populations from a central 'all-seeing' position (see Foucault, 1977), except that rather than a centralized 'big brother,' there are numerous others who may now monitor our behavior.

For the individual, much of privacy is about autonomy and control – the ability to do what you please within your private spaces. This includes sexual freedom, consumer freedom of choice, and freedom to dress your person and decorate your home as you see fit, so long as it does not harm others. The Internet gives us access to a different type of privacy through anonymity. The Internet also gives us potential access to greater physical privacy, but we may or may not have greater informational privacy (Altman, 1975). As Sheller and Urry (2003) argue, the flows and networks linking our public and private personas are altering, due to both those technologically aided mobilities that also have physical form (that is, mobile people, mobile objects, and mobile hybrid humans and machines, such as the car and driver) and those that have informational form (that is, electronic communication via data, visual images, sounds, and texts). The results of these mobilities, as they see it, are new hybrid forms that might be thought of as being private in public (for example, texting in a public place) and being public in private (for example, posting to an Internet forum from home).

Westerners' conceptions of privacy are linked to the notion of individualism and people's rights to non-intrusion. However, the words 'private' and 'public' do not occur in the Qur'an or the oral tradition passed on by the Prophet Mohammad and the word privacy has no exact equivalent in the Arabic language (Vogel, 2003). Although some have suggested that privacy means secrecy in Islam (for example, Asad, 2003; Kadivar, 2003), *hurma* (best translated as sanctity in English) is the concept that is probably closest to the notion of privacy in Arab culture. *Hurma* refers at once to a woman or wife, to the sanctity of religious sites, and also to the sanctity of the home. The home as well as the body or parts of the body are private spaces (*awra*) *par excellence* that should be concealed in public. All are seen as sacred and pure and should be guarded. Another distinctive element in the Islamic construction of private space is its fluidity, in that a public area could be temporarily turned into a private space or vice versa (a private space can temporarily be made public). For instance, a street can be temporarily changed into a private sacred space by occupying it for prayer by men or women (El Guindi, 1999a, 1999b). The home, which is the most private domain, could also be converted to a public space that requires covering by women when a male stranger enters. As such, in the Arab-Islamic world, privacy is very much based on the notion of sanctity and concerns both women and the home (El Guindi, 1999a, 1999b; Secor, 2002). Since the woman is the guardian of collective sanctity of the family and even the nation, the conception of privacy in Islam is not about individualism but is rather collectivist in nature. That is, women's seclusion or covering represents that familial, religious, and sometimes national sense of propriety and sanctity, especially to the extent that it contrasts with alternative practices. It is not the home that is sometimes contested in terms of its gendered spaces, but rather the gendered spaces within the ostensibly public realm (for example, Abisaab, 2005).

The significance of home sanctity in Arab-Islamic culture implies the importance of respecting people's privacy in their homes, for both males and females (Campo, 1991). For instance, a visitor should carefully seek permission to enter someone's private domain and should not intentionally peek into houses. Indeed, Muslim architecture is introverted and has been called the architecture of the veil (for example, Asad, 2003). Surrounded by a simple facade, the courtyard which is the house's most private space is kept hidden. The inward home structure that excludes and protects the private from the public is intended to protect family members' privacy as well as the privacy of the inhabitants of neighboring houses.

The significant need for privacy within many Islamic homes is also related to the concept of modesty in Islam that underlies the Muslim self and particularly the woman's self and her relation to private and public spaces. This need for privacy is also displayed in public spaces via the covered clothing practices of women in the region (Mottahedeh and Stilt, 2003). The sort of body and facial covering found in the Arab Gulf relates to privacy in two distinct ways. The first is that, like gender segregation within the home, it preserves sanctity by hiding the otherwise potentially alluring body. In this sense it provides a mobile private space that the woman carries with her as she travels within public spaces. Secondly, the addition of facial covering, either through facial coverings like a *niqab* or *burka* or by a large scarf-like hood (a *shayla*) and sunglasses, provides anonymity. Anonymity of this sort potentially allows freedom from the surveillance of others, because the woman is not identifiable. It is this lack of identifiability that has caused controversy in other places in the contexts of passports, driver's licenses, and identification cards.

In addition to a person's modest dress in public (physical modesty), modesty should also be observed in conduct, speech and thoughts. Physical modesty is related to the privacy of the body or what must be covered – *awra*. It is 'navel to knee' for men. However, a women's *awra* in public or in the presence of a non-*mahrem* (someone eligible to marry her), consists of her entire body with the exception of her face and hands. This is both to spare the woman embarrassment or shame and to avoid causing *fitna* (chaos, discord) if men were to see her uncovered (Hoffman-Ladd, 1987). Men in the *mahrem* category (that is, husband and kin not eligible for marriage) may see a woman's hair, ears, neck, upper part of the chest, arms and legs. Other parts of her body may only be seen by her spouse. This dress code has traditionally necessitated a unique convenient style in the Arab Gulf, whereby women's living quarters are separated from men's quarters so that women do not have to veil while in their homes. We discuss gender privacy in non-home contexts in the following section before we turn to a more detailed discussion of the issue in the particular context of our study.

GENDERED SPACES

Obviously no society could reproduce itself if there was sufficient gender segregation to ensure the total privacy of men and women from one another. Nevertheless as separate public toilet facilities, dressing rooms, and dormitories suggest, there are venues in which there is an attempt to keep the two sexes separate due to modesty and sexual propriety. There have historically also been a number of organizations, events, and places that have been gender-segregated because of tradition, religious beliefs, gender politics, or gender stereotyping. This includes many secret societies, male and female initiation rites, and sex-specific living quarters. Such separations are often encoded in elaborate mythologies and belief systems and may also involve taboos tied to pollution symbolism, as with the ritual separation of women in some cultures during menstruation and following childbirth (for example, Douglas, 1966; Smith, 2007). There are also professions and activities that tend to be dominated by either men or women based on sex role stereotypes. For example, occupations involving caring, teaching, design, fashion and beauty tend to be dominated by women and sometimes homosexual males, whereas occupations involving manual labor, the professions, combat, management, finance and policing have typically been dominated by men. There are cultural and historical variations in these patterns and gender balance is now increasing. But the stereotypes about gendered occupations still have a kernel of demographic truth. There are also gendered servicescapes (for example, Fischer et al., 1998; Sun et al., 2004; Black, 2004), gendered recreational venues (for example, Fischer and Gainer, 1994; Peiss, 1986), gendered shopping locales (for example, Sherry, et al., 2004; Tuncay and Otnes, 2008), and gendered magazines (for example, Beetham, 1996; McCracken, 1992; Radway, 1984; Scanlon, 1995).

Kwolek-Folland (1997) studied early twentieth-century insurance offices and found that women were increasingly prominent in clerical positions, but that these offices were still gender segregated with women on different floors or in different areas of the buildings. Male executives in these firms tended to replicate the patriarchal arrangements of their homes by including such accoutrements as bearskin rugs, fireplaces and dark wood paneling. Moreover, they transferred their roles as *paterfamilias* from the home to the workplace, creating something of a pseudo-family at work:

> The man with a private office was a man of property. He did not actually *own* the space, but it was nonetheless *his*. In the often noisy, crowded environments of large office buildings, a private space was the most sought-after mark of status. Private offices validated the manhood of those who possessed them by emphasizing individuality and personal freedom. Male workers not blessed with such a space were both lower in status and less manly. Lest anyone should miss the point, private executive offices were shared with female secretaries, who were often referred to as 'office wives' or 'office housekeepers'. (Kwolek-Folland, 1997, pp. 166–67).

Although there is androcentrism evident in such arrangements, gender segregation in the workplace wasn't entirely an act of domination and consigning women to inferior spaces. Rather, there was concern that a woman's moral well-being would be threatened in sexually integrated workspaces (Spain, 1992). Although universities in the US began admitting women in the late nineteenth century, it wasn't until the sexual revolution of the 1920s that the idea of sexual integration of the workplace really began to take hold.

But it was neither offices nor universities that provided the breakthrough to allow women to escape from the confines of the home and to feel at ease in the masculine world of large cities' downtown areas. It was instead the rise of certain retail spaces such as department stores, tea houses, cinemas and restaurants that made it respectable and safe for women to become shoppers in the new spaces of the city (Hutter, 1987; Leach, 1984). The department stores that arose in the late nineteenth century were called 'dream worlds' and 'palaces of consumption' with elegant settings, décor catering to women, deferential sales clerks and an abundance of sumptuous merchandise from around the world (Benson, 1988; Williams, 1982). Reekie (1993) aptly characterizes these luxurious appointments and displays as temptations that 'seduced' female shoppers. With the development of safe public transportation and the increased presence of women in the workforce, women began to claim urban spaces during the late nineteenth and early twentieth centuries in Europe, North America, Asia, and Australia.

But at about the same time, like the office, the feminine 'woman's space' of the home began to become rationalized in the early twentieth century. Sparke (1995) characterizes this as a battle in the sexual politics of taste as masculine science, technology and rationality were imposed in the name of efficiency and drove out the feminine taste, fashion, and superfluity of the Victorian parlor. Healthy children, housekeeping, order and cleanliness became new marks of a good wife and mother. As a result, the home became for a time, less of a feminine domain in Sparke's (1995) view. In seeking a place of their own in the household, perhaps women expressed an equal desire for a time of their own. When asked about where she went to be on her own, a 35-year-old woman with children ages 3, 11 and 14 in a study by Munro and Madigan (1999) replied:

> There isn't really many places in the house that you can go. I mean I've tried going into my room – it doesn't work because the wee one of three, she's in and out – one's doing dishes and that – you know, they'll start arguing and they're in telling me what they're doing and so that doesn't really work. I don't really manage to get any privacy unless they're all out playing and the wee one is asleep. (p. 115).

As this reflection suggests, women as the primary caregivers in the household often subordinate themselves to the needs of others in the household (Miller, 1998) and only occasionally are able to retreat into a 'back region' (Giddens, 1984) where they can 'be themselves.' In *A Room of One's Own*, Virginia Woolf (1929) concluded that in order to be a writer she required 500 pounds a year and a room with a lock on the door. She also realized that this was an impossibility for most women, not least because they could not take the time away from their household responsibilities and the imperative of being care-givers.

Gender partitioning of home spaces exists in many traditional and historic societies (Spain, 1992). In part, this is due to the pollution taboos and fears noted earlier. Part is also due to concerns with sexual propriety. But part is also due to status concerns. Spain (1992) documents how in wealthy nineteenth century British country houses, 'men's' rooms outnumbered 'women's' rooms five to one. There were separate 'men's stairs,' 'bachelors' stairs,' and 'young ladies' stairs' for family and guests, as well as separate stairs for male and female servants. Even to have so many stairways was a luxury that only the wealthy could afford, but the point of relevance here is that privacy and gender segregation are luxuries that are not unique to the Gulf societies to which we now turn.

GENDER AND PRIVACY IN ARAB GULF STATES

The Context

Our research focuses on Qatar and the United Arab Emirates. As the financial, communications and educational crossroads of the Middle East, Qatar and the UAE offer an opportunity to understand what is unique as well as what is common in Arab/Muslim and Western values involving women, privacy, identity and the home. We find that in Qatari and Emirati cultures as well as Gulf States, Islamic identities are reified in the changing material design of homes and the changing designs and uses of covered women's clothing. These spaces and practices not only help shape behavior and encode and express cultural values, they also facilitate and precipitate key family and cultural rituals. They affect patterns of courtship, hospitality, recreation, eating, shopping, education, socializing and more. An understanding of these changing behaviors is vital for successful marketing in the Gulf. In addition, a better understanding of these influences should inform our knowledge of the effects of globalization, culture and religion in an understudied part of the world.

The home is an artifact of culture. The consumption of spaces, places and objects within our homes is expressive of relationships, culture and identity. Such concepts have been extensively studied in the West, but little comparable work has been done in non-Western homes especially in Arab/Muslim cultures. Definitions of private and public spheres are different in Islam than those in Western paradigms. A space is defined as private or public within Islam based on who is present. Compared to the West, we find a more restricted sense of privacy and a sharper distinction between private and public spheres in Qatar, as well as an increasing use of home spaces and objects to encode and express gendered Arab-Islamic identity.

There is no definite obligation in the Qur'an about women's seclusion or segregation in the home and the only stipulation about men's and women's dress is that it be modest. Yet, gendered space, the space that is seen to be the legitimate space of men or women, is highly disciplined in some Muslim societies, and gender sociability may be restricted. Veiling introduces a form of social and symbolic distance between women and men. Such modest dress increases women's mobility and allows them to cross gender borders. Although in countries like Turkey and France veiling has been outlawed in certain public contexts, even in these cases the lack of covering can lead to Muslim women feeling uncomfortable in these spaces (for example, Secor, 2002). While the mandate to wear the *hijab* (head covering) in contemporary Iran has been strongly criticized (for example, Kar, 2003), when the Shah of Iran banned covering in 1936, this too led to women feeling stressed if they ventured into public spaces (Thompson, 2003). By being totally covered, women carry some of the privacy of the home with them. In the Gulf States, this mobile privacy via the black *abaya* (gown), *shayla* (head covering), and sometimes *burqa* (face covering), allows the woman to go places that are male dominated and access spaces they could not otherwise access. Nevertheless, these traditional female coverings have recently started to become much more fashion-driven, including the incorporation of silken embroideries, the attachment of jewels, and the introduction of designer and custom-designed garments. Changes are also occurring in wearing styles that show, rather than hide, parts of the body, hair and jewellery, and the underlying clothing of wearers. Ostensibly these changes invite the male gaze that predecessor versions of these garments seek to deflect. Thus, female garments have become a battleground for global and local cultural influences and controversies abound about what young Gulf women are wearing and about the influence of Western consumption patterns.

Research Methods

Observations and in-depth interviews on the home were conducted in Arabic with adult members of 24 middle-class home-owning families in Qatar, focusing on the meaning and use of home spaces. Women were the primary participants in these interviews, but in several cases we separately interviewed their husbands as well. We asked about meanings of home, favorite areas of the home, situations in which these spaces are used, favorite objects within the home, the meanings of these objects and usage patterns by other family members. We also asked about who had made the decisions regarding home decorating in each room and how the house was selected. Projective probes (for example, if your home were an animal, what kind of animal would it be?) were incorporated in these interviews. In addition we interviewed an architect, a real estate agent and a religious authority as part of this work. We videotaped or audiotaped all interviews and also videotaped and photographed the different rooms of these homes where we were allowed to do so, which was in about half of the home interviews.

We also conducted 24 additional interviews with 17- to 24-year-old university students in Qatar and United Arab Emirates, focusing on women's dress. These interviews were primarily conducted in English, which was the language of instruction at both universities. However when certain thoughts were better expressed in Arabic, the Qatar participants were free to switch from English. Half of the clothing interviews were carried out in Doha Qatar and half in Sharjah, UAE. Interviewers (one non-Muslim male, one covered Muslim female) asked participants about their clothing and grooming practices. Participants were asked to wear one of their favorite outfits to the interview and to talk about it. Following 'grand tour' questions (McCracken, 1988), we asked participants about how they dress for different occasions, what different *abayas* say about them, and how these *abayas* make them feel, as other topics that emerged during the interviews. Projective techniques were also used in these interviews, including visual elicitation based on a set of stimulus pictures of girls wearing different types of *abayas* and displaying different adornment practices. These pictures were chosen to elicit responses toward varying degrees of traditional and modern fashions in different contexts and with different audiences (for example, males, females, Westerners, locals). The favorite outfit that was worn to the interview became a further focus for visual elicitation. Some participants also brought photos of their *abayas*, clothing, and accessories. This research also involved observations conducted at weddings and other female gatherings, including a fashion show. Observations were also conducted at the universities, in shopping malls, and at restaurants. In addition, interviews for the clothing study were conducted with two *abaya* designers, two retail *abaya* shop owners, and one religious scholar. In both sets of interviews related topics such as foods and fragrances emerged and became subjects for further questions. The research was carried out between 2007 and 2009.

All interviews were transcribed and, for the home interviews, translated into English. Coding of interviews and observations was done by both researchers separately and then together in an iterative process. This was facilitated by a computer program (dtSearch). Analysis was hermeneutic and iterative. We use pseudonyms throughout in our account.

FINDINGS

We report our findings first concerning the home and then focusing on clothing and grooming. In both sections the critical concepts are privacy and gender, although the clothing and grooming section is limited to women, where the most contentious and volatile changes are occurring. These sections highlight some of these issues, but are primarily descriptive. The theoretical and practical implications of our studies are discussed in two sections following the findings.

The Home

Our home findings suggest that Gulf homes have different layers of privacy. The street is the exterior public sphere of strangers. The home is the interior private sphere used by

Source: Photo taken by one of the chapter authors.

Figure 5.1   External view of male/female entrances from courtyard

inhabitants and their visitors and is separated from the public sphere by high boundary walls, window screens, and inward facing courtyards, visually encoding a sharp distinction between public and private space. The architect in our study drew the link between the privacy of the home and women's veiling practices:

> Abdullah (architect): Privacy and religious considerations have always been taken into consideration in Qatari homes. Qatari architecture reflects people's lifestyle and values. Being respectful of Islamic religious values in Qatar, Bahrain, Saudi Arabia, the Middle East, Iran, and even Turkey has influenced architecture in these countries and regions. . . . There're a lot of windows but they are equipped with screens, like a woman with veil. She can see but cannot be seen.

This view has also been echoed by others in the literature (for example, Asad, 2003).

A second feature of Qatari homes encoding privacy is the sharp division between men's and women's spaces within the home. Figure 5.1 shows two separate (men's and women's) entrances to the home of one of our participants. The view is from within high courtyard walls. This is consistent with the view that privacy in Islam is based on the notion of sanctity (*hurma*) which applies to both women and the home (El Guindi, 1999a and 1999b). This is the same sanctity that applies to religious sites such as mosques and

Source: Photo taken by one of the chapter authors.

Figure 5.2   A portion of a men's majlis

denotes that which is sacred and inviolable. It has also been a subject of debate within feminist and Muslim discourses, with some (for example, Baron, 1994) seeing greater gender segregation as a rebuke to Western hegemony and others (for example, Nageeb, 2004) seeing it as a form of neo-harem or an instantiation of the lower status of women (for example, Spain, 1992).

This interior sphere is further differentiated into a family/female domain and a male domain (the men's *majlis*). The men's *majlis* is a favorite room of adult males in our study and is considered a cultural symbol of Arab hospitality, pride and honor. Figure 5.2 shows a portion of a men's *majlis* from our study. It is shared by three brothers and also contains an interior entryway with a fountain, a kitchen, and a dining area for about 50 people. As one of our male participants explained:

> Saleh: In [the] *majlis* I meet my friends and old classmates and cousins. [The] *majlis* is a place of prestige and a place of heritage. It has traditions surrounding it. For example, if I host someone I become responsible for him, and nobody may enter [the] *majlis* and insult a guest. These are family traditions.

In contrast, for women, the favorite room within their domain is their bedroom, a place of privacy, retreat, and prayer, as seen in Figure 5.3. Although the interviewee, Aysha, shares this bedroom with her husband, she clearly regards it as her space and regards her husband as a guest there. Husband-as-guest in bedrooms is not a new phenomenon and has been common since Biblical times (Raglan, 1964).

Source: Photo taken by one of the chapter authors.

Figure 5.3 A portion of a woman's bedroom

Although as we noted earlier some call Muslim homes a 'neo-harem' that reduces women's sense of space and sense of control over their lives (Nageeb, 2004), our findings reveal that the home, with the exception of men's *majlis*, can be thought of as a women's kingdom where the wife has power and control over the design, furnishings, and whom she allows to enter. Whereas the men's *majlis* is typically at the front of the house and nearest the street, the woman's bedroom is typically at the rear in a more secluded area. If there is a view other than the interior courtyard, windows are screened in various ways so that the woman may see out, but others may not see in. Reflections like those in the following quotations were typical of women describing their bedroom as their favorite places in their homes:

Mariam: I feel completely free and comfortable in my bedroom. When I'm not with my children, I prefer to be in my bedroom. I do my hair and nails, pray and recite the Qur'an there.

Kawkab: When I want to relax and have privacy and be on my own, I stay in my bedroom. My bedroom is where I stay with myself. I have in the room a small sitting area. It's quiet too, no noise. Every day I must sit by myself one hour . . . when everyone is asleep, after I pray. I like to pray and reflect on the day, children matters etcetera.

Source: Photo taken by one of the chapter authors.

Figure 5.4   Women's majlis

These were the spaces where those studied, far from feeling confined, feel most themselves. They are apt to have a television, telephone, and computer there, so they are not isolated. They usually have walk-in closets, en suite bathrooms, family photographs, oriental carpets, paintings, dressing tables, and religious objects. Some also have decorative fireplaces and exercise equipment. It is their control of their privacy that they value in these spaces. Because bedrooms are almost never shown to guests, their desire is for comfort and privacy rather than status. At the same time, because it is a personal and private space, some do not even let their maids enter the room to clean it.

This is not to imply that women spend all their hours at home in their bedrooms. They also frequent the family room, dining room, and special salons for entertaining other women (sometimes called a women's *majlis* – see Figure 5.4). Five of those studied have jobs outside of their homes and all travel about the city for shopping, socializing, and entertainment. When there are male guests in the home, the separateness of the men's *majlis* keeps non-*mahrem* men (those outside of the immediate family, fathers, and siblings) out of sight of women and vice versa. In some households, adolescent daughters have their own female entertainment rooms so that their guests avoid the gaze of the males in the family. Although several of the couples in our study would entertain other couples in their homes, most would only sanction all-male and all-female gatherings.

The privacy desired by women in their homes extends to immediate neighbors as well. Most Qataris are eligible for free land and money from the government with which to build a home, and many take advantage of the ability to design their homes to be exactly what they want. Mariam explained:

> I started to draw sketches for this house ten years ago during my first pregnancy. The plan is V-shaped, because there is a street in the back overlooking the sea and we wanted to have a swimming pool without the possibility of being seen by neighbors. We wanted the plan to provide freedom throughout the house . . . My home is my kingdom. It's not big and others may consider it small. I wanted a small house with a good plan, reasonable size, easy to control. The important thing is to own my freedom, because we had been fed up with closed places. In many houses in Qatar, the swimming pool is indoors, i.e. without freedom. Ours is outdoors, yet I enjoy both freedom and privacy in it.

Although modesty is an important virtue in Islam, it is evident from our study that the exteriors of recently built homes show an emphasis on status and creating an individually expressive façade. The architect in our study indicated that such embellishments as elevators are also being added by a number of the clients for whom he designs homes. A number of the homes we visited also include expensive artwork, carpets, and antiques. Wedding receptions are another occasion for conspicuous consumption. Men's receptions may host more than 1000 men and are often televised and visible to women at the women's reception typically held in an elegant hotel ballroom. The reverse (men seeing a video of women's gatherings) does not happen as women in the company of other women often remove their covering robes and headgear and parade their finery to the other women, as discussed below.

CLOTHING AND GROOMING

By covering themselves, women carry their privacy with them from the home into the public domain, although many public domains in some Gulf countries such as Qatar are gender segregated to various degrees to accommodate women's need for gender privacy. For instance, public hospitals have different entrances for men and women, and gender-differentiated waiting areas. Qatar national university has different buildings for female and male students. Some banks do not provide gender segregated areas within the building but some Islamic banks have one or more branches for women. Such attempts to control gender relationships in public through demarcating spaces for men and women are an attempt by local governments to reach a compromise between ensuring respect of traditions and women's need for empowerment.

We should reiterate that the clothing portion of our study focused on university women in Qatar and UAE. This is important because there is a sharp generational gap between their clothing and that of their mothers and grandmothers. Moreover, the rate of change is rapidly increasing and many are scandalized by the dress of their sisters who are only a few years younger. The traditional *abaya*, *shayla*, and *burqa* that the young women studied now associate with their mothers and grandmothers is depicted in Figure 5.5. It is plain, black, and covers all of the hair. There is a strong adherence to cultural norms and virtually all Muslim women in Qatar and UAE wear some variation of such garments after puberty. It is a distinctive cultural marker that some also wear on their

Source: Photo taken by one of the chapter authors.

Figure 5.5   Traditional shayla, abaya, *and* niqab

yearly trips abroad, while others merely wear a headscarf or no covering at all when they are outside of their countries. This pattern is consistent with the interpretation that the impetus for the *shayla* and *abaya* is cultural rather than religious.

Although all of those studied wear an *abaya* and *shayla* on a daily basis and increasingly even in the gender segregated buildings of their campuses, their *abayas* are now more colorful, stylish, and revealing, like those in Figures 5.6 and 5.7. Among the influences on new *abaya* styles are the increased wealth from petrodollars, increased exposure to Western television, films, and magazines, and, in Qatar, the 'progressive' dress of Sheikha Moza, the Amir's wife. The influences from global role models and media have been articulated most clearly in women's clothing in the region. Typical accounts of these influences were similar to these:

Suhaila: Those TV shows they put on TV, like for example Gossip Girl, I love it. I really love it. But they exaggerate, like for example when they go to school, they're so . . . it's school even, not university . . . but they're carrying their bags, and their style is, and they're doing their hair and putting on makeup, so girls really get influenced by these.

Khadijah: I don't know. Um, maybe because the society is becoming more open. Like, girls are allowed to go to malls now. They're allowed to hang out with their friends. It's more than, I don't know, 20 years ago. So maybe that's why.

Source: Photo reprinted with the permission of the designer.

Figure 5.6   Contemporary abayas *– I*

A further indication of the popularity of Western desiderata is the Western clothes that these young women wear under their *abayas* and *shaylas*. Although at their universities this is likely to involve jeans, designer shoes and a trendy blouse, at all-female wedding receptions these women are likely to take off their *abayas* and reveal sexy designer cocktail dresses costing as much as several thousand dollars. At such receptions they are in the latest haute couture Western fashions and are heavily made-up and perfumed.

Not only is there increased decoration of the *abayas*, many are by haute couture designers, include elaborate jewels, and are in styles that change rapidly. Moreover, *abayas* increasingly reveal the clothing and heavy makeup worn beneath them. And they are accessorized with jewelry, bags, sunglasses, watches and shoes by Tiffany, Cartier, Prada, Swarovski, Gucci, Louis Vuitton, Hermes, Dolce and Gabbana, Ferragamo, Jimmy Choo and Manolo Blahnik. These accessories as well as *abayas* can be quite expensive. They are also often accompanied by expensive perfumes and elaborate dark makeup. Layla, a UAE woman in the study, estimated that she might have 50 *abayas* in her closet, costing between US$300 and $2000 each. She described the look she was after as 'blingy.' Some young women even have rock star emblems on the backs of their *abayas*. And in light of changing fashions, they might be out of date in a few months. It is little wonder then that the young women studied made comments like these:

Faiza: Yes, every two months there is a new design and something more fashionable and that makes our current one out of fashion, so we have to keep changing to be up to date with the latest fashion in *abayas*.

Umnia: Every time it's just something new, like the long sleeve or the butterfly or I don't know what. They keep coming up with new stuff because if there's no new stuff, people aren't going to keep buying.

Source: Photo reprinted with the permission of the designer.

Figure 5.7   Contemporary abayas *– II*

Mona, one of the *abaya* designers in our study, custom makes garments that cost from $800 to $5000 dollars. As a part of reinventing the *abaya*, she had the following to say about her approach:

I use embroidery in my *abayas* but not like the Indian dull patterns most common here [that] you would see even on the cushions [disgusted smile]. My embroidery style and patterns are inspired from haute couture like Christian Dior and Roberto de Cavalier. I use those patterns but add Swarovski crystals and the base could be velvet. I'm the only one who does this. The challenge is to use haute couture embroidery patterns that set you apart from the rest of designers and give your *abayas* class and style; and women love it because it sets them apart as well . . . *abayas* are usually embroidered around the sleeves and edges of the *shayla* and

'For <u>shaylas</u> with tall padding. This is one good usage of the sunroof in girls' cars.'

Source: Reprinted with the cartoonist's permission.

Figure 5.8   Cartoon mocking 'butterfly look'

these are all very similar. The same patterns keep being used. But mine are different. I do a lot of work on them. I use different cuts, embroidery on the back and front and shoulders. I add some Swarovski crystals, so there is a lot of movement and they look nothing like a modest *abaya*, but they keep to the ethnic look. The main thing is that when my clients wear one of my *abayas* they feel that they are wearing a unique and distinctive piece. So even if the cost of making it is low, I charge 10 times [more]. Some people would come to me and ask me to make some extravagant *abayas*; nothing conventional and not very much accepted. When you look at one of these *abayas*, you either like it or hate it. I usually don't make very funky fashionable *abayas* because fashion fades out and what women pay a huge amount of money for might not be worn for more than three months. Like the butterfly style that came out a few months ago; it has already faded. I'm rather classic in my approach. I only deviate two degrees left or two degrees right.

The butterfly style to which she refers involves putting large butterfly hair clips beneath a *shayla* in order to suggest long hair tied up in a bun beneath. The exaggerated look has been mocked in Gulf States cartoons like the one in Figure 5.8.

In the abaya's evolution from the original style that has prevailed in the Gulf States for several hundred years, the original goals of modesty and anonymous privacy have obviously been jettisoned in favor of sex appeal, status-seeking, and vanity. Although the forces of wealth and Western influences are strong candidates for explaining this shift, what cannot be accounted for from this perspective is why young women continue to wear the *abaya* and *shayla* at all. This is a question we take up in the next section.

DISCUSSION

In both gendered spaces within Muslim homes of the Gulf region and in the clothing and adornment practices of young women, there is an evolving dialogue involving the boundaries between the sacred and the profane, the sexual and the non-sexual, and the private and the public. The chief lines of dialogue have concerned the sphere of the public and the private in terms of theocracy and secularism (for example, Kadivar, 2003; Salvatore and LeVine, 2005; Thompson, 2003) and the volatile issue of the veil or *hijab* (for example, Abu-Odeh, 1993; El Guindi, 1999a, 1999b; Göle, 1996, 2002; Ruby, 2006; Tarlo, 2007). It should come as no surprise that greater tradition is expressed in the home than in the dress of those studied. The women whose clothing and grooming we studied are marking a generational difference from their parents, who make the decisions about the selection, furnishing and decoration of homes. Furthermore, clothing can be changed for different occasions and audiences, for example attending university versus family events. Even these young women's mothers wear haute couture Western fashions under their *abayas* and proudly display them at wedding receptions and other all female events. It is in the volatile world of fashions that the greatest battle is taking place between modernity and tradition. The form of the *abaya* and *shayla* form the traditional framework within which much of battle takes place. Its fashion changes are constant, but to an untrained eye they remain subtle – a wider sleeve here, embroidery there, some jewels sewn into the embroidered pattern for good measure, and a tighter and more shape-revealing cut. One level deeper, a nod toward modern sexuality is made by how these garments are worn: leaving a button of the *abaya* undone, letting some hair show from beneath the *shayla*, wearing dark eye makeup, and accessorizing with designer sunglasses, bags, perfume, and watches. And at a still deeper level the clothing worn beneath the *abaya* is visible to indicate bright Western high-heeled shoes, designer jeans and outfits, and jewellery. These outfits are seldom fully revealed except in the sole presence of other women, but their presence can nevertheless be made unmistakable. Although it is overly simplistic to frame these changes as either the West versus the Middle East or as modernity versus Islam, it is evident that in moving the boundaries of public and private, the young women of Qatar and the UAE are, as Göle (2000) suggests, staking a claim to move out of the private/interior sphere. This has already happened in Egypt (Ghannam, 2002) and is rapidly becoming the case in much of the Gulf region.

More puzzling is why Qataris and Emiratis stubbornly cling to tradition in gender segregation within the home and the covering of men and women, rather than adopt more liberal fashions as in Islamic countries such as Tunisia, Turkey, Egypt, and Lebanon. Each country is different, just as their economies and social situations are different – for instance between Muslim dominant countries like Turkey (for example, Sandıkcı and Ger, 2010), Muslim minority countries like India (for example, Osella and Osella, 2007), and Muslim immigrant countries like England (for example, Tarlo, 2007). But the Gulf States are unique in that the Bedouin Arab Muslim populations are numerically dominated by immigrants to their countries. This is a factor that has relevance to understanding both the stubborn prominence of wearing *abayas* and *shaylas* and the ostentatious gender segregation found in Muslim homes in these countries. Coupled with the Muslim backlash from Western prejudices after the 9/11 attacks, and the increased resources due to surging economies and oil and gas wealth, the swell in Arab nationalism in Qatar and the UAE is also a reaction against the threatened loss of identity in being minorities in their own countries. By proudly sticking to the traditional *abaya* and *shayla* for women and the *ghatra* headcovering and white *thoub* gown for men, there is an assertion of cultural identity. These are cultural rather than religious practices, as even the clerics in our study stipulate. Even though some of the imported labor in these countries is Muslim (for example, maids from Indonesia and Malaysia; construction workers from India), very few of these non-Arab Muslims attempt to wear these distinctive local clothing items. As a result, anyone wearing these clothes is fairly certain to be a citizen (intermarriage is very difficult and there are no other avenues for citizenship by foreign nationals). So a part of these clothing and housing practices is due to cultural pride, as one young woman suggested:

> Umnia: Because there are hardly any locals. We're like twenty per cent or less. And you want to see your own kind in your country, you know? Nothing to do with being racist. I don't mind . . . it doesn't bother me that a lot of people, like expatriates are here and stuff, but you do want to see some people from the country. You want to see people like you.

But there is also a pragmatic side for these young women as well as young men for the sake of the all-important face and honor of their families and clans. As one woman noted in an interview:

> Interviewer: Sometimes I see girls and I can see what they're wearing because it's open or it's just cut open, so the wind blows it open and you can see everything they're wearing.
> Layla: Yeah, then again, they do that on purpose because they want everyone to see it. Like they want guys to see it.
> Interviewer: So why not just not wear the *abaya*?
> Layla: Exactly. I know. Exactly. That's what we all say.
> Interviewer: So why do you think they do wear it?
> Layla: Because they want the attention. Because if you're not wearing the *abaya*, you don't get attention from local guys. They want attention from local guys.

In terms of the ostentation of houses, this is a further arena in which local Qataris and Emiratis can distinguish themselves from the foreigners who are such a presence in their countries. Thanks to being relatively wealthy due to access to prestigious jobs, government grants and subsidies, and the inability of foreigners to own land in Qatar, locals have a distinct advantage in being able to build houses that foreigners could not afford. Furthermore, foreigners are willing to live in apartments and attached housing compounds that locals strive to avoid at all costs. This means that the increasingly impressive houses that Qataris and Emiratis build further set them apart from expatriates in their countries. As with the *abaya* and *shayla*, the basic form of their houses retains the traditional interior courtyard and high walls around their property. However, with air conditioning the inner courtyard has become an enclosed atrium and the former rooftop protected areas for women are gone. House interiors as well as exteriors have become more visibly showy and furnished with more costly artefacts including prestigious brands of Italian furniture, Carrera marble, oriental rugs, expensive incense, and Arabesque paintings. The men's *majlis* is often a showpiece for family antiques and heirlooms and often maintains the Arab tradition of floor seating. Even the popular tent *majlis*, whether within the housing compound, in the desert, or at the sea, is air-conditioned and electrified. Another conspicuous luxury is the ability to maintain gender segregation within the household. Many of the furnishings, appliances, electronics, and fittings of the houses studied are Western or East Asian. In this sense, like the contemporary *abaya* worn by younger women, the home too is experiencing the influence of non-Muslim modernity. And like the insistence on wearing the *abaya* and the *thoub*, the insistence on gender segregation practices within the home is a means of participating in foreign consumer culture while still maintaining a distinctly Arab and Muslim identity. This is not simply a case of using high cultural capital and borrowing from the West (Üstüner and Holt, 2010), nor is it a case of 'glocalization' (adapting the global to the local, Kjeldgaard and Askegaard, 2006). Rather, both *abayas* and gender segregation are anchors for identity – national, ethnic, and religious – that make it possible to freely embrace the global because of the fundamental and symbolically powerful attachment to Arab Islamic values expressed in dress and homes.

IMPLICATIONS

Based on our findings, there are some important implications for marketing in these Arab Gulf countries. What matters in terms of female clothing is what is worn beneath the *abaya*. Sexy underwear (for spouses' eyes only), luxury brands, limited edition handbags, expensive jewellery, and famous global brands of shoes and other accessories are likely to do very well. But outerwear, hats, and low price clothing items are likely to fail with this market. They may well be marketed to expatriates in the country since these are segments that overlap very little with local Arab Gulf customers. They are segments that are partly self-selected based on price affordability. In terms of promotional appeals, the values of the latest fashions and other signs of consumer modernity are likely to be well received, but the values of Westerners per se will not be. Nor will cross-over appeals showing models or mannequins that mix Westerners and Arabs together have much appeal. Although global designer *abayas* already exist and have a market, they are competing against custom-designed local *abayas* rather than lower end products. Sponsoring fashion shows is a good way not only to reach this market, but to help legitimize changes in style in the latest offerings. These need to be all female affairs. If the clothing retailer enters this market thinking that only the most conservative Western clothing is likely to succeed, that retailer has never been to a female wedding reception in Qatar or UAE. Luxury brands will do well if they have the next new thing in limited edition. The competition here is from the European flagship outlets in Paris, Milan and London, to which these customers often travel in the summer. Part of the appeal is using this travel to get goods that are not available locally.

In terms of household furnishings, promoting these products showing mixed sex non-family entertainment or parties is culturally insensitive. Gulf tastes favor heavily upholstered and somewhat baroque and Mediterranean styles that are largely out of fashion in Europe. Ikea stores and Scandinavian furnishings are the antithesis of local styles. Nevertheless styles of furnishing, like styles of clothing, can change. There is now an Ikea store in Dubai and another in Abu Dhabi. While the kitchen is a focus of status in Western homes (for example, Lawrence, 1982), this is not the case in the Gulf. For this and gender segregation reasons it is inadvisable to show people gathering around in the kitchen (kitchens are often outside in order to prevent food odors from entering the house). The house is doused with incense and perfumes before any (same sex) guests arrive as well as at their departure. If non-*mahrem* men are shown, women should be covered. In a women-only or immediate family gathering, this is not necessary, but uncovered local women should never be shown in advertising. Maids and drivers are the norm rather than the exception.

Just as privacy is an important commodity, so is the conflicting norm of hospitality for which Arabs are famous. As Altman (1975) emphasizes, privacy does not mean isolation; it instead involves seeking a balance between being alone and being together. Likewise, it should not be assumed that Gulf women prefer a personal space with large physical distance from others. As Rugh (1985) points out, Western people entering a movie theatre tend to sit far away from one another and give everyone a lot of space. But in many Middle Eastern societies, including those studied, the gender segregated theatres tend to fill up in clumps. The important point is to recognize the different meanings of privacy in these societies and the ways in which the seemingly conflicting values of privacy versus sociality, localness versus globalness, and vanity versus modesty are blended together in the changing cultural patterns of contemporary Arab Gulf societies.

NOTE

* The authors thank Qatar National Research Fund (QNRF) for supporting this research.

BIBLIOGRAPHY

Abisaab, Malek (2005), 'Contesting space: gendered discourse and labor among Lebanese women', in Ghazi-Walid Falah and Caroline Nagel (eds), *Geographies of Muslim Women: Gender, Religion, and Space*, New York: Guilford, pp. 249–74.

Abu Odeh, Lama (1993), 'Post-colonial feminism and the veil: thinking the difference', *Feminist Review*, **43** (Spring), 26–37.

Allan, Graham and Graham Crow (1989), *Home and Family: Creating the Domestic Sphere*, London: Macmillan.

Altman, Irwin (1975), *The Environment and Social Behavior: Privacy, Personal Space, Territoriality, Crowding*, Monterey, CA: Brooks/Cole.

Asad, Talal (2003), 'Boundaries and rights in Islamic Law: introduction', *Social Research*, **70** (Fall), 683–86.

Attfield, Judy (1999), 'Bring modernity home: open plan in the British domestic interior', in Irene Cieraad (ed.), *At Home: An Anthropology of Domestic Space*, Syracuse, NY: Syracuse University Press, pp. 73–82.

Baron, Beth (1994), *The Women's Awakening in Egypt: Culture, Society, and the Press*, New Haven, CT: Yale University Press.

Beetham, Margaret (1996), *A Magazine of Her Own: Domesticity and Desire in the Women's Magazine, 1800–1914*, London: Routledge.

Belk, Russell (1988), 'Possessions and the extended self', *Journal of Consumer Research*, **15** (September), 139–68.

Belk, Russell (1997), 'Been there, done that, bought the souvenirs: of journeys and boundary crossing', in Stephen Brown and Darach Turley (eds), *Consumer Research: Postcards from the Edge*, London: Routledge, pp. 22–45.

Benson, Susan Porter (1988), *Counter Cultures: Saleswomen, Managers, and Customers in American Department Stores, 1890–1940*, Urbana, IL: University of Illinois Press.

Black, Paula (2004), *The Beauty Industry: Gender, Culture, Pleasure*, London: Routledge.

Campo, Juan Eduardo (1991), *The Other Sides of Paradise: Explorations into the Religious Meanings of Domestic Space in Islam*, Columbia, SC: University of South Carolina Press.

Cieraad, Irene (1999), 'Dutch windows: female virtue and female vice', in Irene Cieraad (ed.), *At Home: An Anthropology of Domestic Space*, Syracuse, NY: Syracuse University Press, pp. 31–52.

Douglas, Mary (1966), *Purity and Danger: An Analysis of the Concepts of Pollution and Taboo*, London: Routledge and Kegan Paul.

El Guindi, Fadwa (1999a), *Veil: Modesty, Privacy and Resistance*, Dress, Body and Culture Series, Oxford and New York: Berg.

El Guindi, Fadwa (1999b), 'Veiling resistance', *Fashion Theory*, **3** (1), 51–80.

Fischer, Eileen and Brenda Gainer (1994), 'Masculinity and the consumption of organized sports', in Janeen Arnold Costa (ed.), *Gender Issues and Consumer Behavior*, Thousand Oaks, CA: Sage, pp. 84–103.

Fischer, Eileen, Brenda Gainer, and Julia Bristor (1998), 'Beauty shop and barbershop: gendered service-scapes', in John F. Sherry, Jr (ed.), *Servicescapes: The Concept of Place in Contemporary Markets*, Chicago: NTC Business Books, pp. 565–90.

Florida, Richard (2002), *The Rise of the Creative Class*, New York: Basic Books.

Foucault, Michel (1977), *Discipline and Punish: The Birth of the Prison*, New York: Vintage Books.

Gallagher, Winifred (2006), *House Thinking: A Room-by-Room Look at How We Live*, New York: Harper Collins.

Ghannam, Farha (2002), *Remaking the Modern: Space, Relocation, and the Politics of Identity in a Global Cairo*, Berkeley, CA: University of California Press.

Giddens, Anthony (1984), *The Constitution of Society*, Cambridge: Polity.

Girouard, Mark (1978), *Life in the English Country House*, New Haven, CT: Yale University Press.

Goffman, Erving (1959), *The Presentation of Self in Everyday Life*, Garden City, NY: Anchor.

Goffman, Erving (1961), *Asylums*, New York: Doubleday.

Göle, Nilufer (1996), *The Forbidden Modern: Civilisation and Veiling*, Ann Arbor: MI, University of Michigan Press.

Göle, Nilufer (2000), 'Snapshots of Islamic modernities', *Daedalus*, **129** (Winter), 91–117.

Göle, Nilufer (2002), 'Islam in public: new visibilities and new imageries', *Fashion Theory*, **14** (1), 173–90.

Goodwin, Cathy (1998), 'Privacy as a dimension of service experience', in John F. Sherry, Jr (ed.), *Servicescapes: The Concept of Place in Contemporary Markets*, Chicago: NTC Business Books, pp. 539–64.

Hall, Edward T. (1959), *The Silent Language*, New York: Doubleday.

Hall, Edward T (1966), *The Hidden Dimension*, New York: Doubleday.

Hoffman-Ladd, Valerie J. (1987), 'Polemics on the modesty and segregation of women in contemporary Egypt', *International Journal of Middle East Studies*, **19**, 23–50.

Hutter, Mark (1987), 'The downtown department store as a social force', *Social Science Journal*, **24** (3), 239–46.

Jackson, Maggie (2002), *What's Happening to Home? Balancing Work, Life, and Refuge in the Information Age*, Notre Dame, IN: Sorin.

Kadivar, Mohsen (2003), 'An introduction to the public and private debate in Islam', (introduction to special issue), *Social Research*, **70** (Fall), 659–80.

Kar, Mehrangiz (2003), 'The invasion of the private sphere in Iran', *Social Research*, **70** (Fall), 829–36.

Kira, Alexander (1966), *The Bathroom: Criteria for Design*, Ithaca, NY: Cornell University Center for Housing and Environmental Studies.

Kjeldgaard, Dannie and Søren Askegaard (2006), 'The glocalization of youth culture: the global youth segment as structures of common difference', *Journal of Consumer Research*, **22** (September), 231–47.

Kowinski, William S. (1985), *The Malling of America: An Inside Look at the Great Consumer Paradise*, New York: William Morrow.

Kron, Joan (1983), *Homer-Psych: The Social Psychology of Home and Decoration*, New York: Clarkson N. Potter.

Kwolek-Folland, Angel (1997), 'The gendered environment of the corporate workplace, 1880–1930', in Katharine Martinez and Kenneth L. Ames (eds), *The Material Culture of Gender, The Gender of Material Culture*, Winterthur, DE: Winterthur Museum, pp. 157–79.

Lawrence, R.J. (1982), 'Domestic space and society: a cross-cultural study', *Journal of Comparative Studies in Society and History*, **24**, 104–30.

Leach, William R. (1984), 'Transformations in a culture of consumption: women and department stores, 1890–1925', *Journal of American History*, **71** (2), 319–42.

Lohr, Steve (1997), '"Cubes" vie with "caves" in offices', *International Herald Tribune*, 12 August, 11, 15.

McCracken, Grant (1988), *The Long Interview*, Newbury Park, CA: Sage.

McCracken, Ellen (1992), *Decoding Women's Magazines: From Mademoiselle to Ms.*, London: Palgrave Macmillan.

Menzel, Peter (1994), *Material World: A Global Family Portrait*, San Francisco, CA: Sierra Club Books.

Miller, Daniel (1998), *A Theory of Shopping*, Ithaca, NY: Cornell University Press.

Morley, David (2000), *Home Identities: Media, Mobility and Identity*, London: Routledge.

Mottahedeh, Roy and Kristen Stilt (2003), 'Public and private as viewed through the work of the muhtasib', *Social Research*, **70** (Fall), 735–48.

Munro, Moira and Ruth Madigan (1999), 'Negotiating space in the family home', in Irene Cieraad (ed.), *At Home: An Anthropology of Domestic Space*, Syracuse, NY: Syracuse University Press, pp. 107–117.

Nageeb, Salma A. (2004), *New Spaces and Old Frontiers: Women, Social Space, and Islamization in Sudan*, Lanham, MD: Lexington Books.

Nippert-Eng, Christena (1996), *Home and Work: Negotiating Boundaries through Everyday Life*, Chicago: University of Chicago Press.

Nissenbaum, Helen (2010), *Privacy in Context: Technology, Policy, and the Integrity of Social Life*, Stanford, CA: Stanford University Press.

Osella, Caroline and Osella, Filippo (2007), 'Muslim style in South India', *Fashion Theory*, **11** (2/3), 233–52.

Peiss, Kathy (1986), *Cheap Amusements: Working Women and Leisure in Turn-of-the-Century New York*, Philadelphia, PA: Temple University Press.

Radway, Janice (1984), *Reading the Romance: Women, Patriarchy, and Popular Literature*, Chapel Hill, NC: University of North Carolina Press.

Raglan, Lord (1964), *The Temple and The House*, London: Routledge and Kegan-Paul.

Reekie, Gail (1993), *Temptations: Sex, Selling and the Department Store*, St. Leonards, NSW: Allen and Unwin.

Riley, Terence (1999), 'The un-private house', in Terence Riley (ed.), *The Un-Private House*, New York: The Museum of Modern Art, pp. 9–38.

Romanyshyn, Robert D. (1989), *Technology as Symptom and Dream*, London: Routledge.

Rook, Dennis (1985), 'The ritual dimension of consumer behavior', *Journal of Consumer Research*, **12** (December), 251–64.

Rosenbloom, Stephanie (2010), 'In bid to sway sales, cameras track shoppers', *New York Times*, March 19, online edition.

Rosselin, Céline (1999), 'The ins and outs of the hall: a Parisian example', in Irene Cieraad (ed.), *At Home: An Anthropology of Domestic Space*, Syracuse, NY: Syracuse University Press, pp. 53–59.

Ruby, F. Tabassum (2006), 'Listening to voices of hijab,' *Women's Studies International Forum*, **29**, 54–66.

Rugh, Andrea B. (1985), *Family in Contemporary Egypt*, Cairo: American University in Cairo Press.

Rybczynski, Witold (1986), *Home: A Short History of the Idea*, New York: Viking Penguin.

Salinger, Adrienne (1995), *In My Room: Teenagers in Their Bedrooms*, San Francisco: Chonicle Books.

Salvatore, Armando and Mark LeVine (ed.) (2005), *Religion, Social Practice, and Contested Hegemonies: Reconstructing the Public Sphere in Muslim Majority Societies*, London: Palgrave Macmillan.

Sandıkcı, Özlem and Ger, Güliz (2010), 'Veiling in style: how does a stigmatized practice become fashionable?', *Journal of Consumer Research*, **37** (June), 15–36.

Scanlon, Jennifer (1995), *Inarticulate Longings: The Ladies' Home Journal, Gender, and the Promises of Consumer Culture*, New York: Routledge.

Secor, Anna J. (2002), 'The veil and urban space in Istanbul: women's dress, mobility and Islamic knowledge', *Gender, Place and Culture*, **9** (1), 5–22.

Sheller, Mimi and John Urry (2003), 'Mobile transformation of "public" and "private" life', *Theory, Culture and Society*, **20** (3), 107–25.

Sherry, John F., Jr. (ed.), *Servicescapes: The Concept of Place in Contemporary Markets*, Chicago: NTC Business Books.

Sherry, John F., Jr., Robert V. Kozinets, Adam Duhachek, Benet DeBerry-Spence, Krittinee Nuttavuthisit, and Diana Storm (2004), 'Gendered behavior in a male preserve: role playing at ESPN Zone in Chicago', *Journal of Consumer Psychology*, **14**, 151–58.

Smith, Virginia (2007), *Clean: A History of Personal Hygiene and Purity*, Oxford: Oxford University Press.

Sommer, Robert (1969), *Personal Space: The Behavioral Basis of Design*, Englewood Cliffs, NJ: Prentice-Hall.

Spain, Daphne (1992), *Gendered Spaces*, Chapel Hill, NC: University of North Carolina Press.

Sparke, Penny (1995), *As Long as It's Pink: The Sexual Politics of Taste*, London: HarperCollins.

Sun, Tao, Seounmi Youn and William D. Wells (2004), 'Exploration of consumption and communication communities in sports marketing', in Lynn R. Kahle and Chris Riley (eds), *Sports Marketing and the Psychology of Marketing Communication*, Mahwah, NJ: Lawrence Erlbaum, pp. 3–26.

Tarlo, Emma (2007), 'Hijab in London: metamorphosis, resonance and effects', *Journal of Material Culture*, **12** (2), 131–56.

Thompson, Elizabeth (2003), 'Public and private in Middle Eastern women's history', *Journal of Women's History*, **15** (Spring), 52–69.

Tian, Kelly and Russell Belk (2005), 'Extended self and possessions in the workplace', *Journal of Consumer Research*, **32** (September), 297–310.

Tuan, Yi-Fu (1982), *Segmented Worlds and Self: Group Life and Individual Consciousness*, Minneapolis: University of Minnesota Press.

Tuncay, Linda and Cele Otnes (2008), 'Exploring the link between masculinity and consumption', in Tina Lowrey (ed.), *Brick and Mortar Shopping in the 21st Century*, New York: Lawrence Erlbaum, pp. 153–69.

Turner, Victor (1969), *The Ritual Process*, Chicago: Aldine.

Üstüner, Tuba and Douglas B. Holt (2010), 'Toward a theory of status consumption in less industrialized countries', *Journal of Consumer Research*, **37** (June).

Vogel, Frank E. (2003), 'The public and private in Saudi Arabia: restrictions on the powers of committees for ordering the good and forbidding the evil', *Social Research*, **70** (Fall), 749–68.

Wacks, Raymond (2010), *Privacy: A Very Short Introduction*, Oxford: Oxford University Press.

Williams, Rosalind (1982), *Dream Worlds: Mass Consumption in Late Nineteenth-Century France*, Berkeley, CA: University of California Press.

Woolf, Virginia (1929), *A Room of One's Own*, New York: Harcourt, Brace and World.

6 Being fashionable in today's Tunisia: what about cultural identity?

Fatma Smaoui and Ghofrane Ghariani

Fashion is today an important feature of the contemporary consumer's life. Goods, services and different consumption areas are influenced by the 'fashion system' (Barthes, 1967). Solomon and Rabolt (2009, p. xi) describe fashion as a 'driving force that shapes the way we live – it influences our apparel, hairstyles, art, food, cosmetics, . . . and many other aspects of our daily lives.' By increasing the renewal of forms and the inconsistency of the realm of appearances, fashion enables novelty to be promoted (Lipovesky, 1994). 'It is responsible for consumers changing their wardrobes, music systems, furniture and the cars they drive' (Solomon and Rabolt, 2009, p. 5). Fashion also brings emotion to the purchasing act by adding to the utility function of the product, a hedonic function, related to fantasy and change (Lipovesky, 1994).

The consumer–fashion relationship is complex and goes beyond the mere consumption of goods and services (Davis, 1992; Marion, 2003; Thompson and Haytko, 1997). Fashion meets consumers' hedonist and communication needs and helps with building self and social identities, and expressing individual and cultural values (Marion, 2003; O'Cass, 2001; Sandıkcı and Ger, 2002; Thompson and Haytko, 1997). In fact, fashion reflects society, its culture and how people define themselves (Solomon and Rabolt, 2009). Consumers find in fashion goods symbolic resources which enable them to improve self expression and contribute to their communication with group and culture members. The fashion system is a part of the symbols and meanings characterizing a culture (Craik, 1994; Davis, 1992; Marion, 2003; Solomon, 2004).

Most of the studies dealing with fashion and consumption are conducted in a Western cultural context. Sociologists and anthropologists have associated the emergence of the modern form of fashion with the West (for example Davis, 1992; Finkelstein 1991; McCracken, 1988). Indeed, fashion is intimately related to the emergence of the bourgeois culture in Europe and is inseparable from the competition between classes – between an aristocracy anxious to display its magnificence and a wealthy bourgeoisie eager to imitate it (Lipovetsky and Charles, 2005, p. 4). The development of modern mass consumption was largely enhanced by the fashion system based upon the dismissal of the past (and tradition) and the promotion of novelty and change. Recently, the logic of fashion has been extended to the entire body of the society. Indeed, society as a whole has been restructured in accordance with the logic of seduction, of permanent renewal and marginal differentiation, contributing to the emergence of the postmodern consumer society (Lipovetsky and Charles, 2005). Fashion is thus considered as a Western modern, as well as post-modern institution, characterized by the proliferation of styles and the mass consumption of fashion goods (Lipovetsky, 1994).

Eastern, Arab and/or Islamic consumers are also involved with fashion: the desire to be 'in style' is considered today to be a widespread consumption preoccupation (Abaza,

2007; Hansen, 2004; Jones, 2007; Moors, 2007). Globalization, mass media and the shift towards a mass consumption society have contributed to the diffusion of a global Western consuming culture.

To date, the topic of Islamic and emerging countries' consumption practices is under-investigated (Sandıkcı and Ger, 2002, 2007; Touzani and Hirschman, 2008; Üstüner and Holt, 2007, 2010). Some recent contributions study fashion in Islamic societies, with a focus on fashion clothing, and on Islamic fashion and women veiling (Moors, 2007; Sandıkcı and Ger, 2010; Tarlo, 2007). Anthropological studies try to understand the relationship between fashion and faith through the way Islamic women's dress has changed over the years. Struggle over identity seems to be a central issue in the complex and ambivalent relationship between Islamic consumer and fashion. For example, the desire to enter modernity through fashion consumption is negotiated with personal, local and Islamic values. Nevertheless, the various Islamic nations, even if they all practice the same religion, show cultural, historical or social specificities. Indonesian, Yemenite, Turkish, Egyptian or Tunisian consumers differ in language, ethnic origin and history, which may shape their national identities and determine their consumption patterns.

Tunisia is a small Arab-Muslim country, situated in North Africa. It is part of the 'Maghreb,' the name given by Arabs, which literally means 'sunset' or 'the West' because of its Western position compared to other Arab countries. It is also a Mediterranean country, which has been in contact with several Eastern and Western civilizations because of its strategic geographical location. Formerly colonized by France, Tunisia has undergone, since its independence, important pro-Western reforms that contributed to modernizing the country and to the shaping of a new Tunisian national identity, one that is multicultural and open to Western culture (Abassi, 2005; Bouhdiba, 1978).

How do Tunisian consumers experience fashion? How do cultural, social and religious factors shape their relationship with fashion? And what is the place of identity in the Tunisian consumer–fashion relationship? The objective of the present research study is to explore the consumer–fashion relationship in a Tunisian Arab-Muslim context and to emphasize the particular role played by the identity concept in such a relationship.

FASHION: DEFINITION AND CHARACTERISTICS

Fashion can be defined as a process of social diffusion according to which a new style is adopted by certain groups of consumers (Solomon, 2004). The 'fashion system' (Barthes, 1967) consists of all the persons and organizations involved in the creation of symbolic meanings and their transfer to the cultural consumption products. Lipovetsky (1994, p. 55) dates the development of fashion in its modern form to the second half of the 19th century. Historically, it has been associated with clothing and still is today (Carpenter et al., 2005; O'Cass, 2001; Parker et al., 2004). However, today fashion influences all types of products and services ranging from apparel, books, entertainment, furniture and many other cultural consumption products (Hetzel, 1995). Fashion characterizes modern and postmodern consumption society: 'fashion becomes an exceptional highly problematic institution, a socio-historical reality of the West and modernity itself' (Lipovetsky, 1994, p. 4). Its logic of inconsistency, its great organizational and aesthetic diversity as well as individuals' variety seeking are in line with the increasing individualization of tastes. The development of the 'Western model of fashion' (Davis, 1992; McCracken, 1988), with its cultural images broadcast by advertising and mass media, has been interpreted as a cornerstone of the ideology of consumption, boosting Western capitalist economies (Bocock, 1993; Firat, 1991; Lury, 1996; Peters, 1992). Fashion is regarded as a social phenomenon that affects several people simultaneously, but also as an individual phenomenon exerting a very personal effect on each consumer.

CULTURAL AND SYMBOLIC DIMENSIONS OF FASHION

In the frame of the current consumption context, purchase decisions are often motivated by a desire to be fashionable. Fashion products are aesthetic products rooted in art and history. According to Douglas and Isherwood (1979), consumption is a large information system that allows each individual to position himself/herself in a complex and uncertain world. Consumers do not buy products just to fulfill their needs or display a status, they also engage in the construction of a meaningful personal world. The identification, classification and comparison between owned and used objects make it possible to organize the social relationship and to categorize people and situations (Marion, 2003).

FASHION, IDENTITY AND CULTURE

Identity is intimately related to the self but also operates within the social environment. The symbolic system of objects helps the contemporary individual to shape his/her identity. A concept such as the 'extended self' (Belk, 1988) underlines the importance of objects in the construction of one's individual and social images. Fashion offers a consumption context where the needs for self expression but also for belongingness are rather high (Marion, 2003; McCracken, 1986; Thompson and Haytko, 1997). However, the sensitivity of the identity to fashion is not necessarily common to all (for example Parker et al., 2004). Results of a study undertaken simultaneously in the United Kingdom, Brazil and China (Rocha et al., 2005) showed that young British respondents granted more importance to fashion (as a variable expressing their identities) than did Chinese or Brazilian respondents. This difference could be explained by the existence of a true tradition of innovation in the United Kingdom. Brazilian respondents were much more searching for national identity, while for Chinese individuals traditional values prevail. Every individual develops multiple identities: an individual one, a social one, and also a cultural one. Belonging to a culture is reflected by the acceptance and adherence to its values, codes as well as aesthetic standards, moral and religious values, and historical backgrounds, which all together contribute to the development of the cultural identity of a community and of its members (Mucchielli, 1999). One of the characteristics of the identity is precisely that it has a stable core of values which ensures the essential connection between the individual, his/her culture and the different groups of belonging. The fashion system produces meanings for objects and styles in a specific cultural background (McCracken, 1986) that cannot be reproduced identically in a different culture.

   The complexity and the depth of the relationship between consumers, culture, fashion and identity have been underlined in several research studies conducted mainly in Western cultural settings, and more recently in some Eastern and Islamic countries (Abaza, 2007; Balasescu, 2003; Jones, 2007; Sandıkcı and Ger, 2010). Thompson and Haytko (1997), in the US, and Marion (2003) in France, found that fashion discourse developed by the interviewees translated a complex system of cultural significances specific to the individual. French teenagers' acceptance or rejection of fashion products represents lifestyle choices, contributes to identity formation and expresses their life project. Fashion discourses go beyond fashion consumption to reflect a dynamic dialectic about the meanings of consumption and culture. Thompson and Haytko (1997) found that respondents do not hold a single and stereotyped fashion concept. Rather, they develop personal interpretations according to their system of values, their history and their objectives. The relationship with fashion thus goes beyond the simple identification or rejection and represents instead, a negotiation between the individual and the system of beliefs and values of the social spheres to which he/she belongs. It may also reflect internal tensions, ambiguities and ambivalences contributing to the shaping of individuals' identities and to their ideological and social positioning.

FASHION IN ISLAMIC AND LESS INDUSTRIALIZED COUNTRIES

Understanding the mechanisms and social consequences of consumption practices such as fashion has long been debated and conceptualized in a context of Western developed countries (Bourdieu, 1984; Lipovetsky, 1994; Simmel, 1904). The state of the art in this research subject is largely derived from empirical studies conducted among American and European consumers. A growing interest, however, is occurring in emerging countries' consumers, and in Islamic consumption, in particular. These countries, characterized by fast economic growth and expanding domestic markets differ economically, culturally and historically from Western nations.

Referring to the Turkish consumptionscape, Sandıkcı and Ger (2002) explored existing conceptualizations of consumption practices in a non-Western context. They identified four specific consumption practices: spectacularist, nationalist, faithful and historical, illustrating different consumers' readings of contrasted realities: local/global, East/West and modern/traditional. Sandıkcı and Ger (2002) pointed out the importance of both Western cultural lifestyle and religion in the shaping of consumption patterns and in the negotiation of a traditional–modern identity by Islamic nations' consumers. The cultural globalization literature shows the tremendous cultural power of the West (usually associated with modernity) in a wide range of less industrialized countries. The 'Western lifestyle myth' (Üstüner and Holt, 2010) is central to the construction of some social class status in these countries. Religion and spiritual beliefs may affect the marketplace, demand, and consumption styles (for example clothing, food, leisure, social actions, finance) (Sandıkcı and Ger, 2001, 2007; Jones, 2007; Touzani and Hirschman, 2008; Yakin, 2007). Some consumers in Islamic countries are confronted with how to construct meanings through consumption choices, while balancing tradition and modernity, and faith and contemporary lifestyles.

The literature dealing with Islamic fashion illustrates this negotiation and ambivalence in the experience of fashion (Balasescu, 2003; Hansen, 2004; Moors, 2007). Dealing primarily with clothing and Islamic dress (especially veiling) because of the strong link to fashion and identity building, studies emphasize the effort made by consumers to reconcile fashion and faith. For example, Moors (2007) noted that Islam and fashion are often seen as standing in a tense relationship. Islam is considered as a realm of the eternal spiritual and sacred values and the embodiment of virtues. This conception does not fit easily with fashion, which belongs to the field of surface and form, and is characterized by rapid change (Moors, 2007, p. 320). Exploring the meanings of fashion in an Iranian setting, Balasescu (2003) underlines the problematic relationship between the veil and fashion: 'Since veiling is a practice that does not belong to the "Western" space, and since fashion . . . historically belongs to the West, the veil cannot be fashion' (Balasescu, 2003, p. 47).

Nevertheless, in several Arab-Muslim countries, different and even 'paradoxical' fashion styles can be found. For instance, in Egypt, 'Islamic chic' stands besides 'Western chic' and 'ethnic chic' (Abaza, 2007, p. 281). In other Islamic countries, such as Indonesia, many attempts are made to combine fashion, tradition and religion, especially through women's magazines and stores dedicated to fashionable clothes adapted to the religious, local values (Jones, 2007).

TUNISIA: HISTORY AND CULTURAL IDENTITY

Bouhdiba, a Tunisian sociologist, describes Tunisian society as 'a human cocktail' characterized by cultural pluralism (Bouhdiba, 1978, p. 253). Because of its strategic geographical location at the core of the Mediterranean basin, Tunisia has experienced diverse civilizations through history. The original inhabitants are Berber tribes. In the tenth century BC, Phoenicians settled the north coast and founded Carthage, which became a major and rich city-state competing with Rome. Successive cultures and civilizations shaped the history and identity of today's Tunisia (Slim and Fauqué, 2001): Roman, Vandal, Jewish, Christian, Arab, Islamic, Spanish, Turkish and French, in addition to the contribution of immigrants that settled in Tunisia (Italians, Andalusians, Maltese, and so on). Arabs entered Tunisia in 670, bringing Islam to North Africa and founding the major Islamic city of Kairouan. Different Arab and/or Muslim dynasties have ruled Tunisia since (Aghlabite, Fatimide, Hafiside, Ottoman, Housseinite) (Guellouz et al. 1983; Nabli and Swiderska, 2008).

The contemporary history of Tunisia is marked by the French protectorate (1891 to 1956), seen as a colonization that introduced elements of Western (French) culture. After independence, important pro-Western reforms were introduced by President Bourguiba to modernize the country. The promotion of women's rights and the enhancement of public modern education were the key elements in these reforms. In early 1956, the new Code of Personal Status was promulgated, giving women an unprecedented status in the Muslim-Arabic world; polygamy was forbidden and divorce initiated by women authorized. Later, in 1973, abortion was legalized.

An important issue emerged at the beginning of independence: the new Tunisian national identity (Abassi, 2005). Choices were made for a break with traditional society and a move towards a modern, Western (French) inspired model. Islam remains the official state religion, but the power of religious leaders has been largely reduced, and

Bourguiba encouraged a liberal interpretation of the prescriptions of Islam. In addition, the anchoring of Tunisia in the Mediterranean space was strengthened at the expense of the traditional Arab space (Abassi, 2005).

The question of language was, and still remains, a major issue because of its effect on national identity and access to economic development. Bilingualism (Standard Arabic/French) was deliberately adopted and advocated by Bourguiba just after independence (Abassi, 2005; Messadi, 1958). While Arabic is the official national language, French was considered as the vector of modernization, rationalism and science. The knowledge of European languages and culture has been enhanced by widespread exposure to European media. However the debate was not closed; advocates of 'Arabization' continued to act dynamically to defend their cause and some reforms were introduced, such as the use of the Arabic language in the justice system (Bouhdiba, 1978).

Since the accession of the current President to power in 1987, this movement has accelerated. The only language allowed in all departments of the administration is Arabic. Classes in primary and high schools are mostly in Arabic, while university courses are still mostly in French. French continues to be widely practiced in the business, medical and cultural sectors. It also constitutes a social marker. However, French use seems to be on the decline for the overall population. This is enhanced by the increasing exposure to Middle Eastern satellite TV channels (for example Al Jazeera, Rotana, MBC). The audience of the French TV channels has declined dramatically and seems to be reserved for the intellectual and cultural elite. In parallel, and since the mid-1990s, a return to religious fervor has occurred at many levels of society, coupled with a certain conservatism: women veiling, attendance at mosques and a growing audience for Islamic TV channels. Today, Tunisian society is a mix of lifestyles: traditional, conservative, and Arab-Islamic-culture oriented, or liberal and Western-culture oriented.

METHODOLOGY

A qualitative approach was used to explore the Tunisian consumer's fashion experience and identity relationship. In-depth interviews were conducted with twenty-six Tunisian consumers aged between 21 and 60 to bring variety to the sample in terms of gender, social background and education level. All the respondents were living in the Tunis area and its suburbs (see Table 6.1 for details). Interviews lasted approximately 45 to 60 minutes; they were audio-taped and later transcribed in their entirety. Each informant was invited to speak about his/her perceptions about fashion. The purpose was the generation of ideas and opinions about fashion in general. Then, respondents were asked about their personal relationship with fashion: their motivations, inhibitors, perceptions and attitudes. Finally, interviewees' opinions about cultures, countries, and civilizations in association with fashion were solicited. The fashion–religion relationship issue was not addressed in a direct way. The objective was rather to identify personal experiences from the interviewees' discourses. Careful analysis of the interviews permitted the identification of themes, which were then matched with some pre-defined patterns extracted from literature (Miles and Huberman, 1994).

Table 6.1   Characteristics of the informants

Informants	Gender	Age	Occupation	Educational level
Henda	Female	22	Student	University
Aziza	Female	43	Executive assistant	University
Aïcha	Female	49	Housewife	Elementary school
Emna	Female	23	Student	University
Inés	Female	27	Student	University
Chehrazad	Female	22	Student	University
Mustapha	Male	53	Teacher	University
Ilyés	Male	21	Student	University
Asma	Female	60	Housewife	University
Zohra	Female	40	Worker	Elementary school
Khalil	Male	32	Actor	University
Myriam	Female	19	High school student	High school
Mouna	Female	26	Student	University
Sinda	Female	25	Interior designer	University
Soumaya	Female	24	Student	University
Omar	Male	24	Sales executive	High school
Nesrine	Female	32	Retail sales assistant	High school
Iman	Female	31	Housewife	Elementary school
Faouzia	Female	46	Housewife	High school
Sami	Male	23	Student	University
Zeineb	Female	25	Sales executive	University
Mehdi	Male	30	Businessman	University
Beya	Female	50	Bank executive	High school
Salah	Male	57	Trader	University
Lotfi	Male	30	Lawyer	University

FINDINGS

The analysis of the interview data helped identify several findings that are similar to the themes largely identified and discussed in previous research studies. Fashion appears to be associated with public goods, brands, luxury, modernity, glamour, and novelty (Balasescu, 2003; Lipovetsky, 1994; Marion 2003). It requires money and represents a materialistic vision of life, generating a feeling of frustration. Fashion gives consumers some freedom when it comes to personalizing their choice, but it can also create some instability because of the frequent changes and expenditures it involves (Bordo, 2003; Ewen, 1988; Firat, 1991). Besides this general conception of fashion, the content analysis shows challenging and ambivalent identity dimensions. Indeed, the fashion–respondent relationship and experience imply deep existential questions and tensions about self identity, social identity and particularly cultural identity.

FASHION AND INDIVIDUAL IDENTITY

At the individual level, two major and opposing ideas emerged from the interviewees' discourse: on the one hand, fashion is seen as a means for building and expressing personality; on the other hand, individuals tend to reject it in order to avoid conformity. Differentiation and personalization have been mentioned by respondents. Following fashion and being different from others seems to be more than a goal – it is a source of pride: 'I like standing out from the crowd, with my own style, different from everybody'. The terms 'creativity' and 'innovation' are usually cited by interviewees when speaking about fashion, indicating a tight link between fashion, especially apparel, and the shaping of one's identity and personal opinions and values:

> In our society, clothing has a great importance. It's very important . . . even for people's behavior. I think it's important to be handsome. If someone is handsome . . . well, if he feels handsome, he'll get more confidence, it has a great influence even on his way of speaking, his behavior with people. That's it. So . . . I think it's important. You know, style and colors reflect strongly someone's image! You understand. As I told you, style and audacious colors . . . you know there are people who don't accept to change, they remain on the same stage. It means that . . . for example, with computers, some people stopped at Windows 98, they don't accept Vista. These are . . . er . . . new things. Maybe, for some people change is difficult because it needs some effort. (Sinda, 25 years, interior designer)

However, some informants do not try to stand out through fashion and think even that physical appearance is secondary, regretting that in our society many people judge others by their appearances:

> Unfortunately, we have prejudices about the way people are dressed. If we see someone dressed with Max Mara's shoes or something like that, we look at him/her as someone important because unfortunately, today money consumes us! But someone with high principles won't be influenced easily . . . well, it depends. As far as I am concerned, when someone comes at my office, a customer . . . if he speaks well, introduces himself well, I respect him, I talk to him, I try to understand what he's thinking of, and I treat him the same way he acts. (Beya, 50 years, bank executive)

Constructing an individual identity is one of the most important issues discussed in the fashion literature (Balasescu, 2003; Lipovetsky, 1994; Marion, 2003; Sandıkcı and Ger, 2002; Sennett, 1994, Thompson and Haytko, 1997). Tunisian consumers express the same challenging fashion and self identity building relationship.

However, it is useful to point out that the need for differentiation and peculiarities are not recurrent in the interviewees' discourse, as only a few respondents clearly mentioned these themes. It is also interesting to note a kind of ambivalence. People look to fashion as a vehicle for differentiation, and for personality assertion, but at the same time, this is rejected by others in order to conform to society. Consumers can be prone to internal tensions that can be revealed through their discourse: 'I like being different even if I'm shy'. It seems that this ambivalence regarding the role of fashion is due to the pressure brought by modernity and the rise of 'material culture', where dress, for example, may be regarded as 'armor' (Entwistle, 2000) or as a 'mirror' of identity (Hansen, 2004). Individuals feel the need to give further importance to their appearance in order to be part of society, but also to have their own identity without looking like 'clones': 'fashion articulates a tension between conformity and differentiation: it expresses the contradictory desires to fit in and stand out' (Entwistle, 2000, p. 116). The relationship attire–fashion–self identity is frequently analyzed in the literature. Theorists of fashion work in a paradigm that links clothing, body, and identities, because of clothing's visibility in the public space (Balasescu, 2003; Hansen, 2004) This is particularly true for the case of Islamic dress in both Western and non-Western countries (Jones, 2007; Sandıkcı and Ger, 2010; Tarlo, 2007; Yakin, 2007). Our findings are in line with such results. The Tunisian consumers interviewed show a particular interest in dress and appearance when speaking about fashion. They express their personal values and lifestyle choices through their attitudes to clothing. Particularly, the need for conformity is more largely expressed by interviewees when describing their fashion experience.

FASHION AND SOCIAL IDENTITY DIMENSION

Social identity comprises the parts of a person's identity that come from belonging to particular groups (age, ethnicity, family, religion, gender). It refers to one's way of thinking about oneself and others based on social groupings (Hannum, 2007). Social identity helps individuals categorize people into groups and identify themselves with certain groups. It is through belonging to a particular group, that the individual acquires a social identity and establishes or preserves a difference in favor of his/her own group (Mucchielli, 1999; Tajfel, 1972). The data analysis shows that, for the interviewees, fashion plays an important role in defining their social identity. This can be reflected through a double polarity: a positive meaning and a critical one. The positive meaning can be deduced through the themes of belonging, security, and communication within a group: 'thanks to fashion, people know they belong to a tribe, they are not alone.' Critical meanings can be inferred through themes and expressions such as 'limits,' 'respect,' 'social,' 'constraint,' 'blind imitation' and 'ridiculous.' These refer to the rejection of fashion practices and to people adopting them, in order to be similar to a reference group. One of the respondents pointed out that people following fashion could be easily criticized; 'many people don't respect the limits characterizing our society, they try to follow fashion and that makes them ridiculous.' Others evoke mimicry and exaggeration, arguing that when people try to follow fashion trends and to imitate others blindly, they cannot be respected.

Many interviewees stressed the respect of society and the limits that should not be crossed. According to some of them, following fashion trends should have limits. For example, Myriam chooses clothes to fit both herself and society. Societal approval seems to be very important for the respondents. Having respect and keeping one's society's esteem, by making appropriate choices, is of great importance. Having a pleasant and harmonious relationship with the family is a great concern, for girls notably. Three interviewees even mentioned some conflicts in families, and between generations, related to the non-respect of social standards and decency: 'since I was little, I have acquired some habits in my family. We learned to have respect for family and religion, that's why I don't care about fashion, my parents have no interest in fashion'. Thus, for some respondents, there is a contrast between fashion and 'respect,' 'decency,' 'family conformity and even 'religion'. Because of its association with the West, fashion is frequently considered in Islamic societies to contrast with piety and the tenets of religious morality (Balasescu, 2003; Yakin, 2007). Consumers in these societies are in continuing negotiation between different individual and social limits such as fashion/faith, tradition/modernity, piety/ modernity (Jones, 2007; Moors, 2007, Sandıkcı and Ger, 2002).

The relationship between fashion and social identity construction has been highlighted in several research studies (Cholachatpinyo et al., 2002; Hansen, 2004; Marion, 2003; Thompson and Haytko, 1997). According to Thompson and Haytko, (1997, p. 26), the meaning given to fashion has been used by interviewees as a way of creating differentiation or detachment from the group. It can also be understood as a vehicle for inducing social affiliation and belonging to the group. This dialectic 'need for individualization/need for conformity' is a classical divide concerning the people's relationship with fashion (Barnard, 2002; Douglas and Isherwood, 1979; Marion, 2003). For the Tunisian consumer, the need for conformity and belonging seems to be more important than the need for differentiation. This may be explained by the collectivist dimension of the Arab-Muslim culture, which privileges the group, in particular the family (Hofstede, 2001).

FASHION AND CULTURAL IDENTITY

An important cultural identity dimension emerges from the respondents' discourses. It is illustrated by two main topics, religion and morality, and the dilemma between Eastern and Western cultures.

Identity, Morality and Religion

Religion emerged as a significant component of the whole discourse of interviewees. Different attitudes and interactions were observed. The analysis revealed a positive relationship between fashion and religion, arguing that being fashionable can be completely in agreement with spiritual and religious thought: 'religion is in agreement with fashion as it's in agreement with beauty; God is beautiful and loves beauty' (Faouzia, 46 years, housewife).

Some other respondents tried to have a neutral discourse regarding the relationship between fashion and religion suggesting that religion should be of a subjective and personal consideration and so should fashion be likewise: 'Our relationship to fashion is subjective I think . . . so as long as it's neither shocking nor provocative, it's not bad, you see. After all, religion isn't against beauty, on the contrary. But there are limits we shouldn't cross . . . that's all, not more, not less and everyone sees things in his own way' (Mehdi, 30, businessman).

Nevertheless, most of the respondents emphasized the conflictual relationship between religion and fashion; 'I'm conservative, and it's the same thing for my daughter. I can't let her wear fashionable things: I don't at all allow anything that comes against decency and religion' (Zohra, 40, worker). Other respondents speak about morality. According to some, fashion is a source of immorality, frustration, discrimination, and social stratification. Consumer manipulation is also evoked by some respondents who blame the fashion industry for making money by encouraging consumption in order to increase their profits.

Rejecting fashion can be perceived as a sign of moral virtue (seriousness and self-control) (Thompson and Haytko, 1997). Actually, Western societies have often blamed fashion for its 'materialistic and tyrannical' effect, imposing frequent, stressful, and expensive changes (Bordo, 2003; Ewen, 1988; Lipovetsky, 1994). By contrast, in Islamic societies, rejection of fashion is more often due to its tight link to the West and to modernity (Balasescu, 2003; Jones, 2007). In the present research study, the analysis of respondents' opinions and attitudes shows an ambivalent and multidimensional relationship between moral values, decency, religion and fashion. Religious beliefs seem to have a great influence on individuals' consumption practices and choices, as is the case in other Muslim societies (Abaza, 2007; Moors, 2007; Sandıkcı and Ger, 2007). Indeed several studies show the existence of a variety of practices and styles of consumption in Islamic societies. According to these studies, religion should not be regarded as an obstacle to consumption practices even if some individuals feel a challenge in having a 'faithful' and modern consumption at the same time (Balasescu, 2003; Jones, 2007; Sandıkcı and Ger, 2002, 2010). From the anthropological and historical point of view, Olson (1985) expresses an ideological conflict between secularism and Muslim identity in Turkey that led both orientations to coexist. In modern Tunisia, such a conflict has existed since independence, and the issue of Tunisian identity has been widely debated, notably in relation to the Western/Mediterranean/Arab-Muslim cultural orientation and the language issue (Abassi, 2005; Bouhdiba, 1978). According to Bouhdiba (1978, p. 258) 'The adoption of the Arab language is equivalent to the maintenance of the collective personality and national identity'.

Identity and the West–East Dilemma

In the process of their socialization, individuals submit to standards, values, and representations of their environmental culture that they progressively make their own. In this way, they build a cultural identity, shared with other members of their group. This identity can be composite and intercultural for some people, in the sense that the individual may integrate different cultures at the same time (Arab, Muslim, Mediterranean, French, local, global). Fashion is a consumption context that arouses the cultural identity question for the study's informants. The discourse analysis revealed the complexity of this relationship. Almost all interviewees associated fashion with the West: Western culture produces and diffuses fashion. Some respondents felt uncomfortable with this state of things and blamed blind imitation by the Tunisian consumers of (Western) fashion that can lead to a certain loss of identity; 'teenagers mostly imitate Europeans and this denotes a weak personality', 'fashion encourages neglecting decency and shyness which characterize our Muslim society'. For many interviewees, fashion is a cause for acculturation, an addiction to the West. The subsequent alienation from Islam could also be a form of denial of one's origins. Other respondents mentioned that Tunisians try to imitate the European way of life and that they show preference for Western brands. This relationship with the West may explain the importance of the 'made-in' concept in the perceptions of and choice of fashion products, especially when concerning products originating from Europe or the US. Countries like France or Italy were noted by interviewees as fashion reference countries, followed by Spain and the US. The West is admired by many, thanks to its creative potential, freedom, and way of life: 'We like living like European people'. Some comparisons were made with Tunisian creativity and fashion, revealing some frustration and discomfort regarding Tunisian culture:

> There's a problem with creation in Tunisia, creators rely only on tradition they try to transform . . . the fact that there are no Tunisian creators is problematic, we have to try to innovate, we make fun of those who try to be creative just because they are Tunisian. What comes from the West is admired; we should invest in fashion in order to create a competitive advantage. Tunisia should invent its own fashion. (Lotfi, 30, lawyer)

Imitating Western fashion can be perceived by some consumers, in particular those from Less Industrialized Countries (LIC) or Islamic countries, as a way of accessing a higher social class and modernity. This would explain consumers' interest in foreign brands – European and American ones – that represent important status symbols: 'LIC consumers emulate middle-class consumers of the West, whom they view as the most relevant status group above them. So in this model Western goods operate as powerful global status symbols that citizens of LICs deeply desire and look for' (Üstüner and Holt, 2010). In some Islamic countries, where women wear the Islamic *hijab*, the middle and upper-class women choose to wear headscarves displaying a famous Western designer (Balasescu, 2003, p. 43).

This opinion is shared by many respondents who regret a lack of creativity, especially concerning Tunisian apparel. Interviewees mention traditional clothing and jewelry. Some recognize attempts made by designers in order to modernize traditional crafts through color changes, for example. They note, furthermore, some renewed interest in certain countries towards traditional products. Other respondents wish to see a specific Tunisian fashion that respects their national identity, blaming the fact that most Arab countries are still stuck in traditional ways and use traditional products. However, an exception is made for Lebanon, considered by some respondents as a reference in the field of fashion. Respondents give examples of some famous Lebanese singers and TV presenters; 'most of the Eastern countries are "followers", except Lebanon which has managed to distinguish itself from other Eastern countries' (Myriam, 19, high school student).

Abaza (2007) mentions the need for Egyptians to have a national dress and to focus on their culture and origins. She underlines the success of new Egyptian-ethnic brands in Egyptian high society. Those brands are created by Lebanese designers, who revisited traditional Egyptian dress, jewelry and furniture. Some authors note that fashion is no longer the exclusive property of the West, and that contemporary fashions are created rapidly and in great volume in Latin America, Africa and Asia, redefining both consumption and fashion itself, in a growing globalized world (Hansen, 2004, p. 370).

Some researchers in Islamic countries note the revival of certain traditional practices and rituals such as the 'henna-night ceremony' or traditional dance. These rituals seem to raise people's pride in their history and traditions (Üstüner et al., 2000; Sandıkcı and Ger, 2002). The debate surrounding religion and identity should be related to the question of modernity directly linked to the Western influence (Sandıkcı and Ger, 2001, 2002). The Tunisian interviewees' discourse revealed internal tensions and ambiguous feelings expressed through their fashion-relationship: the West, the main fashion diffuser, is perceived as a source of dream and fantasy, but also as a source of frustration. Some informants assert that they sometimes feel uncomfortable with their own culture, because they have difficulty in defining its boundaries. These boundaries swing between tradition and modernity, and between East and West. Globalization, technological development and mass media exposure has changed the face of societies leading to the coexistence of Eastern and Western culture in many countries. Consumers in Muslim countries often face the dilemma of choosing between access to some products or activities (especially Western ones, usually associated with modernity) on the one hand, and respecting the taboos imposed by religion on the other hand (Balasescu, 2003; Belk et al., 2003; Jones, 2007; Moors, 2007).

Our findings stress the importance of the cultural issue in the Tunisian consumer–fashion relationship and in the building of individual identity. Tunisian interviewees convey through their fashion discourse, their sensitivity to the East–West dilemma and to the question of tradition and modernity, joining thereby other consumers from Islamic or less developed countries (Balasescu, 2003; Jones, 2007). Different attitudes were however identified regarding fashion and Islamic religion; some of the informants find that the Islamic religion is in opposition to fashion (considered as intimately related to the West). Some others, however, perceive a certain harmony between fashion and Islamic religion; they consider that the idea of beauty is linked both to fashion and to God. Other respondents show yet a detachment from the religious issue when considering fashion.

DISCUSSION AND MANAGERIAL IMPLICATIONS

In our research, we explored the fashion universe as a psychological, social, and cultural phenomenon in order to understand the relationship of the Tunisian consumer to fashion. The discourse analysis about the respondents' fashion experience revealed an interesting and complex identity–fashion relationship translating all the ambiguities and tensions of the consumers' relationship with themselves, with modernity, culture, religion, and society.

Indeed, the interviewee-fashion interaction seems to be complex and consists of contradictory feelings of pleasure and frustration, admiration and denigration, identification and rejection. According to Thompson and Haytko (1997), the complexity of the consumer-fashion relationship can be explained by the fact that consumers express their relationship with themselves, with others and with their culture. Tensions, conflicts and ambiguities characterize these relations, but contribute also to assessing consumers' identity. Individuals' perception of fashion reflects their conception of life, of the world surrounding them, and of their identity. Fashion constitutes a means for asserting personality and expressing personal values. It is used by some respondents to fulfill the need for differentiation and the willingness to stand apart from the others, but can also be a means to meet the desire of conformity to a group. This paradox is frequently raised in the literature dealing with fashion (Barnard, 2002; Finkelstein, 1996). According to Brewer (1991), the individual is looking for a social identity that aims to satisfy simultaneously the needs for assimilation and differentiation, in order to reach the highest level of distinction. Yet, our findings show that the relationship of the consumer to fashion seems to be more reflective of 'conformity and membership' than of a quest for differentiation and specificity. In their narrative discourses, the importance of family, respect for social and religious limits, and community belonging are more frequently evoked than the desire for uniqueness and differentiation. This can be explained by the collectivist character of the Tunisian culture as a part of the Arab-Muslim culture, as compared to the individualist character of many Western societies. Hofstede (2001) states that this collectivist culture is manifested through a close long-term commitment to the member 'group' – a family or extended family, or extended relationships. Loyalty in a collectivist culture is important, and frequently overrides most other societal rules. Thus, even though political reforms contributed widely to the modernization of Tunisian society, and even though Tunisian women experienced real emancipation, the original Islamic culture and traditional values still shape deeply Tunisia's national identity and consequently the Tunisian fashion relationship. Pressure for conformity to the group is still an important character of this society. This might be enhanced in the present by a recent surge in interest in religion and a more conservative vision of life by certain categories of the population. This pressure for conformity is, however, probably variable among the different subcultures in Tunisian society, notably urban/rural, conservative/liberal or French culture educated/Arab culture educated.

Furthermore, the respondents' interaction with fashion embodies a significant religious and moral component that seems to be deeply rooted in Tunisians' attitude towards fashion. This dimension is integral to the cultural identity issue. Tunisia is considered as an Arab Muslim society, but it has also historically and geographically a strong relationship with Mediterranean and Western cultures and is considered as sensitive to cultural pluralism (Bouhdiba, 1978). While searching in the West for a modern fashionable lifestyle, the Tunisian consumer remains also attached to his/her national, Islamic and Eastern values. Frustration, discomfort, and ambiguity may then characterize the fashion–consumer relationship. In fact, the fear of marginalization of local culture is a constant preoccupation of Arab, African, and Third World populations (Bouhdiba, 1978; Hansen, 2004). The value systems of the Western world and the world of Islamic countries are different. For instance, Western postmodern culture celebrates difference and personalization, whereas in countries like Tunisia, the influence of social norms, limits, and taboos still prevails and strongly influences the respondents' relationship with fashion.

The cultural identity issue is also manifested through the regret expressed by interviewees about the lack of a 'Tunisian fashion' that would enhance local specificities and identity. Fashion is perceived by respondents as coming primarily from the West. This West is admired for its creativity and freedom in generating fashion styles, but also feared for its ability to blur local particularities. Informants are torn between the Western model, whose lifestyles and values are spread through mass media, and local values. Polhemus (1973) points out that countries evolving towards Westernization can face some uncertainty caused by interactions between Western culture and the national identity. The difficulty of building a modern Islamic identity in a global world is also discussed by some researchers: 'Constructing a "modern" Islamic identity within the local power network involves simultaneously negotiating multiple tensions – the tensions between the West and the East, the secular and the religious, the urban and the rural – and distancing itself from various internal others' (Sandıkcı and Ger, 2001). What characterizes the Arab and

Tunisian societies is that, there is at the same time, a conscious and unconscious attachment to a certain conception of the past as an anchor with the ultimate truth (the Islamic one), and a strong desire to participate in the history of the world, based in large part on the industrialized occidental civilization. 'This is what is very often confusing, because what we call the modern world is not the others' modernity but a rediscovery, in new terms, of oneself with oneself and with others' (Bouhdiba, 1978, p. 211).

Finally, compared to past research on fashion in Muslim countries, our findings also underline the importance of the same main issue: the challenging negotiation between fashion, modernity, West and religion. It seems that, whatever their level of sophistication, their history or ethnic origin, Muslim societies experience, through the fashion relationship, the same dilemma relating to the construction of the self. However, specificities may relate to more practical issues, such as the commodification of Islamic fashion or products and the development of related markets (Islamic appeals, outlets and stores, magazines, dolls). Such markets are, for instance, underdeveloped or nonexistent in Tunisia.

Some managerial implications emerge from the present research study. The launching of Tunisian fashion brands, particularly in the clothing field, can benefit from the positive association made by Tunisian consumers between fashion and Western countries. An option for the company would be to choose a brand name with Western connotations and a Western positioning (communication and store design). Today this kind of strategy seems to be adopted by some clothing and accessories stores: for example, brands like 'Blue Island', 'Dixit' and 'Sasio' are Tunisian, but are positioned solely as European brands. A second implication concerns creativity in the field of fashion. According to the informants' discourse, there is a deep willingness to reconcile Western modern fashion and Tunisian design. It is an important niche that can be filled by Tunisian fashion creators whether in clothing or jewelry and accessories while preserving the product's Tunisian 'spirit' through fabric, design or even communication.

The traditional Arabic-Muslim dimension of the Tunisian identity seems to be exalted in special occasions such as family ceremonies, religious rituals and some national events. Fashion designers can seize these opportunities to propose adapted product lines and, at the same time, making the connection between consumers and their national and cultural identity. Another implication concerns communication of fashion goods. Is it always interesting for advertising agencies to choose 'Western' positioning and Western 'icons'? Which topics should they adopt for fashionable products: differentiation and uniqueness (relating to Western values) or belonging and affiliation (relating to Eastern values)?

Future research perspectives may be proposed. Even if the question of gender seems to be a classical issue, it is particularly interesting in the case of Arab-Muslim countries. The male–fashion relationship in these countries may reveal interesting social representations of the 'modern versus traditional' Muslim male. Fashion is often considered in these societies as part of the women's world. Traditional and religious factors may shape this image. However, globalization and the mass media suggest other male images. How does the Muslim male deal with fashion? Another issue to investigate is the difference between veiled and non-veiled women in their relationship to fashion. The question of the veil has been debated in the previous literature mainly from the point of view of veiled women (Abaza, 2007; Balasescu, 2003; Jones, 2007, Sandıkcı and Ger, 2010). It would be interesting to extend the research question to the experience and attitudes of veiled and non-veiled women relating to fashion in general. Finally, an intercultural research study on the relationship to fashion between Muslim Arab and non-Arab consumers, and between Muslim and non-Muslim consumers could highlight the specificities of each culture or sub-culture regarding fashion experience and could help to elucidate the cultural identity issue.

BIBLIOGRAPHY

Abassi, D. (2005), *Entre Bourguiba et Hannibal – Identité Tunisienne et Histoire depuis L'Indépendance*, Karthala éditions.
Abaza, M. (2007), 'Shifting landscapes of fashion in contemporary Egypt', *Fashion Theory*, **11** (2/3), 281–98.
Balasescu, A. (2003), 'Teheran chic, Islamic headscarves, fashion designers and new geographies of modernity', *Fashion Theory*, **7** (1), 39–56.
Barnard, M. (2002), *Fashion as Communication*, London: Routledege.
Barthes, R. (1967), *Système de la Mode*, Paris: édition du Seuil.
Belk R.W. (1988), 'Possessions and the extended self', *Journal of Consumer Research*, **115** (September), 139–67.
Belk, R., G. Ger and S. Askegaard (2003), 'The fire of desire: a multisited inquiry into consumer passion', *Journal of Consumer Research*, **30** (December), 326–51.
Bocock, R. (1993), *Consumption: Key Ideas*, London: Routledge.
Bordo, S. (2003), *Unbearable Weight: Feminism, Western Culture and the Body*, Berkeley, CA: University of California Press.
Bouhdiba, A (1978), *Culture et Société*, Publications de l'université de Tunis.
Bourdieu, P. (1984), *Distinction: A Social Critique of the Judgment of Taste*, Cambridge, MA: Harvard University Press.
Brewer, M.B. (1991), 'The social self: on being the same and different in the same time', *Personality and Social Psychology Bulletin*, **17** (5), 475–82.
Carpenter, J.M., E. Moore and M. Fairhurst (2005), 'Consumer shopping value for retail brands', *Journal of Fashion Marketing and Management*, **9** (1), 43–53.
Cholachatpinyo, A., I. Padgett, M. Crocker and B. Fletche (2002), 'A conceptual model of the fashion process, part 1: The fashion transformation process model', *Journal of Fashion Marketing and Management*, **6** (1), 11–23.
Craik, J. (1994), *The Face of Fashion*, London: Routledge.
Davis, F. (1992), *Fashion, Culture and Identity*, Chicago: University of Chicago Press.
Douglas, M. and B. Isherwood (1979), *The World of Goods: Towards an Anthropology of Consumption*, Harmondsworth: Penguin.
Entwistle, J. (2000), *The Fashioned Body: Fashion, Dress, and the Modern Social Theory*, Wiley-Blackwell.
Ewen, S. (1988), *All Consuming Images: The Politics of Style in Contemporary Culture*, New York: Basic.
Finkelstein, J. (1991), *The Fashioned Self*, Cambridge: Polity Press.
Finkelstein, J. (1996), *After a Fashion*, Melbourne: Melbourne University Press.
Firat, A.F. (1991), 'The consumer in post-modernity', in R.H. Holman and M.R. Solomon (eds), *Advances in Consumer Research*, vol. 18, Provo, UT: Association of Consumer Research, pp. 70–76.
Guellouz, E., A. Masmoudi and M. Smida (1983), *Histoire de la Tunisie : Les Temps Modernes*, Société Tunisienne de Diffusion.
Hannum K.M. (2007), *Social Identity, Knowing Yourself, Leading Other*, Center for Creative Leadership, North Carolina.
Hansen, K.T. (2004), 'The word in dress: anthropological perspectives on clothing, fashion and culture', *Annual Review of Anthropology*, **33**, 369–92.
Hetzel, P. (1995), 'Le rôle de la mode et du design dans la société de consommation postmoderne : Quels enjeux pour les entreprises ?', *Revue Française de Marketing*, **151**, 19–29.
Hofstede, G. (2001), *Culture's Consequences: Comparing Values, Behaviors, Institutions, and Organizations across Nations*, Thousand Oaks, CA: Sage Publications.
Jones, C. (2007), 'Fashion and faith in urban Indonesia', *Fashion Theory* , **11** (2/3), 211–32.
Lipovetsky, G. (1994), *The Empire of Fashion: Dressing Modern Democracy*, (trans. C. Porter), Princeton, NJ: Princeton University Press.
Lipovetsky, G. and S.Charles (2005), *Hypermodern Times*, Polity.

Lury, C. (1996), *Consumer Culture*, New Brunswick, NJ: Rutgers University, University Press.

Marion, G. (2003), 'Apparence et identité : une approche sémiotique du discours des adolescentes à propos de leur expérience de la mode', *Recherche et Application Marketing*, **18** (2), 1–29.

McCracken, G. (1986), 'Culture and consumption: a theoretical account and the structure of meaning of consumer goods', *Journal of Consumer Research*, **13** (June), 71–84.

McCracken, G. (1988), *Culture and Consumption*, Bloomington, IN: University Press.

Messadi, M. (1958), Opening speech for the freedom of culture, Tunis, 13–18 April (in Arabic).

Miles, M.B. and A.M. Huberman (eds) (1994), *Qualitative Data Analysis: An Expanded Source Book*, 2nd edition, Sage Publications.

Moors, A. (2007), 'Fashionable Muslims: notions of self, religion and society in San'a', *Fashion Theory*, **11** (2/3), 319–46.

Mucchielli, A. (1999), *L'identité*, 4th edn, Paris: PUF.

Nabli, F., and H. Swiderska (2008), *Tunisie, Flash Historique*, Kolekcja Fathel.

O'Cass, A. (2001), 'Consumer self-monitoring, materialism and involvement, in fashion clothing', *Australasian Marketing Journal*, **9** (1), 46–60.

Olson, E.A. (1985), 'Muslim identity and secularism in contemporary Turkey: "The headscarf dispute"', *Anthropological Quarterly*, **58** (4), 161–71.

Parker, R.S., C. Hermans and A. Schaefer (2004), 'Fashion consciousness of Chinese, Japanese and American', *Journal of Fashion Marketing and Management*, **8** (2), 176–86.

Peters, T.J. (1992), *Liberation Management: Necessary Disorganization for the Nanosecond Nineties*, New York: A.A. Knopf.

Polhemus, J.T. (1973), 'Fashion, antifashion and the body image', *New Society*, **11**, 73–76.

Rocha, M.A., L. Hammond and D. Hawkins (2005), 'Age, gender and national factors in fashion consumption', *Journal of Fashion Marketing and Management*, **9** (4), 380–90.

Sandıkcı, Ö. and G. Ger (2001), 'Fundamental fashions: the cultural politics of the turban and the Levis', in M.C. Gilly and J. Meyers-Levey (eds), *Advances in Consumer Research*, vol. 28, Valdosta, GA: Association for Consumer Research, pp.146–50.

Sandıkcı, Ö. and G. Ger (2002), 'In-between modernities and postmodernities: theorizing Turkish consumptionscape', in Susan M. Broniarczyk and Kent Nakamoto (eds), *Advances in Consumer Research*, vol. 29, Valdosta, GA: Association for Consumer Research, pp.465–70.

Sandıkcı, Ö. and G. Ger (2007), 'Constructing and representing the Islamic consumer in Turkey', *Fashion Theory*, **11** (2/3), 189–210.

Sandıkcı, Ö. and G. Ger (2010), 'Veiling in style: how does a stigmatized practice become fashionable?', *Journal of Consumer Research*, **37** (1), 15–36.

Sennett, R. (1994), *The fall of the Public Man*, New York: W.W. Norton.

Simmel, G. (1904), 'Fashion', *International Quarterly*, **10**, 130–55 published in French in G. Simmel, *La tragédie de la culture et autres essais*, Rivages, 1988.

Slim, H., and N. Fauqué (2001), *La Tunisie Antique: De Hannibal à Saint Augustin* Paris: Mengès.

Solomon, M.R. (2004), *Consumer Behavior: Buying, Having, and Being*, 6th edn, Upper Saddle River, NJ: Pearson/Prentice Hall.

Solomon, M.R. and N.J. Rabolt (2009), *Consumer Behavior in Fashion*, Upper Saddle River, NJ: Pearson Education.

Tajfel, H. (eds) (1972), *La Catégorisation Sociale, Introduction à la Psychologie sociale vol. 1*, Moscow and, Paris: Larousse.

Tarlo, E. (2007), 'Islamic cosmopolitanism: the sartorial biographies of three Muslim women in London', *Fashion Theor*, **11** (2/3), 143–72.

Thompson, C. and D. Haytko (1997), 'Speaking of fashion: consumer uses of fashion discourses and the appropriation of countervailing cultural meanings', *Journal of Consumer Research*, **24** (June), 15–42.

Touzani, M. and E. Hirschman (2008), 'Cultural syncretism and ramadan observance: consumer research visits Islam', *Advances in Consumer Research*, **35**, 374–80.

Üstüner, T. and D.B. Holt (2007), 'Dominated consumer acculturation: the social construction of poor migrant women's consumer identity projects in a Turkish squatter', *Journal of Consumer Research*, **34** (June), 42–56.

Üstüner, T. and D.B. Holt (2010), 'Toward a theory of status consumption in Less Industrialized Countries', *Journal of Consumer Research*, **37** (June), 37–56.

Üstüner, T., G. Ger and D.B. Holt (2000), 'Consuming ritual: reframing the Turkish henna-night ceremony', *Advances in Consumer Research*, **27**, 209–14.

Yakin, A. (2007), 'Islamic Barbie: The politics of gender and performativity', *Fashion Theory*, **11** (2/3), 173–88.

7 Consumer acculturation *in situ*: the continuing legacy of French colonization in North Africa
Elizabeth C. Hirschman and Mourad Touzani

INTRODUCTION

Within the consumer behavior and marketing literatures, virtually all studies on acculturation focus upon the adaptive changes made by an immigrant population having arrived within a new country during the present generation or recent generations (see for example Askegaard et al., 2005; Khan, 1992; O'Guinn et al., 1985; Oswald, 1999; Wallendorf and Reilly, 1983). There are some exceptions in which internal migration from rural to urban settings have been the focus of inquiry (Üstüner and Holt, 2007). Yet this research model does not represent the fullness of acculturation as a concept or as an applied form of social science research. Trimble (2003, p. 4–5), for example, states, 'Acculturation may well be synonymous with socio-cultural change . . . The concept now is included in the research agenda of psychologists, psychiatrists, sociologists, social workers and educators [as well as anthropologists]'. Viewing acculturation as a framework that extends beyond immigration studies would also bring it into closer alignment with the post-assimilationist perspective recently espoused by Peñaloza (1994), Oswald (1999), Askegaard et al., (2005) and Üstüner and Holt (2007). As Askegaard et al. (2005, p. 160) point out, 'Post-assimilationist writing challenges the linear acculturation model' between two cultures. Yet, these authors do not actually explore the full ramifications of their statement, instead using as their point of inquiry ethnic migrants to a non-North American country, that is, Inuit immigrants to Denmark. Similarly, Üstüner and Holt (2007) examine the non-linear acculturation responses exhibited by rural Turkish women and their daughters as a result of their migration to urban areas in Turkey. Thus, although acculturation *can* be broadly construed as a social change process involving two or more cultures which come into contact, it has been artificially constrained within the marketing and consumer behavior literatures to apply only to immigration contexts. A review of the acculturation literature emanating from anthropology quickly reveals that its potential applicability is much broader.

The concept of acculturation entered the social sciences during the nineteenth and twentieth centuries in response to the processes of modernization then affecting most nations and cultures (Trimble, 2003). Even prior to this era, however, worldwide patterns of colonization – especially by Western Europeans venturing into the Americas, Africa, the Indian subcontinent and East Asia – had set in motion large-scale events of cultural contact and adjustment (Hollowell, 1945; Berry, 2003). Harley (2001, p. 1) comments that:

> The acculturation process, the borrowing of the values, processes or products of other culture(s) has always existed . . . This process, however, has become much more noticeable in the 20th century, as there are progressively many more forces that make . . . interactions unavoidable . . . Western concepts, values and products are making their way into traditional society . . .

Notably, Askegaard et al. (2005, p. 165) acknowledge this possibility, stating, 'In addition to the institutional forces of home and host cultures, a third acculturative force . . . is the influence of a transnational . . . consumer and communications economy' originating in the West, and especially the United States. Yet the influence of this 'third force' is not examined in depth in their study. Consider this in light of one of the earliest definitions of acculturation:

> Those phenomena which result when groups of individuals having different cultures come into continuous first-hand contact, with subsequent changes in the original cultural patterns of either or both groups . . . (Redfield et al., 1936)

> Acculturation is culture change initiated by the conjunction of two or more autonomous cultural systems. Acculturative change may be a consequence of direct cultural transmission; . . . it [also] may be delayed, as with internal adjustments following the acceptance of alien traits or patterns; or it may be a reactive adaptation of traditional modes of life. (Social Science Research Council, 1954, p. 974)

What we wish to propose in the present study is that acculturation may occur as a continuing legacy of earlier colonization of one country by another country. Even though the colonizer may depart, we propose that cultural influence of the colonizer may linger far into the future, especially when enabled by communication technologies which make possible a virtual form of 'direct contact', in the absence of the actual physical presence of persons from the colonizing culture. The locale for examining this possibility is the North African nation of Tunisia which was colonized from the late 1800s to mid-1900s by the French.

We propose further that the many legacies of colonization around the world may be the greatest untapped reserve of acculturation exemplars available in the social sciences.

TUNISIA

The focus of the present study is the Arab Muslim response to Western, specifically French, acculturation influence. In particular, we will be focusing upon French Colonial and post-Colonial influence on consumption patterns in the North African country of Tunisia. Situated on the east-central shores of North Africa, Tunisia has experienced many episodes of colonization. Among the earliest to arrive were Greek, Carthaginian and other Eastern Mediterranean peoples who used the coastal areas as trade depots; subsequently, Romans settled for an extended period of time, establishing colonies throughout North Africa (Sorel, 1973). However, the post-antiquity history of Tunisia and North Africa, generally, is the legacy of Arab Muslim and then, in the modern era, French colonization patterns. It is to the lengthy and centuries long impact of the arrival of Arabs and Islam to which we first turn.

THE MUSLIM ENTRY INTO NORTHERN AFRICA

Following the passing of the Prophet Muhammad (570–632 CE), the Umayyads took control of Islam (661–750 CE) and ruled from the city of Damascus. Their first caliph,

Mu'awiya, believed that the lands west of Egypt possessed strategic importance to spreading the faith. Over several decades, the Umayyads were able to conquer the northern portion of Africa. The conquest began in 670, with the arrival of an Arab Muslim army under Uqba ibn Nafi. The city of Kairouan ('stronghold' in Arabic) was established as their base. In the late 670s the Arab army defeated the indigenous Berber forces who had not adopted Islam. Over the next few years however, the Berbers regained control of some areas and threatened Muslim Arab dominance. This challenge was overcome in 682, when Uqba ibn Nafi defeated the Berber forces near Tahirt (Algeria), and then proceeded westward until reaching the Atlantic coast (Brahimi, 1996). These campaigns became legendary throughout the Maghrib.[1]

In 705, Hassan ibn al-Nu'man stormed Carthage, leaving it in ruins. Near the ruins of Carthage, he founded Tunis as a naval base. Al-Nu'man was followed by Musa ibn Nusair, who completed the Muslim conquest of al-Maghrib. Ibn Nusair conquered the city of Tangier and appointed the Berber Tariq ibn Ziyad as its governor, helping to consolidate Islam as the religion of all Maghribi inhabitants (Guendouze et al., 1983).

However, during the years preceding the fall of the Umayyad Caliphate, revolts arose among the Kharijite Berbers in Morocco, eventually disrupting the stability of the entire Maghrib (739–772). Direct rule from the East by the Caliphs over Ifriqiya became untenable, despite the establishment of the new Abbasid Caliphate in Baghdad in 750. Further, a local Arab-speaking aristocracy, the Muhallabids, had now emerged in Ifriqiya, which resented the distant caliphate's interference in local matters (Guendouze et al., 1983).

These Arab Muhallabids (771–793) negotiated with the Abbasids to become Governors of the Maghrib. One of the Muhallabid governors was al-Aghlab ibn Salim, the forefather of the Aghlabid dynasty in North Africa. After several decades, the Muhallabid rule became weakened. A minor rebellion in Tunis soon spread to Kairouan, greatly disrupting control over the region (Guendouze et al., 1983).

The leader of the revolt was Ibrahim ibn al-Aghlab, a provincial leader (and son of al-Aghlab ibn Salim), who managed to reestablish regional stability in 797. Later he proposed to the Abbasid caliph Harun al-Rashid, that he be granted Ifriqiya as a hereditary fief, which was granted.

From 800 to 909, Ibrahim ibn al-Aghlab (ruled 800–812) and his descendants, the Aghlabids, ruled in Ifriqiya, as well as in lands to the west (eastern Algeria) and lands to the east (Tripolitania). At this time, there were approximately 100 000 Arabs living in Ifriqiya, with the Berbers still constituting the majority of the population (Arezki, 2004).

The culture of the Maghribi population underwent acculturative change due to both Islamization and Arabization. It should be noted that these two forces did not evolve concurrently. The conversion of the Berbers to Islam required only two centuries, while the adoption of the Arabic language by the majority of the North African population took until the end of the Middle Ages (Arezki, 2004). Further, Arabization did not take the form of racial or ethnic domination. Rather it occurred through the fusion of several cultural contributions in which the Arabic language and way of life served as the dominant template (and following the post-assimilationist model of non-linear acculturation). The end of the Ottoman presence in Tunisia left the country with these two enduring characteristics: Islam and Arabity (Camau, 1989).

FRENCH COLONIZATION IN NORTHERN AFRICA

The foundations of the French colonial empire in North Africa were laid in 1830 with the invasion of Algeria, which was conquered over the next 17 years. The French gradually expanded their hegemony in North Africa, annexing Tunisia in 1881 (Duval, 2009). In subsequent decades, French control was established over much of Northern, Western, and Central Africa, a land area which included the modern nations of Mauritania, Senegal, Guinea, Mali, Côte d' Ivoire, Benin, Niger, Chad, Central African and Republic, and Republic of Congo, as well as the east African coastal enclave of Dijibouti (French Somaliland). In 1911, Morocco became a French protectorate.

In 1954 France's oldest major African colony, Algeria, began to chafe against French rule. The rebellion of Algeria was particularly problematic for France due to the large number of European settlers (or *pieds-noirs*) who had settled there over the previous 125 years. Charles de Gaulle's accession to power in 1958 finally led to independence for Algeria in 1962. Most of the other French African colonies had already been granted independence in 1960 (Duval, 2009).

With the establishment of the French protectorate in Tunisia came a dramatic alteration in culture. This acculturation-in-situ was characterized both by its ambivalence and by ongoing friction between the two dominant cultural models: the Arabic and the French (Fitouri, 1983). The French language, values and way of thinking became widespread throughout Tunisia, despite marked resistance in the major centers more rooted in the Arabic culture: Mahdia, Kairouan and the South. The colonial situation became a cultural battlefield in which the confrontation between these two cultural models led to the diffusion of the French language across the country, while the population also maintained its Islamic religious traditions. The portion of the citizenry choosing to strongly acculturate to the French model came to form a French-speaking community (*communauté francophone*) within Tunisia. It is upon this segment of the Tunisian population that the current study focuses.

METHOD

Our study examines the relationship between Islamic-Arabic culture and French colonial culture in Tunisia. Because of this, we sought out individuals to serve as informants who a priori exhibited acculturative traits drawn from both cultures. To arrive at a set of informants, we first canvassed a sample of 400 Tunisians and measured their level of French acculturation. The acculturation scale developed by Valencia (1985) was adapted and used to identify a continuum of Tunisian-French acculturation ranging from weak to strong. Responses were measured using a 5-point Likert scale. The scale was provided to respondents in both French and Tunisian-dialect Arabic. Any persons who had lived in France were eliminated from consideration, as they would have received the traditional form of immigrant-based acculturation.

From this process, a sample of highly French-acculturated Tunisians was identified and these persons were approached for in-depth interviews. Following the saturation principle (Miles and Huberman, 1994), we continued interviewing until no additional

Table 7.1   Interviewees' profile

Subject number	Gender	Age	Education level	Occupation
1	M	42	College	Pilot
2	F	35	Doctorate	Faculty staff
3	F	37	Doctorate	Veterinary
4	F	55	College	Real estate agent
5	M	42	College	Technical director
6	M	59	College	Forwarding agent
7	F	26	College	Air hostess
8	F	31	College	Secondary school teacher
9	M	29	College	Engineer
10	F	38	College	Primary school teacher
11	M	23	College	Student in computer sciences
12	M	40	High school	Pastry cook
13	F	51	College	Journalist
14	F	44	College	Human resource manager
15	F	49	High school	Home keeper
16	M	35	High school	Clerk
17	F	73	Primary school	Retired
18	M	51	Doctorate	Doctor
19	M	33	College	Entrepreneur
20	F	24	College	Student in management
21	M	36	College	Hotel manager
22	F	48	College	Lawyer
23	F	48	Doctorate	Faculty staff
24	F	22	College	Architect
25	M	25	College	Restaurant manager
26	M	37	College	Accounting clerk
27	M	39	College	Human Resource Manager
28	F	82	Secondary school	Retired
29	F	41	College	Translator
30	F	58	College	Faculty staff
31	F	28	College	Engineer
32	M	54	Secondary school	Driving school owner
33	M	64	Doctorate	Politician
34	F	26	College	Beautician
35	M	53	College	Bank clerk
36	M	60	Doctorate	Dentist
37	M	28	College	Web-manager

themes or examples were being provided by the informants. Altogether a total of 37 informants were interviewed. Their profiles are provided in Table 7.1.

The in-depth interviews were based upon an interactive dialogue approach (Kaufmann, 2006) which was designed to make the respondents feel at ease. Interviews were conducted in Tunisian-Arabic and/or French, occasionally going back and forth between these two languages as the interview unfolded. Interviews took between 45 minutes to two and a half hours. Each was tape recorded and transcribed. For purposes of the present report, the interviews were translated into English except for specific phrases which had no direct counterpart in English. These are given in the excerpts in their original linguistic form, that is, either French or Arabic. To construct our analysis, each transcript was read multiple times, both as an individual response point and also as a corpus of group acculturation themes.

FINDINGS

Language Usage as a Marker of Acculturation

Almost all those we interviewed in the high acculturation group were very fluent in French and used it as their primary language both at home and at work. Because French language usage is associated with Western acculturation within the larger Tunisian population, our interviewees reported that this practice could be off-putting, or even offensive, to Arab-oriented Tunisians.

> At home we speak French, with my wife, my children, my parents, my brother, my sister and all of the rest of the family. Of course, we use some Arabic at times, but mostly we speak French. When we go outside, it's not as easy . . . If we are in our neighborhood, or in some quarters we often go to, we also speak French with clerks working in administration or a salesperson in a shop. However, we have to speak Arabic in several other quarters, because some of the people would not understand the French language, or because it would be considered as something odd, or snobbish to do.

> In some situations when we speak French, everybody looks at us as if we didn't belong to that place, or as if we were doing something bad. So, it generates a feeling of uneasiness . . .

Thus, there is tension between the Western culture of colonization and the 'indigenous' (although historically colonialist also) culture of Arabic speaking Tunisia. There are social class connotations, as well. For example, speaking French is seen within the highly acculturated Tunisian consumer segment as connoting sophistication and cultural superiority: 'When the conversation becomes serious, we move to French.' Those who do not speak French fluently typically are regarded as socially inferior: 'Not speaking French well is a social handicap. When some people who do not speak French very well start to hold higher positions in the political hierarchy, we have contempt for them, in spite of their position'.

This attitude suggests that one of the self-damaging legacies of Western/French colonization is a lingering sense of inferiority for traditional North African, Islamic-Muslim culture. Those seeing themselves as 'more French' regard their Arabic-acculturated countrymen and women as being 'beneath' them. To be 'Arabic' is to be a social inferior even in one's own country, from this Western-acculturated perspective.

French language usage additionally influences the choice of retail stores among our highly acculturated set of interviewees:

> Of course, I prefer places where it is possible to speak French! Sometimes, I can't find the appropriate words in Arabic, and it's easier for me to express my needs or my ideas in French.

And, fortunately, in several shops and stores around here, they recruit salespeople who are fluent in French in order to be able to speak with all the customers . . .

When I'm with my daughter, I avoid going to certain malls or stores. My daughter wouldn't understand some words in Arabic.

I can't imagine myself going to those places where people speak only Arabic. Actually, it's as if we don't belong to the same world. I'll be sincere. We don't really belong to the same class [social class].

Acculturating their Children

One of the quotes above leads to another aspect of French acculturation in Muslim Tunisia. Those consumers who are strongly Westernized also seek to enculturate their children to the same worldview. Within this population segment, Western cultural values were deemed superior to traditional Arab Muslim values:

I put my son in the French school. I think that this school promotes several values that you wouldn't find in the Tunisian educational system. They [the French schools] teach them critical thinking, they give them the opportunity to discuss things, and the way children are managed is based on reaching a consensus. They teach them to respect the environment and nature, and they do it in a very playful and effective manner. You wouldn't find all this in Tunisian schools.

I didn't put my children into a Tunisian school, because I don't want them to be bullied. I want them to blossom. French schools offer the opportunity to develop all their capacities. All the activities are oriented towards helping kids to fulfill themselves. Spontaneity is also very important in a French school. This is not the case elsewhere.

What is especially notable about the above quotes is that they identify a primary agent of Western/French acculturation embedded directly in the Tunisian culture – the French-style educational institutions. Even though the French government has officially left the country for over 60 years, these schools function very effectively as agents of acculturation across generations of Tunisians.

Apparel, Home Décor and other Self-presentation Choices

Among the most strongly marked aspects of the acculturated self are the clothing, hairstyle and facial accessories one chooses to wear. Among upper class Indians in British-colonized India during the mid to late 1800s, for example, adopting English styles of dress signaled their knowledge of and desire for British status markers (Cohn, 1998). Among the first Indian ethnic groups to acculturate to English norms of self-presentation were the Parsis of Bombay, who themselves, had immigrated to India from Persia in the preceding centuries (Cohn 1998, p. 219). By the 1880s, Cohn (1998) reports, the mimicry of British fashion trends became even more widespread across the affluent sectors of Indian society, especially for Indian men educated in Western universities.[2]

In present-day Mexico a similar pattern can be found among acculturated *mestizos*. The most important of these apparel markers, according to Sandstrom (2000), is that those desiring to be viewed as 'Spanish' adopt the wearing of shoes; whereas those who wish to remain identified with their indigenous origins go barefoot. Sandstrom (2000) notes that within Indigenous villages, the more affluent and acculturated consumers have taken to wearing not only shoes, but also 'Western-style clothing' (p. 271).

Closer to the Muslim Tunisian context, Hoffman (2008, p. 62) found Moroccan Berbers who wished to identify with urban Arab culture wore 'polyester warm-up suits, . . . sunglasses, baseball caps, tennis shoes, rode about on mopeds and spoke the Arabic language' instead of wearing traditional Berber apparel and using the Berber language. Further, in rural Berber villages, modern household equipment such as a 'boom box' radio or electric clock served an indexical function, signaling the residents' modernity and Westernization to visitors. Hoffman (2008, p. 68), further states that, 'new market items . . . signaled the user's engagement with the market economy through the male networks that linked country to city . . . The newer, cleaner and more unused an item was, the better . . .'

Among our Tunisian sample, those highly acculturated toward Western/French norms followed the same pattern. Consider the statements below regarding decoration of the home:

> I think that our home décor is different from the one you may find in the average Tunisian house. Yes, definitely. First of all, generally in my family, we avoid all the objects that glitter and glisten that you may find in the other houses. You won't find those huge ceiling lights, but halogen lamps instead . . . You also won't find all of those traditional silver-plated and golden handcrafts that clutter up the Tunisian homes. Yes, their houses are full, cluttered up . . .

> In my home, it's brown, beige and black, and I'm rather happy with them. It's a matter of taste. When I go to all those houses where you find hundreds of colors, red, yellow, green, blue, orange, brown . . . all of those shining colors hurt my vision. [However], it's a matter of taste, and even if I don't like it, I respect their choice.

In these excerpts, the informants never explicitly state that their houses are decorated in the French/Western style, but the contrasting examples they provide make it clear that they are denigrating the traditional Arabic Tunisian style of home décor. For example, the multi-colored interiors and gold and silver items are very much associated with Arabic culture, whereas the more subtle, restrained color palette is indicative of Western/French norms. In essence, the French-acculturated Tunisians are laying claim to Bourdieu's (Bourdieu, 1984) ideology of cultural capital (see Üstüner and Holt (2007) for a discussion of Bourdieu's theoretical applicability to consumer behavior contexts). French culture is believed by them to provide a more ample source of cultural capital than is that of traditional Arab Tunisia.

Western media sources appear to play a strong role in communicating this value system, as noted earlier by Askegaard et al. (2005): 'My main source of inspiration is all the TV programs dedicated to home decoration. There are several of them on the French channels. My mother subscribed to a magazine called *Roche-Bobois*, but times have changed. I use the Internet to get ideas.'

> For decorating the house, we get inspiration from our family and friends' houses, and also from movies, the TV programs in the French channels dedicated to home decoration, and we also buy some French magazines to get ideas. . . . I wouldn't really say that my home has a French style. It's a kind of mélange of different styles. But what is sure is that it's not the traditional style, the one my grandparents used to have. It's more modern, more westernized also.

For decorating the self, these consumers again turned to the Western/French cultural model. As before, there is an explicit statement that this model is not only different from that traditionally found in Tunisia, but also superior:

> Tunisian women have always had a preference for Western fashion. Some find it more practical; others more attractive. This is because Western countries had a head start on us in this area and were able to valorize and promote their clothing heritage, organizing fashion shows and major international fashion events, and using TV and media as a means of promotion.

This respondent insightfully 'sees beneath the surface' and is able to articulate the power of Western ideology as an influence not only on her own choices as a consumer, but also upon Tunisia, as a whole. This, of course, reflects the larger discourse of Western hegemony found throughout the Muslim world (Kassab, 2005). The normative issue, of course, is whether adopting a Western appearance, for one's self and in one's home, means that key aspects of one's ancestral heritage are being abandoned. Or perhaps, is the Arab Tunisian ancestral heritage simply being swallowed up by the powerful wave of Western commodification?

> Today, with all the European stores present in Tunisia, the fashion comes from the West. The Tunisian brands just follow the models brought from elsewhere by these stores. So, I don't think that there's a Tunisian fashion, or a Tunisian clothing style. The only occasions where people still put on Tunisian clothes are the marriages, the circumcisions, the funerals, and the traditional holidays. The government is trying to save the remainder of our clothing patrimony with this 'traditional clothing day', but people didn't follow the initiative, even though the idea is good.

In the passage above, this Tunisian consumer provides a thoughtful discussion of the competing ideologies available, as symbolized through apparel. Indeed, the diffusion of Western chain stores throughout North Africa is another potent agent of acculturation. Together with French-style schools, these retail stores serve as 'embedded' acculturative agents. Tunisians need never leave their home soil to become indoctrinated with the ideals of Western consumer culture.

Recognizing this as a struggle for national ideology, the Tunisian government is making an effort analogous to those found in, say, Indonesia to re-invigorate the traditional national heritage as a means of enhancing national pride (see Harley 2001, p. 3). Harley notes, 'Governments often have been accused of dominating or repossessing ethnic minorities and cultural differences. However, the material culture of minority groups is used often as a symbol of the nation'.

Another informant sees the inflow of French/Western culture as occurring perhaps more subtly through charitable distributions sent to Tunisia.

> What I know is that the big majority of Tunisians buy clothes from the second-hand souks (traditional markets). So, have you ever asked yourself about the origin of these millions of clothes that are sent there? Actually, they come from charity organizations located in developed countries. So, in order to help the Third World, people from those countries give some old and new clothes, and these clothes are sold here at low prices. That looks praiseworthy, no? But, by doing so, the donator gives a part of himself, a part of his own image, and the buyer receives clothes that correspond much more to the donator's image and culture, than to his own. And in the end, if you look at all those clothes, they do not fit at all with our own culture. Maybe they

are a way of changing people's culture to westernize our lifestyle? I don't know if I go too far, but the result is here. Today, everybody is dressed in the Western way.

Thus, charitable donations of culturally coded products represent a third avenue through which Western/French values are transferred to Tunisia. In essence, acculturation arrives with every box of donated goods. The not-so-subtle result may be that the recipient comes to see the donor as having a superior culture, after all, why are things being sent here to Tunisia, instead of our sending things to France?

However, it would be inaccurate to position Western culture, as the only significant influence on Tunisian consumption patterns. It is actually one among many that these consumers may choose from:

> People's sense of aesthetics is very influenced by other cultures . . . Let's take the example of young women you may encounter in the street in Tunis. Some of them are completely connected to Lebanon: they are fascinated by the Lebanese make-up and cosmetics: very red lipstick, bright and shiny effects, eyebrows '*à la libanaise*' . . . it's very fashionable [these days]. Some other young women are rather influenced by the French sense of aesthetics, discreet; they spend hours making-up, but you wouldn't guess that they did so. Finally, the new-comers are those who are influenced by the Gulf countries, those who hide all that under a black integral veil . . . We are far away from our grandmothers' *khol* and *swak* [walnut bark].

Food Preferences and Acculturation

> My grandmother used to spend several hours a day cooking and preparing the different meals for her family. My mother had a French education and didn't follow this model. The way she prepares food is much more Europeanized, and the meals she prepares are healthy, simple, and not time-consuming. My cooking habits are similar to my mother's. However, contrary to her, as soon as I have some free time, especially on Sunday, I prepare some old recipes. Maybe, it's a way of preserving our ancestors' heritage, even though I'm sure that a big part of it has been lost today.

The passage above illustrates well the subtle and non-linear tensions between Western ideology and practices and the traditional Arab Muslim culture of Tunisia and are consistent with the findings of Oswald (1999), Askegaard et al. (2005) and Üstüner and Holt (2007). This woman's description of food preparation documents important intergenerational differences, first, with a shift from traditional Arabic cuisine to French cuisine and now a re-balancing of these two cultures in the present generation. However some Tunisian Muslims are far more oriented toward Western food preparation and ingredients. These tended to be the more cosmopolitan group, who travelled frequently to Europe, especially France.

> When a member of the family goes to France, he/she will bring back different kinds of cheese, wine and champagne. It's for us an opportunity to make a family lunch, such as 'raclette' or 'cheese fondue', in a French way. We also bring sausage, pepperoni or salami. I know that it is supposed to be forbidden by our religion, but it's like this, we can't help it.

> My friends and I always watch TV programs about French cuisine. There are plenty of them . . . Besides, I travel a lot to France. So, each and every time I go there, I bring back new ideas of meals and recipes. So, it's normal that the way we cook and the food that we buy change. Today, we are far away from the traditional cuisine you may find in other households.

Here we see another type of acculturative legacy left after colonialism has officially ended – trips to the former colonizing country result in 'tastings' and 'samples' which are brought back and serve as tempting delicacies. Likely, their forbidden nature makes them even more tantalizing and desirable.

Media Usage Patterns and Acculturation

As has been found often in the marketing and consumer behavior literature, the mass media, especially television programming, is an especially potent source of traditional domestic acculturation (Johnson, 2000; Lee, 1989; Lee, 1993; Lee and Tse, 1994; O'Guinn et al., 1985; Tzu, 1984). However, in the present case, it is programs originating from outside of Tunisia and the Muslim world which are responsible for the strong trend toward Westernization (and see Askegaard 2005; Üstüner and Holt 2007). As a result, traditional, Arabic-language Tunisian television programming was viewed negatively by some.

> When the TV is on a Tunisian channel, I always have the impression that the volume is high, that people are shouting, that they are aggressive . . . it gives me a headache.

> We rarely watch Tunisian TV channels. Actually, the only Tunisian program that my husband would not miss is the Sunday program about football. Generally, we usually watch French TV channels: movies, series, TV shows. For the news, we wait till they broadcast a French-speaking version of them, late at night.

In keeping with post-assimilationist theory (see for example Askegaard et al. 2005), however, Tunisian programming – with its emphasis on traditional Arab Muslim culture – is sought out when the consumer is explicitly conscious of his/her national identity.

> The only period of the year during which we watch the Tunisian and Arabic TV channels is during Ramadan. During this month, we watch all the programs that are broadcast. But during the other months, we rarely watch the Arabic programs. I don't know if it's a good thing, but it's like this. Sometimes we are much more aware of what's happening in Europe than around us, here in Tunisia.

> We watch Tunisian TV channels only when there are special events in Tunisia: when it's snowing, when there are floods, during the elections, and during Ramadan.

Instances of Counter-acculturation

Finally, just as there were Spaniards who 'ran off' and joined Native American tribes in the Americas (Macleod and Rawski, 1998), and Britons who chose to join the Indians in India (Cohn, 1998), there are also Europeans who have adopted traditional Tunisian Arab Muslim consumption patterns. Cohn (1998, p. 210) writes of this counter-acculturation in India, using British General Hearsey, who commanded a division of the Bengal Army, as an example 'Many British thought they had Indian "blood", Hearsey even had his portrait painted in a long, black, oriental-style robe, wearing a richly brocaded cummerbund and holding a scimitar'.

When one of our respondents was asked, 'Do you know of any cases where Westerners/

French have become more Arab/Tunisian – that is, have acculturated in the opposite direction?' he reported:

> Yes. I know several cases. Sabine was born in Tunisia, and when she speaks Arabic, you won't perceive any difference from any other Tunisian. Sabine is French and Christian, but she's so acculturated that when she went to study in France, her French colleagues asked her questions like, 'Do you eat pork?' to know if she's really French or not. Same thing for Christophe, a very acculturated man, who decided to convert to Islam in order to be able to marry Hela, a Muslim Tunisian girl, and to be accepted by her family. Jean-Louis, who was also born in Tunisia, married a Muslim woman and had children, but he didn't need to convert to Islam. Her family was very open. After his divorce from her, he remarried to another French-Tunisian woman, but like him she's very acculturated. He always reminds people in his surroundings: 'I *am* Tunisian'.

Thus, these would be examples of the pattern of acculturation usually studied in marketing and consumer behavior; that is, a person from an ethnic subculture, in this case French, adapts him/herself to the larger, surrounding (in this case Tunisian) culture. The immigration pattern is also present as well:

> If French people have been socialized in France prior to coming to Tunisia, generally their level of acculturation won't be as high. They may adopt several typical Tunisian behaviors, but their acculturation level can't be compared to that of Sabine or Jean-Louis. It is different when it comes to other nationalities. It is possible to find some Italians or Germans that didn't speak a single word of Arabic before coming to Tunisia, and who have been acculturated to the point that you may not be able to distinguish them from a Tunisian.

Possibly, because the French *immigrés* have continuing access to French acculturation agents within Tunisia (for example, television programming), they do not become as fully assimilated to Tunisian culture.

CONCLUSION

Within the marketing and consumer behavior literatures, the concept of acculturation has been mainly studied in conjunction with immigration (see for example Peñaloza, 1994; Oswald 1999), or more rarely, with two groups of consumers evolving within a given national setting and having continuous and direct contact with another (see for example Askegaard et al., 2005; Üstüner and Holt, 2007). The present study is an attempt to broaden both the acculturation concept and its application to the context of formerly colonized countries. We use the case of Tunisia, where large segments of the population have been acculturated without first going abroad, and without necessarily being in physical contact with foreign communities. We call this phenomenon 'acculturation *in situ*'. As a continuing legacy from the colonial period, contemporary Tunisia is characterized by the presence of two cultural models: the Arabic and the French. In some cases, this coexistence results in a stark confrontation between competing and incompatible values, while in others, it can give birth to a harmonious fusion.

Perhaps the most tangible manifestation of acculturation *in situ* is language. Observation in the average Tunisian street reveals the degree to which the blending of Arabic and French cultures is a daily reality. However, those Tunisians who most conform to the

French cultural model desire to enact it in virtually all aspects of their consumer behavior. This translates into their product choices, store patronage, and media exposure, as well as food choice and cooking habits, apparel, home décor, clothing and fashion, aesthetic consumption (for example movies, music, theater) and school choice for their children. Beyond these marketplace choices, acculturation *in situ* has also a tremendous impact on their lifestyle, values, and identity projects not only as consumers, but as people.

Several marketing theory and strategy implications may be drawn from the 'acculturation *in situ*' concept. First, where there are multiple cultural models available to choose from, the individual's degree of acculturation to specific models may be an interesting segmentation criterion, as well as a significant focus for studying identity construction. On the basis of this cultural characteristic, it may be possible to distinguish several homogeneous consumer groups that can constitute relevant potential targets for firms and that may also cohere in terms of their self-image (see Üstüner and Holt 2007). This may permit marketers to direct appropriately adapted goods/services to each group, paying attention to the connotations of brand names, as well as labeling, language, and design. Such efforts may enable multiple clusters of differentially acculturated consumers to best pursue self-creation. Retailers should adapt their assortments to fulfill each segment's desires. For Western acculturated customers, the emphasis should be on goods and services conveying Western ideology and meanings. Further, media selection should be handled with care in order to better reach each target and not create uneasiness among differentially oriented consumers.

This research study has been carried out in the Tunisian context where the acculturation *in situ* phenomenon shows promise from both theoretical and managerial applications. The concept can also be applied to other geographic regions of the world, for instance, to neighboring Maghribi countries such as Morocco or Algeria, and other Arab Islamic nations colonized by countries other than France, for example Egypt or Jordan. Acculturation *in situ* is also applicable to non-Arab post-colonial contexts such as India, South America and Sub-Saharan African countries. It is our belief that acculturation *in situ* may be perhaps the most common and important form of acculturation present in today's world, at both a commercial and a political level. Clearly, attention to this possibility is of large relevance both to theory and in practice.

NOTES

1. An interesting analogy here may be drawn between the Arab Muslim conquest of North Africa and the Incan conquest of indigenous Andean populations during the early 1400s (see Patterson, 2000).
2. Notably, when Gandhi was developing the Indian nationalist movement early in the twentieth century, he explicitly chose to reject British-style apparel and returned to traditional homespun cotton cloth, khadi, as an important symbolic element.

BIBLIOGRAPHY

Arezki, Dalila (2004), *L'Identité Berbère*, Biarritz, Atlantica, Paris: Séguier.
Askegaard, S., E.J. Arnould and D. Kjeldgaard (2005), 'Postassimilationist ethnic consumer research: qualifications and extensions', *Journal of Consumer Research*, **32** (June), 160–70.

Berry, John W. (2003), 'Conceptual approaches to acculturation', in K.M. Chun, P.B. Organista and G. Marin (eds), *Acculturation: Advances in Theory, Measurement and Applied Research*, Washington, DC: American Psychological Association, pp. 17–37.

Bourdieu, Pierre (1984), *Distinction: A Social Critique of the Judgment of Taste*, Cambridge, MA: Harvard University Press.

Brahimi, Abdelhamid (1996), *Le Maghreb à la Croisée des Chemins*, London: The Centre for Maghreb Studies.

Camau, Michel (1989), *La Tunisie*, Presses Universitaires de France.

Cohn, Bernard S. (1998), 'Cloths, clothes and colonialism: India in the nineteenth century', in Murdo Macleod and Evelyn S. Rawski (eds), *European Intruders and Changes in Behaviour and Customs in Africa, America and Asia before 1800*, Aldershot, UK: Ashgate Publishing.

Duval, Eugene-Jean (2009), *Aux Sources Officielles de la Colonisation Française*, L'Harmattan, Paris.

Fitouri, Chedly (1983), *Biculturalisme, Bilinguisme et Education*, Neuchâtel and Paris: Delachaux et Niestlé.

Guendouze, E., A. Masmoudi and M.Smida (1983), *Histoire de la Tunisie*, Tunis: Société Tunisienne de Diffusion.

Harley, Geoff (2001), 'Western influences on the Sasak pottery of Lombok, Indonesia', Working Paper, Centre for Southeast Asian Studies, Monash University.

Hoffman, Katherine E. (2008), *We Share Walls: Language, Land and Gender in Berber Morocco*, Malden, MA: Blackwell Publishing.

Hollowell, A.I. (1945), 'Sociopsychological, aspects of acculturation', in R. Linton (ed.), *The Science of Man in the World Crisis*, New York: Columbia University Press.

Johnson, Melissa A. (2000), 'How ethnic are U.S. ethnic media: the case of Latina magazines', *Mass Communication and Society*, **3**, 229–48.

Jun, S., A. Dwayne Ball and J.W.Gentry (1993), 'Modes of consumer acculturation', in Leigh McAlister and Michael L. Rothschild (eds), *Advances in Consumer Research*, vol. 20, Provo, UT: Association for Consumer Research, pp. 76–82.

Kassab, Mohammed Yacine (2005), *Les Divisions Musulmanes Face à l'Hégémonie Occidentale*, Paris: Éditions palais du livre.

Kaufmann, Jean-Claude (2006), *L'enquête et ses Méthodes. L'entretien compréhensif*, Paris: Armand Colin.

Khalbous, Slim (2003), 'Communication marketing et cultures : une application au cas des consommateurs tunisiens', *Actes du XIXème Congrès International de l'Association Française du Marketing*, May, Gammarth, Tunisia.

Khan, M. (1992), 'Communication patterns of sojourners in the process of acculturation', *Journal of Development Communication*, **3**, 65–73.

Lee, Wei-Na (1988), 'Becoming an American consumer: a cross-cultural study of consumer acculturation among Taiwanese', in *Taiwanese in the Unites States and Americans*, University of Illinois at Urbana-Champaign.

Lee, Wei-Na (1989), 'The mass-mediated consumption realities of three cultural groups', *Advances in Consumer Research*, vol. 16, ed. Thomas K. Srull, Provo, UT: Association for Consumer Research, 771–8.

Lee, Wei-Na (1993), 'Acculturation and advertising communication strategies: a cross-cultural study of Chinese and Americans', *Psychology and Marketing*, **10** (5), 381–97.

Lee, Wei-Na and Tse, D.K. (1994), 'Changing media consumption strategies: acculturation patterns among Hong Kong immigrants to Canada', *Journal of Advertising*, **23** (1) (March), 57–70.

Macleod, M., and Rawski, E.S. (eds) (1998), *European Intruders and Changes in Behaviour and Customs in Africa, America and Asia before 1800*, Aldershot, Hampshire: Ashgate.

Miles Michael and Matthew B. Huberman (1994), 'Data management and analysis methods', in N. Denzin and Y. Lincoln (eds), *Handbook of Qualitative Research*, Second Edition Revised.

O'Guinn, Thomas C., and R.J. Faber (1985), 'New perspectives on acculturation: the relationship of general and role specific acculturation with Hispanics' consumer attitudes', *Advances in Consumer Research*, **12**, 113–17.

O'Guinn, Thomas C., R.J. Faber, and M.D. Rice (1985), 'Popular film and television and consumer acculturation agents: America 1900 to present', in J. Sheth and C.T. Tan (eds), *Historical Perspectives in Consumer Research: National and International Perspectives*, Singapore: National University of Singapore, pp. 297–301.

Oswald, Laura R. (1999), 'Culture swapping: consumption and the ethnogenesis of middle-class Haitian immigrants', *Journal of Consumer Research*, **25** (March), 303–18.

Peñaloza, Lisa (1994), 'Atravasando Fronteras/Bordes crossings: a critical ethnographic examination of the consumer acculturation of Mexican immigrants', *Journal of Consumer Research*, **21** (June), 32–54.

Patterson, Thomas C. (2000), 'The Inca Empire and its subject peoples', in John E. Kicza (eds), *The Indian in Latin American History*, Lanham, MD: SR Books, pp. 1–22.

Redfield, R., R. Linton and M.J. Herskovits (1936), 'Memorandum for the study of acculturation', *American Anthropologist*, **38** (1), 149–52.

Sandstrom, Alan R. (2000), 'Ethnic identity and its attributes in a contemporary Mexican Indian village', in John F. Kicza (eds), *The Indian in Latin American History*, Lanham, MD: SR Books, pp. 269–82.

Smaoui, Fatma (2009), 'Perceived brand name origin: effect on consumer perceptions: the case of emerging market consumers', 8th International Congress Marketing Trends, Paris, 16–17 January.

Social Science Research Council (1954), 'Acculturation: an exploratory formulation', *American Anthropologist*, **56** (6), part 1, 973–1000.

Sorel, Dominique (1973): 'La pénétration romaine en Afrique du Nord dans l'antiquité'. in CIHEAM (eds), *Les échanges méditerranéens*, Paris, pp. 35–39.

Trimble, Joseph E. (2003), 'Introduction: social change and acculturation' in K.M. Chun, P.B. Organista and G. Marin (eds), *Acculturation: Advances in Theory, Measurement and Applied Research*, Washington, DC: American Psychological Assoc., pp. 1–16.

Tzu, Lao (1984), 'Strangers' adaptation to new cultures', in William B. Gudykunst and Young Y. Kim (eds), *Communicating with Strangers: An Approach to Intercultural Communication*, Reading, MA:Addison-Wesley Publishing Company, Inc., pp. 205–22.

Üstüner, Tuba and D.B. Holt (2007), 'Dominated consumer acculturation: the social construction of poor migrant women's consumer identity projects in a Turkish squatter', *Journal of Consumer Research*, **34** (1), 41–56.

Valencia, Humberto (1985), 'Developing an index to measure Hispanicness', *Advances in Consumer Research*, Association for Consumer Research, **12**, 118–21.

Viswanath, K. and Pamela Arora (2000), 'Ethnic media in the United States: an essay on their role in integration, assimilation, and social control', *Mass Communication and Society*, **3** (1), 39–56.

Wallendorf, Melanie and M. Reilly (1983), 'Ethnic migration, assimilation and consumption'. *Journal of Consumer Research*, **10** (December), 292–302.

8 Lifestyles of Islamic consumers in Turkey

Yonca Aslanbay, Özlem Hesapçı Sanaktekin and Bekir Ağırdır

INTRODUCTION

Lifestyle is an interdisciplinary analytical construct introduced in the nineteenth century (Anderson and Golden, 1984). In the 1970s, realizing the significant relationship between consumer choices and lifestyle, marketers operationalized the lifestyle concept specifically to understand consumer behavior. The lifestyle analysis of Wells and Tigert (1971) covers the opinions and interests of people during their daily activities, along with demography and personality, to which Plummer (1974) added feelings and attitudes. Engel et al. (1978) emphasize spending of money and time along with the pattern of living. In the beginning of the 1980s, researchers further enriched lifestyle studies by incorporating the values concept as studies showed a connection between consumers' expected benefits, when consuming a product, and their own personal values (Gutman, 1990). According to Rokeach (1968–69, p. 550) 'a value is a standard or criterion that serves a number of important purposes in our daily lives'. Values have a significant impact upon behavior (Vinson et al., 1977), and thus guide the selection or evaluation of behavior of individuals over their lifespan (Grunert et al., 1989).

Daily practices in life are a means of making up a sense of self. According to Featherstone (1991), one's clothing, leisure, eating preferences, choice of holidays and so on indicate a style of life and imply individuality and self expression. Holt (1997), however, argues that lifestyles are symbolic expressions of collectivities of social categories like gender, age and social class, rather than individual phenomena. Combining the two perspectives suggests that the behaviors and practices within lifestyles are a mixture of voluntary behaviors and conventional ways of doing things shaped by social dynamics. Understanding the impact and restrictions of social surroundings or institutions on lifestyle choices is a neglected area of research. Accordingly, though religion is a factor of culture that is dominant in framing social life, studies examining the relationship between religiosity and lifestyle are rare (Delener, 1994; Assadi, 2003; Lindridge, 2005; Odabaşı and Argan, 2009). Hirschman (1983) explains this inadequacy exists either because researchers are unaware of this relationship, as religion is a taboo subject, or because they overlook religion as it is such an obvious variable that penetrates almost all domains of life (as cited in Mokhlis, 2009, p. 76).

This chapter reports an empirical study that describes the lifestyles of some specified Turkish consumer segments based on religiosity. Turkey is a country with a population of 72.5 million (www.tuik.gov.tr), standing at the crossroads of two continents, Europe and Asia. In Turkey, where the majority of the population is Muslim, Islam has always been a significant symbolic system forming the cultural basis for individual and communal identity (Keyman, 2007; Eser et al., 2007). Additionally, it is a country of unique cultural and religious characteristics, being a secular democratic republic (Küçükcan, 2003). By offering a descriptive approach for understanding the complexity of interactions between the religiosity and the lives of consumers, this study sheds light on how various interpretations in Islam enable different understandings of lifestyle.

LIFESTYLE IN MUSLIM TURKEY

Research has revealed that religion-based values have significant effects on lifestyle and on consumption patterns (Rice and Al-Mossawi, 2002). Religion not only affects lifestyle, but through its adherent practices, it is a part of a lifestyle routine. Religious traditions and institutions can influence the rules of trade: what, where, and when goods are traded (Mittelstaedt, 2002). Sandıkcı and Ger (2007) point out 'what are traded in the marketplace today are not only the products themselves but also their meanings and lifestyle connotations' (p. 191). Baudrillard (1981) states that as mass consumption and the consumer economy developed in the twentieth century, the value of products began to function culturally as signs within a coded system of exchange. Recently, consumption has been studied as a social and a cultural process that includes cultural signs and symbols (Boccock, 1993) and is regarded as a lifestyle marker. Consumption is influenced by the religious codes surrounding the market. Religious codes may either directly influence consumption, or consumption may be affected by religion indirectly through its impact on values. Not only religiosity, but also affiliations with different religions, have an influence on consumption (Essoo and Dibb, 2004). With growing affluence there is an intensification of consumption practices in Muslim countries (Wong, 2007) and Islamic discourses provide different understandings of an identity formation through consumption. On the other hand, although Islam has about 1.5–2 billion believers worldwide (http://pewresearch.org), it is the least researched religion regarding its influence on the lifestyles of consumers (Mokhlis, 2009).

Religion is a recent construct of research in Turkey. Beginning in the 1980s, an emergence of a new lifestyle with a consumption culture has been observed in Turkey, with covered women emerging as a significant market segment (Sandıkcı and Ger, 2007). As Navaro-Yashin noted:

> The most important good that was brought to the marketplace by Muslim business people in Turkey was the veil. More than other consumer items produced in Muslim companies, there was an overload of symbolic interpretation around the veil and its many versions. . . . the rise of Islamist movement in 1980s and 1990s in Turkey was integral to the creation of a market for headscarves, overcoats and veils for women. Several companies sprung up then to produce and sell all sorts of clothing items for women who 'covered' (Navaro-Yashin 2002, p. 225).

An Islamist bourgeoisie with a taste for conspicuous consumption began to emerge while the meaning and style of head covering has been changing (Sandıkcı and Ger, 2005). Indeed, the arguments over women's dresses have occupied a central place within the debates over Turkish modernization ever since the nineteenth century. Now women are the visible actors of contemporary Islam and the covering styles are significant symbols. The new styles of covering seem to be a novel way of holding on to new lifestyles in the sites of modernity, especially in urban areas (Göle, 1991, 2002; Kadıoğlu, 2005; Kentel, 2008).

Turkey has inherited an Islamic past from the Ottoman Empire in which Islam had a great impact on Turkey's social structure. The Ottoman Empire was ruled according to the Islamic laws of *sharia*, which was annulled in Turkey in the twentieth century. After the establishment of the Turkish Republic in 1923, a period of fast and radical change began. Initially, what the republican reformers had predicted was: 'an organized, well-articulated, linear process of modernization through which the whole nation was going to move simultaneously and with uniform experience' (Kasaba, 1997, pp. 16–17). In the 1950s, Turkey began undergoing a transformation in its economic, as well as its cultural environment. The country embarked on a massive industrialization process, and consumption patterns began to change (Sandıkcı and Ger, 2002). The broadcast media started reaching the masses in 1968. Thereafter, the proliferation of TV programs has affected consumption patterns, desires, expectations, and life-styles of the Turkish citizens (Oktay, 1993).

The liberalization of the economy and the transformation processes in the 1980s also caused remarkable changes in society. Turkey's economic structure has been reformed in parallel with the integration process into the global market economy. With the adoption of the principles of a market economy, lifestyles in Turkey have been changing rapidly (Toprak and Çarkoğlu, 2007), influencing individuals and their ways of self-definition within everyday life (Kılıçbay and Binark, 2002). As Navaro-Yashin noted:

> . . . cultural identities were packaged up to be assumed in commodity form. Battles over political difference were waged through the medium of consumption. As Islamists came to forge identities in distinction from secularists, they thought about their habits of use and modified or radically changed the sorts of things that they bought and sold. They wore different clothes, they ate only certain kinds of food, they frequented particular shops, they started special businesses of their own. The rise of Islamist movement in popularity and power is indissoluble from the development of specialised businesses for 'Islamic goods' and the formation of market networks for believers. (Navaro-Yashin 2002, p. 223).

At the end of the 1980s, Turkey began integrating into the global consumer culture. As multinational companies entered the market, many products that were foreign to Turkish citizens became available (Sandıkcı and Ger, 2002). After 1990, Turkey witnessed a string of economic crises, mainly in 1994, 1999, and 2001. Lifestyles and consumption patterns were greatly affected by these struggles. 'In the 1990s social changes such as migration from rural to urban areas, rapid demographic changes, multi-party politics, economic and industrial developments have all affected the rise of Islamic values in Turkey' (Küçükcan, 2003, p. 506). Toprak and Çarkoğlu (2007) revealed that between 1999 and 2006, the percentage of people who consider themselves 'very religious' and those who define their identity primarily as Muslim has increased from 6 per cent to 13 per cent and from 36 per cent to 46 per cent respectively. The formation of a 'conservative' bourgeoisie after the 1980s resulted in urban lifestyles being reformulated in accordance with the demands of the Islamic metropolis (Genel and Karaosmanoğlu, 2006). Islamist media, including newspapers, periodicals, and radio and television programs, emerged and new consumption practices arose. Conspicuous consumption became a symbolic expression for the newly rich (Sandıkcı and Ger, 2002), and for some of the not so rich (Çakar and Yoğurtçuoğlu, 2004). Islamization of urban ways of life permitted the emergence of an Islamic consumption culture (Sandıkcı and Ger, 2001, 2002), including new leisure-time activities for Islamic communities (Kılıçbay and Binark, 2002). Thus, restaurants, supermarkets, entertainment centers, and hotels mushroomed and became visible (Göle, 2000). These cultural changes in Turkey have had a significant impact on the behavior of consumers and on the marketing management of the firms (Eser et al., 2007).

Meanwhile, the huge transformation to urbanization in Turkey has also had a tremendous effect on social life. Making an allowance for its strong influence on lifestyles, the place of living as rural or urban is an important concern of this study. Cities are now sites through which the realization of consumption contributes both to the changing form of the urban consumptionscape and to life practices (Miles and Paddison, 1998). In the second half of the twentieth century, the global spread of information and communication technologies has given rise to rather more homogenous lifestyles on a worldwide scale, affecting also Turkey. Meanwhile, the postmodern fragmented consumer demands began to challenge the unifying dynamics of modern life and the meaning of lifestyle in the urban setting, where consumption is observed to be a means of social change (Ritzer, 1996). In the cities of Turkey, with the increase of the visibility of an Islamic lifestyle, new aesthetic views, habits, consumption and behavior patterns have emerged (Sandıkcı and Ger, 2007). The individuals' pursuit of a balance between the homogenizing tendencies of globalization and the unique characters of localities are expected to have immense implications for the future of urban communities (Featherstone, 1991). The implications of these complexities in the new lifestyles and new consumption culture are areas of interest for several researchers (Bouchet, 1993; Brown, 1993, 1994; Fırat et al., 1995; Fırat and Venkatesh, 1995; Goulding, 2003). The research presented in this chapter covers this broad framework of lifestyle and aims to understand its relationship with religiosity in different places of living in Turkey.

METHODOLOGY

This research draws from data collected through a structured questionnaire which was conducted face to face, in the homes of the respondents by 750 interviewers.[1] The extent of the research is the whole of Turkey. The research aims to expose the lifestyles of Turkish Muslim consumers.

The Sample

To profile the segments, the study analyses the lifestyles based on data from 6236 Muslim subjects, living in both urban and rural areas. Muslim Turkish consumers, aged over 15, were selected by stratified random sampling, using education and employment information in cities and villages. Among the cities, 16 were coded 'metropolis' as defined by the central government.[2] The streets to be visited were selected based on the square meter price information in tax declarations. In each building, only one household was visited conforming to a series of numbers. In each neighborhood, six subjects were surveyed face to face. Quotas of gender and age were used in the selection of the subjects.

The Questionnaire

The questionnaire consisted of structured questions measuring 'religiosity' and 'demographics' on nominal scales, and 'perceived satisfaction of life' and 'lifestyle' on 5-point (1=definitely disagree, 5=definitely agree) Likert scales. The constructs consisted of questions listed as below.

> Religiosity: religion, perception of belief in religion, head covering, and religious sect.
> Perceived satisfaction in life: perceived satisfaction of life in the past and today.
> Demographic profile: age, gender, education (participant and the participants' parents), income and location of living.
> Lifestyle: religious practices, in-house roles, leisure activities (outdoor and vacation), technology adoption, internet consumption, fashion consumption, finance and investment transactions, shopping habits, and possessions.

FINDINGS

The sample size of the current study is 6236 subjects.[3] The mean age of the sample is 38.5; the sample is 51.7 per cent male. Rural households comprise 34.4 per cent of the sample; 23.7 per cent live in small cities (population less than 750 000), 15.4 per cent live in the outskirts of the metropolis and 26.5 per cent live in metropolitan centers.

The Religious Profiles of Religiosity Clusters

Though there are unidimensional definitions in the literature, religiosity is widely accepted to be a multidimensional construct, yet is rarely measured in relation to consumer behavior (Wilkes et al., 1986; De Jong et al., 1976). This study defines religiosity through self definition of the individuals aged over 15. Among the sample, four groups are categorized as non-believers (do not believe in either a god or religion), moderate believers (believe in religion; do not carry out religious practices), high believers (strongly believe in God and religion; often carry out religious practices) and radical believers (strongly believe in God and religion; always carry out religious practices) (1.6, 30.7, 55.0 and 12.7 per cent respectively) (Table 8.1).

The greatest part of the sample is affiliated with the Sunni sect. The second major affiliation is to the Alawite sect. This distribution reflects that of the Turkish population. The majority of the sample is high believers and moderate believers. Although the meaning and forms change over the years in Turkey (Sandıkçı and Ger, 2010), covering is still an important symbol of religiosity among the different levels of religiosity clusters. When the covering of the subjects or their spouse is asked about, the results show that the ratio of covered women to not-covered is 72 per cent. This ratio was found to be 63.5 per cent by Çarkoğlu and Toprak (2006) and 61 per cent by Esmer (2007). There are still non-believers covering their heads, which may be explained as a result of traditions, social affiliation and/or social pressure.

There are contradictory findings in the literature on the relation of religiosity to

Table 8.1   Religion based profiles of clusters

Frequency & Percentages	Religiosity				Total
	Non-believers	Moderate believers	High believers	Radical believers	
Religious Sect (χ^2=421.457; p=.000)					
Sunni Muslim	57	1662	3272	758	5749
	59%	87%	95%	95%	92%
Alawite Muslim	36	191	69	7	303
	37%	10%	2%	1%	5%
Shiah Muslim	0	10	11	5	26
	0%	1%	0%	1%	0%
Other Muslim	4	55	79	20	158
	4%	3%	3%	3%	3%
Head cover of the subject or the spouse (χ^2=834.493; p=.000)					
Not covered	64	790	600	51	1505
	66%	41%	17%	6%	26%
Covered	29	1062	2765	721	4577
	30%	55%	81%	92%	72%
No answer	4	66	66	18	154
	4%	4%	2%	2%	2%
Tota	97	1918	3431	790	6236
	100%	100%	100%	100%	100%

satisfaction about life (Table 8.2), perhaps because it is a subject of interest to researchers from various disciplines (Lewis et al., 1996). In this research, in each of the religiosity clusters, the satisfaction about life today is higher than the perceptions about life in the past. Additionally perceived satisfaction about life both in the past and today significantly increases by religiosity. These results are consistent with the findings of Wilkes et al. (1986) which posit a moderate relationship between life satisfaction and religiosity. The belief in fate in eastern and Muslim cultures may serve as an explanation for these findings.

The Demographic Profiles of Religiosity Clusters

Religiosity is found to be higher among women, the elderly, the less-educated and the low income people (Table 8.3) .

Two findings, higher population of males in lower believing clusters, and increasing degree of religiosity with increasing age, are consistent with previous findings in the literature (Argue et al., 1999; Miller and Hoffmann, 1995). As both education levels and incomes rise, the extent of religious belief decreases. Religiosity is significantly related to the education not only of the respondents, but also of their parents. The results show that the higher the education of the father or the mother, the lesser is the degree of the religious beliefs of the participants. Analysis of the education of the respondents and their

Table 8.2   Perceived satisfaction about life

		Religiosity				Total
		Non-believers	Moderate believers	High believers	Radical believers	
Perceived satisfaction about life						
In past	μ	2.27	2.58	3.00	3.19	2.88
(F= 80.553; p=.000)	Std. Dev.	1.026	1.162	1.171	1.216	1.194
Today	μ	3.30	3.51	3.60	3.72	3.58
(F=14.259; p=.000)	Std. Dev.	.981	.930	.866	.942	.901

parents reveals that, in general, respondents are more educated than their parents. The transmission of values, status and behaviors from one generation to the next has been a central concern of many family sociologists. These findings are in line with an indication of an upwards social mobility of the generations, where several researchers conclude that each successive generation of offspring has higher attainments than the one before (Biblarz et al., 1996). The higher religiosity among the elderly may be the result of an acceptance of religion as a conventional way of living.

Lifestyle Profiles of Religiosity Clusters

Lifestyles are analyzed over different domains of life in terms of religion specific, general and consumption specific daily routines. Religion specific lifestyles are analyzed through religious practices (Table 8.4); general lifestyles are analyzed through the domains of fashion and leisure (Table 8.5), whereas consumption specific lifestyles are analyzed through domains of technology adoption, finance and investment transactions, shopping habits, household decision making roles, possessions and Internet consumption (Tables 8.6 and 8.7).

In general, praying routinely, as a personal practice, is less common as compared to fasting and attending the Friday prayers. The social interaction involved in fasting and the Friday prayers, considering the collectivistic structure of the culture in general (Hofstede, 1980, 1991), may be the explanation of such a variance. As one might expect, daily religious practices are more commonly observed in tight religiosity clusters. On the other hand, there are still some religious practices carried out by the non-believer cluster, which may be explained by traditions, social pressure and/or affiliations as in the covering case.

Articles in some Turkish Islamic women's magazines discuss how fashion is the result of an imposed lifestyle of modern capitalist societies and is contrary to Islamic principles. At the same time, advertisements in these magazines introduce the products of the fashion for covering, which are one of the visible aspects of consumerism experienced as symbolic capital (Kılıçbay and Binark, 2002). Although the controversy about fashion and covering disappears in the everyday practices of today's lifestyles (Gökarıksel and Secor, 2009), following fashion trends is still lower in the high religiosity cluster. Fashion and makeup consumption is more prevalent in the lifestyles of the non-believer cluster.

Table 8.3   Demographic profiles of clusters

	Religiosity				Total
	Non-believers	Moderate believers	High believers	Radical believers	
Gender (χ^2=37.837p=.000)					
Female	33	831	1745	401	3010
	34%	43%	51%	51%	48%
Male	64	1087	1686	389	3226
	66%	57%	49%	49%	52%
Age (χ^2=290.489; p=.000)					
15–24	28	538	641	94	1301
	29%	28%	18%	12%	21%
25–34	32	514	820	129	1495
	33%	27%	24%	16%	24%
35–44	17	445	791	170	1423
	18%	23%	23%	22%	23%
45 and over	20	421	1179	397	2017
	20%	22%	35%	5%	33%
Education of the respondent (χ^2=270.486; p=.000)					
Middle Education	26	1023	2516	668	4233
	27%	54%	73%	84%	68%
High school	35	619	679	94	1427
	36%	32%	20%	12%	23%
University and over	35	268	225	24	552
	36%	14%	07%	3%	9%
No answer	1	8	11	4	24
	1%	0%	0%	1%	0%
Monthly household income (χ^2=143.878; p=.000)					
1500 – TL	59	1458	2933	697	5147
	61%	76%	85%	88%	82%
1501–3000 TL	25	327	363	71	786
	26%	17%	11%	9%	13%
3000 + TL	8	104	84	10	206
	8%	5%	2%	1%	3%
No answer	5	29	51	12	97
	5%	2%	2%	2%	2%
Total	97	1918	3431	790	6236
	100%	100%	100%	100%	100%

Leisure, as an outdoor activity, is generally of low occurrence in the population. The most common leisurely outdoor activity is 'dining out with the family'. The less frequently observed one is 'attending cultural activities' which is most probably a result of the low levels of education in general. There is a significant decrease of outdoor activity when one shifts to the radical believing direction. This difference becomes more visible over 'celebrating the new year', admitted to be more of a Christian-oriented activity. Vacation as a leisure activity is also observed to occur seldom. Visiting one's hometown

Table 8.4 Religion specific lifestyle

Religious Practices		Religiosity				Total
		Non-believers	Moderate believers	High believers	Radical believers	
Pray routinely	μ	1.27	2.16	3.55	4.37	3.19
(F=917.003; p=.000)	Std. Dev.	.757	1.092	1.285	1.068	1.435
Fast routinely	μ	1.63	3.57	4.51	4.76	4.21
(F=542.694; p=.000)	Std. Dev.	1.184	1.465	.930	.707	1.241
Men attend Friday prays	μ	1.55	3.21	4.17	4.53	3.88
(F=398.116; p=.000)	Std. Dev.	1.099	1.525	1.221	1.014	1.416

Table 8.5 General lifestyles

		Religiosity				Total
		Non-believers	Moderate believers	High believers	Radical believers	
Fashion						
Women follow fashion	μ	2.72	2.32	1.94	1.68	2.04
trends (F=85.344; p=.000)	Std. Dev.	1.223	1.194	1.129	1.069	1.167
Women use make-up	μ	3.22	2.60	1.95	1.59	2.12
(F=186.293; p=.000)	Std. Dev.	1.386	1.390	1.211	1.035	1.306
Leisure-Outdoor						
Dine out with family	μ	2.96	2.66	2.35	2.14	2.43
(F= 57.311; p=.000)	Std. Dev.	1.346	1.426	1.388	1.371	1.409
Dine out with friends	μ	3.20	2.71	2.27	2.10	2.40
(F= 84.135; p=.000)	Std. Dev.	1.047	1.215	1.207	1.212	1.232
Attend cultural activities	μ	3.04	2.39	1.92	1.61	2.04
(F= 131.367; p=.000)	Std. Dev.	1.181	1.248	1.151	.976	1.198
Celebrate the new year	μ	4.02	2.84	1.99	1.62	2.24
(F= 264.167; p=.000)	Std. Dev.	1.266	1.531	1.349	1.159	1.470
Leisure-Vacation						
Vacation in the country	μ	2.96	2.66	2.35	2.14	2.43
(F= 36.992; p=.000)	Std. Dev.	1.346	1.426	1.388	1.371	1.409
Vacation in home town	μ	2.48	2.46	2.64	2.58	2.57
(F= 5.129; p=.002)	Std. Dev.	1.501	1.543	1.601	1.638	1.588
Vacation abroad	μ	1.40	1.23	1.18	1.21	1.21
(F= 4.844; p=.002)	Std. Dev.	.886	.701	.660	.756	.690

is more frequent as it is a natural outcome of the high immigration rates from rural to urban areas in Turkey and does not vary among clusters. Going on a vacation either in the country or abroad slightly decreases in frequency according to the increasing degree of religiosity.

Table 8.6   Consumption specific lifestyles

		Religiosity				Total
		Non-believers	Moderate believers	High believers	Radical believers	
Technology Adoption						
Keep up with launched	μ	3.23	2.80	2.47	2.35	2.57
technological products	Std. Dev.	1.237	1.308	1.331	1.332	1.335
(F= 41.479; p=.000)						
Immediately buy the	μ	2.30	2.05	1.85	1.80	1.91
launched technological	Std. Dev.	.959	1.020	.973	1.010	.998
products (F= 26.356;						
p=.002)						
Shopping						
Buy food from	μ	3.37	2.97	2.83	2.72	2.87
big retailers	Std. Dev.	1.202	1.294	1.316	1.383	1.320
(F= 12.767; p=.000)						
Buy food via internet	μ	1.22	1.22	1.19	1.14	1.19
(F= 2.894; p=.000)	Std. Dev.	.633	.700	.676	.604	.674
Buy clothes from	μ	3.15	2.80	2.53	2.42	2.61
big retailers	Std. Dev.	1.286	1.262	1.237	1.280	1.260
(F= 31.010; p=.000)						
Finance & Investment						
Financial transaction	μ	3.87	3.62	3.52	3.53	3.56
via bank	Std. Dev.	1.320	1.498	1.593	1.643	1.568
(F= 3.167; p=.000)						
Financial transaction	μ	1.78	1.48	1.28	1.18	1.34
via internet (F= 37.573;	Std. Dev.	1.235	1.056	.824	.658	.899
p=.000)						
Invest in real estate	μ	1.81	1.85	1.85	1.90	1.85
(F= .477; p=.698)	Std. Dev.	1.253	1.236	1.263	1.353	1.266
Invest in interest banking	μ	2.15	1.84	1.69	1.66	1.74
(F= 11.490; p=.000)	Std. Dev.	1.409	1.233	1.144	1.183	1.185
Invest in non interest	μ	1.27	1.36	1.49	1.51	1.45
banking (F= 8.839;	Std. Dev.	.771	.899	1.077	1.103	1.027
p=.002)						
In House Roles						
Woman buys clothes	μ	3.45	3.46	3.51	3.46	3.49
(F= 0.782; p=.504)	Std. Dev.	1.275	1.145	1.134	1.195	1.147
Man does food shopping	μ	3.29	3.34	3.49	3.59	3.45
(F= 9.659; p=.000)	Std. Dev.	1.241	1.235	1.249	1.310	1.255
Man decides buying car	μ	3.32	3.61	3.75	3.89	3.72
(F= 12.784; p=.000)	Std. Dev.	1.447	1.314	1.329	1.333	1.331
Man decides buying white	μ	2.90	3.17	3.34	3.55	3.30
goods (F= 21.087;	Std. Dev.	1.327	1.257	1.262	1.284	1.270
p=.000)						

Table 8.7 Possessions among clusters

Possessions	Religiosity				Total
	Non-believers	Moderate believers	High believers	Radical believers	
Computer	59	827	1138	173	2197
(χ^2=153.307; p=.000)	61%	43%	33%	22%	35%
Cellular phone	92	1712	2806	580	5190
(χ^2=119.338; p=.000)	95%	89%	82%	73%	83%
Credit card	58	914	1343	222	2537
(χ^2=42.607; p=.000)	60%	48%	39%	28%	41%
Passport	35	332	415	110	892
(χ^2=68.212; p=.000)	36%	17%	12%	14%	14%

The extent of religious beliefs is significantly related to the adoption of technology. With a decrease in religiosity, people seem to be more open to technology. Studies of the adoption and use of technology such as computers have generally shown that education influences technology adoption. Czaja et al. (2006) were able to predict the general use of technology by education along with other variables. Bucy (2000) also revealed that income and education are important social determinants of technology adoption and Internet use; technology use is lowest among members of lower socioeconomic groups. Recent findings also support the previous results on the significant effects of education and income on religiosity.

Although the use of traditional small retailers for food and clothing consumption is more common, big retailers are also a component of shopping for all the religiosity clusters. Buying either food or clothes from big retailers is observed more frequently as religiosity declines. Buying food over the Internet is not a very common practice among the respondents.

Only slight differences are observed among clusters in the use of face to face banking services. People do not make investments widely, which is a result of low income per capita. Nevertheless, investing in real estate is higher than the other types of investments, such as movables; and this is common for all clusters. Turkey is a country that is high on the uncertainty avoidance dimension of Hofstede (1980, 1991), where people are not very tolerant to uncertain, ambiguous situations. The findings regarding the type of investments to which people prefer to allocate their money serve as an understanding of this mechanism of intolerance to uncertainty.

In line with Islamic values, investing in financial tools that incorporate interest rates decreases with a shift to the radical believing direction. The opposite is observed for non-interest investments. The rules of Islam prohibit Muslims from paying and receiving interest. Interest free banking is the result of the religious prohibition of interest on payment or receipt (Okumuş, 2005; Gait and Worthington, 2007). Overall, the number of financial transactions via the Internet is very low. Maycroft (2004) labeled a lifestyle 'digital' when a significant portion of a person's time is devoted to digitalization and consumption of digital goods or services (Maycroft, 2004). This lifestyle is seen more among non-believers in the sample.

Shopping is generally a socially visible behavior, and social referents may affect the patronage behavior of consumers (Evans et al., 1996). Females were expected to do more shopping than males. Recent research, however, suggests that the nature of the behavioral roles of husbands and wives is changing (Lackman and Lanasa, 1993). There is evidence that nowadays the role of shopping has increased in importance for males, while decreasing for females who do not occupy the role of housewives any more (Evans et al., 1996). In Turkey, the majority of women do not work; 66 per cent of the sample consists of housewives. The results show that men are still dominant in the decision making for car and white goods purchases. The dominance of men in decision making for the latter is somewhat lower than for the former. It seems to be the traditional role of women to buy clothes, since there is no significant difference among clusters. As one may expect, in more believing clusters men still have more traditional roles. The interesting point is that from a modern gender relationship perspective, male dominance in food shopping would be expected to be negatively correlated with the male dominance in the purchase decision making of durables and cars. But the findings support an opposite relationship. Further analysis displays that in rural areas of Turkey, going out for food shopping is the traditional role of men, therefore men shop significantly more in the rural areas ($\mu=3.64$), compared to the metropolitan centre ($\mu=3.32$).

The possessions of different clusters are investigated through associations with lifestyle as a reflection of consumption. Significant differences are observed for religiosity and ownership of a computer at home along with cellular phones, credit cards and passports, as the symbols of new lifestyle tools for digitalization, communication, credit using and mobility.

All ownerships are highest in the non-believer cluster and decrease with a shift towards the radical believing direction. One explanation of this finding can be the low income level of high believer groups. The degree to which many households do not have sufficient resources to spend, is almost invisible in the latest consumption literature. In developing countries there is still a considerable number of people whose consumption is shaped by economic assets, rather than lifestyles (Glennie, 1998). Another possible explanation of the finding can be based on Rehman and Shabbir's (2010) finding of a significant reverse relationship between religiosity and new product adoption.

Lifestyle in Interaction with Place of Living and Religiosity

As discussed in the literature, not only the religiosity but also the place of living has a tremendous influence on shaping lifestyles. The analysis above was conducted on the total sample: both rural and urban. To get a comprehensive outlook on the relationship between religiosity and lifestyle according to location, further analysis was carried out. The lifestyle criteria were reduced by factor analysis (Table 8.8).

The resulting two factors were named 'modern life' and 'traditional life' (KMO=0.886; $\chi^2=38.679$; p<.05). Using MANOVA to investigate the interaction between modern and traditional lifestyles with the variables of religiosity and place of living revealed a significant main effect of religiosity in explaining modern lifestyle ($F(3,6232) = 61.323$; p<.05) and traditional lifestyle ($F(3.6232) = 388.063$; p<.05). The place of living is also significant in explaining modern lifestyle ($F(3,6232) = 26.743$; p<.05) and traditional lifestyle ($F(3.6232) = 41.507$; p<.05). Furthermore, place of living and religiosity interact in

Table 8.8 Factor analysis over lifestyle domains

	Loading	Variance	Cronbach Alpha	Item Number
FACTOR 1: Modern life		31.116	.879	12
Dine out with friends	.773			
Dine out with family	.756			
Attend cultural activities	.756			
Keep up with launched technological products	.732			
Immediately buy the launched technological products	.680			
Women follow fashion trends	.678			
Buy clothes from big retailers	.631			
Vacation in the country	.620			
Women use make-up	.620			
Buy food from big retailers	.551			
Celebrate the new year	.534			
Financial transaction via internet	.464			
FACTOR 2: Traditional life		12.821	.680	6
Pray routinely	.749			
Fast routinely	.709			
Men attend Friday prayers	.628			
Man decides buying car	.549			
Man decides buying white goods	.508			
Man does food shopping	.457			
TOTAL VARIANCE		43.936		18

explaining the variance in modern lifestyle ($F(15.6220)= 6.887$; $p<.05$) and in traditional lifestyle ($F(15.6220) = 4.446$; $p<.05$) (Table 8.9).

The results show that within each religiosity cluster, there are significant differences in the modernity of lifestyles changing with the level of religiosity and place of living (rural versus urban). When religiosity increases and place of living is rural, traditional lifestyle increases. When religiosity decreases and place of living is urban, participation in a modern lifestyle increases. However, the existence of low modernity and high traditional patterns of high and radical believers in urban sites is an indicator of the tremendous impact of religiosity on lifestyle, despite the effect of living place.

CONCLUSION

The rhythm of daily life has changed all over the world and this is reflected in consumption. This study is a cross-sectional profiling of the lifestyles of Muslim Turkish consumers, clustered by religiosity. The scarcity of studies about Islam, as well as the relationship between religion and lifestyles, increases the potential contribution of this study to the literature. Significant relationships were found between demographic

Table 8.9   Religiosity and place of living as antecedents of lifestyle

		Religiosity				Total
		Non-believers	Moderate believers	High believers	Radical believers	
Modern Lifestyle						
Rural	μ	2.89	2.09	1.88	1.80	1.93
	Std. Dev.	.799	.705	.676	.677	.698
Urban	μ	3.01	2.69	2.28	2.04	2.41
	Std. Dev.	.668	.829	.768	.694	.815
Total	μ	2.99	2.52	2.14	1.94	2.24
	Std. Dev.	.696	.840	.761	.697	.809
Traditional Lifestyle						
Rural	μ	2.67	3.44	3.95	4.21	3.85
	Std. Dev.	.796	.754	.683	.707	.762
Urban	μ	2.23	3.07	3.71	4.04	3.51
	Std. Dev.	2.32	3.18	3.80	4.11	3.62
Total	μ	2.32	3.18	3.80	4.11	3.63
	Std. Dev.	.743	.786	.715	.684	.821

characteristics and religiosity, as well as between religiosity and lifestyle patterns. Also urbanization in interaction with religiosity was found to have a harmonizing effect over lifestyles, since all religiosity clusters have a more modern lifestyle compared to respondents living in rural sites.

In Turkey, the population in cities rose from five million to 53 million in the years 1950–2008. In this period, although the population multiplied by 3.4, the urban population grew 10.5 times (www.tuik.gov.tr). The outcome was a very fast transformation of the traditional rural to the modern urban lifestyle. Changes in the daily life routines to adapt to the dynamics of an urban context are easily observed. The adaptation to this huge urbanization brought contradictions along with massive problems. The hassle of coping with the problems and the threat of the unknown with any change, resulted in a wave of conservatism. This conservatism is framed not only by religion but also by traditions. The results show a discord between conservative values and modern urban lifestyles. Thus there is a new identity: a conservative outlook based on Islam, but also bearing a relatively close proximity to a modern lifestyle and the consumption patterns of the urban dweller.

The findings are important for marketing decision makers who invest in Islamic countries. Studies of this nature help marketers to obtain insights into the daily lifestyle routines and consumption behavior according to various levels of religiosity. Consumer profiling studies in different cultural environments can elicit generalizable national identity norms as well as a basis for cross-cultural comparisons. More fundamentally, a global perspective on the relationship between market dynamics in different countries and consumer response can be developed systematically to improve global marketing performance.

The findings of this study are based on descriptive research and are subject to the intrinsic limitations of quantitative studies for revealing insights. Yet because of the broad extent of the sample and the versatile frame of the study, the findings will contribute not only to the marketing and consumer behavior fields but also to all other disciplines studying religion, lifestyle, urbanization and consumption.

NOTES

1. The data was collected by Konda Research and Consultancy in two days from 6 to 7 April, 2008, to have control over possible interaction effects of certain variables (such as political movements).
2. Metropolis: Adana, Ankara, Antalya, Bursa, Diyarbakir, Erzurum, Eskisehir, Gaziantep, Istanbul, Izmir, Kayseri, Kocaeli, Konya, Mersin, Sakarya, Samsun.
3. 34.4 per cent of the sample lives in rural areas, 23.7 per cent in small cities (population less than 750 000), 15.4 per cent in the metropolitan center.

REFERENCES

Anderson, W.T. Jr and L.L. Golden (1984), 'Lifestyle and psychographics: a critical review and recommendation', *Advances in Consumer Research*, **11**, 405–11.
Argue, A., D.R. Johnson and L.K. White (1999), 'Age and religiosity: evidence from a three-wave panel analysis', *Journal for the Scientific Study of Religion*, **38** (3), 423–35.
Assadi, D. (2003), 'Do religions influence customer behavior? Confronting religious rules and marketing concepts', *Cahiers du Ceren*, **5**, 2–13.
Baudrillard, Jean (1981), *For a Critique of the Political Economy of the Sig*, St Louis: Telos Press.
Biblarz, T.J., V.L. Bengtson and A. Bucur (1996), 'Social mobility across three generations', *Journal of Marriage and the Family*, **58**, 188–200.
Boccock, Robert (1993), *Consumption*, London, UK: Routledge.
Bouchet, D. (1993), 'Rails without ties. The social imaginary and postmodern culture. Can postmodern consumption replace modern questioning', *International Journal of Research in Marketing*, **11**, 405–22.
Brown, S. (1993), 'Postmodern marketing', *European Journal of Marketing*, **27** (4), 19–34.
Brown, S. (1994), 'Marketing as multiplex: screening postmodernism', *European Journal of Marketing*, **28** (8/9), 27–51.
Bucy, E. (2000), 'Social access to the Internet', *Harvard International Journal of Press/Politics*, **5** (1), 50–61.
Çakar, M. and G. Yoğurtçuoğlu (2004), 'The symbolic expression of consumption with pride: "The car" in the Turkish popular media', *11th Annual ASBBS Conference Proceedings*, **11** (1), 230–35.
Çarkoğlu, Ali and Binnaz Toprak (2006), *Degisen Türkiye'de Din, Toplum Ve Siyaset*, Istanbul, Turkey: TESEV Yayınları.
Czaja, S.J., N. Charness, A.D. Fisk, C. Hertzog, S.N. Nair, W.A. Rogers and J. Sharit (2006), 'Factors predicting the use of technology: findings from the Center for Research and Education on Aging and Technology Enhancement (CREATE)', *Psychology Aging*, **21** (2), 333–52.
De Jong, G.F., J.E. Faulkner and R.H. Warland (1976), 'Dimensions of religiosity reconsidered: evidence from a cross-cultural study', *Social Forces*, **54** (4), 866–88.
Delener, N. (1994), 'Religious contrasts in consumer decision behaviour patterns: their dimensions and marketing implications', *European Journal of Marketing*, **28** (5), 36–53.
Engel, James F., Roger D. Blackwell and David T. Kollat (1978), *Consumer Behavior*, Hinsdale, IL: The Dryden Press.
Eser, Z., S. Mutlu and M. Cakar (2007), 'Changing environment and consumer in Turkey', *Journal of Euromarketing*, **16** (3), 67–79.
Esmer, Y. (2007) *World Values Survey Report*, http://www.betam.bahcesehir.edu.tr/UserFiles/File/sunum/betamsunum7.2.08.ppt, accessed 01 March 2009.
Essoo, N. and S. Dibb (2004), 'Religious influences on shopping behaviour: an exploratory study', *Journal of Marketing Management*, **20**, 683–712.
Evans, K.R., T. Christiansen and J.D. Gill (1996), 'The impact of social influence and role expectations on shopping center patronage intentions', *Journal of the Academy of Marketing Science*, **24** (3), 208–18.

Featherstone, Mike (1991), *Consumer Culture and Postmodernism,* London and Newbury Park, CA: Sage.
Fırat, A.F. and A. Venkatesh (1995), 'Liberatory postmodernism and the reenchantment of consumption', *Journal of Consumer Research,* **22**, 239–67.
Fırat, A.F., N. Dholakia and A. Venkatesh (1995), 'Marketing in a postmodern world', *European Journal of Marketing,* **29** (1), 40–56.
Gait, A.H. and A.C. Worthington (2007), 'An empirical survey of individual consumer, business firm and financial institution attitudes towards Islamic methods of finance', University of Wollongong School of Accounting and Finance, Working Paper Series.
Genel, S. and K. Karaosmanoğlu (2006), 'A new Islamic individualism in Turkey: headscarved women in the city', *Turkish Studies,* **7** (3), 473–88.
Glennie, P. (1998), 'Consumption, consumerism and urban form: historical perspectives', *Urban Studies,* **35** (5/6), 927–51.
Gökarısel, B. and A.J. Secor (2009), 'New translational geographies of Islamism, capitalism and subjectivity: the veiling – fashion industry in Turkey', *Area,* **41** (1), 6–18.
Göle, Nilüfer (1991), *Modern Mahrem,* Istanbul, Turkey: Metis Yayınları.
Göle, N. (2000), 'Snapshots of Islamic modernities', *Daedalus,* **129** (1), 91–117.
Göle, N. (2002), 'Islam in public new visibilities and new imaginaries', *Public Culture,* **14** (1), 173–90.
Goulding, C. (2003), 'Issues in representing the postmodern consumer', *Qualitative Market Research,* **6** (3), 152–60.
Grunert, K.G., S.C. Grunert and S.E. Beatty (1989), 'Cross cultural research on consumer values', *Marketing and Research Today,* **17**, 30–39.
Gutman, J., (1990) 'Adding meaning to values by directly assessing value-benefit relationships', *Journal of Business Research,* **20**, 153–60.
Hirschman, E.C. (1983), 'Religious affiliation and consumption processes', *Research in Marketing,* **6**, 131–70.
Hofstede, Geert (1980), *Culture's Consequences: International Differences in Work-related Values,* Beverly Hills, CA: Sage.
Hofstede, Geert (1991), *Cultures and Organizations: Software of the Mind,* London: McGraw Hill.
Holt, D.B. (1997), 'Poststructuralist lifestyle analysis: conceptualizing the social patterning of consumption in post modernity', *Journal of Consumer Research,* **23**, 326–50.
Kadıoğlu, A. (2005), 'Civil society, Islam and democracy in Turkey: a study of three Islamic non-governmental organisations', *The Muslim World,* **95**, 23–41.
Kasaba, R. (1997), 'Kemalist certainties and modern ambiguities', in S. Bozdoğan and R. Kasaba (eds), *Rethinking Modernities and National Identity in Turkey,* Seattle: University of Washington Press, pp. 15–36.
Kentel, Ferhat (2008), *Örtülemeyen Sorun Başörtüsü,* Istanbul, Turkey: AK-DER Yayınları.
Keyman, E.F. (2007), 'Modernity, secularism and Islam: the case of Turkey', *Theory, Culture and Society,* **24** (2), 215–34.
Kılıçbay, B. and M. Binark (2002), 'Consumer culture, Islam and the politics of lifestyle: fashion for veiling in contemporary Turkey', *European Journal of Communication,* **17** (4), 495–511.
Küçükcan, T. (2003), 'State, Islam, and religious liberty in modern Turkey: reconfiguration of religion in the public sphere', *Brigham Young University Law Review,* **2**, 475–506.
Lackman, C., and J.M. Lanasa (1993), 'Family decision-making theory: an overview and assessment', *Psychology and Marketing,* **10** (2), 81–93.
Lewis, C.A., S. Joseph and K.E. Noble (1996), 'Is religiosity associated with life satisfaction?' *Psychological Reports,* **79**, 429–30.
Lindridge, A. (2005), 'Religiosity and the construction of a cultural–consumption identity', *Journal of Consumer Marketing,* **22** (2/3), 142–51.
Maycroft, N. (2004), 'Cultural consumption and the myth of life-style', *Capital & Class,* **84**, 61–75.
Miles, S. and R. Paddison (1998), 'Urban consumption: an historiographical note', *Urban Studies,* **35** (5/6), 815–23.
Miller, A.S. and J.P. Hoffmann (1995), 'Risk and religion: an explanation of gender differences in religiosity', *Journal for the Scientific Study of Religion,* **34** (1), 63–75.
Mittelstaedt, J.D. (2002), 'A framework for understanding the relationships between religions and markets', *Journal of Macromarketing,* **22** (1), 6–18.
Mokhlis, S. (2009), 'Relevancy and measurement of religiosity in consumer behavior research', *International Business Research,* **2** (3), 75–84.
Navaro-Yashin, Yael (2002), 'The market for identities: secularism, Islamism, commodities' in Deniz Kandiyoti and Ayse Saktanber (eds), *Fragments of Culture: The Everyday of Modern Turkey,* London: I.B. Tauris, pp. 221–53.
Odabaşı, Y. and M. Argan (2009), 'Aspects of underlying Ramadan consumption patterns in Turkey', *Journal of International Consumer Marketing,* **21**, 203–18.
Oktay, Ahmet (1993), *Türkiye'de Popüler Kültür,* Istanbul, Turkey: Everest Yayınları.

Okumuş, H.Ş. (2005), 'Interest-free banking in Turkey: a study of customer satisfaction and bank selection criteria', *Journal of Economic Cooperation*, **26**, 51–86.

Pew Research Center data, http://pewresearch.org (accessed 20 July 2010).

Plummer, J.T. (1974), 'The concepts and application of life style segmentation', *Journal of Marketing*, **38** (1), 33–40.

Rehman, A. and M.S. Shabbir (2010), 'The relationship between religiosity and new product adoption', *Journal of Islamic Marketing*, **1** (1), 63–69.

Rice, G. and M. Al-Mossawi (2002), 'The implications of Islam for advertising messages: the Middle Eastern context', *Journal of Euromarketing*, **11** (3), 1–16.

Ritzer, George (1996), *The McDonaldization of Society*, Thousand Oaks, CA: Pine Forge Press.

Rokeach, M. (1968–69) 'The role of values in public opinion,' *Public Opinion Quarterly*, **32** (4), 547–59.

Sandıkcı, Ö. and G. Ger (2001), 'Fundamental fashions: the cultural politics of the turban and the Levis', *Advances in Consumer Research*, **28**, 146–50.

Sandıkcı, Ö. and G. Ger (2002), 'In-between modernities and postmodernities: theorizing Turkish consumption space', *Advances in Consumer Research*, **29**, 465–70.

Sandıkcı, Ö. and G. Ger (2005), 'Aesthetics, ethics and politics of the Turkish headscarf', in Susanne Küchler and Daniel Miller (eds), *Clothing As Material Culture*, Oxford: Berg, pp. 61–82.

Sandıkcı, Ö. and G. Ger (2007), 'Constructing and representing the Islamic consumer in Turkey', *Fashion Theory*, **11** (2/3), 189–210.

Sandıkcı, Ö. and G. Ger (2010), 'Veiling in style: how does a stigmatized practice become fashionable?', *Journal of Consumer Research*, 37, 15–35.

Toprak, Binnaz and Ali Çarkoğlu (2007), *Religion, Society, and Politics in a Changing Society*, Istanbul, Turkey: TESEV Yayınları.

Turkish Statistical Institute Data, www.tuik.gov.tr (accessed 15 March 2010).

Vinson, D.E., J.E. Scott and M.L. Lamont (1977) 'The role of personal values in marketing and consumer behaviour', *Journal of Marketing*, **41** (2), 44–50.

Wells, W. and D. Tigert (1971), 'Activities, interests and opinions', *Journal of Advertising Research*, **11** (4), 27–35.

Wilkes, R.E., J.J. Burnett and R.D. Howell (1986), 'On the meaning and measurement of religiosity in consumer research', *Journal of the Academy of Marketing Science*, **14** (1), 47–56.

Wong, L. (2007), 'Market cultures, the middle classes and Islam: consuming the market?', *Consumption, Markets and Culture*, **10** (4), 451–80.

APPENDIX: TURKEY – THE DEMOGRAPHICS

Demographics are important indicators of the market structure. Today Turkey has a very young and fast-growing population. It reached 67.8 million in 2000 and 72.5 million in 2009, up from 13.65 million in 1927. In 2009 the growth rate was 1.45 per cent. As a consequence of such a high growth rate, the population profile has a large youth base. In 2009, the population at age 14 and below constituted 26.35 per cent, whereas those between the ages of 15 and 64 constituted 67 per cent of the total. In the same year, 50 per cent of the population was aged below 28.8.

There are wide disparities in the educational level and structure of citizens living in urban and rural areas, in the west and the east of the country as well as between the genders. Educational indicators are better in the cities and in the western part of the country than in the rural and eastern part. In the 2000 nationwide population report, the percentage of illiterate female citizens was reported as 6.16, whereas for male citizens the percentage was 4.05. In 2009, the male illiteracy rate was approximately a quarter of the female illiteracy rate (910 395 vs. 3 730 553, respectively). Even though primary education is compulsory, the female enrollment rate has always been lower than the male enrollment rate. The situation worsens as one moves up the educational ladder. The illiteracy rate in rural areas is higher than it is in urban areas, and the female illiteracy rate goes up as one moves from the west to the east of the country.

In 2000, 47.77 per cent of the population above 25 years of age had completed primary school, whereas 8.23 per cent had completed junior high school or junior vocational school, 12.55 per cent had completed high school or vocational high school and 7.80 per cent had completed higher education. When we look at the statistics for the year 2009, we see that the primary education enrollment rate is 96.5 per cent; the secondary school enrollment rate is 58.5 per cent, and the higher education enrollment rate is 27.7 per cent.

Source: www.tuik.gov.tr.

9 The impact of Islam on food shopping and consumption patterns of Muslim households
Hayiel Hino

INTRODUCTION

Religion is a significant force in the lives of many communities and plays an influential role in shaping individuals' way of life (Delener, 1994; Pettinger et al., 2004). Religious influence often takes two forms (Harrell, 1986): the first is through the direct effect of religious codes of conduct on personal choice; the second is indirect, relating to religion's influence on attitude and value formation (Bailey and Sood, 1993). A household's consumption system is one area in which both forms are prominent. Studies that have investigated the impact of religion on consumption and purchasing decisions of various consumer groups have found that, indeed, religion plays a critical role in consumers' attitudes and behavior (Asp, 1999; Hino, 2010; Just et al., 2007; Mennell et al., 1992; Mullen et al., 2000; Musaiger, 1993; Shatenstein and Ghadirian, 1997; Steenkamp, 1993; Steptoe and Pollard, 1995; Swanson, 1996). Yet research on this topic has been sparse. The sporadic studies that do deal with the influence of religion on consumer behavior report significant differences in shopping and consumption patterns between religious groups (Delener, 1994; Essoo and Dibb, 2004; Mokhlis, 2006), as well as within religious groups – among more and less religious consumers (Choi, 2010; Just et al., 2007; Kaynak and Kara, 2002; Lindrege, 2005; McDaniel and Burnett, 1990). It should also be noted that interpretations of both 'religious affiliation' and 'religiosity' often vary from country to country and beyond that, within social contexts (Essoo and Dibb 2004; Sood and Nasu, 1995).

High levels of religiosity can be indicative of a stronger sense of community, belonging, and commitment to collective standards. This is particularly evident in a religion such as Islam, where faith, law (the *sharia* – Muslim laws and their interpretation) and culture provide values and norms that unify many Muslim communities, the many variations of Islam notwithstanding. And yet, cultural diversity is recognized too, as seen in the Qur'an (49:13) in which God states that He made people into different tribes and nations in order that they would know one other (not hate one another) and that superiority is based on whoever is 'most deeply conscious of Him.'

Indeed, Islam determines for the individual, unequivocal and compulsory rules of behavior in a wide range of areas, regardless of his/her sect affiliation,[1] including family daily life, economics, trade, finance, and social, cultural and personal behavior (Al-Azhari, 2002; Bachar, 1998). The religion's dictates are even interpreted and applied to the specific realm of shopping and consumption patterns, particularly food preparation and eating habits, with rules of conduct laid down that must be adhered to, based solely on membership in Islam (Al-Azhari, 2002; Kabasakal and Bodur, 2002). These values begin with the need for *halal* food – food that is produced in accordance with Islamic religious rites – and the prohibition of products that contain non-*halal* derivatives or that are produced on equipment that is not free from non-*halal* contamination.[2] Recent estimates suggest that about 70 per cent of Muslims worldwide follow *halal* standards (Minkus-McKenna, 2007). The facts that the global *halal* industry is estimated to be worth more than US$580 billion (*Halal Journal*, 2008) and international *halal* food trade exceeds $150 billion a year (Canadian International Markets Bureau, 2001) give us a good idea as to just how profound Islam's role is in Muslim societies, in general, and in food consumption and shopping for food products, in particular.

This chapter employs a conceptual framework to examine the impact of Islam on shopping and consumption patterns of Muslim households for food products. It centers particularly on the influence of Islam on the usage,[3] of modern shopping patterns, whereby consumers make large and concentrated purchases in a 'one-stop shop' at supermarkets and hypermarkets, thus utilizing the economic, personal, and entertainment benefits associated with shopping in large modern stores. Specifically, it asks how Islamic religious values affect the food consumption habits of Muslim households, as well as their store format,[4] choices for purchasing consumables (modern supermarket formats versus traditional food formats, including neighborhood groceries and open markets), and what the proportional division of a household's needs is, based on the various food store types available. In other words, what is the impact of religion on Muslim consumers' shopping patterns, and how do Islamic values, specifically about what is *halal*, affect the degree of use of the various food store types? In this context, there are several recent studies (for example, Bonne and Verbeke, 2008a; Bonne et al., 2007; Hino, 2010), and an earlier one by Yavas and Tuncalp (1984), that identify the *halal* aspects associated with the preparation of food products (such as meat and poultry) and store familiarity as the main reasons for choosing traditional outlets over modern supermarkets and hypermarkets when shopping for food items. These studies, however, do not examine the associated consumer behavior. Large modern food stores can carry a wide assortment of packaged and processed food lines but the *halal* level may be considered questionable, and the processed products may contain ingredients from non-*halal* sources. In such cases, many consumers opt to shop at supermarkets and hypermarkets only for products whose *halal* level is very clear, thus decreasing the proportion of product lines purchased at these food stores (Hino, 2010). This 'selective' use pattern of the supermarket formats illustrates a scenario in which supermarkets are the target of a large proportion of consumers' shopping trips, yet customers do not necessarily buy all of their product needs there; the prevailing consumers' tendency is to buy certain product categories – meat and meat by-products especially – at traditional outlets. This shopping pattern also indicates a failure of the supermarkets to compete in these product categories against the traditional formats and acts as a barrier to the evolution of modern food retail systems. These findings, which reflect the significant impact of religious values on shopping customs, also characterize many Muslim minority communities living in Western/developed economies (Bonne et al., 2007; Bonne and Verbeke, 2008a; Goldman and Hino, 2005).

For the purposes of this chapter, we present a review of the literature that attempts to further the theoretical and empirical understanding of the influential role played by Islam in shaping consumers' shopping and consumption patterns. In particular, we identify Islamic aspects (religious values and norms) that directly pertain to food consumption, review their sources in Islam (specifically the Qur'an and the *sharia*) and highlight their influence on shopping practices employed by Muslim consumers, as well as explaining their impact on modern shopping patterns. This is of major importance to retail firms, public policy makers, and modern retail planners interested in accelerating retail modernization systems, that is, the process by which 'advanced' supermarket technologies replace the 'outmoded' and 'inefficient' traditional food formats and practices. Some scholars (see, for example, Farhangmehr et al., 2001; Goldman, 2001; Goldman and Hino, 2005; Goldman et al., 2002; Kaynak and Cavusgil, 1982; Lo et al., 2001; Maruyama and Trung, 2010; Reardon and Berdegue, 2002; Reardon and Swinen, 2004) view this process as the 'evolution' of modern food retail systems.

THEORETICAL FRAMEWORK

Modern food stores (supermarkets and hypermarkets) have already reached full diffusion in a substantial number of countries around the world. Moreover, most consumers in those countries have adopted the modern store formats, as reflected in their shopping at them regularly. And yet in other countries, many consumers continue to patronize different food formats, including traditional groceries and specialty stores. The dominant shopping pattern of the majority of those consumers is to divide their grocery shopping between two or more stores each week, where supermarkets and hypermarkets supply groceries (packaged and processed product lines), and other food formats – in particular specialty stores – are used to supply selected food items, especially fresh produce (Goldman et al., 2002; Maruyama and Trung, 2007). This selective use pattern means that such consumers have not shifted to the 'one-stop' shop pattern found in many parts of the world.

The phenomenon of shopping at different food formats has been documented in many studies that deal with grocery store shopping behavior (Goldman and Hino, 2005; Goldman et al., 1999, 2002). An examination of these studies points to 'use-adoption gaps' that occur when consumers use supermarket formats to satisfy only a small proportion of their food needs, even when supermarkets are readily accessible and consumers patronize them regularly.

In assessing the antecedents of use-adoption gaps, some recent studies have relied on a number of previous research streams that deal with aspects of the usage phenomena. These include food retail modernization, format development, consumer shopping behavior and retail store choice. Based on this extensive research, several variable sets that may well explain barriers to full use of supermarket formats have been identified; see Figure 9.1 (Hino, 2010).

Religious aspects comprise one of these variable sets. A review of the studies that deal with the impact of religion on consumer behavior point to the significant effects of religious variables, specifically, religious affiliation and 'religiosity' on some aspects of consumer behavior, such as purchasing patterns, store choice and selected aspects of retail store patronage (Choi, 2010; Esso and Dibb 2004; Mokhlis, 2006; Sood and Nasu, 1995). In the context of Muslim communities, these effects are even more prominent, especially where food shopping is concerned. Studies discussing the impact of religious variables report a negative impact of religious aspects, such as *halal* characteristics, on

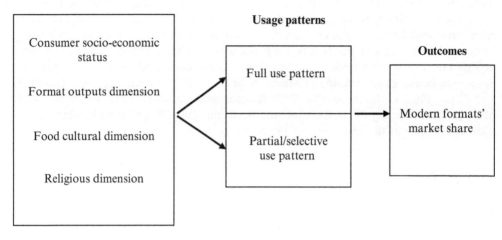

Source: Hino (2010).

Figure 9.1   Sequence of modern food formats' use patterns

shopping for selected food items at supermarkets and hypermarkets, thus decreasing the degree of use of such broad formats (Bonne et al., 2007; Bonne and Verbeke, 2008a; Hino, 2010).

Other variable sets that may well explain the degree of use of supermarkets include: the consumer's socioeconomic status, format outputs, and the consumer's food culture.

Consumer's socioeconomic status: A large number of studies show that socioeconomic status variables such as income, education, and size of apartment affect consumers' shopping propensities. The most relevant perspective is the household production approach (Betancourt and Gautschi, 1986, 1990; Goldman et al., 2002; Hoch et al. 1995; Messinger and Narasimhan, 1997). This suggests that a household's opportunity cost of time (time being more or less valuable), storage costs and consumer ability to buy larger quantities, influence consumers' tendency to shop in modern formats. Consumers high on these variables will conduct fewer shopping trips and buy larger amounts in one-stop purchases.

Format outputs: Variables associated with format outputs provide further insights into format use. They include store location as a factor determining shopping convenience (Craig et al., 1984) and store outputs that constitute functional, social, and entertainment benefits attracting consumers to stores (Bell et al., 1998; Butcher et al., 2002; Carpenter and Moore, 2006; Pan and Zinkhan, 2006; Turly and Milliman, 2000).

Consumer's food culture: Consumers who eat primarily home-cooked meals, use traditional preparation methods and eat traditional dishes often put high value on the use of fresh ingredients. They demand a large variety of fresh produce, are likely to shop frequently for it and to be highly sensitive to the level of outputs and services a store provides. Studies (Oswald 1999; Veeck and Burns, 2005) and anecdotal evidence indicate that these 'traditional' shoppers prefer traditional formats, which they view as better able to supply them with the variety, freshness, price and proximity outputs they require.

THE IMPACT OF ISLAM ON FOOD CONSUMPTION

Many religions impose strict prohibitions on food consumption. This is reflected in a number of rules to which followers adhere in food consumption, from meal preparation to eating. Judaism, Hinduism and Buddhism, for example, all forbid certain foods, usually pertaining to animals; many Catholics abstain from meat on Fridays and during Lent, opting rather for fish. However, the impact of religion on food consumption depends on the religion itself, whether it is part and parcel of the law of state, and on the extent to which individuals interpret and follow the teachings of their religion (Bonne et al., 2007).

Islam, too, determines for Muslims behavioral rules and customs which have a direct bearing on food consumption. These rules are supported by two sources: Islamic religious values and Islamic behavior (Al-Sarieti, 2000).

Islamic Religious Values

The Qur'an and the *sharia* provide the foundations for clear and binding behavior and other rules that are inherent in Islamic religious values. In matters of individual consumption, for example, Islamic values prescribe that Muslims adhere to sensible, balanced consumption and to the prohibition against consuming non-*halal* products. In Arabic, *halal* means 'permissible' (Regenstein et al., 2003), and it refers to anything permitted[5] under Islam. The term *halal,* most frequently refers to food products – whether meat, poultry, fish, or beverages, but it can be extended to all consumer products, including cosmetics, toiletries, pharmaceutical products, or even services (for example, financial services). Having said that, most food and non-food products are considered to be *halal* unless they are specifically prohibited under Islam, in which case, they are considered *haram*, an Arabic term meaning 'unlawful or prohibited.' Products are classified as permitted (*halal*) or prohibited (*haram*) according to the dietary laws. Specifically, those laws prohibit the eating of any meat of animals that have not been slaughtered according to the Muslim methods of ritual slaughter. Furthermore, there are additional conditions that should be taken into account for meat to become *halal*. Bonne and Verbeke (2008b) provide five additional conditions. These refer to the animal itself, which must be of an acceptable species. In addition, the animal must be alive at the time of the ritual slaughter and must die of bleeding rather than as a consequence of stunning. The slaughter of the animal can be carried out by any adult Muslim by cutting the front part of the neck with a very sharp knife and evoking the name of Allah (the Arabic word for God) during the cut, preferably with the animal turned towards Mecca. Fourth, at all times during the slaughter process, Islam advocates the humane treatment of animals: for example, animals should be well nourished, rested, and not stressed before slaughter. Finally, supervised distribution and retailing of *halal* meat is critical to prevent cross-contamination with non-*halal* meat.

Islam also forbids eating the meat of some kinds of animals, specifically carrion, pork or carnivorous animals; where fish is concerned, it must be fresh to be *halal*, meaning that it needs to have been taken out of the water while it was still alive (Qur'an 2:173). As for beverages, Islam forbids intoxicating drinks: the Qur'an is particularly strict on this matter and not only forbids drinking alcohol, including wine (Qur'an 5:90), and eating foods containing alcohol, but also bars Muslim-owned shops from selling any form of alcohol; nor may Muslims work in shops that sell such products. Generally speaking, the Islamic prohibition system is very broad and includes products that are potentially harmful to health (Qur'an 7:157), cigarettes included (Al-Azhari, 2002; Al-Sarieti, 2000).

Regarding 'balanced consumption,' Islam calls for moderate, frugal consumption, according to the individual's essential needs (Al-Azhari, 2002), and is unequivocally against impulsive and lavish spending (Qur'an 7:31 and 25:67). At the same time, Islam calls for balanced consumption based on the individual's financial ability and the benefit of the goods purchased. This is determined by setting clear lists of priorities, the first item being basic necessities, the products most vital to the individual's sustenance. Food that is not absolutely necessary is considered a second priority; this refers to food that a person is able to live without for a while. Luxury items are the lowest priority in terms of consumption and shopping (Qur'an 18:19) (Al-Azhari, 2002).

Islamic Behavior

The other source of Islamic values and norms refers to behavioral conduct, which has a direct link to consumption and eating habits, including food preparation at home. At the individual/family/community level, those norms refer to a number of aspects.

First, the very act of the family sitting together around the table during meals is seen to have social and consumer value, given that group eating requires the preparation of amounts of food sufficient for the entire family. An added value is that group eating is purportedly conducive to saving in the purchase of food products.

Second, food is regarded as 'a gift from heaven' and therefore is not to be wasted or thrown away. Leftovers, if there are any, are to be kept to be eaten at other meals later or the next day (Rosenberger, 1999; Al-Azhari, 2002).

Third, the Muslim consumer is responsible for other family members too. He therefore not only buys food for himself but also for his close family and sometimes even for the extended family, depending on his financial ability (Rosenberger, 1999). The more financial resources he has, the broader his responsibility (Al-Sarieti, 2000). This is an expression of social 'mutual responsibility' which is a typical Islamic value that encompasses, beyond just close and distant family members, neighbors, acquaintances and guests (Kabasakal and Bodur, 2002; Saleem, 1993). It has social and consumer consequences: the assurance of dignified living conditions and life necessities, even for the deprived (Al-Azhari, 2002); a minimized consumption gap between the rich and the poor; and promoting more equal consumption.

Research into the eating and cooking habits of Muslim families points to the clear influence of Islamic religious precepts on consumption patterns in Muslim societies and communities (Kanafani, 1983; Rosenberger, 1999). This is evident in:

(a)   the emphasis on Islamic dietary laws, matching the belief that food is the most important gift that God granted humankind;
(b)   the tradition of eating *en famille* as often as possible;
(c)   the use of spices in cooking, which not only adds taste and aroma but also helps purify meat of impure elements such as blood (Islam regards blood in meat as impure);

(d)   the amount of food cooked for the main meal of the day is beyond that actually needed, in order that there may be enough in case, for example, unexpected guests come to visit at mealtime.

Within the general context of Islamic behavior, many cultural variations of Islam should be noted. Islam acknowledges the diversity in people's customs, race, languages, dress, food, and other cultural expressions. However, it also disapproves of and even condemns those aspects of a culture that contradict its teachings and principles. Some cultural practices[6] are considered acceptable simply because they do not contradict any Islamic principle. An example of this is the preparation of various types of non-prohibited food and drinks. The fact that people have a variety of taste preferences is acknowledged in Islam, and the *sharia* contains provisions for that.

THE IMPACT OF ISLAM ON SHOPPING BEHAVIOR

Studies in the marketing literature suggest that religion greatly influences behavior which in turn affects purchasing decisions (Bailey and Sood, 1993; Delener, 1990; Hirschman, 1981; McDaniel and Burnett, 1990; Wilkes et al., 1986). In the case of Islam – a religion calling for clear and binding consumption patterns – religious aspects are also expected to play an influential role in shaping Muslims' shopping patterns. The key question is how different these behavioral habits are among Muslims in comparison to other communities, especially in Western economies, where consumers who have adopted modern food format shopping buy all of their grocery and food needs in a one-stop shop.

The discussion in this section will consider the influence of Islam on the type of store format in which consumers choose to purchase consumables and to what extent religious values affect shopping at modern food stores. In the context of buying patterns, consumers can choose between two types of store format: traditional, such as local neighborhood groceries, and modern formats, that is, supermarkets and hypermarkets. Many consumers who use only *halal* foods are expected to prefer to shop in stores that are familiar and that they know meet Islamic religious standards. In such cases, consumers may choose to purchase all of their food needs at traditional formats, or at least to split their food purchases between traditional and modern options. The dominant food shopping behavior in the latter scenario is that of the selected use pattern in which modern formats (supermarkets and hypermarkets) operate alongside traditional outlets and supply some types of consumables, while the traditional stores continue to supply most of the food lines, especially those products that must meet *halal* standards.

THE IMPACT OF ISLAM ON STORE CHOICE

Islam strictly forbids the consumption of non-*halal* products and any form of alcoholic drink. It also prohibits shopping in stores that offer such product lines. This necessarily has a direct impact on the purchasing habits of consumers in terms of their choices of food stores at which to shop. In the first place, consumers will only want to buy products such as meat and poultry that are *halal* and then only in stores which certifiably abide by Muslim dietary laws. Those in most cases are traditional local butcher's shops that are either owned by Muslims or employ Muslim workers and, as such, can be trusted to supply authentic *halal* meat. Modern stores such as supermarkets and hypermarkets, on the other hand, offer a wide assortment of product lines which are likely to include product items that are forbidden because they do not abide by *halal* dietary laws. Some consumers – presumably those who are more orthodox – are likely to avoid shopping in such stores, or at least to avoid buying specific items there such as meat and chicken, which they cannot be sure meet the Islamic requirements. Studies that have investigated the determinants of *halal* meat consumption within Muslim minority communities in Europe (see, for example, Bonne and Verbeke, 2008a; Bonne et al., 2007) reveal that Muslim consumers display higher confidence in Islamic establishments, such as Muslim butcher's shops, when it comes to monitoring and controlling the *halal* status of meat. Indeed, the Islamic butcher remains the most preferred place of purchase for *halal* meat even though supermarkets too offer such sanctioned products (Bonne and Verbeke, 2008a). These results are consistent with the findings of Yavas and Tuncalp (1984). In their study on shopping patterns for meat products in Saudi Arabia, they found that one of the reasons consumers prefer buying meat and poultry at traditional channels (the local market) and not at supermarkets is the perceived standard of *halal*. Similar findings were reported in a comparative research that included Muslim populations in Israel and Jordan and investigated the impact of four variable sets on retail formats' usage patterns: consumer economic abilities, retail format outputs, Islamic religious variables (religiosity degree and Islamic religious values) and ethnic-cultural aspects (Hino, 2010). Among other results, the research confirmed that the choice of traditional meat shops resulted in a close familiar and personal relation with butchers or other employees in the store, which in turn served as a risk-decreasing mechanism in purchasing decision making for meat and poultry products. Moreover, religious variables were found in both studies to have a significant impact on consumers' shopping patterns even when there was a difference in consumers' economic status. That is, the effects of religious factors on store choice appear to be high and uniform regardless of socioeconomic standing. The results, however, for consumer economic abilities, retail format and cultural factors were quite different; when consumers enjoy a relatively high economic status, they are more likely to attach importance to the benefits associated with shopping in modern stores. In such cases, format outputs seem to be the most influential factors affecting retail format usage, whereas the impact of economic abilities is relatively small. Furthermore, when consumers climb the social scale, their food consumption patterns are likely to change to a more modern direction. They appear to expand their eating habits (in addition to ethnic/traditional cuisine), and now tend to split their basket according to product category types. That is, they continue to use traditional formats for purchasing fresh products and both modern and traditional formats for non-perishables.

Second, some consumers prefer to shop in stores that do not sell alcohol. This is consistent with findings of studies that deal with shopping behavior of Muslim shoppers in Jordan and Israel (Hino, 2010). Modern stores have a full range of products which typically includes wine and other alcoholic beverages and one could therefore expect that Muslim consumers, especially the more religiously oriented, would steer away from this option in favor of the smaller traditional stores. Although the choice is more limited, they can feel safe in the knowledge that the retailers there can be trusted to abide by the dietary laws and – equally importantly – that the shops or stalls are located within their local neighborhood, making them the preferred option.

The idea that Islamic religious aspects can shape certain shopping patterns has received some recent research attention. A number of earlier studies carried out in Muslim societies (Findlay, 1990; Kaynak, 1985; Kaynak and Cavusgil, 1982; Kumcu and Kumcu, 1987; Miossec, 1990; Othman, 1990; Yavas and Tuncalp, 1984; Zain and Rejab, 1989) documented the tendency of consumers to display food shopping patterns that differ from those of consumers in other countries. Many of those consumers would shop exclusively in traditional outlets rather than in modern supermarkets, or at least they split their food purchases between neighborhood groceries, specialized traditional stores and supermarkets. Similar findings were reported in a recent study investigating the impact of various factors (including religious variables: religiosity degree and Islamic religious values) on the shopping patterns of two Muslim populations, in Jordan and Israel (Hino, 2010). Among other findings, religious variables (Islamic religious values and religiosity degree) were found to have a significant impact on the extent of use of supermarket formats, particularly vis-à-vis fresh products. That is, consumers tend to split their basket according to product category types: they use traditional formats for purchasing fresh products, especially meat and poultry and both modern and traditional formats for non-perishables. This reflects the ultimate commitment of many Muslims to religious values and norms that directly pertain to shopping and consumption patterns. For example, Israeli Muslim-Arab consumers purchase 99 per cent (that figure is 90 per cent in Jordan) of their meat products in traditional outlets, thus underscoring the central role religious values play in their food consumption customs, specifically, the need for *halal* food. However, the empirical results of the study point to the negligible impact of the religious variables on shopping at modern supermarkets and hypermarkets, indicating that these variables do not constitute a barrier to the adoption of these formats. In other words, consumers can shop regularly at supermarkets and hypermarkets, but only for selected product categories.

SUMMARY, CONCLUSIONS AND MANAGERIAL IMPLICATIONS

This chapter has examined the influence of Islam on food shopping and consumption behavior. Specifically, it focuses on the impact of Islamic religious values and norms that apply directly to family life – from food shopping to the kitchen – and, more broadly, to consumption patterns among Muslim populations.

As shown, in Islam, as in other faiths, religion often plays a significant role in outlining an individual's way of life; yet little attention has been given to its impact on the application of modern shopping practices – and better could this be more apparent than in food-related shopping? Thus, the chapter presented a review of Islam's religious aspects, in particular, religious values and behavioral customs that directly pertain to food shopping and consumption, based on the sources of the Qur'an and the *sharia*. In addition, it reviewed the few studies on food retailing that do deal with these topics in the context of Muslim consumer groups.

In conclusion, we can claim that Islam, with its strong code of behavior to which all

Muslims are required to adhere, specifically the prohibition against the consumption of non-*halal* products (which is interpreted to mean that food items should not even be bought in shops that stock products prohibited by Islamic law), has a significant effect on shopping and consumption. This is reflected in the selective purchasing practices found commonly among Muslims (including Muslim minority communities living in Western countries) that differ from those found in non-Muslim Western communities. In particular, many Muslim consumers tend to split their shopping basket according to product category types, though noticeably decreasing their use of modern formats: they tend to patronize traditional formats for fresh products, even though supermarkets and hypermarkets offer these products in a wide assortment, while non-perishables may be bought at both modern and traditional formats. These conclusions lead to some practical implications. First, retailers can encourage the degree of use of the modern store formats by offering broader *halal* product lines. The fact that the vast majority of Muslims worldwide (about 70 per cent) follow *halal* standards highlights the importance of *halal* certification. In this context, kosher foods provide example of a good precedent: kosher products sell well to Jewish consumers for religious reasons and to both Jews and non-Jews because of their perceived quality and the safety considerations associated with certified foods. Food manufacturers and retail companies should thus consider the marketing opportunities that come with *halal* certification to attract new markets for their goods. Moreover, *halal* certification enhances the desirability of a company's products to a broader Muslim customer base and expands opportunities for export to Muslim countries and to Muslim minority populations worldwide.

There are two additional implications that are of major importance to modern retailers and to global retail firms that operate in or plan to enter Muslim markets. Shopping patterns that are manifestations of the partial use pattern whereby consumers divide their grocery shopping between two or more different food formats – modern and traditional – are expected to constrain modern retailers' ability to gain substantial market shares. In other words, we can expect that traditional formats will continue to operate alongside the modern formats and will not be upended by them. If this is the case, modern retailers can positively affect the market share captured by the supermarkets by providing further improvements in format outputs, such as the offering of a wide variety of fresh and non-perishable product lines, thus enabling large purchases in one-stop shops, and the opening of modern stores in an increasing number of locations, making these stores more accessible to consumers.

The other implication deals with the impact of Islam on the process of food retailing modernization. When discussing the influence of Islamic religious values on the appropriation of modern purchasing and consumption habits, such as the shift from buying in traditional food outlets to supermarkets, the question arises whether there is a difference, or a contradiction, between upholding Islamic religious and cultural values and adopting modern consumption habits. Even though topics dealing with modernization and progress[7] in Islamic society are beyond the focus of the present chapter, research into the modernization and development of Muslim society does not show any contradiction between Qur'anic precepts and leading a modern lifestyle, nor does it reveal any other element in Islam that is opposed to modernization. The fact that many Islamic populations have not advanced and remain underdeveloped is attributed to their failure to understand how to apply Qur'anic doctrines (Hafez, 2000). Moreover, that Muslim consumers do purchase selected product lines at supermarkets, demonstrates the choice of modern format, in itself, is not negated by Islamic values and norms (Hino, 2010). This conclusion, which may be indicative of Muslims' attitudes toward the adoption of innovations, is consistent with the findings reported by Esso and Dibb (2004). In their study on religious influences on shopping behavior, Muslim consumers were found to be more practical and innovative in their shopping patterns than other religious groups.

LIMITATIONS AND FUTURE RESEARCH

There are some limitations related to the generalization of the results of this study. First, we draw heavily on research about the impact of Islam on food shopping and consumption patterns of selected Muslim populations. Yet, this research has been sparse. The sporadic studies that do deal with the influence of religion on consumer behavior are not broad enough to make assumptions regarding Muslim populations worldwide. Hence, it is recommended that future research consider a cross-country comparison of Muslim populations. An additional limitation has to do with the correlation between cultural and religious variables. To date no clear distinction has been made between effects attributed to cultural values and effects attributed to Islamic values. This is simply because an overlap exists between the effects of the two sets of variables on the shopping behavior of Muslim consumers. Furthermore, while our study provides some examples of how religious aspects can affect food consumption behavior, more work remains to be done. Certainly there are some patterns of social norms that are consistent across Muslim communities, but it is likely that additional potential determinants, such as family power structures, economic status and other behavioral norms will differ across Muslim populations. Future research could help identify these differences and shed further light on their impact. Finally, in order to get better insights into the influence of Islam on food consumption habits relatively to other religions, a cross-religious study that involves consumers from different religious affiliations and degrees of religiosity is recommended. Such a study would yield research results that are more comparable and would provide a better understanding of the role played by religious values in shaping consumers' consumption systems.

NOTES

1. There are various sects within Muslim populations. Sunni Muslims are by far the majority (approximately 90 per cent of all Muslims in the world are Sunni), with Shi'ites constituting most of the remainder. Sunnis are the mainstream, traditional Muslims who believe in a strict determinism. They base their religion on the Qur'an and the *sunnah* (the 'words and deeds of Muhammad' – Islamic law dictated orally by Muhammad) as understood by the majority of the community. Within the Sunni sects there are also a few subtle differences. Sunnis follow four 'schools of law': *hanafi, maliki, hanbali, shafi'i*. The main difference between these various schools of law is their interpretation of various rules.

   Shi'ites, on the other hand, while accepting the canonicity of the *sunnah* as the second most important source of Islamic law after the Qur'an, do not recognize its decrees as binding. Shi'ism also has its own set of doctrines and practices, which allow more individual freedom in the practice of religion. To sum up, despite differences between the two major Islamic sects in levels of orthodoxy, all Muslims accept the Qur'an as their holy book and adhere to its requirements (Kabasakal and Bodur, 2002). They acknowledge the importance of daily prayer, fasting during Ramadan and paying *zakat* (religious tax). Yet, Islam is as varied as any other religion and since its emergence in the Arabian Peninsula in the first half of the seventh century, it has adapted to the various contexts where it has taken root. Moreover, diversity among Muslims stems from the vast array of contexts where Islam has developed either as the principal religion or as an important presence. In countries where Muslims form the majority population, such as Indonesia and Iraq, or where they constitute large minorities, such as India and Nigeria, a variety of religious institutions, practices, and beliefs have developed over the last 1400 years. Whether within a large country such as Egypt or a small country such as Lebanon, everyday practice among Muslims varies from village to city.

2. This is not to say that all Muslims, even those who have a strong identification with Islam, adhere to all the precepts.

3. 'Usage' refers to consumers' shopping patterns in food store formats; it is defined as the degree of use of the supermarket formats. It will be low when consumers buy only a few of their product needs there out of the total purchased. In this case 'partial' use patterns exist. By contrast, a 'full' supermarket use pattern describes a situation where consumers buy a large proportion of their needs there. This pattern represents the 'one stop' supermarket shopping model.

4. The classification of food retail outlets in this study is based on outlet size of floor space:

    (a) Hypermarkets: over 50000 square feet, usually in out-of-town locations.
    (b) Superstores: between 25000 and 50000 square feet.
    (c) Big supermarkets: between 12000 and 25000 square feet.
    (d) Medium supermarkets: between 5000 and 1200. square feet.
    (e) Small supermarkets: between 1000 and 5000 square feet.
    (f) Neighborhood groceries: 1000 square feet or less.
    (g) Speciality stores: shops specializing in fresh product lines, such as meat and poultry, fish or fruits and vegetables, with a floor space anywhere between 500 and 5000 square feet.

5. The spectrum of permissibility (*halal*) in Islam ranges from what is compulsory/obligatory (*wajib*), to what is recommended (*mandub*) or merely permissible (*mubah*), and to what is discouraged and detested (*makruh*).

6. Other cultural practices encompass traditional verbal greetings, wedding customs, forms of leisure and entertainment, and extend to farming methods and even architecture. Furthermore, many countries have cultural differences, such as polygamy practices or the level of women's participation in society, to mention just two: polygamy is more widely practiced in the Middle East than in Far Eastern countries (India, Pakistan, Bangladesh); meanwhile, in the Far East, women are more active participants in society than their Middle Eastern counterparts. The lower participation of women in Middle Eastern society is not because of the teachings of Islam, but rather due to differences in interpretation of Islamic principles and culture. Under Islamic principles, women have the same right to participate in society as men.

7. There are three theoretical approaches to modernization and progress in the literature dealing with the development of Islamic society (Amarah, 1996). The first unequivocally adheres to Islamic values, history and tradition as the way to achieve progress and to renew the Islamic world's power. According to that approach, Western economies cannot serve as an example for Islam to follow or to adopt. Western economies are not suitable to Islam and it is therefore forbidden to apply their attributes or mimic them (Wilson, 1997). There is, on the other hand, a second approach which supports adopting the Western model as a way to achieve modernization and calls for the general Westernization of individuals and of the entire society, including lifestyle and behavior. The third approach takes the middle path and is the most prevalent. It supports adopting the part of Western modernization that is generally thought to be conducive to the development and progress of Muslim society, while preserving the unique character, tradition and culture of Islam.

REFERENCES

Al-Azhari, M. (ed.) (2002), 'Personal consumption within the context of Islamic economics', Cairo, Egypt (in Arabic).

Al-Sarieti, A. (ed.) (2000), 'Food security and economic development from an Islamic perspective', Egypt: Dar Aljamaah Aljadida (in Arabic).

Amarah, M (ed.) (1996), *Islam and the Future*, Egypt: Dar Al-Rashad (in Arabic).

Asp, E.H. (1999), 'Factors influencing food decisions made by individual consumers', *Food Policy*, **24**, 287–94.

Bachar, Arik (ed.) (1998), *What is Islam?*, Tel-Aviv, Israel: Ahi-Assaf Printing Press.

Bailey, J.M. and J. Sood (1993), 'The effects of religious affiliation on consumer behavior: a preliminary investigation', *Journal of Managerial Issues*, **5** (3), 328–52.

Bell, D., T. Ho and C. Tang (1998), 'Determining where to shop: fixed and variable costs of shopping', *Journal of Marketing Research*, **35** (3), 352–69.

Betancourt, R., and D.A. Gautschi (1986), 'The evolution of retailing: a suggested economic interpretation', *International Journal of Research in Marketing*, **3** (4), 217–32.

Betancourt, R., and D.A. Gautschi (1990), 'Demand complementarities, household production and retail assortments', *Marketing Science*, **9** (Spring), 146–61.

Bonne, K. and W. Verbeke (2008a), 'Muslim consumer trust in Halal meat status and control in Belgium', *Meat Science*, **79** (1), 113–23.

Bonne, K. and W. Verbeke (2008b), 'Religious values informing Halal meat production and the control and delivery of Halal credence quality', *Agriculture and Human Values*, **25**, 35–47.

Bonne, K. I. Vermeir, F. Bergeaud-Blackler and W. Verbeke (2007), 'Determinants of halal meat consumption in France', *British Food Journal*, **109** (5), 367–86.

Butcher, K., B. Sparks and F. O'Callaghan (2002), 'Effect of social influence on repurchase intentions', *Journal of Services Marketing*, **16** (6), 503–14.

Canadian International Markets Bureau (2001), *Canadian International Markets Bureau*.

Carpenter, J. and M. Moore (2006). 'Consumer demographics, store attributes, and retail format choice in the US grocery market', *International Journal of Retail & Distribution Management*, **34** (6), 434–52.

Choi, Youngtae (2010), 'Religion, religiosity, and South Korean consumer switching behaviors', *Journal of Consumer Behaviour*, **9** (May–June), 157–71.

Craig, S., A. Ghosh and S. McLafferty (1984), 'Models of retail location process: a review', *Journal of Retailing*, **60** (1), 5–36.

Delener, N. (1990), 'The effects of religious factors on perceived risk in durable goods purchase decisions', *Journal of Consumer Marketing*, **7** (3), 27–38.

Delener, N. (1994), 'Religious contrasts in consumer decision behaviour patterns: their dimensions and marketing implications', *European Journal of Marketing*, **28** (5), 36–53.

Essoo, N. and S. Dibb (2004), 'Religious contrasts in consumer decision behavior', *European Journal of Marketing*, **28** (5), 36–53.

Essoo, N. and S. Dibb (2004), 'Religious influences on shopping behaviour: an exploratory study', *Journal of Marketing Management*, **20**, 683–712.

Farhangmehr, M., S. Marques and J. Silva (2000), 'Consumer and retailer perceptions of hypermarkets and traditional retail stores in Portugal', *Journal of Retailing and Consumer Services*, **7** (4), 197–206.

Farhangmehr, M., S. Marques and J. Silva (2000), 'Hypermarkets versus traditional retail stores – consumers' and retailers perspectives in Bragar: a case study', *Journal of Retailing and Consumer Services*, **8** (4), 189–98.

Findlay, Allan M. (1990), 'The changing role of women in the Islamic retail environment', in Allan M., Findlay, Ronan Paddison and John Dawson (eds), *Retailing Environments in Developing Countries*, London: Routledge, pp. 215–26.

Goldman, A. (2001), 'The transfer of retail formats into developing countries: the example of China', *Journal of Retailing*, **77** (Summer), 221–42.

Goldman, A. and H. Hino (2005), 'Supermarkets vs. traditional retail stores: diagnosing the barriers to supermarkets' market growth in an ethnic minority', *Journal of Retailing and Consumer Services*, **12** (4), 273–84.

Goldman, A., S. Ramaswami and R. Krider (1999), 'The persistent competitive advantage of traditional food retailers in Asia: wet markets continued dominance in Hong Kong', *Journal of Macromarketing*, **19**, 126–39.

Goldman, A., S. Ramaswami and R. Krider (2002), 'Barriers to the advancement of modern food retail formats: theory and measurement, *Journal of Retailing*, **78** (4), 281–95.

Hafez, K. (ed.) (2000), *The Islamic World and the West*, Leiden: Brill.

Halal Journal (2008), 'ICCI (the Islamic Chamber of Commerce and Industry) to Further Develop Global Halal Industry', available at: http://www.halaljournal.com

Harrell, Gilbert D. (ed.) (1986), *Consumer Behavior*, San Diego: Harcourt, Brace, Jovanovich.

Hino, H. (2010), 'Antecedents of supermarket formats' adoption and usage: a study in the context of non-Western customers', *Journal of Retailing and Consumer Services*, **17** (1), 61–72.

Hirschman, E.C. (1981), 'American-Jewish ethnicity: its relationship to some selected aspects of consumer behavior', *Journal of Marketing*, **45** (Summer), 102–10.

Hoch S.J., B. Kim, A. Montgomery and P.E. Rossi (1995), 'Determinants of store level price elasticity', *Journal of Marketing Research*, **32** (February), 17–29.

Just, R., A. Heiman and D. Zilberman (2007), 'The interaction of religion and family members' influence on food decisions', *Food Quality and Preference*, **18**, 786–94.

Kabasakal, H. and M. Bodur (2002), 'Arabic cluster: a bridge between East and West', *Journal of World Business*, **37** (1), 40–54.

Kanafani, A.S. (ed.) (1983), *Aesthetics and Ritual in The United Arab Emirates – The Anthropology of Food and Personal Adornment among Arabian Women*, The American University, Beirut, Lebanon.

Kaynak, E. (1985), 'Global spread of supermarkets: some experiences from Turkey', in E. Kaynak (ed.), *Global Perspectives in Marketing*, New York: Praeger, pp. 77–93.

Kaynak, E. and T. Cavusgil (1982), 'The evolution of food retailing systems: contrasting the experience of developed and developing countries', *Journal of the Academy of Marketing Science*, **10** (3), 249–69.

Kaynak, E. and A. Kara (2002), 'Consumer perceptions of foreign products: an analysis of product-country images and ethnocentrism', *European Journal of Marketing*, **36** (7/8), 928–49.

Kumar, P. (2002), 'The impact of performance, cost, and competitive considerations on the relationship between satisfaction and repurchase intent in business markets', *Journal of Service Research*, **5** (1), 55–68.

Kumcu, E., and M. Kumcu (1987), 'Determinants of food retailing in developing countries: the case of Turkey', *Journal of Macromarketing*, **7** (Fall), 26–40.

Lindrege, A. (2005), 'Religiosity and the construction of a cultural-consumption identity', *Journal of Consumer Marketing*, **22** (3), 142–51.

Lo, T.W.-C., Lau, H.-F., and G.-S. Lin (2001), 'Problems and prospects of supermarkets in China', *International Journal of Retail & Distribution Management*, **29** (2), 66–76.

Maruyama, M. and L.V. Trung (2007), 'Traditional bazaar or supermarkets: a probit analysis of affluent consumer perceptions in Hanoi', *International Review of Retail, Distribution and Consumer Research*, **17** (3), 233–52.

Maruyama, M. and L.V. Trung (2010), 'The nature of informal food bazaars: empirical results for Urban Hanoi, Vietnam', *Journal of Retailing and Consumer Services*, **17** (1), 1–9.

McDaniel, S. and J. Burnett (1990), 'Consumer religiosity and retail store evaluative criteria', *Journal of the Academy of Marketing Science*, **18** (2), 101–12.

Mennell, S., A. Murcott and A.H. Van Ootterloo (eds) (1992), *The Sociology of Food: Eating, Diet and Culture*, London: Sage.

Messinger, P.R. and C. Narasimhan (1997), 'A model of retail formats based on consumer economizing on shopping time', *Marketing Science*, **16** (1), 1–23.

Minkus-McKenna, D. (2007), 'The pursuit of Halal', *Progressive Grocer*, **86**, 17.

Miossec, Jean-Marie (1990), 'From suq to supermarket in Tunis', in Allan M. Findlay, Ronan Paddison and John Dawson (eds), *Retailing Environments in Developing Countries*, London: Routledge, pp. 227–422.

Mokhlis, Safiek (2006), 'The effect of religiosity on shopping orientation: an exploratory study in Malaysia', *Journal of American Academy of Business*, **9** (1), 64–74.

Mullen, K., R. Williams and K. Hunt (2000), 'Irish descent, religion and food consumption in the west of Scotland', *Appetite*, **34**, 47–54.

Musaiger, A.O. (1993), 'Socio-cultural and economic factors affecting food consumption patterns in the Arab countries', *Journal of the Royal Society for the Promotion of Health*, **113** (2), 68–74.

Oswald, L. (1999), 'Cultural swapping: consumption and the ethno genesis of middle-class Haitian immigrants', *Journal of Consumer Research*, **25**, 303–18.

Othman, Khalifa (1990), 'Patterns of supermarket use in Malaysia', in Allan M. Findlay, Ronan Paddison and John Dawson (eds), *Retailing Environments in Developing Countries*, London: Routledge, pp. 205–14.

Pan, Y. and G. Zinkhan (2006), 'Determinants of retail patronage: a meta-analytical perspective', *Journal of Retailing*, **82** (3), 229–43.

Pettinger, C., Holdsworth, M., and M. Gerber (2004), 'Psycho-social influences on food choice in Southern France and Central England', *Appetite*, **42** (3), 307–16.

Reardon, T. and J. Berdegue (2002), 'The rapid rise of supermarkets in Latin America: challenges and opportunities for development', *Development Policy Review*, **20** (4), 371–88.

Reardon, T. and J. Swinen (2004), 'Agrifood sector liberalization and the rise of supermarkets in former state-controlled economies: a comparative overview', *Development Policy Review*, **22** (5), 515–23.

Regenstein, J.M., M.M. Chaudry and C.E. Regenstein (2003), 'The kosher and halal food laws', *Comprehensive Reviews in Food Science and Food Safety*, **2** (3), 111–27.

Rosenberger, B. (1999), 'Arab cuisine and its contribution to European culture', in M. Saleem (ed.) (1993), *The Moslems and the New World Order*, London, UK: ISDS Books.

Saleem, M (ed.) (1993), *The Moslems and the New World Order*, London: ISDS Books.

Shatenstein, B. and P. Ghadirian (1997), 'Influences on diet, health behaviours and their outcome in select ethno-cultural and religious groups', *Nutrition*, **14** (2), 223–30.

Sood, J. and Y. Nasu (1995), 'Religiosity and nationality: an exploratory study of their effect on consumer behavior in Japan and the United States', *Journal of Business Research*, **34** (1), 1–9.

Steenkamp, J.-B.E.M. (1993), 'Food consumption behaviour', *European Advances in Consumer Research*, **1**, 401–9.

Steptoe, A. and T.M. Pollard (1995), 'Development of a measure of the motives underlying the selection of food: the food choice questionnaire', *Appetite*, **25**, 267–84.

Swanson, L.A. (1996), '1.19850 + billion mouths to feed: food linguistics and cross-cultural, cross-national food consumption habits in China', *British Food Journal*, **98** (6), 33–44.

Turly, L.W. and R. Milliman (2000), 'Atmospheric effects on shopping behavior: a review of the experimental evidence', *Journal of Business Research*, **49**, 361–71.

Veeck, A. and A. Burns (2005), 'Changing tastes: the adoption of new food choices in post-reform China', *Journal of Business Research*, **58** (5), 644–52.

Wilkes, R., J. Burnett and R. Howell (1986), 'On the meaning and measurement of religiosity in consumer research', *Journal of the Academy of Marketing Science*, **14** (1), 47–56.

Wilson, R. (ed.) (1997), *Economics, Ethics and Religion*, New York: NY University Press.

Yavas, U. and S. Tuncalp (1984), 'Perceived risk in grocery outlet selection: a case study in Saudi Arabia', *European Journal of Marketing*, **18**, 13–25.

Zain, O. and I. Rejab (1989), 'The choice of retail outlets among urban Malaysian shoppers', *International Journal of Retailing*, **4** (2), 35–45.

10 Understanding preference formation of functional food among Malaysian Muslims
Siti Hasnah Hassan

INTRODUCTION

Growing awareness concerning health and wellness among consumers has significantly changed their preferences and attitudes towards foods for specific use. The shift to better lifestyles and diets among consumers has created demand for food products that work as preventive measures against lifestyle related diseases and provide health benefits. This type of food is known as functional food. Functional food is believed to offer diverse health benefits beyond basic nutrition (Hilliam, 1996). As individuals become more interested in healthier lifestyles, more functional food brands appear on the market and consumers must select among them.

Food consumption is part of consumer identity, and the process of consumption involves tradition, social commitment, and health (Fischler, 1988; Ikeda, 1999; Lawrence and Germov, 1999). For centuries, it has been believed that foods and herbs have health-giving and curative properties (Sheehy and Morrissey, 1998). There is an old Chinese proverb saying that foods and medicine are isogenic (Arai, 2002). Both are equally important for preventing and treating disease as they come from the same sources; have the same uses; and are based on the same theories (Weng and Chen, 1996). Besides giving basic nutrition, some foods are believed to have a therapeutic effect on human health, which includes prolonging a healthy and active life, boosting physical and mental ability and lowering long-term health care expenses (Ahmad, 1996; Childs and Poryzees, 1997; Diplock et al., 1999; Hassan, 2008; Lawrence and Germov, 1999; Milner, 1999).

Over the past few years, the functional food market has witnessed enormous growth that has transformed it from a niche segment to mainstream. The global market for functional food is growing rapidly. It was estimated at approximately US$73.5 billion in 2005 and is expected to grow considerably (Justfood, 2006). The exact market size for this food is hard to estimate, however, because of the lack of a common definition around the world (Weststrate et al., 2002).

The rapidly expanding functional food market has attracted the medical and scientific communities to investigate how religion might affect health (Levin, 1996). Food is an important part of the religious and spiritual rituals for many faiths. Religious belief and practice influence dietary practice, health behaviour, and wellbeing (Ellison and Levin, 1998; King, 1990; Levin, 1994). The beliefs are complex and varied among individuals and communities, however. Most religions, including Islam, have guidelines regarding the consumption of food but little attention has been given to the relationship between wellbeing and religion. The Qur'an has specific guidelines relating to food and wellbeing, as evidenced in the following verse: 'Then to eat of all the produce (of the earth), and find with skill the spacious paths of its Lord: there issues from within their bodies a drink of varying colours, wherein is healing for men: verily in this is a sign for those who give thought' (Qur'an 16:69).

Muslims must follow certain dictates concerning how to live their lives; one of these is to eat *halal* foods. The market for *halal* food is expanding, amounting to US$346.7 billion annually, which is in tandem with the worldwide growth of an educated Muslim population that has higher purchasing power. Therefore, religion's role in health needs to be examined in a broad context.

Most information about Islam promotes negative stereotypes that characterize Muslims as an out-group (Bunzl, 2005; Laird, de Marrais, et al., 2007). Evidence shows that the existing consumer behaviour models do not yet account for the existence of consumers with differing value systems based on culture and cultural values (Douglas and Craig, 1997; Finucane and Holup, 2005; Hassan, 2008; Hassan et al., 2009). Therefore, the extant models may not be suitable in helping researchers and practitioners to understand Muslim preferences and consumption behaviour.

This study explores how preferences towards functional food formed among the Malay Muslims in Malaysia. The objective is to understand the role of culture and religious dietary practices and provide information for food practitioners and marketers to respect and respond to the needs of Muslim consumers. Malay Muslims in Malaysia are Asian and not of Arab descent. Their food selection is heavily influenced by traditional Malay culture and by the other major ethnic groups in Malaysia that co-exist in close proximity such as the Chinese and Indians. Most of the functional foods in Malaysia are herb-, spice- or marine-based and are directly related to Asian culture and tradition. Thus, there is a need to analyse the Malay culture and Islamic religion to enable marketers to segment the market to address the specific needs, motivations, perceptions, and attitudes shared by members of the cultural group.

DEFINITION OF FUNCTIONAL FOOD

The term functional food was first introduced in Japan in the mid-1980s to distinguish these products from medicine. In Japan, functional food refers to processed foods containing ingredients that aid specific bodily functions, in addition to being nutritious (Arai, 2002). Japan is the first and only country with a specific regulatory approval process for functional foods (Arai, 2002; Hasler, 1998; Kojima, 1996). FOSHU (Foods for Specified Health Use) regulations were introduced in 1991 and are administered by the Japanese Ministry of Health and Welfare (Arai, 1996). Currently Japan has more than 100 licensed FOSHU food products. There is no specific or universally accepted definition for functional food because of the different views held concerning this type of food in various countries, as well as by the respective researchers and food industry practitioners. It is generally agreed that functional food is food that provides health benefits beyond basic nutritional requirements. The International Food Information Council (IFIC) has proposed a simple definition of functional food – a 'modified food or food ingredient that may provide a health benefit beyond the traditional nutrients it contains' (International Food Information Council Foundation, 1998). The American Dietetic Association (ADA) has stated that functional foods include 'whole foods and fortified, enriched, or enhanced foods that have a potentially beneficial effect on health when consumed as part of a varied diet on a regular basis, at effective levels' (ADA Report, 2004, p. 817).

According to Bech-Larsen et al. (2001, p. 1), functional food is 'a concept, which covers foods that are enriched with various kinds of (naturally occurring) components/ substances (for example, vitamins, minerals or probiotic cultures) or modified in a way so that the product provides an additional physiological benefit that may prevent disease or promote health'. In the business context, functional food is an emerging industry that systematically researches, develops, produces and markets health-enhancing food products (Heasman and Mellentin, 2000).

To achieve a certain degree of conceptual equivalence, this study defines functional food as 'a category of food that has health-enhancing properties, and which is not a drug, chemical or vitamin and is not prescribed by doctors or other formally qualified medical practitioners' (Hassan, 2008, p. 2). Food and medicine have the same origin and are both intended to maintain human health; substances in functional food can have medicinal value but medicine itself is not a functional food (Hassan, 2008). Functional food is a food that can be procured like any other food but has health-enhancing properties.

FUNCTIONAL FOOD IN MALAYSIA

All cultures have preferred foods, which include actual and possible food sources in the marketplace. Cultural food preferences and eating patterns shape food choices from childhood (Sobal, 1998), thereby creating demands that influence food product improvement and development. Health food preference is the selection of one type of food that can be obtained from the marketplace over another. Preference plays an important role in the consumer decision making process and is constructed according to the task and context factors present during choice or preference elicitation (Bettman et al., 1998; Hoeffler and Ariely, 1999). The process of preference formation is dynamic, goal-directed and context-dependent (Kahneman and Tversky, 1979; Tversky and Kahneman, 1986), and is considered to be sensitive to the way a choice problem is portrayed (Fischhoff et al., 1980; Kahneman and Tversky, 1979; Tversky and Kahneman, 1986).

Foods with functional properties have been an important part of Asian culture for centuries, even though the term 'functional food' has not been commonly used (Tee, 2004); 'health food' is the usual terminology in most Asian countries. Knowledge of functional foods is often passed from generation to generation through oral traditions. For many years, Malaysians have supplemented their diets with naturally occurring substances. Malaysia has 8000 species of flowering plants (Ahmad, 1996) and about 6000 of these have medicinal value (Muhamad, 1991). Of these, 1200 are used in traditional medicine. Each of the three ethnic groups in Malaysia (Malay, Chinese and Indian) has its own beliefs about food and wellbeing and each has its own popular food with functional properties. The Malays have used herbs and plant roots from the rainforest as traditional dietary supplements for generations (Ahmad, 1996; Anonymous, 2005). Some of the popular Malay foods believed to boost vitality and prevent ageing, cancer, diabetes, and hypertension are mengkudu/noni juice (*Morinda citrifolia*) (Nandhasri et al., 2005; Wang et al., 2002), petai (*Parkia speciosa*) (Wong et al., 2006), pegaga (*Centella asiatica*) (Mohd Ilham et al., 1998), and tongkat ali or long jack (*Eurycoma longifolia*) (Mohd

Ilham et al., 1998). Other functional foods include spices (such as cumin, fennel seeds, pepper and turmeric), herbs such as kacip fatima (*Labisia pothoina*) and misai kucing (*Orthosiphon Stamineus*), various fruits, and vegetables such as peria katak (*Momordica charantia*).

In Malaysia, interest in functional foods is gaining momentum and some products and processes have been patented and commercialized (Ahmad, 1996). There is an increasing array of foods on the Malaysian health food market claiming to boost vitality, reverse ageing or cure and prevent specific diseases. Some of these functional foods are unprocessed, traditional and culturally based, while others are processed functional foods that are modified, fortified, or totally new modern foods. The modern functional food products are easier and more convenient to consume than the traditional functional foods. Examples include foods in liquid, capsule, or powdered forms or sometimes other foods such as instant coffee (3 in1), which are either flavoured or have a therapeutic food added, such as ginseng, lingzhi, black seed, honey, tongkat ali (*Eurycoma longifolia*), or juice enriched with folic acid, vitamin C or calcium.

THE MALAYS IN MALAYSIA

The Malays, who are non-Arab Muslims, constitute over one half of the nation's population and are the dominant ethnic group in Malaysia, both culturally and politically. To be considered Malay, one must be Muslim, speak the Malay language and observe and practice the traditions of the Malay culture.

Malay food and health beliefs are influenced by the Javanese, Indian, Arabic and local indigenous/aboriginal races. Traditional Malay culinary styles, food beliefs and medicines have been greatly influenced since ancient times by traders from Indonesia, India, the Middle East and China. According to Hirschman (1987), there is evidence of extensive contact between the Malays, Indians and Chinese lasting more than a thousand years (Lamb, 1964; Purcell, 1948, 1967). The Straits of Malacca were an early trading route for merchants between China, India and Arabia. These merchants not only traded goods, but also exchanged cultural values and medical beliefs (Laderman, 1983).

Malays classify food on its internal 'hotness', 'coldness' and *bisa* (allergy-causing food or food that makes our bodies feel weak or uncomfortable), These are beliefs that mirror ancient Chinese and Indian traditions and are in line with humoral theories emphasizing the balance of hot–cold and dry–moist oppositions in the diet from Greco-Arabic medicine (Laird et al., 2007).

Malay cooking incorporates ingredients such as spices, lemon grass, pandan (screwpine) leaves and kaffir (lime) leaves. Fresh herbs including daun kemangi (a type of basil), daun kesum (polygonum or Thai basil), nutmeg, kunyit (turmeric) and bunga kantan (wild ginger buds) are also used extensively in Malay dishes. Traditional spices such as cumin and coriander are used in conjunction with the Indian and Chinese spices of pepper, cardamom, star anise and fenugreek. Most of these herbs and spices are also believed to have some medicinal value.

Religious faith is one of the most important factors distinguishing Malays from non-Malays. Islamic values directly and indirectly influence the Malay lifestyle and food consumption. For Muslims there are two documents used as references for the basis of

Islamic law – the Qur'an, the revealed word of Allah (the Arabic word for God); and the *hadith*, a collection of acts and words of the Prophet Mohammed that were compiled after his death. The sayings and living habits of Prophet Mohammed are also referred to as the *sunnah*. Although the Qur'an and *sunnah* provide Muslims with certain food guidelines, ultimately it is the level of individual piety that guides Muslim consumer behaviour in choosing whether to consume a particular food product.

ISLAMIC DIETARY PRACTICE AND HEALTH

The Islamic faith encourages healthy lifestyles; however, research addressing health concerns specific to the Muslim population is rare. To a certain extent, Muslims believe that they are what they eat and that the food they consume will become their flesh and blood. Hence, they are advised to choose their food very carefully. Muslims are constrained by *halal* and *haram* in their food consumption. The Qur'an has specified that Muslims should only choose and consume lawful and wholesome foods: 'Eat of the good things which we have provided for you' (Qur'an 2:173).

Halal foods are permitted and include vegetables and most meat except for pork and its by-products. A product with *halal* certification is deemed to be fit for Muslim consumers. *Halal* foods are visually similar to other foods, but are set apart by their nature, processing, ingredients, handling and slaughter techniques (Canadian Council of Muslim Theologians, 2007; JAKIM, 2009). In Malaysia, the government is investing intensely in *halal* food industries to promote Malaysia as a global hub for *halal* products and services (Muhammad et al., 2009). The food industries in Malaysia follow the *halal* food guidelines for *halal* compliance to enable companies to receive an incentive from the Malaysian government. *Haram* foods, on the other hand, are prohibited in the Qur'an and include pig meat and pig by-products, animals improperly slaughtered or dead before slaughtering, animals killed in the name of anyone other than Allah, alcohol and intoxicants, carnivorous animals, birds of prey, land animals without external ears, blood and blood by-products and foods containing any of the above. See the Qur'an, chapter 5, verses 90–91 for the prohibition on alcohol and the following verse regarding meat: 'Forbidden to you (for food) are: dead animals – cattle-beast not slaughtered, blood, the flesh of swine, and the meat of that which has been slaughtered as a sacrifice for other than God . . .' (Qur'an 5:3).

There are also nine levels of food between *halal* and *haram,* including various designations meaning doubtful or questionable (Eliasi and Dwyer, 2002). These categories include foods containing ingredients such as gelatine, enzymes and emulsifiers, which Muslims are encouraged to avoid consuming. It is important to acknowledge that the concepts of *halal* and *haram* cover all aspects of Muslim life, not just food consumption. They are based on the interpretations of the Qur'an and the *hadith* by learned scholars of Islam – the *ulama*. This study focuses only on the food-related aspects of *halal* and *haram*.

Islam also has a holistic approach to spiritual and physical health. The Qur'an provides guidance on how individuals should treat their bodies with respect and nourish them not only with faith, but also with lawful and nutritious food (Stacey, 2009).

Health-related behaviour is an important issue to understand, to give us insight into behavioural prediction and behavioural change. Consumer health behaviour is dependent on the consumer level of perceived self-efficacy (Conner and Norman, 2005). In other words, human accomplishment and personal well-being are dependent on a strong sense of efficacy. Bandura (1994) defined perceived self-efficacy as 'people's beliefs about their capabilities to produce designated levels of performance that exercise influence over events that affect their lives' (p. 71).

In Islam, health is viewed as a blessing from Allah to mankind. This is evident in the following *hadith*, narrated by Ibn Majah (Yahya 2007): 'Ask Allah for certainty and health, for after being granted certainty, one is given nothing better than health.'

From this *hadith*, it is clear that as a Muslim, one needs to be grateful to Allah for entrusting one with good health and that one should at least try to look after one's health as much as possible. Furthermore, the Qur'an and the *sunnah* instruct all Muslims to protect their health by eating wholesome foods and living their lives in a state of purity. There are numerous examples of this in the Qur'an and *hadith* (see Table 10.1 for examples).

Islam promotes healthy living through eating wholesome and balanced food. A

Table 10.1 Specific food guidelines from the Qur'an

Dimension	Examples of verses
Lawful foods	'Eat of the good things which We have provided for you' (Qur'an, 2:172) 'Eat of what is lawful and wholesome on the earth' (Qur'an, 2:168) 'And He enforced the balance. That you exceed not the bounds; but observe the balance strictly; and fall not short thereof' (Qur'an, 55:7)
Wholesome and balanced foods (carbohydrates, protein, vitamins and minerals – grains, meat, milk, vegetables/ fruits, etc)	'He Who produced gardens, with trellises and without, and dates, and tilth with produce of all kinds, and olives and pomegranates, similar (in kind) and different (in variety): eat of their fruit in their season, but render the dues that are proper on the day that the harvest is gathered' (Qur'an, 6:141) 'And cattle He has created for you (men): from them you derive warmth, and numerous benefits, and of their (meat) you eat' (Qur'an, 16:5) 'With it He produces for you corn, olives, date-palms, grapes and every kind of fruit: verily in this is a sign for those who give thought' (Qur'an, 16:11) 'He Who has made the sea subject, that you may eat thereof flesh that is fresh and tender. . .' (Qur'an, 16:14) 'And verily in cattle (too) will you find an instructive sign. From what is within their bodies between excretions and blood, We produce, for your drink, milk, pure and agreeable to those who drink it' (Qur'an, 16:66) 'And from the fruit of the date-palm and the vine, you get out wholesome drink and food' (Qur'an, 16:67) '. . .and from it (the earth) we produced grain for their sustenance' (Qur'an, 36:33)

healthy nutritious diet must also be balanced, in order to maintain the balance that God has established in all things. Muslims should make sure that they undertake all necessary actions that are conducive to the preservation of good health. However, food must always be consumed in moderation. Direct reference has been made in the Qur'an regarding moderation in eating and drinking. Muslims are required to eat just enough to maintain their health and energy. This is in accordance with the guidance of Allah, as stated in this verse: '. . . eat and drink: But waste not by excess, for Allah loves not the wasters . . .' (Qur'an 7:31).

The Prophet Muhammad was reported (Agwan and Singh, 2006) to have stated that the reason for moderation is that: 'The stomach is the tank of the body and the veins go down to it. When the stomach is healthy the veins come back in a healthy condition, but when it is in a bad condition, they return diseased.'

Each food has specific benefits, therefore variety and moderation are essential for good health. A variety of foods every day will satisfy all the body's needs for carbohydrates, minerals, vitamins, proteins, and fats. Therefore, a balanced diet is not just about foods that one should avoid, it is about foods a person chooses to include. Many modern discoveries that have substantial support in the recent scientific literature signal the contribution of diet towards helping prevent life threatening illnesses.

THE STUDY

To develop an in-depth understanding of consumer experiences in a given culture, an ethnoconsumerist methodology together with constant comparative data analysis technique was used for this study. Ethnoconsumerism is used to study the consumption behaviour from the cultural perspective (Venkatesh, 1995) of Muslim consumers included in the study. This method provides a conceptual framework for studying consumer behaviour using theoretical categories generated within a given culture that allows for the study of cultural phenomena (Meamber and Venkatesh, 2000; Venkatesh, 1995).

Purposeful sampling (Patton, 1990, 2002) and theoretical sampling (Glaser, 1978; Glaser and Strauss, 1967) were carried out to achieve the objectives of the study. Purposeful sampling was used to find willing and suitable participants who consume functional foods and have knowledge of them. The intention was to collect the best data possible with an in-depth description of the culture or phenomenon (Speziali and Carpenter, 2003). In qualitative research the sample size is usually much smaller than in quantitative research (Patton, 1990, 2002). However the interviews were directed by theoretical sampling, which means that it is based on theoretically relevant constructs. In theoretical sampling, data collection is guided by an ongoing process of categorizing, sampling and interviews that continues until theoretical saturation is achieved (Glaser, 1978). Theoretical saturation is the point at which incremental learning is minimal because the researchers are observing phenomena seen before (Glaser and Strauss, 1967). It refers to a situation when no new values, themes, or issues arise regarding a category of data, and when the categories are well established and validated (Glaser and Strauss, 1967). Theoretical sampling cannot be planned before embarking on a theory-building study.

Based on purposeful sampling, middle class Malay Muslim consumers with different backgrounds (in terms of sex, age, education, employment status, experience with functional foods, and so on) were chosen with help from personal contacts. Personal contacts were used to help gain permission to conduct the study in communities and cultural societies. In-depth interviews were conducted to understand Malay Muslim consumers' preference towards functional food. The interviews were conducted until theoretical data saturation was achieved. Thirty-five Muslim informants were interviewed concerning their understanding in choosing and consuming functional foods.

The gathered data were transcribed and transferred to ATLAS.ti software to help manage the many concepts as they emerged from the comprehensive data set. Ongoing, computer-aided, line-by-line in-vivo coding was done each time the data were transcribed. The interview transcripts and field notes were analysed using the constant comparative method. This method is based on Glaser and Strauss's classical grounded theory principle. In this technique, incidents were compared with accumulated knowledge to develop categories and their properties, and delimit and write the theory (Glaser and Strauss, 1967). This is done by integrating incidents into properties. As the constant comparisons proceed, the researcher is able to make theoretical sense that will merge each comparison (Glaser and Strauss, 1967). Both approaches enable this study to be conducted at the emic level, which is within the culture.

Based on the constant comparative technique, all data were carefully examined by selecting individual words, phrases or stories that contained a single unit of meaning. In-vivo codes and code phrases were listed in full and then collapsed into groups of similar code phrases. The code phrases were compared within and between interviews. Similar code phrases were grouped and collapsed into conceptual categories or higher-level concepts (Glaser and Strauss, 1967; Strauss and Corbin, 1990). For the purpose of this chapter, only relevant and related data are discussed and included to provide insight into how the themes were developed.

KEY FINDINGS AND THEMES

Several core categories were identified from the constant comparative analysis. Further analysis included comparing and contrasting the emerging theory with similar existing literature, through which a substantive theory was developed to represent the central themes of the data. The framework (Figure 10.1) explains the link between the factors that directly influence the preference formation of functional food.

According to Wertenbroch and Carmon (1997), dynamic consumer preferences are frequently directed to the task-goal of managing internal or external resources. In this case study of Malaysian Muslims, it is clear that the main goal of consuming functional food is to obtain an ideal health state. However, consumer choice is constrained by the availability of internal resources such as the physiological, cognitive, or emotional resources that consumers bring to the purchase or consumption task. Using the emerging substantive theory, in Figure 10.1, the internal resources can be explained using factors such as cultural values, Islamic values, personal values and knowledge. The three value groups interact with each other to form an individual's values. For Muslims, these factors will undergo a series of considerations to ensure they do not conflict with their religion, customs, or food beliefs. This consideration can be called the value negotiation

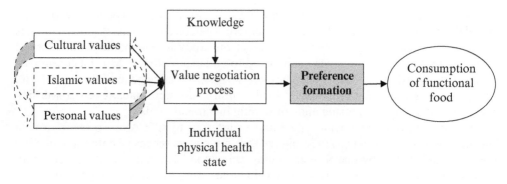

Figure 10.1   Preference formation of functional food

process in this study. Evidence from the literature also states that consumers appear to manage their internal hedonic resources by directly modifying their preferences as a function of whether they expect repeated exposure to hedonic stimuli and as a function of the cost of avoiding aversive stimuli (Gibbs, 1997).

The following section includes a discussion of each of the main themes or core categories identified to develop the substantive theory of preference formation towards functional food among Muslim consumers in Malaysia.

ISLAMIC VALUES

The Islamic religion is an ongoing part of the daily life of Muslims. It is difficult to discuss Islamic values as a separate category from cultural and personal values in this model. This is because the category is ingrained and embedded in cultural and personal values. However, according to Ebady (2004), Islamic values are different from Muslims' (cultural) values because Islamic values are the values portrayed in the Qur'an and the practice of the Prophet Muhammad, whereas Muslims' values are also derived from the cultures of their particular communities.

Malaysian Muslims' functional food practices are mostly created based on their cultural beliefs and customs, which have been passed down from generation to generation. These values will be discussed in the next section. However, recently, because of globalization, there are more functional food products available based on the foods mentioned in the Qur'an and *hadith,* with foods or ingredients mostly found in Arab countries. One of the best-known Islamic-based functional food brands currently on the market is called 'Tok Guru'. 'Tok Guru' literally means 'senior teacher' or Islamic scholar. Tok Guru products are produced locally and the company is owned by local Malays. The products are based on the foods mentioned in the Qur'an and *hadith* and are blessed with an invocation by a famous Islamic religious teacher in Malaysia. A part of the company profits is donated to the 'Development Fund of Religious Schools' in Malaysia.

An example of one of the products is Juice Tok Guru, which is extracted from a combination of seven foods mentioned in the Qur'an and *hadith*, which are pomegranate, raisins, dates, black seed, saffron, honey and olives. Most of these raw materials are from Mediterranean plants and, therefore, are imported from overseas. The juice is believed to increase energy, improve skin complexion, prevent drowsiness and fatigue, strengthen the nervous system, and strengthen memory, especially in children. Another product is Tok Guru Coffee, which is coffee with added black seed (*Nigella sativa*), *Ganoderma*, tongkat ali, and honey. Honey and black seeds are therapeutic foods. *Ganoderma* is a type of mushroom that is thought to have therapeutic effects such as antioxidant, anti-cancer, and antiviral properties. Tongkat ali (*Eurycoma longifolia*) is believed to boost vitality, reduce body fat, and alleviate hypertension (Hamzah and Yusof, 2003; Mohd Ilham et al., 1998).

Evidence from the statements given by the study's informants about Islamic-based functional foods is given below.

My children always have colds and coughs at least twice in a month. Before this I tried many other brands of vitamins and supplements but they do not work. But after taking a delicious strawberry flavoured 'Tok Guru' juice – surprisingly the colds and coughs disappeared for good. Alhamdulillah [Praise be to God] even my children's learning ability has improved. They are stronger now. (Zimah, female, 35)

My child often has a stomach ache, especially in the morning, but after taking the juice he is not sick anymore. I have used four bottles, and I will continue to use Tok Guru products. (Misna, female, 38)

I have a six-year-old child that has difficulty in reading smoothly. At first he did not like the juice but with God's help he started to take the juice. Surprisingly, one day, after coming back from school he was able to read smoothly without any difficulty. After that, we started taking the juice every morning before breakfast. Thanks to Allah who has guided me to take Juice Tok Guru. (Nerina, female, 40)

I am thankful to the management of products of 'Tok Guru' and grateful to Allah; taking the juice has helped me to overcome irregular menstrual cramps. (Sawani, female, 26)

The juice is easy to consume and very powerful although it is a bit sweet. After I took the product I feel more energetic and focused. (Aisyah, female, 36)

From the quotes, it can be seen that the informants trust and believe in Islamic based products because the benefits of these foods are stated in the Qur'an and *hadith*. In the past, it was difficult to obtain plants or fruits from the Mediterranean countries. Normally, it is a tradition for people returning from the *hajj* and *umra* pilgrimages in Mecca to give fruits like dates or figs, and Zam Zam water as gifts to families, relatives and friends. Dates can also be found easily during the Ramadan (fasting) month. Most Muslims will break their fast with dates in accordance with the practice of Prophet Muhammad.

Although the use of these foods is mentioned in the Qur'an and *hadith*, consumers still need to use ingredients in the correct amounts. For example, although honey has considerable efficacy, it has a high glucose content, which might be troublesome for diabetics. This does not mean they cannot use honey at all, as they could apply honey to wounds caused by diabetes, as practiced in ancient Egypt, and in Greek post-operative procedures (Datta et al., 2009; Simon et al., 2008). Honey is not just a sugar, but also a complex combination of enzymes, organic acids, esters, antibiotic agents, trace minerals, and unidentified components that have therapeutic effects (Simon et al., 2008).

The Islamic perspective gives a clue to the therapeutic nature of foods and also teaches moderation in taking the foods. The informants' discourses and practices suggest that invoking the Islamic perspective draws attention to the therapeutic nature of foods and highlights the importance of moderation in taking food. Moderation appears as highly important, especially for consumers already suffering from chronic illnesses.

CULTURAL VALUES

Constant comparative analysis shows that traditional cultural practices reflect the cultural values of Malays, such as their beliefs about food, health, and illness. Cultural values are believed to affect all aspects of food behaviour and form the foundation that motivates food choice and consumption. According to Pachter et al. (2000), Fieldhouse (1986), and Sobal (1998), food, eating, and nutrition are strongly shaped by customs and culture. There are thus cultural value differences among consumers when it comes to issues such as healthy eating, sleeping, exercise and taking supplements or vitamins.

Oral tradition and food beliefs are the two conceptual categories emerging under the core category 'cultural values,' that influence functional food preference. Malays consume traditional foods that are believed to have certain ingredients that promote health. For instance, Malays have used rainforest herbs and plant roots as traditional supplements for centuries. They believe these herbs have natural functional effects. This traditional knowledge is passed on by older generations to younger generations. This is evident from statements given by the informants.

> Some foods are very common in my culture and you can easily get them from the fresh food market. But recently, I noticed the prices of some of these vegetables are getting very high because of their medicinal values. For example, pegaga. I personally know that pegaga is very good to improve memory and youthfulness because it has antioxidant properties and other medicinal values. It is common knowledge in my ethnic group. (Aminah, female, 35)

> I grew up in Kelantan. There are many vegetables and wild plants that I used to eat as *ulam* (plants that can be taken raw like salad) when I lived with my mother. My mother used to tell me all sorts of stories and the benefits of each plant we eat. They all have some kind of medicinal values and are very good for keeping us [women] young, slim and healthy, especially after giving birth. (Cik Yam, female, 45)

From the quotes, it can be seen that the informants obtain knowledge concerning a particular functional food by word of mouth sources including close family members or the Malay community. Oral tradition is a valuable source of learning about one's own culture, and it helps develop cultural values (Chamarik, 1999). Ahmad (1996) states that consumers' traditional food knowledge and their food beliefs are inherited from generation to generation. Bakker (2003) also indicates that the knowledge obtained from oral tradition is the most preferred and trusted source of knowledge.

Malays also tend to classify foods, illnesses, and traditional remedies based on a 'hot' or 'cold' bodily effect. This food belief is evident in a few quotations from the informants. It is clear that an individual must find the food that is compatible with their own body system. This knowledge is passed on verbally and shared among community members. For instance, cold food is believed to have an uncomfortable 'airy effect' on some people. A few informants from the Malay ethnic group said that they would add certain ingredients, such as spices or extra cloves of garlic to balance the airy effect of cold foods. For example, because most plant roots (for example, long jack or tongkat ali) have a heating effect on the body they must be taken with other food that has a cooling effect.

> The processed or modernized traditional food, especially the brand that I am consuming now, has been balanced up (hot and cold) because this food has undergone scientific research and been tested for many years before being commercialized. But individual body systems are different. They have to experience the food themselves before saying which functional food will give the best results. (Zainab, female, 60)

> You cannot take any food in excessive amounts because some foods can be very *bisa* [food that makes our bodies feel weak or uncomfortable]. And the older I get the more foods that I have to avoid. For example, I totally avoid taking jackfruit and certain types of bananas. I have to watch out what I eat and try to understand the effect of each food on my body. (Cik Yam, female, 45)

> If you want to use the pure one (functional food) you must have knowledge of how to prepare it with accurate measurements. But sometimes the traditional practitioners already pack the spices, herbs and plant roots for sale. They are the experts and I trust them. Besides, it makes my life easier. I just have to boil them and drink it. . . . this is because some of the herbs have heat or cold effects and sometimes your body system cannot adjust if the measurement is not right. (Malik, male, 50)

> Only the traditional herbal practitioners know how to balance the different types of food or herbs (cold and hot effect of the foods) so the foods will not affect the harmony of our body system. Sometimes you know about these things from your parents or through personal experience. (Faizal, male, 30)

It is clear from the analysis that oral traditions inherited from previous generations influence functional food consumption by virtue of being an integral part of the medium for transferring or learning culture. This parallels Bakker (2003) who stated that some aspects of culture, customs and traditions are passed on verbally, even though written records of cultures may exist.

PERSONAL VALUES

Personal values were elicited by asking the informants to give their main reason for choosing a particular functional food. The question was based on the specific perceived attributes of functional food and the consequences that the informant wanted to achieve by consuming the food. As stated earlier, consumers use functional food to obtain the desired ends through the benefits yielded by the food's attributes. Because of oral tradition, they also have knowledge, transmitted from generation to generation, of certain culturally embedded functional foods. Desired ends reflect the consumers' personal values.

Rokeach (1973) distinguished between two sets of values: instrumental values and terminal values. Consumers may apply either or both sets of values to achieve their goals. Instrumental values reflect a chosen way of reaching 'end values', for example, behavioural characteristics that are socially desirable. Examples of instrumental values that emerged in the analysis are: independent (taking care of oneself, being self reliant and self sufficient), responsibility (taking care of family, being a good employee, being a good Muslim), obedient (following religion, following cultural/family traditions, being a good mother, wife, or employee), cheerful (feeling healthy or energetic) and loving (being a good mother/wife/child).

Consumers may use terminal values to obtain the desired ultimate modes of life, such as inner harmony or happiness. Results from this study reflect and reveal how consumers may use terminal values to obtain the desired ultimate modes of life, such as inner harmony (peaceful life, maintaining health), being a good person (eating *halal* food, performing prayers and the pilgrimage), happiness (freedom from illness, living a healthy lifestyle), family security (being with loved ones such as family members), freedom (freedom from illness and having the ability to perform prayers), belonging (enjoying more time with family), self esteem (feeling good about oneself) and a comfortable and exciting life (feeling healthy, strong, and energetic, having a clear state of mind, being free from any illness). These terminal values are the end states that informants hope to achieve. Instrumental values are modes of achieving these terminal values. These values were identified from statements made by the informants:

> Health is really important for any human being. People are willing to do anything to have a healthy body and mind state. If consuming functional food can help to achieve good health then why not just take it? (Faizal, male, 30)

> When you are healthy you can do all sorts of things. I am a working mother . . . it means I work 24/7. I need to be strong and stay healthy to look after my family and to be a good employee. (Maria, female, 38)

> . . . if you are sick then you will feel very weak; you become a moody person and so stressful with everyday life. Your face becomes dull and pale. The people near you will also feel the impact and be unhappy because of you. (Latifah, female, 50)

> . . . with good health, I can do my job as an employee of my company and also be a good Muslim. I can do my prayers and go to Mecca to perform the pilgrimage. (Razak, male, 62)

> I'm practicing a modern and healthy lifestyle. . . . I always take and prefer modern health foods that are *halal*. (Faizal, male, 30)

The basic values that all the informants hold are the Islamic values or Islamic way of life. This is because of the specific Islamic guidelines that they have to obey in order to be Muslims. The level of piety concerning the Islamic religion itself is one important factor for this value. Schwartz and Bilsky (1990) asserted that because values are goal-oriented, they are a second facet of fulfilling individual and collective interests until each value is achieved. Personal values are enduring beliefs, preferable states or ideal situations that motivate and guide consumer behaviour, evaluation and decision processes (Rokeach, 1973). These values are often the underlying determinants of consumer attitudes and consumption behaviour (Homer and Kahle, 1988; Scott and Lamont, 1977).

Consumers develop their values throughout their lives. Self-conception, self-esteem, personal experience and changes in society can shape individual personal values (Rokeach, 1979). Malaysia has experienced rapid structural change and social transformation (Embong, 1998), which has created a modern generation quite different from previous generations. According to Yau (1994), consumers may have a few culturally based values, but they acquire hundreds of personal values throughout their lives. This statement is particularly true for functional food consumption. Evidence from the data analysis and the literature shows that informants acquire knowledge of functional foods from various sources and then construct a preference for functional food. Because of economic and social transformation, these values might not be the same as those of previous generations.

INDIVIDUAL PHYSICAL HEALTH STATE

This study's informants were motivated to consume food with functional properties because of its perceived healthiness. Functional foods are believed to provide health benefits beyond basic nutritional needs, such as preventing modern lifestyle diseases. Most Malays believe that foods and medicine are equally important for preventing and treating disease. There is increasing scientific evidence to support the functional role of certain foods in human health. Most of these foods are believed to boost vitality, prevent cancer and other illnesses, for example, turmeric (Krishnaswamy, 1996), mushrooms (Chang, 1996), red yam, mengkudu/noni juice (*Morinda citrifolia*) (Nandhasri et al., 2005; Wang et al., 2002), petai (*Parkia speciosa*) (Wong, et al., 2006), pegaga (*Centella asiatica*) (Mohd Ilham et al., 1998), and tongkat ali (*Eurycoma longifolia*) (Mohd Ilham et al., 1998)

The physical health state of the informants plays an important role in influencing functional food consumption. Nevertheless the motivation to consume functional food products depends on a variety of complex relationships. The perceived benefits of functional food are the major motive for individuals to consume food with functional properties. This is supported by the data analysis of the informants' statements:

I do not have any health problem yet . . . maybe in the future if I have any symptoms of health problems then maybe I will be more concerned and serious in choosing my food choice. Maybe then I will look for functional food. But for the time being, I just take some simple *ulam* (vegetables and herbs) or fruits that have antioxidant and medicinal values. (Maria, female, 38)

I'm afraid of any type of illness. I am getting old each day so I better prevent it, even before it happens. I am 45 years old and I am constantly looking for foods that can improve my health and restore my youthfulness. (Cik Yam, female, 45)

My previous health problems motivated me to look for food that has curative properties that can cure and prevent my health problems other than medicine prescribed from doctors. There are many traditional and modernized traditional functional foods available on the market with good testimony. (Latifah, female, 50)

When I was young I never paid much attention to the food I ate. At home, my wife cooks for me and when I am at work I always eat out with my friends. But now, I suffer from high blood pressure and diabetes. I have to be very careful in my food selection. Nowadays, I only eat at home.

> Besides medicine from the hospital, I also take modern health foods, for example, morinda juice [mengkudu]. This juice is very good for diabetics and for high blood pressure. (Razak, male, 62)

The informants tend to believe advertising claims that traditional and modernized functional foods offer health benefits, especially when these claims are supported by scientific evidence and testimonials from other users. Informants also trust oral traditions about the benefits of functional food, especially when oral traditions and scientific evidence coincide, as show by the following statements:

> Currently I'm taking modernized traditional functional food. Some of these brands have a good reputation and name. These products are specifically formulated for women's health. I do not mind paying a lot of money for them because the products are for my own health and benefit. (Cik Yam, female, 45)

> There are many traditional and modernized traditional functional foods available on the market with good testimony. I did manage to find modern functional foods that are suitable for me. It is really easy to consume, and now I manage to overcome my health problem. (Latifah, female, 50)

Health beliefs clearly play a crucial role in determining the acceptance of functional food. Health is an important motivator for consuming functional food. In this study, informants with current health issues or a family history of health problems were more attracted to functional foods. These people look for foods that might cure or prevent illnesses such as heart disease, diabetes, cancer, hypertension or other debilitating conditions. These informants recognized oral traditions and were interested in culturally based functional food from their own and other cultures. Generally, they were more flexible about accepting traditional or modern functional foods, as long as the food offered curative benefits.

KNOWLEDGE

In general, informants are knowledgeable about functional food. This knowledge is acquired throughout life, commencing in early childhood. The knowledge is likely to be reinforced by experience. Some knowledge may be lost, but some early food experiences can last a lifetime. For example, oral tradition is one of the important sources for each ethnic group for acquiring knowledge concerning traditional functional food. Some of the statements extracted from the transcribed interviews that support knowledge as a core category are:

> I get this knowledge from my mother, grandmother, sister, and friends and sometimes from my own experience and reading. (Cik Yam, female, 45)

> I am afraid of taking pure traditional medicines or food because my knowledge about this food is not good. I do not really know which food is cold and which one is hot [heat effect]. Some say that plant roots and some herbs have heat effect. (Latifah, female, 50)

> . . . but I consumed it because of its health benefits. I think maybe because of my limited knowledge I always take and prefer modern health foods that are *halal*. Besides there are so many advertisements about these products on television, radio and [in] magazines. Sometimes it is

recommended by a friend. You really feel strong and energetic after consuming this drink [3 in 1 long jack and ginseng coffee mix]. (Faizal, male, 30)

I just take chicken tonic/soup from BRAND'S during the confinement period. It will restore your health. It is easy to consume and has a proven track record. Besides it has been on the market for so long. (Mila, female 38)

Knowledge plays an important role in educating the consumer but knowledge alone does not ensure a healthy lifestyle (Nestle et al., 1998). Consumers use nutritional knowledge to link diet to health and change their eating habits. Most of this knowledge is acquired from various sources of information about functional food, including formal and informal learning, mass media and advertising. These sources provide information about the functional foods of their own and other ethnic groups. Some modern functional foods are very common in the Malaysian health food market. The information gained through word of mouth and oral tradition is the easiest to obtain and put into practice. This is information that is normally acquired from trusted people such as close family members or friends.

For example, BRAND'S products have been on the market for more than 100 years and have obtained both *halal* certification and the ISO 9002 manufacturing standard. BRAND'S Essence of Chicken (BEC) was commercially launched as food for children and invalids in 1835. The first shipment of BEC arrived in Singapore in the 1920s. Today the company produces many types of functional food products that enhance health, incorporating traditional Chinese medicine herbs such as American ginseng, lingzhi, tangkwei and cordycpes. Almost all the informants in this study had heard of BRAND'S products, even though they are Chinese-based health tonics. Knowledge about them has passed from the Chinese to the Malay ethnic group via advertising, social interaction and word of mouth. Some other Malay traditional herbal products are also heavily advertised on television, on the radio and in magazines. The promoters stress the importance of inner beauty and appearance (for example, radiant skin, slim figure and youthfulness) and target young women who are concerned about their figures and image.

Knowledge then comes from both personal and impersonal sources. The knowledge gained may not always be accurate and it seems to be acquired passively, rather than actively.

VALUE NEGOTIATION PROCESS

Today, consumers can choose from a variety of modern and culturally based functional foods. Sometimes informants may find that certain foods may conflict with their religion, customs, food beliefs or personal values. In this study, evidence shows that informants subconsciously negotiate or manage their values every time they make a decision to consume or not consume a selected functional food. There are many factors that informants consider before they choose certain functional foods. The informants' statements below illustrate the salient concepts of value negotiation:

I do not totally reject traditional or totally accept modern functional food. Knowledge from reading and talking to others is important. Testimonials and experience from others are also very important in influencing which health or functional food I choose. I need some kind of evidence to make the right choice. (Aminah, female, 35)

Besides *halal*, other important factors that I have to consider whether to consume functional food or not are the taste, smell, price, availability and easiness of preparing the food. (Latifah, female, 50)

I look at the health benefits of the food and suitability of the food to my body type. (Maria, female, 38)

I prefer the modernized functional food in powder form, capsule, fortified or modified so it will not taste bitter. (Cik Yam, female, 45)

. . . if it is ready to eat health food it must be *halal*. (Razak, male, 30)

I prefer to only take traditional food like *ulam* and certain herbs that I know. I have been taking this food since I was small. (Zainab, female, 60)

I take products from BRAND'S. Products from this brand are really good and have a proven track record. (Mila, female, 38)

. . . some of them are processed traditional food. It is still considered as a traditional functional food. Besides, these products are easy to consume. I can take them anywhere I go. However, for me the end result is very important. (Latifah, female, 50)

As illustrated in the above quotes, informants negotiate their values by considering cultural characteristics, such as religion and food beliefs; physical characteristics, such as state of health; and product characteristics, such as price, brand, taste, smell and easiness to consume. Other important factors to consider are individual and contextual influences and personal product experiences in relating to functional foods. Consumers' past choices of and experiences with functional food are important sources of evidence about their choices. Consumer experiences act as a foundation for their preference structures, and the processes associated with such experiences lead to preferences that stabilize over time (Hoeffler and Ariely, 1999).

The results indicate that consumers do not spend much time thinking consciously about their consumption choices, nor are they aware of their values, until they face choices or personal values that are inconsistent with their religion. Value conflicts make it necessary to prioritize values (Connors et al., 2001). In this study, the informants indicated that the chosen functional food must be *halal* before they consider other attributes.

THEORETICAL IMPLICATIONS

This study has examined Muslim consumers' preferences in choosing functional food for the practice of a healthy lifestyle. The research contributes to the existing literature by addressing how Muslim consumers living in multicultural societies develop preferences towards functional food. The model presented serves as a foundation to explore and understand Muslim consumers' attitudes regarding the preference formation of functional food. Studies addressing culture, religion and consumption have not been tailored to the unique facets of the field, as most research has focused on developed countries and has largely ignored the developing world (Douglas and Craig, 1997; Finucane and Holup, 2005; Steenkamp, 2005; Steenkamp and Burgess, 2002). The model offers a new perspective on how Muslim consumers in multicultural societies incorporate their Islamic values in developing preferences towards functional food.

IMPLICATIONS FOR ISLAMIC MARKETING

Studying consumer behaviour is an integral part of successful strategic marketing because it enables marketers to understand and predict how consumers will act (Schiffman and Kanuk, 2002). Preferences are learned and developed over time. A food manufacturer or a marketer needs to understand how consumers, especially specific ethnic groups, construct their preferences for functional foods. Table 10.2 summarizes the specific marketing actions and strategies that could be applied to address each core category developed for this model.

The current study provides us with an understanding of the effects of various interpretations concerning the consumption habits of Malaysian Muslims. The model developed has identified the important factors that consumers consider in forming preferences towards functional foods. Insight into the importance of respective dimensions allows marketers to design value-added functional food products.

The knowledge of Muslim consumers' preferences will help support the selection of appropriate target markets and provide a basis for marketing-controlling activities. In addition, it provides managers with the information necessary for successfully tailoring products to market segments by communicating the benefits of functional food within a specific segment. Insight into segment characteristics in terms of lifestyle supports managerial decisions concerning the selection, combination, and design of communications media to promote functional food products. For example, implementing *halal* signage will show that the products are clean, safe, nutritious and produced under the stringent requirements of Islamic dietary law. As such, a certified *halal* product is not only welcomed by Muslim consumers locally and worldwide but is acceptable to non-Muslim consumers as well because *halal* certified products represent a symbol of quality.

CONCLUSION

This study provides knowledge concerning how Malay Muslim consumers in the multicultural society of Malaysia construct their preferences for functional foods. The predictive power of the theory developed is limited to phenomena in the area from which it was developed; the model can be used as a basis to understand functional food consumption by Malay Muslims. As Muslims, the Malay consumers' main concern is whether the functional foods they consume are *halal*, especially as sometimes the food may originate from other ethnic groups. This attitude reflects the Islamic values the Malays hold as Muslims.

The model developed is limited as it only focuses on Malay Muslims' functional food consumption in Malaysia, which is studied using qualitative methodology. However, the

Table 10.2   Core categories and recommendations for specific marketing action

Core category	Subcategory (Properties)	Marketing action suggested
Cultural values	• Traditional functional food (tradition, common food in the culture and continuity) • Food belief (cold food, hot food) (heating effect to the body), *bisa* (airy food or allergy foods) • Religion (*halal*) • Oral tradition (trusted information, testimony and evidence) • Ethnic tradition/cultural ritual • Roles in the family (leader (husband), mother, wife, daughter, son)	• Marketers may re-position existing products to take into account ethnic culture, traditional knowledge and food beliefs • New product design with attributes that are connected to the cultural values
Islamic Values	• *halal* • Foods mentioned in the Qur'an and *hadith*	• Opportunity for food industry to develop new products based on foods mentioned in the Qur'an and *hadith*. • Alliances with Middle East companies to cultivate new business propositions. This is because most of these foods originate from countries in the Middle East
Health motives	• Ageing, health history and rising chronic diseases and medical cost	• Opportunity for food industry to develop products to cure/prevent specific health problems • Opportunity to develop accurate health promotion information to induce behavioural changes and positive attitude towards functional food products
Knowledge	• Oral tradition, word of mouth, advertisements and mass media	• Communication that emphasizes the benefits and effectiveness of functional foods can give consumers a more accurate and complete view of the product • Marketers could integrate the results identifying their marketing campaigns to improve consumer understanding of the importance of functional foods • Governments could help consumers to improve public health by communicating effectively the benefits of functional food
Personal values	• Education, knowledge, social interaction, socioeconomic change	• Food industry practitioners can build the functional approach to values into their product development and marketing strategies

Table 10.2   (continued)

Core category	Subcategory (Properties)	Marketing action suggested
	• Terminal values – ultimate value in life (comfortable life, happiness, inner harmony, family security, freedom, self-respect, social recognition • Instrumental values – means to achieve ultimate state of life (responsibility, obedient, cheerful, loving, independent and self-controlled)	• Terminal value advertisements should emphasize life-accomplishments and portray 'states of being' or the ultimate goals in life • Instrumental value advertisements should promote the utilitarian and tangible benefits of the product by presenting detailed information to facilitate judgement • Advertising messages can also promote the symbolism of functional food products through metaphors that illustrate the kinds of people and social groups who consume the food • Advertisements should also portray states of being or ultimate goals, which should encourage consumers to judge the product on the basis of their terminal values
Value negotiation	• Health motive • Knowledge • Food belief • Resources • Brand • Price • Time constraint • *halal*	• Food producers would be wise to consider value negotiations, such as how consumers weigh sensory perceptions (taste); monetary considerations (cost of product); and convenience (easy to prepare and consume) • Marketers should integrate the development of personal food choice systems that incorporate value negotiations and behavioural strategies in the marketing campaign for functional food products

model has the potential to be the basis for further exploration. Therefore, it is proposed that the future extensions of the concept could investigate possible additions to the number of dimensions examined in this study. Health benefits associated with functional food seem to have particular significance. The concepts and measures need to be refined and developed in order to better understand the preference of functional food as a source of market value not only for Malaysian Muslims but also for other countries with a Muslim majority population.

REFERENCES

ADA (American Dietetic Association) Report (2004), 'Position of the American Dietetic Association: functional foods', *Journal of The American Dietetic Association*, **104** (5), 814–26.

Agwan, A.R. and N.K. Singh (eds) (2006), *Encyclopaedia of the Holy Qur'an: Medicine – Eating Habit*, vol. 3, India: Global Vision Publishing House, p. 828.

Ahmad, S. (1996), 'Research and development on functional foods in Malaysia', *Nutrition Reviews*, **54** (11), S169.

Anonymous (2005), 'Rainforest herbs: the wisdom of mother nature'. Retrieved 20 January 2005, from http://www.rainforestherbs.com.my/introduction.html.

Arai, S. (1996), 'Studies on functional foods in Japan – state of the art,' *Bioscience, Biotechnology, and Biochemistry*, **60**, 9–15.

Arai, S. (2002), 'Global view on functional foods: Asian perspectives', *British Journal of Nutrition*, **88** (S2), 139–43.

Bakker, E.J. (2003), 'Homer as an oral tradition', *Oral Tradition*, **18** (1), 52–4.

Bandura, A. (1994), 'Self-efficacy', in V.S. Ramachaudran (ed.), *Encyclopedia of Human Behavior*, vol. 4, New York: Academic, Press pp. 71–81.

Bech-Larsen, T., K.G. Grunert and J. B. Poulsen (2001), 'The acceptance of functional foods in Denmark, Finland and the United States: a study of consumers' conjoint evaluations of the qualities of functional food and perceptions of general health factors and cultural values', Aarhus School of Business, MAPP working paper, 73.

Bettman, J.R., M.F. Luce and J.W. Payne (1998), 'Constructive consumer choice processes', *Journal of Consumer Research*, **25** (December), 187–217.

Bunzl, M. (2005), 'Between anti-Semitism and Islamophobia: some thoughts on the new Europe', *American Ethnologist*, **32** (4), 499–508.

Canadian Council of Muslim Theologians (2007), 'Halal guidelines'. Retrieved 23 July 2007, from http://www.jucanada.org/halalguidelines.html.

Chamarik, S. (1999), 'Oral tradition in Thailand: a development perspective,' Paper presented at Collection and Safeguarding the Oral Tradition, a Satellite Meeting of 65th IFLA Council and General Conference, Bangkok, Thailand, 16–19 August.

Chang, R. (1996), 'Functional properties of edible mushrooms', *Nutrition Reviews*, **54** (11), S91.

Childs, N.M., and G.H. Poryzees (1997), 'Foods that help prevent disease: consumer attitudes and public policy implications', *Journal of Consumer Marketing*, **14** (6), 433–47.

Conner, M., and P. Norman (2005), *Predicting Health Behaviour* (2nd edn), Buckingham, England: Open University Press.

Connors, M., C.A. Bisogni, J. Sobal and C.M. Devine (2001), 'Managing values in personal food systems', *Appetite*, **36** (3), 189–200.

Datta, H.S., S.K. Mitra and B. Patwardhan (2009), 'Wound healing activity of topical application forms based on Ayurveda', *eCAM*, 1–10.

Diplock, A.T., P.J. Agget, M. Ashwell, F. Bornet, E.B. Fern and M.B. Roberfroid (1999), 'Scientific concepts of functional foods in Europe: consensus document', *British Journal of Nutrition*, **81**, S1–S27.

Douglas, S.P., and C.S. Craig (1997), 'The changing dynamic of consumer behavior: implications for cross-cultural research', *International Journal of Research in Marketing*, **14** (4), 379–95.

Ebady, A. (2004), 'Islamic values vs. Muslim values', 1 July, available at http://darulislam.info/Article60.html.

Eliasi, J.R., and J.T. Dwyer (2002), 'Kosher and halal: religious observances affecting dietary intakes', *Journal of the American Dietetic Association*, **102** (7), 911–13.

Ellison, C.G., and J.S. Levin (1998), 'The religion-health connection: evidence, theory, and future directions', *Health Education and Behavior*, **25** (6), 700–20.

Embong, A.R. (1998), 'Social transformation: the state and the middle classes in post-independence Malaysia', in Z. Ibrahim (ed.), *Cultural Contestations: Mediating Identities in a Changing Malaysian Society*, London: ASEAN Academic Press, pp. 83–116.

Fieldhouse, P. (1986), *Food and Nutrition: Customs and Culture,* London: Croom Helm.

Finucane, M.L., and J. L. Holup (2005), 'Psychosocial and cultural factors affecting the perceived risk of genetically modified food: an overview of the literature', *Social Science and Medicine*, **60** (7), 1603–12.

Fischhoff, B., P. Slovic and S. Lichtenstein (1980), 'Knowing what you want: measuring labile values', in T. Wallstein (ed.), *Cognitive Processes in Choice and Decision Behavior*, Hillsdale, NJ: Lawrence Erlbaum, pp. 117–41.

Fischler, C. (1988), 'Food, self and identity', *Social Science Information*, **27** (2), 275–92.

Gibbs, J.B. (1997), 'Predisposing the decision maker versus framing the decision: a consumer-manipulation approach to dynamic preference', *Marketing Letters*, **8** (1), 71–83.

Glaser, B.G. (1978), *Theoretical Sensitivity: Advances in the Methodology of Grounded Theory*, Mill Valley: Sociology Press.

Glaser, B.G., and A.L. Strauss (1967), *The Discovery of Grounded Theory*, Chicago: Aldine.

Hamzah, S., and A. Yusof (2003), 'The ergogenic effects of eurycoma longifolia jack: a pilot study', *British Journal of Sports Medicine*, **37** (5), 464–70.

Hasler, C.M. (1998), 'Functional foods: their role in disease prevention and health promotion', *Food Technology*, **52** (11), 63–70.

Hassan, S.H. (2008), *Functional Food Consumption In Multicultural Society*, unpublished PhD, Australian National University, Canberra.

Hassan, S.H., S. Dann, K.A. Mohd Kamal and D. Nicholls (2009), 'Market opportunities from cultural value convergence and functional food: the experiences of the Malaysian marketplace', in A. Lindgreen and M. Hingley (eds), *The New Cultures of Food: Marketing Opportunities from Ethnic, Religious and Cultural Diversity*, Gower, pp. 223–42.

Heasman, M., and J. Mellentin (2000), 'Signposting the way to success in strategic partnerships', Editorial, *New Nutrition Business*, **5** (10), 19.

Hilliam, M. (1996), 'Functional foods: the Western consumer viewpoint', *Nutrition Reviews*, **54** (11), S189.

Hirschman, C. (1987), 'The meaning and measurement of ethnicity in Malaysia: an analysis of census classifications', *Journal of Asian Studies*, **46** (3), 555–82.

Hoeffler, S., and D. Ariely (1999), 'Constructing stable preferences: a look into dimensions of experience and their impact on preference stability', *Journal of Consumer Psychology*, **8** (2), 113–39.

Homer, P.M., and L.R. Kahle (1988), 'A structural equation test of the value-attitude-behavior hierarchy', *Journal of Personality and Social Psychology*, **54**, 638–645.

Ikeda, J.P. (1999), 'Culture, food, and nutrition in increasingly culturally diverse societies', in J. Germov and L. Williams (eds), *A Sociology of Food and Nutrition: the Social Appetite*, Oxford: Oxford University Press, pp. 149–68.

International Food Information Council Foundation (1998), *Backgrounder: Functional Foods*, Washington, DC: International Food Information Council Foundation.

JAKIM (2009), 'Takrifan halal', Retrieved 1 July 2010, from http://www.halal .gov.my/.

Justfood (2006), *Global Market Review of Functional Foods – Forecasts to 2012*: MarketResearch.com.

Kahneman, D. and A. Tversky (1979), 'Prospect theory: an analysis of decision under risk', *Econometrica*, **42** (2), 263–91.

King, D.G. (1990), 'Religion and health relationships: a review', *Journal of Religion and Health*, **29** (2), 101–12.

Kojima, K. (1996), 'The Eastern consumer viewpoint: the experience in Japan', *Nutrition Reviews*, **54** (11), S186.

Krishnaswamy, K. (1996), 'Indian functional foods: role in prevention of cancer', *Nutrition Reviews*, **54** (11), S127.

Laderman, C. (1983), *Wives and Midwives: Childbirth and Nutrition in Rural Malaysia*, Los Angeles: University of California Press.

Laird, L.D., M.M. Amer, E.D. Barnett and L.L. Barnes (2007), 'Muslim patients and health disparities in the UK and the US', *British Medical Journal*, **92**, 922–26.

Laird, L D., J. de Marrais and L.L. Barnes (2007), 'Portraying Islam and Muslims in MEDLINE: a content analysis', *Social Science and Medicine*, **65** (12), 2425–39.

Lamb, A. (ed.) (1964). 'Early history in W. Gungwu', *Malaysia: A Survey*, New York: Praeger, pp. 99–112.

Lawrence, M., and J. Germov (1999), 'Future foods: the politics of functional foods and health claims', in J. Germov and L. Williams (eds), *A Sociology of Food and Nutrition: the Social Appetite*, Oxford: Oxford University Press, pp. 149–68.

Levin, J.S. (1994), 'Religion and health: is there an association, is it valid, and is it causal?' *Social Science and Medicine*, **38** (11), 1475–82.

Levin, J.S. (1996), 'How religion influences morbidity and health: reflections on natural history, salutogenesis and host resistance', *Social Science and Medicine*, **43** (5), 849–64.

Meamber, L., and A. Venkatesh (2000), 'Ethnoconsumerist methodology for cultural and cross-cultural consumer research', in S.C. Beckmann and R.H. Elliott (eds), *Interpretive Consumer Research: Paradigms, Methodologies and Application*, Denmark: Copenhagen Business School Press, pp. 87–108.

Milner, J.A. (1999), 'Functional foods and health promotion', *Journal of Nutrition*, **129** (7), 1395S.

Mohd Ilham, A., A.W. Mahmud and A.K. Azizol (1998), 'Planting of medical and aromatic plants in oil palm plantation', Paper presented at the National Seminar on Livestock and Crop Integration in Oil Palm: Towards Sustainability, Prime City Hotel, Kluang, Johor, 12–14 May.

Muhamad, Z.M.A.M. (1991), *Traditional Malay Medicinal Plants*, Kuala Lumpur: Fajar Bakti Sdn Bhd.

Muhammad, N.M.N., F.M. Isa and B.C. Kifli (2009), 'Positioning Malaysia as halal-hub: integration role of supply chain strategy and halal assurance system', *Asian Social Science*, **5** (7), 44–52.

Nair, M.K.M., P. Vasudevan and K. Venkitanarayanan (2005), 'Antibacterial effect of black seed oil on Listeria monocytogenes', *Food Control*, **16** (5), 395–98.

Nandhasri, P., K.K. Pawa, J. Kaewtubtim, C. Jeamchanya, C. Jansom and C. Sattaponpun (2005),

'Nutraceutical properties of Thai "yor", morinda citrifolia and "noni" juice extract', *Songklanakarin Journal of Science Technology*, **2**, 579–86.

Nestle, M., R. Wing, L. Birch, L. DiSogra, A. Drewnowski, S. Middleton et al. (1998), 'Behavioral and social influences on food choice: discussion', *Nutrition Reviews*, **56** (5), S50.

Pachter, L.M., J. Sheehan and M.M. Cloutier (2000), 'Factor and subscale structure of a parental health locus of control instrument (parental health beliefs scales) for use in a mainland United States Puerto Rican community', *Social Science and Medicine*, **50** (5), 715–21.

Patton, M.Q. (1990), *Qualitative Evaluation and Research Methods* (2nd edn), Newbury Park, CA: Sage.

Patton, M.Q. (2002), *Qualitative Research and Evaluation Methods* (3rd edn), Thousand Oaks: Sage Publications.

Purcell, V. (1948, 1967), *Chinese in Malaya*, Kuala Lumpur: Oxford University Press.

Qur'an (undated), English translation of the meaning, revised version of translation by Abdallah Yusuf Ali, Saudi Arabia.

Rokeach, M. (1973), *The Nature of Human Values*, New York: Free Press.

Rokeach, M. (1979), *Understanding Human Values: Individual and Societal*, New York: Free Press.

Schiffman, L.G., and L.L. Kanuk (2002), *Consumer Behavior* (7th edn), New Jersey: Prentice-Hall.

Schwartz, S.H., and W. Bilsky (1990), 'Toward a theory of the universal content and structure of values: extensions and cross-cultural replications', *Journal of Personality and Social Psychology*, **58** (5), 878–91.

Scott, J.E., and L.M. Lamont (1977), 'Relating consumer values to consumer behavior a model and method for investigation', in T.W. Greer (ed.), *Increasing Marketing Productivity*, Chicago: American Marketing Association, pp. 283–88.

Sheehy, P.J.A., and P.A. Morrissey (1998), 'Functional foods: prospects and perspectives', in C.J.K. Henry and N.J. Heppell (eds), *Nutritional Aspects of Food Processing and Ingredients*, Gaithersburg: Aspen Publishers, pp. 45–65.

Simon, A., K. Traynor K. Santos G. Blaser U. Bode and P. Molan (2008), 'Medical honey for wound care – still the "latest resort"?', *eCAM Advance Access*, **175** (January), 1–9.

Sobal, J. (1998), 'Cultural comparison research designs in food, eating, and nutrition', *Food Quality and Preference*, **9** (6), 385–92.

Speziali, H.S., and D. R. Carpenter (2003), *Qualitative Research in Nursing: Advancing the Humanistic Imperative* (3rd edn), Philadelphia: Lippincott William and Wilkins.

Stacey, A. (2009), 'The importance of maintaining a healthy diet', 1 July, available at http://www.islamreligion.com/articles/1891/.

Steenkamp, J.-B.E.M. (2005), 'Moving out of the US silo: a call to arms for conducting international marketing research', *Journal of Marketing*, **69** (4), 6–8.

Steenkamp, J.-B.E.M., and S.M. Burgess (2002), 'Optimum stimulation level and exploratory consumer behavior in an emerging consumer market', *International Journal of Research in Marketing*, **19** (2), 131–50.

Strauss, A.L., and J. Corbin (1990), *Basics of Qualitative Research: Grounded Theory Procedures and Techniques*, London: Sage.

Tee, E.S. (2004), *Functional Foods in Asia: Current Status and Issues*, Singapore: International Life Sciences Institute.

Tversky, A., and D. Kahneman (1986), 'Rational choice and the framing of decisions', *Journal of Business*, **59** (4), S251.

Venkatesh, A. (1995), 'Ethnoconsumerism: a new paradigm to study cultural and cross-cultural consumer behavior', in J.A. Costa and G. Bamossy (eds), *Marketing in the Multicultural World*, Sage Publications, pp. 26–67.

Wang, M.-Y., J.B. West, C.J. Jensen D. Nowicki C. Su, K.A. Palu et al. (2002), '*Morinda citrifolia* (Noni): a literature review and recent advances in noni research', *Acta Pharmacol Sin*, **23** (12), 1127–41.

Weng, W., and J. Chen (1996), 'The Eastern perspective on functional foods based on traditional Chinese medicine', *Nutrition Reviews*, **54** (11), S11–S16.

Wertenbroch, K. and Z. Carmon (1997), 'Dynamic preference maintenance', *Marketing Letters*, **8** (1), 145–52.

Weststrate, J.A., G. van Poppel and P.M. Verschuren (2002), 'Functional foods, trends and future', *British Journal of Nutrition*, **88** (S2), 233–35.

Wong, S.P., L.P. Leong and J.H. William Koh (2006), 'Antioxidant activities of aqueous extracts of selected plants', *Food Chemistry*, **99** (4), 775–83.

Wu, Y., and D. Wang (2008), 'A new class of natural glycopeptides with sugar moiety-dependent antioxidant activities derived from ganoderma lucidum fruiting bodies', *Journal of Proteome Research*, **8** (2), 436–42.

Yahya, H. (2007), *The Importance Of The Ahl Al-Sunnah*, **190**, Turkey: Global Publishing.

Yau, O.H.M. (1994), *Consumer Behaviour in China: Customer Satisfaction and Cultural Values*, London: Routledge.

PART III

MARKETING PRACTICES

11 Market-orientation and Islamic business practices in Malaysia

Raja Nerina Raja Yusof, André M. Everett and Malcolm H. Cone

INTRODUCTION

This chapter examines the influence of host country culture on the way foreign retail multinational enterprises (MNEs) operate their overseas subsidiaries. The focus is on how the market-orientation culture of foreign retail subsidiaries is influenced by Malaysian Islamic business practices, specifically those that relate to the *halal* and *haram* consumption practices within the Muslim community. As such, the study reported here significantly contributes to the knowledge relating to Islamic business practices within international business management.

Islam is a comprehensive religion that permeates all aspects of life. The religion has been termed a 'civilization' (Huntington, 1993; Mitsuo, 2001), which means 'an advanced stage or system of human social development' (Soanes, 2001, p. 157). It has also been described as a culture in itself (Al-Faruqi, 1982). Thus it comes as no surprise that some of its values and principles influence and affect business organizations. One principle in Islam that has an impact on business firms, especially those in the food retailing industry, is the implementation of *halal* (permitted) and *haram* (forbidden) practices in trade and consumption. According to these practices, a Muslim will only consume foods and drinks that are *halal*, and sourced from animals that have been slaughtered according to *sharia* law (Islamic law). In addition, the practices forbid Muslims to consume *haram* items such as pork and alcohol or products that contain these items in their ingredients. Since food retailing is an industry that handles much of the daily requirements of consumers, especially when it comes to dietary requirements, its operation can be substantially influenced when faced with these particular practices.

This study pursues the question of how the *halal* and *haram* practices in Islam have affected the market-orientation culture of foreign retail subsidiaries in Malaysia. In this study it is assumed that market-oriented culture exists in retail organizations because of the retail industry's emphasis on customers. It is acknowledged that there are different degrees of market-oriented culture in different retail organizations, which play a role in the success rates of retailers in different countries. However, at a minimum, this culture does exist in retail firms due to the nature of their business, which needs to deal with customers' demands.

When a foreign retailer enters a host country, it will bring with it an established corporate culture, including its selected level and style of market orientation. This relates to how the organization strategizes its operations with a focus on satisfying its customers. However, when the host country, such as Malaysia, has a Muslim majority in its population, it is proposed that the market-oriented culture of the retail subsidiaries located there will be influenced by the *halal* and *haram* practices of Islam, and that this will consequently lead to the formation of different types of subsidiary cultures. This study looks at the subsidiary cultures from the convergence-divergence-crossvergence (CDC) framework proposed by Ralston et al. (1997).

The remainder of this chapter is arranged as follows. The next section presents a discussion of literature on relevant topics. The third section briefly highlights the research proposition, and the fourth elaborates on the methodology of this study, examining the implementation of *halal*- and *haram*-related practices by foreign hypermarkets in Malaysia, The fifth section presents our analysis and findings. The concluding section highlights the implications of this study for both managers and academics.

LITERATURE REVIEW

This section discusses selected literature on the topics of multinational enterprises (MNEs) and host country culture, the religion of Islam and its business practices, market orientation within the culture of retail organizations, and the convergence-divergence-crossvergence (CDC) framework.

Multinational Enterprises (MNEs) and Host Country Culture

A multinational enterprise (MNE) is 'an enterprise that engages in foreign direct investment (FDI) and owns or controls value-adding activities in more than one country' (Dunning, 1992, p. 3). The operation of an MNE is particularly interesting compared to a domestic firm because it operates in many different environments and cultures around the world, elevating the importance of coordination of strategy and structure.

Since an MNE has its own 'cultural baggage' (Tayeb, 1997), its subsidiaries are bound to face institutional duality (Kostova and Roth, 2002) or isomorphic pulls (Westney, 2005) when operating in a foreign environment. Adaptation is one way in which an MNE may come to terms with a host country regarding cultural differences. Adaptation is conceptually linked to various constructs underlying MNEs such as multinationalism (Bartlett and Ghoshal, 1989), geocentricism (Perlmutter, 1969), crossvergence (Ralston et al., 1993), and responsiveness in the integration-responsiveness framework (Prahalad and Doz, 1987). Among the theories that support the notion of adaptation are the environmental adaptation theories originating in the organization studies field, including institutional theory, population ecology theory and contingency theory.

Islam and its Business Practices – *Halal* and *Haram*

Islam is the fastest growing religion in the world (Lewis, 2003; Scupin, 2008), with an estimated 1.5 to 1.6 billion Muslims at present (Muslim Population Worldwide, 2009). The teachings in Islam permeate all aspects of its followers' lives, including matters of personal care; relationships between men and women, the environment and God; economics; politics; and health care. To its followers, Islam is holistic in its guidance, leading to an Islamic way of life.

Islam does not practice a separation between religious issues and other matters such as business, politics and economics, as all these issues are believed to be inter-related. Relative to the business world, an occupation in trade is revered and encouraged in Islam, as expressed in the popular claim that trade is two-thirds of wisdom (Ali, 1993). However, like all other aspects of life, business transactions have their own rules and principles in Islam. In general, business people cannot be involved in usury (interest), theft, fraud, speculation, hoarding, gambling-related activities and selling forbidden (non-*halal* or *haram*) items such as alcohol and pork (Ahmad, 2003; Gambling and Abdel Karim, 1991).

The *halal* (permitted) and *haram* (forbidden) practices in consumption are very important concepts in Islam. These practices are integrally related to the business environment and encompass the entire breadth of business activities, from the supply of raw materials through to distribution. As such their impact on the operations of food-based business organizations can be quite comprehensive.

The terms *halal* (permitted) and *haram* (forbidden) are quoted explicitly in the Qur'an. Semantically speaking, the *halal* and *haram* words are related to the Semitic idea of ritual cleanliness (Izutsu, 1966). *Haram* means taboo or forbidden, and it is something that is considered unapproachable, detested and untouchable in the sacred sense (Izutsu, 1966). *Halal* is conceived as everything else that is not taboo. Eating *halal* food is not only obligatory from the perspective of the religion, but it also symbolizes the building up of a person with a character that is pure, fresh and strong.

Basically, Muslims are allowed to eat beef, chicken, mutton and other kinds of meat, but the animals have to be slaughtered in an Islamic way to make them *halal* (see Appendix for details). The rationale for slaughtering in Islam is not only to maintain the physical, moral or intellectual side of a person, but also the spiritual side, whereby the invocation of other than Allah's name during the slaughter symbolizes or is associated with idolatry (Ali, 1973). Muslims are forbidden to eat animals that died of natural causes or in accidents, or that were killed by wild beasts. Furthermore Muslims do not eat pork or consume or even touch any part of a pig that might be in the ingredients of certain products. For example, gelatine is one of the usual ingredients Muslims look out for on food and drink labels. Unless stated to be '*halal*', which generally indicates that the gelatine is vegetable-based or comes from animals (excluding pigs) that have been slaughtered in an Islamic way, gelatine-containing food or drink cannot be consumed by Muslims. To Muslims, pigs, dead animals and blood are *najis*, which means filthy by nature or according to reason or laws (Izutsu, 1966).

Adaptation of Islamic Business Practices (IBP) in Retailing

Little has been written on the topic of adaptation of retail MNEs to Islamic business practices, and even less on the specific topic of *halal* and *haram* practices, which are the focus of this chapter. What can be found prevalent in the literature is the growing awareness of food producers and retailers of the increasing demand for *halal* products, especially in the North American region (Cardwell, 2008; Gallagher, 2006; Minkus-McKenna, 2007).

A retailer is the key intermediary between suppliers and consumers, and thus has responsibilities and commitments towards both parties. *Halal* products or supplies that are sold in a retail outlet come from suppliers, and it is the suppliers' responsibility to ensure that they are indeed *halal*. The retailer has the responsibility to periodically review its suppliers' commitment towards *halal* compliance. Any wrongdoing on their part should be curtailed immediately at the factory using monitoring strategies (that is, audits), and thus it is assumed that only *halal* products will be placed in retail outlets. As such, the bulk of the issues surrounding *halal* supplies lies in the upstream part of the supply chain, between the supplier and retailer.

With regard to non-*halal* (*haram*) products such as pork and alcoholic beverages sold in retail outlets, retailers in a Muslim-dominant society need to be extremely careful and sensitive towards how they display and arrange the sale of the non-*halal* items in their outlets, knowing how much their Muslim consumers abhor and detest these items. Hence, in this sense, dealing with *haram* products is much more of a 'downstream' issue, whereby the retailer–consumer relationship is of importance in assuring that both parties are comfortable and at ease with the arrangement of the *haram* items.

Thus, when retail MNEs invest and set up subsidiaries in Malaysia, they will find themselves having to abide by the Malaysian *halal* and *haram* business practices, which may differ from those in other Islamic countries since Islamic values are subject to different interpretations according to the local environment (for more information on this, see Adas, 2006; Tayeb, 1997). It is crucial for international retailers to be sensitive to the needs of the Muslim population in Malaysia, a country very much involved in developing *halal* standards and championing efforts for ensuring legitimate *halal* products are marketed globally.

Market-oriented Culture and the Retail Industry

Market orientation enthrones customers as the prime interest of organizations (Deshpande et al., 1993; Narver and Slater, 1990). Whether used as a decision-making process (Shapiro, 1988), a market intelligence concept (Kohli and Jaworski, 1990) or a strategic tool (Ruekert, 1992), the main ingredient of market-orientation is the emphasis on customers (Megicks and Warnaby, 2008). Market orientation and the retail industry clearly have a key characteristic in common: customer focus. Pioch (2007) maintained that pricing and products are easily replicated by competitors, so retailers focus more strongly on customers. The focus on final consumers or end users in the retail industry fits comfortably with the market-orientation philosophy because this concept revolves around satisfying consumers' current and future needs (Kohli and Jaworski, 1990) and creating 'superior value for customers' (Narver and Slater, 1990, p. 21).

Lafferty and Hult (2001) pointed out two distinct perspectives arising from the market-orientation concept: the managerial focus and the cultural focus. Our study follows the cultural focus of market orientation as developed by Deshpande and Webster (1989), Narver and Slater (1990) and Turner and Spencer (1997). Deshpande and Webster (1989) were among the pioneers to relate marketing with organizational culture, claiming that the marketing concept paves the way for an organization to have a culture that puts 'the customer in the center of the firm's thinking about strategy and operations' (p. 3). Narver and Slater (1990) discussed market orientation and how it is the key driver for the creation of a culture in an organization. This is evident in how they defined the market-orientation concept as 'the organization culture . . . that most effectively and efficiently creates the necessary behaviors for the creation of superior values for buyers, and, thus, continuous superior performance for the business' (p. 21).

However Narver and Slater (1990) and Kohli and Jaworski (1990) have been criticized for focusing mainly on the behavioral components of market-orientation, an approach perceived as a superficial attempt at recognizing and interpreting the culture. Since scholars of organizational culture agree that culture manifests at different levels, mainly at the values, norms, and behavioral levels, this study adopts market-oriented culture as a concept that encompasses various levels of organizational culture, as operationalized by Homburg and Pflesser (2000). They developed a market-oriented organizational culture model that has four inter-related components of organizational culture: shared basic values, norms, artifacts and behaviors.

This study positions market-oriented culture as a part of the foreign retail MNE's corporate culture, and as such does not consider market-oriented culture as the only culture prevalent in the MNE. This study also assumes market-oriented culture exists in retail organizations because of the retail industry's emphasis on customers. This leads to this study's next assumption, that market-oriented culture should be the dominant culture in retail organizations, although it is acknowledged that this type of assumption downplays the role of other subcultures in the organization (Harris and Ogbonna, 1999).

Convergence-Divergence-Crossvergence (CDC) Framework

Convergence and divergence are opposite explanations for values formation, as related by Webber (Ralston et al., 1997). The convergence view arises from the notion that as industrialized nations become more successful, with developed institutions and modern technology, other nations will gradually follow suit, hence adopting economic and political values similar to those of the industrialized leaders (Gupta and Wang, 2004; Ralston et al., 1997; Rowley and Benson, 2002). This view assumes that these values are merging across boundaries regardless of cultural or historical background differences. On the other hand the divergence view maintains that differences in culture among societies and nations will negate the convergence of economic ideologies (Ralston et al., 1997) as people prefer to preserve their identity and way of doing things despite outside influences.

These views have evolved over time to suit many different areas, including international management, where convergence implies that organizations and managers around the world are 'becoming more similar' (McGaughey and De Cieri, 1999) or 'homogenized' (de Mooij and Hofstede, 2002) in terms of attitudes, practices and behaviors. This view implicitly champions the transfer of 'best practice' management and benchmarking behavior among organizations worldwide (Rowley and Benson, 2002), especially between a parent organization and its subsidiaries (Khilji, 2002). In contrast, proponents of a divergence view insist that managers and organizations in different societies are deeply embedded in their local context, and as a result are 'culturally protected' and immune to outside influences. This will preserve heterogeneity among organizations and employees, who will continue to use their own 'deeply seeded values' (Robertson et al., 2001, p. 226) to transform and develop their organizations.

However these two views posit the extremes of a continuum from pure convergence to pure divergence. People and organizations generally try to be tolerant and accommodate each other to develop harmonious and fruitful cooperation, creating a situation where, in the case of multinational operations, foreign organizations see a need to adapt to some degree to local practices when investing in certain countries (Khilji, 2002). This negates both the convergence and divergence views because it paves a middle path towards accommodating the similarities and differences of the parties (foreign organizations and host countries). The 'crossvergence' term (Ralston et al., 1997) was developed to address the gap and has been quite successful in explaining this alternative view. 'Crossvergence' was formally defined as the situation 'when an individual incorporates both national culture influences and economic ideology influences synergistically to form a unique value system that is different from the value set supported by either national culture or economic ideology' (Ralston et al., 1997, p. 183). This 'cross-bred' value system (McGaughey and De Cieri, 1999), between the two dominant value groups, resulted in the development of the convergence-divergence-crossvergence (CDC) framework (Ralston et al., 1997).

International Retailers and Adaptation to Host Country Culture

In his study regarding the internationalization of retail operators, Dawson (1994, p. 278) concluded that one of the most important aspects of successful retail internationalization is 'adaption of management practices and processes in response to the cultural character of the host country'. There are many examples of international retailers that have failed in foreign markets because of the lack of adaptation, including Royal Ahold, Carrefour, Home Depot and J.C. Penney in Chile (Bianchi and Ostale, 2006) and the case of Marks and Spencer's global market exit in 2001 (Burt et al., 2002).

Evans and Bridson (2005) found that the higher the psychic distance between a retail MNE's country of origin and its host country, the higher the level of adaptation undertaken by the MNE. It seems that when MNEs perceive themselves to be significantly different from the host country in cultural terms, they make more substantial adjustments and changes. This is especially true for dimensions such as market structure, business practices and language. However national culture did not emerge as a significant effect on market adaptation, leading the authors to infer that retailers will prioritize 'obligatory' adaptations (for example, market structure, business practices and language) over those that are 'discretionary' in nature (for example, consumer tastes and values).

A significant part of culture is religion, and in some societies, religion acts as the crux for the core values that underlie the norms and, in certain cases, the regulations within the society. Islam is one such religion, and thus foreign firms that are not familiar with the religion and do not have experience setting up businesses in a Muslim or Muslim-dominant country should expect initial dissonance because of the cultural distance between the MNE's country of origin and host country cultures.

RESEARCH PROPOSITION

This study proposes that the *halal* and *haram* Islamic business practices (IBPs) of the host country will have moderating effects on foreign retail MNEs' corporate cultures, which in turn will result in the emergence of different types of subsidiary organizational cul-

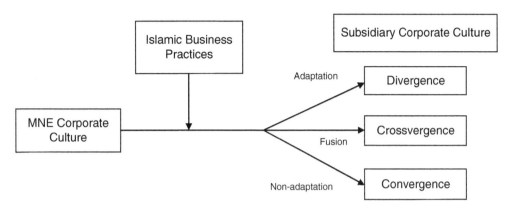

Figure 11.1   Organizing framework for the research proposition

tures. Using the CDC framework developed by David Ralston and colleagues, this study proposes that the interaction of the MNE corporate culture with the IBPs will result in three levels of impacts on the subsidiary's organizational culture. One possibility is that the MNE adapts its corporate culture to IBPs as a condition for it to be accepted by the local population, which results in a divergence subsidiary culture. A second possibility is that the MNE's corporate culture may not be affected by IBPs, and as such requires no adaptation by the MNE to the local IBPs. This type of culture is called the convergence subsidiary culture. The third option proposed here, apart from this potential convergence or divergence of the subsidiary's culture, is that there are subsidiaries that may adapt as well as infuse IBPs into their parent's corporate culture. In other words, there is a crossvergence of an MNE's corporate culture with IBPs. As such, the research proposition and organizing framework (Figure 11.1) for this study are as follows:

The moderating effects of Malaysia's *halal* (permissible) and *haram* (forbidden) IBPs on the market-oriented aspect of a foreign hypermarket retailer's corporate culture should result in the following: adaptation leads to a divergence subsidiary culture, non-adaptation leads to a convergence subsidiary culture, while fusion leads to a crossvergence subsidiary culture.

METHODOLOGY

This section discusses the methodological considerations for the study while laying down justifications for choosing such approaches.

Case Study Approach

This study is portrayed in the form of research case studies, whereby qualitative data from interviews, archival research and observations on the organizations and local context are used for analysis. This study employs a type of cross-case analysis where the proposition is discussed in a section supplemented by information from all organizations included in the study (Yin, 2003). This means that the proposition will be analyzed by extracting evidence in the form of quotations or statements from interview transcripts, facts and figures from documents and observable items from observations.

According to Yin (2003), a case study is 'an empirical inquiry that investigates a contemporary phenomenon within its real-life context, especially when the boundaries between phenomenon and context are not clearly evident' (p. 13). Since this study aims to uncover the phenomenon of 'how' and 'what' pertaining to the influences of Islamic business practices on the corporate culture and strategies of foreign hypermarket operators in Malaysia, an in-depth inquiry on the interaction of the external and internal cultural forces of the organizations is needed. In this instance, the use of the case study method is highly relevant due to its ability to study 'phenomena that are highly complex and/or embedded in their cultural context' (Verschuren, 2003, p. 137).

This approach of utilizing and presenting case studies matches the overall design of the study, which initially put forward a theoretical proposition with the purpose of guiding or focusing the analysis and discussion of the findings (Yin, 2003). Even though a case study is generally known to be more useful for generating propositions or theories (see Eisenhardt and Graebner, 2007; Eisenhardt, 1989), its usefulness as a research method also encompasses the ability to explain, describe, illustrate or explore theoretical propositions (Yin, 2003). Flyvbjerg (2004) supported this particular role of a case study, which he expressed as a method that 'in general can certainly contribute to the cumulative development of knowledge; for example, in using the principles to test propositions' (p. 402). Through case studies researchers have the opportunity to experience first-hand the issue surrounding the research constructs, which enhances their ability to derive examples that support or falsify certain theoretical propositions (Flyvbjerg, 2004; Siggelkow, 2007).

Unit of Analysis

The units of analysis in this study are the Malaysian subsidiaries of foreign retail multinational enterprises (MNEs) which operate hypermarket stores across the country. Foreign MNEs are defined here as 'all non-Malaysian multinational enterprises, excluding those coming from any Islamic or Islamic-majority countries, with non-Muslim or non-dominant Muslim owners', while a hypermarket is defined as a store which consumes an overall space of over 5000m² (Ministry of Domestic Trade and Consumer Affairs, 2005). The hypermarket store format was chosen for this study because it is a relatively new retailing concept in Asia and the players are large multinational chains with already established operations outside the region. As such, these players fit the main target of the research, which is to investigate retail firms that have diversified networks of subsidiaries around the world.

The setting of the research is Malaysia, a country in the South East Asian region. Even though the Malaysian population is multiethnic, the country's majority population is of the Malay ethnicity, most of them practicing Muslims. As such, Malaysia has largely adopted a moderate Islamic approach in its governance and this can be seen in its economic, political and social institutions. The Islamic influence strengthened after Islamization swept across the region during the 1970s and 1980s, raising the awareness of Muslims all over the world (Verma, 2002; Ooi, 2006). Islamic practices encompass every aspect of life; business organizations and transactions are no exceptions. As a result, foreign businesses investing in Malaysia are more or less affected by the Islamic regulations, policies and guidelines produced by the government.

Before describing how the data were collected, it is useful to briefly highlight the background of the sample in this study. All three foreign MNEs operating hypermarkets in Malaysia, constituting the total population of this unit of analysis, are included in the study.

The Carrefour Group of France, which operates under the company name Magnificent Diagraph (Malaysia) Sdn Bhd in Malaysia, was the first multinational retailer to introduce the hypermarket concept to Malaysian consumers, in 1994. Carrefour first internationalized at the end of the 1960s and is currently the number one retailer in Europe and second in the world. It regards itself as an international retailer and sees further growth potential in relatively undiscovered markets such as Brazil, China and Indonesia (Groupe Carrefour, 2009a).

Tesco Stores (Malaysia) Sdn Bhd is the local subsidiary of Tesco plc, headquartered in the United Kingdom (UK). Tesco plc has a long history in the UK, retailing there since the early 1900s before venturing outside the home country. When the company finally internationalized, European countries were its first choice for market development, and only in the 1990s did the multinational retailer enter Asia. However, Tesco plc still regards the UK as its main market, where it has double the number of stores compared to either Europe or Asia (Tesco Annual Review, 2007). Tesco is a late bloomer in Malaysia compared to its competitors, Carrefour and Giant, since it entered the local retailing scene only in 2001.

GCH Retail (Malaysia) Sdn Bhd is the local subsidiary of Dairy Farm International (DFI), a conglomerate based in Hong Kong, which operates the Giant stores throughout Malaysia. The Giant retail company was owned by the Teng family and started off in 1944 as a small local company selling groceries in Kuala Lumpur (Giant, 2009). When acquired in 1999 by Dairy Farm International, the company continued with the 'Malaysian' branding strategy and gradually multiplied the number of stores it operates in Malaysia. DFI itself operates other store formats and brands in Malaysia, such as the Cold Storage stores which also sell food-based groceries and the Guardian store outlets which sell pharmaceutical and health products.

Data Collection Methods

Apart from employing in-depth interviews, this study also utilizes archival research and observations to collect additional data. Interviews for this study were conducted in Malaysia from January to March 2007 and subsequently from July to September 2008 in follow-up sessions with the top managers of selected departments in the hypermarket organizations. Permission for formal interviews was obtained from two of the three retail organizations, namely Tesco Malaysia and Carrefour Malaysia. The third retailer, GCH Retail (which operates the Giant chain of stores), declined to be involved in the research, citing its privacy policy, and supplied an official letter stating its decision. A total of five interviewees from Carrefour and Tesco were identified as suitable resources for this research; quotations from the resulting interviews in this chapter are designated C1–C3 (Carrefour) and T1–T2 (Tesco) to retain interviewee confidentiality. Since Giant did not participate in the interview sessions, data on the organization were gathered through archival research and observations.

FINDINGS AND ANALYSIS

Findings indicate that even though Carrefour, Tesco and Giant possess market-oriented cultures, they have different ways of emphasizing this orientation. This can be seen clearly by the core values they publicly espouse as the backbone of their companies' cultures. However it is acknowledged that what a firm declares in its promotional media may not be aligned with its actions. Hence this study triangulates data from interviews, observations and archives for more solid findings and conclusions.

Market-oriented Organizational Culture of Foreign Retailers

Carrefour presents its core values in a general way, as (1) Freedom, (2) Responsibility, (3) Sharing, (4) Respect, (5) Integrity, (6) Solidarity, and (7) Progress, which the company emphasizes are the 'heritage of all the people and companies that have built the Group' (Carrefour, n.d., p. 8). Apart from the core values, the company's actions are guided by its world view, mission and policies for customers, assets, human resources, merchandising and finance (Carrefour, n.d.). Carrefour also mentions several times that, being a retailer, it is obliged to 'respect the different cultures of the communities in which we do business' (Carrefour, n.d., p. 8) and to establish each store to 'fit seamlessly into its environment in order to build a strong local image' (p. 20). All in all, Carrefour portrays itself as a company that emphasizes adaptation and flexibility in its international operations.

Tesco's 'Every Little Helps' slogan sets the common philosophy for integrating its diverse businesses (Tesco Annual Review, 2006). Tesco's core values are: (1) No one tries harder for customers, and (2) Treat people how we like to be treated. These values guide its work culture and hence the way it does business all over the world. Tesco also has a management tool, the 'Steering Wheel', which resembles the 'balanced scorecard' approach. The 'Steering Wheel' helps the organization to focus and balance its performance on five dimensions: customer, people, finance, community and operations. Each dimension comes with specific Key Performance Indicators (KPIs) which set the targets to be achieved (Tesco Malaysia, 2010). With its 'Steering Wheel' in hand, Tesco portrays itself as a retailer with a set of objectives that it wants its stakeholders to receive or experience. In a way, Tesco's stakeholders match those of Carrefour. However, Carrefour elaborates on them more loosely than Tesco's precise statements on the 'Steering Wheel'. For customers, Tesco has basically given out promises such as 'The aisles are clear', 'I can get what I want', 'The prices are good', 'I don't queue' and 'The staff are great' (Tesco Annual Review, 2006). Tesco, thus, portrays itself as an international retailer that emphasizes the basics of retailing, has detailed visions on what these are and is confident that these basics will work in each and every country it enters. In this sense, the retailer exhibits a global approach to conducting international business.

Dairy Farm International, which operates Giant stores in Malaysia, has a focused mission and goal to be the leading retailer in Asia. In contrast to the other two foreign retail MNEs in Malaysia, Dairy Farm seems to be 'geographically committed to Asia' (Dairy Farm International Holdings Limited, 2008, p. 2). Its goal, 'to satisfy the appetites of Asian shoppers,' implies that Asian consumers have their own preferences or tastes for certain goods and services, and implies that its retail stores are specialized to cater for this type of consumer. Dairy Farm also emphasizes the 'value for money' concept by offering its customers products that are simultaneously low in cost and high in quality.

The values of all three firms are market-oriented, as the bulk of their values and practices focus on their customers. However, findings have shown that there are similarities as well as differences in the way these retail MNEs react to the *halal* and *haram* business practices in Malaysia. In other words, there are certain aspects where the retail MNEs share common reactions to this type of IBP, but there are also certain instances where they differ. These two aspects will be dealt with in turn, beginning with similarities and concluding with differences in practices and policies.

Market-orientation and IBPs: Similarities among Foreign Retail MNEs in Malaysia

Findings from the study indicate that all foreign hypermarkets in Malaysia have similar strategies with regards to three operational aspects.

Offering *halal* goods for all consumers, plus *haram* products for non-Muslims

All foreign hypermarket operators in Malaysia offer non-*halal* products, such as fresh pork and pork-based products, which are put on sale in a separate room inside the store. Only non-Muslim employees are stationed in the non-*halal* room, and they are instructed to use gloves to avoid any contact with liquids from pork meat. Items are packed, bagged, sealed and paid for in the room itself before being brought out. Even though a few of Giant's hypermarket stores do not seem to provide fresh non-*halal* produce, they still sell non-*halal* products that have been processed and packaged prior to placement in their stores. All of the foreign hypermarkets also sell alcoholic drinks, but with the exception of a few of the Giant stores, the alcoholic drinks are segregated into a different room so that Muslim consumers will not be uncomfortable with the upfront sale of these items.

On the other hand, all hypermarkets in the study also offer *halal* products to all of their consumers. It is generally accepted that *halal* products are not specifically for Muslims' consumption only; they are also sold to all consumers in Malaysia regardless of religious affiliation. Moreover, more and more non-Muslims specifically search for *halal* products because of the safety and quality aspects that are emphasized in these kinds of products. Hence, fresh meat and poultry that are sold in these foreign hypermarkets are all *halal*-certified and sold to all customers; there is no separation between *halal*-certified fresh meat for Muslims and non-*halal*-certified fresh meat for non-Muslims (in the case of meat such as chicken, beef or lamb that could be eaten by Muslims if it were to receive *halal* certification).

From these findings, it can be inferred that Carrefour, Tesco and Giant have adapted their corporate values to align with the values of *halal* and *haram* in Islam. In Carrefour's case, its core values of 'respect' and 'freedom' contribute to this particular integration with the *halal* (permissible) and *haram* (forbidden) practices. Respecting one culture does not necessarily mean denying another's right to freedom of choice. That is why, while providing *halal* products to all consumers, Carrefour also provides a range of non-*halal* (*haram*) fresh and processed products for its non-Muslim customers, albeit in a comparable but distinctly separated environment. Tesco is also following its core values and promises to its customers. 'I can get what I want' says it all; that all customers in Tesco will get the products that they want regardless of their background. 'No one tries harder for customers' translates into its efforts to please customers to the best of its ability, thus the effort that it has put into ensuring that both *halal* and non-*halal* products are provided for customers while also considering each culture's sensitivity:

> The non-*halal* section makes sure the doors are closed. Why? Because it is in the Steering Wheel and the core value is that you have customers' satisfaction . . . so [the] Steering Wheel, by virtue of the name itself, [is] what drives the company. (T2, 2008)

As for Giant, its goal to 'satisfy the appetites of Asian shoppers' has been adapted to the *halal* and *haram* IBPs by providing both types of products, attempting to satisfy both its Muslim and non-Muslim customers.

Use of *halal* certification for house brands and locally sourced fresh produce

Both Carrefour and Tesco indicate their commitment to the issue of product quality. Carrefour states in its customer policy that the organization's image depends partly on the quality of its products, especially the firm's house brand products, which it continuously strives to improve in quality (Carrefour, n.d., p. 21). Carrefour requires that 'a product must demonstrate the required quality level before it can be approved for purchase' (Groupe Carrefour, 2009a). Meanwhile, Tesco's aim to 'create value for customers to earn their lifetime loyalty' (Tesco PLC, 2009) translates into having quality products that provide value for money to its customers.

> The Steering Wheel will determine our success, their provision for flexibility, innovativeness, quality, as in all the products must be good. (T2, 2008)

Tesco Malaysia has a Product Development Centre (PDC), situated in Mutiara Damansara (just outside Kuala Lumpur), which conducts consumer research, quality control and improvement as well as public relations work on Tesco products (Tesco Value and Tesco Choice).

> That PDC right there, the processes that they go through as a result of being . . . to improve quality and competence as a result of being in the Steering Wheel. (T2, 2008)

Although not much information regarding Dairy Farm's corporate culture could be obtained, the company has projected its commitment to offer quality goods through its aim 'to offer consumers value-for-money through efficient, low-cost distribution of high-quality fresh foods, and consumer and durable goods' (Dairy Farm International Holdings Limited, 2008, p. 2).

As such, realizing how important *halal* certification is for the Malaysian government and the majority of its consumers, Tesco and Carrefour have made it compulsory for their house brand manufacturers in Malaysia to have *halal* certification before becoming their suppliers.

> For house brand, it's the same thing. All our local house brands, local made, require the JAKIM *halal* certificate. We are aiming for that. (C1, 2007)

> We have requirements where suppliers who would want to supply [for the] Tesco label for instance, for food products, they must get the *halal* certification first. (T1, 2007)

As for Giant, from observation, its house brand products have *halal* logos on them, but it is undetermined whether all of its house brand manufacturers are required to have valid *halal* certification.

Although these retailers come from foreign countries which emphasize different sets of quality indicators, they have accepted *halal* certification as one of the quality indicators for products to be sold in their stores in Malaysia. This illustrates the formation of a local business policy by foreign retailers in Malaysia, which is to require mandatory conformation to the adoption of the *halal* certification for their house brands, as well as a preference for *halal* products in their local stores.

Cooperation with Islamic agencies

Guided by its seven core values, the Carrefour organization has set out to be the retail benchmark for issues pertaining to the 'protection of health, consumer safety and the environment' (Groupe Carrefour, 2009b). The organization's documentation indicates that it is determined for its approach to be globally implemented, while at the same time responding to 'local expectations and to implement a targeted policy that raises local standards while respecting the diversity of cultures and contexts' (Groupe Carrefour, 2009b). Meanwhile, Tesco's core value of 'No one tries harder for customers' can be indirectly perceived as a base for its whole mission to ensure the satisfaction of its customers, and this includes improving aspects of hygiene and safety of its products and operations.

In order to learn effectively about the implementation of *halal* and *haram* procedures in retail settings, foreign retailers maintain good relationships with the Malaysian Islamic Development Department (JAKIM), which is the local government agency responsible for issuing *halal* certificates (the *Halal* Industry Development Corporation, officially abbreviated to HDC, took over the role of certification agency from April 2008 to July 2009, after which it reverted to JAKIM). Since JAKIM is the appointed authority in Malaysia regarding *halal* and *haram* certification, products, and procedures, hypermarket operators frequently refer issues and enquiries that need further clarification to the department.

> We do have people saying . . . this is not *halal* actually. If we get feedback, we will investigate. If we do not know, I will consult JAKIM. I use a couple of JAKIM's officers as a sort of a source to get validation. (C1, 2007)

> We work closely with JAKIM and then we invite JAKIM to Carrefour . . . to give talks to the managers, and also when they come we also bring them around to ask whether . . . is this acceptable or not? (C1, 2007)

> If the government says the HDC are the people we need to liaise with from now onwards, then we are pretty sure that TLT [Trading Law and Technical] people are already with them because that's the point of contact now. (T2, 2008)

By having close relationships with Islamic authorities in Malaysia, the hypermarket operators are acting toward achieving their targeted core values, since the basic values of *halal* and *haram* in Islam are also geared towards achieving the same objectives related to safety and hygiene. This demonstrates adaptation of their cultural values to the Islamic business values and practices in Malaysia.

Market-orientation and IBPs: Differences among Foreign Retail MNEs in Malaysia

Despite the similarities among the foreign hypermarket operators in terms of their market-orientation and Islamic practices synergies, the findings also reveal some differences in terms of the level of conformance and implementation of the *halal* and *haram* standards and procedures in Malaysia.

Carrefour

At the time of the interviews, Carrefour Malaysia was the only foreign hypermarket retailer in Malaysia that had designated one person in the firm to undertake the position of National Halal and Hygiene Coordinator, whose specific job scope was to oversee the *halal* implementation in all stores nationwide. The National Halal and Hygiene Coordinator plays a significant role in the upgrading of Carrefour's hygiene and *halal* standards with the help of relevant government Islamic departments and other related agencies.

> Compared to last time, we have established hygiene standards in the store level, but the momentum is weak. Now we have JAKIM, we have the Health Ministry. The state [Islamic departments] are also coming in when we want to establish *halal*. (C2, 2008)

Carrefour Malaysia informed the researchers that it had submitted an application for its hypermarket store in Putrajaya to be certified *halal* (C2, 2008). At the time of the follow-up interview in September 2008, the application was still pending because of the brief transition of JAKIM's *halal* certification authority to the HDC. However, on the 21 September 2010, JAKIM awarded the Malaysian Halal Certificate to three sections of Carrefour Putrajaya: the salad bar, meat and bakery sections (*Halal Journal*, 2010). In addition, during the 2008 World Halal Forum in Kuala Lumpur, Carrefour and its then Halal and Hygiene Coordinator won the 'Corporate Social Responsibility' Halal Award for their efforts in implementing *halal* procedures in their stores (*Halal Journal*, 2008; International Halal Integrity Alliance, 2009).

According to Carrefour Malaysia, although the majority of the non-*halal* products are segregated into the non-*halal* section, some products, especially those that contain alcohol as one of their ingredients, are seen to be more suitable to be located within their own categories in the general shelves.

> There's a certain type of kicap [soy sauce] like Kikkoman; it contains alcohol. But if we were to take Kikkoman out and put it somewhere else, I think Kikkoman, they won't be happy because you know, you want to see all the sauces together and all that. It's easy for the consumers. If you suddenly put Kikkoman inside the non-*halal* area, of course they will lose sales. Because ultimately if a non-Muslim customer is not going to buy meat for that day, but they wanted to buy soy sauce for example, then they would go there and they won't see Kikkoman and that's it. (C3, 2007)

Carrefour Malaysia decided to label these with a green sticker which says *Mengandungi Alkohol* ('Containing Alcohol') so that Muslim consumers will be aware of the alcoholic ingredients before purchasing the product. This initiative by the firm is said to help its Muslim consumers to be more aware of the ingredients of certain products, even though implementation is time consuming and costly. Along the same lines was the implementation of the special plastic bags for non-*halal* goods in Carrefour Malaysia. Since 2007, the organization has utilized thicker (60 micron) plastic bags to pack the items bought from the non-*halal* room (C1, 2007). The bags cost Carrefour Ringgit Malaysia 27 cents each (instead of 3 cents for the usual one), are pink in color and have the wording 'Non-*halal*' printed below the Carrefour name and logo. The use of the thicker plastic bags was to ensure that contamination does not occur when or if the non-*halal* products come into contact with other products in the store.

The company noted that apart from receiving feedback from customers, it also listens to its employees, especially those working in the stores. Previously, procedures regarding the handling of non-*halal* items were loosely applied but since *halal* and *haram* procedures have been actively applied, steps have been taken to tighten the non-*halal* procedures and make all activities 'proper' according to the Malaysian *halal* standard.

> Pork products, they have their own area, or closed area, they have their own equipment, not mixed, we label them, and then they have their own transporters bringing their own trolley. So, it is not mixed at all. (C1, 2007)

> Let's say if fresh pork comes in, what we do is they have to wrap the whole container or box, up and down before they come into the store . . . non-*halal* will have their own shelves . . . they are labelled non-*halal* . . . even breakage area, one special container for non-*halal* only. (C1, 2007)

Carrefour explained that when fresh or frozen non-*halal* meat comes in, the supplier has to make sure that it is thoroughly wrapped with plastic wrapping before being escorted into the non-*halal* department in the hypermarket by security guards. While in transition, it is not allowed to share the elevator with other products and not allowed to detour or stop by other places except directly to the non-*halal* chillers. Utensils, uniforms, machinery, equipment and materials used for or by the non-*halal* department or employees need to be stored separately and clearly distinguished with blue tape to avoid them being mixed up with other equipment used for other purposes or departments. There are also separate breakage containers to dispose of items related to non-*halal* products or processes. A large part of the internal audits conducted by Carrefour's Halal and Hygiene Coordinator involves the non-*halal* procedures and the audits are designed to monitor whether or not the procedures prescribed by Carrefour Halal Guidelines are constantly being implemented by each of the Carrefour stores in Malaysia.

These findings illustrate how Carrefour Malaysia's Halal Guidelines and Halal Audit System established the foundation for the implementation of *halal* procedures in its stores. These implementation and monitoring systems molded Carrefour Malaysia's culture into one that more deeply emphasizes *halal* implementation in its operations when compared to other foreign hypermarket operators in Malaysia.

Tesco

Tesco Malaysia informed the researchers of a previous action that described its initiative in going beyond the Malaysian government's requirements, with the help of JAKIM, to erase any doubts that its Muslim customers might have regarding its hypermarket operations.

When our non-*halal* deli, which was initially downstairs where we have currently Pizza Hut, because Pizza Hut wanted to come in and then take over the restaurant, take over the space . . . It is not even the government's requirement, but we 'purified' the whole area, we called Selangor Islamic Department, we asked them to help us 'purify' that entire area from A to Z, and we did that with a close cooperation with the government. Then we located [the non-*halal* deli] upstairs at the request of our non-Muslim customers. (T1, 2007)

This example implies that Tesco at that time had thought ahead of the market's reactions to the 'cleanliness' or 'purity' of premises that were once non-*halal* premises. It then decided to take a proactive step to ensure that the Pizza Hut premises would not be doubted by Muslim customers in the future.

Tesco Malaysia has also worked with JAKIM and other Islamic NGOs and government agencies at improving its *halal* and *haram* procedures. In one instance, the retailer invited the Islamic Consumer Association and Islamic officials in the state of Perak to visit its chicken supplier and distribution center (DC) as a gesture of transparency (T2, 2008).

Giant
From observations, the difference between Giant hypermarkets and the other two operators is that a few of its stores do not sell fresh pork meat or fresh pork by-products. These stores do, however, sell canned pork products packaged outside the store. Furthermore, in these stores independent retailers who are tenants in the hypermarket's premises do sell fresh non-*halal* meat to the public.

OVERALL FINDINGS AND DISCUSSION

Overall, the findings indicate that Carrefour Malaysia's market-oriented organizational culture portrays elements of adaptation to the *halal* and *haram* practices. In addition, the firm also seems to go further than the other two foreign hypermarkets in terms of integrating these particular IBPs into its overall operations. This includes establishing guidelines and implementing steps that are additional to the ones that are 'necessary' or obligatory for foreign retail MNEs to be accepted in Malaysia. As such, this study determined that Carrefour Malaysia portrays characteristics that match the crossvergence subsidiary culture, whereby a fusion culture has emerged in the subsidiary as a result of the influence of IBPs on its parent's (MNE) corporate culture. On the other hand, findings have painted a picture of Tesco Malaysia and Giant Malaysia that most suitably categorizes them as possessing the divergence subsidiary culture. Both firms did their part in adapting sufficiently to the *halal* and *haram* basic requirements in Malaysia, but they did not indicate significant additional efforts in implementing or applying more than what was required.

The results that point to the emergence of the divergence and crossvergence cultures in the subsidiaries where some level of adaptation is required to the MNEs' corporate culture are supportive of the argument that localization is one of the retailers' success factors (Wrigley et al., 2005). The local business practices that have emerged in these cultures also imply the underlying motive of gaining legitimacy or 'territorial embeddedness' for these foreign retailers (Coe and Wrigley, 2007; Wrigley et al., 2005). Gaining legitimacy is especially important for a newcomer like Tesco in Malaysia, to attain its stakeholders' approval and acceptance to continue its operations there. On the other hand, for Carrefour and Giant, extensively territorially embedding themselves is their way of competing with newcomers and protecting their interests and advantages as the pioneers of the hypermarket industry in the country. The results that point to the direction of the divergence and crossvergence culture in the retail subsidiaries also highlight the irrelevance of the convergence subsidiary culture (non-adaptation to the IBPs) in this study due to the nature of the retail industry, which is focused on the local market's culture of consumption.

These findings contribute additional knowledge to the body of research into international retailing and corporate culture, as called for by Wrigley et al. (2005). Findings from the study show that even though the MNEs are from the same industry, their corporate cultures, which are influenced by their 'societal embeddedness' (Hess, 2004), do affect the way they localize themselves in the host country. In other words, the background, history and culture of the country of origin of retail firms play crucial roles in molding the firm's culture, which ultimately leads to different localization behaviors.

Although the influence of IBPs on the MNEs' corporate culture has resulted in these divergence and crossvergence subsidiary cultures, the local elements or practices that serve as the basis of these cultures are distinct to only the Malaysian environment, and cannot be generalized to other similar environments, even to other Islamic countries. The reason is that even though Muslims turn to the Qur'an and *sunnah* as the main references of their religion, different regions or countries have different interpretations of the Islamic laws. Thus, foreign organizations need to be aware of various interpretations and implementations in different countries and be careful when generalizing local business practices to other similar host countries. However, as multinational retailers, these corporations do apply the Islamic knowledge that they have gained from operating in Muslim countries in other locations. For example, there was a recent report stating that France's Carrefour 'has a *halal* product coordinator to test that its supply chain is *halal* from farm to fork' (Power, 2008). This indicates that the *halal* practices are also gradually being accommodated in countries where there is an increasing number of Muslims.

CONCLUSION

For many Muslims around the world, their religion has a significant influence over their culture. Taking this into consideration and the fact that the world Muslim population is increasing by the year, it is becoming very important for global corporations to be aware of the different business practices in Islam.

Theoretically, this study has reconceptualized the convergence-divergence-crossvergence (CDC) framework. It conceptually incorporates corporate culture and societal cultural dimensions in a manner similar to previous studies (Andrews and Chompusri, 2001, 2005), but refocused from the broad societal cultural dimension to a specific religious practice in Islam. The same treatment was given to societal culture in which a specific type of corporate culture in retail firms was identified. This ultimately means that the findings of the study are more specific and descriptive of these particular dimensions. In addition, the crossvergence variable in this study is conceptualized not only as a set of 'compromises' or acceptable business practices, but also as including additional practices which portray or imply a firm's acknowledgement of and confidence in its current and potential contributions or benefits towards business performance. This has shifted the perception that crossvergence should be a blend of practices that might not be favored or accepted by a firm but are executed regardless because of the need to achieve a compromise business solution. Crossvergence, in this study, is portrayed to be a firm's voluntary efforts or initiatives to excel in its business segment through compromise and utilization of local culture towards its benefits.

This study contributes to the field of international management and business operations because it incorporates Islamic business practices in the retail industry. Although previous studies have examined Islamic topics in the financial and economic fields, emphasis on Islamic values and principles in the topic of IBP in the retail industry is still lacking. This study addresses the gap by presenting exploratory findings with regard to the implementation of the *halal* and *haram* IBPs in the retail industry. The case studies illustrate and confirm existing arguments on the need for retail MNEs to adapt to local consumption patterns and cultures. Since the nature of the findings is quite detailed, descriptive and explanatory, these findings constitute an essential contribution to the body of knowledge on a topic where little scholarly work so far exists.

This study also shows that managers of retail MNEs should invest extensive efforts in the search for 'new' knowledge embedded in the host-country setting. Retail MNEs' ability to monitor and identify relevant knowledge from the host country is crucial for their competitiveness because they mainly compete in terms of the level of the services they provide to end consumers.

In terms of policy-making, the findings of the study have raised the issue of the need for more than just guidelines to strengthen Malaysia's reputation as a producer of *halal* products and services. There have been cases of the Malaysian *halal* certificate and logo being misused by parties to sell products which have not been genuinely certified *halal*. Hence, the study recommends that a Halal Act be established in Malaysia as soon as possible for better enforcement of the regulations and activities in the industry. A Halal Act will portray the government's seriousness in pursuing the highest credibility for its *halal* certification. It is also an appropriate step for Malaysia since it has a dominant Muslim population which calls for stringent regulations to protect their interests in the country.

REFERENCES

Adas, E. (2006), 'The making of entrepreneurial Islam and the Islamic spirit of capitalism', *Journal for Cultural Research*, **10** (2), 113–37.
Ahmad, K. (2003), 'The challenge of global capitalism: an Islamic perspective', in J. Dunning (ed.), *Making Globalization Good: The Moral Challenges of Global Capitalism*, Oxford, UK: Oxford University Press, pp. 181–209.
Al-Faruqi, I. (1982), 'Islam as culture and civilization', in S. Azzam (ed.), *Islam and Contemporary Society*, London: Longman and Islamic Council of Europe, pp. 140–76.
Ali, M. (1973), *The Religion of Islam*, Lahore: Ahmadiyya Anjuman Isha'at Islam.
Ali, S. (1993), *Social and Economic Aspects of the Islam of Mohammad*, New York: Edwin Mellen Press.
Andrews, T. and Chompusri, N. (2001), 'Lessons in "cross-vergence": restructuring the Thai subsidiary corporation', *Journal of International Business Studies*, **32** (1), 77–93.
Andrews, T. and Chompusri, N. (2005), 'Temporal dynamics of crossvergence: institutionalizing MNC integration strategies in post-crisis ASEAN', *Asia Pacific Journal of Management*, **22** (1), 5–22.
Bartlett, C. and S. Ghoshal (1989), *Managing Across Borders: The Transnational Solution*, Boston, Massachusetts: Harvard Business School Press.
Bianchi, C. and E. Ostale (2006), 'Lessons learned from unsuccessful internationalization attempts: examples of multinational retailers in Chile', *Journal of Business Research*, **59** (3), 140–47.

Burt, S., K. Mellahi, T. Jackson and L. Sparks (2002), 'Retail internationalization and retail failure: issues from the case of Marks and Spencer', *International Review of Retail, Distribution and Consumer Research*, **12** (2), 191–19.

Cardwell, M. (2008), 'New frontiers', *Food in Canada*, **68** (8), 37–39.

Carrefour (n.d.), *Our Policies*, Handbook received during an interview session in 2007.

Coe, N. and N. Wrigley (2007), 'Host economy impacts of transnational retail: the research agenda', *Journal of Economic Geography*, **7** (4), 341–71.

Dairy Farm International Holdings Limited (2008), 'Annual Report 2008', retrieved 29 May 2009, http://www.dairyfarmgroup.com/shareholder/reports/ar2008.pdf.

Dawson, J. (1994), 'Internationalization of retailing operations', *Journal of Marketing Management*, **10** (4), 267–82.

de Mooij, M. and G. Hofstede (2002), 'Convergence and divergence in consumer behavior: implications for international retailing', *Journal of Retailing*, **78** (1), 61–69.

Deshpande, R. and F. Webster (1989), 'Organizational culture and marketing: defining the research agenda', *Journal of Marketing*, **53** (1), 3–15.

Deshpande, R., J. Farley and F. Webster (1993), 'Corporate culture, customer orientation, and innovativeness in Japanese firms: a quadrad analysis', *Journal of Marketing*, **57** (1), 23–37.

Dunning, J. (1992), *Multinational Enterprises and the Global Economy*, Wokingham, UK: Addison-Wesley.

Eisenhardt, K. (1989), 'Building theories from case study research', *Academy of Management Review*, **14** (4), 532–50.

Eisenhardt, K. and M. Graebner (2007), 'Theory building from cases: opportunities and challenges', *Academy of Management Journal*, **50** (1), 25–32.

Evans, J. and K. Bridson (2005), 'Explaining retail offer adaptation through psychic distance', *International Journal of Retail and Distribution Management*, **33** (1), 69–78.

Flyvbjerg, B. (2004), 'Five misunderstandings about case-study research', in C. Seale, G. Gobo, J.F. Gubrium, and D. Silverman (eds), *Qualitative Research Practice*, Thousand Oaks, CA: Sage Publications, pp. 420–34.

Gallagher, J. (2006), 'Halal horizon', *Supermarket News*, **54** (28).

Gambling, T. and R. Abdel Karim (1991), *Business and Accounting Ethics in Islam*, London: Mansell Publishing.

Giant (2009), 'About Giant', retrieved 22 June 2009, http://www.giant.com.my/about_us.html.

Groupe Carrefour (2009a), 'Product safety and quality', retrieved 1 June 2009, http://www.carrefour.com/cdc/responsible-commerce/product-safety-and-quality/.

Groupe Carrefour (2009b), 'Our approach', retrieved 29 May 2009, http://www.carrefour.com/cdc/responsible-commerce/our-approach/.

Gupta, V. and J. Wang (2004), 'The transvergence proposition under globalization: looking beyond convergence, divergence and crossvergence', *The Multinational Business Review*, **12** (2), 37–57.

Halal Journal (2008), 'The Halal Journal Award 2008: honouring outstanding achievements in the halal industry', retrieved 20 May 2009, http://www.halaljournal.com/article/2124/the-halal-journal-awards-2008:-honouring-outstanding-achievements-in-the-halal-industry.

Halal Journal (2010), 'Carrefour Malaysia expansion still on', retrieved 1 November 2010, http://www.halal-journal.com/article/5123/carrefour-malaysia-expansion-still-on.

Harris, L. and E. Ogbonna (1999), 'Developing a market oriented culture: a critical evaluation', *Journal of Management Studies*, **36** (2), 177–96.

Hess, M. (2004), '"Spatial" relationships? Towards a reconceptualization of embeddedness', *Progress in Human Geography*, **28** (2), 165–86.

Homburg, C. and C. Pflesser (2000), 'A multiple-layer model of market-oriented organizational culture: measurement issues and performance outcomes', *Journal of Marketing Research*, **37** (4), 449–62.

Huntington, S. (1993), 'The clash of civilizations?', *Foreign Affairs*, **72** (3), 22–49.

International Halal Integrity Alliance (2009), 'About us – management', retrieved 12 March 2009, http://www.ihialliance.org/about-us/management.html.

Izutsu, T. (1966), *Ethico Religious Concepts in the Quran*, Montreal: McGill University Press.

Khilji, S. (2002), 'Modes of convergence and divergence: an integrative view of multinational practices in Pakistan', *International Journal of Human Resource Management*, **13** (2), 232–53.

Khoo, K. (1991), *Malay Society: Transformation and Democratisation: A Stimulating and Discerning Study of the Evolution of Malay Society Through the Passage of Time*, Selangor, Malaysia: Pelanduk.

Kohli, A. and B. Jaworski (1990), 'Market orientation: the construct, research propositions, and managerial implications', *Journal of Marketing*, **54** (2), 1–18.

Kostova, T. and K. Roth (2002), 'Adoption of an organizational practice by subsidiaries of multinational corporations: institutional and relational effects', *Academy of Management Journal*, **45** (1), 215–33.

Lafferty, B. and G. Hult (2001), 'A synthesis of contemporary market orientation perspectives', *European Journal of Marketing*, **35** (1/2), 92.

Lewis, R. (2003), *The Cultural Imperative: Global Trends in the 21st Century*, Yarmouth, Maine: Intercultural Press.

McGaughey S. and H. De Cieri (1999), 'Reassessment of convergence and divergence dynamics: implications for international HRM', *International Journal of Human Resource Management*, **10** (2), 235–50.

Megicks, P. and G. Warnaby (2008), 'Market orientation and performance in small independent retailers in the UK', *International Review of Retail, Distribution and Consumer Research*, **18** (1), 105–19.

Ministry of Domestic Trade and Consumer Affairs (2005), *Guidelines on Foreign Participation in the Distributive Trade Services Malaysia*, Kuala Lumpur: Government of Malaysia.

Minkus-McKenna, D. (2007), 'The pursuit of Halal', *Progressive Grocer*, **86** (17).

Mitsuo, N. (2001), 'Introduction', in N. Mitsuo, S. Siddique, O.F Bajunid (eds), *Islam and Civil Society in Southeast Asia*, Singapore: Institute of Southeast Asian Studies, pp. 1–30.

Muslim Population Worldwide (2009), retrieved 8 December 2009, http://www.islamicpopulation.com/index.html.

Narver, J. and S. Slater (1990), 'The effect of a market orientation on business profitability', *Journal of Marketing*, **54** (4), 20–35.

Ooi, K. (2006), *Malaysia after Mahathir*, Singapore: Institute of South East Asian Studies.

Perlmutter, H. (1969), 'The tortuous evolution of the multinational corporation', *Columbia Journal of World Business*, **4** (1), 9–18.

Pioch, E. (2007), "Business as usual?" Retail employee perceptions of organizational life following cross-border acquisition', *International Journal of Human Resource Management*, **18** (2), 209–31.

Power, C. (2008), 'Halal goes global', *New Statesman*, **137** (4900), 18.

Prahalad, C. and Y. Doz (1987), *The Multinational Mission: Balancing Local Demands and Global Vision*, New York: The Free Press.

Ralston, D., D. Gustafson, F. Cheung and R.H. Terpstra (1993), 'Differences in managerial values: a study of US, Hong Kong and the PRC managers', *Journal of International Business Studies*, **24** (2), 249–75.

Ralston, D.A., D.H. Holt, R.H. Terpstra, and K.C. Yu (1997), 'The impact of national culture and economic ideology on managerial work values: a study of the United States, Russia, Japan, and China', *Journal of International Business Studies*, **28** (1), 177–207.

Robertson, C., M. Al-Habib, J. Al-Khatib and D. Lanoue (2001), 'Beliefs about work in the Middle East and the convergence versus divergence of values', *Journal of World Business*, **36** (3), 223–44.

Rowley, C. and J. Benson (2002), 'Convergence and divergence in Asian human resource management', *California Management Review*, **44** (2), 90–109.

Ruekert, R. (1992), 'Developing a market-orientation: an organizational strategy perspective', *International Journal of Research in Marketing*, **9** (3), 225–45.

Scupin, R. (2008), 'The anthropological perspective of religion', in R. Scupin (ed.), *Religion and Culture: An Anthropological Focus*, Upper Saddle River, New Jersey: Prentice Hall, pp. 1–21.

Shapiro, B. (1988), 'What the hell is "market-oriented"?', *Harvard Business Review*, **66** (6), 119–25.

Siggelkow, N. (2007), 'Persuasion with case studies', *Academy of Management Journal*, **50** (1), 20–24.

Soanes, C. (ed.) (2001), *Oxford Dictionary of Current English, 3rd edition*, New York: Oxford University Press.

Tayeb, M. (1997), 'Islamic revival in Asia and human resource management', *Employee Relations*, **19** (4), 352–64.

Tesco Annual Review and Summary Financial Statement (2006), received from Tesco during interview session February 2007.

Tesco Annual Review and Summary Financial Statement (2007), retrieved 7 April 2008, www.tescocorporate.com/annualreview07/02_ourmarkets/ourmarkets.html.

Tesco Malaysia (2010), 'Our value', retrieved 1 November 2010, http://www.tesco.com.my/html/corporate_info.aspx?ID=8andPID=33andLID=1.

Tesco PLC (2009), 'Our values', retrieved 1 June 2009, http://www.tescoplc.com/plc/about_us/values/.

Turner, G. and B. Spencer (1997), 'Understanding the marketing concept as organizational culture', *European Journal of Marketing*, **31** (2), 110–21.

Verma, V. (2002), *Malaysia, State and Civil Society in Transition*, Boulder, CO: Lynne Rienner.

Verschuren, P. (2003), 'Case study as a research strategy: some ambiguities and opportunities', *International Journal of Social Research Methodology*, **6** (2), 121–39.

Westney, D.E. (2005), 'Institutional theory and the multinational corporation', in S. Ghoshal and D.E. Westney (eds), *Organization Theory and the Multinational Corporation, 2nd edition*, New York: Palgrave Macmillan, pp. 47–67.

Wrigley, N., N. Coe and A. Currah (2005), 'Globalizing retail: conceptualizing the distribution-based transnational corporation (TNC)', *Progress in Human Geography*, **29** (4), 437–57.

Yin, R. (2003), *Case Study Research: Designs and Methods, 3rd edition*, Thousand Oaks, CA: Sage Publications.

APPENDIX

Sheikh Abdullah Maghribi outlines the principles that are involved in killing animals to make them *halal* (Khoo, 1991, p. 216):

1. The instrument to be used should be a sharp knife with a very keen edge.
2. The slaughterer should face the '*qibla*' and so should the animal.
3. The knife should be held in the right hand of the slaughterer, whilst the left hand should hold the head of the animal, grasping the throat, windpipe and two arteries which run one on either side of the throat.
4. The slaughterer should then utter the name of Allah (God in Arabic), and cut the throat of the animal quickly, severing the windpipe and gullet and the two arteries.
5. After cutting the throat, it should be left on the ground so as to give it ease and comfort in breathing its last and at the same time to allow for the blood to flow out freely, for it is *haram* (forbidden) to consume its blood.

12 An international marketing strategy perspective on Islamic marketing

Sonja Prokopec and Mazen Kurdy

An understanding of the Islamic religious worldview has gained considerable importance in the field of global business and marketing practices, for several reasons. Growing Islamic markets offer enticing potential to companies that are knowledgeable enough to understand Muslim consumers, who constitute approximately one-quarter of the total world population and represent the majority population in approximately 50 countries (Al-Buraey, 2004). An increasing number of Muslim consumers are joining the ranks of the most affluent in the world. These consumers have massive and increasing purchasing power, especially in countries such as Saudi Arabia, the United Arab Emirates (UAE), Qatar, Malaysia, India, Turkey, Kuwait and Bahrain. The purchasing power of Muslim consumers in developed nations is also substantial; a recent study shows that US Muslims' spending power has reached more than $170 billion (Hastings-Black, 2009). Where Muslims constitute a majority (for example Syria, Pakistan, Algeria, Egypt), there appears to be a trend toward greater conservatism and stronger religious commitment that affects all facets of life, including consumption and trade (Rice and Al-Mossawi, 2002; Saeed et al., 2001). According to the US Central Intelligence Agency, US$2.1 trillion worth of *halal* goods and services were exported globally in 2008, representing a huge opportunity not just for multinational corporations but also for small and medium enterprises.

Yet despite this increasing importance of Muslim consumers worldwide, an Islamic perspective on global business and marketing practices has been ignored by most researchers (cf. Alserhan, 2010; Rice, 1999; Rice and Al-Mossawi, 2002; Saeed et al., 2001), leaving gaps in our understanding of international marketing strategies that have Islamic roots and take into consideration Muslim consumers' needs and requirements (Baligh, 1998). The questions of global marketing strategies (standardization versus adaptation) generally and strategies in Islamic markets in particular thus persist. This study therefore explores the extent to which standardization versus adaptation might play a role in Islamic marketing. We introduce Islamic principles that guide the consumption patterns of practicing Muslim consumers and apply them to some core marketing principles. With recent examples from the marketplace, we consider how marketing mix strategies might be adapted for Muslim target markets. Finally, we discuss challenges and opportunities, along with managerial implications, derived from our analysis.

The primary contribution of this chapter is its provision of an overview of Islamic marketing, using an international marketing strategy perspective. Furthermore, this chapter highlights current practices and trends with regards to standardization versus adaptation strategies, and possible implications for Islamic marketing worldwide. It thus provides a starting point for marketers and business consultants interested in understanding the origins, challenges and potential opportunities of Islamic marketing.

THE INTERNATIONAL MARKETING STRATEGY DEBATE

Research in the fields of international business, international marketing and cross-cultural marketing clearly shows that conducting business in different countries poses many challenges, including those related to marketing products and services globally (Young and Javalgi, 2007). One of the first scholars to argue for a standardized approach to marketing, Levitt (1983), suggested the world was undergoing globalization, which he considered a convergence of all cultures toward one common global culture. Furthermore he argued that consumers throughout the world are increasingly motivated by the same desires for modernity, quality and value. Yet standardization may be effective only in homogeneous markets (Jain, 1989); in heterogeneous markets, companies need to rely on adaptation and localization strategies (Duncan and Ramaprasad, 1995). How much standardization versus adaptation is preferred is an important strategic issue for managers around the world (Birnik and Bowman, 2007; Okazaki et al., 2007).

The biggest benefit for firms that standardize products is the resultant economies of scale from a standard product that can sell worldwide. Other benefits of standardization include the presentation of a consistent corporate/brand image across different markets and reduced managerial complexity from better coordination and control (Levitt, 1983). Advocates of the adaptation approach criticize the standardization strategy as an over-simplification of reality. They argue that variations between countries such as different consumer needs, use conditions, purchasing power, culture and traditions, commercial infrastructure and regulations, for example, are too great to be ignored (Terpstra and Sarathy, 2000). Thus it is necessary for the firm to adjust its marketing strategy to each foreign market.

Another strategy, glocalization, views standardization and adaptation as two ends of the same continuum. Advocates of this approach argue that the decision to standardize or adapt the marketing strategy is situation specific and should be based on the analysis of the relevant factors present in a specific market at a specific time (Theodosiou and Leonidou, 2003). Glocalization takes into account that some degree of adaptation is necessary in the real world; therefore, the firm uses a global theme and adapts as necessary to accommodate local tastes and requirements – also referred to as the 'think global, act local' strategy.

The applicability of standardization to consumer goods seems largely limited to products with universal brand name recognition, minimal product knowledge requirements for use, and low information content in advertising. For example, food products are difficult to globalize, because consumers must be able to recognize the product and its contents. Consumer products used at home (for example food and beverages) also tend to be more culturally grounded than products used outside the home (for example automobiles) (Herbig, 1998).

The question that arises when we consider the standardization versus adaptation debate in relation to Islamic marketing is whether the very notion of Islamic marketing simply represents a re-application of a 'standardization' approach to a vast group of consumers. Or, does Islamic marketing mean the adaptation of marketing mix elements to address Muslims? We attempt to address these questions in this chapter, by first examining the principles that guide the Islamic religion.

OVERVIEW OF ISLAM

Muslims number approximately 1.6 billion people worldwide today (Pew Forum, 2009), many of whom engage in consumption activities in the developed world. Contrary to the popular belief that most Muslims live in the Middle East, the majority of Muslims live in Asia, and only 20 per cent live in the Middle East (Pew Forum, 2009). Representing many different ethnic groups and regions throughout the world, Muslims are guided by a faith that usually shapes their moral and ethical behaviours. Despite the heterogeneity of Muslim populations, including their presence as majority and significant minority populations in some 57 countries around the world, Islam bonds these consumers in terms of their daily lives and thus influences their consumption habits (Young, 2010).

Authoritative codes of conduct offer primary authority in Islam, namely, the Qur'an (the holy book of the Muslims) and the *sunnah* (recorded sayings and behaviours of the Prophet Muhammad). The Qur'an is considered the word of God and contains recommendations for living a religiously acceptable life (Fisher and Bailey, 2008). The *sunnah* of the Prophet Muhammad cites his specific words, actions and practices. This is significant for Muslims because these sayings address the proper ways to deal with real-life issues, such as interactions with friends, family, and the government. Finally, *sharia* law is the law by which Muslims abide, which dictates how to deal with topics including, but not limited to, birth, death, marriage and divorce (Fisher and Bailey, 2008). This law is based on the Qur'an and *sunnah* and interpreted by religious authorities, according to Islamic jurisprudence. External observers often express surprise that Islam prescribes rules for entire socio-economic systems, including specific guidelines for managerial tasks such as marketing, commerce, and advertising. However all activities related to business practices, as well as to general daily activities, are broadly categorized as either lawful and permitted (*halal*) or prohibited and forbidden (*haram*). This dichotomy is a foundational element of Islamic ethics, used by most Muslims to determine if something is in accordance with Islam or not in many aspects of life (Rippin, 2005). *Halal* refers not only to a product but also to a way of life, such that it encompasses everything of good quality, from speaking with the right (*halal*) words to *halal* meat to a *halal* way of life.

Also salient are the five pillars of Islam. The first pillar refers to pronouncements of the confession of faith. The second pillar of Islam is the performance of the five daily prayers, or *salah*. The third pillar relates to fasting during the month of Ramadan, when Muslims must fast from dawn to sunset and abstain from food, water, smoking, sex and vice. The fourth pillar revolves around charity, or *zakat*, a yearly charitable requirement that Islamic scholars agree to be approximately 2.5 per cent of a person's wealth. Finally, the fifth pillar involves the pilgrimage to Mecca (*hajj*) once in a lifetime if the person is able (Fisher and Bailey, 2008). *Sharia* law also enforces dietary requirements, such as exclusions of pork and alcohol; guidelines for dressing, such as no sexually provocative clothing permitted in public; and regulations regarding property rights for women and wills, among other legal topics (Fisher and Bailey, 2008).

INTERNATIONAL MARKETING STRATEGY IN ISLAMIC MARKETS

Many marketing and branding decisions affecting Muslim consumers continue to reflect Western management influence and style (Zakaria and Abdul-Talib, 2010).

Understanding Muslim consumers instead requires that the marketing strategy of the firms be assessed and implemented in line with local cultures. However, marketing to Muslim consumers also requires more than just understanding cultural preferences and adapting products to meet them. Religion plays a central role in the decision-making process of Muslim consumers, thus making the Islamic market fundamentally different in terms of motivations, structure and behavior (Young, 2010). For example, recent findings indicate that young Muslim consumers are different from their Western 'Generation Y' counterparts in that they believe that they are more likely to achieve success in the modern world by staying true to the core values of their religion (Gooch, 2010).

The starting point for marketing and branding must be the consideration of the role of *sharia* compliance in the lives of modern Muslim consumers, as well as what they have come to expect from brands in these terms. The Ogilvy and Mather advertising agency recently published the first-ever index of Muslim-friendly brands (Ogilvy and Mather, 2010). The index was based on the perceptions of Muslim consumers from four major Islamic markets: Malaysia, Saudi Arabia, Pakistan and Egypt. The results are considered a representative demographic sample of Muslims worldwide. The findings of this study reveal that Muslim consumers do not give the same level of importance to all product categories in regards to compliance with Islamic values. *Sharia*-compliance is especially relevant for product categories that are closer to the human body, including food, beverage, and oral care brands. These were followed by fashion, personal care, and 'regular' finance. The least important category involved airlines, resorts, financial and insurance products. Muslim consumers also identified *halal/haram* classifications as irrelevant for some categories, such as software (Ogilvy and Mather, 2010). Many companies operating in Islamic markets are taking steps to reassure consumers that all of their products (not just food) are *halal*, by having them officially certified. Thus we argue that marketing to Muslim consumers implies some degree of standardization, separate from the standardization achieved when marketing to global markets. This type of standardization refers to creating a *sharia*-compliant (that is, *halal*) brand; after meeting this requirement, the firm can consider the specific cultural particularities (other than religion) of each market.

It is also important to note that Muslim markets do not represent a single homogeneous market that can be approached in a monolithic way. Although a first prerequisite is understanding the faith and the core Islamic values and making the brand *sharia*-compliant (or *halal*), Muslims represent majority populations in approximately 50 countries around the world. Despite similar beliefs regarding motivations to purchase *sharia*-compliant, or *halal* products, Muslim consumers around the world are geographically as well as culturally diverse. They speak numerous languages and adhere to varying standards of dress and other customs. Therefore understanding the predominant culture, local tastes and preferences, and adapting the *sharia*-compliant brand to these elements is vital. This is in line with previous research on glocalization that states that some dose of adaptation is necessary and situation specific; the difference here is that standardization involves first creating a *halal* brand. If a glocal marketing strategy for Western consumers calls for a 'think global, act local' approach, then a glocal marketing strategy for Muslim consumers should call for a 'think *sharia* (or *halal*), act local' approach.

THE MARKETING MIX AND ISLAM

According to the American Marketing Association, marketing is the process of planning and executing the conception, pricing, promotion and distribution of ideas, goods and services to create exchanges that satisfy individual and organizational goals. It may appear then that Islam is in conflict with many modern Western marketing practices, because Islam does not recognize any division between religious and secular dimensions (Kavoossi, 2000). Nevertheless, in Islam, business activity is a socially useful function; the Prophet Muhammad was involved in trade for much of his life. Islam therefore contains rules governing business conduct, the freedom of the market economy, and problem solving during the trade of goods and services, all of which must be based on maximizing the interests of the individual and the community, as well as non-profit sharing (Al- Buraey, 2004). Some foundational values include honesty, sincerity of intention, respect, kindness, peacefulness, purity, modesty and community. Furthermore, for Muslims, branding cannot be separated from faith (Alserhan, 2010). For example, trade relationships reflect a sincere intention by two business parties to accomplish a good deed, not just obtain apparent material benefits from the transaction (Alserhan, 2010). This logic affects all domains of Islamic marketing: manufacturing, selling, advertising, buying and so on.

The rules of the Qur'an and *sunnah* thus govern the four elements of the marketing mix (product/service, promotion, price and place). In the following discussion, we examine these four Ps in relation to Islam and current marketing practices. Then we examine various industries and product categories, with the goal of highlighting current practices in Islamic marketing from an international marketing strategy perspective.

Products/Services

The quality of production is of paramount importance, because Islamic principles dictate that the production process must be innocent and pure from beginning to end (Al-Faruqi, 1992). A value-maximization approach is favoured over a profit maximization approach (Saeed et al., 2001). Products and services therefore must ensure environmental protection and human safety. The product must be manufactured in an acceptable manner and should not have adverse consequences on the world. In this sense, the principles of Islam are not distant from those of sustainable development. The product also should not cause harm (mental or physical) to an individual or community, as might be the case for cigarettes, alcohol, gambling, weapons or even dangerous games for children. In general, a product must be pure and clean before it can be consumed.

Not all product categories demand the same level of compliance with Islamic values, as previously mentioned. Products rated by Muslim consumers as most important in terms of compliance with their values were food, dairy, beverages and oral care, followed by fashion, personal care and 'regular' finance. We discuss some examples below.

Halal foods

Halal certification means that an animal killed for human consumption has been slaughtered according to Muslim jurisprudence, which requires the animal be killed in a manner that limits pain and allows its blood to drain in a precise way, to avoid harm to the final consumer. *Halal* slaughter is important for Muslims because they believe it is the proper way to kill animals for consumption, as ordained by God. However, *halal* is not merely an approved way to kill an animal; it is also a critical part of the belief system and moral code of conduct, integral for daily living (Wilson and Liu, 2010).

The size of the global *halal* food market is estimated to be approximately $150 billion, $12 billion of which represents just the US market. Moreover, the market for *halal* food is increasing. In Europe for example, it is worth approximately $66 billion and is expected to increase by 20 to 25 per cent in the next decade (Haniff, 2010). France hosts more than 3 000 Muslim butchers, and supermarkets are beginning to take notice of this growing trend. Moreover, France's *halal* market has been increasing by 15 per cent annually, while national food consumption has been decreasing by 2 per cent per year. Even as the overall meat market and food consumption decrease, Muslim food consumption is growing. In the United Kingdom more than six million people consume *halal* food, though there are only two million Muslims ('ECER enters UK *halal* market' 2009). According to organizers of the Third Halal Food Fair in Paris, more than 20 million Muslims in Europe eat some form of *halal* food (Nestorovic, 2007). A 2007 study also revealed that 84 per cent of Muslims in France always eat *halal* meat (Bonne et al.,2007) and in the US, it is estimated that 75 per cent of Muslims follow religious dietary laws (Hussaini, 1993).

Yet growth in the *halal* market can also be attributed to demand from non-Muslims. *Halal* food is perceived as healthier, more environmentally friendly and a better ethical option, because of the way the animals are slaughtered for consumption (Bonne et al., 2007; Bonne and Verbeke, 2006).

There thus is no such thing as the *halal* consumer. Previous research suggests four categories pertaining to consumers' consciousness about this form of consumption: 'natural' *halal* consumers in Muslim countries, who are barely aware of the existence of non-*halal* food; 'conscious' *halal* consumers in non-Muslim countries who are aware of its consumption, because they know that most of the food in the country in which they live is *haram*; 'Western' *halal* consumers who focus on healthy, high quality or pork-free food and therefore choose *halal* but do not necessarily practice Islam; and 'ignorant' *halal* consumers who eat the food without knowing it, because the food industry has switched to *halal* food production to achieve economies of scale. These groups are certainly not clear-cut, in that their boundaries are blurred and some sub-groups likely exist within other groups (van Waarden and van Dalen, 2010).

An increasing number of corporations have developed products to address the dietary preferences of Muslim customers, introducing a wide variety of *halal* foods. A leader in the global *halal* food market, Nestlé produces *halal* food in countries worldwide, with major *halal* markets including Malaysia, Indonesia and Turkey. The company has been producing *halal*-certified products since the 1980s to meet the needs of Muslim consumers. Of the 456 Nestlé factories worldwide, 85 have a *halal* certification. The company established general instructions called 'Guidelines for Intercompany Supply of *Halal* Food' in 1997, which serve as a policy document to help the supplying market understand the mandatory aspects of *halal* qualifications (www.nestle.com.my). Nestlé is a good example of a company that has been able to achieve a level of standardization within Islamic markets by creating a *sharia*-compliant brand. Furthermore, Nestlé has a clear focus on developing local consumer insight and adapting *halal* product offerings to local tastes. Brands that are perceived to be Muslim-friendly are Nestlé's Nescafé and Unilever's Lipton (Ogilvy and Mather, 2010). Nescafé, for example, has an 88 per cent market share in the Gulf Cooperation Council (GCC). Many fast-food chains, including McDonald's, Burger King, Wendy's, KFC, Subway and Dunkin' Donuts have opened stores that offer *halal* foods in Muslim countries. More recently, these companies have recognized the possibilities of providing *halal* offerings to Muslim customers in Western nations. For example, McDonald's began offering *halal* McNuggets in Dearborn, Michigan, in response to repeated customer requests. This area is home to some 150 000 Muslims officially, though unofficial reports suggest the numbers are even higher. Furthermore, sales of the *halal* McNuggets were so good that McDonald's expanded the offering to other locations, including other Western countries such as Australia and the United Kingdom (islam.about.com/od/dietarylaw/a/halalmcd.htm).

Many other examples indicate that companies are grasping the opportunity to enter this growing market, though few of them seem to remain viable for long. A good example is the soft-drink company Mecca Cola. Started in 2002 by a Tunisian-born businessman, Mecca Cola achieved initial success in parts of France and quickly spread to various regions in the Middle East and the Arab and Muslim world. It sold more than 2 million bottles during the course of an early two-month period. Mecca Cola featured a slogan, 'No more drinking stupid, Drink with commitment,' that reflected its commitment to provide 10 per cent of its profits to the Palestinian cause (Bittermann, 2002) and another 10 per cent to local causes. It also claimed to be *halal*, in that the company did not use any pork gelatine ingredients in its production. Yet despite the cola's activist stance and initial success, the brand soon began to fade away from many markets, including France, the UAE and elsewhere.

Another failed soft drink company that marketed to Muslims is Qibla Cola. The name 'Qibla' refers to the direction that should be faced by Muslims when they pray. This company, started in 2003, coordinated its marketing efforts to appeal to Muslims and also donated 10 per cent of its profits to charities. One of its marketing slogans, with the phrase 'it's time to make a choice,' highlighted consumers' choice to drink Qibla Cola or other brands that did not support social causes. The brand received a lot of attention in the United Kingdom and other countries, yet Qibla Cola did not remain a viable company and entered bankruptcy in 2005, blaming anti-competitive practices for its troubles (news.bbc.co.uk/2/hi/uk_news/england/derbyshire/4244508.stm).

Halal fashion

Modesty is an important element of Islam. The Qur'an provides guidelines on how men and women should dress and behave, though references in this regard allow for more or less strict interpretations (Rice and Al-Mossawi, 2002). For example, the Qur'an dictates that a woman should be covered in a way that does not reveal her sexuality in public. Dressing modestly requires wearing clothes that are not tight-fitting, are made of non-transparent material, and do not expose excess skin (Al-Qaradawi, 1995). In addition, Islam invites women to wear a *hijab*, a scarf to cover their hair; however, the Qur'an does not mandate head coverings. Although the four prominent schools of thought in Islam agree that a woman should cover her hair, it has been argued that the Qur'an is not explicit about how to achieve this cover. The *hijab* comes in a variety of styles and can be worn in many ways. In some Islamic cultures, women cover their hair completely, whereas in others, women show some hair, normally just above their face. In countries such as Turkey, the government prevents women from wearing the *hijab* in public, such as on university campuses (Nestorovic, 2007). Since the 1980s though, women in Turkey and elsewhere have adopted the veil voluntarily (Sandıkcı and Ger, 2010).

In the study conducted by Ogilvy and Mather (2010), fashion was ranked as a second-tier product category in terms of importance of *sharia*-compliance. This implies that adhering to Islamic values for a clothing brand is important but not as difficult to achieve as with first-tier product categories (food, beverages and oral care) where the entire manufacturing process has to meet *halal* requirements. The key aspect of *sharia*-compliance when it comes to marketing clothing is that the clothing satisfies the Islamic value of modesty. Furthermore, even within the boundaries of the conservative clothing required by Islam, fashion styles are geographically and culturally diverse, and need to be taken into account when designing Islamic clothing offerings.

Fashion evolves in all parts of the Muslim world. For example, headscarves are often combined with Western or Eastern clothing. This trend partly reflects the lack of high-quality traditional garments available to customers, especially to Muslim women living in Western countries such as the United Kingdom. Few UK retailers of traditional Islamic clothing conduct any market research to determine their customers' needs and thus tend to offer cheap imports from Asia and the Middle East. In addition, online retail sites tend to suffer in terms of image quality, delivery, and customer service (a notable exception is: http://www.shukronline.com/home.html).

Muslim women face similar challenges in the US, where it is very difficult to find *halal* clothes in department stores (La Ferla, 2007). Some retailers appear to be trying to cater to this segment; Nordstrom's was perhaps the first retailer to recognize the unmet needs of US Muslim women to find conservative, fashionable clothing. It hosted the first high-end fashion *hijab* show, sponsored by corporate America, called 'Interpreting Hot Trends for Veiled and Conservative Women.' This fashion seminar took place at the Tysons' Corner mall in McLean, Virginia, home to many well-to-do Muslim families, who live in the suburbs of northern Virginia and increasingly shop at the well-known mall (Nomani, 2005).

The Nordstrom's show may have marked the start of a growing trend, including growth in the veiling fashion industry that is developing internationally. Thus, veiling increasingly is becoming embedded in notions of consumerism (Sandıkcı and Ger, 2007). Some luxury companies recognize the potential of an Islamic clothing market, particularly among women; Hermes, Gucci, Christian Dior and Dolce & Gabbana sell their iconic scarves to fashionable Muslim women. In 2004 Hermes launched a global ad campaign featuring two women with dark hair, dark eyes and olive skin wearing the company's famous scarves wrapped around their heads in the Muslim style of a *hijab* (Nomani, 2005).

Nike also hopes to tap the Muslim market and thus has created a sports *hijab* that does not affect physical movement during sports. Soon after its introduction, the company sold 10000 of the head coverings. Another interesting example is a product innovation, the Muslim swimsuit or Burqini (that is, *burqa* + bikini), invented by an Australian retailer Aheda Zanetti. These polyester swimsuits follow Islamic laws regarding women's modest dress but avoid the risk to women who try to swim in the yards of fabric that make up the traditional *burqa*. Demand for the Burqini is also spreading beyond this target market, in that conservative Christians, cancer patients, and elderly swimmers find it appealing, in countries as diverse as Malaysia, South Africa and the US (Fitzpatrick, 2007).

Halal toys

Barbie is the famous fashion doll manufactured by the US toy company Mattel, Inc., launched in 1959. Barbie has had many different careers, an occasional romantic relationship with her boyfriend Ken and diverse, and at times, liberal fashion apparel. In September 2003 Saudi Arabia outlawed the sale of Barbie dolls, saying she did not conform to the ideals of Islam. A few years earlier, similar actions were taken by religious authorities in Iran and Kuwait ('Iranians slam "satanic" Barbie', 1996). In Middle Eastern countries the alternative to Barbie is called Fulla; she is a similar doll but designed explicitly by a Syrian company NewBoy Design Studio to be more acceptable to Islamic and Middle Eastern countries (news.bbc.co.uk/2/hi/middle_east/1856558.stm). Fulla dresses in a black *abaya* and headscarf for the Saudi market, whereas for more liberal Muslim countries, she has a white scarf and pastel coat. Her outdoor clothes have become more colourful since her introduction in 2003, though her shoulders are always covered and her skirt always falls below her knees. Although Fulla and Barbie are similar in size, height and popularity, they represent very different lifestyles and appearances. Fulla's activities mostly include shopping, spending time with her friends, cooking, reading and praying. She does not have a boyfriend, because Muslims do not believe in non-formal romantic relationships before marriage. Despite her premium price, Fulla has been very popular; for example, in Damascus, where the official average per capita income is approximately $100 per month, the doll sells for $16.

Even though toys have not been specifically ranked as a product category in the study by Ogilvy and Mather (2010), one could think of them as a second-tier product category, similar to personal care or clothing. Therefore compliance with *sharia* law is still relatively important. This example clearly illustrates that toys have to project an Islamic image to be acceptable within Muslim markets. Fulla's clothing as well as activities are all *sharia*-compliant. The adaptations to the specificities of different markets can been seen in adaptation of the attire to suit more conservative Saudi Arabian standards. Thus, Fulla's success appears to be a result of the Syrian company's understanding of Muslim markets and the values of the Muslim consumers.

Promotion/Communication

According to an Islamic perspective, communication between people should be polite, kind and direct, which applies to communication within promotional activities as well. Exaggeration in advertising is considered a form of lying, regardless of whether it works by metaphor or descriptive embellishment (Rice and Al-Mossawi, 2002). A study of advertising conducted in the Arabian Gulf revealed that the emphasis in commercials was mainly on the durability, tradition, quality and overall integrity of the goods and the seller; these researchers observed a distinct lack of exaggeration compared with the level in US advertising (Kavoossi and Frank, 1990). The Islamic faith also does not condone any form of deception in advertising, such that all defects should be disclosed to the buyer before a sale.

Other promotional techniques not allowed by Islam include the use of sex, emotional or fear appeals, false testimonies and pseudo-research appeals (Saeed et al. 2001). These appeals are not permissible because they take advantage of the basic instincts of consumers in an attempt to gain profits and increase market share. In addition, the Islamic faith strictly prohibits stereotyping of women or their use as objects in advertising, as well as suggestive behaviour and language. These principles are implemented by Saudi (Razzouk and Al-Khatib, 1993) and Malaysian (ASA Malaysia, 2008) advertising guidelines, as well as in other more conservative Muslim countries. For example, Rice and Al-Mossawi (2002) point to a billboard advertisement for Davidoff Cool Water Ice perfume that in Western countries featured an apparently naked woman emerging from a lake. It was modified for Bahrain, such that the model's shoulder was covered and only her face was visible. Even with this adaptation, municipal authorities complained that the model's face was too suggestive.

Halal television

A fairly recent project targeting Muslim consumers is the Islam Channel, started in 2004 in the UK for the English-speaking Muslim community there. The founder of the Islam Channel perceived a void in terms of a television station that catered specifically to Muslims; its inception has also created opportunities for companies operating in Western markets to create and advertise products for the Muslim community in the UK. The channel aims to provide programming to both non-Muslim and Muslim communities, such that it includes shows to enlighten those who are not familiar with Islam, and to correct stereotypes and negative preconceived notions. A 2001 UK census indicated that 51 per cent of Muslims in that country had been born there and that most of them were between 25 and 35 years of age. At the start of the century, the UK was home to 1.5 million Muslims (UK Census, 2001); this number now exceeds two million Muslims (Pew Forum, 2009). In turn, 59 per cent of UK Muslims watch the Islam Channel, which thus provides a lucrative opportunity for marketers to communicate about their products. The Islam Channel has also launched in Africa and has plans to expand into North America, which could provide additional opportunities for companies looking to advertise their products to US Muslims. A study by J. Walter Thompson (JWT), an advertising agency in New York, revealed that US Muslims do not feel recognized in current advertisements; 71 per cent said they rarely see people of their own faith or ethnicity in advertising, and 73 per cent said they could not think of one mainstream brand that showed a Muslim in its advertising ('Marketing to Muslims', 2007).

Since the 1990s, the liberalization of broadcasting rules in many Muslim countries has led to the proliferation of *halal* television stations focusing on the Muslim market. Approximately 470 free to air stations exist in the Arab world alone. Although there are many *halal* television stations, ranging from Saudi-based Iqra TV to the recently launched 4Shabab Muslim music channel, each country has its own general standards for what is and is not considered *halal*. Although the rules for *halal* are the same, the degree to which they are applied may vary. Each television station therefore must understand the particularities of each market of interest.

Price, Islamic Banking and the Issue of Usury

In Islam, deceiving the innocent consumer for economic gain is strictly prohibited (Ibn Taymiya, 1982). Islam also prohibits the receipt of profit without working for it, as well as obtaining something too easily without having taken part in labour (Saeed et al., 2001). It is also forbidden to change the price of a product without changing the quality and/or quantity as well. These prohibitions reflect the general idea of not manipulating the consumer. However, it is not forbidden to manipulate the price based on the needs of the market, so if a product becomes scarce, it is permissible to charge a higher price, and it is permissible to set price ceilings on products that have been sold by opportunistic merchants. That is, healthy competition (*munāfasa*) is promoted and encouraged. What is not permitted is the manipulation of consumers based on illicit gain, price manipulation or hoarding (Niazi, 1996).

Halal banking instruments

In accordance with Islamic principles, usury, or a premium obtained from the principal for the use of the funds, is strictly forbidden. In Arabic, the word '*riba*' means increase or expansion, and the two main kinds of *riba* – earning interest on loaned money and providing more of an inferior item for less of a superior item – are strictly forbidden (Alam et al., 2008). Islam teaches that people should use their wealth productively after acquiring it by continuing to circulate wealth and not stopping its momentum. Moreover, one of the five pillars, *zakat* (compulsory charity to the poor) addresses the issue of income redistribution (Rice, 1999).

Many financial instruments have been created to provide services to a growing Muslim population interested in investing their money within an Islamic framework. Common forms of this microfinance market include mutual insurance (*takaful*), in which context adherents have an interest in helping the weaker members of the pool rather than creating profits. This form provides an acceptable way to gain an added amount of economic security. Profit and loss sharing (*musharaka* and *mudaraba*) represent other examples of microfinance. Under *musharaka*, both the entrepreneur and the financier invest funds in the investment and therefore share the risk. *Mudaraba* instead allows the financier to invest the funds while the entrepreneur invests his or her labour. This way, the financier can benefit from the profits while the entrepreneur reaps shares of profit, as well as from the work product. In a cost plus mark-up sale (*murabaha*), the financier buys and sells products to an entrepreneur at a mark-up. The borrower is then responsible for paying back the financier in installments until the loan is paid back. Many of these financial instruments have been in use for more than 1000 years. These forms recently have experienced a resurgence as Muslim economies try to grow without resorting to non-Islamic practices, such as the collection of interest (*riba*) (Imady and Seibel, 2006).

Islamic economics

Generally speaking, there are three forms of Islamic economic systems currently employed in Muslim economies. One in place in approximately 45 Muslim countries is referred to as the 'conventional plus' system. This system is basically a conventional system with a few Islamic banking institutions operating on the fringe of the banking system. Depositors can expect a specific rate of return on their money based on the bank's investments (Mohsin and Mirakhor, 1990). Countries such as Indonesia, Saudi Arabia and many Arabic-speaking countries follow this system; in contrast, Malaysia uses a dual system in which the Islamic banking system operates in parallel with a conventional system. For example, the banks provide a return on investments by pooling their resources and investing them in construction, commodities trading and other businesses that do not generate interest without providing labour and taking part in risk (Parker, 2003). The third type of system is one that totally restructures the economic system of the country. In this case, all economic entities, and banks specifically, are required to operate within a specific code of Muslim conduct. Prime examples of these alternative Muslim economies include Iran, Pakistan and Sudan (Aggarwal and Yousef, 2000).

Islamic banking is expected to grow by approximately 10 per cent per year (Čihák and Hesse, 2008) and currently represents only 0.5 per cent of the world's estimated assets, or \$822 billion dollars (www.economist.com/world/europe/displaystory.cfm?story_ id=14859353). More than 300 Islamic banks function in more than 50 countries, and 250 mutual funds comply with Islamic banking principles. CIMB Group Holdings has stated that Islamic finance is the fastest growing portion of the global financial system and sales of Islamic bonds should increase to approximately \$25 billion in 2010. According to Standard & Poor's Ratings Services, *sharia*-compliant assets reached approximately \$400 billion, though the market potential was near \$4 trillion in 2009 (www.irandaily. com/1388/12/11/MainPaper/3630/Page/5/Index.htm). As a sort of seal of approval, the Vatican put forward the idea that 'the principles for Islamic finance may represent a possible cure for ailing markets' (Totaro, 2009).

Muslim consumers rank personal finance as a second-tier category and financial and insurance products as a third tier category in terms of importance of *sharia*-compliance. This implies that for most of the Muslim consumers it is still important that the operations of a financial institution are in line with the Muslim faith. A recent study published in the *Journal of Financial Services Marketing* also showed that Muslim bank customers preferred banking with a Muslim bank, even if they were not satisfied with the quality of the products and services (Al-Tamimi et al., 2009). Two Western banks currently operating in Muslim countries, HSBC and RBS, were not perceived as Muslim-friendly according to the Ogilvy Noor Brand Index (Ogilvy and Mather, 2010). This dissatisfaction suggests a prime opening for Western banks that may be able to provide more *sharia*-compliant products and services in an Islamic context.

Place

Physical distribution involves the collection of information, people, equipment and organization; it is a process that involves numerous stages, from providing means that enable customers to place an order to final delivery (Bovee and Thill, 1992). Within an Islamic framework, the role of distribution channels is to provide a benefit to the consumer by creating value and increasing the standard of living. This value results from not burdening the consumer with higher prices and delays, and providing ethically acceptable services. Muslim consumers in Western markets are not always protected from paying higher prices for *halal* or Islamically approved products. For example, a persistent problem that many US Muslim consumers face is the high price of meat products and limited selection of *halal* products in most markets. A recent survey revealed that 44 per cent of US Muslim consumers do not feel that their needs are being met by currently available *halal* foods ('Marketing to Muslims', 2007). As mentioned earlier, fast-food chains in the US and Europe regard this opportunity as ideal and have opened *halal*-only restaurants to cater to this niche market. KFC and A&W Hamburger have opened *halal*-only stores in some US locations. Domino's Pizza in the UK offers both *halal* offerings and *halal*-only outlets in certain areas. The stores that serve *halal*-only meats are in areas populated by a majority of Muslim customers (Cooper, 2009). To earn acceptance from the local Muslim community, the franchise needs to be accredited by the Halal Food Authority (HFA) in the UK. KFC has approximately 100 *halal*-only stores in the UK that have been certified by the HFA, Subway has approximately 60 *halal*-only restaurants. A French fast-food chain, Quick, opened 22 *halal*-only stores in France in the summer of 2010 (Heneghan, 2010); it chose to open more stores after its trial stores in eight areas with a strong Muslim population enjoyed a doubling of customers and increased customer spending.

CHALLENGES AND OPPORTUNITIES

Around the world, approximately 1.6 billion people identify themselves as Muslim. Islam shapes their sense of identity, their beliefs and values and their behaviour. From a marketing perspective, the growing influence of Islam is bound to have a widespread effect on Muslim consumption. This scenario provides more marketing opportunities and challenges for Western and non-Western companies to market their products to an interested yet underserved customer base. We thus examine possible opportunities and challenges that companies should address when dealing with Islamic markets and conclude with an analysis of Islamic marketing from an international marketing strategy perspective.

Products/Services

Islam dictates that the products and services offered to the Muslim customer must be innocent and pure, from beginning to end (Saeed et al., 2001). As mentioned previously, opportunities to offer *sharia*-compliant (*halal*) products and services to Muslim consumers are vast yet relatively unexplored by non-Muslim multinational corporations (Alserhan, 2010). Even though the first requirement is that the product is *sharia*-compliant, Muslim consumers are looking for more than just a stamp of religious approval. For example, a 2007 marketing research study conducted by JWT (American Muslim Consumer, 2010) reports that 70 per cent of US Muslim consumers believe that brands play an important role in their purchasing decisions, compared to 55 per cent for average US consumers. Fifty-nine per cent of Muslim consumers say they make a point of knowing which brands are popular (compared to 42 per cent for average US consumers). Finally, JWT found that 55 per cent of Muslims agree that brands make 'life more interesting' compared to 43 per cent for average US consumers. Therefore Western companies with strong brands that can modify their products to the needs of Muslim consumers have an opportunity to develop a loyal customer base, as companies in the fast food industry have done by offering *halal* products and stores. Furthermore multinationals such as Nestlé and Lipton offer a gold standard for marketing to Muslims: Nestlé's *halal* committee and separate facilities for its *halal* products suggest a level of strategic attention that implies a holistic understanding of consumers and an active engagement with Islamic values, across every element of the marketing mix and beyond. In 2008, Nestlé achieved a turnover for *halal* products of US$3.6 billion.

The opportunities for marketing fashion to Muslim consumers are vast, such that the global Muslim fashion industry is estimated to be worth at least $96 billion, based on the assumption that half the world's 1.6 billion Muslims dress conservatively and spend $120 a year on such clothing (Young, 2007).

Although products ranging from colas to financial instruments are currently being marketed to the Islamic world, the real question pertains to their long-term competitiveness. The initial results for products such as Mecca Cola pointed to financial success, along with extensive media coverage. The brand might have connected with some Muslim consumers in response to political momentum, but management could not maintain customer loyalty. Thus, the challenge in serving the Muslim market entails not just obtaining religious approval for the product but also generating the effective level of branding and adaptation to local tastes required by the market.

Promotion

Communication and promotional techniques cannot include manipulative behaviour if they are to meet Islamic requirements. Several brands have found ways to market their products successfully by adapting their commercials (for example Davidoff Cool Water Ice perfume). Opportunities to advertise to Muslim consumers living in Western markets are also increasing, though Muslim consumers still feel underrepresented in modern advertising (JWT, 2007). Opportunities to reach Muslim consumers living in Western markets have expanded with the introduction of the Islam Channel, though the use of this channel may present a challenge because the cultural and religious idiosyncrasies of each Muslim market dictate different promotional and communication techniques (Rice and Al-Mossawi, 2002).

Price

Islam prohibits deception of innocent consumers for economic gain, as well as usury. Many financial instruments are available to Muslim consumers interested in investing their money within an Islamic framework. London is becoming a Western hub of Islamic finance, along with hubs in the Middle East and Malaysia, whereas other countries in Europe are much slower to follow despite their large Muslim populations (for example France, Germany). France also has experienced a backlash regarding Islamic finance; some commentators argue that implementing it contradicts that country's strong secular constitution (Oakley, 2009).

Place

Within an Islamic framework, the role of distribution channels is to provide a benefit to the consumer by creating value and increasing the standard of living by offering ethically acceptable services. Muslim consumers living in Western markets often feel underserved by current offerings, such as *halal* foods that are limited and expensive. As the example of fast-food chains opening *halal*-only restaurants to cater to this niche market shows, opportunities for creating products and services that meet the religious criteria and are accessible to most Muslim consumers in the West are still relatively untapped.

CONCLUSION

This chapter aims to examine Islamic marketing through the lens of the international marketing strategy perspective. We discuss how the Islamic perspective influences international marketing strategies, as well as how it affects marketing mix elements. Furthermore we examine the opportunities and challenges associated with each of the elements. Accordingly this chapter contributes to the extant literature by analyzing Islamic markets from the perspective of an international marketing strategy (standardization versus adaptation of the marketing mix) and by identifying existing practices and trends, as well as opportunities and challenges, in relation to Islamic marketing. This analysis is a necessary step to understand the current state of the field, from both research and managerial perspectives.

Converging evidence suggests increases in the number of businesses catering to Muslim needs, including hotels, finance companies, and butchers (Power and Abdullah, 2009). As the Islamic world explodes economically, the need for value-empathetic brands has increased exponentially too. New *halal* products and services include food and non-food items, originating in the Middle East, Europe and Southeast Asia. Some multinational corporations have successfully penetrated Islamic markets, usually by investing heavily in the cultivation of these markets. As a result of their efforts, such firms often earn up to 90 per cent of the Islamic food, cosmetics and health market. For non-food items or products, for which it tends to be less important to be *sharia*-compliant, reaching Muslim consumers seems easier. For example, cell phone companies are targeting Muslim consumers by offering applications and added features that might attract them; for example, Nokia provides downloadable Qur'an recitations and maps of the major mosques in the Middle East. Such offerings should increase brand loyalty and demonstrate how mainstream brands can appeal to Muslims without changing their core products (Power and Abdullah, 2009).

We argue that it will be helpful for brands to align themselves with the values of Islam to appeal to Muslim consumers. The closer the product category is to the human body, and the more its consumption, the more it must be completely *sharia*-compliant (Young, 2010). Regardless of which Muslim segment the firm is targeting, standardizing the product to be *halal* is a requirement. However, *sharia*-compliant brands cannot simply rely on religion as a driving force for their marketing campaigns. At the end of the day, people will not buy *halal* simply because it is *halal*. They want quality products and products that meet their tastes and preferences. Furthermore, making a brand or a product *sharia*-compliant does not necessarily imply a Muslim brand. In many cases, it is not in the brand's best interest to be associated with religious beliefs, as exemplified by the failures of Mecca Cola and Qibla Cola. These brands did not offer anything other than an Islamic name and some adherence to Islamic principles and thus were not perceived as sincere (Young, 2010). These brands may have misunderstood what it means to be a brand; that is, the need for brand equity and the relationship among brand equity, category benefits and consumer needs. In this chapter we argue that, after the *halal* requirement has been met, firms need to focus on the particularities of the local markets and adapt their *halal* product offerings accordingly. We argue that this is in line with a glocal marketing strategy targeted specifically to Muslim markets, or a 'think *sharia* – act local' approach.

Despite some research efforts cited herein, we still know relatively little about Muslim consumers' buying attitudes and behaviours. Further research should examine the relationship between religious values and buying behaviour, as well as different ways to segment the Muslim markets, which would benefit companies targeting the growing Muslim consumer market, not just in the Middle East, but in Asia and Western markets as well.

BIBLIOGRAPHY

Aggarwal, Rajesh K. and Tarik Yousef (2000), 'Islamic banks and investment financing', *Journal of Money, Credit and Banking*, **32** (1), 93–120.

Al-Buraey, Mohamed A. (2004), 'Marketing mix management from an Islamic perspective: some insights, *Journal of International Marketing and Marketing Research*, **29** (3), 139–52.

Al-Faruqi, Ismail R. (1992), *Al Tawhid: Its Implications for Thought and Life*, Pakistan, Islamabad: IIIT.

Al-Makaty, S.S., G.N. Van Tubergen, S.S. Whitlow and D.A. Boyd (1996), 'Attitudes toward advertising in Islam', *Journal of Advertising Research*, **36**, 16–26.

Al-Qaradawi, Yusuf (1995) *The Lawful and the Prohibited in Islam (Al-halal wal-haram fil Islam)*, trans. Kamal El-Helbawy, M. Moinuddin Siddiqui and Syed Shukry, Kuwait: Al Faisal Press.

Al-Tamimi, Hussein A., Lafi, A. Shehadah and M.D. Uddin (2009), 'Bank image in the UAE: Comparing Islamic and conventional banks', *Journal of Financial Services Marketing*, **14** (3), 232–44.

Alam, S.M., M.A. Khan and A.H. Shaikh (2008), 'Interest – a condemned money and prohibited in the strongest possible terms in Islam', *Economic Review*, 7–8.

Alserhan, Baker Ahmad (2010), 'On Islamic branding: brands as good deeds', *Journal of Islamic Marketing*, **1** (2), 101–6.

American Muslim Consumer (2010), 'A brief about American Muslim consumer', http://americanmuslimconsumer.com/about-2, accessed July 2010.

ASA (Advertising Standards Authority) Malaysia (2008), 'Malaysia Code of Advertising Practice', http://www.asa.org.my/pdf/code eng.pdf.

Baligh, H.H. (1998) 'The fit between the organization structure and its cultural setting: aspects of Islamic cultures', *International Business Review*, 7, 39–49.

Birnik, A. and Bowman, C. (2007), 'Marketing mix standardization in multinational corporations: a review of evidence', *International Journal of Management Reviews*, **9** (4), 303–24.

Bittermann, Jim (2002), 'Boycott battle meets cola wars' *CNN*, http://edition.cnn.com/2002/WORLD/europe/11/05/mecca.cola/, accessed February 2010.

Bonne, K. and W. Verbeke (2006), 'Muslim consumer's motivations towards meat consumption in Belgium: qualitative exploratory insights from means-end chain analysis', *Anthropology of Food*, **5**, 2–24.

Bonne, Karijn, I. Vermeir F. Bergeaud-Blackler and W. Verbeke (2007), 'Determinants of halal meat consumption in France', *British Food Journal*, **109** (5), 367–86.

Bovee, C.L. and J.V. Thill (1992), *Marketing*, New York: McGraw-Hill, Inc. Central Intelligence Agency (2009), The World Factbook, www.cia.gov/library/publications/the-world-factbook/ (accessed November 2010).

Čihák, Martin and Heiko Hesse (2008), 'Islamic banks and financial stability: an empirical analysis', International Monetary Fund, http://www.imf.org/external/pubs/ft/wp/2008/wp0816.pdf.

Cooper, Mathew (2009), 'Domino's pizza defends halal-only outlet', *The Independent*, http://www.independent.co.uk/life-style/food-and-drink/news/dominos-pizza-defends-halalonly-outlet-1607587.html.

Duncan, T. and Ramaprasad, J. (1995), 'Standardization multinational advertizing: the influencing factors', *Journal of Advertising*, **24** (3), 55–68.

'ECER enters UK *halal* market' (2009), *Halal Market News*, Commentary and Analysis, http://halalfocus.net/2009/05/15ecer-enters-uk-halal-market/

Fattah, Hassan M. (2005), 'The new Ramadan: it's beginning to look a lot like . . .', *New York Times*, www.nytimes.com/2005/10/11/world/africa/11iht-islam.html?_r=1, accessed September 2010.

Fisher, Mary Pat and Lee W. Bailey (2008), 'Islam', *An Anthology of Living Religions*, Upper Saddle River, New Jersey: Prentice Hall, 268–308.

Fitzpatrick, Laura (2007), 'The new swimsuit issue', *Time*, http://www.time.com/time/magazine/article/0,9171,1645145,00.html, accessed April 2010.

Gooch, Liz (2010), 'Advertisers seek to speak to muslim consumers', *New York Times*, http://www.nytimes.com/2010/08/12/business/media/12branding.html, accessed November 2010.

'Halal McNuggets a hit in Detroit' (2000), About.com, http://islam.about.com/od/dietarylaw/a/halalmcd.htm, accessed January 2010.

Haniff, Datuk Hussein (2010), 'Brussels: great potential to develop halal market in Europe', http://halalfocus.net/2010/04/02/brussels-great-potential-to-develop-halal-market-in-europe/, accessed 25 July 2010.

Hastings-Black, Michael (2009), 'The overlooked $170 billion of American-Muslim spending power', http://www.huffingtonpost.com/michael-hastingsblack/the-overlooked-170-billio_b_162018.html, accessed 27 July 2010.

Heneghan, Tom (2010), 'French fast food chain expands its halal only outlets', Reuters, http://www.reuters.com/article/idUSTRE67U3BE20100831, accessed September 2010.

Herbig (1998), 'The standardization versus adaptation debate: wherefore art thou now?', in *Handbook of Cross-Cultural Marketing*, New York: The Haworth Press.

Hussaini, M.M. (1993), 'Halal haram lists: why they do not work?' http://www.soundvision.com/info/halal-healthy/halal.list.asp , accessed January 2010.

Ibn Taymiya, Al-Shaykah al-Imam (1982), *Public Duties in Islam: This Institution of the Hisba*, trans. B. Muhtar Holland, Wiltshire: The Islamic Foundation.

Imady, Omar and Hans Dieter Seibel (2006), *Principles and Products of Islamic Finance*, University of Cologne Development Research Center.

'Iranians slam "Satanic" Barbie' (1996), *Gulf Marketing Review*, 25 June.

'Islamic cola firm loses its fizz' (2005), *BBC News*, http://news.bbc.co.uk/2/hi/uk_news/england/derbyshire/4244508.stm, accessed February 2010.

'Islamic derivatives standards set' (2009), *Iran Daily*, http://www.irandaily.com/1388/12/11/MainPaper/3630/Page/5/Index.htm, accessed December 2009.

'Islamic finance in France' (2009), *Economist*, http://www.economist.com/world/europe/displaystory.cfm?story_id=14859353, accessed December 2009.

Jain, S.C. (1989), 'Standardization of international marketing strategy: some research hypotheses', *Journal of Marketing Review*, **53**, 70–79.

Kavoosi, M. (2000), *The Globalization of Business and the Middle East: Opportunities and Constraints*, Westport, CT: Qurom Books.

Kavoossi, M. and J. Frank (1990), 'The language-culture interface in Persian Gulf states print advertisements: implications for international marketing', *Journal of International Consumer Research*, **31**, 5–25.

La Ferla, Ruth (2007), 'We, myself, and I', *New York Times*, http://www.nytimes.com/2007/04/05/fashion/05MUSLIM.html, accessed March 2010.

Levitt, T. (1983), *The Globalization of Markets*, Harvard Business Review, **61**, 92–102.

'Malaysian code of advertising practice' (2008), Advertising Standards Authority Malaysia (ASA), http://www.asa.org.my, accessed September 2010.

'Mapping the global Muslim population: a report on the size and the distribution of the world's Muslim population' (2009), Pew Research Center, Pew Forum on Religion and Public Life, October.

'Marketing to Muslims' (2007), J. Walter Thomson (JWT) advertising agency study.

Mohsin, Khan S. and Abbas Mirakhor (1990), 'Islamic banking: experience in the Islamic Republic of Iran and in Pakistan', *Economic Development and Cultural Change*, **38** (2), 353–75.

'Muslim dolls tackle "wanton" Barbie' (2002), *BBC News*, http://news.bbc.co.uk/2/hi/middle_east/1856558.stm, accessed April 2010.

Nestorovic, Cedomir (2007), *Marketing in an Islamic Environment*, Center for European Management and Marketing.

Niazi, L.A.K. (1991), 'Islamic Law of contract', Lahore, research cell, Dyal Sing Trust Library.

Niati, L.A.K. (1996), *Islamic Law of Contract*, Lahore: Research Cell, Dayal Sing Trust Library.

Nomani, Asra Q. (2005), 'Hijab chic: how retailers are marketing to fashion-conscious Muslim women', Slate, http://www.slate.com/id/2128906/, accessed April 2010.

Oakley, D. (2009), 'The future of Islamic finance: London leads in race to be western hub', *Financial Times*, 4.

Odabasi, Y. and M. Argan (2009), 'Aspects of underlying ramadan consumption patterns in Turkey', *Journal of International Consumer Marketing*, **21** (3), 203–18.

Ogilvy and Mather (2010), 'Ogilvy publishes index of Muslim friendly brands', http://www.ogilvy.com/News/Press-Releases/October-2010-Muslim-Friendly-Brand-Index.aspx, accessed November 2010.

Okazaki, S., C.R. Taylor and J.P. Doh (2007), 'Market convergence and advertising standardization in the European Union', *Journal of World Business*, **42** (4), 384–400.

Parker, Mushtak (2003), 'Malaysia banking liberalization a step in the right direction', *Arab News*, accessed June 2010.

Pew Forum (2009), 'Mapping the global Muslim population', The Pew Forum on Religious and Public Life, http://pewforum.org/uploadedfiles/Topics/Demographics/Muslimpopulation.pdf

Power, Carla, and Shadiah, Abdullah (2009), 'Buying Muslim', *Time International*, **173** (20), 31–34.

Razzouk, N. and J. Al-Khatib (1993), 'The nature of television advertising in Saudi Arabia: content analysis and marketing implications', *Journal of International Consumer Marketing*, **6**, 65–90.

Rice, G. (1999), 'Islamic ethics and the implications for business', *Journal of Business Ethics*, **18**, 345–58.

Rice, G. and M. Al-Mossawi (2002), 'The implications of Islam for advertising messages: the middle eastern context', *Journal of Euromarketing*, **11** (63), 71–97.

Rippin, Andrew (2005), *Muslims: Their Religious Beliefs and Practices*, Routledge: New York.

Saeed, M., Z.U. Ahmed and S.M. Mukhtar (2001), 'International marketing ethics from an Islamic perspective: a value-maximization approach', *Journal of Business Ethics*, Part 2, **32** (2), 127–42.

Sandıkcı, Ö. and G. Ger (2010), 'Veiling in style: how does a stigmatized practice become fashionable?' *Journal of Consumer Research*, **37** (June), 15–36.

Sandıkcı, Ö. and S. Omeraki (2007), 'Globalization and rituals: does Ramadan turn into Christmas?', in Gavan Fitzsimons and Vicki Morwitz (eds), *Advances in Consumer Research*, Vol. 34, Duluth, MN: Association for Consumer Research, pp. 610–15.

'Sharia calling: a political row about Muslim law' (2009), *Economist*, http://www.economist.com/node/14859353, accessed January 2010.

Terpstra, V. and R. Sarathy (2000), *International Marketing*, 8th edn, Fort Worth, TX: Dryden Press.

Theodosiou, M. and Leonidou L.C. (2003), 'Standardization versus adaptation of international marketing strategy: an integrative assessment of the empirical research', *International Business Review*, **12** (2), 141–71.

Totaro, Lorenzo (2009), 'Vatican says Islamic finance may help Western banks in crisis', Bloomberg, http://www.bloomberg.com/apps/news?pid=20601092&sid=aOsOLE8uiNOg&refer=italy, accessed April 2009.

Van Waarden, F. and R.Van Dalen (2010), 'Hallmarking halal. The market for halal certificates: competitive private regulation', Paper presented at the Third Biennial Conference of the ECPR Standing Group on Regulation and Governance, Dublin, 17–19 June.

Wilson, J. and J. Liu (2010), 'Shaping the Halal into a brand?', *Journal of Islamic Marketing*, **1** (2).

Wilson, Rodney (1987), 'Islamic banking: the Jordanian experience', *Arab Law Quarterly*, **2** (3), 207–29.

Young, Robb (2007), 'Muslim fashion designers moving beyond the traditional, *New York Times*, http://www.nytimes.com/2007/09/18/style/18iht-rmuslim.4.7550105.html?-r=1, accessed April 2010.

Young, Miles (2010), 'Muslim futurism and Islamic branding', The Inaugural Oxford Global Islamic Branding and Marketing Forum, Oxford, United Kingdom, July.

Young, R.B and R.G. Javalgi (2007), 'International marketing research: a global project management perspective', *Business Horizons*, **50** (2), 113–22.

Zakaria, Norhayati and Asmat-Nizam Abdul-Talib (2010), 'Applying Islamic market-oriented cultural model to sensitize strategies towards global customers, competitors, and environment', *Journal of Islamic Marketing*, **1** (1), 51–62.

Zoepf, Katherine (2005), 'Bestseller in Mideast: Barbie with a prayer mat', *New York Times*, accessed April 2010.

13 Islamic banking: the convergence of religion, economic self-interest and marketing

Kenneth Beng Yap*

INTRODUCTION

Since time immemorial, religion in its various forms has had a major influence on humanity. The values it attempts to inculcate, which include equality and compassion, can have profound implications for the distribution of welfare in a society. For this reason, religious scriptures and teaching provide prescriptions for the management of human relations and exchange in everyday affairs. In Islam, many such prescriptions relate to the treatment of money and wealth, moral conduct in commercial exchange, ideology on greed and risk-taking, as well as undertaking of charity, among others. The Islamic banking concept encompasses all of these themes and provides a context in which religiosity, economic self-interest and marketing converge. Islamic banking precepts give rise to an alternative banking methodology which has been touted to deliver more equitable welfare distribution (Bjorvatn, 1998; Darrat, 1988; Khan, 1986; Siwar and Karim, 1997; Stiansen, 1995). What started out as a novel experiment in Egypt during the 1960s (Haron and Wan Azmi 2009) has today developed into an entire banking and finance system with over $800 billion in assets (Al-Jasser, 2010).

Despite its rapid market growth and potential contribution to societal welfare, little is known about the marketing of Islamic banking and consumer behavior relating to it. The few studies that have examined Islamic banking from a marketing perspective may have provided some practical suggestions on improving customer satisfaction and service quality at Islamic banks (for example, Gerrard and Cunningham, 1997; Haron et al., 1994; Metawa and Almossawi, 1998; Naser et al., 1999); however, these studies have generally not focused on the unique aspects of Islamic banking that differentiate it from conventional banking. Moreover religiosity has not featured prominently in their work; thus, little is still known about how the religious orientation of a Muslim consumer or investor influences financial decision making, including the decision to adopt Islamic banking. The lack of knowledge in this area leaves other important questions unanswered. For example, what aspects of Islamic banking call upon the religiosity of Muslims in financial decision making? Do more intrinsically religious Muslims have a greater propensity to adopt Islamic banking products? Is there a role for co-religious friends and family to influence a Muslim's adoption of Islamic banking? Does the bank also have to be 'Islamic' in character to promote Islamic banking products effectively?

The knowledge gap is not confined to Islamic banking alone. An extensive literature review revealed that little is known about the influence of religion on marketing. Mittelstaedt (2002, p.6) suggested that 'scholars need to understand the effects of religion on the kind of issues they face in business and, more important, how these issues are defined, informed, and regulated by religion.' Thirty-five years ago, Wilkes et al. (1986)

called for more marketing and consumer research on religiosity; alas, undertakings in this area remain sparse. The ubiquitous presence, power and authority of religious teachings and their effects are too important to continue to be avoided by marketing scholars. This study is a first step in addressing the knowledge gap.

The inclusion of consumer religiosity in the present discourse makes Islamic banking an appropriate vehicle to advance knowledge relating to the role of religion in marketing and consumer behavior. It is the purpose of this chapter to review the marketing literature on Islamic banking and attempt to postulate some preliminary conceptual relationships for future evaluation by marketing scholars and managers. The chapter comprises several sections, starting with an introduction to Islamic banking principles and products. After a discussion of the merits and criticisms of Islamic banking, the chapter lists the features that distinguish Islamic banking from conventional banking, namely profit-and-loss sharing (PLS) arrangements. This is followed by a discussion of how the marketing of Islamic banking has departed from its *raison d être*, which has implications for consumer behavior and marketing scholarship. At the conclusion of the chapter, a research agenda is proposed and several managerial implications are discussed. These implications relate to the promotion and adoption of PLS arrangements in Islamic banking, which incorporate religiosity and Islamic marketing. The research agenda is encapsulated in a conceptual model, which may be a useful point of departure for future research.

ISLAM AND FINANCIAL AFFAIRS

Muslim scholars in general agree that Islam is more than just a religion; it is a comprehensive way of life, prescribed through norms and practices outlined in the Qur'an. The principles and laws of Islam, known as *sharia*, pervade all aspects of a Muslim's life, including financial affairs (Taylor, 2003). The basis of the Islamic law governing economic transactions has its sources in the Qur'an where it is emphasized that all natural means of production and resources have been created by Allah (God); therefore, it is Allah who determines what are lawful (*halal*) and unlawful (*haram*) activities. At its most general level this ancient precept has several striking parallels with Judeo-Christian religions and prohibits liquor, pork, gambling, pornography, usury, as well as anything else that is morally or socially injurious. An individual has the right to property ownership and the right to pursue economic self-interest; however, this must comply with Islamic law. Wealth must be used judiciously and not hoarded or wasted. While surplus wealth can be retained, a portion must be allocated for the well-being of the community as a whole, in order to ensure social justice without inhibiting individual enterprise.

On this general basis, *sharia* is applied to financial matters because Muslims believe that it is Allah who determines the fate of one's financial wealth and endeavors. As a consequence, financial exchanges or transactions should be conducted in accordance with *sharia* if one wishes the outcome to win the approval of Allah. A manifestation of this philosophy is the concept of Islamic banking. In Islamic banking, financial transactions adhere to the rules and injunctions imposed by *sharia* with the intended outcome of improved equality, as well as financial and spiritual well-being. Therefore, in principle, Islamic banking is characterized by compassion for the poor, the sharing of risk, and the abolition of both greed and the exploitation of one class by another (Zangeneh, 1989). Advocates of Islamic banking have argued that this alternative banking model, which adheres to *sharia*, holds the solutions to many economic problems (Bjorvatn, 1998).

PRINCIPLES OF ISLAMIC BANKING

Operationalizing *sharia* in the banking context leads to a very interesting comparison between the Islamic and conventional variety. The key feature that distinguishes Islamic banking from conventional banking is the prohibition of interest. Injunctions against the collection and payment of interest or usury (*riba*) are stated clearly in the Qur'an.[1] The basis of the injunctions is the belief that income should not be generated without labor on the part of the lender and that exchanges based on interest are considered to benefit the rich at the expense of the poor (Noorzoy, 1982). The condemnation of usury is not unique to Islam; it is also frowned upon in Christian and Jewish teaching, as well as by philosophers such as Aristotle (Hardie and Rabooy, 1991). The sentiment against usury among Islamic scholars and religious leaders is aptly captured in the following quote by Taleqani (1983, p. 103):

> The greedy people with the poison of money through usury, extracted the economic blood from the body of the producing classes, which are the active and progressive organs of society, and injected into their fat bodies, which are the parasite of society . . . usury [is] the foundation and root of all or most social and economic problems.

The prohibition of interest in banking may require some explanation. The basic principles underlying a few Islamic banking products can be broadly categorized as either (1) debt-based and lease financing instruments, or (2) equity-based and PLS instruments. There are several other Islamic banking products, which have counterparts in conventional banking such as insurance (*takaful*) and bonds (*sukuk*), but these will not be featured in the present discussion.

The Islamic banking system has products that are the equivalent of debt-based and lease financing instruments in conventional banking; however, they operate quite differently in accordance with *sharia*. As an example, in a home mortgage context, a bank operating in conventional banking lends the homebuyer money and charges interest on the principal. In Islamic banking, however, the bank will buy the house from the seller and resell it to the homebuyer at a mark-up, which is equivalent to the time-value of money and a premium representing the bank's profits. The homebuyer pays the resale price to the bank in installments until it is fully paid up. Until then, the bank retains legal ownership of the house. These two separate transactions – the purchase of the house by the bank and the resale of the house to the homebuyer – help circumvent the injunction on charging interest on the loan. This arrangement is known as *murabaha*, which is analogous to 'rent-to-own' schemes in conventional finance.

The injunction on usury is similarly applied to trade financing where a business owner may be looking to purchase equipment and inventory. In conventional banking, a business owner approaches the bank for a business loan, and upon approval, the bank will provide the loan, which is payable with interest. In Islamic banking, however, the bank purchases the equipment and inventory concerned and sells it to the business owner at a

Table 13.1   Summary of Islamic banking products

Category	Islamic bank product	Description
Debt-based or lease financing instruments	*Murabaha* (home loan)	Repurchase agreement: Islamic bank purchases the house and resells it to the homebuyer at a price that incorporates the bank's mark-up
	Bai bi-thamin ajil (trade financing)	Repurchase agreement: Islamic bank purchases equipment and inventory and resells it to the business owner at a price that incorporates the bank's mark-up
	Wadia (deposit)	Deposit account that repays investor a 'gift' payment that is predetermined
Equity-based or profit-and-loss Sharing (PLS) instruments	*Mudaraba* (equity loan or trust financing)	Bank or investor loans entrepreneur principal which is repayable, in addition to a share of profit. This loan is entrusted to the entrepreneur; bank or investor does not participate in management
	Musharaka (venture capital)	Bank or investor provides venture capital to an entrepreneur and may participate in management in exchange for a predetermined profit distribution schedule.

mark-up, which is equivalent to the time-value of money and the bank's premium. The business owner is allowed to pay in installments until the resale price is fully paid off. Until then, the bank retains legal title of the equipment and inventory. This arrangement, known as *bai bi-thamin ajil*, also overcomes the prohibition of *riba*.

Consistent with this prohibition, banks are allowed to accept deposits from depositors but are prohibited from paying interest to attract or retain such deposits. Similarly Muslim depositors are prohibited from expecting and collecting interest on their deposits. Yet Islam recognizes the need for a banking intermediary. In Islam, when a bank accepts a depositor's money, it becomes a trustee for his or her money. This deposit is available to the depositor at-call and is typically rewarded with a 'gift' payment from the bank in place of interest income. Often this gift payment is equivalent to the time-value of money; however, the bank does not formally predetermine the payment amount. This arrangement, known as *wadia*, is offered and promoted as an alternative to interest-bearing deposits.

The injunction on *riba* is supported by other Islamic principles advocating the sharing of risk, an individual's rights and duties to society, property rights and the sanctity of contracts (Zaher and Hassan, 2001). Of particular importance is the Islamic principle that encourages fellow Muslims to share the risk and fate of financial exchange. Between the bank and the business owner, this arrangement complements the injunction on usury because bank revenue conventionally received in the form of interest charges is now substituted with profit or dividends from its investment in its debtors' business ventures. Participation in this sort of PLS arrangement is greatly encouraged because of its role in achieving and maintaining economic equality, a central tenet of Islam. PLS in commercial enterprise, known as *mudaraba*, is an important feature that distinguishes Islamic banking from conventional banking.

To illustrate the workings of *mudaraba*, let us take an example of a business loan. In conventional banking, the bank loans money to the business owner and this is repayable at the prevailing interest rate, irrespective of the financial performance of the enterprise concerned. In Islamic banking, however, the bank will lend the money to the business owner without charging any interest or fees. If the enterprise is profitable, the bank will receive a share of the profits, proportionate to the loan amount. If the enterprise makes a loss, the bank will bear its share of the losses. This *mudaraba* arrangement will continue until the principal is fully paid up through the bank's share of profits. Effectively, the bank's profit or loss on the loan is equivalent to the enterprise's profit or loss.

Another form of PLS financing greatly encouraged in Islam is the *musharaka* or the joint venture. In this arrangement, Islamic banks perform the role of a venture capitalist by providing capital to entrepreneurs in exchange for a predetermined share of profits, should the venture be profitable. If the venture is not profitable, generally the banks will bear the capital loss. However if it is found that the entrepreneur was negligent or deceitful in the management of the venture, the bank does not have to bear any losses. Ultimately PLS arrangements in Islamic banking are argued to be instrumental in reducing income inequality and class exploitation because they facilitate economic participation from lower socio-economic segments of the population who typically lack access to financing and capital.

All these banking principles conform to the ideal Muslim way of life; however, there appears to be intense debate on the legitimacy and viability of Islamic banking (Ali, 1964. Chapra, 1985, 2000, Sharfi, 2000).

MERITS OF ISLAMIC BANKING

Many scholars have put forth the merits of Islamic banking as an alternative banking system that can potentially reduce poverty and inequality in a society. Since interest rates can have adverse redistributive effects, the prohibition of *riba* seeks to eliminate the indebtedness of the poor to the rich (Wilson, 1982). PLS arrangements effectively eliminate the need for collateral, thereby providing the poor with better access to credit and financing. Better access to credit and financing will, in turn, increase the rate of economic participation and reduce income inequality. Kuran (1996) argued that the PLS feature of Islamic banking is particularly important because many Muslim communities are characterized by sharp inequalities.

Indeed, proponents of Islamic banking argue that PLS arrangements result in several positive benefits to the economy. Chiefly, Islamic banks play an important role in stimulating economic development in rural areas (Bjorvatn 1998, Siwar and Karim, 1997). Stiansen (1995) reported that through PLS arrangements, such as *musharaka*, small-scale farmers can offer a share of the harvest, in exchange for the required financial and physical capital that would not otherwise be obtainable through conventional banking. Caragata (2000) noted that the Indonesian government provides political support for Islamic banking as an alternative to conventional banking for rural entrepreneurs.

The elimination of interest can also have a positive stabilizing effect on the economy. Darrat (1988) and Khan (1986) provided empirical support to attest that in underdeveloped countries, Islamic banking is superior to conventional banking because the prohibition of interest resulted in a more stable financial sector. In addition, Ghannadian and Goswami (2004) indicated that Islamic banking is the most appropriate choice during periods of economic transition. Consistent with historical perspectives of many cultures that view money lending and usury as a parasitic activity, the elimination of interest would serve to minimize class exploitation and civil unrest.

Several authors list other economic benefits of PLS arrangements in Islamic banking. Naser and Moutinho (1997) argue that PLS arrangements forge closer ties between the banks and their customers. In these arrangements, both the borrower and lender have an ongoing interest in the viability of the enterprise. Consequently, the sharing of information about risk between the two parties is increased, thus reducing information asymmetry (Samad and Hassan, 1999), moral hazards, and inequitable returns (Zaher and Hassan, 2001). Zaher and Hassan (2001) argue that through PLS arrangements, Islamic banking improves capital allocation efficiency because interest-based lending tends to award capital to creditworthy borrowers rather than the most productive projects. Another increasingly salient benefit of Islamic banking is its viability as an alternative form of banking. In Muslim countries such as Pakistan, Iran and Sudan where the entire banking system was reformed to conform to Islamic banking principles, observers note that the financial system did not collapse as some skeptics had expected (Khan and Mirakhor, 1990, Pourian, 1995, Zangeneh, 1989). In fact, banking systems in Pakistan and Iran have since recorded significant growth in investment deposits (Khan and Mirakhor, 1990). Nonetheless there is some evidence that the growth in Islamic banking appears to be driven primarily by attractive investment returns, rather than religious obligation or social consciousness (for example, Gerrard and Cunningham 1997; Haron et al., 1994; Metawa and Almossawi, 1998; Naser et al., 1999).

CRITICISMS OF ISLAMIC BANKING

Both the principles and implementation of Islamic banking have attracted criticism. The biggest source of criticism relates to the impracticalities of an interest-free financial system. The interest rate serves as a market-clearing mechanism for capital; therefore, interest income is received as a return on capital risk. Eliminating the interest rate would disable market signals that help investors assess the relative risk/reward of certain investments. Eliminating interest would also reduce the incentive to save, which in turn, limits the funds available for investment and economic development.

Another area of controversy relates to the interpretation of *riba* in *sharia* (Noorzoy, 1982). In Islam, the receipt of earnings on the rental of physical capital is permissible, but *sharia* forbids profiteering from wealth per se, without any form of labor on the part of the lender. Pressing questions arise about the difference between these two revenue streams and which of the two is excessive and tantamount to usury. There is also some ambiguity about whether any form of interest is usury or if zero interest means zero nominal interest or zero real interest. Muslim scholars and clergymen who interpret the spirit of the *riba* injunction would argue that usury refers to excessive profits from increases in real interest rates; in contrast, those who interpret the injunction by the letter would argue that any form of non-zero interest is equivalent to usury.

This quandary gives rise to a range of economic and financial implications for the borrower and lender, as well as the economy in general (Metawa and Almossawi, 1998; Metwally, M.M., 1997, Metwally, S., 1992; Qureshi, 1974; Siddiqui, 1985; Zaher and Hassan 2001). Noorzoy (1982) argued that if *riba* is deemed to be usury associated with excessive profits, then the only changes to the conventional economic model required are the elimination of monopolies and the continual intervention from the state to maintain workable market competition. On the other hand, if *riba* is construed as zero interest, then the entire economic system will need to shift towards stable prices, fixed returns and PLS arrangements.

The third area of criticism relates to whether most Islamic banking offerings are truly interest-free and adhere to the Islamic ideal. In the case of *murabaha, bai bi-thamin ajil* and other similar debt-based instruments, the bank resells property or equipment to the borrower and charges a mark-up comprising the time-value of money and the bank's profit. Critics assert that this mark-up is essentially interest disguised. Defenders of this model claim that Islamic banking is different from interest-charging loans because the bank retains legal ownership until the full sale price is paid, and because the mark-up is fixed between both parties before they enter into the arrangement. Similarly, in the case of *wadia*, critics question the practice of rewarding depositors with gift payments. Even though these payments are not supposed to be guaranteed, they are often promoted to investors with some level of certainty and such gift payments are made at a rate equivalent to the time-value of money (Khan, 1986). Once again, the legitimacy of these mark-up arrangements rests upon the interpretation of the injunction on *riba*.

HOW ISLAMIC IS ISLAMIC BANKING?

The theoretical benefits of Islamic banking remain to be seen because the current interpretation and operationalization of *sharia* governing financial transactions among Muslims makes Islamic banking indistinguishable from conventional banking. With asset portfolios predominantly in mark-up or leasing arrangements (Haron and Wan Azmi, 2009), both Islamic banks and Muslim investors have exhibited an aversion toward PLS arrangements. Yet it is PLS arrangements that adhere more closely to the Islamic ideal of equity and shared risk. Therefore, a critical question is posed: how Islamic is Islamic banking?

Currently, the asset portfolio in Islamic banks is heavily weighted towards short-term financing with an overwhelming majority in mark-up or leasing arrangements, whilst PLS arrangements and long-term financing continue to be a small share of the overall portfolio (Aggrawal and Yousef, 2000; Bjorvatn, 1998; Dixon, 1992; Haron and Wan Azmi, 2009; Khan and Mirakhor, 1990). There are several valid reasons for this lop-sided structure. Firstly, the high monitoring costs involved in PLS projects invariably skew the duration of these arrangements toward the shorter end.[2] Secondly, these costs are exacerbated by the moral hazard that besets PLS arrangements. Many Muslim borrowers have exhibited a history of opportunism and guile. Once the entrepreneur's risk is shared by the bank, he or she has an incentive to underreport the profits of the venture. Khan and Mirakhor (1990) and Sarker (1999) reported that since tax evasion and underreporting are pervasive in PLS arrangements, monitoring costs have become prohibitively high. The financial management of PLS arrangements require more than just religious self-regulation on the part of Muslim borrowers.

Thirdly, if Islamic banking assets were heavily weighted in PLS arrangements, the viability of the banking system might require the support of the government and central banks. A position that relies substantively on PLS arrangements would bring significant volatility to the banks' profitability, as well as the financial returns to its investors and depositors. The government would be called upon to stabilize fluctuations in deposits and liquidity by prescribing a range of return-on-investments rates. These return rates would then converge to a prevailing interest rate, which effectively shifts the portfolio back towards mark-up and leasing arrangements.

Finally, in many countries where Islamic banking co-exists with conventional banking, the 'dividends' of Islamic banks and the interest rates of conventional banks are controlled by central banks and monetary authorities. Governments with a pro-Islamic agenda are in a position to enhance the attractiveness of Islamic banks, which might explain their relatively higher returns (Kuran, 1986). Ironically, governments are using conventional banking mechanisms to prop up the Islamic banking sector and as a result, Islamic banks revert to the conventional mark-up and leasing model to attract deposits and investments.

NOT VERY ISLAMIC

Profit-and-loss sharing arrangements have significant potential to catalyse rural development and increase economic participation from the poor. *Mudaraba* is an ideal source of financing for the rural poor because it does not require collateral from the borrower and the bank shares the risk associated with the venture. Since the bank's return on capital is tied to the profitability of the venture, the borrower's position is less vulnerable to fluctuations in economic conditions. Economic participation among the poor should therefore increase as capital becomes more easily obtainable under these arrangements. The desired effect is a reduction in income inequality. Caragata (2000) reported a successful example of *musharaka*, where Islamic banks act as venture capitalists to small-scale farmers who obtain seed capital for agricultural ventures.

However, the Islamic banks' emphasis on mark-up and leasing arrangements does little to reduce the gap between rich and poor. The ability of the poor to own equity on assets still hinges on both their ability to pay the mark-up and their creditworthiness, both of which deteriorate in tougher economic conditions. Iqbal and Mirakhor (1999) argued that Islamic banks' aversion to long-term financing limits their ability to contribute to economic growth and development. Taylor and Evans (1987) warned that mark-up or leasing arrangements may open a 'backdoor to interest' and urged Islamic banks to shift their emphasis from mark-up and leasing arrangements towards PLS arrangements.

Even the current customer base of Islamic banks indicates that the potential benefits of Islamic banking are not reaching the poor. Research shows that the typical Islamic banking customer is likely to be highly educated, with a high income, and living in the city (Metawa and Almossawi, 1998; Naser et al., 1999; Ratnawati, 2001). Researchers proposed that Islamic banking would have the most positive impact on reducing income inequality by providing financing to the poor in rural areas (Bjorvatn, 1998; Ratnawati, 2001). Yet the coverage of Islamic banks continues to be concentrated in urban areas and is underrepresented in rural areas (Bjorvatn, 1998; Carpenter and Jensen, 2002; Sarker, 1999; Siwar and Karim, 1997).

Banks are promoting debt-based products as 'Islamic' even though they do not adhere to the *riba* injunction. Errico and Farahbaksh (1998) provided several examples where actual Islamic banking practices diverge from the theoretical paradigm. Their investigation showed that all deposits in Islamic banks are often either explicitly or implicitly guaranteed, which would suggest a reversion to conventional banking practices. It is quite suspicious that returns could be consistently promised and paid at a competitive rate to depositors (Kuran, 1995). Kuran also reported that employees of Islamic banks informally promised potential depositors rates of return that are consistently close to the prevailing interest rates. One could infer that the returns on most Islamic banking products are derived from interest-bearing investments (Metwally, 1997; Rammal and Zurbruegg, 2007).

Some critics doubt that Islamic banking adheres to the Islamic ideal of equality and shared risk (Saleem, 2005; Wilson, 1997). It is questionable whether *any* religiosity at all is involved in the promotion and adoption of Islamic banking products today. With the growth in Islamic bank assets worldwide, one might reasonably infer that religiosity and social consciousness among Muslims is also growing. But a closer examination suggests a different phenomenon. The growth in Islamic banking was, in part, attributable to the growth in the number of non-Muslim customers who happen to be seeking higher returns through Islamic banking products (Caragata, 2000; Gerrard and Cunningham, 1997; Naughton and Shanmugam, 1990). Moreover, Haron et al., (1994) indicated that Muslims patronized Islamic banks for the returns they would receive from their investments, instead of fulfillment of their religious duty.

Muslim norms and religiosity may indeed play a role in the adoption of Islamic banking. Since Islamic banking is promoted as banking that complies with *sharia*, the natural target market would be pious Muslims who could apply their religious values to banking. Ironically with mark-up and leasing arrangements, the banks may be using a religious badge to sell products that do not adhere to Islamic ideals. In fact, the growth in mark-up and leasing arrangements and continued aversion towards PLS arrangements makes Islamic banking increasingly less Islamic.

MARKETING ISLAMIC BANKING

The sparse marketing literature on Islamic banking has been confined to studies of customer satisfaction and service quality (for example, Gerrard and Cunningham, 1997; Haron et al., 1994; Metawa and Almossawi, 1998; Naser et al., 1999). As such, these studies do not provide much guidance on understanding the marketing problems and issues that are unique to Islamic banking.

The role of religion in consumer behavior can best be observed if the product concerned is tailored specifically to religious requirements or ideals. A proposition offered here is that Islamic banking products that are similar to conventional banking products, such as mark-up and leasing arrangements in *murabaha* and *wadia*, would not suggest distinct selection criteria that would invoke religiosity or adherence to Islamic ideals. In other words, why would the decision process of a Muslim investor differ from that of a non-Muslim investor choosing between financial products with similar propositions? After all, research suggests that non-Muslim customers would be amenable to Islamic banking products as long as they provided better value or returns (Caragata, 2000; Gerrard and Cunningham, 1997; Naughton and Shanmugam, 1990).

Muslim consumers may appear to be the natural target for Islamic banking products. Some researchers found that the acceptance of Islamic banking among Muslim depositors is motivated by its ability to help them fulfill religious requirements (Kuran, 1996; Metawa and Almossawi, 1998; Naser et al., 1999; Shook and Hassan, 1988); however, Islamic banking products that provide some certainty of return would not require this market segment to compromise their profit objectives for the sake of religion. Since most Islamic banking products are similar to conventional banking products by way of an expected rate of return, any marketing strategies to highlight the 'Islamic-ness' of a product or a bank would be superfluous at best and deceptive at worst. Bank managers may be exploiting the ignorance of Muslim consumers, given that Gerrard and Cunningham (1997) found a general lack of awareness and knowledge of Islamic banking among Muslims.

Wilson (1997) argued that Islamic banking products based on PLS arrangements, such as *mudaraba* and *musharaka*, are closer to the Islamic ideal and would therefore be more relevant to an investigation of the influence of religion on Muslim consumer behavior. Such arrangements have the potential to benefit earnest entrepreneurs who lack access to financing, and to restore equity in the banking function; however, they do not offer customers any certainty in investment return. Islamic banking products of this nature are riskier but adhere more closely to Islamic ideals because the financing risk is shared more equitably and the outcome and profitability of the venture will be what is willed by Allah. Al-Suwailem (2002) explained that in Islam, the proper way to evaluate risk is to first assess whether the appropriate causes for success have been enacted and then attribute the rest to *qadar* (destiny). If a Muslim thought that the cause was worth undertaking in the first place, then he/she might find that the effort was not spent wastefully and failure would not be as hurtful. Investing in PLS arrangements would require Muslims to sacrifice the certainty of investment return but they would do so in exchange for fulfilling both an Islamic ideal and a worthy cause.

Research in the area of ethical investing (Lewis and Cullis, 1990; Lewis and Mackenzie, 2000; Mackenzie and Lewis, 1999; Webley et al., 2001) suggested that ethical investors were willing to forsake the maximum return on capital invested in underperforming ethical funds as long as their ethical objectives were met satisfactorily. Thaler (1985) found that consumers were willing to be flexible in their mental accounting of money in order to feel good about the outcomes. If PLS arrangements are marketed as Islamic banking products, then the increased uncertainty or risk would invoke a decision process that would require adherence to Islamic or ethical ideals. Therefore, a key question for Muslim investors is whether they are willing to accept a greater level of uncertainty in

PLS arrangements as a fulfillment of their religious obligation. It appears that existing literature does not provide much guidance on this important issue.

IMPLICATIONS FOR CONSUMER BEHAVIOR

A review of current Islamic banking marketing practices reveals a departure from the religious ideals governing financial affairs. Unfortunately, this has led to a state where the uniqueness of Islamic banking is diminished, particularly in markets where conventional banking is prevalent. Marketing observers have recommended a reversion to PLS arrangements such as venture capital and entrepreneurial financing as a point of differentiation for banks marketing Islamic banking products (for example, Erol and El-Bdour, 1989; Erol et al., 1990; Wilson, 1997). The focus of marketing activities of most banks has not been in promoting PLS arrangements but on debt-based banking products instead. Metwally (1997) and Rammal and Zurbruegg (2007) noted that indicative 'rates of return' of these debt-based banking products were promoted to customers, thus drawing comparisons with the prevailing rate of return for conventional banking products.

This marketing approach has given rise to several implications for consumer behavior relating to Islamic banking. First, it may have conditioned Muslim and non-Muslim consumers to evaluate the attractiveness of Islamic banking on the same criteria as they would with conventional banking. These common criteria are well documented in the traditional bank marketing literature and include rates of return, service quality, convenience of branch locations and facilities, bank's reputation and image, among others. For this reason, researchers have found that survey respondents can readily assess conventional and Islamic banking products on the same criteria (Erol and El-Bdour, 1989; Erol et al., 1990; Gerrard and Cunningham, 1997; Haron, et al., 1994). It is anticipated that the longer this pattern persists, the harder it will be to uniquely position Islamic banking in the minds of consumers.

The second implication of current marketing practices is that conventional and Islamic banking are for the most part perceived at parity. Studies have documented little differentiation (Erol and El-Bdour, 1989; Erol et al., 1990) and in some cases where there appears to be some differentiation, it is evident that both are interchangeable on many features (Haron et al., 1994) or evaluations were made on the basis of poor knowledge of Islamic banking precepts (Gerrard and Cunningham, 1997). Such a consumer mindset may limit the potential market for truly innovative Islamic banking products in the future.

Thirdly, the failure to differentiate Islamic banking from conventional banking may have deterred consumers from becoming more involved and acquainted with the concept of Islamic banking. Most Muslim bank customers appear to have only a surface understanding of Islamic banking. For instance, there may be a general understanding of what is *halal* and *haram* in the financial context (Rammal and Zurbruegg, 2007), but most studies show that there is little awareness or knowledge of the *riba* injunction (Gerrard and Cunningham, 1997), or the variety of Islamic financing schemes (Metawa and Almossawi, 1998), including PLS arrangements (Naser et al., 1999; Rammal and Zurbruegg, 2007). There is also evidence to suggest that Muslim customers appear to identify only with product features in Islamic banking that are also found in conventional banking (Erol et al., 1990; Metawa and Almossawi, 1998; Naser et al., 1999). Since conventional banking products are often the reference point for Islamic banking products, some level of 'inertia' (or aversion towards Islamic banking) can be expected.

Finally, the lack of differentiation may render religiosity less relevant to the marketing of Islamic banking. Although the Islamic 'badge' may be used to attract Muslim customers as a natural market, there is little evidence to suggest that religiosity or commitment to the Islamic faith has played an instrumental role in product adoption and the consumer decision making process. Erol and El-Bdour (1989) found that religious motives did not account for preferences towards Islamic banks in Jordan. In a study of Islamic bank patronage in Malaysia, Haron et al., (1994) established that religion did not feature prominently in the selection criteria of Muslims. They also found that Muslims and non-Muslims did not differ in their basis for choosing Islamic banks. In both studies, profit was the driving motivation for doing business with Islamic banks; therefore, it appears that the certainty of investment returns in Islamic banking does not require Muslim customers to make any economic sacrifices for religious ideals. As a result, Islamic banking need not apply to Muslims exclusively and any promotional effort to adopt its products on the basis of religious duty or moral obligation would be misguided or superfluous.

The last implication has a significant bearing on the potential for marketing research in Islamic banking. Given the parity between conventional banking and Islamic banking as it stands today, religiosity is hardly invoked in Muslim consumer behavior. This means that there is little value in incorporating religiosity in Islamic banking research. This deficiency limits the advancement of knowledge relating to the influence of religion in marketing and consumer behavior. However, a paradigm shift is proposed here, which might enhance research possibilities in this area. Shifting the research focus towards PLS arrangements in Islamic banking may warrant the inclusion of religiosity. Since investment returns are comparatively less certain in PLS arrangements, the faith required to proceed with venture capital and entrepreneurial financing would invoke commitment to Islamic ideals. To expand on this argument, a research agenda is proposed in the next section, and this may help advance our understanding of the interaction between religion, economic self-interest, and marketing.

TOWARDS A RESEARCH AGENDA IN MARKETING

Mittelstaedt (2002) referred to the influence of religion and religious norms on the marketplace and called for researchers to seek a better understanding of this relationship. In heeding this call, I aim to build a research agenda that incorporates the religious, socio-psychological, and marketing determinants of adopting PLS arrangements in Islamic banking. The adoption of Islamic banking products based on PLS arrangements, such as products relating to *mudaraba* and *musharaka* (or venture capital and entrepreneurial financing), is an important convergence of religion, economic self-interest and marketing. Investments in PLS arrangements as a form of participation in Islamic banking may rely more on a Muslim customer's religiosity than investments in other Islamic banking products because PLS adheres more closely to Islamic ideals on financial affairs. Since investment returns in PLS arrangements are less certain, a trade-off exists between

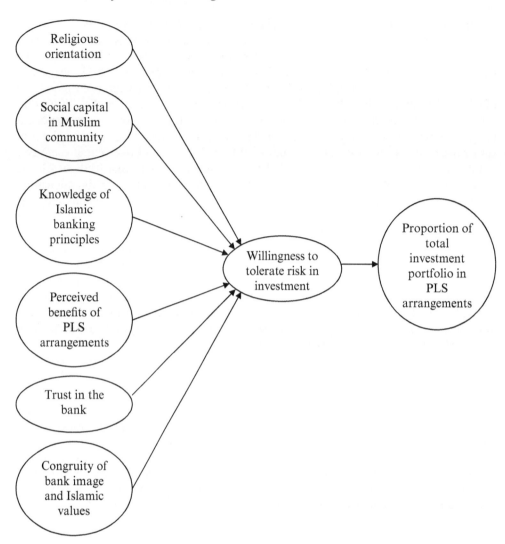

Figure 13.1   Proposed conceptual model

maximizing economic self-interest and compliance to religious ideals. As a result marketing functions may perform an important role in framing this trade-off. On this basis I
would like to pose two key research questions. Which factors influence the propensity of
a Muslim consumer to sacrifice the certainty of investment returns in order to fulfill their
religious duty? And, how do marketing variables feature in this relationship? I propose a
conceptual framework, which is summarized in Figure 13.1.

   This discussion begins with the dependent variable on the right-hand side of Figure
13.1. The dependent variable is the proportion of a Muslim investor's total portfolio in
PLS arrangements. This variable effectively measures the person's adoption of Islamic
banking products that adhere more closely to the Islamic ideal of equitable risk-sharing.
Since information asymmetry and principal-agent problems beset PLS arrangements,

the return on investment is uncertain. Such variance in expected profit represents risk and the extent to which a Muslim investor adopts Islamic banking is related to his/her willingness to tolerate uncertainty or risk. There is some suggestion in the consumer finance literature that risk tolerance is related to the composition of an individual's investment portfolio. Grable (2008) suggested that if an investor holds the majority of his/her assets in equity-based investments where returns are less certain, he/she is deemed to have a higher risk tolerance. Conversely, an investor is deemed to have a lower risk tolerance if the majority of his/her assets are in debt-based investments where returns are more certain. Grable and Lytton (1999) provided a 13-item measure of financial risk tolerance that can be utilized in future research. Accordingly I propose that the proportion of a Muslim investor's total portfolio in PLS arrangements is predicted by his/her willingness to tolerate risk in investment return.

This variable, in turn, is predicted by six explanatory variables: (1) religious orientation, (2) social capital in Muslim community, (3) knowledge of Islamic banking principles, (4) perceived benefits of PLS arrangements, (5) trust in the bank, and (6) congruity of bank image and Islamic values.

Religious orientation is a relevant starting point to examine the effect of religiosity on consumer behavior because religion can prescribe rules of conduct relating to individual choice and/or contribute to attitudes and values concerning consumption and utility (Harrell, 1986). On this basis there are several studies that have established a relationship between religion or religiousness and consumer behavior (for example, Bailey and Sood, 1993; Delener, 1990; Donahue, 1985; Essoo and Dibb, 2004; Hashim and Mizerski, 2010; Vitell et al., 2005; Wilkes et al., 1986). Yet less is known about the relationship between religion and risk tolerance because the evidence is sparse and equivocal. The evidence in some studies appears to suggest that in general, the more religious a person is, the less tolerant they are of risk (Delener, 1990; Irwin, 1993; Wiebe and Fleck, 1980). In the context of consumer durable goods, Delener (1990) established that highly religious consumers have a heightened awareness of risk compared to their non-religious counterparts. Irwin (1993) observed that less religious individuals are likely to have greater financial risk tolerance. Weibe and Fleck (1980) argued that intrinsically religious individuals tend to be more conservative and rigid than those who are extrinsically religious or nonreligious. This body of evidence is consistent with Pascal's wager which maintains that religious conviction itself is an expression of risk aversion.

On the other hand, there is some suggestion that Muslims in particular may not be as risk-averse because of their fatalistic ideology. Essoo and Dibb (2004) surmised that Muslim consumers may be more willing to take risks as consumers because they are perhaps more fatalistic and accepting of Allah's will. Bailey and Sood (1993) provided a concurring viewpoint by suggesting that Muslims are likely to perceive less risk in trying a new product since the outcome is predetermined by Allah. They also found it ironic that this trait may deter them from seeking more information about the product concerned. This is a pertinent observation because the impetuous shopping pattern that Bailey and Sood (1993) referred to, may explain why Muslim customer surveys have demonstrated that there is little perceived difference between Islamic and conventional banking (Erol and El-Bdour, 1989; Erol et al., 1990), as well as generally low levels of awareness and knowledge of Islamic banking precepts (Gerrard and Cunningham, 1997; Metawa and Almossawi, 1998; Naser et al., 1999; Rammal and Zurbruegg, 2007).

A shift in the focus towards PLS arrangements in Islamic banking may prompt Muslim consumers to acquaint themselves with Islamic ideals relating to financial affairs. On the occasion that a Muslim customer is being propositioned with PLS-based banking products, he/she may begin to learn of their social benefits and their relevance to Islam and *sharia* compliance. As I maintained earlier, it is through PLS arrangements that the trade-off between economic self-interest and religious duty becomes apparent, and a Muslim customer's religiosity may be evoked in the decision-making process.

Faced with this trade-off, there is some basis to hypothesize that the more religious Muslim customer is likely to tolerate a greater level of uncertainty in investment return. The mere use of the 'Islamic' label on banking products may naturally attract many Muslim customers but it is expected that only those truly committed to Islamic ideals are likely to tolerate the risk required to invest in PLS arrangements. This suggestion is made on the basis that Muslim consumers who are intrinsically religious (as opposed to extrinsically religious) would show a greater commitment to consumer ethics, religious duty, and Islamic doctrines (Donahue, 1985; Hashim and Mizerski, 2010; Vitell et al., 2005). The operationalization of religiosity utilizing measures of extrinsic and intrinsic orientation was proposed by Allport and Ross (1967). Allport and Ross (1967) described the extrinsically religious as those who 'use their religion', and the intrinsically religious as those who 'live their religion'. This conceptualization of religiosity would be useful in the present research context. On this basis, I propose that a Muslim investor who is more intrinsically religious is willing to tolerate more risk in investment returns of PLS arrangements.

In addition to a Muslim's religious orientation, I propose that his/her religious norms are reinforced by others in the community who share the same orientation. Since it is obligatory for Muslims to help each other practice Islamic teachings, members of a tightly knit Muslim community would be under greater normative pressure to fulfill their religious duty than another Muslim consumer who is not part of the community. There is sufficient research to support the notion that a community that possesses high social capital can more effectively enforce social norms and generate benevolent behaviors (see Banfield, 1958; Coleman, 1988; Portes and Sensenbrenner, 1993; Putnam, 2000). Muslims in a tightly knit community are more likely to have frequent interactions where information on Islam can be exchanged. Hegazy (1995) found that word-of-mouth has a significant influence on Muslim consumers seeking Islamic banking products. Concurring evidence by other authors suggests that co-religious friends, neighbors and relatives play an active role in promoting an awareness of Islamic banking in general or specific banking products (Erol and El-Bdour, 1989; Erol et al., 1990; Metawa and Almossawi, 1998). Thus I propose that higher levels of social capital in the Muslim community will lead to the willingness of an individual member to tolerate greater risk in investment returns.

There are two proposed explanatory variables which relate to consumer knowledge: knowledge of Islamic banking principles and perceived benefits of PLS arrangements to Muslim borrowers. The issue of consumer knowledge is an important one but quite complex in today's context of Islamic banking. Hitherto, most of the growth in Islamic banking appears to have been buoyed by a particular mindset. Muslim investors have been conditioned to expect competitive returns while gaining some satisfaction from subscribing to banking products that relate to their religion or *sharia*. Underlying this mindset is an intriguing phenomenon. In a typical retail encounter, Islamic banking products are often promoted for their investment returns and product features because many Muslim customers, are already familiar with conventional banking products, and can then have some basis to compare both product types. These references to conventional banking counterparts may obscure the fact that many Islamic banking products do not adhere to the true spirit of religious ideals.

Herein lies the conundrum: most Muslim customers have little knowledge of Islamic banking precepts (see Gerrard and Cunningham, 1997; Metawa and Almossawi, 1998; Naser et al., 1999; Rammal and Zurbruegg, 2007) and as long as Islamic banking products provide a competitive return, they appear to have little incentive to inquire further about Islamic banking principles or research the investment methodology concerned. It is possible that the mere branding of these products as 'Islamic' is sufficient for many Muslims to feel satisfied that their investment has complied with religious ideals. Thinking that they have already 'done the right thing', many Muslim customers may feel that their attention or involvement in this matter is no longer required. In other words, consumer involvement (that is, seeking product information, gaining knowledge in Islamic banking principles) in Islamic banking ends when customers feel that they have discharged their religious or moral duty.

There is some evidence in the literature to substantiate this claim. Mackenzie and Lewis (1999, p. 451) found that investors in ethical funds were willing to 'accept the hand of fate, adopt haphazard rules of thumb, and make satisficing accommodations within their consciences'. This implies that if an ethical (or religious) person feels that they have invested money into a worthy cause, then they are likely to apply decision making heuristics and rationalizations that minimize further involvement or perhaps even cognitive dissonance. Many Muslims continue to be Islamic banking customers despite not being aware of the significance of PLS arrangements (Naser et al., 1999; Rammal and Zurbruegg, 2007) and many cite investment returns as a reason for their patronage (Erol and El-Bdour, 1989; Metawa and Almossawi, 1998). This situation persists today because there is some ignorance about Islamic banking principles and bank managers continue to promote debt-based products under the banner of Islamic banking.

In contrast, I argue that if PLS arrangements were promoted, only customers with more intimate knowledge of Islamic banking precepts would appreciate its objectives. In other words, an investor in PLS arrangements is likely to be someone who understands Islamic ideals enough to appreciate the goals and nobility of the undertaking. Someone who lacks this understanding may not be motivated to tolerate the uncertainty inherent in PLS arrangements. I revert to Al-Suwailem's (2002) conception of risk-taking in Islam: if investing in PLS arrangements has been well researched and is considered to be morally worthwhile, then the risk is acceptable and losses can be ascribed to *qadar* (destiny). In addition, Devlin (2002) maintained that customers with a higher degree of financial knowledge are likely to place more emphasis on intrinsic product attributes. It would then be reasonable to infer that a customer knowledgeable in Islamic banking precepts would be more accommodating of the uncertainty inherent in PLS arrangements because it adheres more closely to Islamic ideals. Therefore, I hypothesize that the more a Muslim investor understands the principles and potential benefits of PLS-based Islamic banking products, the more risk-tolerant he/she will be.

The final two predictors of risk tolerance are related to the bank that is promoting

Islamic banking products: trust in the bank and congruity of bank image and Islamic values. The literature is replete with studies citing the importance of trust in a customer's relationship with banks in general. With conventional banking and other services, customers have to trust the bank they deal with particularly if there is significant risk involved (Doney and Cannon, 1997; Morgan and Hunt, 1994). Although the literature offers little guidance on trust in an Islamic banking-specific context, I anticipate that trust would feature more prominently in Islamic banking than it does in conventional banking. The reputation of the bank concerned becomes even more salient in PLS arrangements where information asymmetries and moral hazards can be problematic for Muslim investors. Moreover, if a Muslim investor switches to Islamic banking products where the investment returns are more uncertain, it would be of great comfort for him/her to know that the bank can still be trusted. It should also be noted that if Muslims do indeed exhibit more impetuous consumption patterns as some authors have suggested (Bailey and Sood, 1993; Essoo and Dibb, 2004), then trust may serve as an even more important heuristic cue in financial decision making. Accordingly, the more a Muslim investor trusts the bank marketing PLS-based Islamic banking products, the greater his/her tolerance for investment risk.

The image of the bank should also be congruent with the products it sells; therefore a bank that promotes Islamic banking products may be more effective if perceived as an Islamic-friendly bank. Admittedly this criterion has not surfaced in many customer surveys because the Islamic banking products concerned were predominantly debt-based and were assessed on more secular criteria. Since customers were comparing Islamic banking products to conventional banking products, features such as bank amenities and services, product fees and charges, credit or ATM facilities were given more emphasis than the Islamic credibility of the bank. However in the case of PLS arrangements where religiosity may feature more prominently, the congruity between the bank's image and Islamic values becomes a more salient consideration. A Muslim customer may look to a bank's image and reputation to infer whether it has the credibility and competency to deliver *sharia*-compliant services. The bank's image, in turn, is manifest in its frontline staff and promotional strategies. Since consumers will need a great deal of product education and personal selling, the frontline staff will arguably be the most important component of a bank's image. Hassan et al., (2008) proposed that if the behavior of frontline staff is perceived as Islamic, the bank is also likely to be perceived as Islamic. Elfakhani et al., (2007) reported that banks which offer Islamic banking products often use their promotional material to convey a sense of trust and piety. The use of local *sharia* boards as customer advocates is also a common practice. To reiterate, if indeed the decision to invest in PLS-based products becomes more religious in nature, then increasingly the banks have to be perceived as adhering to Islamic principles (Hegazy, 1995; Metawa and Almossawi, 1998). On this basis, I propose that the more 'Islamic' a bank's image is, the more willing a Muslim investor will be to tolerate risk in investment return.

SUGGESTIONS FOR MARKETING ISLAMIC BANKING

The proposed conceptual model may provide managers with a number of useful suggestions to enrich a marketing program for Islamic banking. This process begins with a commitment to distinguish Islamic banking from conventional banking through equity-based or PLS arrangements. Several observers have urged managers to shift their promotional efforts toward these products, which may provide a source of differentiation and competitive advantage, given the perceived parity between Islamic and conventional banking (Erol and El-Bdour, 1989; Erol et al., 1990; Wilson, 1997). Doing so would require extensive consumer education campaigns and competent sales staff, given the low levels of awareness and knowledge surrounding Islamic banking principles and PLS arrangements. The potency of referrals and word-of-mouth recommendations among co-religious Muslims would suggest that well-placed education seminars and viral marketing campaigns at the community level will prove to be an effective strategy. Suitable locations for these seminars and campaigns may include religious and cultural classes, religious talks at mosques, cultural events and Islamic-themed websites. Market segmentation and targeting activities may help identify a segment of Muslim faithful who may be more predisposed to Islamic banking, specifically PLS arrangements.

Marketing campaigns should also be designed to stir feelings of altruism and religious duty by stressing the relevance of PLS arrangements in Islamic finance. In such campaigns, managers may opt to use case studies and testimonials to emphasize the constraints of debt financing on nascent entrepreneurs or the plight of farmers when they are unable to meet their interest payments. To augment this promotional strategy, managerial decisions relating to distribution should focus on making Islamic banking services more accessible in rural and lower socioeconomic areas. This strategy may appear to be counter-intuitive to the dominant logic of locating banking services at centers of wealth accumulation; however, evidence of social benefits arising from PLS-based Islamic banking products are likely to be most apparent in rural areas (Bjorvatn, 1998; Ratnawati, 2001). Banks that are successful in marketing and implementing Islamic banking in these areas may create a profitable niche market segment which is unlikely to cannibalize market share in conventional banking areas.

Another niche market segment arising from PLS arrangements is microfinancing, where trust financing or *mudaraba* instruments can be used to make micro equity loans to applicants who would otherwise lack access to credit in the conventional banking system. The provision of finance to this market has been proven to improve the welfare of the poor, as evidenced by contributions of Muhammad Yunus and the Grameen Bank which garnered them the 2006 Nobel Peace Prize. Microfinancing is a growth market, which has the ability to attract ethical investors from religious and non-religious backgrounds, and PLS-based Islamic banking products may be suitable vehicles for it.

Community welfare improvements arising from Islamic banking should be documented by the banks and used in the promotion of their image as socially responsible organizations. If indeed the marketing of Islamic banking products requires congruity between the bank's reputation and Islamic ideals, then evidence of corporate social responsibility would certainly help to enhance consumers' impressions of the bank. A healthy corporate image in Islamic banking may even spill over to strengthen the bank's overall image in conventional banking markets.

CONCLUSION

Religion has long been recognized as a major factor in the formation of social structure and human action. Islam in particular is relevant to everyday financial decisions that ultimately shape the well-being of a society. Islamic law is proactive in developing Islamic banking principles designed to guarantee social justice in financial transactions and improve societal welfare (Taylor, 2003).

Islamic banking is a unique characteristic of a major world religion whose effects need to be carefully examined. Islamic ideals concerning financial affairs, risk, and equity in welfare distribution have value in parts of the world where income inequality and injustice are rife. However, it is rather unfortunate that the current development of Islamic banking has diverged from those ideals. The vast majority of investments in Islamic banking reside in products that are indistinguishable from conventional banking products. PLS arrangements adhere to Islamic ideals more closely but both banks and investors are risk-averse. The PLS arrangements in Islamic banking offer a true and attractive alternative to conventional financing and may even find a niche in the microfinance market. Both bank managers and marketing managers have important roles to play in stimulating the demand for these arrangements.

It is my hope that the conceptual framework that I have proposed will establish a research agenda in an area that greatly deserves further development. More importantly, I hope that this chapter will engender more widespread discussion of both the potential of Islamic banking and the promotion of PLS arrangements. The Islamic banking model is truly a unique opportunity to better understand the interaction between religion, economic self-interest, and marketing.

NOTES

*   The author would like to acknowledge Professor Anthony Pecotich for his contribution on an earlier version of this manuscript.
1.   These injunctions are contained in several verses in the Qur'an such as in *surah* (chapter) 2.
2.   The lack of industry expertise combined with profit underreporting and tax evasion by the entrepreneur makes it costly for the bank to monitor the progress of the project

REFERENCES

Aggrawal, K.R. and T. Yousef (2000), 'Islamic banks and investment financing', *Journal of Money, Credit, and Banking*, **32**, 93–120.
Al-Jasser, M. (2010), 'Speech on the overview of the Islamic banking industry', The Fifth Conference for Islamic Banks and Financial Institutions, 15–16 March, Damascus, Syria: Central Bank of Syria.
Al-Suwailem, S.I. (2002), 'Decision-making under uncertainty: an Islamic perspective', in Munawar Iqbal and David T. Llewellyn (eds), *Islamic Banking and Finance: New Perspectives on Profit-Sharing and Risk*, Cheltenham, UK and Northampton, MA, USA: Edward Elgar, pp. 15–39.
Ali, S.A. (1964), *Economic Foundations of Islam*, Calcutta, India: Orient Longmans.
Allport, G.W. and J.M. Ross (1967), 'Personal religious orientation and prejudice', *Journal of Personality and Social Psychology*, **5** (4), 432–43.
Bailey, J.M. and J. Sood (1993), 'The effects of religious affiliation on consumer behaviour: a preliminary investigation', *Journal of Managerial Issues*, **5** (3), 328–52.
Banfield, E.C. (1958), *The Moral Basis of a Backward Society*, Glencoe, IL: Free Press.

Bjorvatn, K. (1998) 'Islamic economics and economic development', *Forum for Development Studies*, **2**, 229–43.

Caragata, W. (2000), 'Islamic finance 101: shariah lenders make headway in Indonesia', *Asiaweek*, 21 July, available at http://www.asiaweek.com/asiaweek/magazine/2000/0721/biz.islamic.html, accessed 26 April 2010.

Carpenter, S.B. and R.T. Jensen (2002), 'Household participation in formal and informal savings mechanisms: evidence from Pakistan', *Review of Development Economics*, **6** (3), 314–28.

Chapra, M.U. (1985), *Toward a Just Monetary System*, Leicester, UK: The Islamic Foundation.

Chapra, M.U. (2000), *The Future of Economics: An Islamic Perspective*, Leicester, UK: The Islamic Foundation.

Coleman, J.S. (1988), 'Social capital in the creation of human capital,' *American Journal of Sociology*, **94** (Supplement: Organizations and Institutions: Sociological and Economic Approaches to the Analysis of Social Structure), S95–S120.

Darrat, A.F. (1988), 'The Islamic interest free banking system: some empirical evidence', *Applied Economics*, **20**, 417–25.

Delener, N. (1990), 'The effects of religious factors on perceived risk in durable goods purchase decisions', *Journal of Consumer Marketing*, **7** (3), 27–38.

Devlin, J.F. (2002), 'Customer knowledge and choice criteria in retail banking', *Journal of Strategic Marketing*, **10** (4), 273–90.

Dixon, R. (1992), 'Islamic banking', *International Journal of Bank Marketing*, **10** (6), 32–37.

Donahue, M.J. (1985), 'Intrinsic and extrinsic religiousness: review and meta-analysis,' *Journal of Personality and Social Psychology*, **48** (2), 400–19.

Doney, P.M. and J.P. Cannon (1997), 'An examination of the nature of trust in buyer-seller relationship,' *Journal of Marketing*, **61** (2), 35–51.

Elfakhani, S.M., I.J. Zbib and Z.U. Ahmed (2007), 'Marketing of Islamic financial products', in M. Kabir Hassan and Mervyn K. Lewis (eds), *Handbook of Islamic Banking*, Cheltenham, UK and Northampton, MA, USA: Edward Elgar Publishing, pp. 116–27.

Erol, C. and R. El-Bdour (1989), 'Attitudes, behaviour and patronage factors of customers towards Islamic banks', *International Journal of Bank Marketing*, **7** (6), 31–37.

Erol, C., E. Kaynak and E. Radi (1990), 'Conventional and Islamic banks: patronage behaviour of Jordanian customers', *International Journal of Bank Marketing*, **8** (4), 25–35.

Errico, L. and M. Farahbaksh (1998), 'Islamic banking: issues in prudential regulations and supervision', *IMF Working Paper WP/98/30*, International Monetary Fund.

Essoo, N. and S. Dibb (2004), 'Religious influences on shopping behaviour: an exploratory study', *Journal of Marketing Management*, **20** (7/8), 683–712.

Gerrard, P. and J.B. Cunningham (1997), 'Islamic banking: a study in Singapore', *International Journal of Bank Marketing*, **15** (6), 204–12.

Ghannadian, F.F. and G. Goswami (2004), 'Developing economy banking: the case of Islamic banks', *International Journal of Social Economics*, **31** (8), 740–52.

Grable, J.E. (2008), 'Risk tolerance', in Jing Jian Xiao (ed.), *Handbook of Consumer Finance Research*, Dordrecht: Springer.

Grable, J.E. and R.H. Lytton (1999), 'Financial risk tolerance revisited: the development of a risk assessment instrument', *Financial Services Review*, **8** (3), 163–81.

Hardie, A. and M. Rabooy (1991), 'Risk, piety, and the Islamic investor', *British Journal of Middle Eastern Studies*, **18** (1), 52–66.

Haron, S., and W.N. Wan Azmi (2009), *Islamic Finance and Banking System: Philosophies, Principles and Practices*, Kuala Lumpur, Malaysia: McGraw-Hill Education (Asia).

Haron, S., N. Ahmad and S.L. Planisek (1994), 'Bank patronage factors of Muslim and non-Muslim customers', *International Journal of Bank Marketing*, **12** (1), 32–40.

Harrell, G.D. (1986), *Consumer Behaviour*, San Diego, CA: Harcourt, Brace, Jovanovich Publishers.

Hashim, N.M. and D. Mizerski (2010), 'Exploring Muslim consumers' information sources for fatwa rulings on products and behaviors', *Journal of Islamic Marketing*, **1** (1), 37–50.

Hassan, A., A. Chachi and S.A. Latiff (2008), 'Islamic marketing ethics and its impact on customer satisfaction in the Islamic banking industry', *Islamic Economics*, **21** (1), 23–40.

Hegazy, I.A. (1995), 'An empirical comparative study between Islamic and commercial banks' selection criteria in Egypt', *International Journal of Contemporary Management*, **5** (3), 46–61.

Iqbal, Z. and A. Mirakhor (1999), 'Progress and challenges of Islamic banking', *Thunderbird International Business Review*, **41** (4/5), 381–405.

Irwin, C.E. (1993), 'Adolescence and risk taking: how are they related?', in N.J. Bell and R.W. Bell (eds), *Adolescent Risk Taking*, Newbury Park, CA: Sage, pp. 7–28.

Khan, M.S. (1986), 'Islamic interest-free banking: a theoretical analysis', *IMF Staff Papers*, 33, International Monetary Fund.

Khan, M.S. and A. Mirakhor (1990), 'Islamic banking: experiences in the Islamic Republic of Iran and in Pakistan', *Economic Development and Cultural Change*, **38** (2), 353–75.

Kuran, T. (1986), 'The economic system in contemporary Islamic thought: interpretation and assessment', *International Journal of Middle East Studies*, **18** (2), 135–64.

Kuran, T. (1995), 'Islamic economics and the Islamic subeconomy', *Journal of Economic Perspectives*, **9** (4), 155–73.

Kuran, T. (1996), 'The discontents of Islamic economic morality', Paper presented at the 108th Annual Meeting of the American Economic Association, San Francisco, CA, January.

Lewis, A. and J. Cullis (1990), 'Ethical investments: preferences and morality,' *Journal of Behavioural Economics*, **19** (4), 395–411.

Lewis, A. and C. Mackenzie (2000), 'Morals, money, ethical investing and economic psychology', *Human Relations*, **53** (2), 179–91.

Mackenzie, C. and A. Lewis (1999), 'Morals and markets: the case of ethical investing', *Business Ethics Quarterly*, **9** (3), 439–52.

Metawa, S.A. and M. Almossawi (1998), 'Banking behavior of Islamic bank customers: perspectives and implications', *International Journal of Bank Marketing*, **16** (7), 299–313.

Metwally, S. (1992), 'The aggregate balance sheet and results of transaction and financial indicators for Islamic banks and financial institutions', *Journal of Islamic Banking and Finance*, 7–61.

Metwally, M.M. (1997), 'Economic consequences of applying Islamic principles in Muslim societies', *International Journal of Social Economics*, **24** (7/8/9), 941–57.

Mittelstaedt, J.D. (2002), 'A framework for understanding the relationships between religion and markets', *Journal of Macromarketing*, **22** (1), 6–18.

Morgan, R.M. and S.D. Hunt (1994), 'The commitment-trust theory of relationship marketing,' *Journal of Marketing*, **58** (3), 20–38.

Naser, K. and L. Moutinho (1997), 'Strategic marketing management: the case of Islamic banks', *International Journal of Bank Marketing*, **15** (6), 187–203.

Naser, K., A. Jamal, and K. Al-Khatib (1999), 'Islamic banking: a study of customer satisfaction and preferences in Jordan', *International Journal of Bank Marketing*, **17** (3), 135–50.

Naughton, T. and B. Shanmugam (1990), 'Interest-free banking: a case study of Malaysia', *National Westminster Bank Quarterly Review* (February), 16–32.

Noorzoy, M.S. (1982), 'Islamic laws on riba (interest) and their economic implications', *International Journal of Middle East Studies*, **14** (1), 3–17.

Portes, A. and J. Sensenbrenner (1993), 'Embeddedness and immigration: notes on the social determinants of economic action,' *American Journal of Sociology*, **98** (6), 1320–50.

Pourian, H. (1995), 'The experience of Iran's Islamic financial system and its prospect for development', *Development of Financial Markets in the Arab Countries, Iran and Turkey,* Economic Research Forum for the Arab Countries, Iran and Turkey.

Putnam, R. (2000), *Bowling Alone: The Collapse and Revival of American Community*, New York: Simon and Schuster.

Qureshi, A.I. (1974), *Islam and the Theory of Interest* (2nd edn), Lahore, Pakistan: S.H. Mohammad Ashraf.

Rammal, H.G. and R. Zurbruegg (2007), 'Awareness of Islamic banking products among Muslims: the case of Australia', *Journal of Financial Services Marketing*, **12** (1), 65–74.

Ratnawati, A. (2001), *Sharia Bank: Potency, Preference and Community's Attitude toward It in West Java*, Jakarta, Indonesia: Bank Indonesia.

Saleem, M. (2005), *Islamic Banking – A $300 Billion Deception*, Bloomington, IN: Xlibris Corporation.

Samad, A. and M.K. Hassan (1999), 'The performance of Malaysian Islamic banks during 1984–1997: an exploratory study', *International Journal of Islamic Financial Services*, **1** (3).

Sarker, M.A.A. (1999), 'Islamic banking in Bangladesh: performance, problems and prospects', *International Journal of Islamic Financial Services*, **1** (3).

Sharfi, A. (2000), *Islam: Between Divine Message and History*, Budapest, Hungary: Central European University Press.

Shook, D.N. and S.S. Hassan (1988), 'Marketing management in an Islamic banking environment: in search of an innovative marketing concept', *International Journal of Bank Marketing*, **6** (1), 21–30.

Siddiqui, K.H. (1985), 'Interest free banking', *Journal of the Institute of Bankers in Pakistan* (June), 57–68.

Siwar, C. and M.Y. Karim (1997), 'Urban development and urban poverty in Malaysia', *International Journal of Social Economics*, **24** (12), 1524–35.

Stiansen, E. (1995), *Islamic Economics: The Experience from the Sudan, 1983–1995*, Uppsala, Sweden: The Nordic Africa Institute.

Taleqani, M. (1983), *Islam and Ownership,* trans. Jabbari and Rajaee. Mazda Publishers.

Taylor, J.M. (2003), 'Islamic banking: the feasibility of establishing an Islamic bank in the United States', *American Business Law Journal*, **40** (2), 385–416.

Taylor, T.W. and J.W. Evans (1987), 'Islamic banking and the prohibition of usury in Western economic thought', *National Westminster Bank Quarterly Review*, (November), 15–27.

Thaler, R.H. (1985), 'Mental accounting and consumer choice', *Marketing Science*, **4** (3), 199–214.

Vitell, S.J., J.G.P. Paolillo, and J.J. Singh (2005), 'Religiosity and consumer ethics', *Journal of Business Ethics*, **57**, 175–81.

Webley, P., A. Lewis, and C. Mackenzie (2001), 'Commitment among ethical investors: an experimental approach', *Journal of Economic Psychology*, **22** (1), 27–42.

Wiebe, K.F. and J.R. Fleck (1980), 'Personality correlates of intrinsic, extrinsic, and nonreligious orientations', *Journal of Psychology*, **105** (2), 181–87.

Wilkes, R.E., J.J. Burnett, and R.D. Howell (1986), 'On the meaning and measurement of religiosity in consumer research', *Journal of the Academy of Marketing Science*, **14** (1), 47–56.

Wilson, R. (1982), 'Economic change and re-interpretation of Islamic social values', *Bulletin (British Society for Middle Eastern Studies)*, **9** (2), 107–13.

Wilson, R. (1997), 'Islamic finance and ethical investment', *International Journal of Social Economics*, **24** (11), 1325–42.

Zaher, T.S. and M.K. Hassan (2001), 'A comparative literature survey of Islamic finance and banking', *Financial Markets, Institutions and Instruments*, **10** (4), 155–99.

Zangeneh, H. (1989), 'Islamic banking: theory and practice in Iran', *Comparative Economic Studies*, **31** (3), 67–84.

14 Market segmentation and buying behaviour in the Islamic financial services industry

Rusnah Muhamad, T.C. Melewar and
Sharifah Faridah Syed Alwi

INTRODUCTION

The Islamic method of banking and financing has become a global phenomenon and has successfully developed into an established industry known as the Islamic financial services industry (IFSI). The industry has generated renewed interest among the players in the financial world amid the recent sub-prime and financial crisis. More importantly, IFSI has emerged as a viable alternative to the conventional interest-based financial services industry (CFSI), and has expanded rapidly over the last two decades with diverse clientele in both Muslim and non-Muslim countries. It is attracting growing interest from global players who are taking increasingly major roles in this industry (Aslam, 2006).

For the past 30 years of its existence, the IFSI has been successful in providing an array of financial products (IDB et al., 2007). However, what is lacking at present is a detailed and classified understanding of consumers' segmentation for the industry, thereby making the strategic positioning and marketing of IFS globally unclear and problematic.

Traditionally, consumer segmentation by banks was largely limited to categories of corporate and retail consumers (Machauer and Morgner, 2001). Corporate consumers are distinguished by their geographic range of activities (regional versus international) or by their sector affiliation. In personal retail banking, externally observed demographic or economic criteria such as profession, age, income or wealth (known as the 'a priori' approach) are often used as dimensions for segmentation (Machauer and Morgner, 2001; Harrison, 1994; Meidan, 1984). Consumers could also be segmented based on a post-hoc approach (for example through benefits sought from products), such as service quality, location, attitudes, lifestyles, and values (Machauer and Morgner, 2001 Harrison, 1994).

The use of the 'a priori' approach alone, however, has been heavily criticized as the use of a single indicator does not address the specific needs and wants of consumers (Machauer and Morgner, 2001); consumers exhibit different personalities, values and lifestyles even within the same category or demographic criteria (Kotler et al., 2009; Meadows and Dibb, 1998); and the profitable segment may be ignored or missed (Harrison, 1994). However, is the same basis applicable in the context of the segmentation of Islamic retail banking and other IFS? Muhamad et al. (2009) explain that in the context of Islamic banking, religion and religiosity appear to explain the underlying motive of consumers when opting for the services and, thus, aid the managerial understanding concerning the type of consumers who will purchase the services. More importantly, the IFSI industry needs to take action to capitalize on the current financial crisis and economic recession, as some economists have suggested that Islamic financial principles may provide an alternative solution for overcoming these problems. Thus, the industry needs to carefully analyse and understand the market segments (pertinently the underlying buying motives in each segment) to appropriately design the marketing and communication strategies for promoting its products.

Muhamad et al. (2009) propose three different market segments for Islamic banking consumers and, accordingly, the main motives underlying the buying behaviour for each segment. These groups are known as the religious conviction group, who are strongly guided by their religious dictates in making their purchase decisions; the ethically observant group, who make decisions based on ethical criteria; and the economic rationality group, whose decisions are solely based on their personal financial gain (economic rationalism). In addition, there is also growing concern regarding the low level of awareness relating to Islamic banking and finance concepts, as well as specific products/services among Muslim and non-Muslim consumers worldwide (Rammal and Zurbruegg, 2007; Okumus, 2005; Karbhari et al., 2004; Bley and Kuehn, 2004; Ahmad and Haron, 2002). Thus, the main objective of this study is twofold:

1. Given the lack of understanding concerning the IFS segmentation, the current study aims to explore the different consumer segments and the underlying motives as proposed by Muhamad et al. (2009), which may be based upon either the a priori or the post-hoc approach. The current findings may be used by the IFS providers to guide their marketing and communication strategies for promoting their products.
2. As there is growing concern regarding the low level of awareness among consumers relating to IFS, the second objective is to determine whether the level of awareness has improved. Therefore, the awareness of IFS is evaluated as perceived by both the key market players and Malaysian consumers (Muslim and non-Muslim).

ISLAMIC FINANCIAL SERVICES INDUSTRY (IFSI)

The IFSI has witnessed a frenetic pace of growth (Saidi, 2009; IDB et al., 2007). It is estimated that the growth rate of the industry over the last decade is between 10 per cent and 20 per cent (McKinsey, 2008; Anon, 2004; Zaher and Hassan, 2001). There are over 300 Islamic financial institutions worldwide across 75 countries. International Financial Services London (2008, 2009) reports that the total projected size of the global Islamic financial assets is US$729 billion and about US$537 billion is in the form of Islamic banking assets. In terms of market share by product, Islamic commercial banks represent the majority of the global Islamic financial assets (74 per cent); Islamic investment banks rank second (12 per cent); and, outstanding *sukuk* issued rank third (11 per cent). Iran has the largest assets (21 per cent), followed by Saudi Arabia (14.3 per cent) and Malaysia (10.3 per cent).

Various factors have fuelled the development of the industry and continue to contribute towards its potential growth, and therefore need to be seriously considered by the key players in the industry. The increasing size of the world's Muslim population, estimated at 1.7 billion in 2009 and expected to increase to 1.9 billion by 2015 (US Census Bureau, International Data Base, 2009), has opened up an opportunity for the IFSI to further progress in what is a largely untapped market. IFS is an attractive alternative for those investors who, in their quest to diversify their portfolios, are looking for new asset classes, new instruments and new products that have low correlation with their existing asset classes and products (Hussain, 2005). Increasing concern for green and sustainable or ethical investment, particularly in European and other Western countries, has also sparked further interest in IFS globally, as the screening criteria used in these investments largely overlap with Islamic finance principles (Saidi, 2009; Ghoul and Karam, 2007). There have even been suggestions that Islamic finance principles may be the best solution for the current global crisis (see for example Maverecon, 2009; Quinn, 2008).

According to El-Sheikh (2008), what makes an economy 'Islamic' is *sharia*: a huge corpus of moral and legal discourses, which were intended by scholars (jurists and theologians) of the second and third Islamic centuries to guide Muslims in their pursuit of a good and virtuous life (El-Sheikh, 2008, p. 116). Therefore, IFS are financial products that are structured in compliance with *sharia* law. The basic principles in designing IFS are prohibition of interest; risk sharing; individual rights and duties; property rights; money as potential capital; prohibition of speculative behaviour; sanctity of contracts; and *sharia* approved activities (Aslam, 2006; Zaher and Hassan, 2001; Loqman, 1999; Iqbal, 1997). Since interest is prohibited in all forms and for all purposes, IFSI has adopted various *sharia* principles, as suggested by Muslim jurists and scholars, in providing services to consumers. In summary, these principles can be broadly classified into four categories, namely: principles that are based on profit-loss sharing (*mudaraba* and *musharaka*), principles that are based on fixed charges (*murabaha, bai'muajjal, ijara,* and *ijara wa iktina*), principles that are based on free charges (*qard hasan*) and, finally, principles that are applicable directly or indirectly to the operation of IFSI (*wadia* and *rahn*) (*Haron,* 1995).

According to Naser and Moutinho (1997), the idea of Islamic banking and finance has grown out of an increasing desire to conduct financial activities in accordance with *sharia* principles. Thus, ensuring the compliance of IFS with the above mentioned guidelines is necessary for the services to be relevant for use by Muslims, thus broadening the public's access to financial services. The IFSI caters to this special need of society. Among devout Muslims the compliance of financial services with *sharia* rules and principles is a primary concern for the users of these services (IDB et al., 2007). Simultaneously, it is also possible to capture demand beyond the Muslim population through the provision of innovative and high-quality IFS. Given its inherent features and the reality of the current economic climate the IFSI has the potential to concurrently achieve the goals of sustainable economic development and just social progress, by offering a competitive alternative to conventional financial services (CFS). The next section presents a brief discussion on the various products offered by the IFSI.

IFSI: BRIEF DESCRIPTION OF PRODUCTS

IFSI successfully offers a range of financial services in a variety of segments including banking, non-bank financial services, insurance and capital markets (IDB et al., 2007). Brief descriptions for each category of products are given as follows:

Islamic Banking

As of today, IFSI is largely composed of the banking sector (Ibrahim, 2006), as Islamic commercial banks represent more than 70 per cent of the global Islamic financial assets (International Financial Services London, 2008, 2009). Worldwide, Islamic banks offer various kinds of products, which may be broadly classified as deposit, investment and financing products. The deposit products include current and savings accounts normally structured under the concept of *wadia yad damaana* (savings with guarantee), *mudaraba* (profit-loss sharing) and *qard* (benevolent loan). The investment products comprise general and special investment accounts that use the concepts of *mudaraba* and *qard*. As for the financing products, we may broadly group these into two main types, namely, personal and trade financing. Various *sharia* concepts are used to structure the different products offered under the financing category, including *mudaraba, musharaka* (joint venture), *murabaha* (cost plus), *ijara* (leasing), *istisnaa* (future delivery), *bai'al dayn* (debt trading), *wakala* (agent), *kafala* (guarantee) and *qard*.

Islamic Non-Bank and Microfinance Institutions (INBMFIs)

The IFSI is largely dominated by banks that specifically contribute towards providing liquidity and access to a safe and efficient payment-settlement system for depositors, thus, there is a need to expand the types of institution and increase the range of products and services to meet the various needs of the Muslim society (IDB et al., 2007). These institutions, collectively known as Islamic non-bank and microfinance institutions (INBMFIs), can be broadly categorized into two main types, namely: the INBMFIs that have counterparts in the conventional financial system, such as finance companies, cooperatives, credit unions, leasing and factoring companies; and INBMFIs that have unique Islamic features such as Tabung Haji and *Al-Rahnu* (Malaysia), *Mudaraba* companies (Pakistan), *Qard Hasan* funds (Iran) and *Waqf* foundations (Turkey and Indonesia). Similar to Islamic banks, these institutions provide deposit and investment facilities, as well as financing products using various Islamic principles, albeit catering for different segments of society.

Islamic Insurance or *Takaful*

Takaful is the Islamic counterpart of conventional insurance, structured as general, life (or family) and *retakaful* (Ali and Odierno, 2008; IDB et al., 2007). There are many types of general *takaful* products including motor vehicles *takaful*, fire *takaful* and miscellaneous *takaful* (examples include personal accident *takaful* and worker's compensation *takaful*). There are two main plans for the family *takaful* products known as the individual plan and mortgage plan. Re*takaful* enables *takaful* operators to spread and share risks with other operators, thereby protecting a primary *takaful* against unforeseen or extraordinary losses (Ali and Odierno, 2008). *Takaful* operations are normally based on the *sharia* concepts of *mudaraba* and *wakala*.

Islamic Capital Market

The development of a well-functioning capital market is critical for a sound and efficient IFSI, as it contributes significantly towards the efficient pricing of assets, risk and liquidity management, and specialized services in resources mobilization and allocation (IDB et al., 2007). Among the products are *sukuk*, *sharia*-compliant securities, *sharia*-based unit trusts, Islamic real estate investment trusts and Islamic exchange traded funds (ETF). *Sukuk* (literally translates as certificate), in essence, is an asset-backed security structured in compliance with the precepts of *sharia*. It is somewhat similar to a trust certificate or bond (Abdel-Khaleq and Richardson, 2007). *Sharia*-compliant securities are securities (ordinary shares, warrants and transferable subscription rights) of a public-listed company that have been classified as *sharia* permissible for investment based on the company's compliance with *sharia* principles in terms of its primary business and investment activities. A *sharia*-based unit trust fund is a collective investment fund that offers investors the opportunity to invest in a diversified portfolio of *sharia*-compliant shares and fixed-income securities, as well as other *sharia*-compliant money market instruments. Islamic real estate investment trusts provide investment opportunities in collective real estate investments through a *sharia*-compliant capital market instrument. ETFs are essentially unit trust funds that are listed and traded on a stock exchange. An Islamic ETF tracks an Islamic benchmark index where the index constituents comprise companies that are *sharia*-compliant.

RELIGIOSITY AND CONSUMER BEHAVIOUR

The effect of religion on consumer behaviour depends on the level of religious commitment of an individual (Mokhlis, 2006). Religious commitment or religiosity is generally described as the degree or extent to which a person adheres to his or her religious belief, values and practices (Worthington et al., 2003; Johnson et al., 2001; Renzetti and Curran, 1998) and this commitment is reflected in the attitudes and behaviour of the individual (Worthington et al., 2003; Johnson et al., 2001; Delener, 1994).

A review of the extant literature reveals that several studies have investigated the relationship between religiosity and various aspects of consumer behaviour. The general conclusion is that there is an association between the two constructs. Wilkes et al. (1986) conclude that religiosity influences several aspects of consumers' lifestyles, which may eventually affect their choices or alternative behaviour. In another study, LaBarbera (1987) found that Christians who are more conservative tend to use Christian broadcast media and have an increased demand for Christian targeted goods and services. Delener (1994) examined the role structure of husbands and wives in automobile purchase decision making; in comparing the Catholic and Jewish households, a strong influence of religiosity on the decision behaviour of households was found.

Several studies found that religiosity correlates with perceived risk and uncertainty (Rehman and Shabbir, 2010; Delener, 1990; Gentry et al., 1988; John et al., 1986). Rehman and Shabbir (2010) investigated the impact of religiosity on the adoption of new products (NPA) and established that religiosity affects NPA among Muslim consumers. They concluded that consumers' beliefs influence how and what products they adopt.

Delener (1990) examined the influence of religiosity on the perceived risk and uncertainty in purchase decisions concerning durable goods and found that the more religious consumers are more sensitive towards the potential negative consequences of their purchase decision. Gentry et al. (1988) established that the more religious consumers perceived a higher level of risk with new products. John et al. (1986) reported a relationship between religiosity and the willingness to try new products and perceived risk.

Other relevant studies on religiosity in consumer behaviour focused on the purchasing and retail patronage behaviour of consumers. These studies include: Choi (2010) who examined the relationship between religious affiliation and the level of religiosity and consumer product and store-switching behaviour among South Korean consumers; Choi et al. (2010) who investigated how consumers' use of various product information sources can differ depending on their level of religiosity (high, low and none); Swimberghe et al. (2009) who investigated the influence of religiosity on store loyalty and complaint intentions; Ahmad et al. (2008) who examined the banking selection among Muslims in Malaysia; Essoo and Dibb (2004) who studied the shopping behaviour of Catholic, Muslim and Hindu consumers in Mauritius; Siguaw et al. (1995) who researched Sunday shopping behaviour of consumers in the US and New Zealand; Sood and Nasu (1995) who investigated the general purchase behaviour of Japanese and American consumers; and McDaniel and Burnett (1990) who considered the importance to consumers of various attributes of retail department stores.

There are also studies that investigated the impact of religiosity on consumers' attitudes towards advertising messages (Run et al., 2010; Michell and Al-Mossawi, 1999; 1995). Run et al. (2010) probed the impact of religiosity on Malaysian Muslims' attitude towards offensive advertising and the reasons that make these advertisements offensive. Michell and Al-Mossawi (1999) examined the influence of religiosity on message contentiousness among Bahraini Muslims. Michell and Al-Mossawi (1995) investigated the mediating effect of religiosity on advertising effectiveness comparing Christian and Muslim consumers in the UK.

The studies mentioned in the foregoing discussion on religiosity and several aspects of consumer behaviour provide evidence that religiosity plays an important role in consumer behaviour. However, there remains a lack of understanding concerning the impact of religiosity on consumer segmentation. In the marketing of products (for example, toothpaste) or services (such as banking) consumers have been commonly segmented according to demographic characteristics such as age, gender, and social class or behavioural characteristics such as user attributes or benefit sought. According to Delener (1994), however, for certain products or services the level of religiosity of an individual is argued to affect consumer purchasing decisions. Specifically, in this study, the religiosity of a consumer might explain his/her behaviour to opt for IFS.

MARKET SEGMENTATION AND PRODUCT POSITIONING IN THE FINANCIAL SERVICES INDUSTRY

Not all consumers are alike and, therefore, trying to provide all things to all consumers is difficult if not impossible in a competitive marketplace. Segmenting identifies consumer subgroups that are smaller and more homogenous than the overall market.

Many financial institutions select a few key target markets and concentrate on trying to serve them better than their competitors (Zineldin, 1996). Institutions offering Islamic financial services (IOIFS) may find this strategy useful to build up their competitiveness in view of their nascent stage.

Theoretically, market segmentation is the process of dividing a market into a distinct group of individuals, who, along with organizations, share one or more similar responses to some elements of the marketing mix (Peter and Olson, 2008; Edris, 1997). Similarly, Dickson and Ginter (1987) described market segmentation as the use of information about market segments to design programmes to appeal to specific segments. Selecting the relevant target market is vital to developing successful marketing programmes (Peter and Olson, 2008). Accordingly, the segmentation process requires that the total market be divided into homogeneous segments, selecting the target segments, and creating separate marketing programmes to meet the needs and wants of these selected segments. Once the appropriate target market and segment groups are identified, the IFS brand can be positioned while, at the same time, managers design the marketing mix that will help form the IFS brand image in consumers' minds (Peter and Olson, 2008). For example, if consumers perceive the image of IFS as ethical and economic then the promotional mix needs to emphasize these messages. Brand positioning can be done using several categories including: (1) product attribute; (2) user or application of the product; (3) product user; (4) product class; and (5) competitors (Peter and Olson, 2008). In the IFS context, a brand could be positioned by (1) product attributes (that is, *sharia* compliant in accordance with the religion of Islam) as well as by (2) competitors, that is, by competing or differentiating between IFS and CFS. However, without a clear understanding of consumers' segmentation and the target market in the IFSI context, the positioning of IFS is rather difficult. The present study hopes to identify the segmentation bases for IFS and thus clarify the positioning of such services.

Substantial literature concerning selection criteria (or patronage) in conventional banking among individual retail consumers is already in place. Gait and Worthington (2008) summarized the following motives, namely: (1) convenience factors such as location and service quality (see for instance, Wel and Nor, 2003; Lee and Marlowe, 2003; Kaynak and Whiteley, 1999); (2) reputation (Almossawi, 2001; Kennington et al., 1996); (3) profitability factors such as low service charges and high interest rates (Kaynak and Harcar, 2005; Ta and Har, 2000; Owusu-Frimpong, 1999); (4) fast and efficient service (Kaynak and Harcar, 2005); (5) security (Gerard and Cunningham, 2001); and (6) professional advice (Devlin, 2002).

Historically, the emergence of IFS in the financial market was propelled by the long-standing necessity of helping the members of Muslim society (*ummah*) who aspire and strive to refrain from indulging in interest (*riba*) while carrying out financial and business transactions (Muhamad et al., 2009). In recent developments, the industry has successfully established a globally diverse clientele and is attracting growing interest from global players, who are not confined to Muslims (Muhamad et al., 2009; Aslam, 2006). Thus, a broader segmentation of the individual retail consumers of IFS has been possible on the basis of religious affiliation such as the Muslim and non-Muslim segments.

Most past studies on IFS focus on Islamic banking institutions, as this is the most significant component of IFSI (International Financial Services London, 2008; 2009). In light of its infancy, as compared to conventional banking, a number of studies have

Table 14.1   Awareness studies in Islamic banking and finance

Prior studies	Findings
Omer (1992)	A high level of ignorance on Islamic finance principles among UK Muslims
Haron et al. (1994)	Most Muslims and non-Muslims in Malaysia have some awareness of Islamic banking basic concepts but are unaware of specific methods and the differences between conventional and Islamic banks
Gerrard and Cunningham (1997)	In Singapore, Muslims are more aware of the nature of Islamic banking than non-Muslims
Metawa and Almossawi (1998)	Most Islamic banking consumers in Bahrain are aware of the fundamental Islamic terms, but are less aware of the more complex financing schemes
Naser et al. (1999)	The majority of Islamic bank consumers in Jordan have a high level of awareness of at least some Islamic methods of finance
Hamid and Nordin (2001)	The majority of bank consumers in Kuala Lumpur know about the existence of Islamic banks in Malaysia but more than 60 per cent of respondents cannot differentiate between Islamic and conventional bank products
Ahmad and Haron (2002)	In a survey administered among 45 financial directors, financial managers and general managers of finance in Malaysia it was found that even though most of them are non-Muslims, most are aware of Islamic banks as an alternative to conventional banks. Most respondents have a low level of knowledge about Islamic banking products, especially the financing products and most of them agree that Islamic banks in Malaysia need to improve on the promotion of their products and services.
Bley and Kuehn (2004)	The knowledge of both graduate and undergraduate students in the UAE on both Islamic and conventional finance methods is relatively low
Karbhari et al. (2004)	A focused interview was conducted with six executives across four Islamic financial institutions in London. Most respondents think that the UK Muslims are generally unaware of Islamic banking products and services
Okumus (2005)	There is a high level of awareness concerning the basic concept of Islamic finance but the level of awareness of the more complicated concepts of Islamic finance is low in Turkey
Rammal and Zurbruegg (2007)	There is a lack of awareness concerning the basic rules and principles of Islamic financing among Muslims in Australia.

been conducted worldwide to examine the level of awareness of Islamic banking and finance concepts as well as specific products/services among Muslim and non-Muslim consumers. Mixed results have been observed from these studies. In countries where Islam is the main religion, such as Malaysia, Jordan, and Bahrain, the level of awareness concerning IFS among consumers (particularly the Muslim consumers) is quite good. In other parts of the world where Islam is not the main religion, such as the UK, Australia, and Singapore, it appears that the level of awareness of IFS is quite low even among the Muslim community/population currently residing in those countries. A summary of findings from various studies on the level of awareness and understanding concerning IFS among consumers is presented in Table 14.1.

In the past, other studies conducted on Islamic banking focused on bank patronage and selection criteria as well as the underlying motives among consumers in purchasing Islamic banking products. Various researchers have focused on individual preference for bank selection factors including both Muslim and non-Muslim consumers (for example, Zainuddin et al., 2004; Gerrard and Cunningham; 1997; Haron et al., 1994). Another category of studies discussed bank selection criteria for individual consumers without showing or giving major emphasis to any explicit classification of consumers along the lines of their religious status (see, for example, Dusuki and Abdullah, 2007; Almossawi, 2001; Metawa and Almossawi, 1998). Consumers' age, income, education, experience and other socio-demographic characteristics have been found to have a significant impact on their buying decision. Gait and Worthington (2008) highlighted two distinct results in their analysis of past studies on the underlying motives in consumers' preferences in selecting a particular Islamic bank. Some studies have found that religion is not the main motivation and that fast and efficient services, the bank's reputation and image, and confidentiality are the primary motives in the decision of consumers to use Islamic banking products and services (see for instance, Hegazy, 1995; Haron et al., 1994; Erol et al., 1990; Erol and El-Bdour, 1989). However in some studies it was found that the majority of consumers in Islamic banks responded that religion was the primary motivation in the use of Islamic banking products and services (Bley and Kuehn, 2004; Al-Sultan, 1999; Metawa and Almossawi, 1998; Metwally, 1996; Omer, 1992).

Although the results of these studies vary, none of them considered religiosity, that is, the commitment to religious ideals and practice, as a potential motive for using/purchasing IFS. While consumers' profiles include information concerning their religion, the intensity of their religious commitment has not been chosen for analyzing how consumers vary in their choice of a particular Islamic bank. Now, the vital question is whether the religiosity of an individual influences his/her decision-making behaviour.

The preceding discussion on religiosity and consumer behaviour established that religiosity influences various aspects of consumer behaviour and, therefore, provides support in the application of religiosity in explaining the underlying motives for IFS. Since the IFSI distinctiveness depends on its offering of financial products/services that are compliant with the basic tenets of *sharia,* the religiosity of consumers then assumes a more important role in segmenting consumers.

Muhamad et al. (2009) offered a fresh proposal on consumer segmentation for the Islamic banking industry based on the segmentation of people in the Qur'an and the segmentation of traders in the *kasb* (earnings) literature. Based on the state of the soul a threefold categorization of human personality can be found in the *Qur'an,* namely, *ammara* (coarse and crude, thoughtless and ill-mannered); *lawwama* (self-reproaching) and *mutma'inna* (the highest level of personality: thoughtful, kind, polite and tender-hearted). Traders in the *kasb* literature are classified into three distinct groups, known as the benevolent-ethical group (wealth is praiseworthy if and only if the wealth is used as a means for seeking salvation in the other world (*al-akhira*)); the rational-moral group (wealth is good in itself and praised for its own sake) and the repugnant-amoral group (trade is an excellent means for the acquisition of wealth). Following these classifications, they subsequently propose a threefold categorization of Islamic banking consumers as given below:

1. The group that is strongly guided by religious dictates is labelled as the religious conviction group;
2. The group that may not be particularly aware or careful of religious dictates but consciously tries to uphold moral values is identified as the ethically observant group; and,
3. The last group, which is indifferent to both religious and moral dictates and is intent on deciding things solely from the perspective of personal financial gain (or economic rationalism), is described as the economic rationality group.

In the above segmentation, consumers are assumed to make purchase decisions based on the ascribed values, namely, religious, ethical, and economic. Values constitute the deepest level of culture and are the most difficult to change (Hofstede, 1980). In Islam, *akhlaq* (morals and values) provide a framework that shapes the moral and ethical behaviour of Muslims in the conduct of all aspects of their life (Ismail, 1990; Saeed et al., 2001) and are expected to have a significant impact on the behaviour of Muslims. Globally, the Islamic resurgence has resulted in an increasing emphasis on *sharia* (Esposito, 1991) and, thus, the IFSI may uncover a profitable consumer segment that makes decisions based on religious values and belief. A similar development occurs in 'ethical consumerism', which is argued to be on the rise (Ismail and Panni, 2008; Auger et al., 2003). Various authors highlight the similarity in the evaluation criteria for ethical investment with the ideals of Islamic banking and finance (see for example, Saidi, 2009; Ghoul and Karam, 2007; Rice, 1999; Wilson, 1997), thus supporting segmentation of IFS based on ethical values.

In order to test the proposal from Muhamad et al. (2009) data were collected from executives holding key positions in the industry. The data were collected from those in managerial positions for the following reasons:

1. The current study's objective – to explore the possible segmentation bases for IFS – is preliminary in nature, as there has been limited research in the past to guide segmentation in the IFS specifically, despite the vast segmentation research done for CFS. The differences in the structuring and operationalization of products/services between CFS and IFS, that is, the element of *sharia* compliance, raised questions on the appropriateness of applying the segmentation bases normally adopted for CFS.
2. The segmentation issues for the IFSI constitute a relatively new area and research on this area is rather limited. Given the newness of these issues, the managerial perspective is considered appropriate (Peter and Olson, 2008). As highlighted earlier, in light of the infancy of the industry, as compared to conventional banking, a number of studies have been conducted worldwide to examine the level of awareness of Islamic banking and finance concepts as well as specific products/services among Muslim and non-Muslim consumers. The findings of these studies established that the level of awareness on IFS is quite low, meaning that collecting data from consumers is less appropriate at this point in time. Therefore, as an exploratory study, insights from the managerial context could help establish the initial base(s) for IFS.
3. The above notion is consistent with previous segmentation research. For example, Wind (1978) suggested that segmentation research could be undertaken based on an 'a priori segmentation approach' in which management decides on a basis for

segmentation such as customer type, loyalty or product purchase (p. 317). Wind (1978) explained that 'the problem at the definition stage usually involves three major considerations and that the first consideration is the managerial requirements, particularly when there is a new product concept involved and the need to determine how the concept differs by respondent groups' (Wind, 1978, p. 318), thus providing support for the selection of the management as respondents. Peter and Olson (2008) highlight the difficulty in establishing the bases for consumer segmentation. They suggest that the initial basis or dimension of segmentation could be developed based on previous purchase trends and managerial judgment. Peter and Olson (2008, p. 370) assert that 'There is no simple way to determine the best bases for segmenting markets. In most cases, however, at least some initial dimensions can be determined from previous purchase trends and management judgment.'

RESEARCH METHODOLOGY

The methodology adopted in this study comprises two stages. To answer the first objective, that is, to explore the different consumer segments and the underlying motives, as proposed by Muhamad et al. (2009), the first stage of data collection is consistent with the notion of Wind's (1978) 'a priori segmentation design'. In stage one, in-depth interviews were conducted with the key market players to determine their opinions concerning the two issues described in Table 14.4. Before conducting in-depth interviews, a secondary literature search was conducted to assist the researchers in formulating the interview guide. Several in-depth interviews were later conducted to gauge the initial dimensions from the managerial perspective to help the researchers further refine the interview guide.

Data Collection Procedure

The sample of respondents (the key market players) was based on three different groups: (1) industry regulators, (2) IFS experts such as *sharia* scholars, IFS consultants and lawyers, and (3) service providers such as bankers, fund managers and *takaful* operators. The sample of respondents includes local (Malaysian) as well as international respondents (from some parts of the Middle East and Europe). The details of the respondents and the nature of organizations that they are attached to are given in Tables 14.2 and 14.3, respectively. The international respondents were interviewed during the sixth Islamic Financial Services Board (IFSB) summit held in Singapore in February 2009.

Each interview lasted between 40 and 90 minutes. All interviews were digitally recorded. The recorded interviews were then transcribed verbatim. The verbal text was analyzed based on the emergent theme in a sentence and coded with a pre-defined coding scheme (Atman and Bursic, 1998). The coding scheme was developed from the proposed consumer segmentation for Islamic banking customers (Muhamad et al., 2009).

An interview guide was developed, as described in the preceding section, so that all interviews could be conducted in a manner to ensure consistent data collection. The two key issues deliberated in these interviews concerned consumers' awareness and how consumers are segmented, as well as their motivation for using/purchasing IFS. Specific questions that were asked during the interview sessions are given in Table 14.4.

Table 14.2 Profiles of interviewees – 1

Job Title	Number of interviewees	Gender		Origin	
		Male	Female	Local	International
Senior management	31	25	6	16	15
Board of directors	8	8	0	6	2
Sharia scholars	5	2	3	2	3
IFS consultants	2	1	1	1	1
Total	46	36	10	25	21

Table 14.3 Profiles of interviewees – 2

Nature of services	Number of institutions
Retail banks	3
Investment banks	2
Takaful operators	1
Wealth management firms	5
IFS consultants	2
Regulators	4
Law firms	3
Media/News agencies	2
Total	22

Table 14.4 Interview guide

Issues	List of questions
Acceptability of IFS	• What is the level of awareness and understanding of the products in general? • What are the measures to improve awareness and understanding among consumers?
Market segmentation and positioning of IFS	• What type of consumers would opt for IFS? • What are the underlying motives for consumers in opting for IFS? Do these motives differ between Muslims and non-Muslims? • Do you have a systematic approach on how you categorize your consumers? In other words, does any specific segmentation exist for your present consumers? • Do you treat consumers as one group? If they are not treated as a group, how do you differentiate them? • Do you think consumer values such as religious, ethical and economic values affect the consumer's purchase decision? • How do you think IFS should be positioned in the global market? • What message should be communicated to these different groups?

The second objective of this study is to identify whether or not the level of awareness concerning IFS has improved. Both qualitative and quantitative methods were adopted. In stage one, where in-depth interviews were conducted with the key market players, consumers' awareness was one of the issues examined. In stage two, a questionnaire survey was administered to determine the present level of awareness concerning IFS, as perceived by Malaysian consumers (Muslim and non-Muslim).

To collect the data, convenience sampling was used (Zikmund, 2000). The selected respondents were working adults in the Klang Valley area who were customers of either Islamic or conventional banks. The questionnaire was prepared in the English language and comprised two main sections. In Section 1, demographic questions, which included age, gender, religion, marital status, level of education, and personal income were posed. In Section 2, respondents were asked to indicate their awareness and understanding concerning the various Islamic banking and finance concepts presented using a 5-point Likert scale ranging from strongly disagree (1) to strongly agree (5). The respondents were informed of what is meant by the words 'know and understand' in all items listed under the 'understanding' section of the questionnaire. A total of 203 usable questionnaires were analysed and respondents were categorized into users and non-users.

FINDINGS AND DISCUSSION

This section presents the findings relating to consumers' awareness of IFS in stages one and two using both qualitative and quantitative methods.

Level of Awareness

IFSI is a relatively young industry and there is growing concern regarding the low level of awareness among consumers concerning the underlying concepts and products offered. It was found that the level of awareness concerning the industry as well as its products remain low, as evidenced in the following interview extracts:

> The level of understanding concerning the products is very low. (CEO Foreign Asset Management firm)

> The level of awareness is very low, if people do not understand, they will shy away from taking an active part in the industry. (Practicing lawyer)

As highlighted by the above respondent, consumers may not opt to use IFS if they do not understand the basic concepts underlying the structuring of the products offered, which may prevent the industry from progressing further. The industry should continue to intensify the educational efforts to improve awareness among consumers, thus increasing the demand for IFS. Therefore, educating the public about the basic concepts and principles of Islamic finance as well as the specific products has become the main priority as emphasized by the following interviewees.

> Considerable effort . . . to educate the public about the Islamic finance industry. (International Regulator 1)

... for *takaful* consumers, they will receive their money back at the end of the year if nothing happens, so, explain this to them, educate the market ... (International Regulator 2)

One respondent even opined that the public should be exposed to financial management knowledge from an early age so that they are familiar with the basic financial concepts to aid them in making better financial decisions; that is, whether to opt for the conventional financial services or IFS.

The whole world needs some level of education in financial management ... The education concerning financial management should start in primary school to expose the youngsters to financial concepts ... therefore, should start educating people to make financial decisions ... (International IFS Consultant)

In conclusion, more needs to be done to educate the market, not only concerning Islamic finance but, more importantly, education regarding basic financial management in general is necessary.

Following the findings obtained from the interviews with the various key market players, as discussed in the preceding section, stage two of the data collection using the quantitative method was conducted. A questionnaire survey was administered in February 2010 to evaluate whether the level of awareness and understanding among

Table 14.5   Profile of respondents

Background variables	Categories	Percentage
User or Non-User (N=203)	User	58.1
	Non-User	41.9
Age	20 and below	0.5
	21–30	33.5
	31–40	36.5
	41–50	23.2
	Above 50	6.4
Gender	Male	45.3
	Female	54.7
Religion	Islam	55.7
	Others	44.3
Marital status	Single	34.0
	Married	65.0
	Divorced	1.0
Education level	STPM and below	33.5
	Diploma	21.7
	Degree	41.9
	Master Degree	3.0
Personal income	RM 2000 and below	19.7
	RM 2001 – RM 4000	51.2
	RM 4001 – RM 6000	19.7
	RM 6001 – RM 8000	6.9
	Above RM 8000	2.5

Table 14.6   Consumer categories – a demographic comparison

Variables	User		Non-User	
	Freq.	%	Freq.	%
Age (χ^2 is not significant, p=0.563)				
20 and below (N=1)	0	.0 (.0)	1	1.2 (100.0)
21 – 30 (N=68)	43	36.4 (63.2)	25	29.4 (36.8)
31 – 40 (N=74)	40	33.9 (54.1)	34	40.0 (45.9)
41 – 50 (N=47)	29	24.6 (61.7)	18	21.2 (38.3)
Above 50 (N=13)	6	5.1 (46.2)	7	8.2 (53.8)
Gender (χ^2 is not significant, p=0.502)				
Male (N=92)	53	44.9 (57.6)	39	45.9 (42.4)
Female (N=111)	65	55.1 (58.6)	46	54.1 (41.4)
Religion (χ^2 is significant, p=0.000)				
Islam (N=113)	94	79.7 (83.2)	19	22.4 (16.8)
Others (N=90)	24	20.3 (26.7)	66	77.6 (73.3)
Marital Status (χ^2 is not significant, p=0.859)				
Single (N=69)	39	33.1 (56.5)	30	35.3 (43.5)
Married (N=132)	79	66.9 (59.8)	53	62.4 (40.2)
Divorced (N=2)	0	.0 (.0)	2	2.4 (100.0)
Education Level (χ^2 is not significant, p=0.173)				
STPM and below (N=68)	44	37.3 (64.7)	24	28.2 (35.3)
Diploma (N=44)	27	22.9 (61.4)	17	20.0 (38.6)
Degree (N=85)	42	35.6 (49.4)	43	50.6 (50.6)
Master Degree (N=6)	5	4.2 (83.3)	1	1.2 (16.7)
Personal Income (χ^2 is not significant, p=0.757)				
Below RM 2000 (N=40)	28	23.7 (70.0)	12	14.1 (30.0)
Between RM 2001–RM 4000 (N=104)	54	45.8 (51.9)	50	58.8 (48.1)
Between RM 4001– RM 6000 (N=40)	21	17.8 (52.5)	19	22.4 (47.5)
Between RM 6001– RM 8000 (N=14)	11	9.3 (78.6)	3	3.5 (21.4)
Above RM 8000 (N=5)	4	3.4 (80.0)	1	1.2 (20.0)

Note: Percentages in parentheses are percentages within the respective demographic variables.

bank consumers (Muslims and non-Muslims) in Malaysia has improved. As explained in the data collection section, a total of 203 usable questionnaires were analysed and respondents were categorized into users and non-users. The profiles of respondents are presented in Table 14.5. Respondents are more or less equally represented in terms of users and non-users, gender and religion. More than half of the respondents are married and the majority are between 21 and 50 years. The chi-square test was conducted to examine whether there is any significant relationship between the different categories of respondents with the various demographic variables. The results presented in Table 14.6 show that only religion (p=0.000) is significantly associated with the different categories of respondents, thereby supporting religion as one of the motives for consumers to opt for IFS. The results show that, in general, the level of, 'awareness' is good, as the mean

Table 14.7   Consumers' awareness

	Mean	S/Dev.
Awareness		
1. I am aware of the existence of the Islamic banking system in Malaysia.	4.07	0.906
2. I am aware of the existence of Islamic banking products and services.	3.87	0.992
3. I am aware of the concept of profit sharing in Islamic banking.	3.42	1.098
4. I am aware of the concept of justice and fairness in Islamic banking.	3.34	1.038
5. I am aware of the concept of the interest-free banking scheme (IBS).	3.26	1.113
6. My overall awareness of Islamic banking, in general, is very good.	3.20	0.955
7. Knowledge concerning Islamic banking is easy to access and acquire.	3.17	0.913
Understanding		
1. I know and understand the concept of *wadia*.	2.88	1.150
2. I know and understand the concept of *mudaraba*.	2.83	1.131
3. My overall understanding of Islamic banking products concepts is very good.	2.73	2.431
4. I know and understand the concept of *bai bi-thamin ajil*.	2.66	1.062
5. I know and understand the concept of *musharaka*.	2.60	1.012
6. I know and understand the concept of *ijara*.	2.45	.950
7. I know and understand the concept of *murabaha*.	2.44	.965
8. I know and understand the concept of *bai'salam*.	2.43	.966
9. I know and understand the concept of *wakala*.	2.43	.938
10. I know and understand the concept of *qard hasan*.	2.38	.950

values of all items ranges from 3.17 to 4.07. However, the level of 'understanding' is still very low as the mean values of all items are less than 3.00. The detailed results are presented in Table 14.7.

MARKET SEGMENTATION

Given the existing level of awareness and the current acceptability of IFS, as discussed above, it is possible to clarify the possible segments that may serve as a guideline to the marketing strategy and communication in the IFSI. This section reports stage one of the qualitative enquiries on the basis and dimension of market segmentation in the IFSI context. Specifically, the verbatim analysis of transcriptions from the in-depth interviews reveals the following market segmentations for the IFSI.

The first objective of this study is to explore consumer segments, as proposed by Muhamad et al. (2009) and explained above, where three types of consumers are considered: the religious conviction group, the ethically observant group and the economic rationality group. Interestingly, the qualitative findings appear to show the existence of another group, who make decisions based on both religious values and economic rationalism, labelled the religious conviction and economic rationality group.

Two important dimensions aided the current understanding of how we segment the IFSI consumers. First, it was based upon beliefs and values (for example religious, ethical or economic values). Second, it incorporated the benefit(s) sought from the product or product or services attributes (such as lower price and good service quality of the IFSI). The next section discusses the detailed findings.

Religious Conviction Group

For this group of consumers, other aspects of IFS such as product options, service quality and attractive pricing may not affect their decision or does not explain the underlying motive for opting for IFS. As argued by Delener (1994), the more religious individuals made decisions based on their religious values. The contention is supported by the findings of various studies on ethical decision making (see for example Muhamad, 2009; Barhem et al., 2009; Muhamad, 2006; Muhamad and Mumin, 2006). Thus, the motive of individuals in the first group to opt for IFS is bounded by their religious commitment. This is reflected by the following comments made by some of the interviewees.

> The way that we profile our consumers is slightly different . . . particularly for people from Kelantan, Kedah or from Terengganu; the religious factor is the main motive in their decision of whether or not to opt for IFS . . . (Malaysian Retail Banker 1)

> The principles would probably be the same. Muslim investors would opt for IFS because of the religious factor . . . (Foreign Investment Bank 1)

This finding is similar to the conclusion made in prior studies, which established that the majority of Muslim customers of Islamic banks have opted for the Islamic banking products and services primarily due to the requirement of their religion (see for instance Bley and Kuehn, 2004; Al-Sultan, 1999; Metawa and Almossawi, 1998; Metwally, 1996; Omer, 1992).

For this group of consumers, the main concern underlying their decision in choosing a financial service is whether it is *sharia* compliant even though they have to pay higher prices, as reflected by the following interviewees.

> . . . there are situations . . . where people only bank with Bank A, even if they have to pay slightly higher rates . . . because Bank A was perceived as very strict in its *sharia* compliance procedures. (Malaysian Retail Banker 1)

This is very much related to the term 'brand fundamentalism' coined by Ambler (2009). He explains that the brand fundamentalists are motivated by their beliefs and emotions, which to him are far more powerful than rationality. He asks questions such as: 'Why do soldiers fight? What made the great religions so influential? and Why were, and are, ordinary people prepared to lose their lives for their religions and/or countries?' He concludes that the answer to all these questions is because belief is more important than knowledge in persuading consumers, and, according to him, without inculcating belief, knowledge will not be retained. Another interviewee provided the same opinion when he said that:

> . . . Bank A has fanatic clients. They refuse to leave bank A. There is nothing you can do to steal them away unless you can stop Bank A . . . They will stay with Bank A simply because of their religious commitment, as they perceive Bank A as being more stringent in its *sharia* compliance procedures. (Malaysian Retail Banker 2)

In segmenting consumers, their religiosity is not only applicable to Muslim consumers, as most of the basic principles of business ethics, as laid down under *sharia* law, are also applicable in other monotheistic religions such as Judaism and Christianity (Muhamad, 2006). This is evidenced in the following interview extracts:

> The level of religious commitment is very relevant in marketing IFS even to the non-Muslims, especially with the Jews and Christians . . . as their religions also prohibit interest . . . when my bank first introduced the housing financing product in the US, I was called by a group of devout Jews to explain the product simply because it does not have an element of interest. (Foreign Retail Bank 1)

We may conclude that for the religious conviction group, IFS should be positioned as *sharia*-compliant products/services, and the term *sharia* compliant should be clearly described. Accordingly, all these features and benefits should be conveyed effectively to consumers to persuade them to purchase IFS and create consumer loyalty.

Religious Conviction and Economic Rationality Group

Interestingly, some of the bankers highlighted that in recent years a new group of consumers has emerged. These consumers combine both religious and economic criteria in their purchase decision. It is suggested that this consumer group has better access to education, has high income, and resides in urban areas. For this group, *sharia* credibility, the reputation of the bank and quality of the services, as well as pricing and returns, may be important motives to opt for IFS. This is reflected in the following interview extracts:

> The second criterion besides *sharia* compliant . . . is the economic values, this is what I think is applicable for the central region, Kuala Lumpur and other parts of the Klang Valley. Consumers are looking more at the economic values instead of the addition in other benefits. (Malaysian Retail Banker 1)

> That is why when we in Bank B started, we decided to concentrate on the *sharia* credibility, and the technological advancement and innovation, as in our opinion both are equally important for some consumers. (Malaysian Retail Banker 2)

> For moderate Muslims, besides *sharia* compliance, they also look for the returns. They will switch to Islamic banks if they can obtain the same benefits as those offered by conventional banks because they can observe the requirements of their religion at the same time. (Foreign Retail Banker 1)

The overlapping of religious and economic rationality is interesting and provides consumer insight to marketers when designing and tailoring their marketing messages. This is akin to the second kind of personality *lawwama,* as described in the Qur'an (75:2), where the angelic element encourages a person to follow in totality the will of God but such a state appears to contain at the same time the evil element that persuades an individual to be selfish and decide things based purely on self-interest. Apparently, this combination or overlapping of values highlights the notion put forward by Wind (1978), where he asserts that clustering consumer segments does not necessarily mean that consumers should be classified in only one cluster (or one segment). He argued that 'conceptually, there are a number of situations in which a consumer can belong to more than a single segment, especially if one considers multiple brand usage, different usage occasion, multiple benefits sought, etc' (Wind, 1978, p. 331). Furthermore, in the context of Islamic banking, Haron et al. (1994, p. 34) explain that, 'consumers view Islamic banks just like any other commercial bank, thus, the service quality and products and services offered must be compatible with those offered by the commercial banks'.

For this newly emerged group, both religious and economic criteria are relevant in their decision to opt for IFS, thus providing an indication to the industry that while *sharia* compliance is critical, other aspects such as quality of services and economic performance should also be emphasized in their marketing messages to consumers.

Ethical Values Group

Another interesting motive that emerged from our qualitative findings is that consumers or investors may consider opting for IFS because this meets the requirements of their ethical beliefs. This is described in the following responses:

> For non-Muslim investors, they are looking to be ethical and honest. I do not think they really care whether it is *sharia* compliant or not . . . most fundamental aspect is that we only invest in ethical investments, and that is not just a religious point of view. (Foreign Investment Bank 1)

> . . . Islamic products are not just for Muslims, we have non-Muslims buying Islamic products. Therefore, to me it is not purely a religious factor . . . one of the drivers is the principles of Islamic finance, which make it appealing to fund managers who want to invest in sustainable or green funds. (Foreign Investment Bank 2)

> In European/Western countries, where ethical/social responsibility funds are emerging and upcoming, IFS may be attractive to this group of investors since the basic principle of Islamic finance is in line with their investing criteria. (Foreign Retail Banker 1)

> I believe that promoting IFS should start through the ethical channel, I am very much involved in ethical investing . . . the Pope is very much in favour of Islamic finance, as published in the daily official newspaper, L'Osservatore Romano . . . to market Islamic finance in western countries, for example, the right thing to do is to portray Islamic finance as an integral part of an ethical approach to finance. (Fund Manager based in Italy and London)

Various authors point out that the evaluation criteria for ethical investing are parallel with the ideals of Islamic banking and finance (see for example, Saidi, 2009; Rice, 1999; Wilson, 1997). Some even went a step further and suggested that Islamic banking and finance principles may be the best solution for the current global crisis (see for example, Farooq, 2009; Maverecon, 2009; Quinn, 2008). A report in AMEinfor.com states that, 'As the global economy creates a new financial architecture, incorporating lessons from the global financial crisis, Islamic banking could emerge as a role model because of its focus on ethical investments'. This was one of the key messages that emerged from a panel discussion on Islamic finance in a forum organized by the Dubai Islamic Financial Centre (DIFC) in 2008. Therefore, IFS could be positioned as one of the alternative choices for ethical investors and the features of IFS that meet the criteria evaluation for ethical/green/sustainability/socially responsible investment should be clearly outlined and effectively communicated to this potential group of consumers.

Economic Rationality Group

For some individuals, Muslims or non-Muslims, the decision to use or not to use IFS is made purely on the economic rationale of minimizing loss and risk and maximizing profit. If investment in Islamic banks can provide good returns and their financing facilities are offered to consumers at a competitive rate, and they are able to provide quality services, then this group of consumers may decide to opt for IFS as highlighted by one of the interviewees: '. . . The bottom line is what is good for their pocket' (Malaysian Retail Banker 1).

Diversification strategy is another reason for consumers in this group in opting for IFS (Hussain, 2005), as the performance of IFS is promising and is argued to be more resilient to economic shocks. One of the interviewees mentioned this reason as the motive for consumers in their decision to opt for IFS.

> . . . the non-Muslim investors would probably opt for it because it is an alternative . . . they see IFS as an arbitrage for the conventional products to minimise risk . . . By investing in both markets, they manage to diversify the credit risk. (Foreign Investment Bank 1)

The ability to provide efficient and innovative products/services that can successfully compete with other available financial products in the market will be necessary to capture the demand from this group of consumers. As stressed by IDB et al. (2007), the IFSI can possibly capture the demand beyond the Muslim population through the provision of innovative and high-quality IFS.

The results of this study exhibit that, in general, practitioners do not have any organized segmentation bases as yet, which may be due to the newness of the issues in the IFSI. Several bases may exist such as geographic (based on regions), socio-cultural (based on religion) and behavioural (based on values). Therefore, we conclude that the most appropriate segmentation, as emerged in this study, could be based on the value dimensions as follows:

1. Religious conviction;
2. Religious conviction and economic rationality;
3. Ethically observant;
4. Economic rationality.

In conclusion, IFS consumers, regardless of whether they are Muslim or non-Muslim, could be segmented into various distinctive groups that may bear a resemblance to either one or more of the suggested groups proposed by Muhamad et al. (2009). A consumer may opt for IFS, not only to satisfy his or her religious requirements but also for certain aspects of economic reasoning (such as returns, price of products and the services quality offered by a bank). Similarly, a consumer may opt for IFS to satisfy these economic rationality requirements but also for the ethical aspects of the bank (such as involvement in social responsibility activities and reputation concerning its ethical stance). Thus, to design marketing communication strategies and messages effectively it is crucial for providers of IFS to understand the different groups of consumers that they are serving, which may suggest a focus on any or a combination of the motives described in the preceding section. The final section discusses the study's conclusion based on the current findings.

CONCLUSION

The results show that the current level of awareness concerning IFS and its products remains low. Theoretically, the current study identifies that the closest possible market segmentation basis for IFS groups are: (1) values (psychographic segmentation), which emphasizes values, opinions and attitudes, activities and lifestyles (Peter and Olson, 2008; Keller, 2000), and (2) benefit(s) sought from product or product attributes. Specifically, it can be concluded that it will be appropriate to position the brand for IFS as based upon values – religious conviction; religious conviction and economic rationality; ethical observance; and economic rationality – and product attributes such as pricing service quality, reputation, and image. These groups bear a resemblance to either one or more of the suggested groups as proposed by Muhamad et al. (2009).

Thus, although the study relies heavily on data collected from executives, the findings provide an interesting theoretical insight into consumer segmentation in the IFS in comparison to the CFS segmentation. Unlike the criticism that surrounds the traditional or CFS segmentation that was based upon a single indicator or 'a priori' approach, the current study suggests that the initial dimensions of IFS segmentation could be based upon a combination of approaches – values (a priori – religion/religiosity) and benefit(s) sought (post hoc).

As for the managerial implication, the study's initial findings could serve as an aid to guide product/brand positioning strategies for IFS when designing marketing communications. For example, if the target group is the religious conviction one, then the message that should be emphasized is the *sharia* credibility of the services provider in ensuring the *sharia* compliance of services and products. In the case of the religious conviction and economic rationality groups, both the *sharia* compliance and economic criteria (such as pricing, returns and services quality) are relevant in consumers' purchasing decisions, and thus should be conveyed to them. Ethical issues such as fairness and justice for all, socially responsible behaviour, accountability, and transparency are among the criteria that may be considered by the ethically observant group in deciding whether to purchase IFS, and therefore these issues should be highlighted to this group of consumers. For the economic rationality group, the only motive in purchasing IFS lies in the economic criteria (such as pricing, returns and services quality) and these attributes should be well communicated to this target group. Furthermore, the overlapping dimension of religious conviction and economic rationality is interesting, as conceptually these overlaps are common in segmentation (Wind, 1978) and to be expected, particularly in the IFSI (Haron et al., 1994). The findings give marketers some insights into the potential of what may be a profitable segment within the IFSI.

It may be concluded that IFS should appeal to both Muslim and non-Muslim groups of consumers who may fall under one or more of these following value groups: religious conviction; religious conviction and economic rationality; ethically observant; economic rationality.

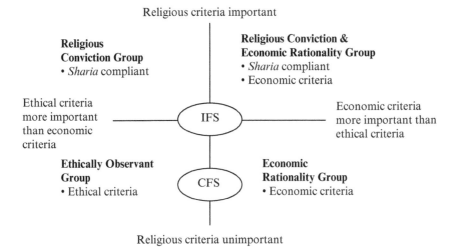

Figure 14.1   Positioning map showing segments for IFS and CFS

In summary, IFS brands should be positioned by the values (Muhamad et al., 2009) and product attributes (Peter and Olson, 2008). The IFSI, in addition to ensuring that all services/products are *sharia* compliant, which is unique to the industry, should also strive to provide quality and innovative services/products with attractive returns to reflect the 'universality' of the IFSI, as it represents the nature of both the Islamic and conventional financial services. The positioning is summarized in Figure 14.1, which is a positioning map showing the possible underlying motives of the different market segments in deciding whether or not to purchase IFS.

The current study examines the market segmentation and positioning of IFS from the perspective of the managerial or key market players. In future, studies may be conducted to examine the issues from the consumers' perspective so that there will be an alignment between what is perceived by the IFS providers and consumers. Thus, the findings of the current study should be interpreted with caution before they have been confirmed through consumer data. However, from the managerial perspective the current findings could be generalized to other regions, such as Europe and the Middle East, as the nature of the data collected covers several countries representing those regions. The present study is exploratory in nature and a larger sample (from both the management and consumer contexts) could be adopted in future studies for the purpose of generalization.

REFERENCES

Abdel-Khaleq, A.H. and C.F. Richardson (2007), 'New horizons for Islamic securities: emerging trends in sukuk offerings', *Chicago Journal of International Law*, **7** (2), 409–25.

Ahmad, N. and S. Haron (2002), 'Perceptions of Malaysian corporate consumers towards Islamic banking products and services', *Journal of Islamic Financial Services*, **3** (4), 1–16.

Ahmad, W.M.W., A.A. Rahman, N. Ali and A.C. Seman (2008), 'Religiosity and banking selection criteria among Malays in Lembah Klang', *Shariah Journal*, **16** (2), 279–304.

Al-Sultan, W. (1999), '*Financial characteristics of interest-free banks and conventional banks*', Phd Thesis, Department of Accounting and Finance, University of Wollongong, Wollongong.

Ali, M.Y. (1992), *The Holy Quran: Text, Translation and Commentary*, Brentwood: Amana Corporation.

Ali, E.R.A.E. and H.S.P. Odierno (2008), *Essential Guide to Takaful (Islamic Insurance)*, Kuala Lumpur: CERT Publication Sdn. Bhd.

Almossawi, M. (2001), 'Bank selection criteria employed by college students in Bahrain: an empirical analysis', *International Journal of Bank Marketing*, **19** (3), 115–25.

Ambler, T. (2009), 'Brand fundamentalism', Keynote address at the 5th International colloquium of Academy of Marketing's brand, corporate identity and reputation special interest group, 1–3 September, University of Cambridge, UK.

Anon (2004), 'Islamic finance is coming of age', *Euromoney*, **35** (422), 2–4.

Aslam, Z. (2006), 'London – key centre for Islamic finance', http://www.nzibo.com/IB2/Islamic_Finance_Jul06.pdf, accessed 25 August 2009.

Atman, C.J. and K.M. Bursic (1998), 'Verbal protocol analysis as a method to document engineering student design process', *Journal of Engineering Education*, **87** (2), 121–32.

Auger, P., P. Burke, T.M. Devinney and J.J. Louviere (2003), 'What will consumers pay for social product features?', *Journal of Business Ethics*, **42** (3), 281–304.

Barhem, B., H. Younies and R. Muhamad (2009), 'Religiosity and work stress coping behavior of Muslim employees', *Education, Business and Society: Contemporary Middle Eastern Issues*, **2** (2), 123–37.

Bley, J. and K. Kuehn (2004), 'Conventional versus Islamic finance: student knowledge and perception in the United Arab Emirates', *International Journal of Islamic Financial Services*, **5** (4), 17–30.

Choi, Y. (2010), 'Religion, religiosity, and South Korean consumer switching behaviors', *Journal of Consumer Behaviour*, **9** (3), 157–71.

Choi, Y., R. Kale and J. Shin (2010), 'Religiosity and consumers' use of product information source among Korean consumers: an exploratory research', *International Journal of Consumer Studies*, **34** (1), 61–8.

Delener, N. (1990), 'The effect of religious factors on perceived risk in durable goods purchase decision', *Journal of Consumer Marketing*, **7** (3), 27–38.

Delener, N. (1994), 'Religious contrasts in consumer decision behaviour patterns: their dimensions and marketing implications', *European Journal of Marketing*, **28** (5), 36–53.

Devlin, J. (2002), 'An analysis of choice criteria in the home loans market', *International Journal of Bank Marketing*, **20** (5), 212–26.

Dickson, P.R. and J.I. Ginter (1987), 'Market segmentation, product differentiation, and marketing strategy', *Journal of Marketing*, **51** (2), 1–10.

Dusuki, A.W. and N.I. Abdullah (2007), 'Why do Malaysian customers patronize Islamic banks?', *International Journal of Bank Marketing*, **25** (3), 142–60.

Edris, T.A. (1997), 'Services considered important to business customers and determinants of bank selection in Kuwait: a segmentation analysis', *International Journal of Bank Marketing*, **15** (4), 126–33.

El-Sheikh, S. (2008), 'The moral economy of classical Islam: a fiqhiconomic model', *The Muslim World*, **98** (1), 116–44.

Erol, C. and R. El-Bdour (1989), 'Attitudes, behaviour and patronage factors of bank customers towards Islamic banks', *International Journal of Bank Marketing*, **7** (6), 31–37.

Erol, C., E. Kaynak and R. El-Bdour (1990), 'Conventional and Islamic banks: patronage behaviour of Jordanian customers', *International Journal of Bank Marketing*, **8** (4), 25–35.

Esposito, J.L. (1991), *Islam: The Straight Path*, New York: Oxford University Press.

Essoo, N. and S. Dibb (2004), 'Religious contrasts in consumer decision behavior patterns: their dimensions and marketing implications', *European Journal of Marketing*, **28** (5), 36–53.

Farooq, M.O. (2009), 'Global financial crisis and the link between the monetary & real sector: moving beyond the asset-backed Islamic finance', Proceeding of the 20th Annual Islamic Banking Seminar: Financial and Economic Crisis and Development of Islamic Banking System of Iran, Iran Banking Institute, Morteza Allahdad (ed.), pp.123–34.

Gait, A. and A.C. Worthington (2008), 'An empirical survey of individual consumer, business firm and financial institution attitudes towards Islamic methods of finance', *International Journal of Social Economics*, **35** (11), 783–808.

Gentry, J.W., P. Tansuhaj, L.L. Manzer and J. John (1988), 'Do geographic subcultures vary culturally?', *Advances in Consumer Research*, **15**, 411–17.

Gerrard, P. and J.B. Cunningham (1997), 'Islamic banking: a study in Singapore', *International Journal of Bank Marketing*, **15** (6), 204–16.

Gerrard, P. and J.B. Cunningham (2001), 'Singapore's undergraduates: how they choose which bank to patronise', *International Journal of Bank Marketing*, **19** (3), 104–14.

Ghoul, W. and P. Karam (2007), 'MRI and SRI mutual funds: a comparison of Christian, Islamic morally responsible investing (MRI), and socially responsible investing (SRI) mutual funds', *Journal of Investing*, **16** (2), 96–102.

Hamid, A.H. and N.Z. Nordin (2001), 'A study on Islamic banking education and strategy for the new millennium – Malaysian experience', *International Journal of Islamic Financial Services*, **2** (4).

Haron, S. (1995), 'The framework and concept of Islamic interest-free banking', *Journal of Asian Business*, **11** (1), 26–39.

Haron, S., N. Ahmad, and S. Planisek (1994), 'Bank patronage factors of Muslim and non-Muslim customers', *International Journal of Bank Marketing*, **12** (1), 32–40.

Harrison, T.S. (1994), 'Mapping customer segments for personal financial services', *International Journal of Bank Marketing*, **12** (8), 17–25.

Hegazy, I. (1995), 'An empirical comparative study between Islamic and commercial banks' selection criteria in Egypt', *International Journal of Commerce and Management*, **5** (3), 46–61.

Hofstede, G. (1980), *Culture's Consequences: International Differences in Work-related Values*, Beverly Hills: Sage.

Hussain, I. (2005), 'Islamic financial services industry: the European challenges', Keynote Address at the Islamic Financial Services Forum by the Islamic Financial Services Board and the Central Bank of Luxembourg on 5 November.

Ibrahim, A.A. (2006), 'Convergence of corporate governance and Islamic financial services industry: towards Islamic financial services securities market', http://lsr.nellco.org/georgetown/gps/papers/3, accessed 15 August 2010.

IDB, IFSB and IRTI (2007), 'Islamic financial services industry development: ten-year framework and strategies', http://www.ifsb.org/docs/10_yr_framework.pdf, accessed 25 August 2009.

International Financial Services London (2008), *Islamic Finance Report*, International Financial Services London Research.

International Financial Services London (2009), *Islamic Finance Report*, International Financial Services London Research.

Iqbal, Z. (1997), 'Islamic financial systems', *Finance & Development*, **34** (2), 42–45.

Ismail, A.H. (1990), 'The teaching of Islamic economics: the practitioner's point of view', paper presented at the workshop on the Teaching of Islamic Economics, International Islamic University, Malaysia, 20–22 July, 1–43.

Ismail, H. and M.F.A.K. Panni (2008), 'Consumer perception on the consumerism issues and its influences on their purchasing behavior: a view from Malaysian food industry', *Journal of Legal, Ethical and Regulatory Issues*, **11** (1), 43–64.

John, J., P. Tansuhaj, L.L. Manzer and J.W. Gentry (1986), 'Fatalism and explanation of the cross-culture differences in the perception of uncertainty in the marketplace', *AMA Workshop on Culture and Subculture*, De Paul University, Chicago.

Johnson, B.R., S.J. Jang, D.B. Larson and S.D. Li (2001), 'Does adolescent religious commitment matter? A reexamination of the effect of religiosity on delinquency', *Research in Crime and Delinquency*, **38** (1), 22–43.

Karbhari, Y., Naser, K. and Z. Shahin (2004), 'Problems and challenges facing the Islamic banking system in the West: the case of the UK', *Thunderbird International Business Review*, **46** (5), 521–43.

Kaynak, E. and T. Harcar (2005), 'American consumers' attitudes towards commercial banks', *International Journal of Bank Marketing*, **23** (1), 73–89.

Kaynak, E. and A. Whiteley (1999), 'Retail bank marketing in Western Australia', *International Journal of Bank Marketing*, **17** (5), 221–32.

Keller, K.L. (2000), 'Building and managing corporate brand equity', in M. Schultz, M.J. Hatch and M.H. Larsen (eds), *The Expressive Organization: Linking Identity, Reputation, and the Corporate Brand*, New York: Oxford University Press, pp. 115–37.

Kennington, C., J. Hill and A. Rakowska (1996), 'Consumer selection criteria for banks in Poland', *International Journal of Bank Marketing*, **14** (4), 35–55.

Kotler, P., K.L. Keller, S.H. Ang, S.M. Leong and C.T. Tan (2009), *Marketing Management: An Asian Perspective*, 5th edition, Singapore: Prentice Hall.

LaBarbera, P.A. (1987), 'Consumer behaviour and born-again Christianity', in Jagdish N. Sheth and Elizabeth C. Hirschman (eds), *Research in Consumer Behavior*, London: Jai Press, pp. 192–222.

Lee, J. and J. Marlowe (2003), 'How consumers choose a financial institution: decision-making criteria and heuristics', *International Journal of Bank Marketing*, **21** (2), 53–71.

Loqman, M. (1999), 'A brief note on the Islamic financial system', *Managerial Finance*, **25** (5), 52–59.

Machauer, A. and S. Morgner (2001), 'Segmentation of bank customers by expected benefits and attitudes', *International Journal of Bank Marketing*, **19** (1), 6–17.

Marshall, G. and M. Johnston (2010), *Marketing Management,* London: McGraw Hill Higher Education.

Maverecon, W.B. (2009), 'Islamic finance principles to restore policy effectiveness', http://blogs.ft.com/maverecon/2009/07/islamic-finance-principles-to-restore-policy-effectiveness/, accessed 22 July 2009.

McDaniel, S.W. and J.J. Burnett (1990), 'Consumer religiosity and retail store evaluative criteria', *Journal of the Academy of Marketing Science*, **18** (2), 101–12.

McKinsey (2008), *The World Islamic Banking Competitiveness Report 2007–08*, Capturing The Trillion Dollar Opportunity, USA: McKinsey.

Meadows, M. and S. Dibb (1998), 'Implementing marketing segmentation strategies in UK personal financial services: problems and progress', *Service Industries Journal*, **18** (2), 45–63.

Meidan, A. (1984), *Bank Marketing Management*, New York: Macmillan.

Metawa, S.A. and M. Almossawi (1998), 'Banking behaviour of Islamic bank customers: perspectives and implications', *International Journal of Bank Marketing*, **16** (7), 299–313.

Metwally, M. (1996), 'Attitudes of Muslims towards Islamic banks in a dual-banking system', *American Journal of Islamic Finance*, **6** (1), 11–17.

Michell, P. and M. Al-Mossawi (1995) 'The mediating effect of religiosity on advertising effectiveness,' *Journal of Marketing Communication*, **1**, 151–62.

Michell, P. and M. Al-Mossawi (1999), 'Religious commitment related to message contentiousness', *International Journal of Advertising*, **18**, 427–43.

Mokhlis, S.C. (2006), 'The effect of religiosity on shopping orientation – an exploratory study in Malaysia', *Journal of American Academy of Business*, **6** (1), 64–74.

Muhamad, R. (2006), 'Islamic corporate reports (ICRs) and Muslim investors: the case of the Islamic banking industry in Malaysia', PhD thesis, University of Malaya, Malaysia.

Muhamad, R. (2009), 'Religiosity, ethical judgments and Malaysian Muslim students', *Journal of Business System, Governance and Ethics*, **4** (1), 53–72.

Muhamad, R. and A.G.A. Mumin (2006), 'Religiosity and moral judgement: an empirical investigation among Malay Muslims in Malaysia', *Jurnal Syariah*, **2** (14), 87–101.

Muhamad, R., A.S.M. Shihabudin and A.M.E. Sukor (2009), 'An analytical review of market segments for Islamic banking industry', Paper presented at the 2009 International Conference Business & Information, Kuala Lumpur.

Naser, K. and L. Moutinho (1997), 'Strategic marketing management: the case of Islamic banks', *International Journal of Bank Management*, **15** (6), 187–203.

Naser, K., A. Jamal, and K. Al-Khatib (1999), 'Islamic banking: a study of customer satisfaction and preferences in Jordan', *International Journal of Bank Marketing*, **17** (3), 135–50.

Okumus, H. (2005), 'Interest-free banking in Turkey: a study of customer satisfaction and bank selection criteria', *Journal of Economic Cooperation*, **26** (4), 51–86.

Omer, H. (1992), 'The implication of Islamic beliefs and practice on Islamic financial institutions in the UK', PhD dissertation, Loughborough University.

Owusu-Frimpong, N. (1999), 'Patronage behaviour of Ghanaian bank customers', *International Journal of Bank Marketing*, **17** (7), 335–341.

Peter, J.P. and J.C. Olson (2008), *Understanding Consumer Behaviour*, Boston, MA: Irwin.

Quinn, B. (2008), 'The land of Adam Smith now teems with a vibrant Islamic banking sector, with even non-Muslims being lured by the model's promise of transparency and stability', http://www.csmonitor.com/World/2008/1128/p06s02-wogn.html/(page)/2, accessed 25 August 2009.

Rammal, H. and R. Zurbruegg (2007), 'Awareness of Islamic banking products among Muslims: the case of Australia', *Journal of Financial Services Marketing*, **12** (1), 65–74.

Rehman, A. and M.S. Shabbir (2010), 'The relationship between religiosity and new product adoption', *Journal of Islamic Marketing*, **1** (1), 63–9.

Renzetti, C.M. and D.J. Curran (1998), *Living Sociology*, United States: Allyn & Bacon.

Rice, C. (1999), 'Islamic ethics and its implications for business', *Journal of Business Ethics*, **18** (4), 345–58.

Run, E.C.D., M.M. Butt, K.S. Fam, H.Y. Jong (2010) 'Attitudes towards offensive advertising: Malaysian Muslims' views', *Journal of Islamic Marketing*, **1** (1), 25–36.

Saeed, M., Z.U. Ahmed, and S. Mukhtar (2001), 'International marketing ethics from an Islamic perspective: a value-maximization approach', *Journal of Business Ethics*, **32** (2), 127–42.

Saidi, T.A. (2009), 'Relationship between ethical and Islamic banking systems and its business management implications', *South African Journal of Business Management*, **40** (1), 43–49.

Siguaw, J.A., P.M. Simpson and M. Joseph (1995), 'Religiosity effects on shopping behaviours: a comparative study of the US and New Zealand', *Proceedings, Institute for Operations and Management Sciences (INFORMS) International Conference*, Singapore.

Sood, J. and Y. Nasu (1995), 'Religiosity and nationality: an exploratory study of their effect on consumer behavior in Japan and the United States', *Journal of Business Research*, **34**, 1–9.

Swimberghe, K., D. Sharma and L. Flurry (2009), 'An exploratory investigation of the consumer religious commitment and its influence on store loyalty and consumer complaint intentions', *Journal of Consumer Marketing*, **26** (5), 340–47.

Ta, H. and K. Har (2000), 'A study of bank selection decisions in Singapore using the analytical hierarchy process', *International Journal of Bank Marketing*, **18** (4), 170–79.

US Census Bureau (2009) 'International Data Base', http://www.census.gov/cgi-bin/ipc/idbagg, accessed 17 April 2009.

Wel, C. and S. Nor (2003), 'The influences of personal and sociological factors on consumer bank selection decision in Malaysia', *Journal of American Academy of Business*, **3** (1/2), 399–404.

Wilkes, R.E., J.J. Burnett and R.D. Howell (1986), 'Meaning and measurement of religiosity in consumer research', *Journal of the Academy of Marketing Science*, **14** (Spring), 47–56.

Wilson, R. (1997), 'Islamic finance and ethical investment', *International Journal of Social Economics*, **24** (11), 1325–42.

Wind, Y. (1978), 'Issues and advances in segmentation research', *Journal of Marketing Research*, **15** (3), 317–37.

Worthington E.L. Jr., N.G. Wade, T.L. Plight, M.E. McCullough, J.T. Berry, J.S. Ripley, J.W. Berry, M.M. Schimitt and K.M. Bursley (2003), 'The religious commitment inventory – 10: development refinement and validation of a brief-scale for research and counselling, *Journal of Counselling Psychology*, **50** (1), 84–96.

Zaher, T. and M.K. Hassan (2001), 'A comparative literature survey of Islamic finance and banking', *Financial Markets, Institutions and Instruments*, **10** (4), 155–99.

Zainuddin, Y., N. Jahya and T. Ramayah (2004), 'Perception of Islamic banking: does it differ among users and non users', *Jurnal Manajemen dan Bisnis*, **6** (3), 221–32.

Zikmund, W.G. (2000), *Business Research Methods*, Orlando, FL: The Dryden Press.

Zineldin, M. (1996), 'Bank strategic positioning and some determinants of bank selection', *International Journal of Bank Marketing*, **14** (6), 12–22.

15 Customer-based brand equity of Islamic banks in Bahrain: an empirical investigation
Omneya Mokhtar Yacout and Mohamed Farid ElSahn

INTRODUCTION

Islamic banking and finance have become a major area of interest in the fields of economics, finance, and marketing. Modern Islamic finance has become a trillion-dollar industry (Clarke, 2009), with various banks offering Islamic financial services in Muslim and non-Muslim countries.

The introduction of Islamic financial products across the world has been in response to the growing need of a significant segment of the marketplace that refused to deal with interest-based instruments (Elfakhani et al., 2007). However Islamic banks have succeeded at the tactical level within the marketing process, while strategic issues, such as brand equity, have suffered (Naser and Moutinho, 1997). This explains why the level of knowledge of Islamic products seems weak across studies that have measured such knowledge. Research findings also show that attitudes toward Islamic financial services are at least partly influenced by religious factors and perhaps other individual characteristics of the consumer (Bley and Kuehn, 2004).

The increasing competitive environment from both Islamic and conventional banks and the changes in customers' perception necessitates assessing the brand equity of these banks. Brand equity reflects the customer response to marketing efforts (Keller, 1993). The merger mania of the 1990s has led brands to be assigned monetary values on the balance sheet, for the purposes of corporate valuation (Morgan, 2000). The escalating cost of brand building (Simon and Sullivan, 1993) requires calculating and tracing return on marketing expenditure, for which brand equity is an important measure (Reynolds and Phillips, 2005).

The purpose of this research is to examine customer-based brand equity of Islamic and conventional banks in Bahrain. This research contributes to the literature in various ways. First, it represents the first attempt to examine brand equity of Islamic banks. In the field of Islamic banks, many studies have been conducted that examine awareness of (Metawa and Al Mossawi, 1998; Hamid and Nordin, 2001; Okumus, 2005), preferences for (Erol and El-Bdour, 1989; Rosly and Abu Bakar, 2003; Bley and Kuehn, 2004; Al-Tamimi et al., 2009) or service quality of Islamic financial products (Ahmad et al., 2010; Othman and Owen, 2001), but none of them examined the brand equity of Islamic financial products. Most Islamic banks clearly describe the Islamic nature in their names, thus examining the brand equity of Islamic banks means examining the customer response to the Islamic identity of the bank reflected in its brand name. Second, services brand equity has received relatively little scrutiny in the academic literature and popular press (Brodie et al., 2002; Brady et al., 2005). Third, it examines the traditional sources of brand equity (brand awareness, brand associations, service quality) as well as brand trust. Brand trust is expected to be a strong predictor of overall brand equity in extended services such as banking. It also examines two outcomes of brand equity, customer loyalty and customer share-of-wallet. Fourth, this research purports to examine the differences between Islamic and non-Islamic banks with respect to top-of-mind awareness, aided recall, unaided recall, associations, perceived service quality, overall brand equity and loyalty. This chapter is organized as follows: we begin with the evolution of Islamic banking, the concept, sources and outcomes of brand equity and brand trust as a source of brand equity. We next discuss the research methodology. Finally, we will end with a discussion of results and implications.

EVOLUTION OF ISLAMIC BANKING

An Islamic banking and financial system exists to provide a variety of religiously acceptable financial services to the Muslim communities (Hassan and Lewis, 2007, p. 2). By definition, an Islamic bank abides by Islamic law, the *sharia* (Algaoud and Lewis, 2007). An Islamic bank is a non-interest-based financial institution that complies fully with Islamic laws, and has creative and progressive financial engineering to offer efficient and competitive banking, investment, trade finance, commercial and real estate financing services (Othman and Owen, 2001).

The main difference between Islamic and conventional banks lies in the fact that the former operates on an equity-participation system in which a predetermined rate of return is not guaranteed, whereas the latter's operations are based on both equity and debt systems that are mainly driven by interest (*riba*) (Abul Hassan and Abdul Latiff, 2008). In such arrangements, funds are channeled to entrepreneurs through sale, sharing and lease contracts (Kahf, 2007).The Islamic bank has to focus on the return on the physical investment, because its own profitability is directly linked to the real rate of return (Algaoud and Lewis, 2007). It is able to undertake direct investments and participate in the management of projects. Indeed this process can potentially help people to obtain finance even if they reside in developing countries and have limited funds but with good projects and ideas (Brown et al., 2007).

Islamic banks should carry out their operations and organize their plans and programs according to this type of general systems outlook of finance with socioeconomic development (Sudin, 1995; Choudhury and Hussain, 2005; Dusuki, 2008; Dusuki and Abdullah, 2007). The social-wellbeing function for Islamic banks is reflected in social security, protection of individual rights and resource mobilization in keeping with the Islamic faith (Choudhury, 2007). Furthermore Brown et al., (2007) posited that Islamic banks have an ethical investment charter. Unethical investments in gambling, alcohol or pornography are avoided in line with the Qur'an. Islamic banks will arrange the payment of *zakat*, or donations to charitable purposes, which is often listed on their financial statements. Islamic banks have a *sharia* board to ensure that practices comply with the Qur'an.

Products and services offered by Islamic financial institutions include: (1) *mudaraba,* the provision of capital to a partial-equity partnership in return for a share of profits, but where the losses on funds lent are borne by the lender; (2) *musharaka,* full-equity partnerships where the provider of funds and the entrepreneur directly and wholly share in the business; (3) *murabaha,* an instrument used for financing the purchase of goods and services where the financial institution purchases these on behalf of the customer; (4) *bai'muajjal*, deferred payments on products encompassed under *murabaha*; (5) *bai'salam*, advance or prepaid sale contracts of goods and services; (6) *istisnaa*, or manufacturing contracts to cover work in progress and paid by the financial institution on behalf of the customer; (7) *ijara*, lease financing in the form of operating leases only; (8) *takaful*, or Islamic insurance in the form of cooperative self-help schemes, and (9) *qard hasan*, benevolent loans offered interest-free (Gait and Worthington, 2009). In these lending arrangements, profits are shared between the investors and the bank on a predetermined basis (Mirakhor and Zaidi, 2007).

Long before the modern Islamic banking system was established, Muslims had an interest-free financial system. Such a system was replaced with an interest-bearing financial system due to many factors, including the increasing complexity and sophistication of Islamic societies and the stagnation of Islamic thought (Elfakhani et al., 2007). Billah (2007) noted that the fundamental basis of modern Islamic banking had been discussed in the mid-1940s. Later, the model of Islamic banking appeared in the mid-1950s, but comprehensive and detailed concepts for interest-free banking appeared only in the late 1960s. The first experiment in Islamic banking was set up under cover in Mit Ghamr, Egypt, in 1963. In the seventies, changes took place in the political climate of many Muslim countries so that there was no longer any strong need to establish Islamic financial institutions under cover (Ariff, 1988). The Islamic Development Bank (IDB) was established in 1974, followed by the Dubai Islamic Bank in 1975, the Faisal Islamic Bank of Sudan in 1977, the Faisal Islamic Egyptian Bank and the Islamic Bank of Jordan in 1978, the Islamic Bank of Bahrain in 1979, the International Islamic Bank of Investment and Development, Luxembourg, in 1980 and Bank Islam Malaysia Bhd (BIMB) in 1983. In Europe, Islamic Banking System International Holding was established in Luxembourg in 1978, followed by Dar al-Mal al-Islami in Switzerland (1981) and Islamic Bank International in Denmark (1983) (Sudin 1995). Even the US Treasury Department has noted the increasing popularity of Islamic mortgages and investment indexes in the US and Europe. It appointed its first Islamic banking scholar-in-residence in June 2004 (Pope, 2005). The Islamic financial sector, though small in global terms, appears to have held up well in the recent financial crisis, with the Asian Development Bank putting annual growth at more than 15 per cent over the next five to ten years (Clarke, 2009).

BRAND EQUITY

Most of the brand equity research in the past 20 years aimed at conceptualizing and operationalizing brand equity. Yet agreement on the definition and operationalization of customer-based brand equity remains somewhat elusive (Punj and Hillyer, 2004).

Two important definitions of brand equity are those of Keller (1993) and Aaker (1996). Keller (1993) defined the term 'customer-based brand equity' as the differential effect of brand knowledge on customer response to the marketing of the brand.

Most of the definitions of brand equity reflect the fact that there is some value added that is uniquely attributable to the brand (Keller, 1993; MacKay et al., 1997; Netemeyer et al., 2004; Bick 2009; Kartono and Rao, 2009a), that this value is the result of marketing efforts (Cobb-Walgren et al., 1995; Yoo et al., 2000), that it leads to some responses on the part of the customer which facilitate future marketing efforts (Keller 1993) and that it positively affects financial performance (Lassar et al., 1995).

The specific effects may be either consumer-level constructs, such as attitudes, awareness, image and knowledge, or firm-level outcomes, such as price, market share, revenue and cash flow (Ailawadi et al., 2003). Thus, there are three different perspectives of brand equity, depending on its effect. The first perspective is 'the customer mind-set' (Keller and Lehmann, 2001). This perspective focuses on assessing the consumer-based sources of brand equity. The customer mind-set includes everything that exists in the minds of customers with respect to the brand – thoughts, feelings, experiences, images, perceptions, beliefs, attitudes and so on (Ambler et al., 2002). It describes how consumers process brand information and develop brand perceptions, and how it motivates their subsequent behavior towards the brand (Kartono and Rao, 2009b).

The strengths in consumer-based approaches lie in their usefulness in aiding specific marketing decisions targeted at different consumer segments, or even individual consumers (Kartono and Rao, 2009b). These measures help managers evaluate their marketing strategies and programs (Ambler et al. 2002; Leone et al., 2006; Sinha et al., 2008; Kartono and Rao, 2009b). Many consumer-based measures are developed based on self-reported data, which may be biased and unreliable, and they are usually not represented in terms of dollar-metric units of the brand's value to the firm (Kartono and Rao, 2009b).

The second perspective is the 'product market brand equity', which measures brand equity by measuring the brand's performance in the marketplace (Keller and Lehmann, 2001). The most commonly used measure is price premium, that is, the ability of a brand to charge a higher price than an unbranded equivalent charges (Aaker, 1996; Agarwal and Rao, 1996; Ailawadi et al., 2003; Netemeyer et al., 2004; Rauyruen et al., 2009), as well as market share (Chaudhuri and Holbrook, 2001).

Finally, the 'financial market perspective' focuses on estimating a monetary value for the brand as a financial asset (Kartono and Rao, 2009b). Such financial benefits could be measured in terms of incremental profit per year obtained by the brand in comparison to a brand with the same product and price but with minimal brand building efforts (Simon and Sullivan, 1993; Srinivasan ct al., 2001).

Neither the product market nor the financial market approach considers the fact that equity can change when consumer perceptions of the brand change (Kartono and Rao, 2009b). These measures provide little or no guidance to managers in implementing and evaluating strategies that help build brand equity (Leone et al. 2006; Sinha et al., 2008; Kartono and Rao, 2009b). However, these measures do not suffer from the self-reporting data of consumer-based brand equity.

Many researchers noted that these different measures are not at odds with each other. For a mature brand, any single measure is unlikely to capture the full range of its equity (Krishnan 1996). Hence, a multitude of measures that reflect several dimensions of equity would be appropriate. Many studies have reported empirical support for the positive effect of consumer-based brand equity on financial measures (Kim et al., 2003; Madden et al., 2006) or on reducing unsystematic financial risk (Rego et al., 2009). Thus, many researchers propose the use of both measures in brand equity research (such as MacKay et al., 1997).

The concept of customer-based brand equity (CBBE) was created by scholars advocating the use of consumer-based measures (Keller, 1993). Yet they have disagreed on the dimensions of CBBE. Keller (1993) defined brand equity as brand knowledge. Brand knowledge is defined in terms of two components, brand awareness and brand image. Brand awareness relates to brand recall and recognition performance by consumers. Brand image refers to the set of associations linked to the brand that consumers hold in memory. Keller (1993) also noted that the different types of brand associations making up the brand image include product-related or non-product-related attributes; functional, experiential, or symbolic benefits; and overall brand attitudes. Aaker (1996) argued that the dimensions of customer-based brand equity include brand awareness, perceived quality, brand associations and loyalty. Such dimensions have been adopted by a number of researchers (Pappu et al., 2005; Pappu et al., 2006; Washburn and Plank, 2002; Buil et al., 2008). Lassar et al. (1995) argued for a five-factor conceptualization comprising performance, social image, value, trustworthiness and attachment. Keller (2003) posited a six-factor model of CBBE that includes brand salience, brand performance, brand imagery, brand judgments, feelings toward the brand, and resonance. A richer conceptualization of brand equity was offered by Netemeyer et al. (2004), who suggested that the core facets of brand equity include perceived quality, perceived value and uniqueness. These three facets affected willingness to pay a price premium. Atilgan et al. (2009) incorporated trust as a possible dimension of brand equity. They reported consistent results in three countries. They argued that trust in global brands may surpass brand awareness and that brand awareness and associations may suffer from lack of discriminant validity. Table 15.1 summarizes the studies that examined the different dimensions of CBBE.

Table 15.1 shows that CBBE conceptualizations could be classified into perceptual and behaviorally based conceptualizations (Cobb-Walgren et al., 1995; Lassar et al., 1995). Punj and Hillyer (2004) posited that brand equity is regarded as being largely attitudinal in nature, composed of beliefs, affect and other subjective experiences related to the brand (brand attitude, brand image, and so on). Conversely Na et al., (1999) suggested that brand equity is more than just a network of brand-related associations. Thus both measures are needed to capture brand equity.

The above discussion reveals that most of the research in the field of brand equity has focused on issues of conceptualizing it. Maintaining or improving this equity over time involves targeting its source – which exists first and foremost in the minds of consumers (Kartono and Rao, 2009a). Understanding the sources of brand equity helps managers understand and focus on what drives their brand equity. On the other hand the outcomes of brand equity help managers understand exactly how and where brands add value (Keller, 2003). The extant literature does not provide a satisfactory measurement method for understanding the sources of brand equity, however (Park and Srinivasan, 1994).

OVERALL BRAND EQUITY: ITS SOURCES AND OUTCOMES

Most of the studies examining brand equity do not distinguish between brand equity and its sources or outcomes, making it difficult to understand how it can be improved. Yoo et al. (2000) noted that because brand equity is the value of a brand name, a con-

Table 15.1   Studies that examined the dimensions of CBBE

Studies	CBBE dimensions
Aaker (1996); Washburn and Plank (2002); Pappu et al. (2005); Pappu et al. (2006); Buil et al. (2008)	Brand awareness, perceived quality, loyalty and brand associations
Kim et al. (2003); Kayaman and Arsali (2007)	Brand awareness, brand loyalty, perceived quality and brand image
Keller (1993)	Brand awareness and brand image
Ambler et al. (2002) and Keller and Lehmann (2006)	Awareness, associations, attitudes, attachment and activity
Agarwal and Rao (1996)	Perceptions, preferences and intentions
Cobb-Walgren et al. (1995)	Awareness, brand associations and brand quality
Atilgan et al. (2009)	Brand associations, perceived quality, loyalty and trust
Sinha et al. (2008)	Brand associations, brand awareness, brand loyalty, perceived quality and organizational associations
Wang et al. (2009)	Service brand associations and service brand loyalty
Broyles and Schumann (2004)	Functional (perceived quality and perceived performance) and experiential dimensions (resonance and imagery)
Myers (2003)	Attribute perceptions and brand associations unrelated to product attributes
Dillon et al. (2001)	Brand-specific associations and general brand associations
Park and Srinivasan (1994)	Attributes and non-attribute components (such as brand associations)
Srinivasan et al. (2005)	Brand awareness, incremental preference due to enhanced attribute perceptions and incremental no-attribute preference
Morgan (2000)	Category-specific component and emotional and intangible issues
Netemeyer et al. (2004)	Core facets: Perceived quality, perceived value, uniqueness and willingness to pay a price premium Related associations: Brand awareness, brand familiarity, brand popularity, organizational associations and brand-image consistency

struct that can be high or low, setting a separate brand equity construct will help us understand how the dimensions contribute to brand equity. They used an overall brand equity construct (OBE), and its sources were perceived quality, brand loyalty, and brand associations with brand awareness. Yoo and Donthu (2001) developed and validated a multidimensional consumer-based brand equity scale (MBE) drawn from Aaker's and Keller's conceptualizations of brand equity. The brand equity scale was found to be reliable, valid, parsimonious and generalizable across Korean and American consumers and across product categories. Washburn and Plank (2002) and Tong and Hawley (2009) also advocated the use of overall equity measures.

Trust was also conceptualized as a possible source of brand equity (for example, Harris and Goode, 2004; Duffy, 2005; Luk and Yip, 2008; Rauyruen et al., 2009). Chiou

(2002) noted that customers have to evaluate several explicit and implicit cues of the service provider to gradually build up trust. Therefore if customers perceive service quality favorably, they will have more confidence in the provider, which in turn will increase their trust in the service provider. Blackston (1992) posited that the total equity of a brand consists of fundamental equities (the classical marketing variables of product, price and packaging, distribution and measured brand image) and the added-value equities, including trust in and satisfaction with the brand.

Trust creates value by (1) providing relational benefits derived from interacting with a service provider that is operationally competent, benevolent toward the consumer, and committed to solving exchange problems, and (2) reducing exchange uncertainty and helping the consumer form consistent and reliable expectations of the service provider in ongoing relationships (Sirdeshmukh et al., 2002). Elliott and Yannopoulou (2007) found that at higher levels of risk the brand needs to develop a relationship of confidence with the brand. Chaudhuri and Holbrook (2001) also noted that the relationship between brand trust, brand affect, and brand commitment depends on aspects of brand-choice risk. Delgado-Ballester and Munuera-Alemán (2001) noted that in contexts of high involvement it may be more appropriate to study brand trust, because in these situations brand trust becomes more central in customers' attitude and belief structures.

Brand trust definitions focus on reliability (Ganesan, 1994; Kumar et al., 1995; Doney and Cannon, 1997; Chaudhuri and Holbrook, 2001; Reast, 2005), integrity (Morgan and Hunt, 1994) and benevolence (Ganesan, 1994; Kumar et al., 1995; Doney and Cannon, 1997).

Trust is primarily formed based on service performance (Chiou et al., 2002; Caceres and Paparoidamis, 2007; Elliott and Yannopoulou, 2007; Briggs and Grisaffe, 2010). The effect of trust on brand loyalty has been demonstrated by a number of studies (Doney and Cannon, 1997; Chaudhuri and Holbrook, 2001; Harris and Goode, 2004; Lau and Lee, 2004; Caceres and Paparoidamis, 2007; Rauyruen and Miller, 2007, for attitudinal loyalty; Sichtmann, 2007; Briggs and Grisaffe, 2010).

The effect of satisfaction on trust is also supported (Ganesan, 1994; Delgado-Ballester and Munuera-Alemán, 2001; Hess and Story, 2005; Caceres and Paparoidamis, 2007; Chu, 2009). Nijssen et al., (2003) and Garbarino and Johnson (1999) noted that trust plays a more important role in forming loyalty for relationally oriented customers (those who consistently patronize the service). Nijssen et al. (2003) noted that in an industry context characterized by customer-perceived sense of control and positive experiences, customer loyalty is based on trust. Banking occupies a role that needs considerable public trust and is heavily regulated. Trust showed the lowest variation between banks. Therefore, the effect of trust on loyalty in this market may be low. Finally, Atilgan et al. (2009) provided empirical support that brand trust is a dimension of brand equity and that its effect may surpass that of brand awareness in the context of global brands.

The outcomes of brand equity have also been examined. Brands with superior equity provide a host of possible benefits to a firm, such as greater customer loyalty and less vulnerability to competitive marketing actions or marketing crises; larger margins; more favorable customer response to price increases and decreases; greater trade or intermediary cooperation and support; increased marketing communication effectiveness; and licensing and brand extension opportunities (Keller, 2001). Generally there are six key outcomes of brand equity: (1) price premiums, (2) price elasticities, (3) market share, (4) brand expansion, (5) cost structure and (6) brand profitability (Ambler et al., 2002). Cobb-Walgren et al. (1995) conceptualized brand equity as an overall measure with various sources. Consumer preferences and purchase intentions were the two outcomes identified in their study.

Adding brand equity outcomes to brand equity models is consistent with the hierarchy-of-effects model because it incorporates overall brand equity as a mediating variable between perceptual variables, such as brand awareness, brand knowledge and brand associations, and perceived quality and behavioral variables, such as accepting higher prices, having lower price elasticity, acceptance of new brands and purchase.

BRAND EQUITY OF ISLAMIC BANKING PRODUCTS

Most of the studies that have examined the marketing of Islamic banks have examined brand-equity-related variables such as patronage, awareness and familiarity, satisfaction and loyalty. The findings of these studies vary from one country to another.

Some of these studies reported that religious belief was the main reason for selecting an Islamic bank (Metawa and Al Mossawi, 1998, in Bahrain; Naser et al., 1999, in Jordan; Othman and Owen, 2001, in Kuwait; Bley and Kuehn, 2004, in UAE; Okumus, 2005, in Turkey; Ackerman and Jacobs, 2008, in South Africa; Al-Ajmi et al., 2009, in Bahrain; Gait and Worthington, 2009, in Libya). In Malaysia, Dusuki (2008) reported that stake-holders of Islamic banks view the industry much more favorably by the social and ethical goals that it serves, rather than the mechanics of its operation. Bley and Kuehn (2004) explained that consumers are making their decisions not on knowledge of the quality and value of the products and services offered, but simply on religious principle.

Conversely, a number of studies found that the religious motives were not promi-nent in the case of Islamic banking (Erol and El-Bdour, 1989 in Jordan; Edris, 1997 in Kuwait; Gerrard and Cunningham, 1997; Rosly and Abu Bakar, 2003 in Malaysia; Al-Tamimi et al., 2009 in UAE).

Studies examining awareness of Islamic banking included two types of awareness. The first type is awareness of the principles of Islamic banking. Some studies reported a high degree of awareness (Erol and El-Bdour, 1989 in Jordan; Bley and Kuehn, 2004 in UAE). Ahmad and Haron (2002) reported lack of knowledge regarding the nature of profit-sharing principles in Islamic banking systems among persons responsible for the financial affairs of the companies listed in the Kuala Lumpur Stock Exchange. Most of them were non-Muslims. Rammal and Zurbruegg (2007) also reported lack of awareness of Islamic banking principles among Muslims in Australia. Gerrard and Cunningham (1997) reported that non-Muslims were completely unaware of Islamic methods of finance; Muslims often fared little better.

The second type of awareness is awareness of Islamic products. Metawa and Al Mossawi (1998) reported a high degree of awareness of Islamic banking products among Bahraini customers. Okumus (2005) reported that Turkish customers were aware of basic Islamic products and services, but not more advanced Islamic financing techniques. Hamid and Nordin (2001) examined both types of awareness and found a high degree of awareness of Islamic banking among Malaysian commercial bank customers. They reported poor self-reported knowledge of specific Islamic products, including poor understanding of the difference between Islamic and conventional banking.

The familiarity, quality and satisfaction with Islamic banking products were examined by some studies. Al-Ajmi et al. (2009) reported that clients of Islamic banks in Bahrain were more familiar with the products that conform to *sharia*. Ahmad et al. (2010) reported that the magnitude of the relationship between service quality and customer satisfaction is greater in Islamic banks as compared to conventional banks. Okumus (2005) reported that more than 90 per cent of Turkish customers in the sample were satisfied with the services and products offered by Islamic banks. Conversely, Metawa and Al Mossawi (1998) reported that in Bahrain, satisfaction with Islamic financial products varied from one product to another. Al-Tamimi et al. (2009) reported that UAE customers preferred banking with Islamic banks but they were not satisfied with the services. Othman and Owen (2001) developed the CARTER measure, which added full Compliance with Islamic law and principles, Assurance, Reliability, Tangibles, Empathy and Responsiveness to service quality dimensions. CARTER included such items as: operated according to Islamic law and principles, no interest either paid or taken on savings and loans, provision of Islamic products and services, provision of interest-free loans and provision of profit-sharing investment products. CARTER was found to be highly valid and strongly linked to customer satisfaction.

RESEARCH FRAMEWORK

The research framework used in this study includes three sets of variables. Overall brand equity is the focal variable whose sources and outcomes are examined. The three sources of brand equity include awareness/associations, perceived service quality (Aaker, 1996; Washburn and Plank, 2002; Pappu et al., 2005; Pappu et al., 2006; Buil et al., 2008; Tong and Hawley, 2009), and brand trust (Atilgan et al., 2009; Rauyruen et al., 2009).

The two outcomes of brand equity include current purchases, or share-of-wallet (Keiningham et al., 2007) and future purchases (Taylor et al., 2007; Tong and Hawley, 2009).

We propose four sets of relationships. First, we propose that there is a relationship between awareness/associations and perceived service quality. Second, we expect that perceived service quality mediates the relationship between awareness/associations and overall brand equity. Third, we propose that brand trust is associated with overall brand equity. Fourth, we expect that overall brand equity is associated with future purchase intentions and share-of-wallet.

With respect to the sources of brand equity, this research framework is based on the two studies conducted by Yoo and Donthu (2001) and Cobb-Walgren et al. (1995). These two studies examined overall brand equity as a separate construct that is preceded by some sources. According to Yoo and Donthu (2001), the sources of brand equity included brand awareness, associations, perceived service quality and loyalty. These findings were supported by Washburn and Plank (2002). Similarly Cobb-Walgren et al. (1995) argued that the antecedents of brand equity include awareness, associations, and perceived quality. Thus the first two research hypotheses are:

H1:   Brand awareness/associations are associated with perceived brand quality.
H2:   Perceived brand quality mediates the relationship between brand awareness/ associations and overall brand equity.

With respect to brand trust, Atilgan et al. (2009) provided empirical support that its effect may surpass that of brand awareness in the context of global brands. Based on this, the third hypothesis was formulated as follows:

H3:   Brand trust is associated with overall brand equity.

It can be argued that since brand equity represents value that results from marketing efforts (Keller 1993), then perceptual and behavioral measures should be included in any model to measure brand equity. Leone et al. (2006) argued that perceptual measures constitute an 'indirect' approach which assesses potential sources of customer-based brand equity by identifying and tracking customers' brand knowledge structures. A 'direct' approach, on the other hand, would measure behavioral measures which reflect consumer response to marketing actions.

Some researchers argue that these perceptual and behavioral elements follow the hierarchy-of-effects model (Keller, 2001, 2003; Washburn and Plank, 2002; Hoeffler and Keller, 2003; Keller and Lehmann, 2006; Tong and Hawley, 2009). Originally introduced by Lavidge and Steiner (1961), the hierarchy-of-effects model argues that customers pass through a set of steps from awareness, to knowledge, to liking, to preference, to conviction and purchase. Hoeffler and Keller (2003) also called for a hierarchy starting from attention and learning stage (building brand knowledge), then interpretation and evaluation of marketing information or brand alternatives (the use of brand knowledge) and the actual choice process (the application of brand knowledge). Biedenbach and Marell (2010) provided empirical support for the use of the hierarchy-of-effects model in understanding the relationship between brand awareness, brand associations, perceived quality and loyalty in a B2B setting.

Empirically, brand preferences were found to be affected by brand awareness, brand associations, and brand quality (Cobb-Walgren et al., 1995), and brand equity (measured in terms of tangible and intangible attributes) (Myers, 2003). Esche et al., (2006) also found that brand awareness affects brand image (that is, brand associations) and that both aspects of brand knowledge are direct determinants of current consumer purchase behavior. Netemeyer et al. (2004) provided empirical support for the effect of perceptions of quality, value and uniqueness on willingness to pay a price premium. Taylor et al. (2007) noted that perceived product quality, perceived value, hedonic, utilitarian and unique brand attitudes affected overall brand equity, which in turn affects customer satisfaction and customer loyalty in the context of financial services. Tong and Hawley (2009) concluded that perceived quality and brand awareness might affect brand equity by influencing brand association and brand loyalty first. Based on this, the fourth and fifth hypotheses are formulated as follows:

H4:   Overall brand equity is associated with current purchases measured in terms of the share of wallet.
H5:   Overall brand equity is associated with future purchase intentions.

Many researchers reported significant differences among customers of Islamic and conventional banks with respect to familiarity (Al Ajmi et al., 2009), preferences and satisfaction (Al-Tamimi et al., 2009). Given that brand awareness exists among customers and non-customers, the sixth hypothesis examines the differences between customers of Islamic and conventional banks with respect to brand awareness of Islamic banks.

H6:   Customers of Islamic banks and customers of conventional banks differ with respect to top-of-mind awareness, aided recall and unaided recall of Islamic banking corporate brands.

Finally, the seventh hypothesis examines the differences between customers of Islamic and conventional banks with respect to awareness/associations, perceived quality, brand trust, overall brand equity, future purchase intentions and share-of-wallet.

H7:   Customers of Islamic banks and customers of non-Islamic banks differ with respect to awareness/association, perceived quality, brand trust, overall brand equity, future purchase intentions and share-of-wallet.

LEVEL OF ANALYSIS

The level of analysis used in this research is the corporate and not the individual brand. Keller (1998) defined corporate brand equity as the differential response by consumers, customers, employees, other firms or any relevant constituency to the words, actions, communications, products or services provided by an identified corporate brand identity (p. 115). He noted that while an individual brand is identified with a certain product category or limited set of products, the corporate brand name evokes associations of common products and their shared attributes or benefits, people and relationships, programs and values and corporate credibility.

Corporate brands were selected because of the nature of Islamic banking services where customers are more likely to form attitudes about the bank, the benefits it provides as an Islamic bank, and its credibility. The individual service brands may be less prominent in this case. Klaus and Maklan (2007) noted that, unlike tangible product brands, service brands should be based on an overall company image driven by the customer experience. This view focuses on the parent company as the major source of brand equity. Gylling and Lindberg-Repo (2006) also noted that corporate branding may be more prominent where the corporate values stretch across the diverse product group, as typically seen with financial service brands.

MEASUREMENT OF RESEARCH VARIABLES

Sources of brand equity constituted the independent variables. These variables included awareness/associations, perceived service quality and brand trust. Keller (1993) noted that brand knowledge consists of brand awareness and brand image. Brand awareness relates to brand recall and recognition performance by consumers. Brand image refers to the set of associations linked to the brand that consumers hold in memory. Two types of measurement are used to measure the awareness and associations variables. The first type of measurement is based on open-ended questions and the second type of measurement is a seven-point Likert scale.

Open-ended questions were advocated by Aaker (1996, p. 62), who noted that there are three levels of brand awareness: (1) brand recognition reflects the ability of consumers to identify a certain brand among others, that is, 'aided recall'. Aided recall is a situation whereby a person is asked to identify a recognized brand name from a list of brands from the same product class. The second level is brand recall. This is a situation whereby a consumer is expected to name a brand in a product class. It is also referred to as 'unaided recall', as consumers are not given any clue from the product class. The third level is top-of-mind awareness. This is defined as the first brand that a consumer can recall among a given class of product.

Based on this, brand awareness was measured using four questions (Cobb-Walgren et al., 1995; Aaker, 1996; Kim et al., 2003). The first question measures unaided brand recall by asking customers to name five brands in a specific product category (in this case, the commercial banks category). Answers are coded as 0 when an Islamic bank is not mentioned or as a number denoting the number of Islamic banks mentioned. The second question measures top-of-mind awareness, whereby the customer is asked to mention the first brand that he or she recalls among a given class of product. The answer is coded as 1 when an Islamic bank is mentioned and 0 when no Islamic bank is mentioned. The third question measures aided recall or brand recognition. It asks the customer to identify Islamic banks among a list of Islamic and conventional banks.

The fourth type of measurement of brand awareness and brand associations was that introduced by Yoo et al. (2000). They used a seven-point Likert scale to measure brand awareness/association. Two items, related to customer recognition of the physical shape of the brand and imagining the product in the customer mind, were deleted since they are not suitable in the context of banking.

Perceived quality was measured using the scale introduced by Netemeyer et al. (2004). According to them, perceived quality is at a higher level of abstraction than any specific attribute, and differs from objective quality as it is more akin to an attitudinal assessment of a brand – a global affective assessment of a brand's performance relative to other brands. Yoo et al. (2000) also argued that perceived quality measures consumers' subjective judgment about a brand's overall excellence or superiority and addresses overall quality rather than individual elements of quality.

Finally, brand trust was measured using the scale introduced by Dimitriadis and Kyrezis (2008) to measure brand trust in a banking context. Brand trust is defined as the willingness of a buyer to rely on the ability of a brand to fulfill the communicated functions and attributes (Morgan and Hunt, 1994).

The dependent variable, overall brand equity, was measured using the scale introduced by Yoo et al. (2000). This scale is based on two considerations. First, the respondent was asked to compare a focal branded product with its unbranded counterpart. Second, in each item, it was emphasized that all brand characteristics other than brand name were identical between the focal brand and its unbranded referent. The only differential information available to the respondents was brand name.

Finally, the outcomes of brand equity included current purchases and future purchase intentions. Share-of-wallet was used to measure current purchases (Keiningham et al., 2007). This measure reflects the stated percentage of total assets held at the bank being rated by the customer. The future purchase intentions were measured using the scale introduced by Yoo et al. (2000).

POPULATION AND SAMPLING

The research population included customers of Islamic and conventional banks in Bahrain. Three hundred and fifty-five questionnaires were distributed to bank customers. Banks selected were top-ranked banks based on stock-market indices. Customers of fourteen banks in Bahrain participated in the survey. These banks included five Islamic banks and nine conventional banks. Islamic banks included in the sample were Kuwait Finance House, Shamel Bank, Bahrain Islamic Bank, Salam Bank and Baraka Bank. Conventional banks included National Bank of Bahrain, Bank of Bahrain and Kuwait, HSBC, Standard Bank, Ahli United Bank, ABC, Khaliji International Bank, Citibank and British Bank. Customers returned 206 completed questionnaires; thus, the response rate reached 58 per cent. Given the fact that banks did not agree to provide the researchers with a list of their customers, a convenience sample was used. Five postgraduate students collected the data. Sixty-nine questionnaires were collected from customers who selected an Islamic bank to be their primary bank, and 136 questionnaires were collected from customers who selected a non-Islamic bank to be their primary bank. One respondent did not report the nature of the bank that he considered to be his primary bank.

Although a convenience sample is not considered a probability sample, care was taken to reduce bias. Three strategies were used to correct most of the problems associated with convenience sampling (Gravetter and Forzano, 2009). The first strategy is to ensure that the sample is reasonably representative. Fourteen banks out of twenty-five retail banks were included in the sample. The second strategy is to use the same technique used in stratified samples. The percentage of Islamic bank customers in the sample reached 18 per cent of the total number of respondents, which is close to the market share of Islamic banks. This market share reached 11.1 per cent of total banking assets in June 2009 (Al-Maraj, 2009). The third strategy is to provide a clear description of how the sample was obtained and who the participants were. Ninety-two respondents had a high-school education or less, 95 respondents were college graduates and 19 respondents had postgraduate degrees. With respect to gender, 123 respondents were males, 81 were females and two questionnaires had missing values with respect to this variable. Ninety-four respondents were below the age of 30, sixty-five respondents were between the ages of 30 and 45, forty respondents were between the ages of 45 and 60, four respondents were above 60 years and three questionnaires had missing values with respect to age. Finally, 201 respondents were Muslims, one respondent was Christian and four questionnaires had missing values with respect to religion.

TESTS OF VALIDITY AND RELIABILITY

Before hypotheses testing, measurement validity and reliability tests were conducted. Content validity was examined before data collection by presenting the scale items to five academics who examined the scale items, and all necessary modifications were made. To examine convergent validity, factor analysis was used. Cronbach's alpha was used to examine reliability. Discriminant validity was examined by comparing correlation coefficients with Cronbach's alpha coefficients.

When factor analysis was performed, the variables of awareness/associations, perceived quality, overall brand equity and loyalty were all univariate. Factor loadings are shown in Table 15.2. All factor loadings exceeded .40 as recommended by Hair et al., (1998) for a sample of size 200. Only one item in overall brand equity had factor loadings of less than .40. This item was related to purchasing the brand in spite of having access to similar brands.

Cronbach's alpha coefficients for perceived quality, overall brand equity, loyalty and trust exceeded .70. The alpha coefficient for awareness/associations was .59. The coefficient rose to .797 when the first item was excluded.

The factor analysis was also performed for the trust construct. As shown in Table 15.3, two factors appear for the trust construct. Items that loaded on two or more factors were excluded. These items included items related to the following questionnaire items: the bank keeps its promises, the bank is always honest, the bank can handle problems, and the bank behaves in the same way in similar circumstances. One item loaded on one factor. This item relates to the bank treating its customers fairly. These items were all excluded from the analysis.

Discriminant validity was examined by the procedure used by Sharma and Patterson (1999) that compares alpha and correlation coefficients for each pair of variables. Although high and significant correlation coefficients were reported, all correlation coefficients were less than the reliability coefficients for the corresponding variables. For example, the correlation coefficient for perceived quality and loyalty was .704 (p<.000), yet the alpha coefficients for these two variables was higher than r, reflecting a high discriminant validity.

HYPOTHESES TESTING

The first five hypotheses were tested using regression analysis. Table 15.5 shows the results of the regression analysis to test research hypotheses.

The first hypothesis examined the association between awareness/associations and perceived quality. R^2 was 16.9, which means that awareness/associations explain 16.9 per cent of the variance in perceived quality (p<.000). This provides support to the first hypothesis.

The second hypothesis examined whether perceived quality mediates the relationship between awareness/associations and overall brand equity. In order to do this, a number of tests were performed as recommended by Preacher and Hayes (2004). This procedure includes the following steps:

Table 15.2　Factor analysis and reliability coefficients of research variables

	Associations Cronbach's alpha =.797	Quality Cronbach's alpha =.871	Overall brand equity alpha=.833	Loyalty Cronbach's alpha =.783
AA1. Some characteristics of X come to my mind quickly	.436			
AA2. I can quickly recall the symbol or logo of X	.880			
AA3. I have difficulty in imagining X in my mind (r)	.89			
PQ1. Compared to other brands of (product), (brand name) is of very high quality		.829		
PQ2. (Brand name) is the best brand in its product class		.811		
PQ3. (Brand name) consistently performs better than all other brands of (product)		.885		
PQ4. I can always count on (brand name) brand of (product) for consistent high quality.		.872		
OBE1. It makes sense to buy X instead of any other brand, even if they are the same			.839	
OBE2. Even if another brand has same features as X, I would prefer to buy X			.881	
OBE3. If there is another brand as good as X, I prefer to buy X			.879	
OBE4. If another brand is not different from X in any way, it seems smarter to purchase X				
LO1. I consider myself to be loyal to X				.836
LO2. X would be my first choice				.862
LO3. I will not buy banking services from other banks if X is available.				.806

Table 15.3 Factor analysis results for brand trust

	Factor 1	Factor 2 Cronbach's alpha =.883
My bank . . .	.307	.614
TR1. . . considers my needs and wishes as very important		
TR2. . . would not do anything against my interests	.763	.218
TR3. . . would not do anything in order to exploit me	.812	.197
TR4. . . keeps its promises	.495	.555
TR5. . . is always honest to me	.529	.421
TR6. . . never claims anything that is not valid	.795	.179
TR7. . . always treats me fairly	.042	.680
TR8. . . has the ability to meet its promises	.422	.438
TR9. . . can properly handle any problem that may occur during my transactions	.654	.398
TR10. . . is remarkably expert and specialized in its field	.763	.225
TR11. . . I never doubt that it will keep its promises	.184	.748
TR12. . . behaves consistently	.664	.168
TR13. . . always behaves in the same way in similar circumstances	.577	.529

Table 15.4 Correlation matrix and alpha coefficients for the research variables

	Associations	Perceived quality	Trust	Overall brand equity	Loyalty
Associations alpha=.797	1.000 —				
Perceived quality alpha=.871	.411**	1.000 —			
Trust alpha=.833	.344**	.689**	1.000 —		
Overall brand equity alpha=.883	.339**	.691**	.587**	1.000 —	
Loyalty alpha=.762	.285**	.704**	.657*	.715**	1.000 —
Share of wallet	.207**	.023	.1	.068	−0.21

Note: ** Correlation is significant at the 0.01 level (2-tailed).

1. To calculate the unstandardized beta coefficients and the standard error for the relationship between the independent variable (awareness/associations) and the mediator (perceived quality).
2. To calculate the unstandardized beta coefficients and the standard error for the relationship between the independent variable (awareness/associations) and the mediator (perceived quality), on one hand, and the dependent variable (overall

Table 15.5   Regression analysis

Hypotheses	R	R^2	SE	F	Sig.
H1: Awareness/associations are associated with perceived quality	.411	.169	1.118	186.679	.000
H3: Brand trust is associated with overall brand equity	.587	.345	1.04	107.419	.000
H4: Overall brand equity is associated with share of wallet	.068	.005	26.54	.935	.335
H5: Overall brand equity is associated with future purchase intentions	.715	.512	.99842	213.927	.000

Table 15.6   Beta coefficients and standard error estimates for the relationship between awareness/associations, perceived quality and overall brand equity

Variables	Unstandardized coefficients	
	B	SE
Independent: Awareness Mediator: Perceived quality	.434	.068
Independent: Awareness Mediator: Perceived quality Dependent: Overall brand equity	.696	.058

brand equity), on the other hand. Table 15.6 depicts the beta coefficients and standard error estimates for the relationship between awareness/associations, perceived quality and overall brand equity.

3. To conduct the Sopel test to examine mediation effects. Using the free statistics calculator (Soper 2010), the result of the Sopel test was 5.63, significant at p<.000 for both one-tailed and two-tailed tests. Thus, the second hypothesis was supported.

The third hypothesis examined the association between trust and overall brand equity. R^2 was 34.5, which means that brand trust explained 34.5 per cent of the variance of overall brand equity (p<.000), thus providing support for the third hypothesis. The fourth hypothesis examined the association between overall brand equity and share-of-wallet. R^2 reached .05 and was not significant. Thus, the fourth hypothesis was not supported. The fifth hypothesis, examining the relationship between overall brand equity and future intentions, was supported. Overall brand equity was found to explain 51.2 per cent of the variance in future intentions (p<.000).

The above results show that both perceived quality and brand trust explain the variance in overall brand equity. Multiple stepwise regression was performed to examine the relative importance of these two variables in explaining overall brand equity. Perceived quality was found to explain 47.8 per cent of the variance in overall brand equity. Both

Table 15.7 Results of multiple stepwise regression

Variables	R	R²	SE	F	Sig.
Perceived quality	.691	.478	.929411		.000
Perceived quality and brand trust	.708	.501	.91052	102.031	

perceived quality and brand trust explain 49.6 per cent of the variance in overall brand equity.

COMPARISON BETWEEN ISLAMIC AND NON-ISLAMIC BANKS

The sixth and seventh hypotheses examine the differences between customers of Islamic and customers of conventional banks with respect to top-of-mind awareness, aided recall, and unaided recall. The Mann-Whitney U-Test was used to examine these differences. Table 15.8 shows the results.

As shown in Table 15.8, the mean rank for Islamic banks is higher than that of non-Islamic banks in top-of-mind awareness, aided recall, and unaided recall, but the difference is not significant in the case of aided recall. This provides partial support for the sixth hypothesis.

T-tests were performed to examine the differences between Islamic and non-Islamic banks with respect to associations, perceived quality, brand trust, overall brand equity, loyalty and share-of-wallet. The means of these variables were higher for customers of Islamic banks than for customers of conventional banks, yet there were no significant differences between the two groups. The only variable with significant difference was brand trust (p<.004). Table 15.9 shows the results of the T-tests for these variables.

Table 15.8 Mann-Whitney U test for top-of-mind awareness, aided recall and unaided recall

Variable	Mean Rank	Sum of Ranks	Test Statistic Mann-Whitney U Test	Asymp.sig (2-tailed)
Top of mind			1499	.000
Islamic banks	149.28	10300		
Non-Islamic banks	79.52	10815		
Aided recall			4001	.067
Islamic banks	113.01	7798		
Non-Islamic bank	97.92	13317		
Unaided recall			1348	.000
Islamic banks	151.46	10451		
Non-Islamic bank	78.41	10664		

Table 15.9   *T-test results for associations, perceived service quality, overall brand equity, loyalty and share-of-wallet*

	Mean	Std. deviation	Std. error mean	Sig. (2-Tailed) Assuming equal variances	Sig. (2-Tailed) Assuming non-equal variances
Association				.518	.503
Islamic	6.0999	1.0724	.12911		
Non-Islamic	5.9889	1.20129	.10301		
Perceived quality			.136	.808	.8
Islamic	4.7703	1.12966			
Non-Islamic	4.72	1.27071	.10896		
Overall brand equity			.151	.154	.150
Islamic	4.9855	1.25432			
Non-Islamic	4.7148	1.29045	.11065		
Trust	5.1567	.96032	.11561	.006	.004
Islamic					
Non-Islamic	4.7148	1.14352	.09806		
Loyalty				.119	.103
Islamic	4.9420	1.28587	.1548		
Non-Islamic	4.6132	1.48235	.12711		
Share-of-wallet			3.9104	.207	.207
Islamic	47.275	26.55902			
Non-Islamic	42.3004	26.57709	3.3693		

DISCUSSION

A number of studies have examined the awareness of, satisfaction with, and loyalty to Islamic banks, but none has examined the brand equity of these banks. This research examines the sources and outcomes of brand equity in banking services and the differences between customers of Islamic and conventional banks with respect to these sources and outcomes. Data was collected from 206 customers patronizing banks in Bahrain. The level of the analysis was the corporate brand and not the individual brand.

The first research purpose was to examine the sources and outcomes of brand equity. With respect to the sources of brand equity, brand awareness/associations was found to be associated with perceived quality, and perceived quality was found to mediate the relationship between awareness/associations and overall brand equity. This supports the contention of Tong and Hawley (2009) that while brand awareness serves as a foundation for brand image and brand loyalty, high quality enables consumers to recognize a brand's distinctiveness and superiority. It also supports Netemeyer et al. (2004) who reported that brand awareness is a nomological correlate of perceived quality. Both perceived quality and brand trust were the most important predictors of overall brand equity. This finding supports Yoo et al. (2000), who reported a positive effect of perceived quality on overall brand equity. Incorporating trust as a source of brand equity is also supported by Harris and Goode (2004), Duffy (2005); Luk and Yip (2008), and Rauyruen et al. (2009).

The association between brand equity and loyalty was also supported, while that on share-of-wallet was not. Customers who report high levels of brand equity also report intentions to repatronize the service in the future. Cobb-Walgren et al. (1995) also reported purchase intentions as an outcome of brand equity. The non-significant effect of brand equity on share-of-wallet may reflect aspects specific to the banking context. Customers might have high brand equity for a particular bank, yet the share-of-wallet may be determined by other variables, particularly the expected rate of return and the propensity to avoid risk. In addition to having a choice among a large number of banks, bank customers have many routes to invest their money, such as mutual funds, investment funds, and so on. Accordingly, the proportion devoted to a particular bank may be determined by factors other than brand equity.

The second purpose of the research was to examine differences between customers of Islamic and non-Islamic banks with respect to top-of-mind awareness, aided recall and unaided recall. Customers who selected an Islamic bank as their primary bank reported higher top-of-mind awareness, aided recall and unaided recall of Islamic banks than those who selected a non-Islamic bank as their primary bank. The difference was significant in the case of top-of-mind awareness and unaided recall. It was not significant in the case of aided recall, however. This finding provides support for the findings related to the sources and outcomes of brand equity. Islamic banks have succeeded in building brand awareness among their customers and among the customers of their non-Islamic rivals, yet their rivals have succeeded in retaining their customers through providing them with higher levels of service. The result has been customers who are aware of Islamic banks, yet patronize non-Islamic banks.

Brand trust was also significantly higher among customers of Islamic banks than those of conventional banks .This means that Islamic banks have succeeded in building brand trust among their customers but not among customers of rival banks.

The finding that Islamic bank customers reported higher, though non-significant, levels of associations, perceived quality, overall brand equity, loyalty and share-of-wallet is consistent with previous studies which reported higher awareness of Islamic banking products in Bahrain (Al-Ajmi et al., 2009; Metawa and Al Mossawi, 1998). This might be attributed to the special nature of the Bahraini Islamic banking industry. Bahrain has emerged as a pre-eminent Islamic financial centre in the Middle East with a highly innovative environment, adapting regulations to the nature of the profit-loss sharing principle and acting as a prime mover in Islamic financial services (Algaoud and Lewis, 2007).

RESEARCH IMPLICATIONS

This research contributes to the study of the fields of brand equity and Islamic banking in various ways. First, it represents the first attempt to examine sources and outcomes of brand equity of Islamic banks. Most of the previous studies examined one or more sources of brand equity of Islamic banks, such as awareness of (Metawa and Al Mossawi, 1998; Hamid and Nordin, 2001; Okumus, 2005), or preferences for (Erol and El-Bdour, 1989; Rosly and Abu Bakar, 2003; Bley and Kuehn, 2004; Al-Tamimi et al., 2009) or service quality of Islamic financial products (Ahmad et al., 2010; Othman and Owen, 2001). Second, it offers a new perspective in examining brand equity. Such a perspective coincides with the hierarchy-of-effects model where customers pass through a set of steps from awareness, to knowledge, to liking, to preference, to conviction and purchase (Lavidge and Steiner, 1961) or from building brand knowledge to the use of brand knowledge to the application of brand knowledge (Hoeffler and Keller, 2003). The finding that awareness/associations is associated with perceived quality highlights the fact that there may be a potential causal order among the dimensions of brand equity (Washburn and Plank, 2002).

This is not to underestimate the importance of brand awareness and brand associations in building brand equity. They do imply, however, that the relative importance of awareness/ associations and perceived quality may differ based on the stage of brand-building efforts as well as the degree of product involvement. If the company is in the first stage of brand-building efforts, and customers do not know the brand yet, all brand-building efforts should be directed to building brand awareness. This is the brand identification stage identified by Lehmann et al. (2008). The second step is to firmly establish the brand meaning in the minds of customers (that is, by strategically linking a host of tangible and intangible brand associations). The third step is to elicit the proper customer responses to this brand identity and brand meaning. This step entails enhancing customer perception of quality. The final step is to convert brand response to create an intense, active loyalty relationship between customers and the brand.

The finding that perceived quality may be more important in brand equity development in the context of banking services sheds light on the role of product involvement in the formation of brand equity and explains why some researchers emphasized the importance of brand awareness/associations (for example, Keller, 2003) while others emphasized the importance of perceived quality (for example, Netemeyer et al., 2004). The relative importance of brand awareness/associations and perceived quality may vary with the degree of product involvement. In this respect Petty et al., (1983) argued that low-involvement products do not stimulate much information processing on the part of customers. In such cases, a person makes simple inferences about the merits of the object and brand awareness and brand associations may be more prevalent. Conversely, high-involvement products require more information processing on the part of the customer. Having purchased the product, the customer engages in some evaluation of the product quality. Such evaluation will be the major determinant of the customer's perception of the brand equity.

Only a small number of studies incorporated brand trust as a possible source of brand equity (Atilgan et al., 2009; Rauyruen et al., 2009). In this research, brand trust was found to be a significant predictor of brand equity. Although its importance in explaining the variance in brand equity was lower than that of perceived service quality, it was still significant. Future research should incorporate brand trust as a possible source of brand equity.

Future research should address the effect of some other variables on the brand equity of Islamic banks. The degree of religious commitment, customer perceived value, personal values and prior experiences are variables that could be incorporated in models examining brand equity of Islamic banks. Furthermore, the brand equity of Islamic banking products could be examined among non-Muslims, especially in Western countries. Future research should use larger and more representative samples.

MANAGERIAL IMPLICATION

This research provides useful insights to marketing managers in general and to marketing managers of Islamic banks in particular. The fact that the importance of brand equity sources varies from one stage to another in brand-building efforts and from one product to another means that there is no one path to enhance brand equity. Specifically, companies in the early stages of brand-building efforts should emphasize issues of brand awareness and associations. This can be achieved through advertising and other integrated marketing communication tools. Once this stage is completed, marketing managers should consider superior quality as the main tool for building brand meaning.

Product involvement is another variable to be considered in examining brand equity sources. In cases of high-involvement products such as banks, customer perceived quality will be the major determinant of brand equity. Conversely, for low-involvement products, brand awareness may be more prevalent, as customers do not intend to invest much effort in processing product information.

Marketing managers of Islamic banks should consider aspects other than creating brand awareness in building their brand equity. Bank customers build equity perceptions and response tendencies based on evaluation of the quality of a bank's service. Efforts directed to the creation of Islamic brand meaning should emphasize quality as the major source for building brand equity.

BIBLIOGRAPHY

Aaker, D.A. (1996), 'Measuring brand equity across products and markets', *California Management Review*, **38** (3), 102–20.

Abul Hassan, A. and S. Abdul Latiff (2008), 'Islamic marketing ethics and its impact on customer satisfaction in the Islamic banking industry', *Islamic Economics*, **21** (1), 23–40.

Ackermann, P.L.S. and E. Jacobs (2008), 'Developing banking products for Islamic corporate clientele', *Southern African Business Review*, **12** (1), 67–88.

Agarwal, M.K. and V.R. Rao (1996), 'An empirical comparison of consumer based measures of brand equity', *Marketing Letters*, **7** (3), 237–47.

Ahmad, N. and S. Haron (2002), 'Perceptions of Malaysian corporate customers towards Islamic banking products and services', *International Journal of Islamic Financial Services*, **3** (4), http://staf.uum.cdu.my/alib/wb3053/perceptions.pdf, accessed 9 December 2009.

Ahmad, A., K. Rehman and M.I. Saif (2010), 'Islamic banking experience of Pakistan: comparison between Islamic and conventional banks', *International Journal of Business and Management*, **5** (2), 137–43.

Ailawadi, K.L., D.R. Lehmann and S.A. Neslin (2003), 'Revenue premium as an outcome measure of brand equity', *Journal of Marketing*, **67** (4), 1–17.

Al-Ajmi, J., H. Hussein and N. Al Saleh (2009), 'Clients of conventional and Islamic banks in Bahrain: how they choose which bank to patronize', *International Journal of Social Economics*, **36** (11), 1086–12.

Al-Maraj, R.M. (2009), 'Islamic Finance Symposium, http://www.bma.gov.bh/page.php?p=islamic_finance_symposium,_nikkei_conference_room,_tokyo,_japan, accessed 10 September 2010.

Al-Tamimi, H., A. Lafi and M. Uddin (2009), 'Bank image in the UAE: comparing Islamic and conventional banks', *Journal of Financial Services Marketing*, **14** (3), 232–44.

Algaoud, L.M. and M.K. Lewis (2007), 'Islamic critique of conventional financing', in M.K. Hassan and M.K. Lewis (eds), *Handbook of Islamic Banking,* Cheltenham, UK and Northampton, MA, USA: Edward Elgar, pp. 38–48.

Ambler, T., C.B. Bhattacharya, J. Edell, K.L. Keller, K.N. Lemon and V. Mittal (2002), 'Relating brand and customer perspectives on marketing management', *Journal of Service Research*, **5** (1), 13–25.

Ariff, M. (1988), 'Islamic banking', *Asian-Pacific Economic Literature*, **2** (2), 46–62.

Atilgan, E., S. Akinci, S. Aksoy and E. Kaynak (2009), 'Customer-based brand equity for global brands: a multinational approach', *Journal of Euromarketing*, **18**, 115–32.

Bick, G.N.C. (2009), 'Increasing shareholder value through building customer and brand equity', *Journal of Marketing Management*, **25** (1/2), 117–41.

Biedenbach, G. and A. Marell (2010), 'The impact of customer experience on brand equity in a business-to-business services setting', *Journal of Brand Management*, **17**, 446–58.

Billah, M. (2007), 'Islamic banking and the growth of takaful', in M.K. Hassan and M.K. Lewis (eds), *Handbook of Islamic Banking*, Cheltenham, UK and Northampton, MA, USA: Edward Elgar, pp. 401–418.

Blackston, M. (1992), 'Observations: building brand equity by managing the brand's relationships', *Journal of Advertising Research*, **32** (3), 79–83.

Bley, J. and K. Kuehn (2004), 'Conventional versus Islamic finance: Student knowledge and perception in the United Arab Emirates', *International Journal of Islamic Financial Services*, **5** (4), accessed 20 December 2009 from http://www.nzibo.com/IB2/CVIF-ME.pdf.

Brady, M.K., B.L. Bourdeau and J. Heskel (2005), 'The importance of brand cues in intangible service industries: an application to investment services', *Journal of Services Marketing*, **19** (6/7), 401–10.

Briggs, E. and D. Grisaffe (2010), 'Service performance–loyalty intentions link in a business-to-business context: the role of relational exchange outcomes and customer characteristics', *Journal of Service Research*, **13** (1), 37–51.

Brodie, R.J., M.S. Glynn and J. van Durme (2002), 'Towards a theory of marketplace equity: integrating branding and relationship thinking with financial thinking', *Marketing Theory*, **2** (1), 5–28.

Brown, K., M.K. Hassan and M. Skully (2007), 'Operational efficiency and performance of Islamic banks', in M.K. Hassan and M.K. Lewis (eds), *Handbook of Islamic Banking*, Cheltenham, UK and Northampton, MA, USA: Edward Elgar, pp. 96–115.

Broyles, S.A. and D.W. Schumann (2004), 'The comparative influence of brand equity's experiential and functional antecedents and its consequences on US and mainland Chinese consumers', AIB-SE (USA) 2004 Annual Meeting, Knoxville, TN, pp. 375–85.

Buil, I., L. de Chernatony and E. Martinez (2008), 'A cross-national validation of the consumer-based brand equity scale', *Journal of Product and Brand Management*, **17** (6), 384–92.

Caceres, R.C. and N.G. Paparoidamis (2007), 'Service quality, relationship satisfaction, trust, commitment and business-to-business loyalty', *European Journal of Marketing*, **41** (7/8), 836–67.

Chaudhuri, A. and M.B. Holbrook (2001), 'The chain of effects from brand trust and brand affect to brand performance: the role of brand loyalty', *Journal of Marketing*, **65** (2), 81–94.

Chiou, J., C. Droge and S. Hanyanich (2002), 'Does customer knowledge affect how loyalty is formed?', *Journal of Service Research*, **5** (2), 113–24.

Choudhury, M. (2007), 'Development of Islamic economic and social thought 21', in M.K. Hassan and M.K. Lewis (eds), *Handbook of Islamic Banking*, Cheltenham, UK and Northampton, MA, USA: Edward Elgar, pp. 21–37.

Choudhury, M. and M.M. Hussain (2005), 'A paradigm of Islamic money and banking', *International Journal of Social Economics*, **32** (3), 203–17.

Chu, K. (2009), 'The construction model of customer trust, perceived value and customer loyalty', *Journal of the American Academy of Business*, **14** (2), 98–103.

Clarke, R.J. (2009), 'Islamic banking: an asset of promise?', *OECD Observer*, 272, 16–17.

Cobb-Walgren, C., C.A. Ruble and N. Donthu (1995), 'Brand equity, brand preference, and purchase intent', *Journal of Advertising*, **24** (3), 25–40.

Delgado-Ballester, E. and J.L. Munuera-Alemán (2001), 'Brand trust in the context of consumer loyalty', *European Journal of Marketing*, **35** (11/12), 1238–58.

Dillon, W.R., T.J. Madden, A. Kirmani and S. Mukherjee (2001), 'Understanding what's in a brand rating: a model for assessing brand and attribute effects and their relationship to brand equity', *Journal of Marketing Research*, **38** (4), 415–29.

Dimitriadis, S. and N. Kyrezis (2008), 'Does trust in the bank build trust in its technology-based channels?', *Journal of Financial Services Marketing*, **13** (1), 28–38.

Doney, P.M. and J.P. Cannon (1997), 'An examination of the nature of trust in buyer-seller relationships', *Journal of Marketing*, **61** (2), 35–51.

Duffy, D. (2005), 'The evolution of customer loyalty strategy', *Journal of Consumer Marketing*, **22** (4/5), 284–86.

Dusuki, A.J. (2008), 'Understanding the objectives of Islamic banking: a survey of stakeholders' perspectives', *International Journal of Islamic and Middle Eastern Finance and Management*, **1** (2), 132–48.

Dusuki, A. and N. Abdullah (2007), 'Why do Malaysian customers patronize Islamic banks?', *International Journal of Bank Marketing*, **25** (3), 142–60.

Edris, T. (1997), 'Services considered important to business customers and determinants of bank selection in Kuwait: a segmentation analysis.' *International Journal of Bank Marketing*, **15** (4), 126–34.

Elfakhani, S.M., I.J. Zbib and Z.U. Ahmed (2007), 'Marketing of Islamic financial products', in M.K. Hassan and M.K. Lewis (eds), *Handbook of Islamic Banking*, Cheltenham, UK and Northampton, MA, USA: Edward Elgar, pp. 116–27.

Elliott, R. and N. Yannopoulou (2007), 'The nature of trust in brands: a psychosocial model', *European Journal of Marketing*, **41** (9/10), 988–98.

Erol, C. and R. El-Bdour (1989), 'Attitudes, behaviour and patronage factors of bank customers towards Islamic banks', *International Journal of Bank Marketing*, **7** (6), 31–37.

Esche, F., T. Langner, B.H. Schmitt and P. Geus (2006), 'Are brands forever? How brand knowledge and relationships affect current and future purchases', *Journal of Product and Brand Management*, **15** (2), 98–105.

Gait, A. and A. Worthington (2009), 'Attitudes, perceptions and motivations of Libyan retail consumers toward Islamic methods of finance', paper presented to the Asian Finance Association 2009 International Conference, Brisbane, 30 June–3 July.

Ganesan, S. (1994), 'Determinants of long-term orientation in buyer-seller relationships', *Journal of Marketing*, **58** (2), 1–19.

Garbarino, E. and M. Johnson (1999), 'The different roles of satisfaction, trust and commitment in customer relationships', *Journal of Marketing*, **63** (April), 70–87.

Gerrard, P. and J. Cunningham (1997), 'Islamic banking: a study in Singapore', *International Journal of Bank Marketing*, **15** (6), 204–16.

Gravetter, F.J. and L. Forzano (2009), *Research Methods for the Behavioral Sciences*, 3rd edn, Belmont, CA: Wadsworth.

Gylling, C. and K. Lindberg-Repo (2006), 'Investigating the links between a corporate brand and a customer brand', *Journal of Brand Management*, **13** (4/5), 257–67.

Hair, J.S., R.E. Anderson, R.L. Tetham and W.C. Black (1998), *Multivariate Data Analysis*, 5th edn, Upper Saddle River, NJ: Prentice-Hall.

Hamid, A. and N.A. Nordin (2001), 'A study on Islamic banking education and strategy for the new millennium – Malaysian experience', *Journal of Islamic Financial Services*, **2** (4), http://www.kantakji.com/fiqh/Files/Research/i%20banking.pdf, accessed 9 December 2009.

Haron, S., N. Ahmad and S. Planisek (1994), 'Bank patronage factors of Muslim and non-Muslim customers', *International Journal of Bank Marketing*, **12** (1), 32–40.

Harris, L.C. and M.H.H. Goode (2004), 'The four levels of loyalty and the pivotal role of trust: a study of online service dynamics', *Journal of Retailing*, **80**, 139–58.

Hassan, M.K. and M.K. Lewis (2007), 'Islamic banking: an introduction and overview', in M.K. Hassan and M.K. Lewis (eds), *Handbook of Islamic Banking*, Cheltenham, UK and Northampton, MA, USA: Edward Elgar, pp. 1–17.

Hess, J. and J. Story (2005), 'Trust-based commitment: multidimensional consumer-brand relationships', *Journal of Consumer Marketing*, **22** (6), 313–22.

Hoeffler, S. and K.L. Keller (2003), 'The marketing advantages of strong brands', *Journal of Brand Management*, **10** (6), 421–45.

Kahf, M. (2007), 'Islamic banks and economic development', in M.K. Hassan and M.K. Lewis (eds), *Handbook of Islamic Banking*, Cheltenham, UK and Northampton, MA, USA: Edward Elgar, pp. 277–84.

Kartono, B. and V.R. Rao (2009a), 'Brand equity measurement: comparative review and a normative guide', Johnson School Research Paper Series No. 24-09.

Kartono, B. and V.R. Rao (2009b), 'Linking consumer-based brand equity to market performance: an integrated approach to brand equity management', Johnson School Research Paper Series No. 23-09.

Kayaman, R. and H. Arsali (2007), 'Customer-based brand equity: evidence from the hotel industry', *Managing Service Quality*, **17** (1), 92–109.

Keiningham, T.L., B. Cooil, L. Aksoy, T.W. Andreassen and J. Weiner (2007), 'The value of different customer satisfaction and loyalty metrics in predicting customer retention, recommendation, and share-of-wallet', *Managing Service Quality*, **17** (4), 361–84.

Keller, K.L. (1993), 'Conceptualizing, measuring, and managing customer-based brand equity', *Journal of Marketing*, **57** (1), 1–22.

Keller, K.L. (1998), *Strategic Brand Management: Building, Measuring and Managing Brand Equity*, 2nd edn, Upper Saddle River, NJ: Prentice-Hall.

Keller, K.L. (2001), 'Building customer-based brand equity', *Marketing Management*, **10** (2), 14–19.

Keller, K.L. (2003), 'Brand synthesis: the multidimensionality of brand knowledge', *Journal of Consumer Research*, **29** (4), 595–600.

Keller, K. and D.R. Lehmann (2001), 'The brand value chain: linking strategic and financial performance', working paper, Tuck School of Business, Dartmouth College.

Keller, K.L. and R.L. Lehmann (2006), 'Brands and branding: research findings and future priorities', *Marketing Science*, **25** (6), 740–60.

Kim, H., W.G. Kim and J.A. An (2003), 'The effect of consumer-based brand equity on firms' financial performance', *Journal of Consumer Marketing*, **20** (4/5), 335–71.

Klaus, P. and Maklan, S. (2007), 'The role of brands in a service-dominated world', *Journal of Brand Management*, **15** (2), 115–22 .

Krishnan, H.S. (1996), 'Characteristics of memory associations: a consumer-based brand equity perspective', *International Journal of Research in Marketing*, **13**, 389–405.

Kumar, N., L.K. Scheer and J.E.M. Steenkamp (1995), 'The effects of supplier fairness on vulnerable resellers', *Journal of Marketing Research*, **32** (1), 54–65.

Lassar, W., B. Mittal and A. Sharma (1995), 'Measuring customer-based brand equity', *Journal of Consumer Marketing*, **12** (4), 11–19.

Lau, G.T. and S.H. Lee (2004), 'Consumers' trust in a brand and the link to brand loyalty', *Journal of Market Focused Management*, **4** (4), 341–70.

Lavidge, R.J. and G. Steiner (1961), 'A model for predictive measurements of advertising effectiveness', *Journal of Marketing*, **25** (1), 59–62.

Lehmann, D.R., K.L. Keller and J.U. Farley (2008), 'The structure of survey-based brand metrics', *Journal of International Marketing*, **16** (4), 29–56.

Leone, R.P., V.R. Rao, K.L. Keller, A.M. Luo, L. McAlister and R. Srivastava (2006), 'Linking brand equity to customer equity', *Journal of Service Research*, **9** (2), 125–38.

Luk, S.T. and L.S. Yip (2008), 'The moderator effect of monetary sales promotion on the relationship between brand trust and purchase behaviour', *Journal of Brand Management*, **15** (6), 452–64.

MacKay, M.M., J. Romaniuk and B. Sharp (1997), 'A typology of brand equity research', Proceedings of the Australia New Zealand Marketing Educators Conference (ANZMAC), Department of Marketing, Monash University, Melbourne, pp.1146–57.

Madden, T.J., F. Fehle and S. Fournier (2006), 'Brands matter: an empirical demonstration of the creation of shareholder value through branding', *Journal of the Academy of Marketing Science*, **34** (2), 224–35.

Metawa, S. and M. Al Mossawi (1998), 'Banking behaviour of Islamic bank customers: perspectives and implications', *International Journal of Bank Marketing*, **16** (7), 299–315.

Mirakhor, A. and I. Zaidi (2007), 'Profit-and-loss sharing contracts in Islamic finance', in M.K. Hassan and M.K. Lewis (eds), *Handbook of Islamic Banking*, Cheltenham, UK and Northampton, MA, USA: Edward Elgar, pp.49–63.

Morgan, R.P. (2000), 'A consumer-oriented framework of brand equity and loyalty', *Journal of the Market Research Society,* **42** (1), 65–79.

Morgan, R.M. and S.D. Hunt (1994), 'The commitment-trust theory of relationship marketing', *Journal of Marketing*, **58** (3), 20–39.

Myers, C.A. (2003), 'Managing brand equity: a look at the impact of attributes', *Journal of Product and Brand Management*, **12** (1), 39–52.

Na, W.B., R. Marshall and K.L. Keller (1999), 'Measuring brand power: validating a model for optimizing brand equity', *Journal of Product and Brand* Management, **8** (3), 170–84.

Naser, K. and L. Moutinho (1997), 'Strategic marketing management: the case of Islamic banks', *International Journal of Bank Marketing*, **15** (6), 187–203.

Naser, K., A. Jamal and K. Al-Khatib (1999), 'Islamic banking: a study of customer satisfaction and preference in Jordan', *International Journal of Bank Marketing*, **17** (3), 135–50.

Netemeyer, R.G., B. Krishnan, C. Pullig, G. Wang, M. Yagci, D. Dean, J. Ricks and F. Wirth (2004), 'Developing and validating measures of facets of customer-based brand equity', *Journal of Business Research*, **5** (2), 209–24.

Nijssen, E., J. Singh and D. Sirdeshmukh (2003), 'Investigating industry context effects in consumer-firm relationships: preliminary results from a dispositional approach', *Journal of the Academy of Marketing Science*, **31** (1), 46–60.

Okumus, H. (2005), 'Interest-free banking in Turkey: a study of customer satisfaction and bank selection criteria', *Journal of Economic Cooperation*, **26** (4), 51–86.

Othman, A.Q. and L. Owen (2001), 'Adopting and measuring customer service quality in Islamic banks: a case study in Kuwait Finance House', *International Journal of Islamic Financial Services*, **1** (3), 6–12.

Pappu, R., P.G. Quester and R.W. Cooksey (2005), 'Consumer based brand equity: improving measurement – empirical evidence', *Journal of Product and Brand Management*, **14** (3), 143–54.

Pappu, R., P.G. Quester and R.W. Cooksey (2006), 'Consumer-based brand equity and country-of-origin relationships: some empirical evidence', *European Journal of Marketing*, **40** (5/6), 696–717.

Park, C.S. and V. Srinivasan (1994), 'A survey-based method for measuring and understanding brand equity and extendibility', *Journal of Marketing Research*, **31** (2), 271–88.

Petty, R.E., J.T. Cacioppo and D. Schumann (1983), 'Central and peripheral routes to advertising effectiveness: the moderating role of involvement', *Journal of Consumer Research*, **10**, 135–46.

Pope, H. (2005), 'Islamic banking grows: with all sorts of rules', *Wall Street Journal*, 3 May.

Preacher, K.J. and A.F. Hayes (2004), 'SPSS and SAS procedures for estimating indirect effects in simple mediation models', *Behavior Research Methods, Instruments and Computers*, **36**, 717–31.

Punj, G.N. and C.L. Hillyer (2004), 'A cognitive model of customer-based brand equity for frequently purchased products: conceptual framework and empirical results', *Journal of Consumer Psychology*, **14** (2), 124–31.

Rammal, H. and R. Zurbruegg (2007), 'Awareness of Islamic banking products among Muslims: the case of Australia', *Journal of Financial Services Marketing*, **12** (1), 65–74.

Rauyruen, P. and K.E. Miller (2007), 'Relationship quality as a predictor of B2B customer loyalty', *Journal of Business Research*, **60**, 21–31.

Rauyruen, P., K.E. Miller and M. Groth (2009), 'B2B services: linking service loyalty and brand equity', *Journal of Services Marketing*, **23** (3), 175–86.

Reast, J.D. (2005), 'Brand trust and brand extension acceptance: the relationship', *Journal of Product and Brand Management*, **14** (1), 4–13.

Rego, L.L., M.T. Billet and N.A. Morgan (2009), 'Consumer based brand equity and firm risk', *Journal of Marketing*, **73** (6), 47–60.

Reynolds, T.J. and C.B. Phillips (2005), 'In search of true brand equity metrics: all market share ain't created equal', *Journal of Advertising Research*, **45** (June), 171–85.

Rosly, S. and M. Abu Bakar (2003), 'Performance of Islamic and mainstream banks in Malaysia', *International Journal of Social Economics*, **30** (12), 1249–65.

Sharma, N. and P.G. Patterson (1999), 'The impact of communication effectiveness and service quality on relationship commitment in consumer, professional services', *Journal of Services Marketing*, **13** (2), 151–70.

Sichtmann, C. (2007), 'An analysis of antecedents and consequences of trust in a corporate brand', *European Journal of Marketing*, **41** (9/10), 999–1015.

Simon, C.J. and M.W. Sullivan (1993), 'The measurement and determinants of brand equity: a financial approach", *Marketing Science*, **12** (1), 28–52.

Sinha, A., N.J. Ashill and A. Gazley (2008), 'Measuring customer based brand equity using hierarchical Bayes methodology', *Australasian Marketing Journal*, **16** (1), 3–19.

Sirdeshmukh, D., J. Singh and B. Sabol (2002), 'Impact of frontline employee behaviors and management practices on consumer trust, value and loyalty in relational service exchanges', *Journal of Marketing*, **66** (1), 15–37.

Soper, D. (2010), Statistics Calculator, http://www.danielsoper.com/statcalc/calc31.aspx, accessed 3 September 2010.

Srinivasan, V., C.S. Park and D.R. Chang (2001), 'EQUITYMAP: measurement, analysis, and prediction of brand equity and its sources', Research Paper No. 1685, Graduate School of Business, Stanford University.

Srinivasan, V., C.S. Park and D.R. Chang (2005), 'An approach to the measurement, analysis, and prediction of brand equity and its sources', *Management Science*, **51** (9), 1433–48.

Sudin, H. (1995), 'The framework and concept of Islamic interest-free banking', *Journal of Asian Business*, **11** (1), 26–39.

Taylor, S.A., G.L. Hunter and D.L. Lindberg (2007), 'Understanding customer-based brand equity in financial services', *Journal of Services Marketing*, **21** (4), 241–52.

Tong, X. and J.M. Hawley (2009), 'Measuring customer-based brand equity: empirical evidence from the sportswear market in China', *Journal of Product and Brand Management*, **18** (4), 262–71.

Wang, C.H., L. Hsu and S. Fang (2009), 'Constructing a relationship-based brand equity model', *Service Business*, **3**, 275–92.

Washburn, J.H. and R.E. Plank (2002), 'Measuring brand equity: an evaluation of a consumer-based brand equity scale', *Journal of Marketing Theory and Practice*, **10** (1), 46–62.

Yoo, B. and N. Donthu (2001), 'Developing and validating a multidimensional consumer-based brand equity scale', *Journal of Business Research*, **52** (1), 1–14.

Yoo, B., N. Donthu and S. Lee (2000), 'An examination of selected marketing mix elements and brand equity', *Journal of the Academy of Marketing Science*, **25** (2), 195–212.

16 Islam and corporate social responsibility in the Arab world: reporting and discourse

Cameron Thibos and Kate Gillespie

Despite a rapidly globalizing world, the scholarly literature concerning corporate social responsibility (CSR) has remained largely focused on the experience of Western firms. This oversight is unfortunate. The emerging markets of the Arab world offer markedly different contexts, constraints and possibilities for CSR activity and research, and many Arab companies stand out in their creative efforts to do good for the communities in which they operate. This chapter adds to the slowly growing body of work on CSR in the Middle East by examining the impact of Islam on CSR reporting and legitimatization discourse in the Arab world.

Academics have had a difficult time agreeing on any one theory of corporate social responsibility. This is due in part to the broad and abstract nature of the concept. For the purposes of this chapter, CSR is defined as any corporate activity designed to benefit society as a whole or in part that may or may not directly benefit the corporation itself. While academic scholarship on corporate social responsibility in a Western context is now extensive, such research in a specifically Middle Eastern context is extremely sparse. Studies on the Levant (predominately Lebanon) dominate the empirical literature of CSR in the Middle East (Jamali and Mirshak, 2007; Jamali et al., 2008; Jamali, 2008; Jamali and Sidani, 2008; Jamali and Keshishian, 2009; Jamali et al., 2009a; Jamali et al., 2009b). However studies also include work on Turkey (Atakan and Eker, 2007; Turker, 2009) and the Arab Gulf (Katsioloudes and Brodtkorb, 2007; Rettab et al. 2009). Williams and Zinkin (2010) conceptually explore connections between Islam and the UN Global Compact. While one study by Jamali et al., (2009b) reports that Islamic principles may play a role in motivating Arab managers to participate in CSR, Islam generally receives little attention in the literature and no study explores the impact of Islam on CSR reporting and discourse.

In this chapter we examine Islam in the context of CSR reporting by large Arab corporations and the Arab press. First, we identify when Islam is referenced in CSR reporting and what subjects are mentioned. Second, we explore how these subjects are described in the discourse. Using an etic paradigm of discourse, we examine the role Islamic authorization and moralization play in the legitimization discourse for CSR initiatives. We also examine two specific categories of CSR initiatives – those aimed at orphans and those aimed at women – specifically identifying the role Islam plays in legitimizing these initiatives and comparing this role to more pragmatic arguments for legitimization that dominate the discourse. Third, we explore how legitimization discourse is framed from an emic perspective. We conclude by enumerating the current findings of our study – identifying how Islam plays both an explicit role and an implicit role in Arab CSR reporting and discourse – and by proposing new questions for research that arise from our findings.

METHODOLOGY

We include in our research of CSR reporting and discourse an analysis of both Arab corporate websites and news articles published by the Arab press. This allows us to capture insights into both corporate and public discourse.

We first examined corporate websites to see what they identify as CSR initiatives and how they present these CSR initiatives. For several practical reasons we limited this survey to the major companies in the Arab world. First, large companies are able to pursue more sophisticated projects and thus represent the pinnacle of Arab CSR achievement. Second, these companies may be more likely to publish their CSR activity because of their links to Western business. Third, large companies are more likely to have a more comprehensive web presence.

We compiled an aggregate list of top Arab companies from four different lists supplied by Internet business news outlets in autumn 2008. These lists comprised the 'Top 100 Companies of the Muslim World' (filtered for Arab companies), the 'Top Forty Arab Brands,' the 'Top 100 Saudi Companies' and the 'Fifty Most Admired Companies in the Gulf Cooperation Council.' We then systematically checked each company for a web presence, and then filtered for websites in English. The decision to focus on English sites increases rather than decreases our sample size. Out of the original list of 192 companies, 179 had English websites, and of these 91 were bilingual. Only one site was available solely in Arabic. Twelve companies did not have a website at all.

We further culled the list of corporate websites to a final sample of 58 companies by only selecting sites with a designated section for CSR activity. This was a reasonable requirement as highly obscured social reporting is not true reporting at all. We proceeded to review each site and record and analyze the issues they covered. The content and length of these sections ranged from a single paragraph or bullet-point list, to many pages of detailed, well-designed content, to downloadable PDF booklets on CSR activity. All references to Islam or religion were noted along with any references to Islam-specific terminology such as Ramadan, *hadith*, *zakat*, and so on.

Bilingual sites were maintained by 64 per cent of the Arab firms in our sample. A comparison of Arabic and English pages on bilingual websites revealed no substantive differences in the treatment of religion, although Arabic pages at times invoked the name of God whereas English pages did not. However this is likely an artifact of the Arabic language. In one case, a Saudi site referred to the 'Islamic religion' on the English page and 'our religion' on the Arabic page.

We then explored how CSR initiatives are reported in the Arab press. After testing several search engines, including the internal search engines of many news sites, we determined Google News to be by far the most appropriate for our purposes. We came to this conclusion for two reasons. First, several of the internal search engines of key Arab news sites did not work or returned results unrelated to the search string. Second, Google News proved successful in identifying CSR-related articles containing the search string on these same media websites.

In November 2008 we searched Google News for the Arabic phrase *'al-mus'uliyya al-ijtima'iyya lil-sharikat'* (CSR) and collected the articles listed on the first five pages of results for the six months between May and November. We checked for false positives and ended with a total of 149 articles published by 27 news sources. Following this we

Table 16.1　Arab CSR reporting and discourse

	Religious/Islamic references	References to orphans	References to women
Websites (N=58)			
Total	14	10	13
No justification	4	5	3
Authorization	7	0	1
Moralization	9	1	2
Instrumental Rationalization	1	5	9
News Articles (N=149)			
Total	5	1	14
No justification	0	0	0
Authorization	5	0	5
Moralization	1	0	0
Instrumental Rationalization	0	1	11

generated a list of 48 Arabic keywords by reading the first five articles from each month. We then used a web browser to highlight each instance of these keywords in the larger dataset, accommodating for the morphological changes inherent in the Arabic language, counted them manually, and tabulated the results. To examine the Islam-related content of newspaper articles, we looked at a series of religion-related keywords in the Arabic text – religion, Islam, *zakat,* Ramadan, Islamic morals/ethics (*ikhlaq*) and so on – and identified when they appeared in these articles.

However, CSR reporting by itself does not explain how companies legitimize their actions to the public or how Islam is used in this legitimization discourse. To explore such legitimization discourse we employed a categorization framework developed by Van Leeuwen and Wodak (Van Leeuwen and Wodak, 1999, and Siltaoja, 2009). Following this framework, we determined if the discourse for each reported CSR initiative or news article sought legitimization of the initiative through authorization, moralization or instrumental rationalization. Authorization denotes specific reference to tradition or authoritative institutions or persons. For example, in the Islamic context this would include reference to the Qur'an, *hadith, sharia,* Ramadan or *zakat.* Moralization is understood to mean specific mention of morality as a basis of the CSR initiative or the specific presentation of a moral argument in its justification. In contrast, instrumental rationalization focuses on the pragmatic and non-religious benefits of the initiative. While authorization and moralization are the two categories appropriate to specific references to Islam, the addition of the category of instrumental rationalization proved useful in examining Islam within the full legitimization discourse, an examination we undertook for CSR projects relating to orphans and women. Each item analyzed could utilize none or one or more of these categories of legitimization. The co-authors independently coded each item into one or more categories. In cases where disagreement arose (three items or 5.3 per cent of total), final coding was determined by further discussion. A tabulation of results is found in Table 16.1.

To augment our etic analysis of legitimization discourse, we examined our data from an emic perspective absent of predetermined categories in order to determine if any new and different themes arose.

THE ROLE OF RELIGION IN ARAB CSR REPORTING

Religion does not play a major role in CSR reporting and discourse in the West. There is very little to be found in the academic literature, and a Google search will quickly reveal that the pairing of CSR with Christianity is found on private and Christian sites rather than on corporate sites – with the exception of special philanthropic initiatives during the Christmas holiday. Even though many academics and managers likely harbor religious sentiments, theological obligation is not presented as a motivation for corporate action. In the United States, this may reflect cultural conditioning related to a vehement defense of the separation of church and state. Alternatively, the phenomenon may reflect the fact that not all stakeholders adhere to one particular faith. Whatever the cause, CSR discourse favors more terrestrial gains such as alleviating social ills and increases to the profits of the firm.

Our research reveals more mixed findings concerning religion and CSR in the Arab world. Similar to discourse in the West, most corporate websites and the majority of news articles do not mention religion, although – as in the West – philanthropic initiatives are associated with a major religious holiday. However, in contrast to the West, mention of Islam does in fact appear as a motivation for CSR on some corporate websites. Furthermore, the likely reason why religion is not invoked more often in the Arab world is probably due to factors very distinct from those that discourage religious mention in western reporting.

Religious motivation for CSR was mentioned 14 times in the corporate database. All companies were located in the Arab Gulf: Saudi Arabia, the United Arab Emirates and Kuwait. For example, the National Commercial Bank, a government-owned Saudi firm, communicates Islamic credentials as part of its public image:

> Through the past decades, NCB has been a major contributor in most areas of social service in a variety of fields such as humanitarian work, charity, education, culture, health, arts and sports. The driving force behind all that was our solid belief in our core values which are derived from the principles of our religion that laid the foundations of social solidarity. (National Commercial Bank website)

Many of the bank's identified CSR initiatives have been religious in nature as well, including the renovation of 25 mosques to receive disabled worshippers. In addition, several companies have created novel, beneficial and worker-sensitive programs that have to do with religion. The National Bank of Kuwait, for example, has an annual field trip for workers who wish to perform *umra*, the lesser pilgrimage to Mecca.

Our news database contains three articles in which the term religion (*al-din*) appears. All three reinforce the notion that 'giving' is an Islamic duty and Islam is the root of philanthropic activities in the Middle East. Our search for the word 'Islam' yielded similarly few results. Of the 11 articles which literally contain the word, only two designate religious motivation for CSR. The others report on businesses connected with religion, such as Islamic finance and educational institutions. One article notes 'a clear social role for the private sector,' as progress in Arabic and Islamic civilizations has historically relied on individuals more than the state (Ghariyaba, 2008). Two other articles contain different comments on the inherently religious nature of CSR from a member of parliament in Abu Dhabi, and the coverage of these comments suggests that the Emirati government is amenable to casting CSR in a religious framework.

ZAKAT AND CSR

Zorzopulos (2006) asserts that *zakat*, a tax mandated by Islam for charitable purposes, and philanthropy are inextricably intertwined in the minds of Muslim managers. *Zakat* is one of the five pillars of Islam and stands equal in priority and importance to professing the faith (*shahadah*), prayer (*salah*), pilgrimage (*hajj*) and fasting (*saum*). Charitable giving is incumbent upon all Muslims and to refuse or ignore the command amounts to disbelief or apostasy (Zysow, 2010). At its core, *zakat* functions to bind together and strengthen the community – be it local, national, or global – through co-dependency and reciprocity. God gave some Muslims the gifts of affluence and success and thus he expects they too will be generous. The poor, who cannot financially return the favor, give back through gratitude and prayer (Kochuyt, 2009).

Zakat is designed to redistribute a small amount of wealth from the relatively well off to needy groups in society. It is neither a strategy for poverty reduction, *per se*, nor an attempt at wealth equalization. Rather, it is a social safety net laid down over 1400 years ago in a region and an era where disadvantaged groups had few places to turn for aid. Its rules are found in the Qur'an, the *hadith* (the sayings of the Prophet Muhammad), and later exposition by Islamic thinkers and jurists. The details of payment are complex, but the threshold of wealth (*nisab*) for paying *zakat* is quite low, making the obligation one that is shouldered by all but the poorest in society.

The Qur'an specifies *zakat* proceeds may go to several different groups. 'Alms are for the poor and the needy, and those employed to administer the (funds); for those whose hearts have been (recently) reconciled (to Truth); for those in bondage and in debt; in the cause of God; and for the wayfarer: (thus is it) ordained by God, and God is full of knowledge and wisdom.' (Qur'an 2008: 9:60). The category designated 'those in the cause of God' was historically understood to comprise fighters of *jihad*. However, more recent interpretations include institutions and projects often targeted by CSR initiatives in both the Arab world and the West, including the financing of mosques, religious foundations, schools, charitable trusts, hospitals, social projects or emergency relief programs worldwide (Kochuyt, 2009).

Throughout most of history paying *zakat* was a personal responsibility. The use of official tax collectors fell into disuse shortly after the Prophet Muhammad's death in 632 CE. However, since the 1940s there has been a revival of interest in adapting *zakat* to the modern world. Today only six countries have enshrined *zakat* collection into law. These are Libya, Malaysia, Pakistan, Saudi Arabia, Sudan and Yemen (Zysow, 2010). Many other Muslim countries that do not require *zakat* by law have government departments standing by to collect *zakat* with high-tech websites, credit card payments and convenient kiosks, in addition to the numerous private organizations that operate independently. Self-reported observance of *zakat* is high throughout the Muslim world (Hassan, 2005).

Two corporate websites specifically mention *zakat.* While this number of explicit mentions is quite low, philanthropy, arguably associated with *zakat,* is extensive, and we particularly observe that many of the projects that are funded by corporations emphasize the traditional recipients of *zakat* funds – the elderly, the disabled, the destitute and orphans.

One of the most popular forms of giving according to this data set is outfitting hospital wards or clinics with the necessary equipment. Companies with no relation to healthcare did this to fill service gaps in their countries. Zain, an Arab multinational telecommunications company based in Bahrain, built a complete hospital, and the Al Faisaliah Group outfitted the Alkhraj Kidney Dialysis Center and donated money to the King Fahd Children's Cancer Hospital (Al Faisaliah Group website; Zain website). Other companies work on a smaller but still valuable scale. Telecom Egypt, for example, paid for the center for the blind at Cairo University's Central Library (Telecom Egypt website). Orascom Telecom, another Egyptian telecommunications company, commissioned four medical supply convoys to the nation's rural areas (Orascom Telecom website).

It should be noted that several companies emphasized their foreign humanitarian aid to other Arab and Muslim countries, confirming the aforementioned idea that charity in Islam works to bind the community together at all different levels. Both the National Holding Company and al-Islami Foods donated aid money to Lebanon after the 2006 war with Israel, and Zain rebuilt universities in Baghdad. SABIC, a Saudi industrial group, highlighted its donations to relief work following the 2004 Asian Tsunami and the 2008 earthquake in Pakistan (SABIC website).

The term *zakat* appears twice in our database of news articles. It is surprising that this potentially powerful concept is so rarely evoked despite strong emphases on related concepts such as volunteerism (74 instances) and morals/ethics (55 instances). Both articles in which *zakat* is mentioned come from the Gulf region. The first article discusses a study that claims Saudi managers are experimenting with new methods of increasing CSR practices. 'The report noted that there is a religious aspect to the corporate Saudi concept of CSR, represented in the necessity of paying the *zakat* which they owe, in addition to charitable associations and helping the poor' (Mahmoud, 2008). The second article covers a speech made by Khalid Abdullah Janahi, the Chairman of Bahrain's Ithmaar Bank, at the World Economic Forum's Annual Meeting for New Champions. Janahi included the concept of *zakat* in his address, stating 'Charitable work is part of our culture in the Middle East. In reality, this issue comes within our precise definition of *zakat* that is one of the pillars of Islam' (Anonymous, 2008a).

RAMADAN AND CSR

Ramadan appears in CSR reporting in a way arguably similar to Christmas in the west. Ramadan, the ninth month of the Islamic lunar calendar, is a holy time in the Muslim world. For all observant Muslims it is a full month of fasting in commemoration of the first verses of the Qur'an being passed down from heaven to the Prophet Muhammad. The Qur'an quite plainly states the historical, spiritual and didactic reasons for requiring the fast in verses 2:183–5. 'O you who believe! Fasting is prescribed to you as it was to those before you, that you may learn self-restraint . . . Ramadan is the (month) in which was sent down the Qur'an . . . so every one of you who is present (at his home) during that month should spend it in fasting.' The fast consists of abstaining from food, drink, tobacco and sex, among other worldly pleasures, from dawn until dusk. Once the sun sets, however, it is a time of celebration and togetherness. Families, mosques, and at times whole communities come together for the nightly *iftar* meal. The end of Ramadan is marked by Eid al-Fitr, a large feast in celebration of all God has given. During Ramadan devout Muslims often donate food to the poor in conjunction with the festivities.

Four corporate CSR websites had specific activities related to Ramadan. Saudi ARAMCO, the national oil company, prepared a pamphlet for its staff detailing how to prepare healthy and nutritional meals during the month-long fast. Several companies provided *iftar* meals to either the community or to the evening shift of workers, as in the case of the Kuwait Petroleum Company:

> In a fitting finale to its Ramadan long charitable contributions, KPC, under the patronage of the Chief Executive Officer Mr. Saad Al-Shuwaib, distributed *sahur* (late night) meals at the Grand Mosque during the last ten days of the Holy Month. This initiative demonstrated the Corporation's social mission, concern to provide all necessary services and ensure the most comfortable atmosphere for worshippers during the blessed ten days at the Grand Mosque. (Kuwait Petroleum Company website)

In our sample of news articles, Ramadan is mentioned twice in association with CSR. One describes a government-corporate partnership to distribute food to the poor during Ramadan (Anonymous, 2008c). The second was a joint project by Jordinvest and Imcan Brokerage and Trading. This firm hosted a series of *iftar* dinners for more than 300 people in communal tents in central Amman. The CEO and Chairman of both Jordinvest and Imcan, Ahmad Tantash, said at the event, 'On these blessed days we call upon all organizations in the private sector to imitate the shared initiative undertaken by Jordinvest and Imcan, not only during the holy month of Ramadan but also to place studied, shared projects on the general agenda' (Anonymous, 2008b).

CSR DISCOURSE: FORMS OF LEGITIMIZATION

CSR initiatives require resources that could alternatively be used to benefit different stakeholders in the firm – higher salaries for employees, lower prices for consumers, and/ or increased profits for investors. Therefore, it is important to analyze how firms and the media legitimize CSR activities in the Arab world. When religion is referenced in our corporate sample, Islamic authorization is utilized to legitimize CSR initiatives in half the cases, while moralization is utilized in 64 per cent of cases. In the news sample, authorization is utilized five times and moralization once. Instrumental rationalization is commonly utilized in Arab CSR discourse as we will discuss further below. However, when Islam is invoked, whether on a website or in a news article, instrumental rationalization is extremely rare.

In sum, discussion of religion is kept brief, and when it does appear in corporate and media discourse it often simply invokes religious tradition or authority to legitimize a

CSR initiative. When religion is invoked in legitimization discourse, mention of additional pragmatic justification is uncommon.

ISLAM AND CSR INITIATIVES TOWARDS ORPHANS AND WOMEN

Up to now we have concentrated on identifying when Islam appears in Arab CSR reporting and how it is used in the legitimization discourse. However, it is also useful to examine the role of Islam in Arab CSR from a different perspective: the role it plays (or fails to play) in legitimizing CSR initiatives in which one might expect Islam to be invoked. These initiatives are those of orphans and women. As noted above, orphans are traditional recipients of *zakat*, and a significant percentage of Arab firms that report CSR programs have initiatives that address the needs of orphans. Many Arab firms also have initiatives that target women, initiatives that are arguably more controversial due to vastly different interpretations of the role of women across the Muslim world.

ORPHANS AND ISLAM

Orphans hold a special place in Islam. The Prophet Muhammad was raised by his grandfather and uncle after being orphaned at the age of six (Harwazinski, 2010). In addition to this intimate connection, orphans and society's responsibility to care for them constitute an important theme for the Qur'an with 23 mentions in the Yusuf Ali translation. Repeatedly and in no uncertain terms Muslims are commanded to look after these vulnerable children and to protect their property rights. Not surprisingly, the *Encyclopaedia of the Qur'an* claims that dealing justly with orphans is one of the most important duties of Muslims and that this theme has greatly influenced Islamic law and ethics (Giladi, 2010).

In our sample of corporate CSR sites, ten Arab firms (17 per cent of total) reported programs specifically relating to the needs of orphans. Additionally, there was one mention in our media sample of a CSR initiative relating to orphans. Despite the apparent popularity of orphan-related projects, Islam was never invoked as a legitimizing factor in the discourse justifying these projects. In half the cases a project was mentioned with no justification. In the remainder of projects, instrumental rationalization was utilized. Moralization was only employed once and did not specifically mention Islam.

For example, the National Commercial Bank in Saudi Arabia reports of its Al Ahli Orphans Program:

> NCB provides support and sponsorship specifically for orphans, in collaboration with the relevant societies and organizations, either with financial aid or through well-designed programs to fulfill their material needs such as stationery, school bags, clothes, medical care and other requirements. The objective is to compensate these members of the society for the loss of their parents and the lack of family life. This will help to protect them from vagrancy, uncertainty and other negative effects so that they can grow in a decent environment and have a successful future. (National Commercial Bank)

Although moral argument is presented for this project – orphans deserve compensation for loss of parents and family life – Islam is not invoked. In addition the project is justified via instrumental rationalization by the utility derived by society (the prevention of vagrancy).

Another example of instrumental rationalization comes from the Savola Group's orphan training program.

> In this program, a number of the orphans were trained in cooperation with the International Vocational Education and Training Association to perform printing jobs. Thirty orphans were trained on the modem printing and publication methods to attain self-reliance principle, and to acquire the necessary experience needed for their involvement in the job market'. (Savola Group website)

The utility exacted from this CSR project resides in orphans who attain gainful employment and for society which enjoys an increase in the overall pool of skilled labor.

However, given the Qur'an's emphasis on providing for the needs – especially the material needs – of orphans, the question remains as to why Islam is not invoked in the context of CSR projects involving orphans. We suspect there are two possible reasons for this omission. The first is that the directive to care for orphans is so engrained into Muslim society and ethics that it is not perceived as necessary to mention Islamic authority or morality for this directive. The religious connection is implicit and consequently understood by a Muslim audience. A second possible reason may be that these largely bilingual corporate websites are designed as much for non-Muslim foreigners as they are for Arabs. Designers may have decided that caring for vulnerable children is a universally accepted moral imperative. By not mentioning religion as a motivating factor, the message remains neutral for all audiences while not obscuring the religious overtones immediately perceptible to their domestic and/or co-religionist audiences.

WOMEN AND ISLAM

One of the key findings in the survey of corporate websites was a relatively large number of programs specifically targeting women. Women in the Arab and Islamic worlds (which are by no means synonymous and monolithic) are a historically and currently disadvantaged group. Unfortunately one finds in the Arab countries some of the least educated and least economically active women in the world. However, World Bank statistics for Arab countries reveal literacy rates for women vary greatly across the region, from 93 per cent in Kuwait to 40 per cent in Yemen, with a 16-country average of 75 per cent. The average participation rate for women in the workforce is only 27 per cent[1] (World Bank, 2009).

Nonetheless, feminism has existed in the Arab world since at least the nineteenth century, maturing alongside national and anti-colonial movements (Al-Hassan Golley, 2004). Muslim feminists suggest that the treatment of women in the Arab world is a complicated picture that exists in the gray areas between religion, the practice of religion, patriarchal tradition and history. Furthermore, these feminists seek a path to equality that does not compromise their religious devotion or relegate spirituality to a separate sphere, as has been done in the United States. They argue that the Islamic religion itself is not the problem but the misogyny and patriarchy that pervade its practice today. For example, female Arab writers as early as the mid-1800s studied Islamic texts and were surprised to learn that veiling and gender segregation were not essentially Islamic (Al-Hassan Golley, 2004).

However, since men have monopolized Qur'anic learning since the early days of Islam in the 7th century, they have inevitably included in their interpretations their own moral codes and traditions. A traditional, patriarchal interpretation exists in many parts of the Islamic world, such as in Saudi Arabia where the government and the puritan Wahhabi strain of Islam are inextricably intertwined. The activities of women are strictly monitored and controlled, to the extent of a prohibition on driving, all in the name of defending the undoubtedly temporal issue of family honor. As Al-Hassan Golley explains, 'women's bodies . . . have been "traditionally" constructed as "trustees of family (sexual) honour"' (Al-Hassan Golley, 2004). Traditional practices and inequalities are taken to such extremes and given such leeway that a Saudi man was able to divorce his wife legally by text message (Anonymous, 2009).

Given the controversy concerning the place of women in modern Islam, it is interesting to note that many of the Arab corporations in our survey present themselves as strong advocates for women's empowerment. Mention of Arab CSR initiatives towards women appear on the websites of thirteen companies, over 22 per cent of our sample, even outpacing initiatives aimed at orphans. However, Islam is rarely invoked as justification for CSR initiatives aimed at women. Three websites offer no justification for the initiative, two present a moral argument and one invokes Islamic authorization.

The sole company to invoke Islamic justification is the National Commercial Bank of Saudi Arabia. The discourse on the company's education programs for women utilizes authorization: 'The Islamic religion and traditions urges [sic] all Muslims to learn and to teach.' However, it also utilizes instrumental rationalization: '[This program will] provide job opportunities to the maximum number of Saudi nationals to enable them to be productive and contribute to the development of the society' (National Commercial Bank website).

In fact, the most common form of justification for women's programs is instrumental rationalization and these arguments come overwhelmingly from Saudi Arabian firms. This is partially explained by Saudi Arabia's dominant presence in the survey. However, it might also reflect the explicit policy of 'Saudization' championed by the government and promoted by the kingdom's private sector. This policy, effective since 1975, was designed to curtail the kingdom's heavy reliance on imported labor. The Saudi government has channeled significant resources into educational and employment programs for the past three decades in order to remedy this situation (Mackey, 2002, pp. 184–85). Many companies have taken up the banner as well and proudly promote their commitment to training and hiring nationals. These programs draw on the national discourses of capacity building, self-sufficiency and development.

For example, the Saad Group, a privately owned holding company, created a women-only nursing school to staff its private hospitals (Saad Group website). A program such as this empowers women, increases the quality of healthcare in the kingdom and transforms Saudi youth into productive members of the workforce. Not only does this program serve to educate women but it also provides them with direct employment opportunities. Numerous other firms have also endowed various university professorships, scholarships, computer literacy centers, entrepreneurial workshops, and educational institutes in one form or another.

Among the news articles that mention women, many report on the launch of a new CSR program by a company and simply note that both females and males are intended as beneficiaries. For example, one article about Zain states that the company gave scholarships to 116 male and female students. There is no justification given for why both sexes were included, simply that they were. It is common in Arabic to use the masculine versions of nouns to refer to mixed-sex groups, so this parsed manner of writing is not absolutely necessary for the inclusion of women. Thus, while this phrase may to an extent be stylistic it is also a conscious choice to emphasize the diversity of the group.

Similar to what we observe on corporate websites, religious references in relation to CSR and women are rare in the news articles in our sample. Islam is only referenced once in an article in which the authority of the Amir of Mecca is invoked (Anonymous 2008f). No moralization (involving Islam or not) is presented in the articles. Oddly, of the five times that authorization is utilized to justify a women's initiative, Islam is invoked once while Queen Rania of Jordan and her public campaign for women's empowerment are invoked four times.

In fact, the vast majority of the 14 articles that discussed women's CSR initiatives come from Jordan, a finding partially attributable to a public campaign headed by Jordan's royal family, especially Queen Rania. For example, one article reports that the queen chaired a conference to promote the progress of women in society and gave several speeches to this effect. Another article reports on the success of Tamweelcom, the micro-credit branch of the Noor AlHussein Foundation (headed by the dowager Queen Noor). Without the articles covering the activities of Jordan's royal family, news coverage linking women with corporate social responsibility would be extremely scant.

Similar to the corporate websites, most articles from our newspaper sample provide an instrumental rationalization as justification for a women's CSR initiative. For example, one article reports on the Saad Group's several private schools for men and women, including the female-only nursing school, noting: 'Responding to a clear need within Saudi Arabia, the College was founded with the mission of becoming a leading academic institute for young Saudi women wishing to pursue a career in the nursing profession' (Saad Group).

EMIC INSIGHTS INTO ISLAM AND ARAB CSR REPORTING AND DISCOURSE

Our emic analysis of our data tended more to support and expand our prior findings than to present us with very different findings. This may be due to the fact that the discourse is often brief and perfunctory. Nonetheless we do observe, arising from the data, the emphasis of CSR as philanthropy and what may be described as a *respect* for philanthropic CSR as opposed to strategic CSR.

The concept of strategic CSR is promoted by Porter and Kramer (2002) who argue that companies should not simply donate to philanthropic causes (philanthropic CSR) but develop strategic CSR programs to improve the competitive context of the community. Specifically, firms should design initiatives, such as in-house training programs, that reflect their own business goals and draw upon their expertise. Similarly, van de Ven (2008), summarizing nearly 20 years of empirical research on CSR, concludes that firms should select causes with a high fit to their core competencies and communicate to consumers, who may be skeptical of solely philanthropic initiatives, that CSR actions will benefit both society and the firm.

However, there is no indication that Arab firms consider philanthropic CSR to be inferior to strategic CSR. Recurring words on the websites were philanthropy and charity. Also recurrent was the reference to initiatives aimed at 'the needy.' In addition, four companies describe the causes they support or the deeds that they do as 'noble', as exemplified by the language of the National Bank of Kuwait.

> Locally, our deep commitment to the community by far exceeds the role normally expected from a banking institution and embraces a broad spectrum of social and philanthropic involvement. We proudly boast that we have fully shouldered this noble and sublime responsibility right from the earliest days of the Bank's inception in 1952. (National Bank of Kuwait website)

Only four companies draw a strategic link between social responsibility and commercial success, and these links are tentative, emphasizing generalities and not firm specifics. For example, as the National Bank of Kuwait states, 'Today, it has become quite infeasible for successful organizations to create value or maximize the return for shareholders on a continuous basis if, at the same time, they do not respect the social and humanitarian values that are of interest for the public and therefore the market' (National Bank of Kuwait website).

We discovered some Arab companies did in fact undertake projects that could qualify as strategic CSR. These comprised public projects that were related to the firms' core competencies, and most involved the establishment of training institutes that could possibly create new employees for the firm. However, firms never framed these initiatives in terms of strategic CSR per van de Ven's (2008) suggestion. All instances of strategic CSR reporting (10 websites and 10 news articles) emphasized the benefits for the target group and pointedly ignored or severely downplayed the benefits to the firms themselves. Instead the discourse focused on investing in the students rather than in the company, with perhaps a small aside regarding how future employment with the firm will be of further benefit to the student. For example, Saudi Oger, a large, diverse firm, operates a training center and notes on its CSR site that,

> In 2007 we officially inaugurated 'Saudi Oger Training Institute', a nonprofit organization, at a cost of more than 45 million dollars that caters to train young Saudi males and females and prepare them for employment in various sectors by providing them the education and the on hands training in four sectors Hospitality, Technical, Construction and Continued training. (Saudi Oger website)

The reporting neglects to mention that Saudi Oger has extensive expertise and interests in these sectors, and will likely indeed benefit from its own benevolence.

These emic findings likely arise from an inherent secrecy surrounding *zakat*. The intention (*niyya*) underlying the charitable gift is an important component of *zakat*. Donating to charity is seen as an act of worship itself, so it must be done correctly, with altruistic motives. The Qur'an distinguishes between giving money in order to profit and giving for a good cause. The latter act will be reciprocated by God and the giver's wealth will increase (Qur'an 2008: 30:39). However, the Qur'an also warns that giving conspicuously casts doubt on one's intentions. To make a show of philanthropy implies ulterior motives and vanity. However, if no one knows about the gift it must have come from the heart. 'O you who believe! Cancel not your charity by reminders of your generosity . . . like those who spend their substance to be seen of men, but believe neither in God nor in the Last Day' (Qur'an 2008: 2:264).

From a theological point of view this command is hard to overstate. In the record of his sayings (the *hadith*), the Prophet Muhammad also pronounces the importance of keeping philanthropy secret.

> The Prophet said, Seven people will be shaded by Allah under His shade on the day when there will be no shade except His. They are: . . . (6) a person who practices charity so secretly that his left hand does not know what his right hand has given (i.e. nobody knows how much he has given in charity). (Bukhari)

The reason for this secrecy is that unseen charity is construed as pure altruism whereas giving that promotes the economic, social or political standing of the giver does the opposite. This is important because the gift is not only an act of worship but, once again according to the *hadith*, 'Allah has made *zakat* obligatory simply to purify your remaining property' (Abu-Dawud).

This notion of purity is inextricably tied up with *zakat*. This is one reason why we argue that there is a strong cultural and religious unwillingness toward publicizing CSR initiatives. A further lens with which to view the depth of this relationship is linguistic. Unlike in English, where charity can be defined as 'benevolence to one's neighbors, especially the poor' (OED 1989), the definitions of *zakat* and its more general cousin *sadaqa* (voluntary alms giving) have different emphases and connotations. *The Hans Wehr Dictionary of Modern Written Arabic*, a standard in the field, defines these words in conjunction with their roots and related terms. *Zakat* comes from the root *zaka*, meaning 'to thrive; to grow, increase; to be pure in heart, be just, righteous, good.' *Zakat* itself is defined as 'purity; justness, integrity, honesty; justification, vindication; alms-giving' (Wehr, 1994, p.441). *Sadaqa* comes from the root *sadaqa*, which Wehr defines as 'to speak the truth, be sincere.' He confines his definition of *sadaqa* itself to alms-giving, but related to this word are *sidq* and *sadaqa*, meaning truth and friendship, respectively (1994, p.594).

These definitions suggest that charity connotes different concepts in Arabic than in the English language. At a linguistic level, and thus also at a cultural level, the emphasis on purity and the innocence of intention is salient. When one gives *zakat* one is being pure of heart. *Sadaqa* relates to friendship and one is not supposed to exploit friends. Indeed, one is supposed to be sincere, honest, and treat them with integrity. Thus Zorzopulos's (2006) statement that *zakat* and philanthropy are inseparable in the minds of Muslim managers probably holds true at more levels than that of personal faith and can be strong even in the less devout. These cultural connotations may help explain why both pious and secular businessmen and women in the Arab world might avoid the publicity usually associated with CSR projects and wish to downplay any strategic gains associated with them.

One last insight arose from our emic investigation: evidence of the blending of Western and Islamic themes. Kudu Arabia, a Saudi quick-service restaurant chain, presents in its website a somewhat odd combination of Western CSR discourse associated with green initiatives and sustainability and Islamic dietary propriety. The nature of Kudu's business, food preparation, combined with its location in the heartland of Islam likely requires Kudu to communicate that its production methods and meat sourcing are *halal*, or in accordance with Islamic dietary laws. The website states under a section entitled Islamic Values 'that all products within the supply chain conform [to] Islamic laws, that they are *halal*, and do not contain genetically engineered ingredients.' In addition it states that 'our products do not cause harm for the current or future generations' (Kudu website).

CONCLUSIONS AND SUGGESTIONS FOR FURTHER RESEARCH

CSR is a modern Western concept that has been adopted by many corporations in the Middle East. With this adoption, however, has come transformation. In this chapter we have attempted to explore how Islam in particular impacts CSR reporting and discourse in the Arab world in both explicit and implicit ways.

The explicit use of Islam in Arab CSR reporting and discourse is arguably limited. When Islam is referenced, the reference is brief. It ranges from short mentions of a CSR initiative associated with Ramadan to a statement that Islam is the foundation of a firm's CSR program. The former is not unlike the appearance of Christmas initiatives in the west. The latter appears to be a more unique phenomenon of the Islamic context.

When Islamic terminology is utilized in Arab CSR reporting, the discourse is absent of stories or in-depth moral arguments. Authoritative legitimization is relatively common – possibly suggesting that mere referencing of Islamic authority or tradition, such as the Qur'an, Ramadan, or addressing the needs of orphans, is sufficient to establish legitimacy in the eyes of a Muslim audience. Individuals in the United States are increasingly unable to understand religious references in discourse due to a significant decrease in religious literacy in the past generations (Prothero, 2007). However, this may not be the case in the Arab world.

Ramadan initiatives provide a good example of the terseness we observe when religious themes appear on Arab CSR websites. References to Ramadan initiatives only briefly mention projects and no religious sentiment is evoked through pictures or print beyond associations readers themselves would connect to the word Ramadan. In contrast, companies throughout the Arab world expend substantial resources on elaborate television commercials to associate themselves and their products with the fast and subsequent celebration. For example, one television commercial by Zain, a telecommunications company in our sample, depicts a crowded Arab street. People are passing by an old shopkeeper as they wish their friends a happy Ramadan. The shopkeeper invites people into his humble sweets shop, but nobody notices him. He becomes downcast and begins to close up shop. A well-dressed boy sees him, positions himself in front of the shop door and begins to sing a song about God and the joys of Ramadan. A crowd gathers, and when the boy is finished singing, the crowd surges into the store. Later that night, the man gives the boy a jar of candy, which the boy shares with his friends. At the end of the commercial the phrase 'may God answer your prayers' appears, followed by the Zain logo (Zain Commercial). This advertisement utilizes story-telling and encompasses themes of sharing and concern for the poor by the rich. In addition the use of an innocent and religious child evokes Islamic family values. The final statement is suggestive of the reciprocity of *zakat*. Blessings from God should be acknowledged by giving to others. While advertisements and websites are not directly comparable, the contrast is still stark.

Our findings also give rise to the possibility that Islamic reference may be curtailed in Arab corporate CSR reporting and discourse because different audiences – both Muslim and non-Muslim Westerner – are targeted by these websites. As previously noted, all 58 of the companies in our corporate sample possess an online presence in English, however only 64 per cent felt the need to maintain a bilingual website. As the majority of Arabs do not speak fluent English, the conscious choice to exclude a large portion of the region's population suggests that the primary audience of these websites is likely limited to the educated elite of the Arab world and foreign investors. The choice to include a foreign, and presumably largely non-Muslim, target audience may partially explain differences between Ramadan discourse commonly found in Arabic-language advertisements and that found on bilingual corporate CSR websites.

It is less clear why public discourse in the Arabic language media has little explicit reference to Islam. One possible explanation is the relationship of government and media in Arab countries. The majority of Arab news outlets are either owned and operated or censored and influenced by the government. According to Reporters Without Borders Annual Index of Press Freedom, Egypt ranked 143rd out of 175 in 2009, Saudi Arabia 163rd, Jordan 112th, Lebanon 61st, Syria 165th, and the United Arab Emirates 87th (Reporters Without Borders, 2009). Therefore, it is appropriate to view the Arab media as proxies for their respective governments rather than as opinion makers in their own right. While Arab governments are not hostile to Islam, and some in the Arab Gulf base their legitimacy on Islam, these governments may want to associate the benefits of CSR with the economic development of their particular nation state. Therefore media discourse is dominated by the more practical and less spiritual instrumental rationalization.

We also discovered one corporate CSR website that invoked Islamic morality as supporting the education of women, although the many other firms that undertook CSR initiatives for the training of women avoided any association with Islam, possibly due to controversy surrounding women in the workplace that likely exists across a Muslim audience.

Our findings that both Islam and strategic CSR play only a small role in the CSR reporting of major Arab firms appears to support the findings of Jamali and Mirshak (2007) whose study of CSR in Lebanon discovered that the vast majority of CSR activity was philanthropic in nature and not undertaken for the sake of increased profitability. However, our findings contradict two qualitative studies by Jamali and colleagues and a survey by the Sustainability Advisory Group. One study by Jamali et al; (2009b) reports that Islamic principles were frequently cited by Arab managers as motivations for CSR, and a study by Jamali et al. (2009a) reports that Arab managers are aware of strategic CSR and a significant number support the idea. Another study by the Sustainability Advisory Group presented at the 7th CSR Summit in Dubai reports that 75 per cent of 100 Arab corporate leaders surveyed believe that CSR could attract new investment, capture new markets, and increase market share (Anonymous, 2010).

One explanation is that there is a difference between what Arab managers say and what they do. Several authors have argued that there is a divergence between the ideal of Islamic teachings concerning business and actual business practices in the Muslim world, and this divergence accounts for the prevailing belief in Muslim societies that businesses are basically unethical (Tsalikis and Lassar, 2009). However, another explanation could be the fact that CSR reporting is essentially a foreign concept to Arab culture. Fassin (2008) notes that formalization of CSR reporting can be viewed by a firm as a counter-productive administrative burden, thus its absence does not imply that the firm is not behaving responsibly.

A final explanation may lie with Islamic tradition itself. If the explicit role of Islam in Arab CSR reporting and discourse is limited, our study argues for a more significant implicit role. A cultural connection between CSR and *zakat* likely affects reporting and discourse in four ways.

First, a connection between *zakat* and CSR likely impacts the choice of recipients of CSR initiatives as reported on corporate websites. As we have noted, many of these recipients are traditional recipients of charitable giving associated with *zakat*. In particular, we observed many programs aimed at orphans. Second, CSR reporting is dominated by the concept of philanthropy. Despite arguments in the West that mere philanthropy is a more naive form of CSR, CSR discourse in the Arab world does not appear to feel ashamed by philanthropy, often utilizing vocabulary related to philanthropy and referring to philanthropic actions as noble. Third, in contrast to CSR practice in the West, Islam teaches that charitable giving should not be publicized. Fourth, a connection between *zakat* and CSR may make Arab managers uncomfortable with the concept of strategic CSR. In our study we observe that CSR discourse on corporate websites avoids identifying strategic initiatives as being strategic.

Consumer skepticism of CSR motivations exists in the West (see, for example, Mohr et al., 2001; Sen and Bhattacharya, 2001). However, the sentiment that publicizing corporate philanthropy is inherently wrong may be even more pronounced in Muslim societies. During interviews with Lebanese managers, Jamali and Mirshak (2007) found a propensity for businesses to practice 'silent CSR.' Silent CSR occurs when a company does not publicize projects or outcomes, because it fears sullying its altruism with charges of whitewashing and advertising.

A 2009 report by the Sustainability Advisory Group noted that Arab Islamic culture believes that 'to promote or discuss charitable donations is regarded as vulgar, as individuals are seen to be capitalizing on this societal obligation for self gain, a large step away from the view of the West' (Anonymous, 2010). Similarly, Mouza al-Atibah, a member of parliament in Abu Dhabi, is reported to remark on the existence of silent CSR.

> She pointed to the fact, of which there is no doubt, that Gulf companies display positive agreement with regard to social responsibility and with an individual feeling of responsibility. Most of what is completed is performed in secrecy and comes from a moral and religious starting point. (Anonymous 2008d)

> [al-Atibah] added that volunteerism, charitable work, and helping society without waiting for compensation – this is the true translation of the pillars of *our* true religion . . . (Anonymous 2008e)

If this tendency to practice silent CSR is a religiously based cultural trait shared throughout the region, it may explain why only 58 of 192 (30 per cent) of companies in our aggregate list believed it beneficial to publicize their CSR activities on their websites. In all likelihood many of the other 70 per cent of organizations are engaged in various types of CSR as well, and one should not assume CSR is rarely practiced in the Arab world simply because a minority of Arab companies choose to publicize their activities.

Our study has limitations. By its very nature a study of the Arab world is constrained by differences between countries. As noted above, articles on CSR and women are predominately a Jordanian phenomenon. Also our corporate sample comes largely from the Arab Gulf. Our methodology is also limited to the examination of extant written sources.

Further research could help us to better understand the connection between Islam and CSR in the Arab world as well as elucidating similarities and differences that might exist among Muslim communities. To date research on Arab CSR has focused on the perceptions of managers and has utilized case studies, interviews, and observation. Future case research might help determine who the envisaged audiences in fact are for Arab CSR reporting, who makes decisions concerning CSR reporting, and when and how decisions to invoke Islam are made. In addition, the specific motivations for and perceptions of CSR initiatives towards women should be a fruitful area of research given their popularity with Arab firms.

However, future research should also incorporate studies of consumer behavior. Behavioral research could better elucidate how different audiences respond to religious references and particularly examine if Muslims respond differently than audiences of different religious affiliations. Differing levels of religiosity among respondents could also be measured to help determine if religiosity and not simply religion affects responses to CSR reporting. In addition, levels of religious literacy could be measured and compared to understanding of religious reference in CSR discourse. Future cross-cultural research could also help determine if different attitudes do in fact exist toward strategic CSR initiatives and the publicizing of CSR initiatives.

Participants at the 3rd Middle East CSR Summit held in Dubai concluded that CSR and CSR reporting in the Arab world would need to evolve to meet the expectations of international investors. Yet for this to be successful, Arab CSR must find a way to harmoniously integrate global business practices with the cultural and religious factors of the Middle East (Anonymous, 2006). Najeeb Mohammed Al-Ali, Executive Director of the Dubai Centre for Corporate Values, remarked, 'Giving to society is deep-rooted in Islamic tradition and a cornerstone of positive CSR. By bringing international and local companies together with government support, a model can be formed that will embrace local culture and international corporate standards' (2006). Our study captures at a point in time the already present influence of Islam in Arab CSR. It is possible that its influence will become even more apparent in the future, as Islamic tradition continues to be fused with Western conceptions of corporate social responsibility.

NOTE

1. All data come from the 'Beyond 20/20 World Development Indicators,' September 2009 edition. Most of the data are for 2007. However, as not all data are available for that year, some are for 2004, 2005 and 2006.

BIBLIOGRAPHY

Abu-Dawud, 'A partial collection of the ahadith in Sunun Abu-Dawud, 9:1660', www.usc.edu/schools/college/crcc/engagement/resources/texts/muslim/hadith/abudawud/009.sat.html, accessed 5 November 2010.

Al Faisaliah Group, www.alfaisaliah.com/index.asp?id=148, accessed 16 March 2009.

Al-Hassan Golley, Nawar (2004), 'Is feminism relevant to Arab women?', *Third World Quarterly*, **25** (3), 521–36.

Anonymous (2006), 'Islamic culture key to regional CSR model', *AMEinfo.com*. www.ameinfo.com/97560.html, accessed 2 April 2010.

Anonymous (2008a), 'Khalid Janahi participates in the World Economic Forum', *AME Info*, 15 October 2008.

Anonymous (2008b), 'Jordan Investment Trust and Imcan Brokerage and Trading present charity dinners in the blessed month of Ramadan', *Al-Ra'i*, 11 July.

Anonymous (2008c), '"Imana" delivers the first disbursement of food packages among needy families', *Ad-dustour*, 5 August.

Anonymous (2008d), 'Increased Giving Initiative kicks off the national program for social responsibility', *Emirates News Agency*, 2 August.

Anonymous (2008e), 'The Giving Hands Initiative was released as the first attack on treating the ills of the nation', *Emirates News Agency*, 22 June.

Anonymous (2008f), 'Schools and companies take students to the region of Mecca to attend the exhibition "Al-Faisal", *Asharq Al-Awsat*, 8 November.

Anonymous (2009), 'Saudi man divorces wife by text message', *Daily Telegraph*, http://www.telegraph.co.uk/news/worldnews/middleeastlsaudiarabia/5132754/Saudi-man-divorces-wife-by-text-message.html, accessed 1 April 2010.

Anonymous (2010), 'Middle East: CSR valued, but rarely reported', *Business and the Environment ISO 14000 Updates*, July, **21** (7), 6–8.

Atakan, M. and Eker, Tutku (2007), 'Corporate identity of a socially responsible university', *Journal of Business Ethics*, **76** (1), 55–68.

Bukhari, 'A collection of the ahadith in Sahih Bukhari 2:24:504', http://www.usc.edu/schools/college/crcc/engagement/resources/texts/muslim/hadith/bukhari/024.sbt.html, accessed 5 November 2010.

Fassin, Yves (2008), 'SMEs and the fallacy of formalizing CSR,' *Business Ethics: A European Review*, **17** (2), 364–78.

Ghariyaba, Abraham (2008), 'Corporate social responsibility: is it possible to found an organization for social accomplishment and development around the economic work of companies?', *Islam Today*, 8 September.

Giladi, Avner (2010), 'Orphans', in Jane Dammen McAuliffe (ed.), *Encyclopaedia of the Qur'an*, Leiden: Brill, http://www.brillonline.nl/subscriber/entry?entry=q3_SIM-00311, accessed 23 August 2010.

Harwazinski, Assia Maria (2010), 'Muhammad', in Kocku von Stuckrad (ed.), *The Brill Dictionary of Religion*, Leiden: Brill, http://www.brillonline.nl/subscriber/entry?entry=bdr_COM-00296, accessed 23 August 2010.

Hassan, Riaz (2005), 'On being religious: patterns of religious commitment in Muslim societies', *RSIS Working Papers*, No. 80, Singapore: Institute of Defense and Strategic Studies.

Jamali, Dima (2008), 'A stakeholder approach to corporate social responsibility: a fresh perspective into theory and practice', *Journal of Business Ethics*, **82**, 213–31.

Jamali, Dima and Ramez Mirshak (2007), 'Corporate social responsibility (CSR): theory and practice in a developing country context', *Journal of Business Ethics*, **72**, 243–62.

Jamali, Dima and Yusef Sidani (2008), 'Classical vs. modem managerial CSR perspectives: insights from Lebanese context and cross-cultural implications', *Business and Society Review*, **113** (3), 329–46.

Jamali, Dima and Tamar Keshishian (2009), 'Uneasy alliances: lessons learned from partnerships between businesses and NGOs in the context of CSR', *Journal of Business Ethics*, **84**, 277–95.

Jamali, Dima, Asem M. Safieddine and Myriam Rabbath (2008), 'Corporate governance and corporate social responsibility: synergies and interrelationships', *Corporate Governance: An International Review*, **16** (5), 443–59.

Jamali, Dima, Yusef Sidani and Khalil El-Asmar (2009a), 'A three country comparative analysis of managerial CSR perspectives: insights from Lebanon, Syria and Jordan', *Journal of Business Ethics*, **85** (2), 173–92.

Jamali, Dima, Mona Zanhour and Tamar Keshishian (2009b), 'Peculiar strengths and relational attributes of SMEs in the context of CSR', *Journal of Business Ethics*, **87** (3), 355–77.

Katsioloudes, Marios I. and Tor Brodtkorb (2007), 'Corporate social responsibility: an exploratory study in the United Arab Emirates', *SAM Advanced Management Journal*, **72** (4), 9–20.

Kochuyt, Thierry (2009), 'God, gifts and poor people: on charity in Islam', *Social Compass*, **56** (1), 98–116.

Kudu, http://www.corporate.kudu.com.sa/index.php?page=social, accessed 16 March 2009.

Kuwait Petroleum Company, http://www.kpc.com.kw/indexz.htm, accessed 16 March 2009.

Mackey, Sandra (2002), *The Saudis: Inside the Desert Kingdom*, New York: W.W. Norton.

Mahmoud, Ibrahim (2008), 'Study presented at the climate conference in Sanaa . . . Saudi management adopt new concepts in dealing with corporate social responsibility', *Dar al-Hayat*, 31 October.

Mohr, Lois A., Deborah J. Webb and Katherine E. Harris (2001), 'Do consumers expect companies to be socially responsible? The impact of corporate social responsibility on buying behavior', *Journal of Consumer Affairs*, **35** (1), 45–72.

National Bank of Kuwait, http://www.nbk.com, accessed 19 March 2009.

National Commercial Bank, http://www.alahli.comlcontent/csr.asp, accessed 16 March 2009.

OED (1989), 'Charity', *Oxford English Dictionary* (2nd edn), Oxford: Oxford University Press.

Orascom Telecom, http://www.otelecom.comlCSRlPrograms.aspx, accessed 15 March 2009.

Porter, Michael and Mark Kramer (2002), 'The competitive advantage of corporate philanthropy', *Harvard Business Review*, December 56–68.

Prothero, Stephen (2007), *Religious Literacy,* San Francisco: Harper.

Qur'an (2008), trans. Abdullah Yusuf Ali, New York: Tahrike Tarsile Qur'an, Inc.

Reporters Without Borders 'Press freedom index 2009', http://www.rsf.orglfr-classementl00l-2009.html, accessed 2 April 2010.

Rettab, Belaid, Anis Brik and Kamel Mellahi (2009), 'A study of management perceptions of the impact of corporate social responsibility on organisational performance in emerging economies: the case of Dubai', *Journal of Business Ethics*, **89** (3), 371–90.

Saad Group, http://www.saadgroup.comimainsite/DisplayInfo.aspx?pid=20&lang=en, accessed 16 March 2009.

SABIC, http://www.sabic.comlcorporate/en/ourcommitments/default.aspx, accessed 16 March 2009.

Saudi Oger, http://www.saudioger.comlcorp.html, accessed 16 March 2009.

Savola Group, http://www.savola.com/SavolaE/index.php, accessed 16 March 2009.

Sen, Sankar and C.B. Bhattacharya (2001), 'Does doing good always lead to doing better? Consumer reactions to corporate social responsibility', *Journal of Marketing Research (JMR)*, **38** (2), 225–43.

Siltaoja, Marjo (2009), 'On the discursive construction of a socially responsible organization', *Scandinavian Journal of Management*, **25**, 191–202.

Telecom Egypt, http://ir.telecomegypt.com.eg/csr.asp, accessed 15 March 2009.

Tsalikis, J. and Walfried Lassar (2009), 'Measuring consumer perceptions of business ethical behavior in two Muslim countries,' *Journal of Business Ethics*, **89**, 91–98.

Turker, Duygu (2009), 'How corporate social responsibility influences organizational commitment', *Journal of Business Ethics*, **89** (2), 189–204.

Wehr, Hans (1994), *The Hans Wehr Dictionary of Modern Written Arabic, Student Edition*, J.M. Cowan (ed.), 4th edn Ithaca: Spoken Language Services.

Williams, Geoffrey and John Zinkin (2010), 'Islam and CSR: a study of the compatibility between the tenets of Islam and the UN Global Compact', *Journal of Business Ethics*, **91**, 519–33.

World Bank (2009), 'Beyond 20/20 World Development Indicators', http://www.esds80.mcc.ac.uk, accessed 26 March 2010.

van de Ven, Bert (2008), 'An ethical framework for the marketing of corporate social responsibility', *Journal of Business Ethics*, **82** (2), 339–52.

Van Leeuwen, Theo and Ruth Wodak (1999), 'Legitimizing immigration control: a discourse-historical analysis', *Discourse Studies*, **1**, 83–118.

Zain, http://www.zain.com/muse/obj/portal, accessed 16 March 2009.

Zain Commercial, http://www.youtube.com/watch?v=cBOf_SJtmhk, accessed 4 November 2010.

Zorzopulos, Santiago (2006), 'Corporate social responsibility in the United Arab Emirates: a preliminary assessment', Dubai Ethics Resource Center.

Zysow, A. (2010), 'Zakat', in P. Bearman et al. (eds), *Encyclopaedia of Islam*, Second Edition, Leiden: Brill Online, http://www.brillonline.nl/subscriber/entry?entry=islam_COM-1377.

17 Exploring marketing strategies for Islamic spiritual tourism

Farooq Haq and Ho Yin Wong

INTRODUCTION

Business and sociology researchers are showing increased interest in spirituality and related issues (Pesut, 2003; Hill, 2002; Cimino and Lattin, 1999; Konz and Ryan, 1999). The rediscovery of spirituality as a cure for humanity's ills has been credited to the rise in commercialism and individualism in almost all societies of today's world (Kale, 2004; Piedmont and Leach, 2002; Lewis and Geroy, 2000). This global change and attention to spirituality has been appreciated and embraced by various industries (Mitroff and Denton, 1999). For example, the tourism industry has welcomed this growth of interest in spirituality (Tilson, 2005; Mitroff and Denton, 1999; Cohen, 1972 and 1992).

Spirituality and related issues are also gaining significance among Muslim communities around the world (Azam, 2010; Francesconi, 2009; Rustom, 2008; Maneri, 2006). Increased curiosity about Islamic spirituality is evidenced in the study conducted by the Pew Global Organization (2005), which concluded that the majority of Muslims around the world were prouder of being called Muslims than of being nationals of a particular country. A shift towards religiosity and spiritual awareness among young Muslims residing in different countries is noticeable (Alserhan, 2010; Azam, 2010; Poynting and Mason, 2006). Young Muslims are showing interest in various facets of Islamic spirituality, including tourism.

As a branch of tourism marketing, spiritual tourism marketing has started to attract attention from academia and business practitioners. Some empirical studies have examined the role of promotional campaigns in spiritual tourism (Tilson, 2005), some have tried to understand the motivations and experiences of Western tourists visiting a particular place (Sharpley and Sundaram, 2005), and some have explored the impact of spiritual tourism on a community's economy (Tilson, 2001). In addition a few conceptual studies have investigated the role of spirituality in tourism marketing (Li and Petrick, 2008; Kale, 2004; Buhalis, 2000; Redfoot, 1984). Despite some progress in spiritual tourism marketing research, it is still in its infancy. As suggested by Kale (Kale, 2004, p. 93), 'as of now, our understanding of the demand and supply patterns associated with the spiritual needs of consumers remains fairly rudimentary'. Similarly, researchers have even argued that tourism marketing, an important research area, remains largely unexplored; the lack of empirical research in the area has been noted (Li and Petrick, 2008; Buhalis, 2000; Riege and Perry, 2000). Therefore, there is a need to study spiritual tourists' buying decisions in order to provide them with an appropriate combination of tourism products and services.

The purpose of this chapter is to examine what fundamental issues affect spiritual tourists' buying decisions. It discusses the global emergence of marketing of Islamic products and services, with particular focus on spiritual tourists' destination selection and buying motivations, followed by a presentation of the research methodology and findings.

SPIRITUAL TOURISM: BACKGROUND

Cohen (1972) is known as a pioneer who studied various dimensions of tourism; he presented religion, spirituality and the pilgrimage as significant phenomena in tourism. Similarly, Mitroff and Denton (1999) stressed the growing significance of spirituality in daily life and suggested that traveling was a significant form of spiritual expression or identity. Cohen (1992) separated the pilgrimage experience into the popular and the formal. The formal pilgrimage represents the pilgrim's motives to fulfill religious commitments, while the popular pilgrimage is identified with the non-religious, but with personal development and wellness-oriented goals (Cohen 1992). Cohen's studies present a classification of religious tourists and pilgrims and their motivation for traveling; his research did not focus on the factors that influence the decision-making by travelers for religious/spiritual tourism or pilgrimages.

The literature provides a definition of a spiritual tourist that is adopted in this chapter: 'someone who visits a specific place out of his/her usual environment, with the intention of spiritual meaning and/or growth, without overt religious compulsion, which could be religious, non-religious, sacred or experiential in nature, but within a Divine context, regardless of the main reason for travelling' (Haq and Jackson, 2009, p. 145). This definition covers tourists who visit sacred places and events seeking a Divine presence, even without classifying themselves as followers of a religion. There are many people, for example belonging to the New Age groups, who call themselves non-religious, but believe in God, a High Spirit or a Supreme Being (Digance, 2003; Tucker, 2002).

The above mentioned definition of a spiritual tourist could be used to identify a Muslim spiritual tourist as someone who travels for his or her spiritual development by seeking closeness with Allah (the Arabic word for God). For example, *hajj* is compulsory for Muslims who are capable of making the journey to Mecca, but many *hajjis* (people who have performed the *hajj* pilgrimage) have indicated that their intention for *hajj* was not to fulfill the religious obligation but to seek proximity to Allah, thereby qualifying them as spiritual tourists (Haq and Jackson, 2009). This definition lays a foundation for us to explore further Muslim spiritual tourists' buying decisions.

Islamic Spiritual Tourism

Muslims are recognized as the most rapidly growing religious group in the world (Catholic News Service, 2008; Poynting and Mason, 2006). Among other religious practices, they also constitute the largest spiritual tourism market, which includes the pilgrimages to Mecca known as *hajj* and *umra*. The current research in this area advocates that pilgrimage and religious tourism are subsets of spiritual tourism (Finney et al., 2009; Geary, 2008; Rountree, 2002).

Spiritual travels and tourism in Islam can be divided into three types: the *hajj/umra, rihla* and *ziyara* (Timothy and Iverson, 2006; Bhardwaj, 1998; Kessler, 1992). *Hajj* is the essential, if viable, visit for all Muslims to the holy city of Makkah. A Muslim can under-take the spiritual trip of *umra* any time during the year, but he/she can perform *hajj* only during the specific dates of 9th and 10th of the month of *Dhul-Hijja* (Haq and Jackson, 2009; Clingingsmith et al., 2008). A Muslim's spiritual journey in search of knowledge, commerce, health or research has been defined as the *rihla* (Kessler, 1992). Famous Muslim travelers such as Ibn Battuta are renowned around the world for their *rihla,* which has motivated many other Muslim spiritual tourists (Morgan, 2001). The spiritual journeys of Muslims visiting the mausoleums, mosques or monasteries belonging to spiritual Muslims of the past are called *ziyara* (Timothy and Iverson, 2006; Bhardwaj, 1998; Kessler, 1992).

Ziyara has been categorized into two kinds of spiritual travels. First are the journeys to meet Islamic religious and spiritual scholars, to attend Islamic festivals, events, seminars or gatherings, or to follow in the footsteps of the prophets, sufis and spiritual celebrities (Bhardwaj, 1998). Second are journeys to holy places in search of spirituality to improve their quality of life (Timothy and Iverson, 2006; Bhardwaj, 1998). An example of the first type of *ziyara* is the *tabligh*, which is gaining popularity among young and professional Muslims around the world (Sikand, 2006; Timothy and Iverson, 2006; Bhardwaj, 1998). Sikand (2006) explained *tabligh* as a practice of Muslim men who visit and reside in dif-ferent mosques in different geographic locations, where they meet with local Muslims and teach them about Islam and its spiritual practices. The *tabligh* groups organize annual *ijtima* (get-togethers) where Muslim men meet and stay in a large mosque for three days to learn and teach Islamic spirituality and practice Islamic brotherhood and equality. The annual *ijtima* in Pakistan is held in Raiwind where more than two million Muslims meet. Similar travels, but *ijtima* on a lesser scale, are organized during Easter holidays in the Australian cities of Sydney, Melbourne, Brisbane and Perth.

Another example of the first type of *ziyara* is the recent development in Muslim spiritual tourism of various international festivals, seminars and conferences that are being organized to draw Muslims together to integrate their scholarly, spiritual and commercial abilities (Haq and Wong, 2010; Raj and Morpeth, 2007). These events attract Muslims from diverse backgrounds to travel, attend and participate in the latest self-created spiritual destinations. The numerous Islamic Trade and Travel Expos, *Halal* Product Expos, Muslim youth or women's seminars and Sufi symposia are a few of the many examples to be noted. In this study, any Muslim, on any kind of travel (*hajj, umra, rihla* or *ziyara*); with the intention of spiritual development and connection with Allah, is considered as a spiritual tourist.

Tourism Marketing

An examination of the literature on tourism marketing has identified three perspectives: firstly, consumer-oriented, secondly, competitor-oriented and thirdly, trade-oriented (Li and Petrick, 2008; Buhalis, 2000; Riege and Perry, 2000). With the purpose of this chapter in mind, we adopted the consumer-oriented perspective, which focuses on individual or groups of tourists, their behaviours and attitudes. The consumer-oriented approach for tourism marketing focuses on the destinations and motivation of tourists, and factors affecting their decision making (Poria et al., 2004; Buhalis, 2000; Chon and Olsen, 1990). Understanding tourists' buying decisions is a prime issue in tourism marketing.

There has also been broadly based research into tourists' motivations in destination choice, mode of travel, expectations, information sources used and the effect of socio-demographic characteristics on motivation (Poria et al., 2004). Destination research, theoretical and applied, has been embraced by tourism marketers. While destinations are interwoven with the formation of values, beliefs and habits, people for whom they play the primary role are in the minority (Poria et al., 2004; Buhalis, 2000). Pilgrimage and religious tourism have a religious dogma motivation, though people also travel to religious destinations for other motives, such as education, knowledge and awareness (Andriotis, 2009; Cochrane, 2009; Finney et al., 2009; Cohen, 1992). Destinations linked to Islamic spiritual tourism are not only religious places, but they include Islamic events and gatherings where people feel spiritually fulfilled (Haq and Wong, 2010). The review of the literature on Muslim journeys categorizes spiritual tourism as a pilgrimage and a religious practice depending upon the intention of the tourist.

A number of studies indicate the different motivations of tourists to select a place or an event for their tours. Moutinho (1993) offered a comprehensive model to study consumer behavior of tourists and concluded that personality, culture, social class, reference groups, and families play important roles in motivating tourists to make tourism decisions. Legoherel (1998) discovered that financial costs and number of travelers are the key factors. The role of media has been described as the fundamental tool to turn any tourism destination into a business success (Morrison, 2002; Poria et al., 2004). Tourism research conducted by Morrison (2002), Poria et al. (2004), Legoherel (1998) and Moutinho (1993), studied different aspects of tourists' behavior and motivation, but they did not focus on Muslim spiritual tourists.

In spite of the extant literature trying to understand the buying decisions of tourists and pilgrims, very limited studies have specifically explored the Islamic spiritual tourists' buying decisions. This study attempts to fill this gap in the literature by providing empirical evidence about such decisions. The guiding research question was: what are the issues affecting Islamic spiritual tourists' buying decisions?

METHODOLOGY

A qualitative methodology was considered appropriate because of the exploratory nature of the research. The ontology of critical realism was embraced to conduct this study and report the findings. Critical realism takes the view that while there are multiple perspectives and 'realities' in the environment, and in the minds of the researchers and the participants, it is necessary for the authors to take a 'critical' position in terms of doing everything possible to increase the objectivity and scholarship within the research (Pegues, 2007; Lincoln and Guba, 2003; Perry et al., 1999).

The research problem was addressed by conducting face-to-face interviews with Muslim spiritual tourists residing in Australia and Pakistan, since tourism marketing could be best understood by getting the insights directly from the tourists. Only Muslim spiritual tourists residing in Australia and Pakistan were included in this study; a balance among the respondents was sought according to gender, social status and educational background.

There are three main reasons that we chose these two countries. Firstly, non-probability sampling is suitable for exploratory studies (Lincoln and Guba, 2003; Cavana et al. 2001). Considering the exploratory nature of this study, samples from the two countries would enrich the information collected. Secondly, an empirical study previously used Australian and Pakistani samples to explore their differences from the strategic tourism point of view (Haq and Jackson, 2009). The findings suggest that there are differences between these two groups of samples. Thirdly, Australia is a majority-Christian country whereas Pakistan is a majority-Muslim country; comparing and contrasting the responses from the samples of these two countries should provide insightful ideas.

Individuals who were requested to participate in this research were qualified according to preset criteria: if they fitted into the definition of spiritual tourists provided previously; if they accepted themselves as Muslim spiritual tourists; and finally, if they consented to be interviewed.

Convenience and purposeful sampling methods, supplemented by the snowballing technique as the study progressed, were used to identify interviewees (Alam, 2005; Browne, 2005; Stake, 2005). Initially, religious organizations and groups were asked to identify Muslim spiritual tourists in Australia and Pakistan. After some initial questions with the interested candidates, the respondents were then qualified or not, according to the set sampling criteria.

The focus in this study was on the richness, and not the quantity, of the data. Hence the sample size was determined using the criterion of 'saturation:' the position where the collected data became saturated after achieving a thorough understanding of diverse experiences related to the research issue (Gibbs et al., 2007; Alam, 2005). When additional research participants could not provide any new knowledge leading to the recognition of further ideas, the data collection process was saturated, thereby fixing the size of the sample (Lincoln and Guba, 2003). The final sample consisted of 36 respondents, 16 from Pakistan and 20 from Australia. Five of the Australian Muslims were recent converts to Islam.

The five research questions provided in Appendix 1 were used as a guideline in the interviews to probe the respondents' experience and understanding with respect to spiritual tourism. The transcripts were read many times by both authors for the cross-case content analysis, searching for the thoughts expressed by the respondents relevant to the discussion in this chapter (Stepchenkova et al., 2009). The content analysis used data coding that was steered by the research questions and which directed the authors towards insights pertaining to the overall research objective (Alam, 2005; Miles and Huberman, 1994). The initial coding of the two sets of transcript information from the interviews with respondent groups in both countries was undertaken as separate exercises for the cross-case content analysis, as suggested by Miles and Huberman (1994). However, the same procedure was applied to both groups and memos were placed on the transcripts to identify strong ideas emerging from the interviews regarding the marketing of Islamic spiritual tourism.

Australian respondents were coded as A1 to A20, while the Pakistani respondents were coded as P1 to P16. The details of each respondent are provided in Appendix 2. The content of the interview transcripts that was related to the spiritual tourists' buying decisions was highlighted and analyzed separately to get insights that could help to solve the research problem. The analytical framework for cross-case analysis presented by Miles and Huberman (1994) was adopted; responses of spiritual tourists to the research questions in both countries were placed separately and linked to the five emerging themes of this study. Investigator triangulation was adopted: the first author analyzed the data; the second author conducted a separate analysis; then the emerging insights were triangulated to reach the analysis outcomes (Alam, 2005; Yin, 1994). This approach facilitated the emergence of ideas reflecting upon the Islamic tourism buying behavior decisions.

RESEARCH FINDINGS

The findings of this study emerging from the data analysis are illustrated by quotations. Three emerging themes, Islamic spiritual tourism destinations, motivation for travelers, and their decision making constructs, are discussed separately below. The themes are extracted from the data analysis based on the respect given to the direct words of spiritual tourists interviewed in both countries.

The Islamic Spiritual Tourism Destinations

The content analysis indicated that the favorite destinations for Muslim spiritual tourists in both countries were the holy cities of Mecca and Medina. Australian respondents mentioned Jerusalem as well; because of visa restrictions in Israel, Pakistani tourists were precluded from visiting Jerusalem. Muslim spiritual tourists preferred to visit sites signifying the past and present glorification or spirituality of Islam. Some interviewees talked about Sufi Rumi and their desire to visit his shrine in Konya (Turkey), or the shrines of other Sufi scholars in India and Pakistan, such as Ali Hajveri in Lahore (Rustom, 2008; Huda, 2000).

> I am always ready to visit the tomb of the Prophet in Medina, tomb of Sufi Rumi in Konya, and the tomb of Sufi Hajveri in Lahore. (A10)

> I try to visit every mosque in any new city I visit, I feel as the guest of Allah in any mosque. (A16)

> If I cannot visit the Kaaba in Mecca, then the tomb of Daata ji (Sufi Hajveri) is my beloved place. (P1)

> For me the best place to be close to Allah is His house in Makkah. (P8)

Islamic events tied to specific destinations and religious obligations were also valued by the interviewees in both countries. Most respondents aspired to visit Mecca and Medina during the *hajj* event or at least during the month of Ramadan. Many Australian respondents in this group referred to various Australian events that were organized by Australian Muslim societies and organizations. Some of them discussed their personal or family plans to visit such events, considered to be important for Muslim unity and community building in Australia.

> If possible I try to participate in the Open Days of all mosques anywhere in Australia. (A7)

I feel spiritually fulfilled to travel to Brisbane to join the CresWalk [annual walk organized by Muslim Youth Group of Brisbane where all are invited to meet Muslims and learn their faith] organized by local young Muslim brothers and sisters. (A4)

My family and I love to go to both Eid festivals [Eid-ul-Fitr and Eid-ul-Adha] in Sydney. I am happy meeting other Muslims. My wife enjoys shopping and the kids like to play. (A14)

I wish I could be in Mecca in every Ramadan. (P5)

I try my best to attend the *ijtima* in Raiwind every year. (P16)

The respondents in both countries expressed religious loyalty and described Mecca and Medina as primary spiritual destinations and Sufi shrines as the secondary destinations. Comparatively, Australians were observed to be keener to locate or organize new venues to practice spiritual tourism. Similarly, the Australians evidently thought of more occasions based on national holidays for spiritual tourism, compared to Pakistanis who followed conventional sacred days based on the Islamic calendar.

Motivation for Muslim Spiritual Tourists

The respondents in both countries pointed out self-identity or self-recognition as one of the key motivations in spiritual tourism. Self-identity, their understanding about who they were, developed their sense of belonging, while self-recognition indicated their individual needs for self-fulfillment from spiritual tourism. In their search for self-identity, Australian Muslim spiritual tourists were vocal about the lack of service quality or poor attitude of the people involved. The Pakistani respondents expressed more patience and tolerance towards the challenges faced and unfriendly attitudes of the people involved with Islamic spiritual tourism.

Whatever I do, my identity as a professional Muslim woman is very important for me, [with a smile] that is why I always wear my *hijab* (head-scarf). (A1)

I consider my own spiritual tourism for self-recognition, but I teach the students in my college that self-identity is a key issue faced by the Muslims in Australia. (A10)

How can I purchase a ticket to Mecca from someone who is not a righteous Muslim? (A3) [the informant saw the Hajj agent smoking and decided not to buy the package from him]

I recognized myself when I first time went to the *ijtima* in Raiwind. (P1)

I recognized the truth of life when I saw the Kaaba in Mecca. (P6)

Islamic spirituality begins with forgiveness, I never mind any troubles or mistreatment during my *hajj* or *umra*. (P11)

The Australian respondents specified their quest for self-identity and Muslim unity that could be achieved through spiritual tourism. Since most Australian Muslims were born overseas, they feel that they have lost their identity. Even Muslims born in Australia, including the recent converts to Islam, had the impression of being different from others. Most respondents expressed their goal from Islamic spiritual tourism as finding self-identity. For example, the majority of Australians who went to *hajj* claimed the strengthening of their self-identity from *hajj* (Haq and Jackson, 2009). On the contrary, Pakistanis were observed to be more enthusiastic about gaining self-recognition. They perceived an invaluable increase in their personal well-being derived from their spiritual tourism. Most respondents looked forward to spiritual tourism as a means of attaining self-recognition.

Among the motivating factors for Islamic spiritual tourism, the source of the spirituality was recognized, which was based on faith or knowledge sought by tourists. Many interviewees described themselves as Muslim spiritual tourists because they perceived themselves as travelling to develop their spirituality, motivated by their knowledge or faith, or improving their knowledge, or strengthening their faith. It was noticed from the data analysis that Pakistani respondents referred more to faith as a motivating factor, compared to the Australians who found more inspiration to travel as Muslims in order to gain knowledge.

For Muslims faith is the theory and knowledge is the practice of Islam. (A9)

I have travelled to mosques in every continent of this planet to gain knowledge, which has boosted my faith in Islam. (A13)

Not sure about faith – I am in search of spiritual knowledge that takes me to various places. (A19)

Knowledge develops the faith and there would be no need for knowledge if there was no faith. (A4)

I went to *hajj* to improve my faith; my knowledge could be improved by watching the *hajj* on TV. (P6)

I think faith and learning are similar from an Islamic perspective and they both can be improved by travelling, that is why the Holy Qur'an advises us to travel in the land of the Lord to see His blessings and learn from them. (P8)

I think in spiritual affairs, theory is knowledge but faith is the practice, my life and travelling is a practice not a theory. (P10)

I think spirituality or connection with God starts with faith and develops with education, and the best school for education is travelling. (P12)

The data analysis indicated that interviewees in both countries agreed about their Islamically based motivation. However, Australian Muslims expressed more motivation from knowledge about Islamic spirituality, while Pakistanis thought their faith in Islam was the major inspiration. Australian Muslims reported being in a quest for self-identity; Pakistanis were in search of self-recognition from spiritual tourism.

Factors Influencing Decision Making for Islamic Spiritual Tourism

The influence of historical and religious characters on Islamic spiritual tourism was apparent. The love and devotion towards the Prophet of Islam, Muhammad, identified him as the opinion leader for the Muslim spiritual tourists in both countries. The Pakistani respondents also referred to their love for various Islamic scholars and Sufis.

> Like most Muslims, Prophet Muhammad is by far my favorite personality and I try to copy all his actions and travel in his footsteps. (A9)

> After becoming a Muslim I have been most impressed by the personality and travels of Rumi; his poetry was written in the thirteenth century and still has impact. (A16)

> Prophet Muhammad is my role model and I would not have been to *hajj* if he had not been there. (P10)

> Sufi Rumi is probably my favorite personality not only due to his spiritual writings but also his diverse personality that is known globally and his philosophy that applies to all times. (P14)

The respondents in both countries agreed that Prophet Muhammad was their major opinion leader, followed by some Muslim Sufis and scholars. Likewise, almost all interviewees talked about the significance of the spiritual destination service providers, the people who were serving them or guiding them. A key difference between the two groups of interviewees was that Muslims in Pakistan placed little importance on the tourism operator who booked their spiritual travels. By contrast, Australian Muslims commented on the effect of the behavior and attitude of the tourism operators. The majority of Pakistani respondents refrained from complaining about any aspect of the service during their spiritual tourism, including the behavior and capability of the people.

Usually the site veneration attaches itself to the person who is a guide or a tour assistant telling the tourists about the historical and spiritual depth of the place. However a number of Pakistani Muslim tourists (P2, P5, P11) mentioned their disappointment at various Sufi shrines in Pakistan where the local guide could not provide details regarding the writings and the public spiritual impact of the particular Sufi. Some of the respondents (P5, P15, P16) also raised their concerns about the inadequate linguistic skills of the people who represented the place. Meanwhile, the Australians (A5, A6, A15, A19) gave examples of travels to destinations in Pakistan, Iraq, Jordan, Egypt and Turkey, where the local guides could not provide the relevant information in 'proper' English.

The financial cost involved in Islamic spiritual tourism was an important theme that emerged in this study. Most respondents discussed issues related to financial costs; however, many did not acknowledge that it affected their decision making.

> Islam teaches economic management; hence I work on the travel costs and find the best prices for my spiritual travels. (A3)

> I learnt from my spiritual visit to Mecca that service quality is irrelevant, but the financial costs need to be carefully managed. (A18)

> Money is not a problem [regarding spiritual tourism], for me the cost is the sacrifice and value is the quality of faith. (P13)

> Regarding my spiritual journeys, all money related issues are irrelevant. (P9)

The Pakistani respondents did not refer to pricing and costs as critical factors involved in their spiritual tourism decisions, though only a few mentioned that they were not concerned with financial costs. It is likely that a cultural embargo on overtly discussing money matters and linking them to religious affairs created reluctance to mention price and cost among them. By contrast, the Australian respondents were specific and outspoken about their preference for low cost spiritual tourism packages. Muslim spiritual tourists in Australia gave considerable priority to low-priced spiritual tourism products in their decision making. They also perceived that Islam stressed good economic and financial management and that economic prudence should be reflected in spiritual tourism decision making.

All interviewees in both countries expressed their thoughts on the role and influence of media in their spiritual tourism. They mentioned the importance of Islamic literature, in the Qur'an and *hadith*, Sufi poetry, and modern day electronic media, motivating them to engage in spiritual tourism. Communication channels such as radio, print media, the Internet and public relations were favored by all interviewees. Australian Muslims did not rely on local television since they found few specific programs that they could watch. In Australia, a fortnightly newspaper called the *Muslim Times* is published in major cities and is considered reliable in communicating about Islamic spiritual tourism. Local Islamic radio stations in major Australian cities are also popular since they broadcast Islamic programs for all age groups, for example, channel 92.1FM in Sydney. The Internet is commonly used by Australians to search and book spiritual tourism packages. Pakistanis watched and listened to religious programs and documentaries on TV and radio, which motivated them towards tourism.

> The spiritual pleasure and motivation to travel from the poetry of Sufi Rumi or Hajveri cannot be matched by a TV program or a website. (A1)

> Now I am getting motivated to travel by reading the Qur'an and following its explanations on the Internet. (A18)

> For me the Holy Qur'an is the best medium for any spiritual guidance. (P9)

> A virtual tour on the Internet about a spiritual destination is a must before actually visiting the location. (P15)

Table 17.1 is a summary of the findings with regard to the differences between the Australian and Pakistani Muslim spiritual tourists in terms of the emerging themes.

Although there were differences between the two national groups of interviewees, there were some common themes emerging from both samples as presented in Table 17.2.

DISCUSSION

This study makes a contribution to the literature by providing new empirical evidence in relation to spiritual tourism marketing. Differences in the cultures of Australia and Pakistan, the countries from which the participant sample was drawn, have been reported (Franke et al., 1991). Documenting the differences and similarities with respect

Table 17.1   Differences between Australian and Pakistani Muslim spiritual tourists

Emerging themes	Findings from Australian Muslim spiritual tourists	Findings from Pakistani Muslim spiritual tourists
Islamic destinations and events	Jerusalem as a famous destination	Did not refer to Jerusalem (due to visa restrictions from Israel)
	Australian Mosques at Open Days, Islamic charity events and multi-faith gatherings	Did not mention any multi-faith gatherings
	Input from tourism operator preferred if from similar ethnic background	Tourism operator is not relevant to spiritual tourism decisions
	Expect fair treatment and justice during spiritual tourism	Not concerned with treatment, more forgiving during spiritual tourism
Financial costs	Prefer low-priced packages	No pricing preferences
	Cut costs using tour wholesalers and agents, Internet distribution	Costs determined by retail travel agents, no Internet booking opportunities
	Comprehensive travel packages required	Partial packages with limited services required
The role of media	No influence from TV	Positive influence from TV
	Paper media preferred: Holy Books or publications such as 'Muslim Times'	Paper media not preferred, except the Holy Books
Self-identity and recognition	Seek self-identity and a sense of belonging	Seek self-recognition and knowledge of the inner self
	Vocal about their issues and ready to complain about the quality of services and attitude of locals	Hesitant to discuss any problems arising during spiritual tourism. Did not complain as part of the sacrifice during the spiritual tourism
Faith and knowledge	Seeking knowledge from spiritual tourism	Seeking faith from spiritual tourism
	Good knowledge can strengthen faith	Pure faith can develop knowledge

Table 17.2   Similarities between Australian and Pakistani Muslim spiritual tourists

Emerging themes	Findings from the Australian and Pakistani Muslim spiritual tourists
Opinion leaders and other people	Prophet Muhammad and some Muslim Sufis and scholars
Islamic destinations and events	Mecca, Medina and some overseas Sufi shrines
	Travel for *tabligh*
	Service providers and tour guides at destination are significant
The role of media	Use of the name of Islam, brotherhood and Prophet Muhammad
	Reliance on the Internet as a promotion tool
	Influenced by the Holy Books

to attitudes to spiritual tourism across these two reportedly different countries is a significant outcome from this research study. The findings of this research identified a distinctive product and illustrated the development of a marketing strategy.

The Muslim spiritual tourists displayed strong loyalty in their travels to the preferred spiritual destination irrespective of the costs. Most Australian participants talked about their visits or future plans to see the mosques and Islamic centers in different Australian cities to maintain their spiritual relationships. They were happy to travel to Open Days organized in Australian mosques. They also considered it to be their duty to attend various multi-faith festivals and conferences to represent Islam and Muslims. The Pakistani responses were more traditional in site selection and preferred conventional destinations such as Mecca, local *ijtima* or famous Sufi shrines. Most Sufi shrines have annual festivals to celebrate the anniversary of the Sufi, which have a high level of attendance from the devotees.

Spiritual tourists in both countries were loyal in buying spiritual tourism products in their own ways. Pakistanis reported that their families as a customer group, which included multiple generations, were accustomed to purchasing their *hajj* and *umra* packages from a particular operator. The respondents in Australia also had a loyal attitude towards their travel agents. However spiritual tourists tend to buy from operators who are of the same country of origin as themselves. For example, Pakistani tourists bought from Pakistani operators, Turks bought from Turkish operators and Indonesians bought from Indonesian operators (Kotler and Gertner, 2002).

All respondents indicated their attraction towards messages promoting closeness with Allah, obedience to Prophet Muhammad and the Islamic brotherhood. Most participants showed solemn devotion towards Prophet Muhammad and his words. The Australian Muslims further stressed that marketing communications need to indicate the development of their self-identity, discovering themselves and knowing who they are through spiritual tourism. Meanwhile, Pakistani Muslim spiritual tourists preferred the communication message to emphasize achieving self-recognition and Muslim unity through spiritual tourism.

There is little trust among Pakistanis in booking and paying online for tourism products. The economic prosperity and visa access of Australian Muslims who find the spiritual destinations appealing allows them to easily make up their minds to visit these destinations.

The Australian respondents expressed satisfaction from the tour wholesalers who were reported to be well organized in their business. In order to capitalize on the exclusive market of *hajj* and *umra*, the operators need to be able to get a license to act for the Saudi Arabian Embassy and adopt the role of tour wholesalers and travel agents simultaneously. The distribution channels for Pakistani Muslim spiritual tourists are always through retail travel agents, as no dedicated spiritual tourism agents or agencies exist.

MANAGERIAL IMPLICATIONS

The findings of this study lay a foundation for tourism operators to understand their customers that in turn can assist them to develop an appropriate marketing strategy. To develop a consistent marketing strategy, products designed to target Muslim spiritual tourists need to focus on the similarities and differences identified between Australian and Pakistani Muslim spiritual tourists. The Pakistani tourism operators need to leverage the findings about self-recognition, individual and family spiritual education, character development and closeness to Allah when targeting the spiritual tourist. Within Australia, the marketing strategy that spiritual tourism operators need to adopt for Muslims is to position their offerings as a means of supporting the achievement of the objectives of self-identity, unity and integration among Muslims. Therefore, a focus on the development of family spirituality and self-identity, along with Muslim unity, is the key to effective marketing communications. Likewise, the providers of public and private spiritual tourism should be careful in their selection of local guides. The training of guides should include the history, spiritual depth and impact of the site. The guides should also be fluent in different languages, particularly the languages commonly spoken by visiting spiritual tourists.

The Australian tourism operators could partner with Australian Muslim societies and organizations to promote programs for more, similar, events throughout the country. The partnerships could facilitate wider promotion of the events and provide access to a combined usage of resources (Wuyts et al., 2009). Such events could be collectively promoted as milestones along the road leading towards Muslim unity and cohesiveness and the operators could offer reasonably priced bundled packages for individuals and families to travel to and attend such events.

The maintenance of public relations is vital for marketing Islamic spiritual tourism. Muslims have been recently targeted by media and the public in Muslim-minority countries. There have been some reports on the *hajj* as a ritualistic and orthodox exercise where Muslims practice extreme and violent measures by throwing stones in groups, causing stampedes, killing animals, and creating health problems (Ahmed et al., 2006). As pointed out by many interviewees, the media linking Islam to terrorism and violence have motivated Muslims to be more steadfast spiritually. They now travel more frequently to specific Islamic destinations, with the purpose of learning Islam and improving their inner selves. Tourism operators can turn negative publicity around to use it to encourage Muslims to travel more often to Mecca and other Islamic spiritual destinations.

CONCLUSIONS AND FUTURE RESEARCH

This study distinctively defined the concepts of Islamic spiritual tourism and Muslim spiritual tourists that have been overlooked in the extant literature. The Islamic spiritual tourism product has been defined as a combination of various types of religious travels and pilgrimage taken by Muslims for the past 1400 years. The unique nature of these definitions strengthens the theory of Islamic marketing and sheds light on a new area for valuable research into Islamic commerce and tourism, in specific, and tourism and marketing, in general.

The study contributes to theory by identifying the commonalities and differences of two groups of spiritual tourists' buying decisions. Understanding the spiritual tourists' underlying buying decisions can assist tourism operators to better deploy their marketing strategies. Key similarities and differences were observed for Islamic spiritual tourism in Australia and Pakistan based on the understanding and practices of the participants. Three major themes emerged from the data analysis: destinations, tourists' motivations and factors affecting tourists' decision making. These themes were based on sub-themes such as: opinion leaders, Islamic destinations and events, financial costs, self-identity and recognition, spirituality based on faith or knowledge and the role of media. The themes were studied and the similarities and differences between both samples were noted.

This chapter concludes that the Australian and Pakistani spiritual tourists are different. Consequently marketing strategies targeting these two groups of spiritual tourists should be adapted accordingly. Although future research is indicated to test the validity of the definitions offered, this study has contributed to Islamic marketing theory. Confirmatory research is required before the terminology adopted in this study is widely accepted. The efficacy of adapting the proposed marketing ideas for Islamic spiritual tourism globally should be evaluated in further studies. Different groups could be recognized among the Muslims in both countries, for example, followers of different sects in Pakistan, and migrants or converted Muslims in Australia. A future study to analyze the distinct behavior of such groups could be conducted to identify new insights in the area of Islamic spiritual tourism.

REFERENCES

Ahmed, Q.A., Y.M. Arabi and Z.A. Memish (2006), 'Health risks at Hajj', *Lancet*, **367** (1), 1008–15.

Alam, I. (2005), 'Fieldwork and data collection in qualitative marketing research', *Qualitative Market Research: An International Journal*, **8** (1), 97–112.

Alserhan, B.A. (2010), 'On Islamic branding: brands as good deeds', *Journal of Islamic Marketing*, **1** (2), 101–06.

Andriotis, K. (2009), 'Sacred site experience: a phenomenological study', *Annals of Tourism Research*, **36** (1), 64–84.

Azam, M. (2010), 'Religious behaviors in Pakistan: impact on social development', *Journal of Conflict and Peace Studies*, by Pakistan Institute for Peace Studies, **3** (3), 59–80.

Bhardwaj, S.M. (1998), 'Non-Hajj pilgrimage in Islam: a neglected dimension of religious circulation', *Journal of Cultural Geography*, **17** (2), 69–87.

Browne, K. (2005), 'Snowball sampling: using social networks to research non-heterosexual women', *International Journal of Social Research Methodology*, **8** (1), 47–60.

Buhalis, D. (2000), 'Marketing the competitive destination of the future', *Tourism Management*, **21** (1), 97–116.

Catholic News Service (2008), 'World has greater number of Muslims than Catholics', http://www.catholic.org/international/international_story.php?id=27384 (accessed 15 July 2008).

Cavana, R.Y., B.L. Delahaye and U. Sekaran (2001), *Applied Business Research: Qualitative and Quantitative Methods*, Milton: John Wiley and Son.

Chon, K.S. and M.D. Olsen (1990), 'Applying the strategic management process in the management of tourism organisations', *Tourism Management*, **11** (3), 206–13.

Cimino, R. and D. Lattin (1999), 'Choosing my religion', *American Demographics*, **21** (4), 60–65.

Clingingsmith, D., A.I. Kwaja and M. Kremer (2008), 'Estimating the impact of the Hajj: religion and tolerance in Islam's global gathering', Harvard Kennedy School, Faculty research working chapter series, http://ksgnotes1.harvard.edu/Research/wchapters.nsf/rwp/RWP08-02 (accessed 09 September 2008).

Cochrane, J. (2009), 'Spirits, nature and pilgrimage: the other dimension in Javanese domestic tourism', *Journal of Management, Spirituality and Religion*, **6** (2), 107–20.

Cohen, E. (1972), 'Towards a sociology of international tourism', *Social Research*, **39** (1), 164–82.

Cohen, E. (1992), 'Pilgrimage centre: concentric and excentric', *Annals of Tourism Research*, **18** (1), 33–50.

Digance, J. (2003), 'Pilgrimage at contested sites', *Annals of Tourism Research*, **30** (1), 160–77.

Finney, R.Z., R.A. Orwig and D.F. Spake (2009), 'Lotus-eaters, pilgrims, seekers, and accidental tourists: how different travelers consume the sacred and the profane', *Services Marketing Quarterly*, **30** (2), 148–73.

Francesconi, D. (2009), 'Sufism: a guide to essential reference resources', *Reference Services Review*, **37** (1), 112–24.

Franke, R.H., G. Hofstede and M.H. Bond (1991), 'Cultural roots of economic performance: a research note', *Strategic Management Journal*, **12** (1), 165–73.

Geary, G. (2008), 'Destination enlightenment: branding Buddhism and spiritual tourism in Bodhgaya, Bihar', *Anthropology Today*, **24** (3), 11–14.

Gibbs, L., M. Kealy, K. Willis, J. Green, N. Welch and J. Daly (2007), 'What have sampling and data collection got to do with good qualitative research?', *Australian and New Zealand Journal of Public Health*, **31** (6), 540–44.

Haq, F. and J. Jackson (2009), 'Spiritual journey to Hajj: Australian and Pakistani experience and expectations', *Journal of Management, Spirituality and Religion*, **6** (2), 141–56.

Haq, F., and H. Wong (2010), 'Spiritual tourism as a new strategy to market Islam: an exploratory study of Australian Muslims', *Journal of Islamic Marketing*, **1** (2), 136–48.

Hill, B.J. (2002), 'Review of: Tourism and Religion, by Boris Vukonic', *International Journal of Tourism Research*, **4** (4), 327–28.

Huda, Q. (2000), 'Celebrating death and engaging texts at Data Ganj Bakhsh's "Urs"', *Muslim World*, **90** (3–4), 377–94.

Kale, S.H. (2004), 'Spirituality, religion, and globalization', *Journal of Macromarketing*, **24** (2), 92–107.

Kessler, C.S. (1992), 'Review essay for "Pilgrim's progress: The travellers of Islam"', *Annals of Tourism Research*, **18** (1), 147–53.

Konz, G.N.P. and F.X. Ryan (1999), 'Maintaining an organizational spirituality: no easy task', *Journal of Organizational Change Management*, **12** (3), 200–10.

Kotler, P. and Gertner, D. (2002), 'Country as brand, products and beyonds: a place marketing and brand management perspective', *Journal of Brand Management*, **9** (4/5), 249–61.

Legoherel (1998), 'Toward a market segmentation of the tourism trade', *Journal of Travel and Tourism Marketing*, **7** (3), 19–39.

Lewis, J.S. and G.D. Geroy (2000), 'Employee spirituality in the workplace: a cross-cultural view for the management of spiritual employees', *Journal of Management Education*, **24** (5), 682–94.

Li, X. and J.F. Petrick (2008), 'Tourism marketing in an era of paradigm shift', *Journal of Travel Research*, **46** (3), 235–48.

Lincoln, Yvonna and Egon G. Guba (2003), 'Paradigmatic controversies, contradictions, and emerging confluences', in N.K. Denzin and Y.S. Lincoln (eds), *The Landscape of Qualitative Research*, California: Sage Publications, pp. 253–91.

Maneri, M. (2006), 'The philosophical fundamentals of belief in the mystical poetry of Rumi and Donne', *Religious Studies and Theology*, **25** (2), 137–60.

Miles, Matthew B. and A. Michael Huberman (1994), *Qualitative Data Analysis – A Source Book of New Methods*, 2nd edn, Sage, Newbury Park, CA.

Mitroff, Ian and Elizabeth Denton (1999), *A Spiritual Audit of Corporate America: A Hard Look at Spirituality, Religion, and Values in the Workplace*, California: Jossey-Bass Inc.

Morgan, D.O. (2001), 'Ibn Battuta and the Mongols', *Journal of the Royal Asiatic Society*, **11** (1), 1–11.

Morrison, Alastair M. (2002), *Hospitality and Travel Marketing*, 3rd edn, New York: Delmar Thomson Learning.

Moutinho, I.. (1993) 'Consumer behaviour in tourism', *European Journal of Marketing*, **21** (10), 5–44.

Pegues, H. (2007), 'Of paradigm wars: constructivism, objectivism, and postmodern stratagem', *Educational Forum*, **71** (4), 316–30.

Perry, C., A. Riege and L. Brown (1999), 'Realism's role among scientific paradigms in marketing research', *Irish Marketing Review*, **12** (2), 16–23.

Pesut, B. (2003), 'Developing spirituality in the curriculum: worldviews, intrapersonal connectedness, interpersonal connectedness', *Nursing and Health Care Perspectives*, **24** (6), 290–94.

Pew Global Organization (2005), 'How Muslims see themselves and Islam's role', Pew Global Attitudes Project, http://pewglobal.org/reports/display.php?PageID=813 (accessed 21 September 2007).

Piedmont, R.L. and M.M. Leach (2002), 'Cross-cultural generalizability of the spiritual transcendence scale in India', *American Behavioral Scientist*, **45** (12), 1888–1901.

Poria, Y., R. Butler and D. Airey (2004), 'Links between tourists, heritage, and reasons for visiting heritage sites', *Journal of Travel Research*, **43** (1), 19–28.

Poynting, S. and V. Mason (2006), 'Tolerance, freedom, justice and peace? Britain, Australia and anti-Muslim racism since 11 September 2001', *Journal of Intercultural Studies*, **27** (4), 365–91.

Raj, Razaq and Nigel D. Morpeth (2007), *Religious Tourism and Pilgrimage Festivals Management: An International Perspective*, Oxford: CABI Publishers.

Redfoot, D. (1984), 'Touristic authenticity, touristic angst, and modern reality', *Qualitative Sociology*, **7** (4), 291–309.

Riege, A.M. and C. Perry (2000), 'National marketing strategies in international travel and tourism', *European Journal of Marketing*, **34** (11/12), 1290–1305.

Rountree, K. (2002), 'Goddess pilgrims as tourists: inscribing the body through sacred travel', *Sociology of Religion*, **63** (4), 475–96.

Rustom, M. (2008), 'The metaphysics of the heart in the Sufi doctrine of Rumi, *Studies in Religion*, **37** (1), 3–14.

Sharpley, R., and P. Sundaram (2005), 'Tourism: A sacred journey? The case of Ashram tourism, India', *International Journal of Tourism Research*, **7** (3), 161–71.

Sikand, Y. (2006), 'The tablighi jama'at and politics: a critical re-appraisal', *Muslim World*, **96** (1), 175–95.

Stake, Robert E. (2005), 'Qualitative case studies', in N.K. Denzin and Y.S. Lincoln (eds), *Handbook of Qualitative Research*, Thousand Oaks, CA: Sage Publications, Inc, 443–66.

Stepchenkova, S., A.P. Kirilenko and A.M. Morrison (2009), 'Facilitating content analysis in tourism research', *Journal of Travel Research*, **47** (4), 454–69.

Tilson, D.J. (2001), 'Religious tourism, public relations and church-state partnerships', *Public Relations Quarterly*, **46** (3), 35–39.

Tilson, D.J. (2005), 'Religious-spiritual tourism and promotional campaigning: a church-state partnership for St. James and Spain', *Journal of Hospitality and Leisure Marketing*, **12** (1/2), 9–40.

Timothy, Dallen J. and Thomas Iverson (2006), 'Tourism and Islam: considerations of culture and duty', in D.J. Timothy and D.H. Olsen (eds), *Tourism, Religion and Spiritual Journeys*, New York: Routledge, pp. 186–205.

Tucker, J. (2002), 'New Age religion and the cult of the self', *Society*, **39** (2), 46–51.

Wuyts, S., P.C. Verhoef and R. Prins (2009), 'Partner selection in B2B information service markets', *International Journal of Research in Marketing*, **26** (1), 41–51.

Yin, Robert K. (1994), *Case Study Research: Design and Methods*, 2nd edn, Thousand Oaks: Sage Publications.

APPENDIX 1

The Research Questions Asked in the Interviews

The interviews with Muslim spiritual tourists focused around the following research questions:

RQ 1.   What do you understand by the term 'Islamic spiritual tourism?' Do you consider yourself as a Muslim spiritual tourist? Please elaborate why.

RQ 2.   As a Muslim spiritual tourist what do you think are the products of Islamic spiritual tourism: place and events? Which places and events have you travelled to as a spiritual tourist? Please discuss your experiences.

RQ 3.   What issues related to costs and convenience did you face when purchasing an Islamic spiritual tourism product?

RQ 4.   What type of promotion convinced you to purchase the spiritual tourism product? Please explain why.

RQ 5.   Please elaborate on the role and attitude of the people involved in delivering the Islamic spiritual tourism product.

APPENDIX 2

Demographic Profile of Australian Muslim Spiritual Tourists:

A1:   Young female with family, PhD student
A2:   Young and single, postgraduate student at university
A3:   Middle-aged businessman living with family
A4:   Young and single, graduate with a Masters degree
A5:   Young house manager with husband
A6:   Young house manager with family
A7:   Mature age with family, active in funds collection for mosques and organizing Islamic seminars for the Australian public, has been for *hajj.*
A8:   Mature age with wife, a medical practitioner and active in promoting relationships between various Australian faiths, has been for *hajj* and *umra.*
A9:   Mature age with family, a medical specialist, active in developing relationships between Muslims and Australians of other faiths, has been to Mecca
A10: Mature age with family, PhD from Al-Azhar University in Cairo, Imam in mosque and educationalist at an Islamic College, extensive spiritual tourism experience
A11: Young with family, Imam in a mosque, very active in organizing and presenting at multi-faith gatherings, has been for *hajj.*
A12: Mature age with family, a medical practitioner in Sydney, every year travels with his group to various cities within Australia for *tabligh.*
A13: Mature age with family, former cricket coach and now a Sydney business man, a regular *tabligh* group member
A14: Mature age with family, IT professional and businessman in Newcastle, a regular *tabligh* group member
A15: Young with family, businessman in Melbourne, *tabligh* group member
A16: Young and single, writer living on the Sunshine Coast, converted to Islam from Christianity/Hinduism/Buddhism, travels to all multi-faith gatherings
A17: Young businesswoman with husband, converted to Islam from Buddhism, has been for *umra* and visits multi-faith gatherings
A18: Young technician with family in Queensland, converted to Islam from Catholicism, active in relationship building among various Australian faiths
A19: Young with family, working on the Sunshine Coast, converted to Islam from Christianity and has travelled to many places to learn spiritual and cultural values of different people in Bali, Thailand and Japan
A20: Young with family, born in Japan, residing on the Sunshine Coast, converted to Islam from Buddhism/Christianity, travelled to many places to learn spiritual values of different people in Bali, Thailand and Japan

Demographic Profile of Pakistani Muslim Spiritual Tourists

P1:   Young and single, software engineer. Visits the Sufi shrine in Lahore
P2:   Young and single, vice-chairman of a private university. He has travelled to many countries and enjoys visiting local churches and temples for spiritual knowledge

P3: Young and married, software business owner. When gets a chance he visits holy sites of other religions for spiritual understanding

P4: Young and married, mother, manages her own software export company. She went for *hajj* twice, once with her father and then with her husband

P5: Young and married, Major in the Pakistani Army. Was a high-involvement spiritual tourist and voluntarily came for the interview after hearing about the research. Visits various Sufi shrines in Pakistan

P6: Young and married, open source specialist (IT). Travelled to many countries and went for *hajj*

P7: Middle aged, housewife, blind. She lived for a while in Dubai and went for *hajj*

P8: Middle aged, housewife. She lived for a while in the UK and has been for *hajj* and *umra*. She visited some churches and temples in the UK but did not feel any spiritual presence

P9: Middle aged, female doctor who lived and practiced in the US and recently moved back to Pakistan after her husband's death. She performed *hajj* and has been teaching Islamic faith practices for women

P10: Middle-aged, single, eye-specialist. Was a high-involvement spiritual tourist and came for the interview from another city after hearing about the research. Travelled for *hajj* many times and had a research and learning perspective in his spiritual tourism

P11: Retired diplomat, lived and worked in many countries. Supported inclusive spiritual tourism and also appreciated various religious sects that had different spiritual tourism destinations and perspectives.

P12: Middle-aged, married, professor, PhD from Japan. Appreciated temples and spirituality in Japan. Recently joined a university in Saudi Arabia to be closer to Mecca and Medina

P13: Middle-aged Minister of Sports of Pakistan. An educationist who had travelled to many countries and also been for *hajj*

P14: Young, single, female officer in the Ministry of Railways, travelled to many countries, visited many holy destinations, likes to be an independent Muslim woman; considers that pilgrims are extremists and spiritual tourists are moderates

P15: Middle-aged, single, banker and businessman living in Dubai. Believes in Islam but too busy for the daily practice of his religion, spiritual tourism is for self-actualization

P16: Young and married. Property business owner, loves nature and travels for nature. Went for *hajj* and to various religious and natural sites in Pakistan; considers visiting any natural site is spiritual tourism

18 A digital media approach to Islamic marketing
Mohamed El-Fatatry, Stephen Lee, Tariq Khan and Vili Lehdonvirta

INTRODUCTION

Around the world, digital media are taking hold as a key brand-marketing interface with consumers. Digital media reach across geographical and cultural barriers, opening opportunities in niche markets that could only be cost-effectively addressed as an invisible part of the wider audience by mass media channels. The personal use of digital media and the wealth of information available via the Internet are both an opportunity and a challenge for the corporate marketer. This is often because the messages and use of digital media require a significant change in the old push advertising model. The effective use of digital channels requires listening and being part of the conversations other people create. These are critical unexplored elements for many traditional advertisers and agencies. For an industry that is used to dominating and pushing its messages through one-way channels, using digital and particularly social media represents a completely new way of thinking. A solid digital strategy also represents a gateway to new markets such as the Muslim consumer.

The emerging Muslim consumer market, especially in regions with high Internet penetration, represents a prime example of a large untapped niche market that can be addressed with the effective use of digital media. The development of strategies to address this emerging multicultural market requires basic understanding both of the successful use of digital media and of how they apply to brand communication with Muslim consumers.

Digital channels have not changed the central concept of brand. The basic idea of 'commitment to brand' is still a central part of consumer purchasing behavior. According to research by John Story and Jeff Hess (2009) in the *Journal of Product and Brand Management*, '[c]ustomers' behaviors toward a brand change as they become committed to the brand. They shop less, consider fewer brands, and are willing to pay more . . . The implications of these results are that, when a brand does a great job of satisfying customers and building trust, commitment develops' (p. 240). This also 'increases the ethical burden on the brand' (p. 240). It requires the brand to be closer than ever to the values and needs of the consumer. Ethics framed in the teachings of the Islamic faith provide the backbone for the consumers' value system not only for their religious practices but for their lives. Combining the earlier Story and Hess research with our own current findings and cases, this chapter concludes that trust, personal connection, satisfaction and functional connection all lead to stronger and longer-lasting commitment from customers. Connecting with people through the ethical framework of their faith is a logical avenue to develop, but as Story and Hess note, it carries a higher responsibility to deliver value and quality.

The recognition and chance to gain the trust of the Muslim consumer leads to the question of cost-effective methods of addressing the market. The birth of the opportunity for brands to address the Muslim consumer starts from the core Internet trends that have unlocked the potential of many different niche groups. The Long Tail phenomenon is a concept introduced by Chris Anderson. The idea is based on the unlimited choice provided by Internet access that brings together groups of like-minded consumers who can be addressed at a very low cost (Anderson, 2006, p. 53). In application, this means that whether it is for products or information, even minimal demand is worth addressing, as the cost to do so is also nearly negligible. Anderson also argues that an unlimited number of small purchases eventually add up to a large amount of money, giving businesses a good reason to address the Long Tail. This has changed the relationship between consumers of all types, and companies with products and services. Services like Facebook and Google have also led the way to a shift from an older model – where vertical information flows originate at the producer and are mediated by marketing before terminating at the consumers – to a model where information is exchanged in networks between individuals and organizations (Scoble and Israel, 2006, p. 27).

The change to network-based communication is one of the observed trends that provide the framework for this chapter. Researchers such as Story and Hess have demonstrated the need for a new, more personal relationship with consumers, beginning with the necessity of becoming part of the consumer social conversation. From a marketer's viewpoint, the goal becomes fostering positive communication and a sense of community around the brand rather than simply broadcasting messages (Story and Hess, 2009). 'The web introduced the idea of unhindered communication between the brand and the consumer and among consumers themselves. Buyers can and do now communicate with each other, learn from each other, and help each other' (Gobé, 2009, p. 243).

Among the members of the Muslim community, few things are more significant to them than their faith. According to the Pew Research Center's US Religious Landscape Survey (2008), more than 91 per cent of US Muslims polled believe in God with an opinion of 'absolutely certain' or 'fairly certain.' On the 'importance of religion in their lives,' Pew found that for 90 per cent it was either 'very important' or 'somewhat important.' This relationship is emotional and long-lasting. Faith provides not only an ethical bond but also one of the most emotional bonds. For marketing purposes, according to studies by Mangold and Faulds (2009), 'People tell others about things to which they are emotionally connected. Organizations can leverage emotional connections by embracing one or more causes that are important to their customers.' Mangold and Faulds further describe how social and digital media can be used to harness these emotions. Consumers make associations through both personal and seemingly personal connections with virtual friends they have never met face to face. Today, through services like Facebook, trust is built via common experience and background. This is where information is gathered and choices are made. Vollmer and Precourt (2008) underscore this in their book *Always On.* They note that in the era of social media 'consumers are in control; they have greater access to information and greater command over media consumption than ever before' (p. 5).

All of this leads back to the need for a closer connection with users. Because of its mass reach into fragmented markets and relatively low upfront costs, digital media often provide the most efficient opportunity to access these groups. The question becomes how digital media are best harnessed to reach the Muslim consumer. Globally, Muslim consumers are online using both mainstream and Muslim-specific media. This chapter examines how growing Internet usage and social media have opened the door to the Muslim consumer. We address elements of digital strategy that companies need to consider combined with examples of implementation of digital media that brands are already implementing towards Muslim consumers. Unless otherwise noted, case studies presented in this chapter are based on the original research and corporate records of Muxlim Inc. Muxlim is an integrated media company offering a range of services that engage, communicate with and access the global Muslim market. Muxlim.com is an online Muslim lifestyle network run by Muxlim Inc., utilized for both delivering customer campaigns and collecting data on trends and content consumption among Muslims online. We also include tools and methods currently used by Muxlim for comparing and measuring marketing digital communication as part of the marketing mix.

THE DIGITAL ISLAMIC MARKETING LANDSCAPE

The Muslim consumer market represents one of the most attractive emerging markets in today's world. It is estimated that in 2010 there were 1.6549 billion Muslims globally, growing at a rate of 1.555 per cent annually (Kettani, 2010). Estimates for the buying power of this segment range from $1 trillion (Power, 2009) to over $2 trillion (Bladd and Ferris-Lay, 2010). This buying power is situated in countries such as Turkey and Saudi Arabia but also in Western and Muslim-minority countries such as the US, France and the United Kingdom (Pew Research Center, 2007, p. 25). Furthermore, the profile of Muslim consumers in these countries with high buying power often includes a large number of younger and more educated consumers, which makes them one of the preferred targets for digital media marketing. Muslim digital media audiences have also reached critical mass, and are reachable through many destinations such as Muxlim, Facebook (Muslim groups), YouTube (Muslim channels), Naseeb, and many others.

For example, in Muslim-minority countries where Muslims rank highly in terms of buying power, digital media can bridge fragmented demographic segments that are challenging or impossible to reach using traditional means. With today's consumers more in control of the messages they receive, companies and brands that harness digital media to develop loyalties with individuals, communities and niches are at an advantage.

The rules of engagement have changed and consumers are now earned, not acquired. Consumers are in the driver's seat, and the most successful companies are the ones that can adapt to this new reality. In the US market during the early 1980s, consumers who wanted to do banking were told that banks are open from 9am to 3pm, are located on Main Street, require two ID documents, and offer service only in English. Today, consumers can dictate that they are interested in doing business only if they can get all their questions answered on their laptop, at midnight, in a language other than English – and the services need to be *sharia*-compliant. In fact, several institutions would be interested in providing this customer with a variety of services, including home financing, investment planning, retirement planning, education planning, and estate planning.

Companies now have to deal with a consumer-centric world where people are more educated and demanding, know that they can get whatever they want and however they want it, and expect brands to have a conversation with them.

DIGITAL MARKETING AND MUSLIMS TODAY

Rather than looking like a melting pot, our world today is a multicultural mix similar to a salad bowl, where people from different cultures, faiths and lifestyles proudly stand out in their own way. As a result, many mature multicultural segments, such as the Hispanic, African American, and Asian markets in countries like the US, receive vigorous marketing attention. For the Hispanic market alone in the US, more than four billion dollars was spent on advertising in 2008 with $225 million of that going to digital media (Ad Age Data Center, 2009). The money shift indicates a power shift away from traditional mass marketing and renders emerging and multicultural markets extremely important. These new markets are causing top line population growth, with Asia and Africa in the lead. According to UN reports, 60 per cent of the world's population lives in Asia and almost 15 per cent lives in Africa. Islamicpopulation.com states that 30 per cent of Asian populations and 52 per cent of African populations are Muslim. Meanwhile, Internet World Stats reports that 42.4 per cent of the world's Internet users come from Asia alone. The world's largest Muslim populations are also living in Asia. Furthermore, while the 'Muslim consumer' has existed for a long time, he/she was mostly confined to countries or regions heavily populated with Muslims. Now opportunities exist in both Muslim-majority and Muslim-minority countries. Digital communication is the reason for this changing opportunity.

Table 18.1 notes the estimated top Muslim populations online. The data includes per capita income estimates from the International Monetary Fund (IMF, 2010) and the UNDP's Human Development Index data (UNDP, 2009a); it gives a snapshot of the potential online marketing opportunity within the global Muslim community.

The information in Table 18.1 helps marketers look at the digital opportunity in both emerging and established online Muslim communities. Using the ranking of estimated Muslims online as a base, the understanding of PPP adjusted per capita income helps us understand the average individual buying power of the society. This assumes that Muslims operate as a part of their larger society within a country. In applying the Human Development Index (HDI), the UNDP notes on their website that: 'Human Development is a development paradigm that is about much more than the rise or fall of national incomes. It is about creating an environment in which people can develop their full potential and lead productive, creative lives in accord with their needs and interests' (UNDP, 2009b). HDI of 1.00 represents a perfect score, with Norway being the highest performing country in 2009 (HDI = 0.971). We use the HDI to give insight as marketers on the general society or country in which Muslims are living and particularly to help evaluate whether it is prone to promoting innovation and new thought. Innovation and new thought in communication are the key elements of digital growth, which makes HDI a good measurement within this context.

In employing this table, a marketer could look, for example, at the US and ask the following questions:

Table 18.1   Estimated Muslims online: top countries (June 2010)

Rank	Country	Average Muslims online*	Per capita income ($ PPP, 2009)	UNDP HDI**
1	Turkey	33 113 025	$12 476	0.81
2	Iran	30 797 712	$11 172	0.78
3	Indonesia	24 485 549	$4 157	0.73
4	Nigeria	20 707 717	$2 249	0.51
5	Pakistan	17 243 720	$2 661	0.57
6	Egypt	15 835 658	$6 123	0.70
7	India	10 882 991	$2 941	0.61
8	Morocco	10 456 545	$4 604	0.65
9	Malaysia	10 329 863	$13 769	0.83
10	China	9 602 766	$6 567	0.77
11	Saudi Arabia	9 343 835	$23 221	0.84
12	Russia	9 313 708	$14 920	0.82
13	Algeria	4 581 092	$6 869	0.75
14	Uzbekistan	4 174 884	$2 807	0.71
15	Azerbaijan	3 708 510	$9 564	0.97
16	United States	3 429 801	$46 381	0.96
17	Tunisia	3 419 720	$8 254	0.77
18	Syria	3 340 521	$4 887	0.74
19	France	3 332 693	$33 679	0.96
20	United Arab Emirates	3 113 418	$36 537	0.90
21	Sudan	3 010 050	$2 380	0.53
22	Germany	2 798 558	$34 212	0.95
23	Kazakhstan	2 730 109	$11 693	0.80
24	Kyrgyzstan	1 718 166	$2 253	0.71
25	Philippines	1 572 615	$3 521	0.75
26	Jordan	1 558 832	$5 620	0.77
27	United Kingdom	1 302 263	$34 619	0.95
28	Thailand	1 293 960	$8 060	0.78
29	Kuwait	1 088 228	$38 304	0.92
30	Oman	1 055 844	$25 110	0.85

Notes:
*   Estimated average number of global Muslims online is 268 892 827.
**   United Nations Development Programme Human Development Index.

Source: Table developed by the authors using data from UNDP, IMF and World Bank PPP per capita income data. The research sources for the population and usage data in the report include: http://religions.pewforum. org/, http://www.islamicpopulation.com/source.html, data published by Nielsen Online, by the International Telecommunications Union, by GfK, and data from the following sites: http://www.state.gov/, http://www. factbook.net/muslim_pop.php, http://www.nationmaster.com/graph/rel_isl_pop-religion-islam-population, http://www.Internetworldstats.com/stats.htm, https://www.cia.gov/library/publications/the-world-factbook/.

- Is this Muslim market large enough to address with online media?
- Can we speculate that the customers have enough to spend?
- Is there potential for high growth and potential for new communication ideas that will connect with the Muslim consumer or is the market still more likely to use traditional marketing communication media?

If the marketer believes the US is a big enough target and the other values are high, this could justify looking closer at further factors in using digital as a medium to address the market. It should be noted that this comparison is offered simply as an improved look at the global data – one practical element to be considered in the strategic decision-making of media choices towards the Muslim consumer. It should also be noted that the data do not specify if Muslims in some societies are in upper or lower classes of that society, have varying education levels or have other indications of higher or lower Internet usage. Nor do we suggest that there should be any differences. In the US for example, Pew Research has already found that most Muslims are middle class and mainstream with higher than average incomes and education levels (Pew Research Center, 2007). Similar data would be useful in exploring other countries and specific regions of countries that would interest a marketer.

DIGITAL MARKETING IN MUSLIM-MAJORITY COUNTRIES

Naturally, Muslim-majority countries have always been sensitive to their population's needs. Companies marketing in countries like Malaysia and Indonesia have always marketed to the lifestyle of Muslims. There is little need to ask in these places if a product is *halal* as Muslim culture is all around the consumer at all times and marketers are sensitive to that. Many global brands including Coca-Cola, Burger King, HSBC, Ikea, Nestlé, Pepsi, Starbucks and others are quite familiar with and experienced in advertising in Muslim markets from Turkey to Malaysia – using messaging and customization that cater to Muslim needs and attitudes. Brands have seamlessly incorporated Ramadan (the Muslim month of fasting) and the two Eid holidays within their local marketing campaigns. In September 2008, across its Middle East outlets, Starbucks offered and marketed special traditional Arabian coffee blends coupled with pastries to commemorate the holy month of Ramadan. These special treats were positioned to be enjoyed while breaking the fast at sunset and received rave reviews from both the local media and the social media spheres.

Still, brands are only now making the first small steps in attempting to utilize some of the most modern marketing techniques and services, even with huge numbers of Muslims online in these countries. Traditional methods combined with a taste of the new tools are finding their way into Muslim-majority country advertising mixes. Nevertheless, companies marketing in countries such as Indonesia and Malaysia continue to spend almost all of their ad money on traditional media like TV, magazines, and newspapers (Haymarket Media, 2010). Advertisers in Indonesia spent nearly two billion dollars in the first quarter of 2010 but almost none of that money is attributed to digital advertising. Both examples below highlight the desire of brands to try new digital methods, sometimes even with high quality production, but they still seem to lack the understanding of the best ways to create a genuine success story by using digital for mass appeal.

Heineken Launches Fayrouz around the World

Given the continued rise of popular culture within the Muslim lifestyle context, the Heineken global beverage distributor has launched their Fayrouz non-alcoholic malt beverage in many countries across the world. Along with campaigns using mostly traditional media, a Flash website caters to the younger online generations and promotes the trendy activities around music and dance (Fayrouz, 2010). In addition to the alcohol-free angle for the product, all images and videos on the site are done within the social and moral context of the target customer. Although this is a good demonstration of the use of some of the latest tools, the site does tend to be very basic, with little depth. It is not clear, for instance, why the site is in English rather than the different languages of the countries represented (Peterson, 2010).

Attempts at Viral Video

In June 2010 Apple initiated an online and mobile viral campaign to help sell Apple's iPod Touch during the Fifa World Cup (Arab Business Machine, 2010). It was shot around Dubai during the run-up to the competition and was called 'Have you got the Touch?' The video is professionally produced and features some very talented local footballers. The attempt by Apple had very little impact and few views but shows some first attempts to use the leading viral techniques popular in Western culture. Other viral video attempts include well-produced but minimally viewed videos for Nestlé KitKat candy bars, featuring the acrobatic group the Chunky Boys (JWT Dubai, 2009). The videos gathered less than 10000 views during their one-year run on YouTube and under 1600+ Facebook likes to the accompanying Facebook fan page.

DIGITAL MARKETING IN MUSLIM-MINORITY COUNTRIES

Today, Muslim consumers in Muslim-minority countries have also reached critical mass, have very high buying power and are growing faster than any other faith-based consumer segment (Kerbaj, 2009). Multicultural marketing and segmentation is growing rapidly, especially in the US, as marketers deepen their understanding of the importance of reaching out to different ethnic groups. Across many consumer industry sectors, companies are strategically establishing relationships with consumers and developing a more intimate understanding of their lives in order to improve the entire market consumption of their services and products. For example, the Coca-Cola Chief Marketing Officer announced that the company will spend nearly 33 per cent of its marketing budget on multicultural targets in 2010.

The idea of marketing digitally to Muslims in European and North American countries has taken hold much faster than it has in regard to Muslims in other parts of the world. This may be due to generally higher Internet availability and penetration percentages across society as a whole, along with a more advanced culture in online social networking. A Western society's Internet usage habits and average income levels clearly seem to have an influence on digital marketing. For example, the most successful viral brand videos of all time are for the most part from the US (Learmonth, 2010), where digital marketing is a strong component of most major consumer-products companies' media mix. In the US, the brands that have targeted Muslims tend to be ones that have been targeting Muslims for many years across the world. This has started to help them to recognize the growing American Muslim market opportunity. This trend, however, is still in its infancy, not from a technology usage or media point of view but rather in its direct approach to the segment. Negative media attention to global events involving Muslims has also contributed to confusion among brands attempting to address Muslim consumers. In addition, Muslim lifestyle-focused digital outlets that have mass appeal and that focus on the subject matter brands would like to be associated with – for instance, outlets like Muxlim.com – are only now emerging. Some examples of such campaigns and target marketing are explored here.

MoneyGram

MoneyGram International is a leading global payment services company providing consumers with payment services that are meant to be affordable, reliable and convenient. The diverse array of products and services enables consumers, most of whom are not fully served by traditional financial institutions, to make payments and to transfer money around the world, helping them to meet the financial demands of their daily lives.

The nature of the transaction business positions MoneyGram as an important natural connection between many people in different countries and cultures. Over the years, the company has recognized that the Muslim community represents one of the key customer segments using its services. The Muslim population has migrated globally. Millions live in the US, Europe, and around the world but maintain their connection with friends and family in their mother country through traditions and holidays. As a result, MoneyGram explored and launched strategic marketing efforts towards these consumers, particularly during the religious celebrations of Ramadan and Eid. All case studies in this chapter come from the Muxlim Report and/or from Muxlim's company records.

According to Zainab Ali, senior marketing manager at MoneyGram: 'We see a large increase of remittances from the US and Canada to South Asia and the Middle East during the time of Ramadan. With our more than 203 000 locations across the world, we are able to meet the needs of Muslims everywhere who want to send funds to their family.'

During Ramadan 2010, MoneyGram launched a global Ramadan and Eid promotion across Asia Pacific, Canada, Europe, and the US in which customers had a chance to win $1000 per week. Customers who sent money with MoneyGram were given a chance to win with every transaction.

The goal of the campaign was to increase transaction volumes and create awareness of the MoneyGram brand among Muslim consumers. With many alternatives in the market, the company needed to engage and interact with customers to reach its goals. Joining in the celebration of these important traditions provided an opportunity to show appreciation and to share with customers, continuing the development of a long-term connection with the community.

In line with these goals and in order to increase the visibility of the campaign, MoneyGram looked to connect with users through social media. The company launched an effort that encouraged people to share stories of kindness across the Muslim community with a social media campaign called 'Ramadan Kindness.' Muxlim.com was used, along with Twitter and Facebook, to develop and spread passionate heartwarming stories highlighting Muslims doing extraordinary acts for others. Information sharing was catalyzed through daily postings to the different channels to draw more people to the pages and encourage them to post their own stories. MoneyGram banner ads were also posted on a series of high traffic Muslim sites as part of the campaign.

Wilson Basketball

Wilson is the world's leading manufacturer of sporting goods equipment. Wilson's sporting focuses are tennis, baseball, American football, golf, basketball, softball, badminton, and squash. As a global brand, Wilson enjoys strong distribution and channel relationships. Wilson was incorporated in 1913 as Ashland Manufacturing Company, and is now a fully owned subsidiary of Finland-based Amer Sports. Headquartered in Chicago, Wilson employed 1919 people at the end of 2006, and serves customers in over 100 countries. Its business is structured along three general business areas: racket sports, team sports, and golf.

In 2010, Wilson Basketball launched a campaign on the Muxlim network encouraging Muslim basketball enthusiasts to share stories centered around players in the NCAA National Tournament. The user community rated, commented on and promoted the campaign across different social media including Muslim-focused Facebook groups and Twitter. Online Muslim sports groups engaged with the campaign and contributed further information for consumption by the community. The objective of the campaign was to introduce Wilson as a brand of choice for Muslim consumers through the association with things they cared about. Muslim basketball players often do not get significant exposure within the mainstream media, and Wilson was able to bring their stories to the eyes of Muslims across the US and around the world. The aim was to build brand affinity with Muslim youth through supporting and enhancing their passion for NCAA Basketball.

Best Buy

With operations in the United States, Canada, Europe, China, Mexico and Turkey, Best Buy is a multinational retailer of technology and entertainment products and services with a commitment to growth and innovation. The Best Buy family of brands and partnerships collectively generates more than $49 billion in annual revenue and includes brands such as Best Buy, Best Buy Mobile, Audiovisions, Carphone Warehouse, Five Star, Future Shop, Geek Squad, Magnolia Audio Video, Napster, Pacific Sales, and Phone House.

In November 2009, Best Buy, along with its regular Thanksgiving Day sales circular advertising, included a note saying 'Happy Eid Al-Adha,' which refers to a holiday of sacrifice for Muslims. This was greatly welcomed by Muslim consumers, who reacted with positive comments and word-of-mouth praise on their holiday being recognized and celebrated by a national brand. At the same time, some non-Muslims criticized Best Buy for the note, and Best Buy responded with a brief statement on its website: 'Best Buy's customers and employees around the world represent a variety of faiths and denominations. We respect that diversity and choose to greet our customers and employees in ways that reflect their traditions.' This strong statement of support not only won the hearts of Muslims, but Best Buy's December 2009 sales compared to 2008 actually went up, showing no negative impact from the 'Eid Greetings' campaign. Digital channels no doubt contributed to this growth as a strong word-of-mouth effect (on Facebook, Twitter, Muxlim and other online networks) was created and Muslims nationwide were made aware that Best Buy was reaching out to them.

HSBC

HSBC Group, one of the world's most globally active banks, is headquartered in London. The Group serves customers worldwide from around 8000 offices in 87 countries and territories. With assets of $2418 billion as of 30 June 2010, HSBC is one of the world's largest banking and financial services organizations. HSBC is marketed as 'the world's local bank.'

HSBC Amanah is the global Islamic financial services division of the HSBC Group. Established in 1998, with more than 300 professionals serving the Middle East, Asia-Pacific, Europe and the Americas, HSBC Amanah represents the largest Islamic financial services team of any international bank.

In September 2009, HSBC launched the HSBC Amanah Bankwide Campaign, promoting a range of products to cater to a wide spectrum of Muslim customers with different financial and lifestyle needs. Additionally, in conjunction with the holy month of Ramadan, breaking fast activities were held at various HSBC Amanah branches. Both efforts were propagated through HSBC's digital properties and mailing lists.

WHY DIGITAL?

Today, consumers are more proactive and less reactive (Gabriel and Lang, 1995). We are living in an increasingly consumer-generated and consumer-controlled media society. Already, many popular ads have bypassed TV broadcast and gained popularity via the Internet. In 2008, Google had 173.1 million unique visitors, with an average of 208.3 minutes per user (Ad Age Data Center, 2010). Especially in the west, we have become quite dependent on our digital connections. In the developed countries and in several emerging countries, people conduct many transactions online, from ordering food to buying expensive items such as cars. People born after 1990 cannot imagine that the world existed without the Internet and mobile phones. They are starting to join the fulltime workforce and becoming important target customers for many businesses. Marketers should clearly understand that the preferred medium for these customers is digital and that in some cases, digital is the only way to reach them.

As noted in the introduction, a digital medium tends to be one of the most emotional media forms, because it is made up of people's thoughts and feelings, experiences and stories, interactions and reactions. Therefore, it is arguably the most powerful, cost-efficient tool for marketers to engage with faith-based and lifestyle customers such as the Muslim market. In December 2008, an article in the *Guardian* newspaper noted: 'Marketers have sleepwalked past what is possibly the largest and most wealthy emerging global market. What they lack is an introduction to that community' (Chiswick, 2008). While many brands may have contemplated reaching out to Muslim consumers in the past, the initial bridge towards them has been missing.

Targeting

In today's consumer-centric environment, consumers themselves have become marketers. Business schools taught B2C (business to consumer) and B2B (business to business) marketing, but now we are seeing C2C (consumer to consumer) marketing every day on eBay. In this environment, it is very difficult to use a generic marketing strategy to reach out to a mass audience, let alone a target segment such as Muslim consumers. Most companies used to define their target consumer as 'people ages 25 to 65 generating X income in Y cities' (some companies still do it that way). However, more recently marketers have come to recognize that consumers are extremely diverse. They have a wide range of cultures, lifestyles and preferred engagement mediums, among other differences. One person may like to be contacted via email in Spanish; the second may prefer Facebook; the third may watch ethnic TV; the fourth is on MySpace; the fifth is best found on Twitter; and the sixth wants to read an Arabic local newspaper. They may all live in the same neighborhood. So how can marketers plan an effective campaign that will reach all of them? One way is to sub-segment their target group and divide them based on affinity and lifestyle. From there it is possible to develop an integrated communication strategy that can provide a brand maximum exposure through multiple channels.

With the mainstream adoption of consumer Internet services in developed countries since the late 1990s, digital marketing quickly became a key topic in the academic marketing discipline (Kotler and Keller, 2006). Early literature on digital marketing highlighted the superior targeting and customization capabilities as unique benefits of the so-called 'new media' (Kierzkowski et al., 1996). While traditional mass media rely on the concept of audiences with broadly similar characteristics to target marketing messages to selected segments, digital marketing channels allow marketers to target large numbers of individual consumers based on known characteristics such as location and interests. Digital channels also allow messages to be tailored based on each individual's characteristics, as deduced from observed usage behavior. With the recent rise in popularity of social networking services, individuals are revealing even more information about themselves online than before (Boyd, 2008). This has allowed for increasingly better targeting and customization of marketing messages, but has also created new privacy concerns.

Measurability

Another aspect of digital marketing highlighted as superior by the early literature is measurability (Kierzkowski et al., 1996). While traditional mass media use panels and surveys to estimate the number of contacts achieved by a marketing message, in digital channels it is typically possible to record every single instance of a message being displayed to a user. This allows better tracking of campaign objectives and better awareness of what kind of consumers the message is reaching (Kotler and Keller, 2006). Due to the combination of efficient tracking and measuring abilities, it is frequently argued that digital marketing is a cost-effective and low-risk method to reach consumers, especially when communicating with niche segments (Urban, 2003).

MEASURING DIGITAL AND SOCIAL MEDIA CAMPAIGNS

Digital offers marketers the opportunity not only to communicate but also to listen and measure the responses from their audiences. It is an opportunity to see real conversation and exchange in order to develop an ongoing discussion with the customer. This unique feedback can then be used to recognize trends, develop better marketing and further engage with the consumer. To see this in practice, we again refer to the MoneyGram Ramadan Kindness campaign of 2010.

Case: MoneyGram International

The Ramadan Kindness MoneyGram campaign results encompassed a series of social media metrics including Facebook 'Likes', Muxlim and Facebook fans, Twitter followers, comments, sharing, and views. It also provided insight into the click performance of banners associated with the campaign on sites directly tied to the social media campaign and on those with no exposure to social media.

To launch and feed the social media activity, 20 professionally written stories with MoneyGram branding were originally posted to and shared with Muxlim.com over the course of the Ramadan holy month. The Ramadan Kindness social media campaign resulted in thousands of views and 'likes' on Facebook and Muxlim.com. In its first five weeks, the MoneyGram Ramadan Kindness Facebook page surpassed the company's own fan page by 57 per cent with currently over 2500 likes. (The MoneyGram company Facebook page has been up for more than one year.) There were 40 894 content views directly via Facebook and Muxlim.com as of 7 September 2010. There were 919 comments and 31 078 shares and likes in the period on the Ramadan Kindness and Muxlim Facebook pages. This did not include the many thousands of shares and likes of the content on other fan pages such as 'I Love Allah,' which alone received 5603 likes and 163 positive comments on the MoneyGram Ramadan Kindness post for 24 August 2010. During the project, Muxlim.com analyzed some 655 Facebook comments, the majority of which were positive to neutral in tone. Comments included:

> I love seeing what we Muslim do in other parts of the world. This is awesome – may Allah bless them!! (23 similar mentions)

> MoneyGram, one of the companies that transfers money, just launched a website on the occasion of Ramadan. (37 similar mentions)

In addition, banner ads that were combined with the social media campaign had a 0.31 per cent clickthrough rate (CTR) versus an average of 0.07 per cent on other sites without social media. In this campaign, every content view was accompanied by MoneyGram branding and banners. Originally, the campaign was targeted to provide one million banner impressions but the overwhelming response and popularity resulted in Muxlim.com's decision to deliver nearly 2.5 million impressions primarily during the six-week campaign while still maintaining the high CTR.

INTERACTIVITY AND IMMEDIACY

As the practices of digital marketing developed, later marketing scholarship focused on the interactivity and immediacy of digital media (Urban, 2003). Thanks to the two-way nature of online communications, marketers learned to use the medium not only to disseminate their messages, but also to obtain feedback from their customers in a relatively low cost way. Furthermore, in addition to presenting product information and building awareness, Internet campaigns were used to allow customers to immediately act upon calls-to-action by completing purchases online or signing up for further direct marketing (Kotler and Keller, 2006). These aspects also apply strongly to mobile marketing – marketing, sales and payment through consumers' mobile phones (Lehdonvirta et al., 2009).

Internet retail channels also scale better to offer a wider selection of goods and thus cater to a wider selection of tastes (Anderson, 2006). For example, while a typical Borders bookstore offers a selection of 100 000 books, Amazon.com has an inventory of 3.7 million book titles (Anderson, 2006). A similar situation prevails in several other industries and product categories. The massive selection is made possible by the low cost of listing products in an online store, as well as by efficient searching and browsing features that allow customers on the Web to find what they seek. A consequence of the huge selection is that consumers' purchases can be distributed over a much wider range of products than was previously possible, enabling greater divergence and fragmentation in tastes and styles.

EMOTIONAL ENGAGEMENT AND COMMUNITY BUILDING

The combination of the above factors that make digital channels easy and low-cost platforms for marketers can result in oversaturated digital marketing environments. To gain consumers' attention and trust in such conditions, many marketers find it necessary to be increasingly open, honest and even 'intimate' in their marketing communications, and to listen very carefully to the consumer's response (Scoble and Israel, 2006; Tapscott and Williams, 2006). Corporate blogs or blogs maintained by company members, micro-blogs, profiles on social networking sites and other so-called social media applications are some of the most commonly used tools that marketers use to become intimate with online consumers.

Perhaps more importantly, the technologies that enable marketers to be more intimate with their customers have given consumers themselves unprecedented ability to connect with other like-minded consumers. This has been the topic of much enthusiastic discussion and authorship in recent years, under such rubrics as Web 2.0, remix culture, and participatory consumption (Benkler, 2006; Scoble and Israel, 2006; Surowiecki, 2005; Tapscott and Williams, 2006; Lehdonvirta, 2009). The basic claim is that certain new technologies and new ways of designing online services have led to a radical empowerment of the consumer in certain processes of production and consumption. Technologies and design techniques such as blogs, RSS feeds, tags, social networking, web applications, Creative Commons licensing, and peer-to-peer networking have permitted users to change from uninformed shoppers to discerning connoisseurs, from passive consumers to active producer-consumers, and from isolated individuals to consumer communities.

This paradigm shift, as it is portrayed in the literature, could be conceptualized as a shift from a model where vertical information flows originate at the producer and are mediated by marketing before terminating at the consumers, to a model where information is exchanged in networks between individuals and organizations. From a marketer's point of view, the goal becomes fostering positive communication and a sense of community around the brand rather than broadcasting messages (Scoble and Israel, 2006). 'The web introduced the idea of unhindered communication between the brand and the consumer and among consumers themselves. Buyers can – and do – now communicate with each other, learn from each other, and help each other' (Gobé, 2009). Muslims use many different channels to connect with their communities. Some of them are similar to those used by the general population while some are special-interest channels closely tied to their Muslim lifestyle.

Individuals are no longer tied to only one network. Facebook must connect with Twitter and YouTube. Muxlim and other niche sites integrate Facebook Connect and ShareThis to bring more people into their experiences. The 'walled-garden' approach is no longer effective and marketers must look for a larger share of voice by triggering positive word-of-mouth and building sub-communities around their brands.

UNIQUE BENEFITS OF DIGITAL MEDIA IN ISLAMIC MARKETING

In this section, we look at the unique benefits and roles of digital media when applied to Islamic marketing. The objective of the section is to show that these benefits and roles go beyond the traditional ones discussed in the previous section.

Today an estimated 250 to 287 million Muslims are online.[1] The largest Muslim Facebook group, called 'I am Muslim and I am Proud,' has over 1 million fans. Muslims utilize the Internet to share and enrich all aspects of their lifestyle. Entertainment, food, fashion and education are just some of the topics Muslims discuss, share and explore online. Muslims use online networks such as Facebook.com, YouTube.com and Twitter. com, as well as specialized Muslim networks such as Muxlim.com. The Internet has made it possible for this geographically fragmented segment to be addressed as a unified consumer market. Muslim women are also very active online, which allows marketers to reach them in ways that are not possible using traditional media or offline. For example, according to profile data from Muxlim Inc., 51 per cent of its users online are women.

UNIFYING GEOGRAPHIC AND ETHNIC FRAGMENTS INTO ADDRESSABLE AUDIENCES

Companies like Vodafone (UK), Shoes.com (US), Nokia (Finland), Mobily (Saudi Arabia) and others are connecting with Muslims digitally. What is driving these brands to choose the digital route to access this market? What makes digital media especially interesting from a Muslim consumer's perspective? Muslim communities are a cross-section of all socio-economic classes, age groups, nationalities, and races; a fact that makes the community harder and more expensive to target and reach as a mass market.

Digital media are able to negotiate around the segregation between different Muslim sub-communities (for example Arab, Asian, and so on), and bring on new ways of communicating with Muslims as a group that is not necessarily attracted by the same messages as the mass market. It enables reaching all sub-communities simultaneously where marketers can easily deliver messages to each community in its own language and style.

For example, the Muxlim.com website reaches Muslims in more than 4500 cities in the US alone. Without this digital channel, surveying users across such a vast geographical region would be costly and time consuming. But online networks can now reach even the most remote users, and online properties become virtual hubs where people of similar interests and backgrounds congregate, making them an easier target for marketers.

Like any other consumer group, Muslim consumers have some major sub-groups that are quite different from one another. However, there are opportunities to connect with them on a global scale. For example, the holy month of Ramadan is celebrated at the same time by Muslims all over the world. Ramadan provides an excellent opportunity to connect with them in a very emotional context, such as HSBC organizing *iftar* in their branches to connect with their Muslim customers. No global marketer would miss the month of December and thus not take advantage of consumer spending before Christmas – yet that's exactly what they are missing during the Ramadan season.

There also may be a misconception that focusing on Muslim consumers unnecessarily alienates other customers. When done completely in mass media within Muslim minority countries, this has indicated some negative reactions from those outside the community such as in the case of Best Buy. But the use of digital channels has the opportunity to focus targeted messages to the correct audience, allowing also for stronger, more emotional messages to be created. MoneyGram and HSBC are examples of companies that understand their customers and needs along with the multicultural media they use. This led to a popular and positive response to their campaigns.

REACHING AUDIENCES THAT OTHER CHANNELS HAVE DIFFICULTY REACHING

Media coverage of conflict in Muslim countries and society's general consumption of the media have painted a picture of Muslim communities that does not match the daily lives of most Muslims in the world today. As a result, Muslims now have a stronger distrust of mainstream media than other audiences do (Young, 2010), which makes it difficult to reach some Muslim consumers through traditional media.

Marketers who use digital channels have the great advantage of directly addressing potential Muslim consumers through trusted Muslim-focused or ethnic media. This type of media allows marketers to communicate messages that are targeted specifically towards the Muslim consumer. These actions help not only gain the trust of Muslim consumers and create a reputation-safe scenario but also target the message to the consumer who best understands and values it. Digital channels further make it easy to hone the message and interact in a direct manner with all those engaging with the brand over the long term. This allows brands to directly manage their relationship and continuous communication with their loyal and potential customers.

For other reasons, two Muslim sub-segments are particularly difficult to reach via traditional channels: Muslim women and Muslims in emerging market countries. The women's market in general has been ignored for many years. It is finally getting some of its due share but is still far from being fully explored. Several research projects have shown and validated that the majority of buying decisions in the developing as well as the emerging world are made or influenced by women – however, the majority of the marketing efforts are still directed towards men. The role of Muslim women in particular is becoming more interesting for marketers, especially with the digital generation consumer. Brands that will connect with this growing segment may experience a long-term beneficial relationship. Today, Muslim women consumers are welcomed as being smart, vocal, increasingly responsible for buying decisions and very brand conscious. More and more, they share their opinions with friends online through digital networks. Also, mobile penetration is growing rapidly in emerging markets, many of which are Muslim countries, suggesting that one unique use for digital mobile marketing in Islamic marketing is to reach emerging market consumers who have little access to any other media.

One of the most effective types of marketing is word-of-mouth. Hence, the goal for many marketers is to have an established relationship with customers and to get those customers to talk about their products with their friends. These relationships, however, need to be initiated and maintained by marketers for the effect to last. Because the digital world is a place where we seek both companionship and answers, brands have an opportunity to engage with consumers, providing them with information, services and entertainment that enhance their lives. This generates valuable brand exposure, develops a positive relationship with consumers and maximizes the chances for word-of-mouth. Therefore, developing a solid relationship with members of an online community and allowing them to be the mouthpiece for the company is an effective way to generate brand exposure. Consumers are changing rapidly and they are becoming quite vocal about their opinions and preferences (both positive and negative). Easy ways to share interesting information help create a word-of-mouth snowball that spreads to both online and offline consumers.

Digital media have created an opportunity for marketers to develop a genuine conversation and relationship with the Muslim consumer that is partially shaped by interactions with the brand's messages. By taking a single common entry point (lowest common denominator) and then listening carefully to how consumers react to it and shape it, marketers can understand and cater to all sub-identities in their marketing messages, thus maximizing their appeal among Muslim consumers.

Accordingly, consumers can socially endorse the product or capture the attention of their friends (who may not be necessarily interested at first) by interacting with a brand digitally.

For example, Wilson Basketball has always focused on relationship building and has succeeded by being part of their customers' lives through their products. As one of the pioneering companies in reaching Muslim consumers, Wilson is currently using digital channels and specifically social media as the catalyst for many online conversations. In a campaign called the 'Dream Team' launched on Muxlim.com, the company initiated conversations with users about basketball with avid fans within the Muslim community. They utilized expertise in an area where they had authority and thought-leadership, to get people talking about a subject they love. The company also engaged leading bloggers and individuals within the Muslim community to spread these discussions to other Muslim websites and Muslim basketball groups on Facebook. It is clear that creating relationships with influential individuals who already have a reputation within a community was one of the core elements of the campaign's success. They created an easily shareable personal endorsement of the brand, making an even clearer case for digital channels as the most cost-effective way to develop consumer-brand relationships.

STARTING RELATIONSHIPS THAT CONTINUE TO OTHER CHANNELS

As discussed above, some traditional channels have managed to alienate many Muslim consumers. Traditional channels may also lack the necessary degree of customizability to target messages to Muslim consumers and build trust. For this reason, we propose that the third unique benefit of digital marketing in Islamic marketing is that it can be used as an initial tactful contact point between a brand and the consumer. Once the trust is established, the relationship can continue in other channels.

Before brands start engaging with a completely new market such as Muslim consumers, digital channels allow them to collect data and trends to help them understand the consumers they are targeting. Online panels can provide marketers with deep insights into best practices and help them refine campaign ideas, while anonymous consumer data can help them identify the best channels and tactics to execute. And what better way for consumers to be introduced to a brand, when they are not being sold something, but rather asked how they can be served better?

Some brands have successfully leveraged digital media to appear as a market leader building consumer trust and loyalty, without ever making a product pitch. This can be achieved by harnessing digital channels as a broadcasting tool to establish thought-leadership and add value to consumers' lives outside of the context of a transaction. Transactions may happen once consumers view the brand as trustworthy and genuinely interested in supporting the community. This can make a world of difference during buying decisions, especially if consumers have developed a solid premeditated preference towards a certain brand due to their exposure to the brand's ideas and messages.

Additionally, the richness of digital media allows marketers to create a complete and contextual experience for consumers, instead of simply talking about their products. Marketers can use a whole tool box, including rich media (audiovisuals, animations), games, social contacts, and behavioral targeting, to create wholesome consumer experiences. Better yet, consumers may enjoy those experiences and start sharing them with their friends and friends of friends, thus acting as brand ambassadors, and quickly propelling the brand's message into a large mass of consumers. This way, digital marketing can act as a launch pad for a comprehensive marketing strategy that includes both digital and non-digital channels to reach Muslim consumers. This also includes the cross-over impact and reach of mainstream media versus ethnic media versus Muslim-specific media. Integrated marketing is becoming a core component of many corporate marketing strategies. Many businesses around the world have challenged their advertising, marketing, and public relations agencies to develop measurable integrated marketing and communications frameworks. This is partly due to budget cuts and enhanced multi-channel distribution, as well as the wide diversity of today's consumers.

Another huge advantage of digital marketing is the ownership of consumer data. Today, Google and MySpace have a personal database of over 300 million consumers, mostly gathered in less than 10 years. Some of the leading companies in the world have not been able to gather a similar database in over 100 years. Consumers would never agree to sign on for the same disclosures in print as they do digitally.

The US is the largest consumer market in the world in terms of revenue. Over 100 million multicultural consumers reside there with over $2.5 trillion in buying power.

Many of these consumers are better reached through non-traditional digital and ethnic media. Today, the most successful agencies may not buy spots on prime-time TV or radio stations. Instead, they execute an integrated promotional mix which includes advertising, sales promotions, public relations, personal selling, direct marketing and most importantly a digital strategy in a language and medium preferred by their target consumers, not the brand client.

CHALLENGES FOR THE ISLAMIC DIGITAL MARKETER

In this section we reflect on key challenges that marketers must overcome to successfully use digital media to address Muslim consumers.

Digital Media and the Muslim Identity

Muslims' motives to buy products and engage with brands are as wide and diverse as their geographies, ethnicities and languages. However, aspects of their religious affinity have common factors that hold true for the majority of Muslims, such as dietary preferences, modesty, social responsibility, financial services, education, spirituality, and so on.

According to a JWT report (JWT, 2007), Muslim Americans said they felt ignored by big brands and that they would like to be acknowledged as Muslims in marketing campaigns. Furthermore, 70 per cent of Muslims felt that brands played an important role in their purchasing decisions, as opposed to 55 per cent of other Americans surveyed. Similarly, 59 per cent of Muslims stated that they made a point of knowing which brands are popular, compared with 42 per cent of the general sample. Clearly, brand affinity is an important driver in decision-making for Muslims.

Al-Jazeera has become a global news and information source and gained market share quickly by focusing on building a brand within the Muslim market. While several global brands have succeeded by focusing on Muslims in Muslim-majority countries, there are also over 300 million Muslims in Muslim-minority countries. Muslims exhibit a wide range of affinities towards Muslim lifestyle offerings. Muslim consumers' ethnic affinities also affect their product and media consumption habits.

Digital channels allow marketers to carefully target Muslim consumers without over-using their 'religious' identity to attract their attention. Consumers may feel their identity being over-used if marketers single them out in mass marketing whereas digital media can subtly integrate brand messaging among lifestyle content. Digital marketing can take into account consumers' sub-identities from sports to fashion, from technology to entertainment, and can provide instant value to the consumer, thereby initiating and cultivating a relationship at a very low cost.

The next generation of Muslim consumers does not shy away from expressing its feelings and preferences. Younger Muslims are becoming quite conspicuous in displaying their identity and are evidently proud of it. Indeed, many young Muslims in the US, who go to schools with very few Muslim classmates, proudly announce themselves as Muslims and are widely accepted as Muslim Americans by friends and teachers. The million plus 'I'm Muslim and I'm proud' fans on Facebook is a sign of their confidence. These young men and women will control a significant portion of consumer spending in the years to come. Any brand connecting with them now has a better chance of retaining them as a profitable consumer in the future. And digital channels are clearly where these young consumers are today (North et al., 2008).

As mentioned earlier, there is a critical mass of Muslims who live as minorities in countries around the globe. It has been observed that the minority Muslims are concerned about the next generation's connection with their religion. Muslim immigrants in the Western world make extra efforts to take their children to Sunday Islamic school, mosques and other social events that may bring the next generation closer to their culture and religion. These Muslims are also looking for online options as an alternative way to keep their families connected to their religion. This provides an outreach opportunity for brands to make contact with a desirable audience through a unique medium.

Gaining the Muslim Consumer's Attention in the Digital Environment

The age of Google has put more power in the hands of the consumer. Where messages could be channeled through a select group of media in the past (for example. broadcast TV, newspapers, radio), inventions like TiVO and the ability to search for what one is looking for have caused a massive power shift away from marketers. Consumers now have the ability to ignore messages from marketers completely, and Muslim consumers are not any different. They want to be addressed, entertained and informed by the media they watch. As a result, marketers are becoming content producers.

The strategic creation of content for the Muslim consumer is a key relationship-building tool that gives consumers what they are interested in, rather than the product or the company itself. It is not necessarily expensive to develop such a relationship, but it must be of high quality. The starting point of the relationship should illustrate to the potential customers that the company not only knows what they like but is ready to show its interest by investing in the relationship. To do this effectively, companies must take the time to study and explore how their specific products and services fit into the Muslim lifestyle. They should also study the online conversations within sub-communities around the product category or industry segment to gather valuable insight on types of content that would be appropriate and appealing to the consumers. Thus, a company can also learn about the required levels of product customization (if any) to address a particular need and the time when the consumer is ready to hear the company's message.

The nature of the Internet means that content can come in many forms. It includes blogs, news, video, images, interactive games, polls and more. Companies have an opportunity to combine these digital tools with interests in all different lifestyle categories to produce compelling content that attracts Muslim customers. If executed properly, the content is shared and goes viral among the community on multiple platforms, reaching both online and offline potential customers. By being the owner or sponsor of the content, the brand becomes associated by the community with a source of expertise that understands their needs. The other method is finding content or content producers that have a pre-existing relationship with the community and associating closely with their content, including cross-references to reinforce the affiliation.

Content distribution should also be strategic and well managed. Targeting the Muslim community means using trusted media for that community. Popular mainstream channels like YouTube and even television networks may be less trusted by the Muslim community when discussing topics related to them. Providing the right content on Muslim-friendly media channels opens the door to positive dialog with the community and a long-term conversation that can be followed with targeted advertising to generate transactions and direct response.

Case: Wilson Basketball

Returning again to the case of Wilson Basketball, Wilson has been engaging Muslim consumers through content they would find attractive. Through their Dream Team campaign on Muxlim.com (www.muxlim.com/dreamteam), the company was able to engage with users about basketball within the context of Muslim players in the NCAA. Initial study of the online conversations showed an extremely positive association with basketball within the Muslim lifestyle context. Muxlim analyzed each post for words that expressed the emotional context of that post, using an algorithm that noted the terms within a certain range of the word 'basketball.' 'Right,' 'Good' and 'Love' emerged as the top emotional-context words within more than 550 blogs, Twitter and Facebook posts mentioning basketball during February 2010. Using this and other data about Muslim lifestyle conversations related to basketball, a campaign was launched to explore the use of messages and content-creation based on these findings. During the campaign, and through experimenting with posts that had no Muslim references versus ones that did have Muslim references, 10 to 20 times more activity and interest (for example views, shares and comments) were generated on posts that referenced Muslim players within the NCAA, according to Wilson Basketball. The related ad campaign clicks on banners surrounding the content averaged 0.14 per cent CTR in comparison to Google's standard ad CTR of 0.04 per cent.

CONCLUSION

Digital media have enabled the most fragmented of markets to be crafted into lucrative opportunities, including substantial opportunities in the Muslim consumer market. The world is rapidly becoming more digital, and as many as 250 to 287 million Muslims are online today. Since Muslim consumers have been strategically engaged before in only a minimal fashion, brands can build loyalty and gain competitive advantage within this emerging market by utilizing the emotional powers of digital media. Looking at the combination of growing Internet penetration among Muslims and combining that with data about Muslim buying power can help indicate the best digital marketing opportunities within the global Muslim community and also follow those opportunities that emerge in the future.

To do this, digital can be applied as both a broadcast and listening opportunity for brands to develop the emotional relationship with the Muslim community, using the techniques that are best suited for social media. This requires a change in the way brands and companies address the Muslim consumer, starting with a move away from the traditional broadcast methods.

Mangold and Faulds (2009) describe the shift towards a form of engagement similar to that practiced in the 2010 MoneyGram campaign. They note: 'Managers must learn to shape consumer discussions in a manner that is consistent with the organization's mission and performance goals.' They continue: '[Methods] include providing consumers with networking platforms, and using blogs, social media tools, and promotional tools to engage customers.'

For companies marketing to Muslim consumers, the true nature of harnessing the social web today is in using multiple media types. For example, the MoneyGram campaign combined the use of Muxlim.com, Facebook and Twitter, each having its own advantages for sharing and communication. Not only were messages originally posted and pushed to the community, but also these tools were used to listen and respond to users, creating further opportunities for sharing and interaction.

This does not, however, mean that marketers need to impose overt religious messages through digital channels. The digital universe is a place where people come to enjoy and emotionally connect within the context of their values. Marketers must use the digital opportunity to engage honestly and within the context of their brand.

In conclusion, digital and especially social media represent the key to launching new opportunities for marketers towards becoming the category brand or product of choice for the Muslim consumer. The digital path can also be an affordable chance to address a large global niche market with products and services based on the brands' demonstrated understanding of Muslim lifestyle and the common thread this lifestyle weaves between people of many nations.

Suggested Further Research

In observing the fast-growing Muslim consumer market, observations should be started now to track the emerging channels and trends in this market. These studies can be used to successfully harness other emerging markets as they are recognized.

Some specific areas of study are also suggested to improve the understanding of the true behaviors of Muslims online. This chapter assumes that Muslim Internet adoption and subsequent behavior are similar to those of others in the population within the specific country where they live. In places where the majority of the population is Muslim, it is easy to assume that Muslim Internet usage is representative of that country's population. But in Muslim minority countries, does being a Muslim imply that a person is more or less likely to be online? Is there a class difference between Muslims and non-Muslims in the society that would result in a significant difference in Internet usage or availability? In India, Muslims are often in the upper classes. In the US, the Pew Research Center reported that Muslim Americans are primarily 'middle class and mostly mainstream' (Pew Research Center, 2007), which would suggest that they fall in line with most of the American population on other behaviors. It is our opinion that studies and funding have focused unduly on the radicalization of the Internet by a small minority. Few scientific studies if any have comprehensively sought to understand the average Muslim usage of the Internet in Muslim minority countries, which is where studies have already shown that much of the buying power and marketing opportunity lie.

NOTE

1. Muxlim Report (2010). The research sources for the population and usage data in the report include: http://religions.pewforum.org/, http://www.islamicpopulation.com/source.html, data published by Nielsen

Online, by the International Telecommunications Union, by GfK, and data from the following sites: http://www.state.gov/, http://www.factbook.net/muslim_pop.php, http://www.nationmaster.com/graph/ rel_isl_pop-religion-islam-population, http://www.Internetworldstats.com/stats.htm, https://www.cia.gov/ library/publications/the-world-factbook/.

BIBLIOGRAPHY

Ad Age Data Center (2009), *Hispanic Fact Pack*, New York: Crain Communications.

Ad Age Data Center (2010), 'Digital family trees 2010', *Advertising Age*, available at http://adage.com/digital-familytrees2010/.

Anderson, C. (2006), *The Long Tail: Why the Future of Business Is Selling Less of More*, New York: Hyperion.

Arab Business Machine (2010), 'YouTube user "iloveipodsandmusic". *Have you got the touch? Dubai Football – Viral Video*', YouTube, available at http://www.youtube.com/user/iloveipodsandmusic, http://www.facebook.com/iloveipods.

Benkler, Y. (2006), *The Wealth of Networks*, New Haven: Yale University Press.

Bladd, J. and C. Ferris-Lay (2010), 'Planet Islamic: the $2trn battle for the halal market', *Arabian Business*, 9 September, http://www.arabianbusiness.com/planet-islamic---2trn-battle-for-halal-market-348084.html

Boyd, D. (2008), 'Why youth ♥ social network sites: the role of networked publics in teenage social life', in, D. Buckingham (ed.), *Youth, Identity, and Digital Media* Cambridge, MA: MIT Press, pp. 119–42.

Chiswick, L. (2008), 'In a virtual world of their own', *Guardian* (UK), 11 December.

Fayrouz (2010), 'Fayrouz: who are we?', available at http://www.fayrouz.com/aboutus/ (2010).

Gabriel, Y. and T. Lang (1995), *The Unmanageable Consumer: Contemporary Consumption and its Fragmentations*, London: Sage.

Gobé, M. (2009), *Emotional Branding: The New Paradigm for Connecting Brands to People*, New York: Allworth Press.

Haymarket Media (2010), *Campaign Asia Pacific*, Hong Kong/Singapore: Haymarket Media Ltd., available at http://www.campaignasia.com/Page/AdSpend.aspx.

IMF (International Monetary Fund) (2010), http://www.imf.org/external/data.html.

JWT (2007), *Marketing to Muslims*, New York: JWT.

JWT Dubai (2009), Vimeo user 'pullbeard', *The Chunky Boys play FootBasketball*, Vimeo website, http://vimeo.com/5611338.

Kerbaj, R. (2009), 'Muslim population rising 10 times faster than rest of society', *Times* (UK), 30 January.

Kettani, H. (2010), 'World Muslim population 2010,' in *Proceedings of the 8th Hawaii International Conference on Arts and Humanities, Honolulu, Hawaii, January 2010*, available at www.pupr.edu/hkettani/papers/ HICAH2010.pdf.

Kierzkowski, A., S. Mcquade, R. Waitman and M. Zeisser (1996), 'Marketing to the digital consumer', *McKinsey Quarterly*, (2), 180–83.

Kotler, P., and K. Keller (2006), *Marketing Management* (12th edn), New Jersey: Prentice Hall.

Learmonth, M. (2010), 'The top 10 viral ads of all time', *The Ad Age Viral Video Chart* online, available at http://adage.com/digital/article?article_id=145673.

Lehdonvirta, V. (2009), *Virtual Consumption*, Publications of the Turku School of Economics (A-11:2009), Turku: Turku School of Economics.

Lehdonvirta, V., H. Soma, H. Ito, T. Yamabe, H. Kimura and T. Nakajima (2009),'UbiPay: minimizing transaction costs with smart mobile payments', in *Proceedings of the 6th International Conference on Mobile Technology, Application and Systems (Mobility 2009)*, New York: ACM.

Mangold, W., and D. Faulds (2009), 'Social media: the new hybrid element of the promotion mix', *Business Horizons*, **52** (4), 357–65.

Muxlim website homepage (2010), http://www.muxlim.com.

North, S., I. Snyder and S. Bulfin (2008), 'Digital tastes: social class and young people's technology use', *Information, Communication and Society*, **11** (7), 895–911.

Peterson, M.A. (2010), 'Agents of hybridity: class, culture brokers, and the entrepreneurial imagination in cosmopolitan Cairo', in Donald Wood (ed.), *Economic Action in Theory and Practice: Anthropological Investigations (Research in Economic Anthropology, Volume 30)*, Bingley, UK: Emerald Group Publishing Limited, pp. 225–56.

Pew Research Center (2007), *Muslim Americans: Middle Class and Mostly Mainstream*, Report of the Pew Research Center, available at http://pewresearch.org/assets/pdf/muslim-americans.pdf.

Pew Research Center (2008), *U.S. Religious Landscape Survey*, The Pew Forum on Religion and Public Life, available at http://religions.pewforum.org/comparisons#.

Power, C. (2009), 'Halal: buying muslim', *Time*, 25 May, available at http://www.time.com/time/magazine/article/0,9171,1898247-1,00.html#ixzz0tAmj1tUr.

Scoble, R., and S. Israel (2006), *Naked Conversations: How Blogs are Changing the Way Businesses Talk with Customers,* New York: Wiley and Sons.

ShareThis website homepage (2010), http://sharethis.com/.

Story, J., and J. Hess (2009), 'Ethical brand management: customer relationships and ethical duties', *Journal of Product and Brand Management*, **19** (4), 240–49.

Surowiecki, J. (2005), *The Wisdom of Crowd*, New York: Anchor Books.

Tapscott, D. and A. Williams (2006), *Wikinomics: How Mass Collaboration Changes Everything*, New York: Portfolio.

UNDP (United Nations Development Programme) (2009a), *Human Development Report 2009*, including HDI Human Development Index, New York: Palgrave Macmillan, available at http://hdr.undp.org/en/reports/global/hdr2009/.

UNDP (2009b), 'The Human Development Concept', website description accompanying *Human Development Report 2009*, available at http://hdr.undp.org/en/humandev/.

Urban, G. (2003), *Digital Marketing Strategy*, New Jersey: Prentice Hall.

Vollmer, C., and G. Precourt (2008), *Always On: Advertising, Marketing, and Media in an Era of Consumer Control*, New York: McGraw-Hill.

Young, S.W. (2010), 'Insights into interfaith potential from a two-year study of the Islamic society of oston', JewishMuslim.org website, available at http://www.jewishmuslim.org/articles/Young_article_Interfaith_Relations.doc

PART IV

GLOBALIZATION, POLITICS AND RESISTANCE

19 Serving God through the market: the emergence of Muslim consumptionscapes and Islamic resistance

*Sultan Tepe**

The Second Islamic Clothing, Fashion, Apparel and Accessories Fair, 'the only fair of this genre ever organized in the world', in the words of its organizers, opened its doors in İstanbul, Turkey in April of 2010.[1] The fair was popularly referred to as the *tesettür* fashion fair.[2] With a 400 per cent increase in total participation over one year the fair displayed the dynamism of Islamic fashion amidst the attending producers' praise for the insatiable customer appetite and an astonishing potential for further growth within the Islamic fashion market. Attesting to this potential, not only committed producers of Islamic fashion eagerly participated in the fair, but also some non-religious clothing companies had their stands ready, having never invested in Islamic fashion before. At the entry of the exhibition center there was another unexpected scene; a group of women stood in their *tesettür*, vehemently protesting against the convention with Turkish and English signs: 'Are Qur'anic Surahs [on *tesettür*] out of Fashion?' 'Do not be the object

Source: Haksöz Haber, Tesettür Modası Protesto Edildi, 12 April 2010. Özgür Açilim Platformu, 12 April 2010, http://ozguracilim.net/page/5/.

Figure 19.1   A group of protesters at the Second Islamic Clothing, Fashion, Apparel and Accessories Fair, İstanbul, 11 April 2010

of capitalism.' 'What is fashion? Creating (Dis)conformities.' 'Wake Up, Resist, Free Yourself.' The scene, with its unexpected tensions and actors, presented a microcosm of new faith-based consumptionscapes where both miraculous economic success stories and strong yet muted reactions to them create a vibrant market space that defies conventional patterns and explanations.

The Islamic fashion industry's exponential growth has not been an exceptional case in the country. In fact, since the early 1990s, Turkey has witnessed the emergence of an Islamic consumptionscape which provides a diverse range of faith-approved (or faith-based) goods and services ranging from alcohol free perfumes to luxurious gender segregated resorts. It is this unprecedented meeting of Islamic ideas and market forces that mesmerized many observers not only in scholarly circles but beyond. A quick review of the existing literature identifies three main phases through which studies of the emerging Islamic consumptionscapes have expanded yet also have been confined to the dominant views of various disciplines. Enchantment by the unexpected blending of Islam and capitalism marked the first genre of the literature (mid-1980s and early 1990s) (for example, Birtek and Toprak, 1993; Kedourie, 1996). In this early stage, studies often described the emerging market as a paradoxical mélange where the Islamic community met its other, Western capitalism. The second genre (late 1990s) moved beyond the bewilderment of the initial discovery and paid more attention to the unfolding creolization and hybridization, and started to explore the plurality marking this expanding market as a *bricolage* (for example, Göle, 1999a; Navaro Yashin, 2002; Sandıkcı and Ger, 2001, 2005, 2010). As the studies on hybridization alone seem to give us an incomplete assessment of how and with what implications consumptionscapes emerged, a burgeoning third genre has turned its attention to the ways in which Islamic identities and consumption practices are formed, contested, and transformed, through a comprehensive analysis of Islamic consumers, producers, and marketplace discourses (for example, Göle, 2000; Buğra, 2002; Adaş, 2006; Tepe, 2008; Gökarıksel and Secor, 2009).

Building on existing studies, this analysis falls into the third genre by exploring consumers and dynamics of faith-based markets *on their own terms.* To this end, it explores how Turkey's faith-based market sits at the intersection of class and identity politics and serves as one of the most important venues to better understand the transformation of market structure, social processes and economic relations in Turkey. In order to demonstrate how these class and identity politics play out in and through the Islamic consumptionscape, the arguments presented focus on the rather unique case of Tekbir – one of the most successful and internationally renowned Islamic clothing firms in Turkey. Due to its central role in the *tesettür* market, its unprecedented transnational success, and its radical innovations, Tekbir presents an excellent case that embodies the transformation of Islamic markets and commodification of Islam as well as the Islamic resistance to it. More specifically, this chapter delves into the court case that a group of Muslim theologians brought against the company – on the grounds that it misused sacred values – to analyze the nature of Islamic markets as well as their critics. In fact, while the company's name, Tekbir, is popularly referred to as 'Allah's tailor' or the 'Prophet's Couturier', Tekbir literally refers to the statement *'Allahu akbar'* (God is Great) – expressing one of the key beliefs of Islam. Given its market position and pronounced ability to tap into the Islamic symbols, the legal case against Tekbir displays intricate class-based and exegetical tensions that mark the Islamic community – a community which is often described as homogeneous.

To capture the pluralistic nature of the Islamic consumptionscapes, the subsequent discussion introduces us to the intricate relations among the producers, goods, consumers, and contestants of Islamic markets. To better understand the role of 'faith' the analysis explores the broader context of faith-based markets and the ways in which different interpretations of Islamic sources are offered, as well as variant approaches to the religious values of piety and righteousness in the marketplace are presented. It contends that only through understanding such contexts and approaches can we fully grasp how customers view faith-based products and how resistance to the Islamic market from within plays out. Understanding the consumers of faith-based products is especially important given that despite its importance for marketers and consumer researchers, Islamic resistance largely remains an underexplored terrain in the literature. Existing studies mainly address the phenomenon within the framework of the Islamic–secular conflict and as a reaction to cultural modernization (Norris and Inglehart, 2004; Sandıkcı and Ekici, 2009). While these studies have provided valuable insights regarding Islamic resistance to the global consumer culture and its products, they implicitly assume that all Islamic marketplace inventions are welcomed by Islamic actors and fail to address the multiplicity of ways in which Islamic consumers react to the Islamic market's offerings and innovations. Therefore, the missing analyses of Islamic reactions and resistance to faith-based consumption goods and services amounts to a significant theoretical and empirical lacuna in the rapidly growing literature on Islamic consumer markets.

Against this background the analysis explores Tekbir as a heuristic case to explain the ways in which (1) faith-based brands establish themselves not only in Turkey's growing and competitive market but also in the booming Islamic transnational markets; (2) new Islamic consumption practices are launched and perceived; and (3) the emergence of these new brands has been accepted and contested among Muslim consumers. In an effort to locate these issues in a broader historical context, the first section provides a brief description of Turkey's expanding Islamic consumptionscape and traces its transformation over the last three decades. The following sections include a review of the intricate foundations and rules in Islamic exegeses that lie at the center of Islamic internal debates on Islamic consumptionscapes and the content and reactions to the court case against Tekbir. The findings draw on diverse sources such as a set of interviews with Tekbir managers and two plaintiffs and their legal advisor who took the company to court on the grounds that it misused sacred values, as well as a review of consumer reactions to Tekbir expressed by diverse groups, by paying special attention to the reaction of women who wear the headscarf, in various newspapers, including pro-Islamic newspapers, and several meetings such as the ones held by the Beykoz and Pendik Municipalities in İstanbul or sponsored by Özgür-Der, an Islamic Human Rights Association.[3] At the theoretical level, this close review of Tekbir allows us to identify the competing demands of various Islamic groups that seek to assert their version of Islam over others, a process that can be defined and analyzed as competition over authoritative authenticity.

The use of authenticity in this analysis offers several advantages. Given the dearth of studies on the customers of faith-based markets, viewing the debates on Islamic consumptionscapes through the lens of authenticity enables us to capture the idiosyncrasies of Islamic markets in particular as well as the trends that mark consumptionscapes in general. In a global society, where identifying the nature, locus and acceptable representation of marginalized and tainted identities and ideas defines many political and social puzzles, the term 'authentic' is used profusely both to present and distinguish authoritative claims and distinctive experiences that individuals perceive as original, 'loyal to its source,' or the 'real deal' in many areas. Reflecting what appears to be a new global battle over the best representation of the original, the term 'authenticity' serves as a defining idiom not only in marketing (for example, Leigh et al., 2006; Gilmore and Pine, 2007; Outka, 2009; Beverland and Farrelly, 2010), but also in philosophy, political theory (for example, Trilling, 1972; Ferrara, 1998; Taylor, 1991), ethnic studies, nationalist movements, (for example, Bendix, 1997; Lee, 1997; Cheng, 2004; Lindholm, 2008) and more importantly in religious movements (for example, Deemer, 1997; Chidester, 2005). Although it has become a common currency in many disciplines, authenticity is a complex and elusive term consisting of two parts – *auto* (self) and *hentes* (being and doing). The term serves to validate the claims to capture the true essence. Yet such assertions are inherently self-appraising, prompting others to question the user's ability and credentials to represent the claimed original idea. Due to this dialectical tension intrinsic to 'authenticity', many view the term as holding antithetical ideas. Yet perhaps because of its nature to provoke questions, the term has particular significance in the faith-based market. As the discussion below shows, each faith-based product faces the test of authenticity, tackling the questions of whether and how it is acceptable within the boundaries of religion. Disentangling debates in faith-based consumptionscapes through the lens of authenticity illuminates the ways in which these parallel debates (for example, globalization, cultural, social, market and religiously centered) converge in the production of faith-based markets and helps to capture the critical contestation over the meaning of Islam's distinctive self and representation.

THE TRANSFORMATION OF TURKEY'S FAITHFUL BUSINESSMEN AND FAITH-BASED MARKETS

A review of the metamorphosis of Tekbir from a local neighborhood store in İstanbul in the early 1980s to an international brand name in the early 1990s shows that, despite its remarkable success, Tekbir's rise is not an accidental triumph against all odds. Instead, placing Tekbir in a broader context shows that the company has risen on the tide of Islamic political and economic movements as well as its special ability to advance a unique approach to Islamic clothing. A careful look at Tekbir's context helps us tease out how the transformation of state policies, bourgeoisie, and political ideologies often go hand in hand, and, more significantly, how consumptionscapes are nested within many divergent currents. It is important to note that although faith-based markets have gained salience in recent years, Islamic bourgeoisie have always existed as the owners of provincial, small-to-medium size enterprises (SMEs). These provincial and decentralized SMEs started to carve out more space in Turkey, and later in international markets, as the Turkish economy has been transformed from its initial state controlled form (from the early 1930s to the early 1960s), to an export oriented market (the mid 1960s and the early 1980s), and finally to a more open market economy (from the mid 1990s to the present). In part due to their initial state-dependent growth, and later to their close relations to the state, Turkey's big industrialists are often seen as the supporters of Turkey's official policies and its secularism. Thus Turkey's main business organization, the Association of Turkish Industrialists and Businessmen, TÜSİAD, came to be seen as a secularist institution catering to big business interests and marginalizing faith-based production.[4]

When international factors and internal domestic crises forced the state elite to revise its state-centered economic policies, some new economic actors were formed and new political alliances were forged. Attesting to the close ties between Turkey's political Islamic movements and economic changes, Turkey's first openly Islamic party's leader, Necmeddin Erbakan, was elected to the board of chambers, an institution that represented the mostly provincial private sector.[5] It was only after losing his position on the board that Erbakan embarked upon his political career. Under Erbakan's leadership, Turkey's first wave of political Islamists spoke of a 'just order,' and advocated promoting a local version of economic growth informed by Islamic values against the West. It was only after his party became a part of the ruling coalition government in 1997 that Erbakan's views faced strong criticism from Islamic groups. As explained below, a new group that relied less on the state to create a liberal just system was formed under the leadership of Recep Tayyip Erdoğan. The popular slogan 'commitment to a just order' was replaced by one pledging allegiance to conservative democracy and a commitment to the power of non-state and free enterprise. Thus the strengthening of Islamic social movements since the early 1990s and the state economic reforms towards launching a free market based and export oriented economy altogether helped to form a fecund environment for provincial Islamic entrepreneurs to make gains against established big industrialists (Göle, 1997; Buğra, 1998; Keyder, 2004; Demir, 2004).

In this political context, the establishment and growth of the Independent Industrialists and Businessmen Association, known by its Turkish acronym MÜSİAD, exemplifies the remarkable remaking of Turkey's economic sphere and subsequent boom of faith-based markets. MÜSİAD was formed in 1991 with an acronym that was popularly assumed to refer to its 'Muslim' outlook. The group's name and the members' geographical location suggested that MÜSİAD was formed to promote a nascent Islamic bourgeoisie that could not be represented in the established TÜSİAD.[6] As the TÜSİAD controlled the export and financial sectors, MÜSİAD members focused on the local markets. The same entrepreneurs that took a lead in the establishment of MÜSİAD also played an important key role in Turkey's Islamic parties' electoral gains. It is important to note that such interactions between the state, Islamic bourgeoisie, and parties cannot be reduced to a linear causal relationship. Instead they often affect and are affected by each others' positions and their relations are also altered by external global factors. For instance, MÜSİAD was initially opposed to EU membership, but the 1996 European Custom Union Agreement (CUA) turned the SMEs into one of the main beneficiaries of the agreement thanks to substantial subsidies and new market opportunities in Europe. It is not surprising therefore, that in the mid-1990s Turkey's then most popular Islamist party, the Welfare Party (WP), revised its anti-EU position. The sea-change among the Islamic groups further encouraged MÜSİAD to not only alter its skeptical position on the EU but also to invest in the West, as well as other markets. The growing appeal of Islamic movements, the electoral success of Islamic parties, and the changes in international markets under neo-liberal policies altogether created an unprecedented environment for faith-based markets to expand and the community of faithful businessmen to grow. Attesting to the confluence of these conductive factors, MÜSİAD has undergone a drastic transformation from a modest business association with limited membership to a transnational business union, by expanding its membership from dozens to 4700 members operating more than 12 000 companies whose production amounted to 15 per cent of Turkey's GDP in 2009.[7]

The emergence of Turkey's currently ruling Justice and Development Party (JDP) offers another illuminating example of the close relations between political and economic Islam and the transformation of Islamic movements from within. The WP's astounding victory in the 1996 national elections raised the expectations of the Islamist groups and business elite regarding Islamic reforms. However, while in power the WP not only failed to promote the interest of Islamic groups but also endorsed a set of policies which popularly came to be known as the 1997 soft military coup that sought to curb the power of Islamic groups, and an internal revolt quickly followed.[8] When the group, which sought to take a more active role in politics and economics, popularly described as 'reformist,' lost in the primaries, they split to form the JDP. The JDP's leadership represented a broad range of interests with a noticeable presence of the Islamic business elite. It is no coincidence that since its inception a significant number of the JDP's founding members were 'merchants' or 'business owners' (more than half of its 50 founders), whereas engineers formed the majority of the Erbakan-led Prosperity Party's Central Committee. With this business centered perspective, the JDP used its electoral gains to form the foundation of a globally oriented, open domestic market. As such, among many other business friendly bills, the party passed the 2004 law that loosened the reporting requirement on businesses (that is, a law initially introduced to prevent tax fraud), and the 2005 banking law that asked major banks to allocate a certain percentage of their loans to SMEs. Other laws that sought to attract foreign direct investment established neo-liberal market practices, thereby offering a supportive environment for SMEs to establish themselves as major players in the global markets (Buğra, 1998; Öniş, 2005; Demiralp, 2009).

It is important to note that the changes in the business world and political sphere were rooted in and have parallel shifts at the societal level. While transformations at the societal level can be more elusive and hard to measure, one of the most comprehensive surveys on Islamic clothing, entitled 'Religion, Secularism and the Veil in Daily Life Survey,' offers a foundation to observe some of the most pronounced shifts.[9] The trends identified by the report indicate that from 2003 to 2007, in a span of four years, there has been a significant increase in headscarf use.[10] The percentage of women who cover their heads increased from 64 per cent to 69 per cent. The survey classifies headscarf users into three groups: those who use the most habitual traditional headscarf, *başörtü*, the more conservative who wear the *türban,* and the most conservative, the *chadur* users. When these different forms are taken into account, the numbers of those who wore the *türban* has increased drastically from 3.5 per cent to 16.2 per cent. The overall trends not only suggest that wearing the headscarf is becoming a more common practice but also that those who cover their heads increasingly prefer the *türban*. The results also show that the increase in *türban* use has been highest among the youngest group (18–28 years of age) with an increase from 4 per cent to 20 per cent.[11]

The recent shifts in population indicate that Tekbir's domestic market, Islamic clothing, not only constitutes one of the fastest growing markets in the country with a very dynamic customer profile, but also poses the question of how its production is shaped and influenced by unfolding changes. While the vibrancy of the domestic market is remarkable, it is also important to note that within Turkey's notable growth rate (an average growth rate of 5.2 per cent between 2003 and 2009), the textile market plays a critical role. As such, in 2002 clothing exports constituted 21.8 per cent of the country's total exports and in 2006 this contribution increased to 26 per cent. The textile sector includes many large companies with world-wide operations, yet the majority of the firms are small and medium sized. Notwithstanding these supportive trends the subsequent discussion elaborates on, Tekbir's rise cannot be attributed solely to the Islamic movements and business's upward swing. Instead it becomes clear that the company sits at the intersection of many clashing and reinforcing forces and that its resilient expansion is anything but inadvertent.

It is important to note that the unprecedented growth of the Islamic consumption market in Turkey is not a *sui generis* process. Instead it can be seen as a reflection of similar processes unfolding in other Muslim countries at the global level. In fact, the increasing political and social appeal of Turkey's Islamic movements since the early 1970s mirrors comparable processes in other countries ranging from Egypt to Indonesia (Öniş,1997; Buğra, 1998; Tepe, 2008). Furthermore, while Turkey has followed some global patterns it has also played an important role in defining some of these patterns – especially those pertaining to the formation of the global Islamic consumption market. For instance, one of the most important international organizations for Muslim countries, the Organization of the Islamic Conference (OIC) was established in 1969. OIC has grown to include 57 countries and plays a significant role in spearheading changes in the Muslim world. A fact neglected by many observers is that OIC's main committee on economic cooperation, the Standing Committee for Economic and Commercial Cooperation (COMCEC) was established during its Third Islamic Summit in 1981. Only after the nomination of the Turkish president as the COMCEC president in 1984 did the committee start to function and manage to take the first steps towards strengthening the economic and commercial capacity of individual members and cooperation between them. Attesting to the pivotal role played by the committee under Turkey's leadership the committee established itself as a platform in the 1990s to develop shared standards for all Islamic products. To this end COMCEC formed the Standardization Experts Group (SEG) which prepared three key documents that exert critical influence on Muslim consumptionscapes, namely 'the OIC General Guidelines on Halal Food,' 'Guidelines for Bodies Providing Halal Certification;' and 'Guidelines for the Authorized Accreditation Body Accrediting Halal Certification Bodies' in 2009.[12] Turkey's leading role in the identification of the Islamic standards for emerging faith-based markets is further consolidated due to the SEG's current efforts to develop international implementation mechanisms of the OIC Halal Food System.

As the above review illustrates when placed into its broader context, Turkey's faith-based consumptionscape sits at the cross-section of a wide range of local and global currents and offers an excellent environment to understand how these currents interact and define the shape of Muslim consumptionscapes. Accordingly our inquiries about the Tekbir case form an important venue to understand the nature and consumer of faith-based markets not only in Turkey but beyond. Given the forces shaping its broader environment, untangling Tekbir's reinvention from a small store in Fatih, a conservative neighborhood in İstanbul, to a global brand in world fashion offers important insight to the remarkable transformation of pro-Islamic small merchants into global market players. A quick review of the company's history shows that Tekbir's owner, Mustafa Karaduman, got his first job in the textile sector as an ironer in 1969, the same year that Necmeddin Erbakan, the leader of Turkey's first Islamic party, embarked upon his political career. Karaduman, according to his own account, was irked by Fatih's clothing stores, as they displayed outfits blatantly exposing women's bodies. After opening a clothing store serving women looking for religiously acceptable attire in 1982, he was well positioned to take advantage of the forthcoming boom in Islamic economic political and social movements and women's demand for Islamic clothing. Although Tekbir's business venture was first launched in Fatih, a mixed community mostly populated by religiously conservative middle and lower middle class residents, its first expansion was in 1992 to Osmanbey, a liberal upscale neighborhood in İstanbul. This captured both Tekbir's ability to successfully expand and its desire to cater to the tastes of faithful and middle and upper middle class consumers.

The mutually supportive relation between Tekbir and Turkey's Islamic groups was strained when the company held its very popular yet controversial *tesettür*, or Islamic clothing fashion shows.[13] Hiring a designer from Germany and enlisting models who declared that they opposed *tesettür* in their personal lives, blending Ottoman martial music with on-stage symbolic prayers performed by the models, Tekbir, for some of its observers, exemplified the ability of Islamic businesses to expand in a market society, while for others the company demonstrated ultra-pragmatism in its use of Islamic symbols.[14] In part due to the clout of such reactions, Tekbir distanced itself from Turkey's first Islamic movement and forged close ties with the JDP. Parallel to the growth of the Islamic bourgeoisies and the second generation of Islamic political movements, Tekbir reinvented itself from a local to a national and later an international brand, as the company began designing the clothes of the wives of the Islamic political elite. From its humble beginnings, in the present day Tekbir has become a powerful international franchise with 92 branches, in addition to hundreds of franchised stores in Turkey, and distributors in a wide range of countries from Europe to the Middle East.[15]

Beneath the company's business success, one can find that the owner of Tekbir's rather basic yet powerful religious approach echoes an increasingly widespread market-centered approach to Islam. According to Karaduman, engaging in commerce, taming market forces and being successful is not contradictory to, but instead one *sine qua non* of becoming a pious Muslim, for example:

> Islam has five pillars. Three of them are about beliefs and body, and two of them ultimately pertain to conducting business. After all, if you don't run a successful business you cannot go to pilgrimage and if you don't do business you can't give to charities. You need to have money to go to pilgrimage and give to charity . . . If I were a journalist I would write only Islamic content, if I were a writer I would write to serve Islam. Since I am in textiles I serve my faith by making Islamic clothing.[16]

What distinguishes Tekbir from others, according to Karaduman, is its strict allegiance to Islamic requirements in its pursuit of making Islamic clothing more attractive for consumers. For instance, although rather profitable, the company would not produce *haşema*, the generic term used to describe Islamic full body swim wear. According to the founder, *haşema* does not have 'two layers;' thus it needs to be seen as an undergarment. 'If we had made this for women to wear in a mixed environment, it could be sinful because it isn't exactly an outer garment. In the Qur'an the Prophet says to his wives and other women from among the believers; when you go outside you should wear an extra covering.'[17]

Similar explanations offered by Karaduman reiterate that it is his interpretation of the Qur'an that guides his business decisions. As a result, according to the company, although Tekbir pushes the boundaries of fashion with its fashionable *tesettür*, or its Islamic clothing, at the end of the day it remains firmly within the boundaries of an Islamic framework.[18] Yet the company's commitment to religious authenticity and its efforts to protect authentic Islam manifest themselves in some important symbolic actions. For instance, Tekbir agrees to sell *haşema* but refuses to produce it due to its questionable nature within Islam. Likewise, to explain the foundation of its fashion shows, Karaduman states that the decision was not rushed but instead was discussed with well respected religious leaders, and was sanctified on the principle 'that what is permissible, or *halal* to produce and use, is also *halal* to introduce and promote' thus marketing tools can be used freely.[19] Although such exegetical ventures play an important role, they beg the question of if and how such approaches carry any weight and what impact, if any, they might have on Turkey's Islamic movements and their advocates. Thus, what makes the Tekbir case most intriguing, and a critical venue in which to understand the future of Turkey's faith-based consumptionscapes, is that the company's main product, Islamic clothing, sits at an area where religious and market forces blend and clash most visibly. With its remarkable success, and multifaceted nature, understanding the case of Tekbir enables us to explore the new faces of Islamic markets and their paradoxes not only in Turkey, but also beyond.

COMPETITION OVER AUTHENTICITY: REDISCOVERING VERSUS REINVENTING

As Islamic goods production and consumptionscapes expand exponentially, one of the questions facing both producers and consumers of faith-based markets is what makes a product Islamic. Although such questions are ostensibly simple in many cases, Islamic consumer items face the manifold demanding test of being religiously acceptable.[20] What makes Islamic clothing in general and the headscarf in particular such an area of contention is that Islamic rules are perhaps open to interpretation. For instance, commonly cited Qur'anic verses from *surah an-nur* (chapter 24, verse 31) and *surah al-ahzab* (chapter 33, verse 59) do not offer a set of specific rules about the clothing but offer only general guidelines and the intentions behind them. Thus applying these guidelines requires an authoritative interpretation of not only the texts but also a review of the Islamic tradition.

It is important to note that such interpretations of the Qur'an and the pluralism of approaches are not inconsistent with Islamic epistemology. In fact, areas that require interpretation are not limited to issues related to Islamic attire. Instead, contrary to some religious movements' claims of certainty (or of the lack of ambiguity in religious rules), in the Qur'an one can find highly abstract principles and metaphors that allow for starkly diverse interpretations and pluralistic practices. For instance, *al imran*, one of the most cited *surahs*, says: 'He it is who has sent down to thee the Book (Qur'an): In it are verses basic or fundamental (of established meaning); they are the foundation of the Book: others are allegorical, none will grasp the Message except men of *understanding* [emphasis added] (Qur'an, 3:7–8).' In fact, a closer look quickly shows that many of the messages in the Qur'an are delivered through parables, allegories and metaphors; thus discussions of religious terms and ideas are not outside Islam's own language. In light of the Qur'an's self-identification, some of these verses are called *muhkam* or decisive (which are termed as 'mother of the Scripture' [*umm ul kitab*]), while others are called *mutashabih,* that is, allegorical or idiomatic. As *mutashabih* explanations invite readers to engage critically, a plurality of interpretations are inherent to Islamic discourse; therefore the claim for 'authenticity' is one of the driving forces in debates.[21]

What makes Islam's relation to market practices rather intricate is the significance of exegetical exercises in applying the Qur'anic principles not as isolated injunctions but instead as in their relation to Islam's overall meaning-system. As such, while the Qur'an's allegorical parts cannot be read in any way one pleases, an informed reader's engagement is required to understand their details and meaning. Perhaps the paradox of the Qur'an is that if *mutashabih* explanations are left beyond the scope of continuing hermeneutical and interpretative exercises, the entire Qur'an is effectively treated as *muhkam* – going against the Qur'an's own self-identification. However, undertaking interpretations creates the multiplicity of practices that might contradict something *muhkam*. It is against this background that the expansion of Islamic faith-based consumptionscapes inevitably faces the question of who has authority in applying Islamic ideas to new practices, and how and when some interpretations transcend the boundaries of faith and start eroding the essence of Islamic messages, ideas, and symbols from within. For instance, when do authenticity claims guide religiously antagonistic demands?

TESETTÜR FASHION: A LOST CAUSE OR AN AUTHENTIC APPEARANCE OF ISLAM?

Perhaps due to the nuanced nature of the relevant Qur'anic verses and the room for authoritative interpretation, many Islamic clothing companies advertising one way or another refer to the religious foundations of the headscarf. A Tekbir advertisement conveys the religious approach it espouses by evoking the image of the modern-female Muslim and asking, who is a modern Muslimah?[22]

> The modern Muslimah strives to show her devotion to her creator through the study of *din*. She honors the scholars as inheritors of the prophets, and struggles to discipline her *nafs* [desires]. She cares as much about social justice as she does about homemaking, she has a voice and she isn't afraid to use it. The modern Muslimah isn't afraid to wear the *hijab*, and she isn't about to apologize for it either. She integrates the grand history of Islam into a contemporary Western lifestyle, without sacrificing the integrity of the *din*. Who is the modern Muslimah? She's you, sister.[23]

Such marketing appeals are rather new in that they not only openly embrace hybrid structures but reintroduce these very hybrid structures as being authentically Islamic in

Source: Personal archive.

Figure 19.2   Window display of Tekbir's store in Üsküdar, İstanbul

a changing social environment. The Western lifestyle emerges not as a cultural setting to avoid, but instead as an area to explore and conquer with an Islamic approach. Women, in these new social contexts, keep their traditional roles (homemaking) with a renewed interest in global issues (attention to global justice issues). Likewise, she honors the Prophet and resists her desires. Perhaps symbolizing women's ability to combine what appear to be clashing forces, the Islamic clothing transforms the image of women's fashion from the act of one simply throwing on a formless garment to carriers of Islamic aesthetics. In fact, the owner of Tekbir views this very new fashionable look in Islamic appearance as the main factor that encourages many to wear the headscarf and other Islamic clothing, thereby facilitating their entry into the Islamic world. Corollary to such statements, for Tekbir's owner the headscarf not only expresses faith but more importantly serves as a venue to instill faith. Karaduman states, for instance: 'We received a call from a family in Bostancı [an affluent secular neighborhood in İstanbul]. They were trying to convince their daughter to wear Islamic clothing for years. Only after she saw our fashion show she told them this is beautiful, I can cover up now.'[24]

Although Tekbir takes pride in its ability to serve God by making modest clothing also fashionable, for many the very idea of 'fashionable modesty' is a contradiction in terms. While faith-based items seem to conquer markets, they also allow market powers to substitute religious authority and consumption decisions for meaning-seeking actions. Thus whether Tekbir is able to walk the fine line of creating an authentic expression of Islam in a market society or whether their products mark the limits of the Islamic bourgeoisie's religious imagination elicits many reactions and invites us to look at their arguments further to avoid coming to a cursory or deductivist answer.

Source: Personal archive.

Figure 19.3   Window display of Tekbir's store in Üsküdar, İstanbul

'ONE AND ONLY': TEKBİR'S FAITHFUL CONSUMERS AND CONTESTANTS

Tekbir has been in the public eye through its fashion shows which first launched in 1992. These shows stirred broad interest and garnered widening support and criticism, attesting to the firms' ability to shape the Islamic clothing sector and its constant hybridization of Islamic ideas and modern fashion. Although such reactions and support for the company are often expressed in newspaper columns and in local discussions, a group of Islamic intellectuals took a rather unprecedented step and opened up an unusual case against Tekbir in May 2008. The chair of the Qur'anic Exegeses section from Ankara University's Theology Department, İlhami Güler, and the founder and general manager of one of Turkey's most respectable Islamic periodicals, *İslamiyat*, Süleyman Bayraktar, brought a court case against Tekbir.[25] The case centered on the very name Tekbir, questioning its acceptability as a brand name under the current laws guiding the Court for Intellectual and Property Rights. The application resorted to an existing law, Law 556 on the protection of patent brand names, which forbids the commercial use of names 'imbued by society with a moral value and religious symbols.'[26] According to Güler and Bayraktar:

> The word Tekbir which is an expression of the idea of *tawhid*, the unity of God, and a part of daily prayer, has been turned into a commercial brand by the defendant company. The use of *tekbir* in trade damages the spiritual meaning of the term, allowing the company to accrue income by capitalizing on religious convictions and initiating unfair competition by applying a sacred name to a brand name.[27]

The court case, according to the plaintiffs, seeks to set a precedent for other similar company or business names that advance a predatory expansion of Islamic markets by appropriating Islamic names. Given the mushrooming of trademarks that use Islamic names (*uhud*, *tekbir*, and so on) and the establishment of faith-based markets, according to Güler, it is religious groups which need to object to the abuse of sacred religious symbols by those who claim to act in the name of religion.

Ironically, nowhere in the complaint did the plaintiffs mention the company's products. Yet they question the company's attempt to claim authority over the meaning and the shape of Islamic dressing. In other words, it is not the product per se but the owner's messages and his association with the religious meaning of his brand that constitutes the real challenge:

> In our petition we contend that the products this brand produces fall in the realm of *tesettür* (covering) in Islam. However, the owner of the brand, instead of introducing his own products alone, talks about the religious rules behind the covering with an all inclusive authority. He often claims that no one knows the rule of Islamic covering, *tesettür*, better than he does. This means that he associates his brand with a religious belief by ignoring individuals' different choices. He makes others feel bounded by his own choice. However, covering is up to the discretion of individuals.[28]

What makes such conflation between the producer's identity and religious norms behind a product alarming, according to Güler and Bayraktar, is the continuous narrowing of the meaning of religious symbols and their random redefinition by producers that are guided more by their own market driven visions than by their religious convictions. During the course of his successful marketing campaign, the owner of the company has claimed and been associated with Tekbir, the brand name, but also the popular name for the statement that 'God is Great'. The owner seeks to attribute religious authenticity to his actions, words, and attitudes, reinforcing the idea that Tekbir's approach to Islamic clothing is a genuinely Islamic one. Such a predatory association, Güler and Bayraktar contend, puts 'the people who share the same religious beliefs in a difficult position vis-à-vis other (non-practicing) people. It affects us directly.'[29] The company's strategic selection of its name has both intended and unintended consequences. Despite its variant meanings, in popular use Tekbir first evokes the religious idea of unity and the supremacy of God, thus the company capitalizes on the name's meaning by declaring an authentic understanding and experience. However, it is the transfer of a religious term to the market world that damages religious ideas and the sensibilities of the faithful. The resulting religious injury needs to be seen as the main reason why such brands need to be questioned. In other words, the producer's claim of religious authority and increasing monopoly over the meaning of religious symbols risks, by using these terms, instigating a process that blurs the lines between the images of commodities and the ideas of the Qur'an, thereby subsuming prophetic ideas under profitable merchandise.

While Güler and Bayraktar center their complaints on the company's business-driven intrusions to the domain of religious meanings, Tekbir's own defense further exemplifies how Islamic brand names create increasingly complex discursive spheres and how faith-based groups differ in their approaches to the relations between faith and consumption. As such, Tekbir's defense states that

> the name Tekbir per se cannot be reduced to a religious symbol. It is derived from the root of *t-k-b*. whose derivatives mean great. Other words derived from the same root like *kabir* (great), *kubra* (greater), or *akbar* (greatest) can be translated to Turkish as gratification or glorification. Tekbir in Turkish also means 'one and only.' As the word only refers to the idea that 'there is nothing which resembles it,' it is an important expression but not a religious symbol.[30]

Besides Tekbir's argument that its name is not a religious term, the company's defense challenges the very core of the law by raising the question of who incurs potential damages if sacred values are used commercially. Not only can such questions not be settled easily, but given that such laws are designed to protect business, Tekbir's defense lists undue damages to the company in the case of brand-name change. After all, Tekbir has become not only a domestically but an internationally recognized name and its image generates reflexive reactions. Given its international and domestic recognition, any change to the brand will result in significant financial damages. More importantly, Tekbir's defense takes the argument further, stating that even if Tekbir was a religious term, the plaintiffs cannot complain to the court as they did not incur any damages due to the company's use of the term. Not only was the case unable to be substantiated against Tekbir, but the plaintiffs also filed the case after the time allowed for the filing of objections to a name, following its registration. Given the case's lack of merits on all dimensions, it needed to be dismissed.

Notwithstanding the growing interest in Tekbir and the case, the court did not release its detailed decision until 22 months after it received the defense. The initial decision given to the plaintiffs indicates, however, that the courts cannot be the best venue to question faith-based brands' relation to religion.[31] As such, accepting Tekbir's own arguments and after long deliberations, the court ruled against the plaintiffs on the grounds that they did not incur direct real damages and did not meet the procedural requirement of such cases.[32] Although the official detailed verdict had still not been announced when this chapter was written, the lawyer of Güler and Bayraktar, Yakup Erikel, expressed interest in appealing the case and publicly questioning the rationale behind the decision, as in similar cases when threats to nationalism evoked the protection offered by Law 556. All believers, after all, 'need to oppose any hollowing out of religious symbols and values' and thus 'their interests and religious sensibilities need to qualify them as part of this dispute. Given the law's promise to protect sacred social values, Muslims should be able to resort to legal protection in the face of serious damages to religious ideas and symbols.'[33]

MUSLIM CONSUMPTIONSCAPES, FAITH-FULL PRODUCTS, AND ISLAMIC RESISTANCE?

Although the case against Tekbir failed on the judicial front, it evoked unprecedented public discussions within Islamic circles and led three main periodicals to dedicate their issues to reflect on the discussions among the religious elite.[34] The level of these reactions can be attributed to the positions of the petitioners, well known experts of Islam, as well as the case's overtly stated goals of instigating broader criticism of the commercialization of the sacred and unfair competition as well as Tekbir's increasing ability to shape the *tesettür* market. The reactions of consumers can be grouped based on their main rationale and level of support/opposition to the product. To better analyze these reactions, diverse views can be further grouped based on their (1) organizational focus (individual vs. collective), (2) goals (reformist to radical), (3) tactics (directed at marketing or changing the meaning behind products), or (4) economic location (within or beyond the market) that seek to initiate change.[35] Placing the reactions to Tekbir under the lenses of these groups illustrates that, despite the brand's remarkable success, the reactions directed at Tekbir are rather multifaceted and create intense debates among the faith-based consumptionscapes. The following discussion identifies four groups (see Table 19.1) that range from a complete commitment of Tekbir to spread Islamic values, to a holistic rejection of the brand due to its predatory commodification to Islam.

More specifically, the reactions to the Tekbir case can be grouped under the following four labels, which summarize the prevailing views of customers on the relations of consumption to Islam. Under these summary labels, explained in detail below, we can see both converging and clashing views marking Turkey's faith-based consumptionscapes: (1) consuming to spread faith; (2) consuming in light of faith; (3) consuming at the expense of faith; (4) consuming by hollowing out faith.

(1) Consuming to spread faith   According to this group, marketization of Islamic ideas only serves religion. As a result, the expansion of faith-based products needs to be celebrated as a sign of increasing faith in the society. More specifically the consumers' reactions that fall into the first category view Tekbir's hybridization as not a defeat by monopolizing ideas such as what is fashionable and what constitutes Western style, but instead as conquering the West by creating a genuinely Islamic visibility in areas not only excluding Islam but also excluded by Islam. In this regard, Tekbir's activities amount to changing Western standards from within through an Islamic outlook, thus the company's actions should be endorsed. Tekbir's success sends out the message to others that an Islamic life style can accommodate the aesthetic expectations of others. The arguments of Güler and Bayraktar, for the consumers of this group, remain 'hypotheses,' or crude speculation at best, given that both scholars' assertions do not have evidence to support them. In fact, turning their criticism to Güler and Bayraktar, some even suggest that it is the lack of strong evidence of Tekbir's misuse of religion which forced two Islamic intellectuals to resort to the court's coercive power to challenge the company. Rather than damaging religion, Tekbir's commercial success is an important step towards spreading the idea of Tekbir (that is, God's greatness). Similar arguments also point out that Islamic scholars should not have any role and say in such market-based debates. Given that there are so many brands such as Ankara's Noah pasta, they ask, if the purification of Islamic terms starts, then where would it end?[36]

(2) Consuming in light of faith   According to this group, faith-based consumption needs to be approached carefully. Yet even in cases where marketization can be questionable, resistance to such practices might inadvertently encourage anti-Islamic enforcements.

Table 19.1 A summary of reactions to Tekbir as a brand of Islamic fashion

Customer position on faith-based consumption	Consumer reactions	Main rationale	Organizational focus (individual/collective)	Tactics	Goals (or targeted effect)	Economic location of reactions
Consuming to spread faith	Supportive	Spreads faith	Collective	Consuming more	Increase saliency of faith-based products	Reformist/Within market
Consuming in light of faith	Supportive/ Critical	Faith consumption can enhance or hamper faith	Individual	Selective responsible consumption	Use individual religious values to decide	Reformist/Within market
Consuming at the expense of faith	Critical	Faith consumption increases market's hegemony, needs to be challenged	Individual	Refuse to buy	Changing the terms/Meaning of consumption	Reformist/Radical/ Seeks to modify market
Consuming by hollowing out faith	Rejectionist	Faith-based consumption hollows out religion, a new free market consistent with Islam needs to be promoted	Collective	Refuse to buy and protest the market in general	Changing approach to faith-based production	Radical/Seeks to redefine market

Thus the marketization of Islamic products should be challenged only through the market and through individual reactions undertaken vigilantly. Those whose reactions fall into this second category find both the reasoning behind the Tekbir case and the involvement of the state's judicial forces as most perturbing. According to this group, the critics of Tekbir insist on 'preventing misuse of religion for commercial purposes.' Such statements echo the secularist motto that secularism's main goal is to 'prevent misuse of religion for political purposes.' True to its motto, the state enacted many laws and institutions to prevent such presumed misuse. These laws paved a way for the implementation of coercive practices, such as the banning of the headscarf. Given the state's exclusionist policy towards covered women, using a similar rationale and resorting to 'the secular state's court' only reinforces state coercion. Therefore, such judicial actions appear to be detrimental to the unity of Islam and its efforts to promote Islam openly in the public sphere. Thus even though the practices of Tekbir are questionable, according to those who fall in to this group, secular state institutions cannot be used to subvert the company's practices. Muslims can refuse to buy from Tekbir and they should know that Tekbir's approach cannot be equated to the approach of the Qur'an.[37] Given that the case against Tekbir was filed two months after the chief prosecutor took the JDP to court demanding its closure on the grounds that it had become the center for anti-secularist activities, the criticisms of this group centered on forming a unified Islamic block against any state involvement in religion.

(3) Consuming at the expense of faith   Reactions summarized under this group contend that in any form, commodification of faith-based items in essence is detrimental to faith and needs to be resisted by using existing institutions (for example, opening a court case, organizing customer resistance, and so on) Offering an excellent example of arguments that fall under this third group, some columnists, such as Fatma Barbarosoğlu, frame the question of Tekbir as more of a question about fashion's relation to individual experiences and beliefs. In her series of books on the topic, namely *Fashion and Mentality* (*Moda ve Zihniyet*, 2002), *Show and Private* (*Şov ve Mahrem*, 2006) and *Image and Deep Religiousness* (*İmaj ve Takva*, 2009) Barbarosoğlu invites consumers in general, and faithful consumers specifically, to call into question the ways in which the patterns of consumption promoted by the market society affect its Muslim consumers. Fashion, for Barbarosoğlu, owes its presence to modernization, and it establishes its authority by cultivating the idea of an *unquestionable* nature of fashion. It is this new approach to fashion that changed the definition of beauty and aesthetics. Diminishing the role of the individual, this modern nature of fashion makes what is fashionable into what is beautiful (not vice versa). 'As masses wear the same thing, the fashion designers became the tailor for the naked king.'[38] In comparable contexts, according to Barbarosoğlu, there are some '*türbanists*'. While *türbanists* seem to be defending or promoting women and wearing the headscarf, in fact they are trying to restore and advance their positions, careers, and world views through their '*türbanist* manners'. Tekbir in Turkey, just like its secularist counterpart, centers its attention on Islamic clothing and reifies the women in them. Thus the company acts both as a conduit for fashion's role in reinventing female Muslim identities, rendering women the object of Islamic clothing, not as independent agents who are free to make choices and exercise their will. To express their repulsion towards the brand, women in this group do not shy away from referring

to Tekbir as *'müstekbir'* a Qur'anic term in Turkish that refers to unfair, exploitative actions.[39]

(4) Consuming by hollowing out faith   According to the reactions that fall under this group, a resistance rooted in theology is needed not only to tame the Islamic consumptionscape and production sphere, but also to create an alternative to the global predatory consumerism to which Islam seems to fall prey. Without such resistance the encroachment of market ideas in the religious sphere risks turning Islam into a commodity of the market society. Although it is hard to draw the line between the ideas put forward by the consumers in the third and fourth groups, what distinguishes those in the last group from the others is their emphasis on theology and their reflections on the complex relations between the market society and Islam. Those that fall into this group warn consumers against their misplaced loyalty. For instance, while struggle against un-Islamic groups is emphasized in Islam, according to Bayraktar, one of the most vocal critics in this last group, what is equally important is the struggle against corruptive groups *within* Islam. As such Islam also invites the believers first and foremost to struggle against corruption within their own community. Failing to resist corrupt practices, thus, amounts to not following one of the most important Qur'anic orders: 'Let there be such a group among you, that they may call towards goodness and command what is just and forbid evil' (Qur'an 3:104). Corollary to that, the corruption of Islamic values in the name of protecting Islamic groups and treating them all as serving religion, is rather anti-Islamic.[40] How current groups neglect the potential of 'harmful groups within Islam' and stop questioning 'what is really Islamic' lies at the heart of many issues that corrupt Islam from within.[41]

It is important to note that those who fall under this fourth group seek to show that their views do not amount to a simple rejection of consumerism or relentless productionism. Instead they emphasize the urgency of placing the market society in an Islamic paradigm, and oppose the trend embodied by Tekbir – the placement of Islam in a market society. After all, many contend that the Qur'an was revealed in Mecca – a free trade center – and thus since its inception, the Qur'an has embraced market practices yet also condemned Mecca's bourgeoisie, who committed to ideas and practices strongly resembling those of today's bourgeoisie. Yet, although there are ownership and property rights in Islam, they cannot be seen as absolute rights (or an end in themselves). Property and ownership have their functions – they enable human existence (to eat, drink, and have shelter) and help the poor. Limitless consumption, production and earning without helping others translate to a monopoly, meaning a shortage, not abundance. The motto of capitalism is production, distribution, and consumption using limited economic sources to satisfy the unbounded 'needs' of people. In this regard, capitalism approaches humanity's endless desires and fantasies as 'needs' and seeks to meet them by creating a heroic and hedonist structure. As the market society expands and changes Islam from within, the fourth group concludes by stating, '[W]e need to expose this ongoing violence that disguises its presence under the sacralization of human desire, resist it, and present an alternative.'[42]

Perhaps due to their broad global assessment, the fourth group's criticisms often center on Tekbir's place in its broader historical context. As such for this group as political Islamism has spread, it has also gained supporters – bourgeoisie and merchants.

These businessmen stated their will to give Islamic names to their companies and products, on the one hand, and to promote their ideologies on the other hand to make other believers their customers. Therefore, the Islamic bourgeoisie's activities are not driven by their religious ideas, nor are they strictly based on business. The very intersection that these groups straddle explains why their claims for using Islam need to be questioned and better embedded in Islam. The business centered uses of Islamic symbols and names undermines their original importance and makes them increasingly hollowed out conduits of market practices.

> In this trend many Islamic names, except the name of the Prophet and God, had their shares. Among others, there are companies named Islam (book store, funeral services), Tevhid (book store), Tekbir (clothing), İhlas (Corporation), Medine (tourism company, and dates), Hicret (clothing, book store), Miraç (elevators), Cihad (restaurant), Zemzem Mekke (cola), Hicab (Clothing) İffet (Clothing) Seriat (swimwear) . . . Even though it appears the name of God and prophets have been protected in this trend, in reality this predatory trend appears to not have a limit. For instance, one company sent a report to its shareholders stating that 'our biggest shareholder is God.' Shortly after the report was sent out, the company had to declare bankruptcy due to business misconducts and corruption. Thus shall we infer that God also had a bankruptcy?[43]

According to Güler, a resistance theology is needed to better approach the dominant market society and questions posed by Tekbir. Such theology rooted in Islam does not mean that Islam is against trade or, in today's terms, against a market society.[44] In fact, the Qur'an liberally uses the language of trade such as accounts, registering, balance, weighting, price, damage, payment, loss, commerce, profit trade, and loan. Such terms are used not only to provide examples to explain the benefits of trade, but also to curb an individuals' ungratefulness, negligence and forgetfulness, and to increase a moral awareness by encouraging the faithful to refuse greed and seek greatness. Thus the very terms and ideas of a market society are part and parcel of Islam. But just like any other religion, Islam needs to reinforce certain overarching values and keep an eye on the weaknesses of market society. In fact, the critics within the last group contend that historical events suggest that individuals have a universal tendency to make market use of religious values and abuse religious values. It is not a coincidence that Jesus' big revolt took the form of his rejection of the transformation of Jerusalem's temples to places of commerce. His harshest reaction was to try to throw the salesmen out of the temple. It is also no coincidence that only after such a revolt did the key religious leaders want to capture Jesus. The same moral values introduced by Jesus were corrupted later to the extent that the church sold the property rights to places in heaven.

An overall review of reactions to Tekbir serve as evidence that consumers'assessments of faith-based products are not simple questions of approval and disapproval, but instead form a multidimensional matrix. As summarized in Table 19.1, the consumers in the first group view Islam's commercialization as its victory, and the second group calls for individual responsibility to keep their market decisions in check under the light of Islamic teaching. For the third and fourth groups the advocates of Islamic market society fail to see that commodification of Islam does actually lead to its decay. While the critics in the third group center their attention on the ability of a predatory market society and modernization to undermine the capacity of individuals in general and women specifically, the fourth group sees it as a broader problem that is faced by many religions. In contrast to the second and third groups' emphasis on individual actions, both the advocates and critics of market society (namely the first and fourth groups) stress the importance of collective action. While other groups seek to remain within the limits of market society or find a place for an Islamic paradigm in the global market society, the last group stresses the importance of putting the market society within an Islamic paradigm. Ironically, while companies like Tekbir turn to the West to compete, conquer, and form alliances to promote their business, its critics, such as the advocates of resistance theology, look to the religious foundations of resistance in the West, such as liberation theology. All in all, with their drastically different yet increasingly vocal views on how Islam needs to be approached in Turkey's consumptionscapes, consumers' responses constitute an increasingly important force in the country's faith-based markets.

LIMITS OF ISLAMIC MARKETS? A SEARCH FOR STANDARDIZATION OF AUTHENTICITY

When Tekbir's case is placed in a broader context, one might argue that due to the diversification of the faith-based market we see more organized attempts to regulate Islamic production and consumption.[45] In fact, the plaintiff's challenge to the name Tekbir also includes a call for a better regulation of brand names that capitalize on the world of Islamic symbols. Their suggestions also included that a branch in the Directorate of Religious Affairs should take a more active role in monitoring the registration of such brand names. While the critics of Tekbir focus on the name and the producer's claims, there have been other, more active and successful attempts to regulate Islamic production spaces in different ways. In the area of Islamic banking, for instance, the institutions that claim to offer Islamic banking products and services are expected to have a *sharia* supervisory board to ensure that activities are in compliance with *sharia* principles.[46] Yet the decisions of these boards create not cohesive but instead a multiplicity of rules as the sectors' expansion introduces new problems without clear answers. For instance, how much risk taking is acceptable, and at what point does the level of risk taking resemble gambling? These form important questions for financial sectors while the Islamic boards' decisions impact the market actions and consumer decisions drastically.[47]

A review of similar boards that seek to set Islamic standards acceptable to a plethora of Islamic groups that approach the tradition differently in the market indicate that while attempting to ensure authenticity they inevitably also face new issue areas such as neo-liberalist policies on genetic modification or potentially environmentally hazardous processes. Facing such new issues the supervisory boards engage in a new level of Islamic interpretation and redefine traditional terms. For instance, the Association for Inspection and Certification of Food and Supplies (AICFS), founded in 2005,[48] defines its goals as to inspect whether the ingredients are consistent with *halal* (that which is religiously permissible) and whether the production process was hygienic and is transparent in the reporting of its activities. The association's list of 'the items to exclude' as not *halal* contains products that are treated with hormones or genetically modified.[49] In fact, through the announcements of the group one can see how such regulatory bodies seek to appeal to a transnational audience while also striving to create acceptable Islamic standards. For instance, an international conference held by AICFS summarizes its target audience in the following way: '*halal* food is not only fit for Muslim consumption, it is also fit for Muslims and non-Muslims alike. Integral to the meaning of *halal* is that it is clean, natural, and nutritional.'[50] AICFS's description of its goals and criteria for issuing a *halal* certificate suggests that they also include in their review not only the production process but also the conduct of the producers. As such the group's *halal* criteria states that to ensure whether an item is *halal*, the association ensures that the composition of products during the manufacture, and all individuals, companies, and firms that supply all raw, processed, and half-processed materials after production, do not display conditions that are overtly in conflict with Islamic faith and life style.

It is important to note that creating institutions for standardization is rather new in Turkey and in the Muslim world in general and reflects not only the demands, but also the changing opportunity structure of Islamic consumptionscapes at the national and global levels. Ironically, how Islamic standards are debated and discussed within national platforms formed by these incipient institutions demonstrates the ways in which these efforts have been facilitated by transnational forces. For instance, according to the reports released after the second International Halal Food Conference held in Turkey, the *halal* food sector accounts for 17 per cent of the global food market amounting to a US $642 billion share of the market after 2010.[51] As the global world market grows more accepting, *halal* standards would be further enforced by the Trade Preferential System among the Organization of Islamic Conference (OIC) countries. Such efforts, according to participants, not only supply dependable faith-based consumption items but also allow the OIC countries to tap into the growing *halal* market which is currently dominated by non-Muslim countries. Thus competition over authenticity emerges as an important area where Islamic values and market forces meet and facilitate market segmentation. Yet how Islamic standards will be debated remains to be seen and has the potential to pull participants in different directions. While new advisory boards appease the anxieties of Muslim consumers by ensuring compliance with Islamic rules, such regulatory intervention also creates safe markets and consumptionscapes that offer advantages to selected companies. Yet as new issue areas emerge and Islamic rules are debated openly, the institutions of authentication have the potential to serve sites that can both advance but also prevent the advancement of consumer reaction such as those called for by the advocates of resistance theology.

CONCLUSIONS: CONSOLIDATION OF ISLAMIC MARKETS AND THE LIMITS OF SEARCHING FOR THE AUTHENTIC?

With its ability to conjure up paradoxical images from the appearance of being a market jihadist to an agent of Islam's deterioration, Tekbir's success epitomizes the dynamics and dilemmas of faith-based markets. Understanding the reactions to Tekbir opens a new door to the inner workings of faith-based markets and helps us better conceptualize the ongoing process of commodification of religious symbols and ideas and consumer resistance in general. It is important to note that consumer resistance is often used as an umbrella term to describe a range of reactions to old and new consumer products, producers and the market. Perhaps due to the term's emphasis on the unexpected reactions of customers it often instigates studies that focus on consumer *decisions* and *choices* in isolation. More often than not collective or organized resistance is studied at the expense of more diffused resistance and unconventional challenges to the market. As a result, the existing approaches tend to privilege individual choices over the impact of institutional and societal factors (for example, Foxall, 1998; Laukannen et al., 2007) or the importance of the intended goals over the processes (for example, Tormey, 2007; Webb, 2005). Such studies often fail to shed light on how exactly the resistance is formed and why it takes a certain form and yields intended and unintended consequences. Given the lacuna marking the existing literature, the analysis of the Tekbir case and Turkey's faith-based consumptionscape presented in this chapter affords us a critical vantage point to explore not only how producers and individuals are embedded in their political social environments but also the ways in which they strive to both define and alter the meaning of faith-based consumption objects.

Unraveling the rise of and reactions to Tekbir shows us that what makes consumer reactions to faith-based products more intriguing and challenging is that such reactions not only draw on the ongoing debates over the authentic meaning of religious symbols and ideas but also are affected by the role of religion in the social, political and economic system. When religion is given a different role in these spheres it presents a complex decision making environment for customers. For instance, while the economic system endorses rapid liberalization of the market and opens up more opportunities for faith-based consumptionscapes, and many producers are driven to invest in faith-based products, how faith should be positioned in a liberal economy poses an unprecedented contention. When religious symbols are constrained and questioned under a political system such constraints might alter customer reactions due to strategic reasoning. Likewise, the legal or judicial framework might offer alternative venues of customer resistance unavailable to others. When religion and religious choices are fiercely contested in a society, it is not only faith-based products that are challenged. Their producers, who claim an authoritative understanding of Islamic values or attribute religious credence to their products, are also questioned, thereby influencing customer reactions to their products. Subsequently, the discussions on faith-based products include a myriad actors, from the average consumers, to producers, to religious experts. Their claims and resistance both reflect and become an important part of debates on how religious symbols and rules need to be experienced nationally and globally. For consumers of religious products, faith-based products are not external to their faith or dispensable consumer items but, on the contrary, such products are seen as a main constituent of their religious experiences. Therefore faith-based products constitute a unique venue to better analyze both how religious symbols are commodified in an ever expanding national and global market society, and how this commodification is framed, adapted, negotiated, and contested by its producers and users.

Although faith-based consumptionscapes are often approached as uniform and less prone to consumer resistance by their faithful consumers, the above analysis reveals that consumer views of Tekbir and reactions to Tekbir vary widely – some view the company as a modern agent of *dawa* (that is, spreading religion). Others see it as a company serving God through trade, while some others argue that the company's ruthless commodification of values merits a revival of resistance theology to save Islam from its perennial challengers, the vices of market-based ideas. Tekbir's impressive growth demonstrates that faith-based companies, on the one hand, have a unique advantage of serving a market that continues to develop due to existing social, political, and demographic changes. On the other hand, as such companies make inroads to the global markets, faith groups question their Islamic qualifications and their impact on Islam more stringently. When viewed from the perspective of the literature on consumer resistance, attending to these underlying currents of the faith-based markets constitutes an important step towards better explaining both the multiplicity of actors and micro foundations of consumer resistance by continuously questioning their position within their broader context. Therefore, a closer look at Tekbir's customer reactions presents us, not with an idiosyncratic account, but with a heuristic case, thereby enabling us to gain insight to how social, political and market forces effect, interact and shape consumer practices in many other faith-based consumptionscapes. Such a multi-layered approach is especially important given the limited efforts to develop holistic and dynamic models of consumer resistance, most noticeably in faith-based consumerscapes, with some rare exceptions (for example, Sandıkcı and Ger, 2007; Brickell, 2002).

As faith-based consumption continues to expand, resistance to faith-based products can be seen as a critical force that affects the ways in which Islamic consumptionscapes are formed or reformed. The unprecedented court case brought against Tekbir and the protests in front of the last *tesettür* fair exemplifies that resistance to Islamic consumptionscapes effectively blends unconventional and conventional venues of resistance and is affected by national and global changes. Although these resistance movements are positioned differently, ultimately they have a strong bearing on the changing forms and offerings of new products within this market. As such the challenge of sustaining the Islamic core in inventing new images and services amounts to the unique challenge of presenting and discerning the Authentic New, or the 'modern Islamic.' How these dilemmas facing the producers and consumers alike will be addressed is critical to the future of faith-based markets not only in Turkey but beyond.

As the above review of Tekbir indicates, the company's success lies in its ability to reintroduce the traditional with a new face. The owners of Tekbir pride themselves on their ability to challenge the image of Muslim women, who are often perceived to sit at the crossroads of two life styles rooted in modern and anti-modern views, by promoting a 'modern Muslimah.' This image resonates with many who want to carve out space (or see a space carved out) beyond the prevalent tensions, offering a place to those who feel that they belong to neither world but feel at home within these hybrid structures. It is no coincidence, for instance, that for some consumers Islamic fashion is a venue for the 'normalization of the images of Muslim women,' in that by being fashionable they encounter others on equal terms within the similar parameters of aesthetics.[52] Ironically, the very nature of these hybrid products and the characteristics of Islamic beliefs nested within them holds these brands to the test of authenticity by many others.

As captured by the debate on Tekbir's claims to be the most authentic yet chic *tesettür* option for Muslim women, the very question of 'what is authentic?' evades definite answers and generally creates a competitive discursive sphere. In Turkey's faith-based consumptionscapes 'how Islamic is Islamic fashion?' is a question that spurs more questions and fierce claims defending variant positions. Looking beyond the façade of these positions draws our attention to the impact of differential assessments on political context and the perceived role of Islam, as well as contesting inferences elicited from the main Islamic texts. It is important to note that although faith-based products seek to shelter faith in an increasingly pluralistic and fragmented political and economic environment, they also become susceptible to their own influences. As exemplified in the reactions to the case against Tekbir in faith-based markets, consumer responses take rather intricate forms based on the customers' perception of the position of Islam not only within the market system but also in political life. For instance, expressed rationales behind the assessment of Tekbir's products indicate that those who view Islam's role as marginalized in the political system tend to oppose any questioning of Islamic brands regardless of their personal (dis)satisfactions. Likewise, those who believe that Islamic political movements and markets have reached a certain maturity invite Muslims to engage in a more critical assessment within the faith-based markets. Such conclusions invite us to explore the unintended influence of political contexts on consumer calculations further.

When the perceived role of faith is taken into account a different picture emerges. Tekbir's claim to spread faith by selling products in unexpected areas and by pioneering an aesthetic look appealing to a Western sense of style with Islamic meanings disarms some potential resistance in the name of serving religion. Although many customers express apprehension about Tekbir's 'questionable Islamic practices,' what is often publicly questioned is the company's high price tags and limited designs – an a-religious area to voice – concerns, not its Islamic ventures. The concerns are presented as individual assessments, not framed as collective grievances, and other brands are often mentioned to diffuse individual responsibility. Such conclusions reveal that in faith-based markets, the idea of spreading faith not only by consuming but through protecting the sale of faith-based products highlights an important component of a consumer's relations to brand, product, producer, and their consumer resistance strategies. Similar to the impact of political context in a social environment where faith and its symbols are seen as 'under attack' and subjected to 'ill-intended scrutiny,' consumer reactions can be further muted. By the same token, when the social environment is perceived to be divided, faith-based consumers reveal less publicly discernible forms of resistance and/or center their reactions on readily acceptable areas.

Although the literature on consumer reactions directs our attention to products and the production process, as captured in the Tekbir case, the producers play unexpected roles due to the intricate ways faith-based products declare their authenticity. The religious authenticity of Tekbir's products rests on its owner's personal authority or discretion to define what is both Islamic and acceptable. Although in small companies such claims face less scrutiny, as the markets grow and products change their shapes and forms, the relation between customers' expectations and a company's own Islamic quality assurance becomes more contested. Perhaps it is the elusive nature of some Islamic assertions that prompts the consumers of faith-based products to look for authoritative interpretations. As a result, just like the increasing need of the producer to claim religious authenticity in the world of production, in the consumer's world Islamic scholars emerge as unexpected and key players considering the critical role of the interpretation of tradition in selecting authentic Islamic products. Therefore, the owner of Tekbir's claims of authority over Islamic sources, and Güler and Bayraktar's resorts to extreme measures to prevent it, are not surprising. Such efforts can be seen as a reflection of a deeper debate rooted in objections to increasing reinterpretation of Islamic values based on or drawn from a business model, and redefinition of the authentic experience of Islam in a global context defined by market society.

While the *tesettür* sector faces the question of what is Islamic, the recent developments in other sectors such as food and finance show that, ironically, their expanding production makes faith-based companies rely on experts more and more to substantiate their declared authenticity. Such reliance only grows as they become international in scope and face more intricate questions. It is not surprising, therefore, that faith-based companies' workforces include supervisory and advisory boards, including Islamic experts, to confirm the Islamic essence of daily business decisions. Therefore, faith-based markets create institutions that serve to reconcile both the homogenizing market forces and the quest of experts to protect Islamic tradition against such forces. As experts try to define when risk taking (religiously admissible) starts becoming gambling (religiously not permissible), they also gain disproportionate power over the inner workings of the faith-based markets.

It is important to note that despite the challenges to Tekbir's approach to Islamic clothing, the company remains the primary provider in a market which it invented – *tesettür* fashion. Attesting to its adaptable and effective marketing policies and despite the country's financial crisis, its recent sales campaign (for example, offering customers a second item for just one Turkish lira) increased its sales volume dramatically, making the brand more accessible to women from lower income groups. More importantly the company's influence on other brands in the industry, such as İclal ve Aydan *tesettür* clothing, have been remarkable. Not only does each company seek to expand its customer base to Europe and beyond, but they also use similar marketing approaches. Despite the strong criticism leveled against Tekbir's fashion shows, Aydan has recently staged its first fashion show, though it was presented as an alternatively modest fashion show without the glamour and the symbolic representation of Islam featured in Tekbir's events. Ironically, these companies also adopt the increasingly vocal Islamic critique of *tesettür*. For instance, while Aydan follows in the footsteps of Tekbir, it also states that it does not bring Islam to fashion but fashion to Islam.

Despite the effectiveness of the critiques against Tekbir, it is important to note that reactions against the company do not translate to a full fledged consumer resistance movement. However, within the rapidly changing landscape of Islamic consumptionscapes, the ideas proposed by scholars such as resistance theology, although they are in their incipient stage, constitute one of the most potent areas for new customer reactions. Given that resistance theology first appeared in 2006 and was addressed more publicly in 2008, its effects on consumers have been remarkable. A symbolic protest at the entrance of the country's second *tesettür* fair used many of the arguments from the court case against Tekbir, suggesting that the case has already successfully framed ongoing reactions. The prevailing appeal of the ideas articulated by the case against Tekbir over a short period of time suggests that they carry a great potential towards changing the configuration of faith-based markets. These currents of change imply that as political and market forces collectively allow faith-based products to conquer new areas with new products, it is religious experts and consumers who will play a significant role and retain a significant degree of influence in defining the course of events as well as the limits of faith-based markets.

NOTES

*   The author thanks Andrew S. Mcfarland, Andrew Swanson, İlknur Karaaslan, Fatma Ünsal, the editors, Özlem Sandıkcı and Gillian Rice, and the anonymous reviewers for their invaluable support, research assistance and insightful comments. Without the input of the participants this analysis would not have been possible.
1.   The Demos Fair Company organized both fairs that took place in İstanbul. Author's interview with the company representative, 12 April 2010.
2.   *Tesettür*, spelled in the Turkish way, is an Arabic term '*tasattur*,' which means 'cover'. It has been used by the Islamic movements in Turkey to refer to full, modest covering that is different from traditional covering. The term became popular in the mid 1990s to refer to the deliberate embrace of an Islamic clothing style.
3.   Subjects are selected using a purposive selection to include women from different cultural and economic backgrounds in İstanbul and Ankara. Subjects consisted of 40 women and semi-structured interviews centered on the use and marker of the headscarf. The answers informed the main arguments presented here. The questionnaire included questions that delved into the respondents' demographic characteristics, buying habits, familiarity and reactions to different Islamic clothing brands. To better represent the participants' choices and opinions, open ended questions were used to explore the ways in which they approach different brands without constraining their answers to a limited number of options. The information gathered from the survey is used in conjunction with the information gathered through the author's visits to Tekbir stores as well as in-depth interviews with the managers in and marketing consultants to the *tesettür* companies.
4.   Ziya Öniş and U. Türem (2001).
5.   For more see Ayşe Buğra (1998).
6.   While 70 per cent of TÜSİAD businesses were based in the country's major cities, most MÜSİAD members are located in the provincial cities of Antep, Bursa, Kayseri, Konya or Maras.
7.   For more see musiad.org.tr
8.   For more on the reactions of Islamic groups to the 1997 decisions see Sultan Tepe (2008) p.154.
9.   *Religion, Secularism and the Veil in Daily Life Survey*, Konda Araştırma, 2007.
10. The survey is based on 5291 interviews selected by using the 2000 General Census and the 2002 General Election results. It reflects the changes in both urban and rural Turkey by including 46 797 neighborhoods and villages selected randomly. For more, see, Konda, (2007).
11. Ibid.
12. http://www.comcec.org/
13. For an example of Islamic groups' reactions to Tekbir's fashion show see 'White Turks', *Akşam*, 22 April, 2008.
14. Tekbir's designer, Heidi Beck, is well known and specializes in 'haute couture.' Her own business in Cologne specializes in evening clothes. Ironically while she views herself as the only European woman in Tekbir, her designs for Tekbir are inspired mostly by Ottoman history. For a detailed description of her views see Frank Lorent (2008).
15. Information gathered by author from interviews with Tekbir representatives.
16. Interview with Mustafa Karaduman, November 2006. For more see Dominic Ozanne (2006).
17. Ibid.
18. Karaduman refers to surah an-nur 31, sura al-ahzab 59. His other explanations on the issue often refer to the same verses and his own interpretation.
19. Ümit Kızıltepe (2007).
20. Many of the Islamic rules set up general guiding principles that require careful interpretation. For instance, *gharar*, or sales with high risk, are forbidden in Islam, yet how the degree of risk is determined and 'high risk' is defined remains a source of controversy.
21. For a review of *muhkam*, see Oliver Leaman (2006), p.93.
22.   Muslimah is used to refer to a Muslim woman.
23. From Tekbir's clothing advertisements distributed in the United Kingdom, 5 January 2010.
24. Ümit Kızıltepe (2007).
25. For an extensive discussion on the role of Islamic journals and intellectuals see Esra Çifci Dindar (2010).
26. For the law see http://www.turkpatent.gov.tr/dosyalar/mevzuat/MarkaKhk.pdf.
27. 'Case Filed Against Tekbir' *Akşam*, 5 April 2008.
28. Süleyman Bayraktar, 'Religious people should prevent the abuse of religion,' *Zaman*, 11 May 2008.
29. Author's interview with Süleyman Bayraktar, 5 April 2010.
30. Rezzak Oral, 'Tekbir is not a Religious Symbol,' *Akşam*, 28 July 2008.
31. Author's interview with Yakup Erikel, the plaintiffs' lawyer, 2 April 2010.

32. Ibid.
33. Author's correspondence with Süleyman Bayraktar, 1 April 2010.
34. For instance see *Haksöz*, no. 207, June 2008 or *Doğudan*, no.15, April 2010.
35. 'Organizational focus' refers to the expected social location of broader reaction.
36. Ali Atıf, 'Questions to Ilhami', *Bugün*, 8 May 2008.
37. Personal interviews with a Tekbir consumer, 28 January 2010.
38. Fatma Barbarosoğlu, 'Tekbir's search to save the rental bodies,' *Yeni Şafak*, 13 May 2008.
39. Personal interview with a consumer critical of Tekbir, 4 April 2010.
40. Author's interview with Süleyman Bayraktar, April 2010.
41. Personal interview with a consumer critical of Tekbir, 12 March 2010.
42. İlhami Güler 'Transformation of Tekbir to a textile brand,' *Radikal*, 4 May 2008.
43. For a comprehensive account of Resistance Ideology see İlhami Güler (2010).
44. Ibid.
45. For an analysis of standardization, see Franck Cochoy (2006).
46. Clement M. Henry and Rodney Wilson (2004). For a more detailed discussion see Murat Ünal (2009). Scholars' involvement is especially noteworthy considering that there was one Islamic bank in 1975; the number of these banks increased to 300 operating in more than 75 countries. Ünal's study shows that 180 scholars serve on nearly 1000 *sharia* consulting boards, creating a complex relation between scholars and Islamic sectors.
47. In the words of Agil Natt, chief executive of the International Centre for Education in Islamic Finance, 'Islam encourages you to manage your risk but when does risk management end and gambling begin?' Such questions demand interpretations that draw on some clear rules and broad guidelines. For instance, there is agreement that excessive uncertainty (*gharar*) can invalidate a contract, but it is also agreed that businesses involve *some* level of risk. Indeed, one can point to the Qur'an's unequivocal approval of trade (Qur'an, 2:275) as a sign that balance needs to be achieved. Yet finding this balance is the very puzzle to the consumers and providers of this sector. For more see *Islamic Banker*, May 2009.
48. For more information about AIFS visit http://www.gimdes.org/
49. AIFS Halal Standards interview with the AIFS representatives, February 2010.
50. AIFS, International Halal Food Conference official invitation letter, 23 March 2009.
51. *Muslim Weekly*, 8 November 2009.
52. Personal interview with a Tekbir customer, January 2010

BIBLIOGRAPHY

Adaş, E.B. (2006), 'The making of entrepreneurial Islam and the Islamic spirit of capitalism', *Journal for Cultural Research*, **10**, 113–37.
Ahluwalia, R. (2000), 'Examination of psychological processes underlying resistance to persuasion', *Journal of Consumer Research*, **27** (2), 217.
Amato, S. (2009), 'The white elephant in London: an episode of trickery, racism and advertising', *Journal of Social History*, **43** (1), 31–66.
Barborosoğlu, Fatma (2002), *Fashion and Mentality (Moda ve Zihniyet)*, İstanbul: İz Yayıncılık.
Barborosoğlu, Fatma (2006) *Show and Private (Şov ve Mahrem)*, İstanbul: Timas Yayıncılık
Barborosoğlu, Fatma (2009) *Image and Deep Religiousness (İmaj ve takva)*, İstanbul: Timas Yayıncılık.
Barger, Rick (2005), *A New and Right Spirit: Creating an Authentic Church in a Consumer Culture*, Herndon, VA: Alban Institute.
Baudrillard, Jean (1988), *Selected Writings*, Stanford, CA: Stanford University Press.
Bayraktar, S. (2009), 'Who would benefit from abusing "the case against abusing Islam"?', *Haksöz*, 209, August.
Ben-Porat, G. and Y. Feniger (2009), 'Live and let buy? Consumerism, secularization, and liberalism', *Journal of Comparative Politics*, **41** (3), 293–313.
Bendix, Regina (1997), *In Search of Authenticity: The Formation of Folklore Studies*, Madison, WI: University of Wisconsin Press.
Beverland, M.B. and F.J. Farrelly (2010) 'The quest for authenticity in consumption: consumers' purposive choice of authentic cues to shape experienced outcomes,' *Journal of Consumer Research*, **36** (5), 838–56.
Bilici, M. (2000), 'Caprice hotel: transforming Islam on the Aegean coast', *ISIM Review*, **6** (30).
Birtek F. and B. Toprak (1993), 'The conflictual agendas of neo-liberal reconstruction and the rise of Islamic politics in Turkey: the hazards of rewriting modernity', *Praxis International*, **13** (2), 192–212
Brickell, C. (2002), 'Through the (new) looking glass: gendered bodies, fashion, and resistance in postwar New Zealand', *Journal of Consumer Culture*, **2** (2), 241–2.

Brownlie, D. and P. Hewer (2009), 'Cultures of unruly bricolage: "debadging" and the cultural logic of resistance', *Advances in Consumer Research*, **36**, 686–87.

Buğra, A. (1998), 'Class, culture, and state: an analysis of interest representation by two Turkish business associations', *International Journal of Middle Eastern Studies*, **30** (4), 521–39.

Buğra, A (1999), *Islam in Economic Organizations*, İstanbul: Türkiye Ekonomik ve Sosyal Etüdler Vakfı (TESEV)/Friedrich Ebert Foundation.

Buğra, A (2002), 'Labor, capital, and religion: harmony and conflict among the constituency of political Islam in Turkey', *Middle Eastern Studies*, **2** (38), 187–204.

Bulaç, A. (2006), 'Bilgi ve Hikmetten Servet ve Iktidara' ('From knowledge and wisdom to wealth and power'), *Bilgi ve Hikmet*, http//:www.bilgihikmet.com/, accessed 22 February 2010.

Çamurcu, Kenan (2005), *AKP'nin Stra'Trajik Meseleleri (Strategic Issues of the Justice and Development Party)*, İstanbul: Sehir Yayinlari.

Cheng, Vincent J. (2004), *Inauthentic: The Anxiety Over Culture and Identity*, New Brunswick, NJ: Rutgers University Press.

Chidester, David (2005), *Authentic Fakes: Religion and American Popular Culture*, Berkeley, CA: University of California Press.

Cochoy, Franck (2006) 'Industrial roots of contemporary political consumerism: introducing the evolution standardization,' in M. Micheletti, A. Follesdal and D. Stolle (eds), *Politics, Products and Markets*, New Brunswick, NJ: Transaction Publishers.

Craig, M. (2009), 'To be or not to be: understanding authenticity from an existential perspective', *Journal for the Society of Existential Analysis*, **20** (2).

Deemer, Robert Lee (1997), *Overcoming Tradition and Modernity. The Search for Islamic Authenticity*, Boulder, CO: Westview Press

Demir, Fırat (2004), 'A failure story: politics and financial liberalization in Turkey, revisting the revolving door hypothesis', *World Development*, **32** (5), 851–69.

Demiralp, S. (2009), 'The rise of Islamic capital and the decline of Islamic radicalism in Turkey', *Journal of Comparative Politics*, **41** (3), 315–35.

Dindar, E.Ç. (2010) 'The Islamic journals after 1980', *Hak Soz*, 13 April.

El-Gamal, Mahmoud A. (2006), *Islamic Finance: Law Economics, and Practice*, Cambridge, MA: Cambridge University Press.

Featherstone, Mike (1991), *Consumer Culture and Postmodernism*, Thousand Oaks, CA: Sage Publications.

Ferrara, Alessandra (1998), *Reflective Authenticity: Rethinking the project of Modernity*, Loudon: Routledge.

Fischer, E. (2001), 'Rhetorics of resistance, discourses of discontent', *Advances in Consumer Research*, **28**, 123–4.

Foxall, Gordon (1998), 'Radical behaviourist interpretation: generating and evaluating an account of consumer behavior', *Behavior Analyst*, **21**, 321–54.

Genel, S. and K. Karaosmanoğlu (2006), 'A new Islamic individualism in Turkey: headscarved women in the city', *Turkish Studies*, **7** (3), 473–88.

Gilmore, J.H. and B.J. Pine II (2007), *Authenticity: What Consumers Really Want*, Boston, MA: Harvard Business School Press.

Gökarıksel, B. (2009), 'Beyond the officially sacred: religion, secularism, and the body in the production of subjectivity', *Social & Cultural Geography*, **10** (6), 657–74.

Gökarıksel, B. and A.J. Secor (2009), 'New transnational geographies of Islamism, capitalism, and subjectivity: the veiling-fashion industry in Turkey', *Area*, **41** (1), 6–18.

Göle, Nilüfer (1997), *The Forbidden Modern: Civilization and Veiling*, Ann Arbor, MA: University of Michigan Press.

Göle, Nilüfer (1999a), *Melez Desenler: Islam ve Modernlik Üzerine (Hybrid Patterns: On Islam and Modernity)*, İstanbul: Metis.

Göle, Nilüfer (1999b), *Islam in Economic Organizations*, İstanbul: Türkiye Ekonomik ve Sosyal Etüdler Vakfı (TESEV)/Friedrich Ebert Foundation.

Göle, Nilüfer (2000), *Islamın Yeni Kamusal Yüzleri (The New Public Faces of Islam)*, İstanbul: Metis

Güler, İlhami (2010), *Direniş Teolojisi (Resistance Theology)*, Ankara: Ankara Okulu Yayınları.

Hebdige, Dick (1979), *Subculture: The Meaning of Style*, New York: Routledge.

Henry, Clement M. and Rodney Wilson (2004), *The Politics of Islamic Finance*, Edinburgh: Edinburgh University Press.

Hooper, B. (2000), 'Globalisation and resistance in post-Mao China: the case of foreign consumer products,' *Asian Studies Review*, **24** (4), 439–70.

Kedourie, Elie (1996), *Turkey: Identity, Democracy, Politics*, London and Portland, OR: Frank Cass.

Kemahlıoğlu, O. (2008), 'Particularistic distribution of investment subsidies under coalition governments: the case of Turkey', *Journal of Comparative Politics*, **40** (2), 189–207.

Keyder, Çağlar (2004), 'The Turkish bell jar', *New Left Review*, **28**, July–August.

Keyman, F. and B. Koyuncu (2004), 'AKP, MÜSİAD, ekonomik kalkınma ve modernite' ('Justice and Development Party, MÜSİAD, economic development and modernity'), *Dusunen Siyaset*, **19**, 125–45.
Kızıltepe, Ü. (2007) 'Custom barrier to Tekbir', *Yeni Asya*, 15 May.
Kleijnen, M., N. Lee and M. Wetzels (2009), 'An exploration of consumer resistance to innovation and its antecedents', *Journal of Economic Psychology*, **30** (3), 344–57.
Konda (2007), *Religion, Secularism and the Veil in Daily Life Survey*, İstanbul: Konda Arastirma.
Laukkanen, T., S. Sinkkonen, M. Kivijärvi and others (2007), 'Innovation resistance among mature consumers', *Journal of Consumer Marketing*, **24** (7), 419–27.
Laukkanen, P., S. Sinkkonen and T. Laukkanen (2008), 'Consumer resistance to Internet banking: postponers, opponents, and rejectors', *International Journal of Bank Marketing*, **26** (6), 419–27.
Leaman, Oliver (2006), *The Qur'an: An Encyclopedia*, London: Routledge.
Lee, Robert D. (1997), *Overcoming Tradition and Modernity: The Search for Islamic Authenticity*, Boulder, CO: Westview Press.
Leigh, T., C. Peters and J. Shelton (2006), 'The consumer quest for authenticity: the multiplicity of meanings within the MG subculture of consumption', *Journal of the Academy of Marketing Science*, **34** (4), 481–93.
Lewis, D. and D. Bridger (2001), *The Soul of the New Consumer: Authenticity: What We Buy and Why in the New Economy*, Boston, MA: Nicholas Brealey Publishing.
Lindholm, Charles (2008), *Culture and Authenticity*, Malden, MA and Oxford: Blackwell Publishing.
Lorent, Frank (2008), 'Mode für moderne Musliminnen', *Welt*, May.
Mcfarland, Andrew and Michele Micheletti (2009), *Creative Participation: Responsibility-Taking in the Political World*, Boulder, CO: Paradigm Publishers.
Navaro-Yashin, Yael (2002), *Faces of the State: Secularism and Public Life in Turkey*, Princeton, NJ: Princeton University Press.
Norris, Pippa and R. Inglehart (2004), *Sacred and Secular: Religion and Politics Worldwide*, New York: Cambridge University Press.
Outka, Elizabeth (2009), *Consuming traditions: modernity, modernism and commodified authentic*, Oxford University Press.
Öniş, Z. (1997), 'The political economy of Islamic resurgence in Turkey: the rise of the Welfare Party in perspective', *Third World Quarterly*, **18** (4), 743–66.
Öniş, Z. (2001), 'Political Islam at the crossroads: from hegemony to coexistence', *Contemporary Politics*, **7** (4), 281–91.
Öniş, Z. (2003), 'Domestic politics, international norms and challenges to the state: Turkey–EU relations in the post-Helsinki era', *Turkish Studies*, **4** (1), 9–34.
Öniş, Z. (2005), 'Entrepreneurs, citizenship and the European Union: the changing state of state–business relations', in Ahmer Içduygu and Fuat Kayman (eds), *Turkey Challenges to Citizenship in a Globalizing World*, London: Routledge.
Öniş, Z. and U. Türem (2001), 'Business, globalisation and democracy: a comparative analysis of Turkish business associations', *Turkish Studies*, **2** (2), 94–120.
Ozanne, D. (2006), 'After a fashion: a tale of two Turkeys', *This World*, 16 November.
Palazzo, G. and K. Basu (2007), 'The ethical backlash of corporate branding', *Journal of Business Ethics*, **73** (4), 333–437.
Pavia, T. and M. Mason (2007), 'Space, the final frontier: consumer adaptation, resistance and redefinition of spatial limitation in the marketspace', *Advances in Consumer Research*, **34**, 590.
Pine, B.J. and J.H. Gilmore (1999), *The Experience Economy: Work Is Theater & Every Business a Stage*, Boston, MA: Harvard Business School Press.
Ram, S. (1989), 'Successful innovation using strategies to reduce consumer resistance: an empirical test,' *Journal of Product Innovation Management*, **6** (1), 20–34.
Ritson, M. and S. Dobscha (2009), 'Marketing heretics: resistance is/is not futile', *Advances in Consumer Research*, **26**, 159.
Roy, D.A. (1986), 'Islamic banking: rapid growth and moral dilemma', *Middle East Executive Reports*, **9** (4), 8–13.
Rudnyckyj, D. (2009), 'Spiritual economies: Islam and neoliberalism in contemporary Indonesia', *Cultural Anthropology*, **24** (1), 104–41.
Russo, Michael V. (2010), *Companies on a Mission: Entrepreneurial Strategies for Growing Sustainably, Responsibly, and Profitably*, Stanford, CA: Stanford University Press.
Sandıkcı, Ö. and A. Ekici (2009), 'Politically motivated brand rejection', *Journal of Business Research*, **62** (2), 208–17.
Sandıkcı, Ö. and G. Ger (2001), 'Fundamental fashions: the cultural politics of the turban and the Levi's', in Mary C. Gilly and Joan Meyers-Levy (eds), *Advances in Consumer Research*, Vol. 28, Valdosta, GA: Association for Consumer Research, pp. 146–50.
Sandıkcı, Ö. and G. Ger (2002), 'In-between modernities and postmodernities: theorizing Turkish

consumptionscape', in Susan M. Broniarczyk and Kent Nakamoto (eds), *Advances in Consumer Research*, Vol. 29, Valdosta, GA: Association for Consumer Research, pp. 465–70.

Sandıkcı, Ö. and G. Ger (2005), 'Aesthetics, ethics, and politics of the Turkish headscarf', in Susanne Küchler and Daniel Miller (eds), *Clothing as Material Culture*, Oxford: Berg, pp. 61–82.

Sandıkcı, Ö. and G. Ger (2007), 'Constructing and representing the Islamic consumer in Turkey', *Fashion Theory*, **11** (2/3), 189–210.

Sandıkcı, Ö. and G. Ger (2010), 'Veiling in style: how does a stigmatized practice become fashionable?', *Journal of Consumer Research*, **37** (June), 15–36.

Seubsman, S., M. Kelly, and P. Yuthapornpinit (2009), 'Cultural resistance to fastfood consumption? A study of youth in Northeastern Thailand', *International Journal of Consumer Studies*, **33** (6), 669–75.

Taylor, Charles (1991), *The Ethics of Authenticity*, Boston, MA: Harvard University Press.

Tepe, Sultan (2008), *Beyond Sacred and Secular*, Stanford, CA: Stanford University Press.

Tormey, S. (2007), 'Consumption, resistance and everyday life: ruptures and continuities', *Journal of Consumer Policy*, **30** (3), 263–80.

Trilling, Lionel (1972), *Sincerity and Authenticity*, Boston, MA: Harvard University Press.

Ünal, M. (2009), 'Shariah scholars in the GCC – a network analytic perspective', *Research on Islamic Banking*.

Walsh, M. and J. Lipinski (2008), 'Unhappy campers: exploring consumer resistance to change', *Journal of Travel & Tourism Marketing*, **25** (1), 13–24.

Webb, D. (2005), 'On mosques and malls: understanding Khomeinism as a source of counter-hegemonic resistance to the spread of global consumer culture', *Journal of Political Ideologies*, **10** (1) 95–119.

Yalkin, C. and R. Elliott (2009), 'Adolescents yet again speak of fashion: an account of participation and resistance', *Advances in Consumer Research*, **36**, 532–33.

Yankaya, D. (2009), 'The Europeanization of MÜSİAD: political opportunism, economic Europeanization, Islamic Euroscepticism', *European Journal of Turkish Studies*, **9**, http://ejts.revues.org/index3696.html, accessed 18 April 2010.

20 The Arab consumer boycott of American products: motives and intentions
Maya F. Farah

INTRODUCTION

Whether boycotted for acting against well-established human rights, against the environment, or even against animal rights, companies increasingly face the risk of consumers voting through their wallets for the type of societies they want to live in. Boycotts can target the goods produced by a particular company or they may target all the companies of a specific country for political reasons. By withholding purchases from companies or countries that they perceive as abusive, consumers expect to increase corporate and governmental sensitivity to their economic, environmental, political and social concerns (Sen et al., 2001).

This area of research is of particular importance for a number of reasons including (1) the growth in boycott frequency accompanying the trend toward less governmental regulation of business (Friedman, 1985), (2) the sophistication of boycott organizers, who are increasingly adopting high-tech methods such as computerized mailing lists and large databases of consumers' mobile numbers (Garrett, 1987), and (3) the growing recognition of boycotts as a legal form of social protest, whereby promoters and participants are not held liable for financial damage inflicted on targeted companies (Garrett, 1987) .

An extensive review of the literature reveals that only a few attempts have been made to tackle the variables that influence consumers' individual boycott decisions (for example, Klein and John, 2003; Klein et al., 2004; Kozinets and Handelman, 1998). This study aims to fill the gap by exploring the various beliefs that lie at the core of those decisions by adopting an established socio-psychological model, namely, the Theory of Planned Behaviour (TPB, Ajzen, 1991).

CONSUMERS' BOYCOTTING MOTIVES

A boycott describes 'the attempt by one or more parties to achieve certain objectives by urging individual consumers to refrain from making selected purchases in the marketplace' (Friedman, 1999, p. 4). Though a limited number of studies tackle consumers' drive to participate in micro- or corporate-level boycotting campaigns, studies on consumers' motives to participate in macro-level campaigns are scarce. Macro-boycotting campaigns are usually directed against a country's brands due to military, political or diplomatic conflict (Abosag, 2010). Numerous micro-boycotting motives discussed in the literature may be significant in the conceptualization of the drives motivating consumers' participation in macro-boycotting campaigns, such as the boycott studied in the context of this study.

Research suggests that the perceived egregiousness of an entity's actions is the chief motivation for boycott (Smith, 1990). This perception is highly dependent on each individual's value system, culture and the context in which the campaign occurs. In all cases, the more egregious a consumer perceives a behaviour to be, the more likely is his or her participation in the boycott (Klein et al., 2004). Klein et al. (1998) tackle this behaviour at a macro-level where a country's policies lead to a boycott of all products from that country. The egregious act may in such situations not be committed by the target itself, but the campaign is expected to ultimately affect that actor.

Boycott participation can also be motivated by one's need to vent anger or outrage, by way of maintaining or enhancing self-esteem (Brewer and Brown, 1998; Pittman, 1998). Though much of the literature refers to participating in boycotts as a social activity, this behaviour may also be 'the expression of an individual's uniqueness' motivated by a drive for moral self-realization (Sen et al., 2001). Boycott participation can thus be considered a self-enhancing act (Brewer and Brown, 1998; Klein et al., 2002), as one's self-esteem can be enhanced by one's sense of remedying of a corporate wrongdoing.

Moreover, participating in a boycott called for by a group with which one identifies strongly is a common way of relating to fashionable attitudes and moral values. One may choose to participate in a specific boycott merely to satisfy the need for group belonging, provided that one's self-concept derives partly from that group (Tajfel, 1982).

In addition to perceived social pressure, an individual's own feeling of moral obligation to participate in the boycott is important. Feelings of citizen-efficacy (Tyler and McGraw, 1983) can be significant drivers in this context. An individual's perception that his or her influence can be non-negligible may lead to the presumption of a strong link between one's boycott participation and the potential outcomes of the campaign. Besides, led by the thrill of victory, people may like to be part of a successful boycott, in which case both the free-rider and the small-agent effects disappear.

However, the free-rider and small-agent (Hardin, 1968; Olson, 1965) effects can be significant in limiting the incentive to participate. People may consider that they would reap the benefits of a successful boycott whether or not they participate; thus some may be motivated to free-ride upon the boycott actions of others. In the case of an instrumental boycott which typically has specific, quantifiable aims since the protesters' intentions are generally to compel the target to make an explicit behavioural change (Friedman, 1999), greater participation by others may discourage individual participation.

In addition, a number of consumers may think that they are relatively small compared to the market and hence that their actions are likely to have a negligible impact. This belief is based on the idea that their individual participation would most probably not yield any instrumental benefit and is thus unworthy.

Several noteworthy factors can also restrain one's incentive for participation. These are mainly the costs associated with such a behaviour, which will differ considerably from one boycott or individual to another (Klein and John, 2003). It is commonly assumed that potential participants will not join a boycott if their personal cost of participation is high. In this cost-benefit approach, the first cost is related to consumers' preference and loyalty for the boycotted product (Klein et al., 2004); the second is associated with the unavailability in the marketplace of suitable and affordable direct substitutes (Sen et al., 2001). Another barrier to participation may be the perception that such campaigns may have negative outcomes, such as increased unemployment (Klein et al., 2004).

GAPS IN THE LITERATURE

Though boycotts of various place and time considerations, objectives, corporate targets (Friedman, 1985) and level of participation attract increased attention in contemporary consumer research (Herman, 1992; Peñaloza and Price 1992), the review conducted allows the uncovering of three main gaps in the literature on the motives behind boycott participation. First, the majority of the existing research on boycotting is related to the impact of these campaigns on the revenues and profits of companies, with only a few studies focusing on the conceptualization of the motives behind it (Klein and John, 2003; Klein et al., 2004; Smith, 1985). Second, although there are some indications that many boycott campaigns are taking place in non-Western markets, most of the existing studies have been conducted in Western contexts. Third, the few studies on boycott motives conducted can be methodologically criticized for their over-reliance on convenience samples, usually university students. The findings of these studies are often not generalizable to the overall population.

In light of how little is known conclusively about the antecedents of consumer boycotting behaviour, the development of an extensive inventory of boycott motives and the use of a sounder theoretical framework in consumer behaviour research appears to be essential. Accordingly, this study aims to foster research in the consumer boycotting field from a behavioural perspective.

THE ARAB BOYCOTT OF AMERICAN PRODUCTS IN THE LEBANESE MARKET

The Arab boycott of American products as a sign of protest against the US policy in the Middle East is used as an ideal case for this study. An extension of the 1951 Arab boycott against Israel, the boycott of American companies started in 1999. Boycotts of US products have been pursued by various Arab civilians ever since in response to the perception widely held by consumers sympathetic to the Palestinian and other Pan-Arab causes that the US has been taking the side of Israel in its conflict with the Palestinians, and lately because of the American government's actions in Iraq and its overall foreign policy in the region. The effect of this boycott is not well known, yet the fact that 300 million Arab citizens could be reached and persuaded even partially to boycott is a cause for concern for many US companies.

The choice of Lebanon for the purpose of this study is related to the noteworthy involvement of the Lebanese citizens in this boycott. Though there is no empirical data on the actual material losses incurred by US companies operating in Lebanon, evidence of such effects can be inferred from the call of numerous companies for financial and marketing consultants to examine the consequences of these campaigns. Rather than looking at the financial impact of the boycott, this study aims to contrast the rationales used by the various Lebanese social and religious groups to justify their boycotting behaviour.

Situated on the eastern coast of the Mediterranean Sea and bounded on the north and east by Syria and on the south by Israel/Palestine, Lebanon is a country of visible contradictions. If any one word defines Lebanon, it is 'social diversity'. The Lebanese society is constituted of two main religious groups, Muslims and Christians, further divided into 18 sectarian groups. Each of these sects plays a significant role in shaping the Lebanese social structure and affecting its national culture and political life. According to recent statistics in the CIA World Factbook (2010), 59.7 per cent of the Lebanese population is Muslim, while 40 per cent is Christian. The Maronites, associated with the Roman Catholic Church, are the largest Lebanese Christian community, representing roughly 25.2 per cent of the population. The Maronites have always had good relations with the Western world, especially France and the Vatican. The second largest Christian community, representing 7.8 per cent of the Lebanese population, is that of the Greek Orthodox who have often been recognized for their pan-Arab leanings. The remaining Christian groups constitute 7 per cent of the population (Greek Catholics, Protestants, Roman Catholics, among others). The Muslims are broadly divided into Shiite, Sunni, and Druze. The Shiite sect is the single largest Lebanese community accounting for 35 per cent of the population, while Sunnis represent 20 per cent and Druze 5 per cent of locals.

The campaign calling for the boycott of American products brings together various local non-governmental organizations (NGOs), unions, student groups, religious figures and political parties. Although commercial circles and a number of politicians are conservative vis-à-vis the above-mentioned boycott, local statistics show significant recurrent participation by the citizens. A survey undertaken by Information International (research consultancy firm, member of the Market Research Association) in May 2002 and sampling 600 people in the Greater Beirut area reveals that 45 per cent of the surveyed sample had boycotted US products in solidarity with Palestinians (Information International, 2002).

Rather than analysing the financial consequences of the campaign, this study adopts a socio-cognitive approach to identify and investigate the behavioural, normative and control beliefs underlying consumers' intention to boycott and to test the relationships between these beliefs and the direct TPB measures, namely, attitude, subjective norm and perceived behavioural control (PBC). The research intends to differentiate between the beliefs motivating the participation of Muslim versus Christian consumers. The identified beliefs are valuable targets for businesses planning to design counter-boycott participation interventions.

AN APPLICATION OF THE THEORY OF PLANNED BEHAVIOUR TO BOYCOTT BEHAVIOUR

The TPB framework (see Figure 20.1) is adopted for the purpose of this study to define the beliefs underlying consumers' attitudes towards participating in a macro-boycott, subjective norms and PBC. According to the TPB, human action is guided by three kinds of considerations, namely, behavioural beliefs, which relate to the likely outcomes of the behaviour and the evaluations of these outcomes, normative beliefs associated with the expectations of others and the motivation to comply with these expectations, and control beliefs concerning the presence of factors that may facilitate or impede performance of the behaviour and the perceived power of these factors (Fishbein and Ajzen, 1975).

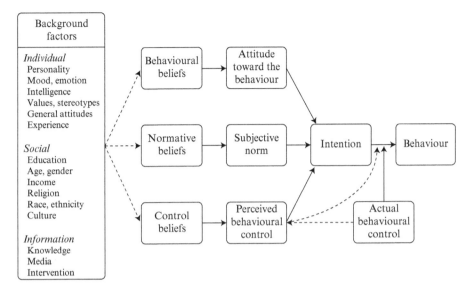

Source: Ajzen (1991).

Figure 20.1   The Theory of Planned Behaviour model

Behavioural beliefs and attitude toward the behaviour

People's attitudes toward participating in the boycott are determined by their accessible behavioural beliefs. The attitude is measured by both the salient beliefs about the outcomes of participating in the boycott and the individual's evaluation of the outcomes resulting from that action. The consumer is likely to have a more positive attitude toward participating in the boycott if the behaviour is believed to have positive consequences.

Normative beliefs and subjective norm (SN)

Normative beliefs refer to the perceived behavioural expectations of important referent individuals or groups, such as the consumer's family, friends, the campaigning group, or society in general. These beliefs in combination with the person's motivation to comply with those expectations determine the subjective norm, which is generally understood as the perceived social pressure to engage in the boycott or not. Research suggests that people's consumption decisions are strongly influenced by their reference groups (Childers and Rao, 1992). By extrapolation, boycotting behaviour could be similarly influenced.

Control beliefs and perceived behavioural control

Control beliefs are associated with the perception that certain factors may facilitate or impede one's participation in a boycott. These beliefs, as well as their perceived power, determine one's behavioural control, namely, one's perception of one's ability to participate/engage in a boycott.

Background factors
In the TPB model, individual (personality traits, experience and values) and social (education, age, gender and religion) factors are considered background factors. They are assumed to influence intentions and behaviour indirectly by affecting behavioural, normative or control beliefs.

Behavioural intention
Intentions are generally an indication of how hard people are willing to try to perform a given act. In this study, intention represents a consumer's readiness to participate in the boycott, and it is considered to be the immediate precondition of behaviour.

THE PRESENT RESEARCH

The present research is divided into two studies. The first study aims to delineate through a series of interviews the beliefs at the basis of the Lebanese consumers' decision to participate or not in the boycott of American products. The use of interviews is based on Creswell's (1994) indication of the adequacy of such a method given (a) the exploratory nature of the research, (b) the number of variables still to uncover, (c) the importance of the context where the boycott is taking place and (d) the lack of an agreed-upon theoretical framework for the study of boycott motives.

The second study is based on a survey whereby a questionnaire, including the most frequently cited beliefs drawn from the interviews, is distributed to a sample of Lebanese consumers. In this quantitative study, the analyses aim to test whether consumers' indirect beliefs toward boycotting US products are related to their attitude, subjective norm and perceived behavioural control. The data collection conducted has led to the use of a confirmatory and deductive logic, whereby both descriptive and analytic statistics were generated.

STUDY ONE: INTERVIEW METHODOLOGY

Based on the guidelines provided by Ajzen and Fishbein (1980), an interview methodology was adopted for the first study. Thirty people were interviewed face-to-face in order to generate the list of beliefs that Lebanese consumers hold regarding boycotting US companies. Their behaviour was defined in terms of (1) the action (boycotting, as a sign of protest against US policy in the Middle East), (2) the target (American companies, especially those producing consumer goods), (3) the context (Lebanon), and (4) the time (until a change in US policy in the Middle East occurs).

Method

Participants
The data were collected during the second half of June 2005 from interviews with 30 consumers living in Beirut, the capital of Lebanon. Interviewees included (a) four activists belonging to NGOs advocating the boycott of American products, (b) a consumer behaviour lecturer at the American University of Beirut, (c) a psychology lecturer teach-

ing at the Lebanese University, (d) a salesman working at BHV shopping mall, (e) an employee working at McDonald's, (f) a journalist, (g) ten university students and (h) eleven housewives typically engaged in daily household shopping. The sample included 13 male and 17 female participants. Ages ranged from 26 to 62 years (Mean age = 41 years, SD = 9.1 years). The interviewees came from diverse backgrounds, and as such, were likely to represent the views held by most Lebanese consumers. The sample size was determined on the basis of data saturation principles.

Procedure
The semi-structured interviews meticulously followed the guidelines prescribed by Fishbein and Ajzen (1975). Each interview lasted 30 to 50 minutes. Interviewees were guaranteed anonymity. Audio-taping facilitated the transcription, coding and grouping of the statements into the categories suggested by the TPB.

Interview questions
The open-ended questions were designed to elicit Lebanese consumers' salient behavioural, normative and control beliefs. Salient beliefs, the few that the consumer can entertain at the time of the interview, are considered to be the only immediate determinants of the consumer's attitude, subjective norm and PBC.

Elicitation of behavioural beliefs
In order to grasp the salient beliefs underlying their attitude toward boycotting American companies, the respondents were asked the following: 'What do you believe are the advantages/disadvantages of your boycotting American companies in Lebanon until a change in US policy towards the Middle East has occurred?'

Elicitation of normative beliefs
To elicit the identity of those people affecting their decision to boycott, the interviewees were asked: 'Are there any individuals or groups who would approve/disapprove of your boycotting US products?'

Elicitation of control beliefs
In order to draw up the list of factors that may facilitate or impede one's participation in the boycott, the interviewees were asked the following: 'What factors or circumstances would enable you or make it difficult for you to participate in a boycott?'

Results

The interviews were analyzed semi-quantitatively: interviews were content-analyzed and described using theme frequencies. As a result of the interviews conducted, a list of constructs related to consumers' motivation to boycott was compiled and an explanation of the statistical results generated by the survey of the second study was given.

Behavioural beliefs
Careful consideration shows that the elicited behavioural beliefs related to boycott participation were predominantly positive, with only one main negative belief related

Table 20.1   Identification of modal salient behavioural beliefs

Participating in the boycott would. . .	Frequency	Percentage of respondents expressing each belief
Endanger the jobs of local workers who work for American companies	20	66.67
Help me express my Arab identity	20	66.67
Help me preserve my sense of belongingness with my community	20	66.67
Allow me to act according to my social values	20	66.67
Help me release my anger in a peaceful way	20	66.67
Make me feel a winner if the campaign is successful	20	66.67
Satisfy my sense of responsibility towards the Arab Community	18	60
Help the campaign achieve its ends	18	60
Raise the effectiveness of the campaign by encouraging others to boycott	18	60
Be useless as I can enjoy its outcomes without personally participating	15	50
Help me express my religious beliefs	15	50
Help the people affected by the US policy in the Middle East	15	50
Make companies rethink their operations/decisions	15	50
Make the American Government reconsider its policies	15	50
Increase trade of products between Arab World countries	5	16.67
Help re-launch the local industries and therefore boost local economy	3	10

to the fact that the boycott could put the jobs of many locals working in US companies operating in Lebanon at risk. Based on Ajzen and Fishbein's (1980) recommendations, the beliefs mentioned by at least 20 per cent of the interviewees were included in the salient beliefs set. The most commonly cited beliefs were expressed in statements reflecting the 14 beliefs that are likely to affect consumers' attitude toward boycotting US products. The validity of a number of those constructs was confirmed by the existing literature on boycotting. Adopting the beliefs cited by at least 20 per cent of the sample resulted in selecting all but the following beliefs: 'increase trade of products between Arab World countries' and 'help re-launch the local industries and therefore boost local economy.'

Normative beliefs
Since the referents cited were very similar for all interviewees, five sources of social pressure were identified, namely, family, close friends, colleagues/co-workers, the community to which one belongs and the religious leader of one's community.

Control beliefs
Interviewees expressed both inhibiting and facilitating control beliefs about participating in the boycott. The most frequently expressed beliefs were related to (a) the respondent's preference of American companies' products over all other products, (b) the dependence on US products and (c) the unavailability of substitutes at reasonable or competitive prices.

Discussion

The interviews conducted showed that participants' views regarding the boycott were mainly based on behavioural beliefs. Although normative beliefs were brought up by almost every interviewee, still these did not appear to be at the basis of the decision of whether to boycott or not. Moreover, the interviewees emphasized only three control beliefs related to boycott participation. These were related to the existence of substitutes as well as to the price and quality issues at the basis of not only their preference but often their dependence on US products.

In line with Dickinson and Carsky's (2005) findings, interviewees who boycott or intend to do so generally believe that this act is an expression of the sovereignty that they hold in the marketplace. The conversations reveal that although the participants' decision to engage in a boycott is an individual decision, they often consider themselves to be part of a larger group, all voting in the same way. Generally speaking, this group holds at heart the notion of responsibility in matters of consumption and believes in voicing its objection to American policy in the Arab world in the hopes of reversing that policy. Although participation in the boycott instilled in many of the interviewees the notion of responsibility to act as consumer citizens, some were aware that, as individuals, they possessed a limited degree of sovereignty determined by available choices and information. In fact, many interviewees recognized that for it to be effective, the boycott has to be a collective action. Among those who boycotted for a period then renounced, a psychology lecturer at the Lebanese University asserted:

> My family and I participated in the boycott for a few months in 2002 after the military operations that took place in the West Bank, then again when Iraq was invaded in 2003. But a few months later, we felt like we were acting alone. We saw little enthusiasm from people around us, let alone from the Arab community as a whole. I am not saying that mass movements did not take place. But for it to work, the rallies should have been of a greater scope and for longer periods of time. So we gave up!

Moreover, it is worth noting that some respondents who are still boycotting understand that such campaigns may have a negative impact on the local economy by jeopardizing the jobs of the employees of the targeted companies. These results reveal that people may hold both positive and negative beliefs related to boycotting US companies operating in Lebanon. The literature shows that such ambivalence can result either from the existence of simultaneous conflicting cognitive beliefs or from a conflict between cognition and affect (Eagly and Chaiken, 1993).

The small agent effect explained earlier appears also to be among the strongest beliefs discouraging people from boycotting. Among the explanations given by respondents who affirmed never to have boycotted, a middle-aged housewife clarified that not only does she find such an endeavour useless and ineffective in terms of changing the US government's stance, but also that a change in her purchasing habits is very complicated. She explained, 'Why would I penalize myself by deciding to stop purchasing a product that I need and I am used to? How would my purchases affect the United States? Not in any way, I can assure you!'

In general, interviewees who claimed to be boycotting explained their behaviour in terms of either their religious or political orientations. Accordingly, a discussion of these two factors shaping the behaviour of local citizens with regard to the boycott appears to be valuable to the understanding of such consumer behaviour.

The Effect of Political Orientation on Boycott Participation

The political inclinations of local consumers affect notably their individual views on the campaign mainly promoted by the Arab Nationalist Party and its various affiliations as well as by the Lebanese Communist Party due to their historical contempt for US foreign policies.

Arab Nationalism as a dogma started with Abdel Nasser, the President of Egypt, from 1954 to 1970. Abdel Nasser was famous for his Arab nationalist policies promoting action on the part of Arab states to confront what was seen as the 'imperialist West' (Stephens, 1972). Arab nationalism has evolved from a sense of identity to a formal political party with a particular stance regarding boycotting US products based on the American government's alleged support of the state of Israel. The Arab Nationalist Party regroups today a number of citizens who still take the Arab cause to heart. It is crucial to note that since the creation of the republic in 1943, the Lebanese have disagreed over the identity of the state. While Muslims favoured a close association with the Arab world, Christians, particularly the Maronites, opted for linking Lebanon culturally and politically to the West. In fact, a faction of the Christian community, especially among Maronites, were uneasy about the Taif agreement reached in September 1989, which for the first time declared Lebanon as an Arab nation in loyalty and identity (Christiansen, 2005). This disparity with respect to sense of identity between the different Lebanese citizens has not only shaped the structure of the Arab Nationalist Party, but has also affected the composition of the groups participating in the boycott in support of the Arab cause.

In line with this stream of thought, a medical doctor in his mid-60s who affirmed in the interview to be boycotting some American products, explained:

> When I boycott American products, I boycott the ones supporting Israel not all American products. I try to differentiate and do a small enquiry on the pharmaceutical company. Nowadays, access to information is easy especially with the Internet. I can know where the company operates, who its main investors [are], its philanthropic contributions and lots of other details that help me decide. In the last years of Israeli occupation here in Lebanon before 2000 and a bit later in 2002 when the situation in Palestine worsened I used to boycott all American products that had substitutes, but later due mainly to price reasons, I decided to differentiate among US companies that support Israel or the operations in Iraq and those that don't. With some of my colleagues, we exchange information on companies and products to be avoided. We tend to work together among groups of doctors who take the Arab cause at heart. I think each of us can and should do something.

The Lebanese Communist Party is another political party that has intermittently supported the boycott. This party brings together a number of intellectuals and young people of all religions yearning for the institution of a classless society and fighting against the capitalist values highly endorsed by the United States. Though based on a different set of motives than those promoted by the Arab Nationalist Party, the Lebanese Communist party's campaign against US products is sponsored by a number of NGOs who have a communist orientation.

The Effect of Religious Orientation on Boycott Participation

Religion has traditionally been of overriding importance in defining the Lebanese population, its political views and the loyalty of Lebanon's citizens to the numerous local political groups, as well as their recognition of their Arab identity. A number of NGOs promote the boycott of American products based on the *fatwa* rulings, in other words, the Islamic teachings preached by prominent religious figures of the two major Islamic sects: Shiites and Sunnites. The comprehensive review of the calls for boycotting reveal a concurrence between the Sunnites' and the Shiites' outlooks.

In this context, in his *fatwa* of 28 November 2000, Ayatollah Al Sayyed M. Fadlallah, a prominent Shiite religious leader in Lebanon, called on all Muslims to boycott all Israeli and American companies, basing his case on the Prophet Muhammad's sayings, that 'whosoever does not care about Muslims' affairs is not a Muslim' and 'whosoever hears Muslims calling for help without answering that call is not a Muslim' (Fadlallah, 2002). Likewise, *fatwa* no. 8822, dated 27 February 2002, of Imam Al Sayed Ali Khamenei, the religious leader of the Islamic Republic of Iran, stipulated that 'any transaction with a company whose profits are for helping the enemies of Muslims or for supporting the Zionist regime is not permissible' (Khamenei, 2002). Similarly, Ayatollah Al Sistani, the Shiite religious leader in Iraq, proclaimed that 'it is not permissible for a Muslim to buy products manufactured in countries that are in a state of war with Muslims' (Al Sistani, 2002, p.146). These Shiite religious figures emphasize openly that answering a Muslim's calls for help either as an individual or as a group is an integral part of the teaching of Islam. Repeatedly, these religious leaders have preached that the least that the members of the Islamic world could do in order to support other Muslims is to boycott all those who support the enemy, implicitly referring to the American government.

The religious discourse provided by Sunni representatives parallels that of their Shiite counterparts. In fact, Sheikh Al Qaradawi of Egypt emphasized the role of women in the success of this boycott campaign, declaring:

> Our sisters and daughters who control the houses have a role to play, which may be more important than that of the man, because women supervise the needs of the house . . . She plants the Jihadic spirit in the children and educates them in what they must do for their *ummah*, especially in terms of boycotting (Al Qaradawi, 2002).

The approach of these religious leaders seems to be based on the Muslim Prophet's saying that 'the Muslim is a brother to the Muslim; he can't oppress him, can't give him up and can't let him down.' This quote is often used by religious leaders to stimulate the sense of belonging and unity within the Islamic nation and the moral responsibility towards other members of the community. Some religious personalities go as far as declaring the act of buying American goods, when there is an alternative from other countries, as *haram*, which refers to the act of committing a major sin against God's law. The spread and impact of these messages is made even more important through the use of chat rooms and blogs as a platform for fervent boycott calls.

Affected by such discourses, an old southern woman interviewed about her boycotting stance and status, passionately revealed:

> I am an old-school boycotter from the heydays of the Aqsa uprising, got the habit and never dropped it. Whether boycotting is effective or not is irrelevant. It's a personal choice. It satisfies my sense of moral responsibility. Even more, I believe it is a religious obligation. I am an Arab and a Muslim. If I forget what has happened to us in Lebanon, to our houses, sons, daughters, I can't allow myself to see what is happening to other Muslims and not help. That is my only means of helping. I teach my sons and their wives and my daughters to boycott US products. If each of us explains to the others around the importance of such an act, perhaps we will manage to change something. If we don't, we would at least have acted according to the Prophet's teachings. I am not boycotting out of romanticism. I think we Muslims can and must do something. It's both a human and religious duty!

This account reflects the responses given by various Muslim interviewees who believed that participating in the boycott satisfies one's sense of moral responsibility towards other citizens of the Arab World affected by the US policy in the Middle East and that this participation in itself is a religious duty.

In sum, religious calls for boycott participation have been significantly more recurrent and decisive among the various Muslim communities than among Christian ones, as such calls by priests appear to be quasi-nonexistent. Sporadic sermons in Sunday masses in the local Orthodox Church calling for boycott participation are considered exceptions and can be explained by the deep sense of Arab identity of this community. Such views can be controversial in the Maronite church to which the majority of the Lebanese Christian community adheres, given an equivocal view of the Arab identity of the latter group. Most Christian consumers interviewed preferred to have a good product at a good price regardless of the country of origin. Many of them showed little if any intention to participate in the boycott saying that the problems that exist in the rest of the Arab World are irrelevant to them. These respondents were mostly favourable to the role that the US is playing in the Middle East. The Christian interviewees who expressed interest in the boycott often did so either because of their affiliations to one of the two political parties referred to above or because of reports aired by the media that brought the topic to their attention in a vivid and concrete manner. It should be noted at this point that ethical views in the context of such boycotting campaigns are very subjective due to the differences in how consumers evaluate the US policy in the Middle East based on their own individual religious and political orientations.

STUDY TWO: SURVEY METHODOLOGY

Hypotheses

Previous research based on the TPB has found that behavioural, normative and control beliefs are generally positively related to attitude, subjective norms, and PBC, respectively (Fishbein and Ajzen, 1975). The following hypotheses were tested to investigate whether the relationships between the belief-based measures extracted from the interviews and the direct measures of the TPB are positive:

H_1: There is a positive relationship between behavioural beliefs and attitude.
H_2: There is a positive relationship between normative beliefs and subjective norm.
H_3: There is a positive relationship between control beliefs and PBC.
H_4: There is a positive relationship between behavioural beliefs and intention.
H_5: There is a positive relationship between normative beliefs and intention.
H_6: There is a positive relationship between control beliefs and intention.

Method

Participants

A questionnaire was filled in the presence of an investigator by a sample of 500 consumers chosen so as to be representative of the Lebanese population. The data were collected during the months of July and August 2005. Each encounter lasted 15 to 20 minutes.

The study was based on a multi-stage systematic-random sampling methodology. First, the country was stratified according to the five existing conglomerates: Southern Lebanon, Beqaa, Greater Beirut, Mount Lebanon and Northern Lebanon. The sample of people to survey in each conglomerate was computed in proportion to the corresponding number of residents. The adoption of a conglomerate-based stratification procedure was decided upon because people from the same religion typically cluster by geographical zones.

The respondents were systematically selected from the local household telephone directory (that is, the white pages). Because numbers are more stable than names, the unit of sampling from the directory was set to be the phone number available in the houses or flats contacted; hence, the total frame from which the sample was selected comprised the 650 000 households over which the local fixed lines are distributed. The process started with the calculation of the number of telephone lines to sample.

Targeting a sample size of 500, the figure was enlarged by 50 per cent to allow for refusals, ineligible numbers and numbers which are not answered. The sample size was estimated based on the following three measures: the size of the population, considered at this stage to be the 650 000 fixed non-business telephone lines distributed locally and which could be assumed to mirror the number of Lebanese families; an error level or confidence interval of 4.5 per cent, and a level of confidence of 95 per cent (Zikmund, 1994, p 408).

In order to sample from the household telephone directory, a specific line from each nth line column was selected. The number of the column chosen depended on the calculation for each conglomerate. This multi-stage sampling allowed us to decide which dwellings were to be sampled rather than which people to survey. One respondent from each household contacted was sampled based on the age criteria. Any person aged 16 years and above living in the household contacted qualified for the study.

Of the original 750 contacts selected, 721 qualified as eligible housing units and produced either a completed face-to-face interview with a randomly selected

Table 20.2   Response rate per conglomerate

	Beirut	Mount Lebanon	Northern Lebanon	Southern Lebanon	Beqaa	Total
Number of contacted persons	63	309	174	104	71	721
Number of respondents	49	191	113	89	58	500
Response rate (%)	77.77	61.81	64.94	85.57	81.69	69.35

Table 20.3   Distribution of respondents by area of residence and religious affiliation

	Frequency	Percentage	Muslims	Christians	Muslims %	Christians %
Beirut	49	9.8	29	20	59.18	40.82
Mount Lebanon	191	38.2	26	165	13.61	86.39
Northern Lebanon	113	22.6	63	50	55.75	44.25
Southern Lebanon	89	22.8	74	15	66.99	33.01
Beqaa	58	6.6	40	18	68.97	31.03
Total	500	100	232	268	46.40	53.60

respondent from that household (69.35 per cent), or a non-response (30.65 per cent). The latter group included refusals to participate or unavailability at home at the time agreed upon for the interview. The response rate per conglomerate is shown in Table 20.2.

The significant difference in response rates among the conglomerates is explained based on two essentials. Firstly, people living in areas that were under Israeli forces' occupation prior to the year 2000, chiefly southern Lebanon, showed enthusiasm in expressing their beliefs and explaining their behaviours regarding the boycott. Secondly, the conglomerates where the population consisted of a large Muslim community (southern Lebanon and Beqaa) showed higher response rates, possibly due to the religious implications of the boycott.

Forty-six per cent of the respondents were Muslims. The religious distribution of the sample by area of residence (Table 20.3) fairly mirrored the figures presented in the governmental study, 'Mapping of living conditions in Lebanon, 2004' (2005).

Measures
The questionnaire administered in the second study was developed based on Study 1. Designed to measure the TPB constructs as applied to the study of the motivational factors behind boycott participation, items assessing both belief-based and direct measures of attitude, subjective norms, PBC and intentions, were included in the questionnaire. A complete list of items is presented in the Appendix. The inclusion of the indirect measures was based on the assumption that individuals can seldom give a summary estimate of their global attitude. The use of indirect measures also presupposes that people can both accurately report their beliefs in a probabilistic way and

rationally report their relative weightings. Another intricacy related to these measures is the assumption that the researcher has included in the research instrument all the items which together have sufficient content validity to correlate significantly with the direct measure.

Attitudes toward boycotting were directly assessed by asking the respondents to evaluate the behaviour on the following form of stems: 'My participation in the boycott against US companies in the Arab World, as a sign of protest against US policy in the Middle East, would be . . .' The items were rated on six semantic differential scales with the following endpoints: useless–useful, bad–good, unreasonable–reasonable, not beneficial–beneficial, undesirable–desirable and unfair–fair. In order to have an indirect measure of participants' attitudes to boycotting, the 14 behavioural beliefs elicited in the first study were included to be rated on a 7-point scale with endpoints labelled 'extremely unlikely' and 'extremely likely'. Respondents were asked to assess the likelihood that their boycotting would lead to each of the outcomes, then to estimate each of the latter on a bipolar evaluative scale. Accordingly, 14 evaluative items were added requiring respondents to estimate how good or bad the cited outcomes would be.

Two items were included to assess the direct measure of subjective norms. The first scale required participants to rate the likelihood that most people who are important to them would encourage them to boycott, whereas the second asked respondents whether most of the people important to them boycott US companies. In addition to the direct measure of subjective norms, the five salient referents identified at the interview stage were adopted in order to assess the normative beliefs. These were family, close friends, colleagues/co-workers, members of the community to which one belonged and the religious leader of this community. With respect to each of these referents, two items assessed normative belief strength and motivation to comply.

Two rating scales were included to provide a direct measure of PBC assessing respondents' ability to refrain from buying the products if desired, and the likelihood of their having total control over the decision of whether or not to boycott. To measure control-belief strength, respondents were to rate their preference and dependence on the boycotted products and the likelihood of finding viable substitutes for the boycotted products at a reasonable or competitive price. Three corresponding scales were designed to gauge the perceived power of the different factors.

Subjective norms and normative beliefs, PBC and control beliefs, as well as the two items that were designed to elicit respondents' intentions to boycott were all assessed on 'strongly disagree – strongly agree' 7-point semantic differential scales.

The final part of the survey solicited respondent demographics, including age, gender, conglomerate of residence, religion and, lastly, boycotting status; in other words, whether they are boycotting American products or not.

The internal reliability of all the direct measures scales was checked through the computation of their related Cronbach alpha coefficients and proved to be satisfactory as each largely exceeded the cut-off point of .7 proposed by Kline (1999). In fact, the Cronbach alpha coefficients for the attitude, subjective norm, and PBC scales were as follows: $\alpha_{ATT}=.93$, $\alpha_{SN}=.92$, $\alpha_{PBC}=.74$ and $\alpha_{Intentions}=.90$ (Farah and Newman, 2010).

Results

Descriptive analysis
At a demographics level, the analysis of the relationship between the respondents' conglomerate of residence and their boycotting status brought up interesting results. The highest percentage of respondents who were boycotting at the time of data collection was among those living in the Bekaa area (34.5 per cent) with slightly fewer in the southern area of the country (32.59 per cent). This rate was roughly similar in Beirut (30.6 per cent). It is worth mentioning that these areas have the largest percentages of Muslim citizens and include not only those who were the most affected by the Israeli invasion from 1975 to the 1980s, but also those who live or used to live on the borders with Israel before migrating to the Beirut area. Moreover, boycott participation differed notably between the two religious sub-groups studied. While only 23.38 per cent of the surveyed Muslim respondents had never participated in the boycott, 61.71 per cent of the Christian respondents had not participated. These figures can be explained by the following three main facts: (a) the Lebanese areas that faced most of the confrontations on the Lebanese-Israeli borders were inhabited by Muslim communities; (b) the existence of stronger feelings of sympathy with the Palestinian cause within this Muslim subgroup, and (c) the presence of the strongest activists advocating boycott participation in the guise of Muslim religious figures.

Bivariate correlation analysis and variances explained
The indirect measure of attitude was obtained by multiplying each of the belief-based items by its corresponding outcome evaluation. The same procedure was adopted to obtain the indirect measure of subjective norm, whereby each of the normative beliefs was multiplied by the respondent's motivation to comply with the related referent expectation. Similarly, each of the three control beliefs' strength was multiplied by its matching control belief perceived power to obtain an indirect measure of PBC. For each category of beliefs, the product terms were summed up to obtain a final indirect measure of attitude, subjective norm and PBC, respectively. For the direct measure of attitudes, subjective norm and PBC, a composite measure was calculated for each by averaging out the answers on the various scales measuring each. The correlation between the belief-based measure of the TPB and its corresponding direct measure was then computed. The results are shown in Table 20.4.

The strong and statistically significant correlations between belief-based measures of attitude and subjective norm and their direct corresponding term (R = .790 and R = .656, respectively, both significant at $p < .001$) provided support for H1 and H2. However, the negative and weak correlation between the control belief-based measure and PBC (R = −.379, $p < .001$) disproved/negated H3. It should be noted that this negative correlation is linked to the idea that, while control belief measures are designed to assess the barriers preventing the respondent from participating in the boycott, such as 'I generally prefer US products to all other products', 'I depend heavily on US products' and 'I cannot find substitutes to most US products at reasonable or competitive prices', the PBC items gauged one's control over the boycotting decision.

The strong and significant correlation between the behavioural belief-based measure and intention (R = .868, $p < .001$) demonstrated support for H4. Moreover, as predicted

Table 20.4 *Bivariate correlations between the belief-based and the direct measures of the TPB*

Belief-based measures	Direct measures			
	1 Attitude	2 Subjective norm	3 PBC	4 Intentions
1 Behavioural beliefs	.790***	.634***	.825***	.868***
2 Normative beliefs	.235***	.656***	.282***	.331***
3 Control beliefs	.165***	.321***	−.379***	−.342***

Note: N = 500, *** $p < .001$ (correlation is significant at the .001 level (2-tailed)).

Table 20.5 *Analysis of belief-based versus direct measures of the TPB model: variances explained and F-tests*

	R^2	F
OLIKs*OEVs vs. Attitude	.622	515.367***
OLIKs*OEVs vs. Intention	.753	953.939***
NORMs*MTCs vs. Subjective norm	.428	178.433***
NORMs*MTCs vs. Intention	.106	29.083***
CBSs*CBPPs vs. PBC	.140	33.297***
CBSs*CBPPs vs. Intention	.113	26.235***

Note: N = 500, *** $p < .001$.

by H5, the correlation between the normative beliefs measure and intention was positive and statistically significant, yet quite weak (R = .331, $p < .001$). Like the correlation between the control beliefs measure and PBC, the correlation between the control beliefs measure and intention was not only weak but also negative (R = −.342, $p < .001$). This finding disproved H6.

The related coefficients of determination (R^2) were subsequently investigated in order to evaluate how much these beliefs accounted for the variance in their corresponding direct measure, and subsequently, in intention. Table 20.5 showed that behavioural beliefs account for 75.3 per cent of the variability in intention while normative and control beliefs account for 10.6 per cent and 11.3 per cent, respectively, of that variability.

DISCUSSION

By using a combination of qualitative and quantitative methods in a complementary manner, the researcher was able to triangulate the data obtained from the literature, the interviews, and the questionnaire survey in order to test the validity of the information collected from various sources. In fact, both the qualitative and the quantitative studies were important as they revealed different aspects of an empirical reality.

The expectancy-value model on which Fishbein and Ajzen's (1975) work is based rests on two main assumptions. First, it assumes that humans are inherently rational and therefore inclined to think and act in a logical and consistent way. Second, it presumes that each person may simultaneously hold a number of beliefs about a given behaviour, each associated with an evaluative response. The subjective value of each attribute contributes to attitude in direct proportion to the strength of the belief. According to Ajzen (1991), if the expectancy-value concept at the basis of the TPB is valid, the belief-based measure of attitude should theoretically correlate well with its corresponding direct measure. This postulation is supposed to hold true both for the measure of subjective norm and for the PBC measure.

The above-mentioned analyses have revealed that the belief-based multiplicative terms did contribute to the variance not only in the direct measures of the TPB model, but also in intention. Accordingly, the study has provided evidence to support the use of the multiplicative assumption of belief-based attitude, subjective norm and PBC formation, thereby confirming the validity of the underlying theoretical principle of expectancy-value that underpins the TPB.

More interestingly and from a practical point of view, the survey has also demonstrated that behavioural beliefs may be the most useful targets for business interventions designed to reduce boycott participation. Changing the beliefs underpinning the attitude toward boycotting is likely to lead to a change in behavioural intention and ultimately in boycotting behaviour. In fact, campaigns can be planned so as to reinforce the belief strength relative to the boycott negative outcomes by, for instance, increasing the perceived risk that such an act would put local workers' jobs in danger. An alternative would be to weaken the belief that boycotting would have an impact on the operations of the boycotted companies or the US government's stance.

THEORETICAL CONTRIBUTIONS AND MANAGERIAL IMPLICATIONS

Though the subject of boycotting is attracting increased consideration in modern consumer research, most studies tackle boycott motivation mainly from a conceptual perspective. While some researchers have begun to draw on theoretical perspectives to guide their inquiry, these contributions are the exception rather than the rule (Klein et al., 2002; Klein et al., 2004). Accordingly, to fill these theoretical shortcomings, this research has adopted the theory of planned behaviour as a theoretical framework to study the effect of an undeniable threat that businesses are increasingly facing.

Indeed, international news abounds with examples of targeted companies, which find themselves unexpectedly and arguably for no justified reason at the centre of geopolitical, religious and commercial turmoil. Research by Ettenson et al. (2006) establishes that no one company is really protected against such societal boycotts launched by consumers against companies of a certain country. The potential harm of such campaigns is often longer lasting than company-specific boycotts whose consequent drops in sales are usually transitory. This clearly shows the significance of this work on a managerial level.

This research has implications on how businesses can respond to consumer boycotting in such a way as to reduce the impact of the boycott on their operations and revenues. In order to discourage consumers from boycotting, it is important for businesses to understand the mechanisms by which consumers' decisions are made. More specifically, the findings of this study are of significance for American companies being targeted by the campaign in Lebanon and which seek to evaluate its adverse consequences. In fact, in light of the recurrent hostilities in the region, risks related to potential revivals of boycotts persist and compel companies to build solid counteractive plans to escape unscathed and to reduce damage to their sales and reputation. The findings of this study can be tested for applicability to other boycott campaigns, and hence could be helpful in designing interventions in different boycott contexts.

Based on the identified beliefs at the basis of consumers' boycott intentions, this study can assist targeted businesses in choosing among the various methods available to discourage boycotters and promote change in their behaviour. Since all the TPB components that predict intention and behaviour are cognitive, the methods used to design change interventions are to be largely based on information and persuasion. The interventions can be mainly built upon the transmission of information about the non-political orientation of the targeted companies and their rejection of the violence targeting civilians in the Middle East, or on the risks related to boycotting companies operating locally and employing nationals.

Besides the traditional use of media channels, the dissemination of information countering the beliefs that drive the public to engage in boycotts can occur through the company's sponsoring of community events. Such persuasive means of communication, including written messages disseminated through various media channels and involvement in public events promoting discussion, are among the most effective techniques designed to discourage boycotting. Though persuasion is the main technique used to achieve such an end, a wide range of clarification techniques can be successfully used to change cognitions, including the use of audio-taped, audiovisual, or printed messages. The latter can be disseminated through informative advertisements, talk shows in universities, or public conferences, all of which could be broadcast through mass media channels.

The analyses conducted show that behavioural beliefs account for the highest explained variance in boycott intention. Therefore, behavioural beliefs would appear to be the most effective target. The interventions could change people's accessible beliefs by asking them to think about the positive and negative aspects of boycotting. From this perspective, the managers of the targeted companies could change consumers' accessible beliefs by asking them to think about the consequences of participating in a boycott that could have negative consequences. Another approach proposed by Levine et al. (1996) is to make intending boycotters think about the reasons for holding their attitude toward boycott participation. This process may help distort respondents' attitudinal judgements and disrupt the attitude-behaviour relation.

In conclusion, by increasing the understanding of the beliefs at the basis of consumers' boycott intentions, this study can help targeted companies to minimize the damage caused by the boycott, by identifying the most appropriate strategic responses. Ettenson et al. (2006) argue that 'when animosities run high, traditional approaches such as price promotions for increasing sales will have little effect' (p. 6). Accordingly, alternative solutions that targeted companies can consider include (a) de-emphasizing the country-of-origin aspect of the product, (b) repositioning brands to look as if they were local by forming joint-ventures with local companies, or (c) addressing directly the source of the hostility (Ettenson et al., 2006). The present research is particularly helpful for companies adopting the third approach. In this case, the beliefs underpinning consumers' attitudes and boycott intentions could be dealt with openly through messages designed to counteract them.

LIMITATIONS AND FURTHER RESEARCH

Despite their limitations, these two studies undoubtedly present opportunities for future research. Although the application of the TPB to the boycotting behaviour area was particularly successful, the acknowledgment of the limitations of this study may allow its replication in different contexts, thereby improving the validity of the findings. A first limitation related to such a theoretical framework adaptation is linked to the reliance on respondents' own reports. Reliance on these reports was the only feasible method for obtaining information on participants' daily behaviour due to the complexity of the context of study, whereby observation in shopping settings would not have been safe or permissible.

Another limitation is that the sample selected for this research relied solely on Lebanese consumers, and while it is indicative of the region, generalizing the findings to all consumers in the Arab world should be done cautiously. Subsequent studies may validate the results of the developed model in different countries of the region and test the usefulness of the developed research instrument to study consumers' behaviour in other boycott contexts. A current application could have resulted from the 'Burn the Qur'an on the ninth anniversary of 9/11' campaign launched by Terry Jones, the Pastor of a church in Gainesville, Florida. Calls for the boycott of American products had started to spread in many Muslim countries and could have led to immeasurable consequences if the situation had not been properly controlled by the American government.

This study has investigated the intention to boycott US companies selling locally in general, yet has not investigated the effect of the type of products boycotted on the boycotting intentions. It is possible that the boycotting of necessity goods may have a different psychology from the boycotting of luxury items and may have a different psychological impact on the decision. As there has been little investigation into the impact of type, price of substitutes, and lack of alternative products on consumers' boycotting attitudes, beliefs and intentions, this appears to be a fruitful area for future research.

Future studies could also explore more fully the difference in underlying beliefs that are most salient for the Muslim and Christian sub-groups. These may reveal a number of differences based on religious and socio-cultural backgrounds, the understanding of which can help in the design of tailored business interventions to prevent the threat and outcomes of boycotts. Lastly, on a managerial level, further experimental research is needed to investigate the most effective methods for changing consumers' beliefs, attitudes and ultimately their intention to participate in the boycott.

CONCLUSION

Understanding why consumers choose to participate in boycotts is an important issue for both social scientists and management who develop strategy that attempts to address such attitudes. Despite the importance of understanding the antecedents of this behaviour, with few exceptions, most of the literature related to this topic has lacked theoretical analyses. This research is a unique application of a socio-cognitive approach to this particular consumer behaviour area. In light of how little is known about consumer boycott motives, especially at a macro-level whereby countries are targeted, the extension Theory of Planned Behaviour has allowed for a considerable advancement in the understanding of the beliefs behind consumer boycott intentions.

REFERENCES

Abosag, I. (2010), 'Dancing with macro-boycotters: the case of Arla Foods', *Marketing Intelligence and Planning*, **28** (3), 365–73

Ajzen, I. (1991), 'The theory of planned behaviour', *Organizational Behaviour and Human Decision Processes*, 50, 179–211.

Ajzen, I. (2001), 'Nature and operation of attitudes', *Annual Review of Psychology*, **52**, 27–58.

Ajzen, I. and M. Fishbein (1980), *Understanding Attitudes and Predicting Social Behaviour*, Englewood Cliffs, NJ: Prentice Hall.

Al Qaradawi, Y. (2002), 'Islamic Fatwas on the Arab Boycott of Israeli and American Products', 4 April, available at www.inminds.com/boycott-fatwas.html (accessed 22 June 2006).

Al Sistani, A. (2002), *A Code of Practice for Muslims in the West*, London: Imam Ali A.S. Foundation.

Armitage, C. and M. Conner (2000), 'Attitudinal ambivalence: a test of three key hypotheses', *Personality and Social Psychology Bulletin*, 26, 1421–32.

Brewer, M. and R. Brown (1998), 'Inter-group relations', in D.T. Gilbert , S.T. Fiske and G. Lindzey (eds), *Handbook of Social Psychology*, Boston, MA: McGraw-Hill.

Childers, T. and A. Rao (1992), 'The influence of familial and peer-based reference groups on consumer decisions', *Journal of Consumer Research*, **19** (2), 198.

Christiansen, D. (2005), 'Arab and Christian: It's a complex identity in the Muslim mid-east', March 11, *National Catholic Reporter: The Independent Newsweekly*.

CIA World Factbook (2010), 'Lebanon People – 2010', available at http://www.cia.gov/library/publications/the-world-factbook/geos/le.html#People (accessed 1 September 2010).

Creswell, J. (1994), *Research Design: Qualitative and Quantitative Approaches*, Thousand Oaks, CA: Sage.

Dickinson, R. (1996), 'Consumer citizenship: the United States', *Business and the Contemporary World*, **8** (3–4), 255–73.

Dickinson, R. and M. Carsky (2005), 'The consumer as economic voter ', in R. Harrison, T. Newholm and D. Shaw (eds), *The Ethical Consumer*, London: Sage, pp. 25–36.

Eagly, A. and S. Chaiken (1993), *The Psychology of Attitudes*, New York: Harcourt Brace and Company.

Ettenson, R., C. Smith, J. Klein and A. John (2006), 'Rethinking consumer boycotts: recent events provide five key lessons for the post 9/11 era', *MIT Sloan Management Review*, **47** (4), 6–7.

Fadlallah, M.H. (2002), 'Islamic Fatwas on the Arab boycott of Israeli and American products', November 28, available at http://www.inminds.com/boycott-fatwas.html (accessed 22 June 2006).

Farah, M. and A. Newman (2010), 'A socio-cognitive approach to exploring consumer boycott intelligence', *Journal of Business Research*, **63** (4), 347–55.

Fishbein, M. and I. Ajzen (1975), *Belief, Attitude, Intention, and Behaviour: An Introduction to Theory and Research*, Reading, MA: Addison-Wesley.

Friedman, M. (1985), 'Consumer boycotts in the United States, 1970–1980: contemporary events in historical perspectives', *Journal of Consumer Affairs*, **5**, 1–23.

Friedman, M. (1999), *Consumer Boycotts: Effecting Change through the Marketplace and the Media*, New York: Routledge.

Garrett, D. (1987), 'The effectiveness of marketing policy boycotts: environmental opposition to marketing', *Journal of Marketing*, **51** (2), 46–57.

Hardin, G. (1968), 'The tragedy of the commons', *Science*, **162**, 1243–48.

Herman, R. (1992), 'The tactics of consumer resistance: group action and marketplace exit', in L. McAlister and M. Rothschild (eds), *Advances in Consumer Research*, Provo, UT: Association for Consumer Research, pp.130–34.

Information International (2002), 'Lebanese consumers and the boycott of American products', May, available at http://www.information-international.com/iimonthly/issue2/opinion.html (accessed 12 June 2005).

Khamenei, A. (2002), 'Islamic Fatwas on the Arab Boycott of Israeli and American products', February 27, available at http://www.inminds.com/boycott-fatwas.html (accessed 22 June 2006).

Klein, J. and A. John (2003), 'The boycott puzzle: consumer motivations for purchase sacrifice', *Management Science*, **49** (9), 1196–1209.

Klein, J., R. Ettenson and M. Morris (1998), 'The animosity model of foreign product purchase: an empirical test in the People's Republic of China', *Journal of Marketing*, **62**, 89–100.

Klein, J., N. Smith and A. John (2002), 'Exploring motivations for participation in a consumer boycott', *Advances in Consumer Research*, **29** (1), 363–69.

Klein, J., N. Smith and A. John (2004), 'Why we boycott: consumer motivations for boycott participation', *Journal of Marketing*, **68** (3), 92–109.

Kline, P. (1999), *The Handbook of Psychological Testing* (2nd edn), London: Routledge.

Kozinets, R. and J. Handelman (1998), *Ensouling Consumption: A Netnographic Exploration of the Meaning of Boycotting Behaviour*, vol. 25, Provo, UT: Association for Consumer Research.

Levine, G., J. Halberstadt and R. Goldstone (1996), 'Reasoning and the weighting of attributes in attitude judgments', *Journal of Personality and Social Psychology*, **70**, 230–40.

'Mapping of living conditions in Lebanon 2004' (2005), Central Administration of Statistics of the Republic of Lebanon, January, available at http://www.cas.gov.lb (accessed 1 June 2005).

Olson, M. (1965), *The Logic of Collective Action: Public Goods and the Theory of Groups*, Cambridge, MA: Harvard University Press.

Peñaloza, L., and L. Price (1992), 'Consumer resistance: a conceptual overview', in L. McAlister and M. Rothschild (eds), *Advances in Consumer Research*, Provo, UT: Association for Consumer Research, pp. 123–28.

Pittman, T. (1998), 'Motivation', in Daniel T. Gilbert, S.T. Fiske and G. Lindzey (eds), *Handbook for Social Psychology*, Boston, MA: McGraw-Hill.

Sen, S., Z. Gurhan-Canli and V. Morwitz (2001), 'Withholding consumption: a social dilemma perspective on consumer boycotts', *Journal of Consumer Research*, **28** (4), 399–417.

Smith, C. (1985), 'Ethical purchase behaviour and social responsibility in business: an investigation of pressure group influence on purchase behaviour particularly in the use or threat of consumer behaviour, Cranfield: School of Management, Cranfield Institute of Technology.

Smith, C. (1990), *Morality and the Market: Consumer Pressure for Corporate Accountability*, London: Routledge.

Stephens, R.H. (1972), *Nasser: A Political Biography*, New York: Simon and Schuster.

Tajfel, H. (1982), *Social Identity and Inter-group Relations*, Cambridge, UK: Cambridge University Press.

Tyler, T. and K. McGraw (1983), 'The threat of nuclear war: risk interpretation and behavioural response', *Journal of Social Issues*, **39**, 25–40.

Zikmund, W. (1994), *Business Research Methods* (4th edn), Fort Worth, TX: The Dryden Press.

APPENDIX: TPB-RELATED ITEMS INCLUDED IN THE SURVEY INSTRUMENT

Intention

- I intend to start/keep on boycotting American products
- I will try to start/keep on boycotting American products

Attitude

- My participation in the boycott against US companies in the Arab World, as a sign of protest against the US policy in the Middle East, would be . . .: *useless–useful, bad–good, unreasonable–reasonable, not beneficial–beneficial, undesirable–desirable, unfair–fair*

a. Outcome likelihood

- My participation in the boycott of American products would have an impact on the operations of the boycotted companies.
- My participation in the boycott would raise the effectiveness of the campaign by encouraging people around me to boycott.
- Boycotting would help me release my anger in a peaceful way toward the US policy in the Middle East.
- Boycotting would help me act according to my personal values.
- Boycotting would allow me to help the people affected negatively by the US policy in the Middle East.
- Boycotting would help me preserve my sense of belonging with my community.
- My participation in the boycott would have an impact on the US government stance.
- Boycotting would help me express my religious beliefs.
- Boycotting would help me satisfy my sense of responsibility toward the Arab community.
- I could enjoy the final outcomes of the campaign without personally boycotting.
- Boycotting would help me express my Arab identity.
- By boycotting, I would be helping the campaign to achieve its objectives.
- Boycotting US companies operating locally would put local workers' jobs in danger.
- I feel I am a winner when I participate in a successful boycott.

b. Outcome evaluation

- For me, having an impact on the operations of the boycotted companies is
- For me, raising the effectiveness of the campaign by encouraging people around me to imitate me and boycott is
- For me, releasing my anger in a peaceful way toward the US policy in the Middle East by participating in the boycott is

- For me, maintaining a consistency between my personal values and my actual behaviour by participating in the boycott is
- For me, to help the people affected negatively by the US policy in the Middle East by participating in the boycott is
- For me, to preserve my sense of belonging with my community by participating in the boycott is
- For me, to have an impact on the US government stance is
- For me, to express my religious beliefs by participating in the boycott is
- For me, to satisfy my sense of responsibility towards the Arab community by participating in the boycott is
- For me, to enjoy the final outcomes of the boycott without personally participating in it is
- For me, to express my Arab identity by participating in the boycott is
- For me, helping the campaign achieve its objectives by participating in the boycott is
- For me, to boycott US companies operating locally and providing work for a large number of citizens is
- For me, to feel I am a winner when I participate in a successful boycott is

Subjective norm

- Most people who are important to me boycott American companies.
- Most people who are important to me think that I should boycott.

a. Normative belief strength

- My family thinks that I should boycott American products.
- My close friends think that I should boycott American products.
- My colleagues think that I should boycott American products.
- Most of the members of my community think that I should boycott.
- The religious leader of my community thinks that I should boycott.

b. Motivation to comply

- When it comes to purchasing choices, I generally want to do what my family thinks I should do.
- When it comes to purchasing choices, I generally want to do what my close friends think I should do.
- When it comes to purchasing choices, I generally want to do what my colleagues think I should do.
- When it comes to purchasing choices, I generally want to do what most of the members of my community think I should do.
- When it comes to purchasing choices, I generally want to do what the religious leader of my community thinks I should do.

Perceived behavioural control

- If I want I can refrain from buying American products.
- I have total control over whether I do or do not boycott.

a. Control belief strength

- I generally prefer American products to all other products.
- I depend heavily on American products.
- I can find substitutes to most American products at reasonable prices.

b. Control beliefs perceived power

- My preference for American products prevents me from boycotting
- My dependence on American products prevents me from boycotting.
- The availability of substitutes to most of the American products at a reasonable price enables me to boycott.

21 Moments of departure, moments of arrival: how marketers negotiate transnationalism in Muslim markets

Chae Ho Lee and Jennifer D. Chandler

If [we] were to look at culture, the first thing that we would think of is people: the communication of people together . . . culture is a social creation. (Franklin, Lebanon)

. . . you have to keep in mind that you are probably talking to people from 30, 40 different countries. I won't say it makes it difficult to create advertising, actually it makes it simpler. We have to find the common denominator. (Raj, India)

The purpose of this chapter is to make salient how marketers negotiate transnationalism in a Muslim market. Specifically, we explore how marketers act as guardians of continuity when they negotiate transnationalism through an evolving dialectic that encompasses notions of the global and the local (Hannerz, 1996; Wilk, 1995). We focus on marketers in the city and emirate of Dubai, in the nation of the United Arab Emirates.

Dubai was chosen as an example of a progressive Muslim market that has experienced phenomenal economic and social growth (Pacione, 2005). Part of this growth has stimulated increased national, ethnic, religious, and social diversity. We refer to this diversity as transnationalism because many Dubai residents affiliate with more than one nation. Transnational individuals (that is, transnationals) who live and work in Dubai may maintain strong ties with the nation of their birth, the nation within which they currently live, or the nation where their families currently reside. Their lives take them back and forth among multiple markets, forcing them to travel space, place and time in many different ways on a variety of occasions.

We explore how marketers negotiate transnationalism to extend its discussion in the consumer behavior and marketing literature. Most recently, transnationalism was examined as a convergent Asian identity influenced by the consumption of Asian brands (Cayla and Eckhardt, 2008). We extend this discussion by drawing from anthropology (Kearney, 1995) and focusing on transnationalism through the lenses of marketers who live and work in the Muslim market of Dubai. This sheds light on a broader conceptualization of transnationalism that is important for the cultural production work involved in the design and creation of cross-cultural marketing or advertising (Alden, et al. 1999; Ger and Belk, 1996; Penaloza and Gilly, 1999 et al.).

Specifically, based on interviews with marketers in Dubai, our findings highlight that transnationalism gives Dubai a cultural complexity that requires a deep and more nuanced negotiation of culture (Cook, 2006). The findings suggest that marketers negotiate transnationalism as cultural complexity in two ways. Sometimes, marketers negotiate this cultural complexity by *adapting* cultural elements, which we refer to as 'moments of departure' (Chatterjee, 1993; Penaloza, 2001). Other times, marketers negotiate cultural complexity by *allowing* cultural elements to stand untouched on their own, without alteration or change, which we refer to as 'moments of arrival'. An example of a moment of departure would be a modern re-design of the traditional *abaya* that is worn throughout Dubai; the *abaya* as a cultural garment may be adapted in color, beading, adornment or length, for example, in order to fit within a contemporary space and time. An example of a moment of arrival would be the inclusion of original linguistic scripts (that is, Arabic, Indian, English) on print advertisements; the linguistic scripts remain in their original typefaces yet are included together, for example, in an advertisement. These moments influence cultural production, but are based on marketers' individualized experiences that assist them with tying notions of the local and the global together in their work.

Based on this, we argue that moments of departure and moments of arrival are together integral for the negotiation processes that facilitate cultural production. Marketers interviewed for this project express how they continually traverse their own sense of local, contrast it with the Dubai sense of local and compare these both with the global. This is similar to processes that enable diverse subcultures to thrive within larger populations (Schouten and McAlexander, 1995), as has been shown in glocalization (Kjeldgaard and Askegaard, 2006), hybriditization or creolization (Ger and Belk, 1996), global structures of common difference (Wilk, 1995), or cosmopolitanism (Thompson and Tambyah, 1999). Such processes enable marketers to assert their own experiences based on their individualized sense of a 'local' culture and scale these experiences to facilitate cultural production on a global level.

As will be discussed, this occurs because marketers retain, rather than reject, their local experiences when based in different nations; marketers are deemed valuable on marketing teams because of this (McLuhan and Powers, 1989). On teams, marketers draw on each other's cultural expertise to create marketing and advertising work that resonates with multiple national audiences. In this way, addressing transnationalism necessitates that marketers negotiate local divergences and global convergences, rather than opting solely for a homogeneous sense of global culture (Haugerud, et al., 2000; Inda and Rosaldo, 2008; Jameson and Miyoshi, 1998; Ritzer, 2004). As Kemper (2001) explains, the role of marketing 'as a site of cultural production in a network that links every place with every other place makes it the transnational profession par excellence, a site where the relationship between things and their meanings is always under construction, always responding to imagination and economic interest (p. 2).'

Moments of arrival and moments of departure can be viewed as 'domaining' practices, or processes by which cultural elements become distinct from one another (Vora 2008). In domaining practices, marketers negotiate how cultural elements are distinctive from others, which cultural elements are similar to one another and which cultural elements can be modularized and adapted for the work of cultural production. Domaining practices seldom occur when marketers work in isolation from one another, or in isolation from the markets to which they communicate. Rather, domaining practices are facilitated when marketers work on teams because cultural production benefits from the increased diversity of cultural knowledge made salient through domaining practices. Our approach thus emphasizes how marketers negotiate transnationalism in Muslim markets through domaining practices, thereby acting as guardians of continuity in time and space, between the global and the local (Hannerz, 1996).

We begin by outlining the socioeconomic background and importance of Dubai. Especially because many Dubai residents regularly return to their nations of origin, our findings suggest that there is less acculturation and adaptation, especially when compared to other cities that elicit permanent immigration of their residents. We follow with an extended conceptualization of transnationalism, an outline of our findings and a discussion that relates our findings to the general marketing and consumer behavior literature, as well as the broader transnationalism literature.

DUBAI AS A MUSLIM MARKET

The Emirate of Dubai

The city of Dubai is also an emirate within the nation of the United Arab Emirates (UAE), a federation made up of seven emirates: Abu Dhabi, Ajman, Dubai, Fujairah, Ras- al-Khaimah, Sharjah and Umm al-Quwain. Before the creation of the United Arab Emirates in 1971, Dubai was part of a territory referred to as the Trucial States, a loose confederation of tribal groups based in the Arabian Peninsula along the coast of the Arabian Gulf. The humble economic beginnings of the Trucial States relied heavily on the husbandry of camels (as a food source and to transport goods), hunting, fishing, date cultivation, pearling and the collection of guano (Heard-Bey, 2007).

The emirate of Dubai began as a small fishing village but due to its winding creek – which extends from the sea to its inland areas – Dubai quickly became a primary port of trade in the region, as well as a center for the pearling trade. Dubai's growth (see Tatchell, 2009 for a detailed examination) can also be attributed to the income and foreign workers that entered the city about the same time as the UAE discovery of oil around 1935. Dubai itself did not export oil until 1969, seven years after Abu Dhabi, which was much later than other emirates (Heard-Bey, 2007). Continuing its aggressive growth at the turn of the twenty-first century, Dubai's post-oil focus has been stimulated particularly by import-substitution industrialization, real estate, global financial investments, luxury tourism and cultural initiatives.

Rapid growth in the UAE and most of the Gulf region has been heavily dependent on international labor provided mostly by lower class laborers from the Indian subcontinent, the Arab world, the Philippines, Australasia and Europe. Living and working in the Emirates continues to require the sponsorship of an Emirati partner, municipality, or specialty 'freezone' authority. The employment of non-UAE citizens at both higher-class executive levels and at lower-class laborer levels is not possible without such sponsorship. In some cases, there is a lack of regulation in labor recruitment agencies, which has led to human rights infringements; this being said, laborers often work in hazardous conditions, including intolerable heat and humidity, and incur significant debts in relocating to the UAE. To repay these debts, laborers provide long years of servitude with recruitment agencies, which often withhold laborers' passports and wages to ensure compliance. However, multinational corporations and the UAE government have begun to improve labor policies and conditions. For example, administrators associated with New York University (NYU) restrict companies building the NYU UAE campus from withholding laborer passports, and also require companies to provide health insurance, overtime compensation, 30 days leave and other benefits that are not typical of most laborers' contracts in the UAE (Human Rights Watch, 2010).

Despite this, Dubai and the UAE are epicenters for economic development in the region and in the world economy. Dubai World, Dubai's main government-run holding and administration company, extends its reach into a wide variety of investments ranging from financial investments and services, enormous real estate and urban development projects, to transportation and logistical services. For example, Dubai World is the third largest port operator in the world, with assets that include companies such as Drydocks World, Economics Zones World, Istithmar World, Nakheel and a majority ownership of the international maritime terminal operator DP World. Dubai World first made headlines as an owner of American properties in February 2006, when it was forced to sell its stake in US port operations due to US security concerns (King and Hitt, 2006). Dubai World also invested $5 billion dollars in the MGM Mirage, one of the world's largest hotel and gaming companies, with over 17 multi-billion dollar properties in the US alone (Stutz, 2007).

Economic crisis
In recent years, due to the global economic downturn, Dubai World has been forced to restructure its debts and investments in the Emirates and throughout the world. Yet the flexibility with which this restructuring has occurred demonstrates how Dubai continuously attracts capital of many forms to its shores. Dubai's current debt liabilities are estimated at over eighty billion dollars (Butters, 2009). At the beginning of 2010, Dubai World requested a six month-suspension of debt repayment. In response to this request, global stock markets in the United Kingdom, Germany, France and Tokyo plummeted over 3 percentage points (Jolly and Galbraith, 2009). Still, in May 2010, Dubai World restructured $23.5 billion dollars of this debt by negotiating with 90 different lenders (Thomas, 2010). Dubai's financial security was also supported by its neighboring emirate, Abu Dhabi, one of the Organization of the Petroleum Exporting Countries (OPEC) top five oil producers, and the Abu Dhabi Investment Authority, the world's largest investment institution.

In response Dubai halted many real estate and construction projects and instead focused on expanding its profile as a global hub for aviation, particularly as a stopover on Asia–Europe routes. The Al Maktoum International Airport is the world's largest airport, designed to handle 120 million passengers annually. Emirates, the national airline of Dubai, plans to expand toward India and China by building a fleet of 90 Airbus A380 superjumbos, challenging the market dominance of international carriers such as Air France, KLM, Lufthansa and Singapore Airlines. Dubai's continued expansion of its airport and flight routes has ensured its place as an international travel hub and, by doing so, has secured its location as a hub for tourism, trade and financial industries in the region.

Culture and national identity in Dubai and the UAE
When a sense of national identity is expressed in the UAE, it is often reserved for individuals who are considered 'locals'. Stated differently, locals are typically individuals who have obtained UAE citizenship. National identity in the UAE is an act by locals to preserve and distinguish their culture from that of residents not born or raised in the UAE. Thus, UAE citizenship is both exclusive and protectively guarded. In the UAE, citizenship can be appealed through contractual labor laws with set residency deadlines

and termination clauses, rather than through open immigration laws and policies. Emirati citizens see their culture as distinct from every other nation; individuals who are not born to an Emirati or married to an Emirati male cannot obtain citizenship – no matter how many years they have lived in the country.

UAE nationals differentiate themselves from others most visibly through their outward appearance. For the wearer, the unique public appearance of the UAE national dress grants a level of social prestige and protection. At the same time, the UAE national dress prohibits wearers from entering bars and nightclubs because of strictly enforced rules regarding head and open-toe foot wear. The national dress consists of garments and accessories such as the *kandura* or *dishdash* (white or colored cloak) with *kerkusha* (string neck ornament) often worn with sandals and *guthra* (headscarf) with *egal* (black rope) for men, and *abaya* (black gown), *shayla* (head covering) and possibly *burqa* (head covering exposing only the eyes) or *gishwa* (black veil) and *gafaaz* (gloves) for women.

This being said, nationhood is still a new development in the country and the UAE government realizes that creating a stable national identity and protecting its current ethnic mixture requires promotion of the country as a whole, rather than small groups of individuals or tribes. This is of special concern in the UAE because its citizens continue to tie themselves to family and close-knit tribal bonds despite active efforts by the UAE government to highlight national traditions and identity. In April 2008, a UAE National Identity Conference was held in Abu Dhabi to respond to these concerns about the dissonance that Emirati citizens carry toward nation-level traditions and culture. One such institution that is intended to reconcile this dissonance is the celebration of the annual 'UAE National Day' on 2 December during which large-scale heritage competitions occur in almost every emirate.

Of all the emirates, Abu Dhabi – Dubai's neighboring emirate – is the largest in terms of natural resources, oil revenues and land area. However, at the time of writing, Dubai is the largest emirate based on population, which is more than double that of Abu Dhabi's. Despite their dominance, Dubai and Abu Dhabi are similar to the other emirates in that they are all heavily influenced by Muslim practices and laws. All emirates in the UAE adhere to a mixture of civil, criminal and Muslim law, known as *sharia* law, which is implemented by a federal judiciary. *Sharia* law plays a significant role in Muslim practice because there are no juries or lawyers present in a *sharia* court of law; there is only a judge (*qadi*) who presides over the court and renders a final judgment based on the reading of *sharia* law. *Sharia* law is based on four sources: the Qur'an, *sunnah*, *ijma* and *qiyas*. The Qur'an is the primary source for the law. The *sunnah* (habit or usual practice) is a record of the words and the deeds of the Prophet Muhammad. The *ijma* is ideally a consensus of the interpretation of the Qur'an and *sunnah* by religious Muslim scholars. In difficult cases, the *qiyas* (analogical reasoning) is applied in consideration with the other three sources. Muslim law is particularly strict and outlines significant penalties for adultery, apostasy (rejection or desertion of Islam), fornication, homosexuality, and theft (Hallaq, 2005).

Transnationals in the UAE

Islam is the state religion and there exists a prevalence of Sunni mosques that are sponsored by the UAE government, which also employs Sunni Imams. Although waves of immigration have occurred in Dubai, most of the population remains Asian, mainly from India, Bangladesh, Pakistan and the Philippines. Westerners constitute a small population in the emirates with some reports at 3 per cent of the total population. Due to the large number of laborers from the Indian subcontinent, the population in Dubai remains predominately Muslim. Local UAE citizens who are true to their Muslim faith and culture remain tolerant of others whose beliefs differ.

Sharia law does not appear to be a deterrent for 80 per cent of Dubai's residents, who are transnationals and non-UAE citizens. Because the oil industry is slowly being replaced by industries associated with cultural production (including advertising, marketing, and public relations that are mostly centered on tourism), transnationals who can affiliate with the residents of Dubai, understand the culture of the UAE, and also bridge Dubai with global perspectives, are important to the modern evolution of the emirates. Abu Dhabi, for example, has created partnerships with international cultural and educational institutions such as the Louvre, Guggenheim, Sorbonne and New York University. Meanwhile, Dubai has become a center for trade, manufacturing, advertising, marketing, broadcasting and media through the development of numerous free zones such as the Dubai Airport Free Zone, Jebel Ali Free Zone and Dubai Media City.

In the 2007 census, Dubai's population consisted of more than 1.5 million residents, of which only 10–15 per cent were UAE citizens. Because of this, Dubai – traditionally thought of as a homogeneous Muslim market – is actually quite diverse. The population of Dubai differs from those of other emirates because of its transnational resident base and the resulting cultural diversity. In fact, Dubai's cultural diversity ranks among those of other world-class cities such as Toronto, Amsterdam and Miami (Benson-Short et al., 2005). The majority – more than 80 per cent – of Dubai's population is comprised of transnationals from over 100 nations, employed in occupations ranging from conscripted labor working in adverse conditions to corporate executives living in luxury accommodations (Dubai Statistics Center 2007). Many transnationals are migrant laborers from the Indian subcontinent who work on enormous construction projects throughout the city and constitute the physical labor force and the nation's domestic help and service industry. However, the immense residential towers and communities built predominantly in Dubai (but also throughout the rest of the Emirates) are intended to accommodate future residents, complete with residency visas included in the purchase price of a property.

To demonstrate, the languages spoken and written in Dubai are so numerous that it is difficult for a majority language to emerge. Some of the languages frequently spoken in the United Arab Emirates include: Arabic (Standard), Baluchi (Southern), Bengali, Danish, English, Farsi, French, German (Standard), Goanese Konkani, Greek, Hindi, Italian, Japanese, Korean, Malay, Malayalam, Panjabi (Eastern and Western), Pashto (Northern and Southern), Polish, Russian, Serbian, Shihhi, Sinhala, Somali, Soqotri, Swahili, Swedish, Tagalog, Tamil, Telugu, Thai, Turkish and Urdu (Gordon 2005, p. 150). This list does not include the variety of dialects and differences in vernacular that are also present in spoken Arabic as used throughout the nation. The spoken forms of *Khaliji* (Gulf Arabic) are extremely difficult to understand even for individuals fluent in standard Arabic.

Although Dubai is perhaps one of the most culturally diverse markets in the Middle Eastern region, it is probable that other Muslim markets may follow in its footsteps. To a large extent, other Middle Eastern nations (for example, Bahrain, Kuwait, Qatar) already share environments that are influenced by both transnationalism and Muslim faith because of similar migration patterns to these nations from diverse parts of the world including, for example, India, Pakistan, the Philippines, Malaysia, England, Sudan and Indonesia. Dubai exemplifies how transnationalism de-territorializes a Middle Eastern market that is strongly influenced by Muslim faith, life and culture but within which varying subcultures and ethnicities thrive. Still, many marketing studies examine overseas Muslim markets as homogeneous in cultural and religious make-up. For this reason, we focus on transnationalism in Muslim markets as an aspect of Muslim marketing that is often overlooked in the consumer behavior and marketing literature.

TRANSNATIONALISM AND MARKETERS

Transnationalism in the Marketing and Consumer Behavior Literature

Our findings suggest that transnationalism in Dubai extends beyond individuals simply maintaining multiple connections to different nations and cultures; transnationalism involves individuals negotiating place, space and time such that their affiliations with other nations remain intact while they reside in Dubai to participate in the global market. Because of their work in cultural production, marketers play an important role in Dubai because they negotiate the bounds of transnationalism to appeal to both Dubai-based locals and transnationals (Cook, 2006). Yet, the role of marketers in negotiating transnational culture has received little attention in the consumer and marketing literature (for an exception, see Penaloza and Gilly, 1999).

Transnationalism has been discussed in the marketing and consumer behavior literature in the context of brands that assist individuals with severing the link between themselves and their narratives of national conflict, a liberation that theoretically allows them to participate in a global marketplace (Cayla and Eckhardt, 2008). Specifically in the context of their study, an 'imagined Asia' emerges in part because of convergent, shared consumption of 'urban, modern, and multicultural' Asian brands (see also Anderson, 1991). Cayla and Eckhardt (2008) argue that transnational brands assist consumers in moving their thinking beyond affiliation with one nation, to thinking about affiliation with multiple nations in a broader 'imagined community.' They emphasize how Asians, regardless of national orientation, share the notion of an 'imagined Asia' because of cultural convergence via shared consumption.

Based on the proposed framework of moments of arrival and departure, it can be seen that their emphasis on a 'unified field of communication' and a 'sense that readers [experience] the same kinds of social change' (Cayla and Eckhardt, 2008, p. 216) implies that moments of departure (that is, when cultural elements are adapted) are more important than moments of arrival (that is, when cultural elements remain untouched). In other words, their notion of transnationalism is based largely on smaller national subcultures converging with a larger homogeneous transnational culture.

We extend their discussion by emphasizing that such liberated individuals, although they participate in global marketplaces, may not necessarily reject their nations of origin. Whereas Cayla and Eckhardt (2008) emphasize transnationalism in the context of cultural *convergence* via imagined communities, we emphasize transnationalism in the context of cultural *divergence* via physical communities (Ger and Belk, 1996; Kjeldgaard and

Askegaard, 2006; Ozanne and Saatcioglu, 2008; Penaloza and Gilly, 1999). Cultural divergence refers to the proliferation of diverse national cultures in a market rather than, as in the case of cultural convergence, the adaptation of diverse cultures to a homogeneous market. Transnationalism in an imagined community may veer closer toward cultural convergence implied by Cayla and Eckhardt (2008), but transnationalism in a geographically based community such as Dubai may veer closer toward cultural divergence as examined here.

RESEARCH DESIGN AND DATA

Data were collected in the emirate of Dubai due to its centrality for marketing and advertising in the region. Twenty-one marketers in small- to large-sized advertising agencies, marketing firms and corporations were interviewed in English at their places of employment over the course of one to three hours (Kjeldgaard et al., 2006; McCracken, 1998). The participants varied in gender, ethnicity and nationality. Over 60 per cent of the participants were individuals who held European citizenship, most with extensive travel and experiences working abroad. Fifteen per cent of participants were Emirati citizens, mostly women, who were just entering the marketing and design field. When requested, female Emirati participants were accompanied by their elders at the interview.

Interviews were conducted by the two primary investigators separately and sometimes together, with a general line of questions regarding the work and roles of the participants within their companies and brand projects. Primary questions focused on participants' work-related tasks, collaborations and their perceptions of Dubai culture. Toward the end of the interview, participants were asked to specifically define 'culture' and their perceptions of its impact on their work.

Both investigators have extensive industry experience in and around marketers and advertising agencies, and are thus familiar with the general flow of marketing/advertising tasks. One of the investigators lived and worked in Dubai for close to a decade. And both investigators are transnational, either with ties to both the United States and Korea, or with ties to both the United States and the Philippines. One investigator is male, and one investigator is female.

The research comprises a multi-sited ethnographic market study by following those people who are engaged in transnational activities (Kjeldgaard et al., 2006). Data were analyzed using grounded theory, including subjecting the data to open, axial and selective coding processes (Strauss and Corbin 1997). The research procedure can be likened to similar studies based on marketers in India (Mazzarella, 2003) and Sri Lanka (Kemper, 2001).

FINDINGS

How Marketers Negotiate Transnationalism

To restate, we conceptualize transnationalism as it occurs beyond an 'imagined community' (Anderson, 1983; Cayla and Eckhardt, 2008; Kearney, 1995). Transnationalism as a complex concept requires deeper problematization for many reasons. Generally speaking, individuals maintain ties to multiple nations, often for reasons – sometimes positive, sometimes negative – beyond their control. To better understand transnationalism, we explore the processes by which cultural divergence influences cultural production in the work of marketing. In Dubai particularly, marketers create work that appeals to transnationals especially because of the unlikelihood that residents become UAE citizens.

Based on our findings, we develop and extend the 'ideological sieve' of Chatterjee (1993) that suggests a process by which cultural divergences are sifted and negotiated. We conceptualize moments of departure based on Chatterjee's notion of borrowing, which refers to the adaptation of different ideas, concepts or practices. And we conceptualize moments of arrival based on Chatterjee's notion of difference, which refers to the retention of pre-existing ideas, concepts or practices.

These moments were salient in four fundamental areas that, according to our findings, affect cultural production in the work of marketing. We first discuss moments of departure within these four fundamental areas: the visual aesthetic of Dubai, the language of Dubai, the market policy of Dubai and the collaborative style needed to succeed in Dubai. Second, we discuss moments of arrival according to the same four fundamental areas. Each is described below.

Moments of Departure

The term moments of departure refers to moments when ideas, concepts, or practices are adapted or changed for the purposes of cultural production in the work of marketers (Chatterjee, 1993; Kemper, 2001). Culture, as described by Hannerz (1996), can move from anywhere to anywhere, from anybody to anybody. In this sense, moments of departure occur when a cultural element departs from a previous idea, concept, or practice, or when a cultural element is adapted or changed. Examples of these moments are discussed below.

Adapting to the visual aesthetic of Dubai

In negotiating transnationalism, the visual aesthetic of Dubai appears to play an important role for marketers. One of the most prominent themes from our interviews was the marketers' recall of the visual aesthetic of Dubai. When asked to describe what Dubai 'looked like', many participants chose to describe the people seen walking in the street. In this way, many marketers relate the visual aesthetic of Dubai to the diversity of its residents, often recounting differences and similarities among ethnic groups. Participants described the visual aesthetic of Dubai relative to their own hometowns (that is, their own sense of local) and sometimes inadvertently referred to their own national affiliations through their efforts to describe Dubai:

> A very large amount of the population is Indian, or Pakistani. Then there are also Filipinos here, mostly in the helping, domestic services. And then of course we have the so-called expats which are probably, mostly Anglo Saxon, but not just British . . . also a large population of South Africans and Australians. Only a few non-Anglo Saxons, and I'm one of them. (Evan, United Kingdom)

As shown, the descriptions of Dubai often refer back to the participants' own experiences or affiliations, as based on their own local experiences in different markets or nations. Marketers seem to desire an adaptation of their aesthetic sense to one that is a closer match to the aesthetic of Dubai. Evan, for example, recognizes the visual differences in the population before finally referring to himself as one of 'a few non-Anglo Saxons'. Like many of the other marketers, it seems that Evan does not feel connected to the other groups that he describes. He is adapting his own sense of local to the Dubai sense of local.

The salience of this local diversity and the visual prominence of different types of people contribute to the Dubai aesthetic in a way that is surprisingly evident in the interviews. That is, the visual diversity of Dubai's residents seems to supersede the visual impact of architectural or national landmarks. Consider for example that such architectural presences as the Burj Al Arab, one of the finest hotel properties in the world, which is shaped like the sail of a boat, as well as the Burj Khalifa, the tallest building in the world, were not mentioned by the marketers. This may be because marketers considered such architectural wonders as more appropriate for tourists, rather than for residents. In this way, it is evident that marketers are cognizant of the resident market base, rather than tourists, as the targets of their work.

Interestingly, there is little explicit description of the local Emirati population as an element in the visual aesthetic of Dubai. This can be partially attributed to the very fast pace at which Emirati citizens have adapted to the increasing prevalence of Westernized city life. In the following passage, Zora – one of the marketers of Arab ancestry who was raised in the Arabian Gulf – describes the impact that these changes have had on UAE citizens. Zora begins the description by referring to traditional Emirati cultural icons such as the Bedouin woman, the bronze mask (traditional Emirati *burqa*), and the *abaya*. Later in the passage, when referring to modern day Dubai, Zora refers to Westernized icons such as bright green Lamborghinis and mobile phones:

> Dubai is probably one of the quickest changing societies I've lived in. When I'm walking down the road into the older parts of town and there is an Emirati, or Bedouin woman, with the bronze mask and the abaya and everything, she might only be 40 or 45 – but she is hunched over as though she's 70. In her life span she's seen pearl diving, trading camels and goats, and living a nomadic life through the desert, to everybody having a bright green, pink and yellow Lamborghini, people on their mobile phones. Especially in the older parts of town you see quite a lot of that. That's what makes it really evident to me. I think my life has changed, but for them . . . in one lifetime, even one place. (Zora, Bahrain)

The moments of departure described in this passage make explicit how UAE citizens move through time and inadvertently borrow aspects of Westernized modern life at a rapid pace. In many ways, UAE citizens constantly negotiate ideas, concepts, or practices that are not their own in order to participate in the modern global marketplace that has become their home. Respondents who are UAE citizens expressed an obligation to be tolerant of other cultures, but to simultaneously retain their own sense of values and traditions.

Adapting language in Dubai

As described previously, many languages are spoken in Dubai. To accommodate such linguistic diversity, many marketers are hired for proficiency in multiple languages. It is as if the ability to accommodate linguistic diversity facilitates the ability to negotiate cultural elements. In some cases, Emirati marketers are sent abroad to learn and adapt to Western ways, then return to Dubai to help close different types of cultural and linguistic gaps:

> . . . corporations themselves are finding that Arabs from the Levant region in particular, who are trained and educated in the States so therefore they're bilingual, are more of use to them than a Westerner like myself or an American who is not bilingual. We are a dying breed in Dubai. (Steve, United Kingdom)

Not only do marketers adapt and borrow ideas, concepts or practices, they actively learn and study ideas, concepts and practices that are not their own. Although English serves as a primary language for communication, the work of marketers requires knowledge of different cultures and mindsets. This demonstrates a deeper negotiation of cultural diversity, especially due to the code-switching involved in social behavior and interaction. The ability to speak multiple languages and adapt to varying situations is seen as an asset for marketers who must address multiple diverse audiences. Often, the ability to overcome differences across multiple perspectives helps marketers to succeed in Dubai, even in small nuances across distinctive social situations. As many participants describe, even slight adaptations or changes in accent may change with the formality of a business situation:

> Also it's different because people are working. If you met a local guy during working hours and if you met him after working hours, there is a very big difference in the way he dresses, even in the way he acts. During work hours he's very formal, strict kind of. Then, right after you finish work they would go to coffee shops or something and they would be wearing their jeans. They would be less formal, more casual. They even hang out with non-locals. Even the accent changes: the accent during work hours and off work hours. It is more formal at work, there is less English, less interference of other languages. (May, Palestine)

Adapting policy and infrastructure in Dubai

Due to its position as an international port, Dubai is economically and politically important to the region and exploits this advantage by actively trading with worldwide partners. By doing so, Dubai has been able to adapt to the cutting edge of logistics management, a feat that allows Dubai and any merchants based there to remain intensively competitive. Because the United Arab Emirates is a Muslim nation and bases its laws on the Qur'an, marketers must be conscientious of laws, rules and prohibitions that determine the form and conditions under which marketing messages may be sent. For transnational marketers, this often entails adapting an existing marketing strategy to fit within the realm of *sharia* law:

> Obviously it's a Muslim country. It's *sharia* law. In some Western countries you can differentiate between culture and religion, whereas here the culture is very much led by the religion because it is Muslim law, and you have to respect that. That's not a bad thing, it's just a new way of learning to live. All the influences are with respect to the *sharia* law. (Zora, Bahrain)

Adapting collaborative styles in Dubai

Generally speaking, marketers must develop a connection with the audience to which they are communicating. Although Dubai residents are not always able to attain citizenship, permanent residency is reserved for the few individuals able to purchase a home with a long-term residency visa included in the package. Most Dubai residents live temporarily in the nation, determined by contracts with fixed lengths. Marketers are aware of this and significantly adapt their strategies for this environment. To address these audiences and develop the necessary diversity in knowledge and skills to do so, firms seek marketers who are open to learning about audiences from different nations. A South African of European descent, working in Dubai, notes how he copes with diversity:

> For me personally, having worked in advertising out here, I've had to learn a lot about Asian cultures, or about Arabic cultures in order to make sure that we are communicating in the right way. As a company we do promote having as many cultures as possible within the company to serve that purpose. (Mark, South Africa)

Here, Mark expresses a lack of confidence in his knowledge of Asian and Arab cultures, but reaffirms the importance of proper communication with these audiences. He acknowledges that he seeks to learn about these communities and discusses this moment of departure and how it affects the entire company, as well as his own ability to adapt in Dubai. Similarly, an Armenian marketer recognizes her own identity and its importance in influencing her work:

> I'm Armenian and I'm outside my home country because of whatever happened. I'm part of a diaspora and I have this identity crisis. Personally I always fight to keep my culture, to keep my language, to keep my ethnicity. So that's why I always have the tendency to put whatever I can, the colors, the feel, the texture . . . I kind of relate it to Armenian cultures . . . I try to infiltrate it in my work. (Kalia, Armenia)

In this way, each marketer's experience and identity helps to connect other marketers and cultural production to diverse national audiences. These moments are marked by adapting the work of marketing in different ways, including collaboration and learning with other marketers. Because marketers are aware of their individual-level inability to connect with nations that are not their own, they rely on one another as sources of cultural knowledge. In this way, collaborative styles that facilitate cultural exchange are important when marketers negotiate transnationalism:

> Working with people helps a lot. We got about 55–60 people here and there are about 20 different nationalities. Immediately, if there is something happening in Sri Lanka it affects their families directly, then of course I care for my colleagues and I'm interested in what happens. Elections in Hungary or Serbia, it becomes immediate and you absorb the information as you go. (Zora, Bahrain)

Moments of Arrival

In contrast to moments of departure as described above, we use the term moments of arrival to refer to moments when cultural elements remain untouched on their own, without alteration or change, with regard to cultural production (Chatterjee, 1993, Kearney, 1995). These are discussed below.

Retention in the visual aesthetic of Dubai

Our findings reveal that the retention of culture through moments of arrival is pervasive in Dubai. That is, there is not typically an expectation of cultural adaptation, which puts marketers a little more at ease with marketing to a Dubai-based audience. This is particularly true with regard to the visual aesthetic of UAE-specific decor in the general environment of Dubai – that is, outside of the Emirati home. In the city landscape, the visual aesthetic of Dubai looks like a modern city similar to New York or Manila, but there are small Muslim influences seen in the presence of mosques, Muslim motifs and Arabic script on buildings. Small but important elements of UAE and Muslim culture are retained in the city landscape.

Inside the typical Emirati home, however, Arabian and Persian inspired architecture is part of the expression of a 'local' identity. Such architecture has been modernized however so that piers, beams and wind towers act as pure visual reminders of UAE culture, while true functionality is replaced with concrete beams and modern air conditioners. For example, traditional *al hush* (courtyards) and *al sathi* (roof terrace) can be seen inside many Emirati homes, but only traces of these types of traditional architectural motifs may be seen on external window frames or roof tops. In this way, visual culture specific to the UAE is not pervasive in either the city landscape or outside of the Emirati home. Most non-UAE citizens only view architecture specific to the UAE culture when invited *inside* the Emirati home. A marketer at a locally owned advertising and marketing agency describes encounters with the UAE culture:

> As an [expatriate] you have to look for the culture. Apart from hearing the Imam call to prayer four or five times a day, walking past the mosques all the time, Muslim designs on buildings, you really have to look for it. They have a wonderful culture and a wonderful history but it's quite short. (Zora, Bahrain)

There is a sense of loss for the local culture on a visual scale as Zora describes the need to actively look for culture because it is not easily available. Zora acknowledges Muslim practices and sights that are common to other Muslim markets, but expresses disappointment with an inability to easily find visible UAE culture. However, from the perspective of another marketer who is outside of the UAE culture, the family-oriented culture of UAE citizens provides a different type of aesthetic that is again based on the presence of people:

> The micro family is one of the most important things to a UAE national. The wife, the son, the daughter, as opposed to grandparents, uncles and so forth. The family is very key to their culture. The West sometimes forgets about family. They [Emiratis] have their grandparents living with them and so on. (Steve, United Kingdom)

The importance of family and small social groups or tribes is important for UAE citizens, and transnationals seem to understand this. Like the example above in which a marketer describes Dubai by describing the different types of people who live there, descriptions of Emirati families as seen together throughout the city tend to provide the fundamental visual reminder of being in Dubai. In this way, retaining the importance of families and the importance of selectively sharing the 'inside' of Emirati culture plays into the visual aesthetic of Dubai.

Retention of language in Dubai

Marketers appear to struggle with the extreme diversity of languages spoken in Dubai. As a result, they find themselves collaborating with individuals who speak and understand more than one language. Especially for those marketers attempting to connect with Gulf Arab communities outside of Dubai (for example, Saudi Arabia, Bahrain, Qatar and Kuwait), it is important to connect with citizens respective to each of those markets as well as the overwhelming majority of transnationals. For marketers that are fluent in only one language, it is difficult to communicate to an audience that is diverse and constantly changing:

> If we go out where the creative people are sitting, people are probably talking three or four different languages because you also have a transient population. So what brand image are you going to build? Five years from now those people won't even be here. If I am advertising in India I can focus on brand imaging because I have a stable population, they are not going anywhere. They are going to grow up there, they are going to live there, they are going to die there. That is not the case in this city. (Raj, India)

The ability to retain languages in their original forms is important in Dubai. But for marketers, as Raj describes, along with the difficulty of creating marketing and advertising to reach very different types of markets, it is important to realize how the retention of language – even over time – affects the work of marketers, especially in building brand image. Marketers are challenged by the fact that Dubai residents often carry with them different brand notions that originate from different national experiences; as a result, creating meaningful connections among brands and residents is extremely difficult. Often, one marketer alone is not able to distinguish between varying levels of brand awareness. For this reason, interaction among marketers again plays an integral role in successful marketing work. It is evident that a moment of arrival occurs every time that a boundary of one's cultural knowledge is reached; that is, marketers retain a sense of local but then work to bridge the boundary in order to engage in cultural production. Many respondents credit their marketing work as a catalyst in this way. Most were especially proud of the diversity within their organizations.

> You never see a British guy hanging out with a Sri Lankan boy or an Indian boy. I don't think so. There is no interaction, there is always – 'we are in this group and you are in that group'. Sometimes there are exceptions. Me here in my company, I don't face that. We are like a whole group with different nationalities. In general it is not the case. (Franklin, Lebanon)

Franklin expresses that his personal experience and cultural knowledge are valued by his advertising agency and the clients that he serves. He acknowledges the diversity of his firm. In this way, moments of arrival facilitate and catalyze collaboration in the work of marketing.

Retention of policy and infrastructure in Dubai

Dubai policy makers appear to have successfully borrowed knowledge and skills from individuals outside its national borders, yet have minimized political or social disturbances that deter other cities from reaching the same level of diversity. It is not entirely clear what makes this possible, but many participants agree that the cultural diversity of Dubai is supported by the global marketplace:

> I would say that the one thing that unites everybody in this city is the pursuit of money. That's why all of us have come here. Money and everything that goes with money: lifestyle, living well, buying and spending. That is a very important element of the culture in Dubai . . . I didn't come here for the theater or art, I came here to make money. (Raj, India)

Based on the pursuit of money, there seems to be an emphasis on building Dubai into a world-class city and an international center for commerce, rather than – contrary to popular thinking – a source for natural oil. Open trade policies and a well developed infrastructure in Dubai help create a market that is tolerant of cultural diversity. Travelers to Dubai are welcomed; its international airport has become the 16th busiest in the world and the 11th busiest in the world by cargo traffic (Gale, 2008). Emirates Airlines is one of the largest carriers in the region, making it more convenient for Dubai residents to leave and return to the emirate. This has expanded financial and social networks among Middle Eastern cities, European cities, and other cities around the world.

Retention of collaborative styles in Dubai

As discussed above, diversity significantly affects cultural production in marketing. Thus, marketers seek different mixes of colleagues to enhance their team's ability to address diverse audiences:

> When we are hiring we try and get that mix because it's a necessity more than anything else. I have to have Arabic designers. I have to have Indian people as well because I'm talking to those audiences, as well as other people that can write English copy. It's a necessity that we do mix it up. I think it's a good thing anyway. Ideas are referenced by different people in different ways. (Mark, South Africa)

Cultural differences among residents are explicit to marketers in Dubai and they recruit team members who can successfully address these differences. This allows marketers to draw on their own cultural experiences and affirms each marketer's unique value as based on national associations. As some of the respondents describe, however, there can be prejudices within the teams stemming from favoritism and affinity for their own cultural bases:

> Every ethnic group that comes here comes with their own set of biases. For instance, let us say you get a marketing manager from New York. He has a certain understanding of what is good advertising, what is not, and who can create this advertising. So a marketing manager from New York may not respond favorably to an advertising agency executive who is from Bangladesh. What do Bangladeshis know about creating advertising? (Raj, India)

In the same way, these moments of arrival are also important for managing clients that request marketers who are similar in ethnicity or culture. An Arab marketer shares his perspectives on how his perceptions of Dubai are affected by the differences in economic status between himself and an imported laborer.

> If you segregate a group of people you are creating multiple cultures that are isolated and you stop being able to see the big picture. For me, if I'm looking at a picture I probably see it differently than someone who is stuck in the sun constructing Burj Dubai or from someone who has been living at Burj Dubai for the past year. Your view on culture will change and the perception of it will change. (Franklin, Lebanon)

As seen, Franklin acknowledges his own bias yet is aware that he integrates this bias into much of his work. Marketers like Franklin realize they are experts on their own cultures and thus have worldviews that are different from others. A South African marketer notes the importance of diversity in his company:

> At any given time in our company we can have five or six different nationalities in a small company like this. I didn't feel I was exposed to that anywhere else that I've worked in the world including South Africa. I think it broadens your view of the world. You have to bear in mind what those cultures believe in. If we do an ad that is for the Saudi market, we've got to make sure that there are certain ways that we do and don't do things. It's not a single minded way of approaching anything where you can tend to have that in more homogenous markets. (Mark, South Africa)

Similarly, a permanent resident of Dubai notes the difficulty of addressing her own culture because it is such a small percentage of the overall population and highlights the importance of retaining a distinct local emirate culture:

> Only seven per cent of the UAE [are] locals, so how can you expect that seven per cent to actually still be focused on what their culture is when 94 per cent occupies their land? It's very, very hard. Of course they get excited as soon as they see something cultural. (May, Palestine)

DISCUSSION

Beyond 'Imagined Communities'

Previous discussions of transnationalism in the consumer behavior and marketing literature do not comprehensively address the reality of diverse cultural communities living in the same geographical and physical marketplace. This often occurs in markets all over the world, including Muslim markets such as Dubai. We extend this discussion of transnationalism by emphasizing that individuals participating in global marketplaces may not necessarily reject their nations of origin. And, we underscore the role that marketers play in facilitating this phenomenon.

Our findings suggest that the process by which marketers negotiate transnationalism in Dubai occurs because diversity is maintained and valued, rather than being replaced with an assumption of cultural homogeneity. This differs from the approach of Cayla and Eckhardt (2008) who discuss transnationalism as convergence of culture based on Anderson's (1983) original conceptualization of 'imagined communities' in Spanish-speaking Creole communities in Southern and Central America. In Anderson's conceptualization, transnationalism is made salient by a 'new consciousness' that is homogeneous among marginalized Creole communities; and in Cayla and Eckhardt's (2008) conceptualization, transnationalism is made salient by the homogeneous consumption of Asian brands. Different from both of these conceptualizations, transnationalism in our study is made salient because of shared residence in the same geographic market (that is, Dubai).

Marketers in Dubai recognize that people from different nations, subcultures and communities come together in real time and real space in Dubai. This occurs largely because Dubai allows participation in the global market, which is perhaps the only common element among its residents. Aside from this, the place, space and time in Dubai emphasizes that transnationals retain ties to their nations of origin because they are not permitted to become UAE citizens. Many transnationals are in fact residents of Dubai only because of temporary economic arrangements with UAE-based employers.

Rather than negotiation based on convergent notions of marginalization (as in the Anderson model) or convergent notions of consumption (as in the Cayla and Eckhardt model), the negotiation of transnationalism by marketers in Dubai is based on convergent physical space and time in a global marketplace and divergent affiliations with multiple nations. For example, Anderson describes how declining dynastic and religious legitimacy encourages a stronger culture among smaller sub-communities (Anderson, 1983). However, in Muslim markets such as Dubai, dynastic and religious legitimacy helps to shape a more unified national culture. For example, Dubai's government continues as a constitutional monarchy ruled by Mohammed bin Rashid Al Maktoum. The six other emirates in the UAE are also ruled by monarchies, or an Emir (the Emir is the monarch) with an elected President and Prime Minister, both of which offices are based on hereditary lines. In this way, the strength of religious legitimacy adds to the strength of the national culture. Sheikh Al Maktoum and his family have shaped the financial and cultural destiny of Dubai for decades. The image of the Sheikh and his family is placed daily in local newspapers and magazines, adorned in storefronts, and enlarged to drape across buildings so that it can be seen from highways.

On another note, in his discussion of transnationalism, Anderson (1983) emphasizes how common vocabularies, or languages, give life to a convergent culture (see also Loomba, 1998). However, in some Muslim markets, the negotiation of culture is based on fragmented language, often because written text forms cannot be replaced by vernacular language. While Anderson (1983) sees national identity as an inclusive phenomenon, UAE nationals see national identity as exclusive. Emirati consumers do not want to be portrayed as just Arab and Muslim; they have their own unique history, culture and future, separate from those of other Gulf countries such as Bahrain and Qatar.

CONCLUSION

Transnationalism in Muslim markets further complicates the already complex process of negotiating among social, economic and cultural worlds in Dubai. Dubai is an ever changing market-within-markets and its residents are global citizens and economic nomads. For instance, it is not uncommon for a resident to hold several passports and live in different nations throughout the year. Dubai also expands its borders annually and creates new communities, further diversifying its population. Furthermore, different waves of immigration and tourism change the social, economic and cultural make-up of the city. The city seems to be bursting during the convention and trade show season, while it appears to be a ghost town when heat reaches nearly 110 degrees Fahrenheit and 100 per cent humidity during the summer months.

Because of this, social, cultural, and geographic boundaries bend in Dubai. A European marketer in Dubai may be allowed to enter the economic world of an Emirati, but never gain access to his or her private and personal networks. Co-workers in a company may share a meal and socialize outside of work, but will fly home for arranged marriages that are overseen by their families. Tolerance for social and cultural diversity is embraced as long as *sharia* law is not broken.

Although similar social, economic and cultural environments exist for marketers in Middle Eastern cities such as Abu Dhabi, Manama and Doha, none of these cities has gained the amount of international media attention and exposure received by Dubai. At the time of writing, Dubai stands in the world spotlight as a place by which to measure the successes and failures of other financial, economic and cultural centers in the Middle East. Dubai is not the largest Muslim market, by far, but at the time of writing it is probably one of the most influential.

In this way, marketers shape the way in which Dubai is presented to the world. Marketers in Dubai are asked to communicate not only their intentions and ideas to the public, but also to demonstrate their social and cultural knowledge to each other and their clients. It is common for marketers to be asked to identify themselves as part of a nation, religion, tribe or culture in an environment that is always in flux. For instance, the question of 'Where are you from?' is not easy to answer in Dubai because most marketers in Dubai are not typically from one place, nor do they typically identify with only one social or cultural group. It is automatically assumed that an Emirati citizen is Muslim and that a person who appears to be of European descent is not Muslim. After these assumptions are made, other cultural elements are more difficult to decipher. Unwritten rules of behavior in the Emirate and country, along with the social and cultural capital one gains from building relationships, remain important navigational tools to understanding Dubai's mix of several hundred nationalities.

Because of this, Dubai-based marketers must demonstrate a particular type of proficiency – an 'ideological sieve' – for negotiating culture (Chatterjee, 1993). They do this through moments of departure and moments of arrival specific to cultural production in the work of marketing. These two types of moments do not stand in opposition to one another, but are dialogically related.

In moments of arrival that are associated with the retention of existing cultural elements, transnationalism may act as a constraint for Dubai-based marketers because these marketers must continuously update their understanding of Dubai and its residents, including clarification of national origins, garnering of diverse historical and cultural knowledge, and reconciliation of brand associations across many nations. Because there is not an expectation of acculturation to a mainstream market culture in Dubai, transnationals emphatically retain connections to the UAE and to other nations. Also, the UAE citizen population seeks to maintain a traditional sense of nation, as well as its ties to ancient tribes and families. Marketers develop this particular type of domaining practice by identifying cultural elements that should remain unchanged because they are important to each of these diverse audiences. These cultural elements remain untouched during moments of arrival.

On the other hand, in moments of departure that are associated with adapting existing cultural elements, transnationalism acts as a resource when Dubai-based marketers are knowledgeable enough to modularize culture and understand which cultural elements can be adapted for their marketing work. Our findings suggest that, to address transnationalism in Dubai, marketers develop cultural brokerage skills, or the ability to modularize, adapt, and integrate cultural elements. Domaining practices inherent in cultural brokerage draw on transnationalism as a resource because diverse cultural elements provide potential malleable inputs to cultural production processes. This is elaborated in the following paragraph.

Whether culture acts as a constraint or a resource depends on marketers' abilities to negotiate cultural differences in Dubai. When marketers come together on teams, they draw on different streams of cultural knowledge and experiences to find cultural domains within the fuzzy but vivid culture of Dubai. Determining which cultural elements should stand on their own through moments of arrival, or which cultural elements can be adapted through moments of departure, is a cultural brokerage skill or domaining practice that marketers in Dubai appear to master. This is not a small task; deciphering the importance of Muslim cultural elements is especially important in Muslim markets and marketers must be cognizant of acceptable adaptations.

Our findings also reaffirm that marketers become changed when they participate in cultural production (Penaloza and Gilly, 1999). They bridge notions of the local and the global, both within their own personal experiences and also through participation in marketing teams (Hannerz, 1996; Wilk, 1995). By drawing on studies of transnationalism from anthropology (Kearney, 1995), we underscore that the same consumers studied as transnationals in the consumer behavior literature are also marketers who influence cultural production (Ger and Belk, 1996; Kjeldgaard and Askegaard, 2006; Schouten and McAlexander, 1995; Thompson and Tambyah, 1999; Wilk, 1995).

Through the work of marketing, Dubai-based marketers integrate their localized lives into a collective narrative that scales the Dubai experience to a global level. Because of this, further research is needed to clarify parallel processes of cultural divergence, rather than singular trajectories toward cultural convergence. Furthermore, the role of transnational individuals as marketers requires deeper investigation because individual-level processes inevitably impact firm-level performance. Marketing practitioners and theorists can explore other processes of transnationalism by examining the often overlooked heterogeneity in Muslim markets and other international marketplaces.

The purpose of this chapter was to explore how marketers negotiate boundary and space issues within Muslim markets through their experiences of transnationalism. Our findings suggest that this occurs either through the adaptation of cultural elements in moments of departure, or through the acknowledgement of difference among cultural elements in moments of arrival. Most important, we find that the marketing 'team' is an integral component of cultural production and reaffirm how marketers become changed through the work of marketing in Dubai.

BIBLIOGRAPHY

Abdullah, Muhammad, Morsy (2007), *The United Arab Emirates: A Modern History*, Abu Dhabi: Makarem G Trading and Real Estate LLC.
Alden, Dana L., Jan-Benedict Steenkamp, and Rajeev Batra (1999), 'Brand positioning through advertising in Asia, North America and Europe: the role of global consumer culture', *Journal of Marketing*, **63** (1), 75–87.
Anderson, Benedict (1983), *Imagined Communities: Reflections on the Origin and Spread of Nationalism*, London and New York: Verso.

Benton-Short, L., M.D. Price and S. Friedman (2005), 'Globalization from below: the ranking of global immigrant cities', *International Journal of Urban and Regional Research*, **29** (4), 945–59.

Butters, Andrew Lee (2009), 'Will Dubai's financial problems spread?', available at http://www.time.com/time/business/article/0,8599,1943212,00.html (accessed 20 December 2010).

Cayla, Julien and Giana Eckhardt (2008), 'Asian brands and the shaping of a transnational imagined community', *Journal of Consumer Research*, **35** (August), 216–30.

Chatterjee, Partha (1993), *The Nation and its Fragments: Colonial and Postcolonial Histories*, Princeton, Princeton, NJ: Princeton University Press.

Cook, Daniel T. (2006), 'In pursuit of the "inside view": training the research gaze on advertising and market practitioners', in Russell Belk (ed.) *Handbook of Qualitative Research Methods in Marketing*, Cheltenham, UK and Nothampton, MA USA: Edward Elgar, pp. 534–546.

Gale, I. (2008), 'Dubai world's sixth busiest airport', *The National* (UAE online edition), 30 April, accessed 7 March 2010.

Ger, G. and R.W. Belk (1996), 'I'd like to buy the world a Coke: consumptionscapes of the "less affluent world"', *Journal of Consumer Policy*, **19** (3), 1–34.

Gordon, Raymond G. Jr (2005), *Ethnologue: Languages of the World, Fifteenth Edition*, Dallas: SIL International.

Hallaq, Wael B. (2005), *The Origins and Evolution of Islamic Law*, Cambridge: Cambridge University Press.

Hannerz, Ulf (1996), *Transnational Connections*, London: Routledge.

Haugerud, Angelique, M. Priscilla Stone and Petter Little (eds) (2000), *Commodities and Globalization: Anthropological Perspectives*, Lanham, MD: Rowman and Littlefield Publishers.

Hawley, Donald (1971), *The Trucial States*, London: George Allen & Unwin Ltd.

Heard-Bey, Frauke (2007), *From Trucial States to United Arab Emirates*, Dubai, UAE: Motivate Publishing.

Human Rights Watch (2010), 'UAE: NYU's Labor Rights Provisions, Break New Ground', available at http://www.hrw.org/en/news/2010/02/03/uae-nyu-s-labor-rights-provisions-break-new-ground?print (accessed 16 July 2010).

Inda, Jonathan and Renato Rosaldo (2008), *The Anthropology of Globalization: A Reader*, 2nd edn, Oxford: Blackwell.

Jameson, Frederic and Masao Miyoshi (eds) (1998), *The Cultures of Globalization*, Durham, NC: Duke University Press.

Jolly, D. and K. Galbraith (2009), 'Dubai's move on debt rattles markets', available at http://www.nytimes.com/2009/11/27/business/global/27dubai.html?sq=dubai&st=cse&scp=7&pagewanted=print (accessed 27 November 2009).

Kearney, M. (1995), 'The local and the global: the anthropology of globalization and transnationalism', *Annual Review of Anthropology*, **24**, 547–65.

Kemper, Steven (2001), *Buying and Believing: Sri Lankan Advertising and Consumers in a Transnational World*, Chicago and London: University of Chicago Press.

King, N. Jr. and G. Hitt (2006), 'Dubai ports world sells US assets: AIG unit buys operations that ignited controversy as democrats plan changes', available at http://online.wsj.com/article/SB116584567567746444.html (accessed 3 January 2010).

Kjeldgaard, Dannie and Soren Askegaard (2006), 'The glocalization of youth culture: the global youth segment as structures of common difference', *Journal of Consumer* Research, **22** (September), 231–49.

Kjeldgaard, Dannie, Fabian F. Csaba and Guliz Ger (2006), 'Grasping the global: multi-sited ethnographic market studies', in Russell Belk (ed.), *Handbook of Qualitative Research Methods in Marketing*, Cheltenham, UK and Northampton, MA, USA: Edward Elgar, pp. 523–33.

Landon, T. Jr. (2009), 'Abu Dhabi tightens its grip as it offers help to Dubai', available at http://www.nytimes.com/2009/12/15/business/global/15dubai.html?sq=dubai&st=cse&scp=3&pagewanted=print (accessed 9 December 2009).

Loomba, Ania (1998), *Colonialism – Postcolonialism*, London: Routledge, 186–92.

Mazzarella, William (2003), *Shoveling Smoke: Advertising and Globalization in Contemporary India*, Durham, NC: Duke University Press.

McCracken, Grant (1998), *The Long Interview*, Newbury Park, California: Sage.

McLuhan, Marshall and Bruce R. Powers (1989), *The Global Village: Transformations in World Life and Media in the 21st Century*, Oxford; New York and Toronto: Oxford University Press.

Ozanne, Julie L. and Bige Saatcioglu (2008), 'Participatory action research', *Journal of Consumer Research*, **35** (October), 423–39.

Pacione, M. (2005), 'City profile Dubai', *Cities*, **22** (3), 255–65.

Penaloza, Lisa (2001), 'Consuming the American West: animating cultural meaning at a stock show and rodeo', *Journal of Consumer Research*, **28** (December), 369–98.

Penaloza, Lisa and Mary C. Gilly (1999), 'Marketer acculturation: the changer and the changed', *Journal of Marketing*, **63** (July), 84–104.

Ritzer, George (2004), *The Globalization of Nothing*, Thousand Oaks, CA: Pine Forge Press.

Schouten, John W. and James McAlexander (1995), 'Subcultures of consumption: an ethnography of the new bikers', *Journal of Consumer Research*, **22** (1), 43–61.

Smith, Simon C. (2008), *Britain's Revival and Fall in the Gulf: Kuwait, Bahrain, Qatar, and the Trucial States, 1950–1971*, London and New York: Routledge Curzon.

Strauss, Anselm, and Corbin, Juliet (1997), *Grounded Theory in Practice*, Thousand Oaks, CA: Sage.

Stutz, H. (2007), 'MGM mirage deal: Dubai buys into Strip', available at http://www.lvrj.com/business/9328871.html (accessed 20 December 2010).

Tatchell, Jo (2009), *A Diamond in the Desert*, London: Hodder & Stoughton Ltd.

Thomas, L. Jr. (2010), 'Dubai World reaches deal to restructure its debt', available at http://www.nytimes.com/2010/05/21/business/global/21dubai.html (accessed 5 June 2010).

Thompson, C. and S. Tambyah (1999), 'Trying to be cosmopolitan', *Journal of Consumer Research*, **26** (3), 214–41.

UAE Interact (2008), 'Dubai World's 6th busiest airport', available at http://www.uaeinteract.com/docs/Dubai_worlds_6th_busiest_airport/29804.htm (accessed 5 May 2008).

van Agtmael, Antoine W. (2007), *The Emerging Markets Century: How a New Breed of World-Class Companies is Overtaking the World*, New York: Free Press.

Vertovec, S. (1999), 'Conceiving and researching transnationalism', *Ethnic and Racial Studies*, **22** (2), 447–62.

Vora, N. (2008), 'Producing diasporas and globalization: Indian middle-class migrants in Dubai', *Anthropological Quarterly*, **81** (2), Spring, 377–406.

Wilk, Richard (1995), 'Learning to be local in Belize: global systems of common difference', in Daniel Miller (ed.), *Worlds Apart: Modernity Through the Prism of the Local*, London: Routledge, pp. 112–33.

22 Cultural diplomacy and the United Arab Emirates: the emergence of a sovereign wealth fund nation on the international art world stage

Rula Al-Abdulrazak and Derrick Chong

INTRODUCTION

Writing in *Foreign Affairs*, Peter van Ham (2001) discusses the 'rise of the brand state' as indicative of the current climate of international relations marked by 'the postmodern politics of image and reputation'. French philosopher Nicolas Bourriaud (2009) uses the term altermodern as the title for the exhibition he curated for the Tate Triennial 2009: '*A new modernity is emerging*, reconfigured to an age of globalisation – understood in its economic, political and cultural aspects: an altermodern culture' (emphasis in the original). In some respects one detects the influences of both Edward Soja (1989) and Fredric Jameson. Jameson (1990) articulated a reading of postmodernism as the cultural representation of multinational or finance capital. This (cultural) logic of late capitalism – with reference to Ernest Mandel's third phase of capitalism – views postmodernity as a world of mesmerizing surfaces, seductively addictive, but depthless. As a pioneering human geographer, Soja (1989) sought to reassert the significance of space – not least of all cultural spaces in flux – in critical social theory.

One might cite so-called sovereign wealth fund (SWF) countries[1] – representing globalized and totalizing spaces of the new world system – as an example of Bourriaud's altermodernity that is consistent with Jameson's view of multinational capital and Soja's examination of why and how societies use space for social purposes. Viewed as a new form of competitive capitalism certain countries are prominent for SWFs, namely the Gulf States (such as the Kuwait, Qatar, Saudi Arabia and the United Arab Emirates), China and Singapore. For example, the Abu Dhabi Investment Authority (ADIA) is the biggest; in 2008 Sheikh Mansour bin Zayed Al Nahyan, brother of the ruler of Abu Dhabi, purchased Manchester City, a leading English Premiership football club; and as part of the global financial crisis, attention has focused on the economic fortunes of Dubai World. Themes of globalization and postmodernism appear – some might say have become naturalized – in any mix of the United Arab Emirates (UAE), culture and marketing. How is the UAE seeking economic diversification beyond natural resources to become a destination site? The stakes can be high if one assumes that the UAE is susceptible to the so-called resource-curse economy label. Is there a case that the UAE seeks to bypass a conventional industrial/manufacturing process as part of its economic development? Liquid capital due to natural resources – petrodollars as a consequence of SWF status – is being used to fund infrastructure projects. We draw on cultural projects of international significance in this chapter.

Explicit reference to cultural diplomacy in the chapter title – alongside the UAE –

means that we are located in the context of nation branding, a marketing topic of relatively recent origin as the role of branding widens its reach. With the inclusion of nation states, branding starts to encroach on terrain traditionally the preserve of international relations and foreign affairs. Softer terms such as public diplomacy and cultural diplomacy have received mixed reviews; supporters consider this new language as a conceptual break from the grip of corporate branding principles and practices; on the other hand, critics remain skeptical – it goes without saying – citing the links to propaganda. Bourriaud's altermodern narrative is one way to help frame what proceeds. Addressing the UAE, both a Muslim Arab nation and a former colony of the UK, as a site to explore cultural diplomacy, adds a layer of complexity relevant to Islamic marketing. What is the nature of exchange – a key concept of marketing – in a post-colonial context? What are the similarities and differences in how nations approach cultural diplomacy?

The chapter begins with two sections on the role of place. First is the perspective of Edward Saïd (1935–2003) on Orientalism. Though Saïd is not normally associated with marketing, the Islamic dimension of the handbook project invites his critical gaze. Second, the post-colonial formation of the UAE four decades' ago and its economic rise can be viewed as part of the reorganization of space and flows of multinational capital. Such a consumer culture representation of the UAE recognizes how the most prominent emirates, Dubai and Abu Dhabi, have staged experiences as part of competitive capitalism, against the likes of Doha, Singapore and Shanghai, to become an international hub.

Attention then turns to cultural diplomacy, a form of exchange, and the branded nation. This recognizes the interconnectedness of nations. Cultural diplomacy, a term of recent origin, has been adopted to describe how cultural expression can help to shape international opinion of a nation. The literature associated with branding a nation has been prominent alongside international relations and foreign affairs. Fostering common values – a tenet of cultural diplomacy – is examined based on the case of UAE's emergence on the international art world stage during the latter half of the 2000s, with key projects to emerge in the 2010s. The business of art is prominent, namely the role of auction houses and art fairs, to attract (wealthy) art collectors from the Gulf States and south Asia; the visual and performing arts projects initiated by the Government of Abu Dhabi, as part of Saadiyat Island, have the potential to create a major cultural attraction for the region and to shape international opinion of the UAE. A comparative analysis of how and why New York's Guggenheim Foundation and France's Louvre are treating the UAE as a cultural space is offered in the penultimate section. Differing agendas are apparent which contribute to the theorization of nation branding. Implications for Islamic marketing are discussed in the final section.

EDWARD SAÏD ON ORIENTALISM

Orientalism by Edward Saïd (1978) is considered a watershed text by both supporters and critics (Halliday, 1993; Prakash, 1995). Though critiques of something called 'the Orient' pre-date Saïd's *Orientalism*, the book had a subversive effect; moreover, it helped to stimulate post-colonial criticism. Saïd adopted a postmodern approach with reference to Michel Foucault, namely a conception of Orientalism as a discourse of power

(Prakash, 1995, p. 211): 'By inserting the domination of the Other into the very constitution of the West, Saïd identified a deep fissure in the operation of Western hegemony'. Saïd (1978) focused on Orientalist descriptions of the Islamic world in the Middle East; moreover, he argued that the original reason for European attempts to deal with Islam as if it were one giant entity was polemical. Islam was considered a threat to Christian Europe and it had to be fixed ideologically, according to Saïd (1978, p. 204): 'Orientalism is fundamentally a political doctrine'. As European empires – namely Britain and France – developed, knowledge of Islam was associated with control and power. Islam was thus something to judge harshly, to dislike and therefore to be on guard against.

Culture and Imperialism provided Saïd (1993) with an opportunity to expand on *Orientalism*. Saïd identified two factors behind the text: a general worldwide pattern of imperial culture; and historical experience of resistance against empire. Connections to cultural diplomacy and the UAE, not least of all the emergence of the UAE as part of the international art world, offer opportunities for a post-colonial (re)assessment.

Yet there are significant hurdles. For example, difficulties in establishing and sustaining democracy have been cited as a mainstay of the Middle East: 'Democracy in any real sense of the word is nowhere to be found in the still "nationalistic" Middle East: there are either privileged oligarchies or privileged ethnic groups', according to Saïd (1993, p. 363). A similar point is made by Fred Halliday (1993, p. 152), another sympathetic commentator: the Middle East is marked by '[d]ifficulty or impossibility of change, particularly if this is seen to be in a direction more like the liberal, secular and in broad terms rational democracies of the West'. During the Cold War, America's ideological battle was with the Soviet Union. Since September 11, 2001 – now depicted in shorthand as 9/11 – misconceptions about Islam have emerged, including religious clichés that Islam is violent, anti-modernist and monolithic. The following chain of associations – 'Islam = Muslim = Arab = Terrorist' – is an outcome, according to A.N. Ahmad (2010) in *Third Text*. This represents a conflation of the Arab world with Islam (even though the non-Arabic speaking world of Islam such as Indonesia, Pakistan and in Europe is significant in size). It goes without saying – but needs to be said – that the Arab and Muslim worlds are misunderstood (and hence contentious) terms. Certainly there is a conceptual distinction between Islam as a religion and a lived Muslim history, culture and experiences.

Writing in the West on the Middle East has focused on particularisms with religion as the most important mainstay, according to Halliday (1993, p. 151): 'The issue of Islamic religion is the most important, as Islam, as defined by its classical texts and traditions, can be seen not merely as a phenomenon pervading most life in the Middle East, but also as an independent variable, an explanatory factor'. Halliday cites examples such as sociology of Islam, the Islamic arts, Islam and madness, Islam and sexuality, and Islam and capitalism. Ahmad (2010) acknowledges the suspicion by some of the term Muslim and its usage in relation to cultural forms. Indeed Islamic and/or Muslim art and culture is uncomfortable to many. Does it represent an oppressive and unnecessary cultural classification? Are there pitfalls in trying to describe the aesthetic and spiritual influences of Islam (or for that matter Judaism, Christianity or Buddhism) on art – or even marketing? This is to suggest that Halliday's particularisms of religion may apply to Islam and marketing or Islamic marketing. Is Islamophilia a well-meaning but simplistic exoticism, as suggested by Ahmad (2010)?

CONSUMER CULTURE REPRESENTATION OF THE UAE

New patterns of dominance based on consumer culture have emerged due to the reorganization of space and increased flows of multinational capital. The role of branding as a commercial practice adopted by all sorts of institutions has become naturalized. Branding can be considered a form of corporate storytelling (Salmon, 2010; Twitchell, 2004). This acknowledges that in everyday English a brand can be likened to reputation (that is, what is generally said or believed about a person's or thing's character); this means that branding is a plan for earning that reputation, and for making consumers know about it and believe in it too. The brand can be an instantly recognizable logo – an outward symbol and name – or an immediate association or emotional resonance. 'The brand is a prefix: the qualifier of character. The symbolic associations of the brand name are often used in preference to the pragmatic description of a useful object' (Pavitt, 2000, p. 16). Douglas Holt (2003, p. 43) discusses 'myth making' as helping to explain how 'some brands become icons'. 'Inventing traditions' is an apt term proffered by two prominent historians to include both 'traditions actually invented, constructed and formally instituted and those emerging in a less easily traceable manner within a brief and dateable period – a matter of a few years perhaps – and establishing themselves with great rapidity' (Hobsbawn and Ranger, 1983, p. 1). Reality matters, but it is possible – for those with vested interests – to help shape what is perceived as real.

The UAE was created in 1971 – following the end of formal protectorate status by the UK and its complete withdrawal from the Gulf region – as a federation of seven states (emirates): Abu Dhabi, Ajman, Dubai, Fujairah, Ras-al-Khaimah, Sharjah and Umm al-Quwain.[2] The UAE is a federal presidential elected monarchy, a federation of seven absolute monarchies. (The ruler of Abu Dhabi, Sheikh Khalifa bin Zayed Al Nahyan, is the President and Head of State of the UAE; the ruler of Dubai, Sheikh Mohammed bin Rashid Al Maktoum, is the Prime Minister and Head of Government of the UAE.)

There was a brief ascendancy of the Arab oil-producing states in the 1970s; however, this was eclipsed by Japan's international power, unparalleled in the 1980s and into the 1990s (Saïd, 1993). The Gulf Cooperation Council (GCC) – with the UAE as one of six countries located in the Arabian Gulf including Bahrain, Kuwait, Oman, Qatar and Saudi Arabia – was formed in 1981. As with other members of the GCC, the UAE has a predominately Muslim Arab population. Moreover, the GCC is now positioned to be the powerhouse behind the emergence of MENASA (Middle East, North Africa, and South Asia) as a regional group, according to McKinsey & Co (De Boer et al., 2008).

Material wealth amongst the GCC – as measured by GDP per capita (purchasing power parity in US$) – has accrued due to oil and natural gas reserves: the UAE at $41 800 ranks third behind Qatar ($121 400) and Kuwait ($55 800) (USA CIA, 2010). (By way of comparison: Singapore ($50 300), the USA ($46 400) and Switzerland ($41 600).) Other measures of relative national success can also be cited. Transparency International (2010) ranks Qatar (no. 22) and the UAE (no. 30) as the only two countries from the Middle East and North Africa to make the top thirty in its Corruption Perceptions Index 2009. Kuwait (no. 31), Qatar (no. 33) and UAE (no. 35) are included in the highest of four categories based on the United Nation's Human Development Index of 182 countries (UN HDR, 2009). (By way of comparison: Switzerland (no. 9), the USA (no. 13) and Singapore (no. 23).) The UAE – particularly Dubai – has been an attractive site for elite workers from around the world.

There has been a desire by the UAE to diversify its economic platforms beyond natural resources that has included self-promotion as an attractive regional and international destination for tourists and investors. For example, Abu Dhabi and Dubai are already listed as international (tourist) cities by *Time Out* (2010); the UAE represent two of fifty-five (with Bahrain, Beirut, and Doha rounding out the Middle East contingent). Another ten are from Asia, so this signals that geographical or territorial assumptions of assigning centrality to the Atlantic world and congenital – with delinquent peripherality to non-Western regions – are starting to give way.

Experience economy is a term proffered by the co-founders of Strategic Horizons, Pine and Gilmore (1998, p. 97): 'While prior economic offerings – commodities, goods, and services – are external to the buyer, experiences are inherently personal, existing only in the mind of an individual who has been engaged on an emotional, physical, intellectual, or even spiritual level'. Staging an experience includes developing a theme – one that is both concise and compelling – in order to drive a storyline that captivates key stakeholders such as tourists and investors. In many respects, the UAE is represented by city-state identities, namely Dubai, Abu Dhabi and Sharjah, with particular points of comparison: inter-emirates competition includes money and building projects. Of course this can be reductive as far as cultural depth of the UAE is concerned. For example, the UAE is described as a stage for Dubai: 'glitzy, glam, over-the-top' and 'materialistic beyond anyone's wildest dreams' (Lonely Planet, 2010); 'Shiny, new, over-scaled, scaleless, pompous, obscene, tasteless, but very real, Dubai is utopia without ever using the word' (Basar, 2006). Dubai has promoted an image of progress and dynamism via building the biggest and most opulent structures to attract the affluent (for example, Burj Al Arab opened in 1999 as the world's tallest hotel; and Burj Khalifa opened in 2010 as the world's tallest building). Sharjah is positioned as 'the anti-Dubai' (Lonely Planet, 2010) and promotes itself as the cultural capital of the UAE. Abu Dhabi is the capital of the UAE and the most powerful emirate, not least of all due to wealth from being home to 10 per cent of the world's oil reserves; moreover, the ruling Al Nahyan family has been selective in development projects such as Saadiyat Island (see below).

'Modernization is not entirely the product of some determinative inner logic of capitalism, but neither is it a rootless and ineluctable idealization of history': this is how Soja (1989, p. 27) has wrestled with the new geographies of space. The UAE does not operate in a vacuum. The nature of competitive capitalism, with an increasing number of so-called emerging economies vying for attention, includes the flow of multinational or finance capital. London's Architectural Association uses the phrase 'cities from zero' with particular reference to the cases of Dubai and the rapid urbanization of China (Basar, 2007). The subtext is that 'vision plus money, plus historical circumstances equals unapologetic expressions of new-found economic – and therefore political prowess in the 21st century' (Basar, 2007). Moreover, they are successful examples of eschewing participatory democracy – promoted as an American ideal – and espousing a form of state-controlled free market capitalism. One result is a growing emphasis on a market-based populist culture of consumerism. This is to suggest that consumer preferences converge (homogenization of tastes) alongside a growing demand to consume (pluralization of consumption). These so-called instant cities – that is, instant in that they are the product of a super-fast urbanism – are unlike major capital cities such as London, Paris, Berlin, and New York, shaped through a long process of evolution (Bagaeen, 2007).

Other prominent examples of competitive capitalism can be cited. Post-colonial Singapore, essentially a city-state, is described as retaining Asian values of social rules alongside adopting an open business environment associated with Western economies. This has resulted in a highly economically competitive and materially successful nation combining business with tourism. The emphasis on shopping and eating started to ease in the mid-1990s with greater promotion of Singapore as a hub for culture and creativity. The enduring success of Switzerland throughout the last century and into the present one – say 'as a hub for money and a hub for art as the two aspects complement and reinforce one another' (Guex, 2003) – is a significant model for the UAE as it emerges as a core player in the international art world.[3] In each case, a specific history and institutional reasons help to account for why a particular form of capitalism has evolved, though one can cite that these examples have a common feature of highly centralized activities.

CULTURAL DIPLOMACY AND THE BRANDED NATION

The potential for cultural expression to shape international opinion about a nation strikes at the core of cultural diplomacy's ambition. Cultural diplomacy is considered a sub-set of public diplomacy. Both draw on the literature associated with branding a nation (as a particular place). The interconnectedness of nations means that nations both compete and collaborate in the global community.

The application of corporate branding principles and practices to nations has been advanced (Anholt 1998, 2002, 2003, 2007, 2009; Dinnie 2008; Kotler and Gertner 2002; Moilaneu and Rainisto 2009; van Ham 2001;). This includes international consultancy firms, such as Wolff Olins and Interbrand, in the business of offering help to governments in what the national brand should stand for and how it should be promoted. Branding a nation as a marketing operation includes attracting tourists, investors and skilled and talented knowledge workers – that is, to visit, invest, and work-live – which may require separate branding messages. There is a potential to enhance exports, an essential aspect of country-of-origin literature in marketing that serves as a base for nation branding (Dinnie, 2008). Moreover, success can win the approval of other governments and international public opinion. As an example of convergence theory in practice, van Ham (2001) noted how former satellites of the Soviet Union (such as Poland, Hungary and the Czech Republic) sought to lose the 'post-communist' label by repositioning themselves as 'pre-EU' in the run-up to European Union (EU) membership (with the EU 'brand' being viewed as a beacon of civilization).

However, criticisms of the nation as a brand have been noted. O'Shaughnessy and O'Shaughnessy (2000, p. 56) are skeptical of the application of corporate branding to nations as 'a nation is not a product, and the national image is very much bound up with the social concept of the nation'. More trenchant is the view of Halsall (2008, p. 17), who considers 'nation branding' – as advanced by consultant Simon Anholt, who established a journal, *Place Branding and Public Diplomacy* (Palgrave Macmillan, 2010) in 2005, by proffering the need of 'countries, cities and regions [to] manage their reputations' – as the ultimate stage of 'post-colonial capitalism'. Halsall (2008) challenges the cultural discourse of the 'brand state' – such as expressed by the consultancy Placebrands (2010) which mixes 'brand management and development policy' – as the redefinition of the nation purely as a business location. 'The tendency to see the nation as brands', according to Halsall (2008, p. 26), 'stems largely from ignorance, from the fact that contemporary consumers of the global media actually know very little if anything about other nations and cultures'. This means that '[n]ation branding is not just the benevolent application of marketing tools to improve the images of nations' (Halsall 2008, p. 27); rather it adopts an ideological perspective that assumes a nation should be run like a company.

A bi-polar Cold War environment has been replaced by the uncertainties of a multipolar, post-9/11 world. Public diplomacy – that is, 'diplomacy directed at people rather than other diplomats', according to the think tank Demos (Demos Projects 2009) – has risen in significance. The Association for Place Branding and Public Diplomacy (2010), a nonprofit organization, posits public diplomacy as 'the public face of diplomacy'.[4] The UK's Foreign Policy Centre (FPC) notes that 'the image and reputation of a country are public goods which can create either an enabling or a disabling environment for individual transactions' (Leonard, 2002, p. 9). 'Governments need to present their policies to entire populations, not just in private to other governments; the way that they present the whole country (its products, its culture and its people as well as its government's policies) to the outside world', according to Anholt (2010). Public diplomacy is about long-term trust: it may be non-specific such as promoting liberal internationalism. On the other hand, how places attract tourists (that is, what they want to market and to whom) and factories and companies (as representing new investments) addresses short-term trust in that it is transactional and specific. In practice there is an expansion of the conventional foreign policy focus of governments presenting their policies in private to other governments.

Of course critics cite a perceived affinity between public diplomacy and propaganda. Is public diplomacy a euphemism for propaganda (which depends to a certain extent on a closed society and control over the sources of information reaching the target)? What is the effective balance in the relationships between culture and politics?

Whereas cultural exchange has been intertwined with the pursuit of foreign relations throughout history, cultural diplomacy has emerged (within public diplomacy): 'We should think of culture as *providing the operating context for* politics' (Bound et al., 2007, p. 20; emphasis in the original). Cultures are meeting, mingling and morphing so there is potential for cultural expression to shape international opinion about a nation. However it is recognized that 'cultural diplomacy is not easily defined' (Bound et al., 2007, p. 16). The Berlin-based Institute for Cultural Diplomacy (2010) cites American political scientist Milton Cummings (2003, p. 1) – as do others including a former American diplomat (Schneider, 2006) – who described cultural diplomacy as 'the exchange of ideas, information, values, systems, traditions, beliefs, and other aspects of culture, with the intention of fostering mutual understanding'. The ICD elaborates:

> This cultural exchange can take place in fields including art, sport, literature, music, science and the economy. Such exchange implies communication and respect between the cultures involved, based on a sounder understanding of respective values and a reduced susceptibility to stereotypes. The potential of such an improved knowledge is to enable improved interaction and cooperation. Cultural diplomacy is the initiation or facilitation of such exchange with an aim to yielding long-term benefits, whether they promote national interest, build relationships or enhance socio-cultural understanding. (Institute for Cultural Diplomacy, 2010)

This means the use of creative expression and exchanges of ideas, information, and people to increase mutual understanding. 'As identity politics exert an increasing influence on domestic and international exchange, these attributes make culture a critical forum for negotiating and a medium of exchange in finding shared solutions' (Bound et al., 2007, p. 11).

Fostering common values is a key tenet of cultural diplomacy. The case of the UAE as a cultural hub – namely one that is emerging on the international art world stage – accentuates this theme. Before proceeding to the next section, it is instructive to elaborate Bourriaud's (2009) 'hypothesis of the end of postmodernism, and the emergence of a global altermodernity':

> Travel, cultural exchanges and examination of history are not merely fashionable themes, but markers of a profound evolution in our vision of the world and our way of inhabiting it. . . . Altermodernity is characterised by translation, unlike the modernism of the twentieth century which spoke the abstract language of the colonial west, and postmodernism, which encloses artistic phenomena in origins and identities.

Eight themes of altermodernity are posited: archive ('exploring history as a new terra incognita . . . remix, re-present and re-enact, using the past as part of an understanding of the present'); borders ('contemporary culture can no longer be seen as a single totality, but as an interrelated network'); docu-fiction ('truth and fiction and fiction are presented side by side, in modes traditionally associated with the authentic'); energy ('energy consumption can be seen as an indicator of a particular cultural era'); exiles ('with an increase in enforced and voluntary geographical exile or nomadism and globalisation of goods . . . interrogating what cultural identity is, questioning these traditional ideas of origin and immigration'); heterochronia ('a chaining or clustering together of signs from contemporary and historical periods which allows an explosion of what is now'); viatorization ('from Latin for travel or traveler . . . navigation between the signs, often almost in the form of hypertext'); and travel ('as global travel has become more attainable, the act of travelling has become a medium itself').

UAE'S EMERGENCE ON THE INTERNATIONAL ART WORLD STAGE

During the latter half of the 2000s, the UAE started to become a site of increasing interest for elite art world players – auction houses, art dealers and public art museums – seeking to enter emerging markets in a manner that challenges art world assumptions:

> An art world is undeniably materializing in the UAE but, oddly, in the reverse of the traditional trajectory, and perhaps even at the expense of a full-fledged art scene. The elements that typically preceded market activity – schools, critics, and curators – are all but absent. (Azimi, 2008)

A notable exception is the Sharjah Biennial, established in 1993, under the directorship of Sheikha Hoor Al Qasimi, daughter of the ruling skeikh, which has emerged as a showcase for contemporary art in the Middle East (with ambitions to be a cultural event in the vein of German-based Documenta). In 2009, 'building on the pioneering role Sharjah has played in the artistic and cultural development of the UAE and the region' and 'recognizing the central and distinctive contribution that art makes to society', the Sharjah Art Foundation (2010) was established to 'focus on the production and presentation of the contemporary visual arts'.

Since Negar Azimi's article (cited above) in the 'Art and Its Markets' issue of Artforum, the UAE appeared for the first time at the Venice Biennale, in 2009, with two pavilions.[5] One, a national pavilion under the UAE banner, bore the provocative exhibition title 'It's Not You, It's Me', and featured Dubai-based artist Lamya Gargash, who presented photographs of 1* (one-star) hotel bedrooms in Dubai; the curator proffered that the title was a comment that it is no longer about European and American art, though some critics interpreted it as a message from Dubai to the other emirates. Another pavilion was organized by the Abu Dhabi Authority for Culture and Heritage (ADACH 2010) – established in 2005 as the cultural authority of the Government of Abu Dhabi – which presented a wider selection of artists from the UAE and included Abu Dhabi's ambitious cultural projects.

In the UAE the business of art as opposed to the artists themselves may be an answer to the question 'what is art?' (see Currid, 2010). Likewise the production of art is less significant – at least presently in the UAE – relative to the impact of art on the economy.[6] (Cairo, Beirut and Tehran have been centers of production in the Middle East, with London and Paris as sites for diaspora artists.) This focus on the business of art means attracting high net worth individuals (HNWIs) and ultra high net worth individuals (UHNWIs) – terms borrowed from private wealth management to represent individuals or family groups with investible assets of $1 million, or $30 million for the ultra status – as collectors (Capgemini and Merrill Lynch, 2008). In a similar vein of target marketing, Basar (2006) includes 'invite the super-rich to visit and move-in first' (as one of the 'critical steps to sudden success').

International Art World System

In order to appreciate the UAE's emergence, key aspects of the international art world deserve notice. Artist and critic Martha Rosler (1997, 20–21, n. 1), writing in *Art Bulletin* on money, power and contemporary art, offers a 'thumbnail definition' of the '*high* art world'

> as the changing international group of commercial and nonprofit galleries, museums, study centers, and associated venues and individuals who own, run, direct, and toil in them; the critics, reviewers, and historians, and their publications who supply the studies, rationales, publicity, and explanations; the connoisseurs and collectors who form the nucleus of sales and appreciation; plus the artists living and recently dead who supply the goods. (emphasis in the original)

In many respects, Rosler's representation of the circulatory network of art fits a conventional industrial economic flow model of 'production – intermediation – consumption'.

Art schools and nonprofit galleries are crucial to support contemporary – that is, living – artists, who represent production. Key intermediaries are dealers (who collaborate in the case of art fairs) and auction houses. Collectors of art – representing an intense form of consumption – include private individuals, business corporations and public art museums. Art collecting, which has historically been an elite recreational activity, makes an explicit appearance in the tenth edition of *World Wealth Report* (Capgemini and Merrill Lynch, 2008) as a so-called passion investment.[7] More importantly, the role of the public art museum is crucial to the circulation of art, as it represents an idealized and final resting place (and serves as a basis for primers in art history). Indeed museum quality is a term used by dealers and auction houses as part of their sales patter to high net worth individuals.[8]

Rosler's definition continued with an identification of the core art world: 'This art world, if it needs to be said, is based on the advanced industrial countries of the West, along with outposts like Australia and the quasi-Western country of Japan'. Economies of agglomeration with core-periphery patterns remain. However, the market for art, not least of all contemporary art, has become more globalized in the decade since Rosler's article appeared. This helps to account for the UAE's emergence for those interested in the business of art such as auction houses, art fair organizers and public art museums.

Several of Bourriaud's (2009) altermodern themes are instructive in appreciating UAE's emergence on the international art world stage. Exiles feature in post-colonial representations of the UEA as a country – particularly in the case of migration to Dubai – even if the 'traditional ideas of origin and immigration' remain resolved. Patterns of travel, as part of growing transnational perspectives, have started to serve the UAE, which continues to develop its appeal as a destination site for international art world players, from auction houses to public art museums. Moreover, interrelated networks associated with borders – such as crossing physical and psychological borders – can be cited with the emergence of Muslim Arab locations. In addition there is a breach of traditional cultural borders of practice when the activities of the public art museums are examined.

Auction Houses

Locations of salesrooms of the two largest auction houses – Christie's (owned by François Pinault, founder of the French luxury goods conglomerate PPR and a major art collector) and Sotheby's (listed on the New York Stock Exchange) – recognize the significance of New York and London as key to the art market. Other existing core centers for Christie's and Sotheby's include EU cities, namely Paris, Amsterdam and Milan. Non-EU Switzerland – in particular Geneva and Zurich – is notable for the same reasons private wealth management is attracted to the country. (In the case of contemporary art, Basel is home to Art Basel, the most prominent modern and contemporary art fair, and in Germany, post-unification Berlin has developed a reputation for artists, with reasonable rental spaces serving as a draw.) Seeking growth opportunities by following pockets of affluence, both Christie's and Sotheby's have established salesrooms in Hong Kong. In a similar manner, Dubai and Doha (capital of Qatar) have taken lead roles as sites for auction houses. It is telling that Bonhams, a distant third as an international auction house (with key salesrooms in London and New York) have opened salesrooms in Hong Kong and Dubai.

International auction houses have identified four key hubs: the current dominant markets of New York and London, alongside the considerable potential over the next decade of Hong Kong and Dubai/Doha. The three international auction houses entered the Middle East between 2006 and 2009. Dubai and Doha – both desire to be viewed as centers for culture – offer access to a new generation of collectors, dealers and artists. As a Middle East hub, Dubai/Doha serves as an alternative to travelling to London for collectors from the Gulf states, India and Pakistan, for example; it also allows more focused attention on particular art market categories such as modern and contemporary art from the region (including Iran, India, Pakistan, Egypt and Iraq). Christie's was the first entrant to reflect the emergence of 'Modern and Contemporary Arab, Iranian, and Turkish Art' as an art market sector; as such the first sale in May 2006 focused on 'International Modern and Contemporary Art'. Bonhams followed Christie's into Dubai, as a joint venture with the Al Tajir family. Bonhams' first sale, in November 2007, included contemporary Iranian artist Farhad Moshiri's *Eshgh (Love)* (2007) – the canvas is dominated by a monumental script in Farsi of the word love, using Swarovski crystals and glitter so the work plays with the purity of the concept of love alongside commercialization of culture in an age of mass consumerism – being sold for over $1 million, a record at auction for an artist from the Middle East. Sotheby's was the last of the three auction houses to enter the region, with its first sale in March 2009. Sotheby's cited the Museum of Islamic Art (designed by I.M. Pei) as well as other museums planned in the city as a factor to locate in Doha.

Art Fairs

Paco Barragán (2008), in *The Art Fair Age*, uses the example of Art Basel Miami Beach – which opened in December 2002 as an offshoot of Art Basel – to epitomize the emergence of art fairs in the 2000s as 'Urban Entertainment Centers' (UECs). In doing so, Barragán draws on the work of Pine and Gilmore (1998) to view the art fair as staging an experience. Of course, there has always been a performative element to the art world: the term 'art scene' suggests both parts in a drama to be performed and celebrity notions of being seen. This suggests that a successful art fair as UEC is more than a trade show (as a meeting place between leading dealers of modern and contemporary art and collectors). There is intense networking to generate sales and to build and sustain relationships.[9]

Art Dubai, now a subsidiary of Dubai International Finance Centre (DIFC), was established in 2007 as the DIFC Gulf Art Fair. (The DIFC describes itself as an 'onshore hub for global finance' that 'bridges the time gap between the financial centers of Hong Kong and London and services a region with the largest untapped emerging market for financial services'.) The art fair was initiated with grand ambitions to 'become one of the top five contemporary art fairs worldwide within three years' and viewed itself as part of the first stage in the development of Dubai as an important center for 'art commerce' likely 'to rival London and New York within a decade' (Art Dubai, 2007). Prominent dealers were attracted to the first edition. The initial desire to break into the top five fairs devoted to modern and contemporary has not been realized by the time of the fourth edition in 2010.[10] However, one significant result has been the emergence of Abu Dhabi Art, which was launched in 2009 (following the collapse of artparis-AbuDhabi, part of the Paris-based artparis series of art fairs, which ran in 2007 and 2008). Organized by the Tourism Development and Investment Company (TDIC, 2010) – established in 2006 as a tourism asset management and development arm to encourage inward investment strategy – and the ADACH, with the Crown Prince of Abu Dhabi as patron, the Patrons

Committee of Abu Dhabi Art included international artists Jeff Koons and Sudobh Gupta (both represented by Gagosian, a participating dealer, along with other elite dealers such as Acquavella, Hauser & Wirth and White Cube), architect Norman Foster, François Pinault and government ministers. Taken in tandem Art Dubai and Abu Dhabi Art indicate that the UAE should be considered as part of the international art fair scene; moreover, the Sharjah Biennial has become one of the most established and prominent cultural events in the Middle East.

Public Art Museums

The TDIC, with Sheikh Sultan Bin Tahnoon Al Nahyan as chairman and sole equity stakeholder of the Abu Dhabi Tourism Authority (2010), a statutory body established in 2004 under the Government of Abu Dhabi's economic diversification strategy), is master developer behind the transformation of Saadiyat Island. The ambitious project was announced in 2006. Saadiyat Island (2010), located off the coast of Abu Dhabi (and linked by highway bridges), is proposed as a 'multi-faceted island offering a great variety of attractions to many different people', and organized into seven districts (cultural, beach, retreat, reserve, marina, promenade and lagoon):

> A buzzing business hub for international commerce; a relaxed waterfront home for residents; a cultural magnet for arts aficionados; the home of dazzling architectural icons; a pristine beachfront tourism destination and a focal point for compelling sporting experiences, such as the Gulf's only tidal and ocean golf courses. It will also be the only place in the world to house architecture designed by five individual Pritzker prize winners. Saadiyat Island will be an irresistible magnet attracting the world to Abu Dhabi – and taking Abu Dhabi to the world. This unique place will offer an entirely unique invitation to the discerning traveller. The island is infused with a richness that serves its visitors and residents cultural, social, emotional and environmental rewards. Indeed Saadiyat is positioned to become, an international destination of desire, a flagship for Abu Dhabi, a treasure for the world.

Saadiyat, which is Arabic for 'isle of happiness', can be considered as an extreme example of a flagship cultural project (of large-scale museum and performing arts complexes) intended to spur investment and consumption throughout the surrounding area of the GCC and MENASA. Central to Saadiyat, with a reported initial budget of $27 billion (essentially state funding), are the cultural district's five projects, each associated with an acclaimed architect. The Frank Gehry-designed Guggenheim Abu Dhabi is massive at 450000 sq ft, making it the largest and most complex Guggenheim project to date; it takes precedence over the smaller museum building Jean Nouvel has been commissioned to design as the Louvre Abu Dhabi. In addition to these two lead projects, which draw on international museum partnerships, a performing arts centre is being designed by Zaha Hadid, and Tadao Ando has a commission for a maritime museum. Finally, Norman Foster's Foster + Partners is designing the Zayed National Museum, dedicated to Sheik Zayed bin Sultan Al Nahyan, founder and long-time ruler of the UAE, who died in 2004. One can read the appointment of architects, who are from different cultural backgrounds, as fitting altermodern themes such as exiles and borders. Yet conservatism is also at play in naming five 'starchitects' from the current Pritzker fraternity. In a similar manner, Saadiyat Island's use of energy – another altermodern theme – seems to bypass the crisis in energy, namely that fossil fuel energy is not limitless, and sustainability in energy.

UAE AS CULTURAL SPACE FOR THE GUGGENHEIM AND LOUVRE

As an Enlightenment project, the public art museum – as opposed to the private art collections of royalty and the church – remains, at least for some, a symbol of democratic values. The Louvre has a central role: as a royal palace it was transformed into a public art museum as part of the formation of democracy in post-Revolution France (Carrier, 2006; McClellan, 1999). Moreover the principles of equality and elitism embodied in the Louvre remain an idealized representation of France.

Interest in Abu Dhabi by the Guggenheim and the Louvre – in separate but related projects – can be considered as part of an overall strategy of the UAE to become an international cultural hub. Indeed Saadiyat Island may become a secular pilgrimage to complement the Islamic holy cities of Mecca and Medina, located in Saudi Arabia, as the most significant and visited sites in the Middle East.[11] For example, the UAE is keen that Saadiyat Island (2010) 'is positioned to become an international destination of desire'. This attention on 'material civilization' can be viewed as part of rethinking Islam, according to Mohammed Arkoun (1987/2003, p. 37; my emphasis): 'The social-historical space in which religions emerged, exercised their function, and shaped cultures and collective sensibilities is being replaced by the *secular positivist space*'. There is the potential to establish a global cultural brand.

Though the UAE serves as a common space of entry, there are differences in how and why the Guggenheim and the Louvre approach the UAE as a cultural terrain for museum projects.[12] The Guggenheim operates as a private and local arts organization, which represents a standard governance model in the USA, and has served as a trendsetter of museum branding. This is part of the Guggenheim's search for a competitive position against other museums of modern art (including New York's Museum of Modern Art, the Centre Pompidou in Paris and London's Tate Modern). On the other hand, the Louvre is a national institution (of the state) such that a French government delegation is required to finalize any arrangement. This suggests that France considers its museums as valuable assets to further national interests as part of cultural diplomacy initiatives.

Some view these cultural projects as a welcome sign as part of cultural diplomacy, not least of all by the UAE. It affords the UAE an opportunity to diversify its economic platforms; in doing so, by entering the world of high culture, it is able to draw the attention of an influential target segment of art collectors and affluent tourists from the region and internationally. It can be read as a way for the UAE to soften the harder aspects of the UAE's brand. On the other hand, critics suggest imperialist ambitions behind such attempts to establish global brands by Western art museums seeking to shape what are perceived to be empty cultural spaces. Early critics informed by the free-market spirit of the 1980s, such as Rosalind Krauss (1990), noted that art in the permanent collection was being treated as trading capital. 'The notion of the museum as a guardian of the public patrimony has given way to the notion of the museum as a corporate entity with a highly marketable inventory and the desire for growth' (Philip Weiss cited in Krauss, 1990, p. 5). Thus the current situation of hazards associated with standardization of cultural attractions, and art as the handmaiden of cultural tourism.

The Guggenheim and Louvre projects validate the term 'superstar museum', coined in the late 1990s by cultural economist Bruno Frey (1998) to describe a particular category of museum then taking shape: a must for tourists, which suggests high brand recall or top-of-mind recognition; attracts a large number of visitors, as such a headline figure of popularity serves to measure success in the absence of financial performance metrics; has famous artists and art works (as found in art history texts) in its permanent collection; the architecture of the museum building is an artistic feature, which has fostered a starchitect mindset as an essential ingredient for museum development projects; and commercially aware of both internal revenue spaces for merchandising and catering and external impact measures on the local economy.[13] Superstar museums have sought ways to attract audiences and promote identity such that they behave akin to 'power brands', marked by 'personality' (that is, extending beyond a functional relationship so that there is an emotional bond) and 'presence' (that is, high visibility and recognition that is attractive to consumers due to national or international scale), as described by McKinsey & Co (Court et al., 1997, 1999), and seek ways to exploit brand value. This fits a period marked by 'eclecticism', according to Jean-François Lyotard (1984, p. 76), which he describes as 'the degree zero of contemporary general culture'. Lyotard (1984, p. 76) elaborates:

> But that this realism of 'anything goes' is in fact that of money; in the absence of aesthetic criteria, it remains possible and useful to assess the value of works of art according to the profits they yield. Such realism accommodates all tendencies, just as capital accommodates all 'needs', providing that the tendencies and needs have purchasing power. As for taste, there is no need to be delicate when one speculates or entertains oneself.

Thomas Krens, during his tenure as chief executive officer of the Solomon Guggenheim R. Foundation (between 1988 and 2008), questioned and challenged the ideals and principles that gave rise to the public art museum.[14] This included expanding the conventional boundaries of the museum beyond one physical site, including operations outside of the country-of-origin. That the Guggenheim Foundation 'realizes its mission through exceptional exhibitions, education programs, research initiatives, and publications, and strives to engage and educate an increasingly diverse international audience' is unremarkable. However, the remainder of the Guggenheim's mission statement – 'through its unique network of museums and cultural partnerships' – reflects the mindset of a cultural institution with expansionist tendencies. Krens (2006) elaborated on the Guggenheim's mission:

> The whole idea here is about a free exchange of commentary and ideas. It's a discourse on an international scale. In a contemporary society for contemporary art, with everything becoming ever more interconnected, I think it's an essential aspect of how museums have to confront the world.

According to art historian David Carrier (2006, p. 217), Krens should be 'praised for understanding that only when high art is as popular as mass culture can it compete'.

Precursor to Saadiyat Island

With an eye to replicating the success of Bilbao, the Guggenheim responded to a call, in 2005, by the West Kowloon Cultural District (WKCD) in Hong Kong. The Guggenheim Foundation (2005) established a partnership with the Pompidou and property developer

Dynamic Sun International. The WKCD was part of a 40-hectacre waterfront site being developed by the Government of Hong Kong to create 'an integrated arts, cultural, and entertainment district' that offered 'an exciting possibility for cultural exchange, sharing, and dialogue'. Krens (2006) described the WKCD proposal in terms of size: 'Now this is a colossal scale. This [is] probably four or five times the scale of Bilbao'. Partnering with the Pompidou was used to justify the Guggenheim's globalization strategy: 'And more and more, you see the French museums adopting this direction as a matter of national policy' (Krens, 2006).

Krens objected to critics who perceived the Guggenheim exporting a commodity that was somehow the same wherever the Guggenheim was situated. The notion of franchising, with its fast-food connotations, was not used by Krens. Rather he talked about mutual exchange and the 'free exchange of commentary and ideas'. 'Pioneering' is how Krens (2006) categorized the various partnerships with other institutions: 'The fact that these institutions would choose to work with us and enter into a long-term agreement to share collections, to share staff, to share programming, in effect, to regard ourselves as a kind of – how would you say – *free trade zone or strategic alliance* of some kind I think is significant' (my emphasis).

A Secular Pilgrimage?

Almost immediately following the cancellation of the WKCD project by the Government of Hong Kong in 2006, the Guggenheim announced a joint project in Abu Dhabi to establish a museum as part of a much bigger cultural project. 'What I have planned in Abu Dhabi is so much bigger than what I've done so far. It'll be the kind of thing we've never seen before. The only expression I can think of to describe it is pharaonic', according to Krens (2008), making a reference to the Egyptian pyramids. Krens (2008) has referred to Chartres Cathedral when discussing what he wanted Gehry to design at Bilbao:

> In the Middle Ages, when someone came to the city from a village, they had never seen buildings with more than one story before and then they stood in front of this massive cathedral. That's the effect I wanted to achieve. It's technology, cosmology, science and religion, all thrown together. Breathtaking.

According to the Louvre (2009), 'The Louvre Abu Dhabi project grew out of the wish to share France's cultural heritage with the Emirate of Abu Dhabi by creating a pioneering new museum. Under the Louvre name, the Louvre Abu Dhabi represents the best of all French museums'. 'Pioneering' echoes Krens, yet a national perspective – 'France's cultural heritage' and 'the best of all French museums' – is apparent.

Henri Loyrette, director of the Louvre (2009), has described the project as a 'scholarly and cultural benchmark for museums all over the world and a blueprint to museums in the twenty-first century'. An 'intergovernmental agreement' (between the governments of the UAE and France) was signed in March 2007. However, the initial announcement, in 2006, of a proposal to establish the Louvre Abu Dhabi – revenue from the project is €1 billion over thirty years (including €400 million for the rights to use the name) to directly benefit the Louvre and other French museums taking part in the project – raised the ire of many art professionals in France and abroad. This included a petition, 'Les musées ne sont pas à vendre' in Le Monde (13 December 2006), that invited Didier Rykner (2006, 2007c) to use his website, La Tribune de l'Art, in a concerted effort to scupper the proposal.

Both the Louvre's proposed regional branch in Lens (announced in 2003 as Louvre-Lens, citing Tate Liverpool and Guggenheim Bilbao as examples of museums playing a part in local regeneration, with a proposed opening in 2012) and a three-year partnership between 2006 and 2009 with Atlanta's High Museum of Art, under the exhibition banner 'Louvre Atlanta', were criticized, though the Louvre Abu Dhabi was the real target. In short, according to Rykner, the UAE project is not based on research or increasing the understanding of works of art. Rather than culture being central, it is an example of two nefarious interests: economic ones of mercenary commercialization, that is, selling national heritage to generate private funds; and political ones of expansionist policies, namely foreign affairs associated with oil and military defence contracts. Rykner has responded to criticisms of snobbery and anti-globalization prejudice (see, for example, Bronitsky, 2007). 'The Louvre is not a storage place where you can pick up works of art with diplomatic or political reasons', according to Rykner (2007b), as the real reasons to oppose the Louvre Abu Dhabi are artistic, not political. A more general statement appeared on his website: 'We believe that museums must not be used for diplomatic, political or financial reasons to reach objectives that would jeopardize a museum's integrity and we will fight against any such eventuality' (Rykner, 2007a).

Particular French issues are raised by the Louvre Abu Dhabi. The legacy of republican values – *le patrimoine republicain* – suggests that money for the Louvre should come from the state. Laïcisme – a form of strident secularism adopted by the French state such that expressions of religiosity are to be kept outside of the public sphere – means that self-censorship is more controversial. What can be exhibited in the UAE? Local laws reflect that the UAE is a Muslim country. There is zero tolerance for drugs and alcohol. Cultural differences need to be respected such as avoiding bad language, rude gestures, or public displays of affection; the UAE also has strict laws banning sex outside of marriage. Yet self-censorship is essentially a minor issue as the Louvre Abu Dhabi is viewed as a new and bigger step towards a policy that the French government has been leading. For example, Agence France-Muséums (2010) was established in 2007 to coordinate the expertise of government-owned cultural institutions (including the Louvre and the Pompidou, along with others such as the Musée d'Orsay, the Château de Versailles, the Musée Rodin and the Musée du Quai Branly) with a commitment to the Louvre Abu Dhabi and new international partners.

However, one is invited to reflect how France's engagement with the wider Islamic world sits alongside its domestic home policy. In January 2010 a French parliamentary committee suggested a ban of the Islamic full face veil inside of public buildings – including access to services offered in such buildings – that has the support of President Nicolas Sarkozy. Over five million Muslims live in France – more than any other EU nation – with only approximately 2000 women wearing the *niqab* (which is distinct from the *burqa* that covers the entire face and body). Supporters of a ban cite that it is contrary to republican principles of secularism and equality and invites negative connotations (such as repression of women and religious fundamentalism); however, any proposed ban may be unconstitutional.

Commercial and competitive tones are apparent in Saadiyat Island's two main museum projects. First, Saadiyat Island's publicity speaks of being an 'international destination of desire'. As such, it is not surprising that there is a link between real estate projects (money) and museum projects (culture). Saadiyat Island benefits the UAE as a nation by creating what may become a 'secular positivist space'; at the same time, it serves as Abu Dhabi's cultural marker to the other emirates. Second, both the Guggenheim and the Louvre can be said to be leveraging artistic assets; however, the treatment of the UAE by the Guggenheim and the Louvre is shaped by how the US and France, respectively, treat arts institutions. The US has supported private and local initiatives in the arts, thus the Guggenheim competes against other museums of modern art based in New York (for spectators and patrons); when Krens makes reference to the 'free exchange of commentary and ideas', he is evoking a particular American rhetoric – certainly used during the Cold War with Abstract Expressionism – that artistic freedom is linked to political democracy. As an effective arm of the French state, the Louvre may be guided by the interests of foreign affairs. This can be controversial if expansionist policies are perceived, including oil and military defence contracts.

POTENTIAL ADVANCES IN ISLAMIC MARKETING

This chapter on cultural diplomacy and the UAE has several implications. It contributes to a discussion of different parts of the Islamic world – more heterogeneous than many assume – within a single volume. It invites consideration of the nature of exchange in a post-colonial context, as the brand state or nation branding. It reflects an intersection of a postmodern political discourse and a neo-liberal marketing rhetoric (Halsall, 2008). Finally, the case of the UAE, as it emerges as a player in the international art world, contributes to the development of cultural diplomacy.

First, the case of cultural diplomacy and the UAE needs to be read within the context of a handbook on Islamic marketing. That is to say, it contributes to a discussion of different parts of the Islamic world within a single text. Reading this chapter alongside others may highlight that different parts of the Islamic world do not necessarily have more in common with each other, other than they do with other countries in Europe, North America or Asia. For example, the UAE can be viewed as core to any popular representation of the Islamic world, as a state in the Gulf region. Yet the UAE is a particular Muslim Arab nation, even within the Gulf Cooperation Council, comparable to Qatar in some respects (such as high material wealth and a desire to develop a reputation as a cultural hub of regional and international significance), yet also different in having city-states (like Dubai and Abu Dhabi) with distinct identities. To compare – as readers of the handbook are likely to do given their interests in both the Islamic world and marketing – is not to conflate, but rather to underline differences. It is possible that each chapter is a contribution for readers to educate themselves in how complex and intertwined cultures and religions really are.

Second, political dimensions with reference to Saïd's *Culture and Imperialism* (1993), namely the general worldwide pattern of imperial culture, pose challenges. Can this post-colonial example of Western entry of key art world players from auction houses to public art museums to the Middle East be viewed as a dialogue? It has been suggested that the

UAE, as representing the new Middle East market for art, can allay critics in the West of oil-rich rulers buying culture:

> ... at its best, it stands to pioneer a new sort of cosmopolitanism, linking the cultural capitals of Cairo and Beirut – to each other and to the rest of the world – and to reinvigorate a region that has been subject to one too many narratives of failure. (Azimi, 2008)

Azimi's 'new sort of cosmopolitanism' – a perspective of seeing the Middle East not as 'Other', following Edward Saïd's thesis in *Orientalism* (1978) – opens out to the world. It offers many benefits. It suggests a union of global democracy and world citizenship. This is consistent with Bourriaud's altermodern thesis. In addition, John Urry (1995) has proffered 'aesthetic cosmopolitanism', as an extension of the Enlightenment tradition, to acknowledge that tourists of all kinds can develop more cosmopolitan or far-reaching tastes. Certainly there is a potential to present Islamic art – not least of all in the UAE – that may be a way to overcome stereotypes, particularly if there is a focus on searching for varied experiences and a delight in understanding the contrasts between societies. It serves as a counter to the globalization of markets thesis advanced by Theodore Levitt (1983). This is to suggest that Abu Dhabi will be a more important cosmopolitan place and setting in the future. At the same time, the nature of royal assent under a state-controlled system of free market capitalism may come under pressure.

Third, a cultural diplomacy perspective offers an opportunity to delve into these issues. Cultural diplomacy in practice is complex, raising knotty issues, often marked by tension or conflict. 'Every place has its preconditions, history, culture and people which is represented through multiple and often contested identities: political groups, civil initiatives stakeholders from all areas a place can offer. Political changes challenge the demand for brand consistence and coherence', according to the Association for Place Branding and Public Diplomacy (2010). Using 'competitive identity', as an updated version of 'nation branding', Anholt (2007) acknowledges the importance of national identity, politics and the economics of competitiveness alongside conventional corporate branding. It is difficult to view cultural diplomacy as politically neutral, even if the political agenda is not always in the foreground.

The UAE is an example of a Muslim Arab government devoting resources to a proactive cultural policy that puts across a favourable representation of Arab and Muslim culture. It represents finance capital and the use of space for social purposes. This means a competitive marketplace between nations marked by large-scale capital projects. The UAE is positioning itself to exploit the advantages of cultural diplomacy including tourist dollars and a battle for hearts and minds alongside the likes of Qatar, Singapore and Shanghai. Saadiyat Island is an obvious case. But it is also important to acknowledge the role of the Sharjah Biennial in fostering important links to the contemporary art world of New York, London, Basel and Berlin. Moreover, the commercial trade in art, namely auction houses and art fairs, has established roots in Dubai and Abu Dhabi. Identities of the individual emirates are better known than the UAE as a nation. A recent *Artforum* diary entry affirms this situation: 'At least three of the country's seven emirates [with reference to Sharjah, Dubai and Abu Dhabi] are pushing hard to become the region's singular cultural hub, and they often seem more opaquely competitive than transparently collaborative' (Wilson-Goldie, 2010). A similar case was mooted following the UAE's first Venice Biennale appearance in 2009. However, such examples of inter-emirates rivalry can benefit the UAE as a branded nation, without necessarily negating the benefits associated with a coordinated and centralized approach.

What the UAE is proposing – to perform at the highest level of the international art world – is rooted in reality. There are key champions, not least of members of the various royal families, who operate via face-to-face interactions with key stakeholders. The UAE has adopted a non-traditional approach to cultural diplomacy by emphasizing commercial culture associated with the art market trade (of buying and selling art) – that is, the business of art – thus key intermediaries of auction houses with salesrooms in the country and art dealers visiting to participate in major art fairs. Flagship cultural projects associated with public art museums trail behind, yet have the potential to be much more significant: 'One of the primary aims of Saadiyat Cultural District is to foster greater understanding and appreciation of the arts, as part of this strategy a programme of innovative artistic and cultural events has been developed to engage and inform a local and regional audience.' Converting the wealth accruing from natural resources into cultural projects is an opportunity for the UAE to carve out its own space in the new world system alongside the differing agendas of the Guggenheim and the Louvre.

However, vulnerabilities are associated with the UAE case. This is to say that any branded nation also seeks to obscure. There is an absence of a political discussion and social purpose of elite cultural projects. Privileged oligarchs are the key beneficiaries. From the perspective of target marketing and cultural diplomacy, income (of the art collectors and cultural tourists) is a prime variable, which does cast some doubt on the use of space for social purposes. The lack of civil society – a component alongside government and business Anholt (2007) has identified as important – means that it is difficult to pose ethical issues of who gains the most. For example, how do citizens benefit relative to business interests? Furthermore the working conditions and treatment of a migrant labour and service class and the unsustainable use of resources – to create ecologies that have no resemblance to the natural climate – have been noted by many critics (see, for example, Basar, 2006).

Notwithstanding these problems, the case of cultural diplomacy and the UAE, as part of a wider discussion of Islamic marketing at this particular point in history, helps to break down walls of economic insularity, nationalism and chauvinism.

NOTES

1. A sovereign wealth fund is a state-owned investment fund composed of financial assets such as stocks, bonds, real estate or other financial instruments – often based in foreign countries – that is funded by foreign currency reserves but managed separately from official currency reserves. It is a way to manage government wealth in order to generate a profit (though some have raised concerns that political power is what is being bought when investing in foreign companies). Commodities are a source of sovereign wealth; current account surpluses are another source.
2. Other UK protectorates, Qatar and Bahrain, became independent nations.
3. Switzerland's success factors include neutrality (determined non-involvement in both World Wars and absence from supranational organizations such as the European Union), extraordinary political stability (including a lack of major strikes, and moderate political parties), banking secrecy and a secured niche in the capital markets by becoming the prime manager of mobile assets for high net worth individuals (Guex, 2003).
4. Note that the Association for Place Branding and Public Diplomacy is not linked to the journal of the same name published by Palgrave Macmillan.

5. By way of comparison, China made its Venice Biennale debut in 2005.
6. There have been recent developments with elite universities offering visual culture, such as New York University and the Sorbonne, establishing sites in Abu Dhabi; Virginia Commonwealth University has a site in Doha.
7. Other passion investments include luxury collectibles (e.g., automobiles, boats and jets) and sports investments (e.g., sports teams, sailing and racehorses).
8. The market for art – not unlike the market for office towers – is a thinly traded market. The overwhelming majority of dealers and auction houses are privately held firms so the public disclosure of accounts associated with publicly listed companies does not take place; there is no reliable method to verify transactions between dealers and sellers (or buyers). Each work of art is a unique item, so it is difficult to estimate the price prior to sale, and the price is inherently subjective. Authenticity, quality, rarity, condition, provenance and value are characteristics to consider when buying art, according to the Art Dealers Association of America (2007). Uniqueness and relative illiquidity of art serve as risk factors that invite art to be promoted as an alternative asset class.
9. Modern and contemporary art fairs need to establish a brand position relative to other fairs: this includes competitive entry selection criteria (i.e., peer review to assess quality of exhibiting dealers) to ensure dealers and artists from a variety of countries of a global orientation, which is considered appealing to collectors. Staged entry access to elite contemporary art fairs – not just a private view before the general public, but how privileged is private view – can be used as markers of social distinction. A cultural programme, to balance the commercial imperatives of an art fair, can include a curated section, including performance art and large-scale installations that many consider highly creative, seminars and round table discussions, book launches, etc. Private lounges at art fairs sponsored by investment banks during the boom years of the mid-2000s followed the segmentation models of airport lounges and so-called VIP sections in nightclubs.
10. The top fairs devoted to modern and contemporary art are Art Basel (and Art Basel Miami Beach), London's Frieze Art Fair, New York's Armory Show and Paris's FIAC; other strong art fairs in Europe include Madrid's ARCO, Art Berlin and Art Cologne, Shanghai's ShContemporary is the most respected art fair based in Asia.
11. In terms of prominent cultural pilgrimages, one can cite the Piero della Francesca trail and the Bayreuth Festival.
12. UK's Tate has been cited by Krens (2006) as an example of doing nationally – with two museum sites in London and two more in Liverpool and St Ives – what the Guggenheim was attempting on a global scale: 'it is an opportunity to use its collection and to reach a wider audience, and that's essentially what is driving us'. Moreover, in July 2009, the British Museum signed a ten-year contract to help launch the 130000 sq ft Zayed National Museum, which is scheduled to open in 2012/13. The BM will lend works of art, help organize the gallery space, and curate exhibitions. The venture represents the BM's biggest overseas venture, which has been initiated to help fund its £135 million expansion, and reflects the institution's stance to work with partners as opposed to mounting outposts.
13. It goes without saying – but needs to be reiterated – that the Guggenheim Bilbao, which opened in 1997, was manufactured to be a museum with high brand values to generate popular appeal in order to regenerate the disused port town of Bilbao, in the Basque region of Spain (see, for example, Twitchell 2004; Cuno 2004; Carrier 2006; McClellan 2007). Bilbao changed the perception of cultural projects and economic regeneration. Its success has given rise to the so-called Bilbao Effect, namely that an industrial town can be transformed into an international tourist destination; it has become a powerful metaphor for the contemporary way to do cultural business, namely by becoming an international tourist destination.

    Architect Frank Gehry's museum building remains the key drawing card. The opening also featured Jeff Koons, who created *Sky Puppy*, a large-scale public sculpture. Koons, represented by Gagosian, modelled for Hugo Boss. In turn, Hugo Boss, one of the Guggenheim's major corporate sponsors – including the Hugo Boss Prize, a biennial award established in 1996 to recognize a significant achievement in contemporary art – was keen to advance the German-based fashion label in the USA.
14. Though the Solomon R. Guggenheim Foundation was established in 1937, the emergence of the Guggenheim brand really dates from 1959, when Frank Lloyd Wright's spiral building was opened as the Solomon R. Guggenheim Museum. In 1979, the Peggy Guggenheim Collection – which had been established in 1951 in Venice – came under the control of the Guggenheim Foundation. At the end of Krens's reign, the Guggenheim Foundation had ownership of two museums – the flagship site in New York, the Guggenheim Museum, designed by Frank Lloyd Wright, and the Peggy Guggenheim Collection in Venice – and provided curatorial direction and management services to two museums, Guggenheim Museum Bilbao and Deutsche Guggenheim in Berlin. Furthermore, an ambitious project in Abu Dhabi had been announced in 2006. Many other proposed projects such as the West Kowloon Cultural District in Hong Kong failed to materialize. In addition, sites had opened and closed: the Guggenheim SoHo

(1992–99), which was criticized for requiring entry to the galleries via the museum's store, and the Guggenheim Hermitage Museum in Las Vegas (2001–08).

Concern was first mooted by a significant patron and board member, Peter Lewis, that too much attention was devoted to the Guggenheim's spokes (or satellites) with insufficient attention to the hub in New York. As such, Guggenheim Abu Dhabi may be a pyrrhic victory for Krens (2008) who, in a post-director interview, noted the risks of being considered a 'pioneer': 'They're the people in a group who walk at the very front, who are the first to fall face down in the mud and the first to be shot in the back with an arrow'.

BIBLIOGRAPHY

Abu Dhabi Art (2009), 'Abu Dhabi Art launch', press release (14 July), http://www.abudhabiartfair.ae/en/Press/3.aspx, accessed 1 September 2010.

Abu Dhabi Tourism Authority (2010), http://www.abudhabitourism.ae/en/main/about-adta.aspx, accessed 1 September 2010.

ADACH (2010) (Abu Dhabi Authority for Culture and Heritage), http://www.adach.ae/en/default.aspx, accessed 1 September 2010.

Agence France-Muséums (2010), http://www.agencefrancemuseums.fr/en/home/, accessed 1 September 2010.

Ahmad, A.N. (2010), 'Is there a Muslim world?', *Third Text*, **24** (1), 1–9.

Anholt, S. (2010), http://www.simonanholt.com/, accessed 1 September 2010.

Anholt, S. (2009), *Places: Identity, Image and Reputation*, Houndmills, UK: Palgrave Macmillan.

Anholt, S. (2007), *Competitive Identity: The New Brand Management for Nations, Cities and Regions*, Houndmills, UK: Palgrave Macmillan.

Anholt, S. (2003), 'Elastic brands', *Brand Strategy* (February), 28–9.

Anholt, S. (2002), 'Foreword', *Brand Management*, **9** (4–5) (April), 229–39.

Anholt, S. (1998), 'Nation-brands of the twenty-first century', *Journal of Brand Management*, **5** (6), 395–406.

Arkoun, M. (1987), 'Rethinking Islam today', originally published as an occasional paper, Washington, DC: Georgetown University, Center for Contemporary Arab Studies, reprinted in *Annals of the American Academy of Political and Social Science* (July 2003), 18–39.

Art Dealers Association of America (2007), *Collector's Guide to Working with Artists*, New York: ADAA.

Art Dubai (2010), 'Art Dubai 2010 presents its strongest programme to date', press release (1 March), http://www.artdubai.ae/press/documents/2010_highlights.pdf, accessed 1 September 2010.

Art Dubai (2007), 'Dubai International Finance Centre (DIFC) enters partnership with the Gulf Art Fair (8–10 March 2007)', press release (1 February), http://www.artdubai.ae/downloads/news/010207.pdf, accessed 1 September 2010.

Association for Place Branding and Public Diplomacy (2010), http://www.nationbranding.de/site_english/about.php, accessed 1 September 2010.

Azimi, N. (2008), 'Trading places: the new Middle East market', *Artforum* (April), http://www.artforum.com/inprint/issue=200804&id=19758, accessed 1 September 2010.

Bagaeen, S. (2007), 'Brand Dubai: the instant city; or the instantly recognizable city', *International Planning Studies* (May), 173–97.

Barragán, P. (2008), *The Art Fair Age*, Milan: Charta.

Basar, S. (2006), 'Dubai: self-help for those wanting to build a 21st century city', *Static* (November), http://static.londonconsortium.com/issue04/basar_selfhelp.php, accessed 1 September 2010.

Basar, S. (ed.) (2007), *Cities From Zero: Vision plus Money plus Historical Circumstances Equals Unapologetic Expressions of New-Found Economic – and Therefore Political – Prowess in the 21st Century*, London: Architectural Association.

Bound, K., R. Briggs, J. Holden and S. Jones (2007), *Cultural Diplomacy*, London: Demos.

Bourriaud, N. (2009), 'Altermodern: Tate triennial 2009' (3 February to 26 April), London: Tate Britain, http://www.tate.org.uk/britain/exhibitions/altermodern/manifesto.shtm, accessed 1 September 2010.

Bronitsky, J. (2007), 'For their eyes only', *The American: The Journal of the American Enterprises Institute* (26 March), http://www.american.com/archive/2007/march-0307/for-their-eyes-only, accessed 1 September 2010.

Capgemini and Merrill Lynch (2008), *World Wealth Report*, Capgemini and Merrill Lynch.

Carrier, D. (2006), *Museum Skepticism: A History of the Display of Art in Public Galleries*, Durham, NC and London: Duke University Press.

Court, D., A. Freeling, M. Leiter and A. Parsons (1997), 'If Nike can "just do it" why can't we', *McKinsey Quarterly* (no. 3), 24–34.

Court, D., M. Leiter and D. Loch (1999), 'Brand leverage', *McKinsey Quarterly* (no. 2), 100–116.

Cummings, M.C. (2003), *Cultural Diplomacy and the United States Government: A Survey*, Washington, DC: Center for Arts and Culture.

Cuno, J. (ed.) (2004), *Whose Muse? Art Museums and the Public Trust*, Princeton, NJ: Princeton University Press.

Currid, E. (2010), 'Symposium introduction: art and economic development: new directions for the growth of cities and regions', *Journal of Planning Education and Research*, **29** (3), 257–61.

De Boer, K., C. Figee, S. Jaffar and D. Streumer (2008), *Perspective on the Middle East, North Africa and South Asia (MENASA) Region*, Dubai: McKinsey & Co.

Demos Projects (2009), 'The new public diplomacy' (project), London: Demos, http://www.demos.co.uk/projects/thenewpublicdiplomacy, accessed 1 September 2010.

Dinnie, K. (2008), *Nation Branding: Concepts, Issues, Practice*, Oxford: Butterworth Heinemann.

Finn, H. (2003), 'The case for cultural diplomacy: engaging foreign audiences', *Foreign Affairs*, **82** (6) (November/December), 15–20.

Frey, B. (1998), 'Superstar museums: an economic analysis', *Journal of Cultural Economics*, **22** (2–3) (June), 113–25.

Guex, S. (2003), 'Greek statues and tomatoes: the Swiss art market in the twentieth century', in E. Walliser-Schwarzbart (ed.), *Art Market Switzerland*, Passages: the cultural magazine of Pro Helvetia (no. 35), Zurich: Arts Council of Switzerland Pro Helvetia, pp. 38–42.

Guggenheim Foundation (2008), 'Thomas Krens to step down as director of Guggenheim Foundation', press release (2 February), http://www.guggenheim.org/new-york/press-room/press-releases/press-release-archive/2008/1806, accessed 1 September 2010.

Guggenheim Foundation (2006), 'Abu Dhabi to build Gehry-designed Guggenheim Museum', press release (8 July), http://www.guggenheim.org/new-york/press-room/press-releases/press-release-archive/2006/3326, accessed 1 September 2010.

Guggenheim Foundation (2005), 'Centre Pompidou and the Solomon R. Guggenheim Foundation announce partnership for Hong Kong proposal', press release (28 October).

Halliday, F. (1993), '"Orientalism" and its critics', *British Journal of Middle Eastern Studies*, **20** (2), 145–63.

Halsall, R. (2008), 'From "business culture" to "brand state": conceptions of nation and culture in business literature on cultural difference', *Culture and Organization*, **14** (1) (March), 15–30.

Hobsbawn, E. and T. Ranger (eds) (1983), *The Invention of Tradition*, Cambridge: Cambridge University Press.

Holt, D. (2003), 'What becomes an icon most?', *Harvard Business Review* (March), 43–49.

Institute for Cultural Diplomacy (2010), 'What is cultural diplomacy', http://www.culturaldiplomacy.org/index.php?en_culturaldiplomacy, accessed 1 September 2010.

Jameson, F. (1990), *Postmodernism, or, the Cultural Logic of Late Capitalism*, Durham, NC: Duke University Press.

Kotler, P. and D. Gertner (2002), 'Country as brand, product, and beyond: a place marketing and brand management perspective', *Brand Management*, **9** (4–5) (April), 249–61.

Krauss, R. (1990), 'The cultural logic of the late capitalist museum', *October*, **54** (Fall), 3–17.

Krens, T. (2008), 'Krens' museum for global contemporary art [interview]', *Spiegel Online International* (27 March), http://www.spiegel.de/international/world/0,1518,543601,00.html, accessed 1 September 2010.

Krens, T. (2006) 'Thomas Krens, director of the Solomon R. Guggenheim Foundation, talks about the role of museums and the mission of the Guggenheim Museum [interview]', *Charlie Rose Show* (3 January), http://www.charlierose.com/view/interview/596, accessed 1 September 2010.

Leonard, M. (2002), *Public Diplomacy*, London: Foreign Policy Centre.

Levitt, T. (1983), 'The globalization of markets', *Harvard Business Review* (May–June), 92–102.

Lonely Planet (2010), 'Introducing United Arab Emirates', http://www.lonelyplanet.com/united-arab-emirates, accessed 1 September 2010.

Louvre (2009), *Magazine: the Louvre Abu Dhabi* (1 September), http://www.louvre.fr/llv/dossiers/page_magazine.jsp?CONTENT%3C%3Ecnt_id=10134198674151899&CURRENT_LLV_MAGAZINE%3C%3Ecnt_id=10134198674151899&bmLocale=en, accessed 1 September 2010.

Lyotard, J.-F. (1984), 'Answering the question: what is postmodernism?', trans. R. Durand, in *The Postmodern Condition: A Report on Knowledge*, Minneapolis, MN: University of Minnesota Press.

McClellan, A. (2007), *The Art Museum From Boullee to Bilbao*, Berkeley, CA and London: University of California Press.

McClellan, A. (1999), *Inventing the Louvre: Art, Politics and the Origins of the Modern Museum in Eighteenth-Century Paris*, Berkeley, CA and London: University of California Press.

Moilaneu, T. and S. Rainisto (2009), *How to Brand Nations, Cities and Destinations: A Planning Book for Place Branding*, Houndmills, UK: Palgrave Macmillan.

O'Shaughnessy, J. and N. O'Shaughnessy (2000), 'Treating the nation as a brand: some neglected issues', *Journal of Macromarketing*, **20** (1) (June), 56–64.

Palgrave Macmillan (2010), *Place Branding and Public Diplomacy*, Houndmills, UK: Palgrave Macmillan, http://www.palgrave-journals.com/pb/about.html, accessed 1 September 2010.

Pavitt, J. (ed.) (2000), *Brand.new*, London: V&A Publications.

Pine, J. and J. Gilmore (1998), 'Welcome to the experience economy', *Harvard Business Review* (July/August), 97–105.

Placebrands (2010), 'The principles of place branding,' http://www.placebrands.net/principles/principles.html, accessed 1 September 2010.

Prakash, G. (1995), 'Orientalism now', *History and Theory*, **34** (3) (October), 199–212.

Rosler, M. (1997), 'Money, power and contemporary art', *Art Bulletin* (March), 20–24.

Rykner, D. (2007a), 'The Art Tribune is born', *The Art Tribune* (15 September), http://www.thearttribune.com/La-Tribune-de-l-Art-a-quatre-ans.html, accessed 1 September 2010.

Rykner, D. (2007b), 'A reply: firing back on the Louvre Abu Dhabi', *The American: The Journal of the American Enterprises Institute* (29 March), http://www.american.com/archive/2007/march-0307/a-reply-firing-back-on-the-louvre-abu-dhabi/?searchterm=rykner, accessed 1 September 2010.

Rykner, D. (2007c), 'Non', *La Tribune de l'art* (7 January), http://www.latribunedelart.com/non-article00193.html, accessed 1 September 2010.

Rykner, D. (2006), 'Pétition', *La Tribune de l'art* (14 December), http://www.latribunedelart.com/petition-article002280.html, accessed 1 September 2010.

Saadiyat Island (2010), http://www.saadiyat.ae/en/Content/about_saadiyat_island.aspx, accessed 1 September 2010.

Saïd, E. (2002), 'Impossible histories: why the many Islams cannot be simplified', *Harper's* (July), http://www.mtholyoke.edu/acad/intrel/crisis/said.htm, accessed 1 September 2010.

Saïd, E. (1993), *Culture and Imperialism*, London: Chatto and Windus.

Saïd, E. (1978), *Orientalism*, New York: Random House.

Salmon, C. (2010), *Storytelling: Bewitching the Modern Mind*, trans. D. Macey, London: Verso.

Schneider, C. (2006), 'Cultural diplomacy: hard to define, but you'd know it if you saw it', *Brown Journal of World Affairs* (Fall/Winter), 191–203.

Sharjah Art Foundation (2010), http://www.sharjahart.org/, accessed 1 September 2010.

Soja, E. (1989), *Postmodern Geographies: The Reassertion of Space in Critical Social Theory*, London: Verso.

Tate Britain (2009), 'Explore altermodern', http://www.tate.org.uk/britain/exhibitions/altermodern/manifesto.shtm, accessed 1 September 2010.

TDIC (Tourism Development and Investment Company) (2010), http://www.tdic.ae/default.aspx, accessed 1 September 2010.

Time Out (2010), http://www.timeout.com/, accessed 1 September 2010.

Transparency International (2009), 'Corruption perceptions index 2009: regional highlights: Middle East and North Africa', http://transparency.org/policy_research/surveys_indices/cpi/2009/regional_highlights, accessed 1 September 2010.

Twitchell, J. (2004), *Branded Nation: The Marketing of Megachurch, College, Inc., and MuseumWorld*, New York: Simon and Schuster.

UK FCO (United Kingdom Government, Foreign and Commonwealth Office) (2010), 'Travel advice – United Arab Emirates', http://www.fco.gov.uk/en/travel-and-living-abroad, accessed 1 September 2010.

UN HDR (United Nations, Human Development Report) (2009), 'Human Development Report 2009 – HDI rankings', http://hdr.undp.org/en/statistics/, accessed 1 September 2010.

Urry, J. (1995), *Consuming Places*, London: Routledge.

USA CIA (United States Government, Central Intelligence Agency) (2010), *The World Factbook*, https://www.cia.gov/library/publications/the-world-factbook/rankorder/2004rank.html, accessed 1 September 2010.

USA Department of State (2005), *Culture Diplomacy: The Linchpin of Public Diplomacy*, Report of the Advisory Committee on Cultural Diplomacy, Washington: Department of State.

van Ham, P. (2001), 'The rise of the brand state: the postmodern politics of image and reputation', *Foreign Affairs*, **80** (5) (September/October), 2–6.

Wilson-Goldie, K. (2010), 'March in time', *Artforum* (March), http://artforum.com/diary/archive=201003, accessed 1 September 2010.

PART V

THE FUTURE

23 The future of Islamic branding and marketing: a managerial perspective

*Paul Temporal**

INTRODUCTION

Before I address the future of Islamic branding and marketing, I would like to define exactly what I am writing about. I will start with a question I was asked recently which was, 'Is Islamic branding and marketing a myth or reality?' My answer to the question was that Islamic branding is a reality and not a myth. My reasoning was that there are substantial markets seeking products and services that are either *sharia* compliant, or demonstrate that they understand Islamic values and principles, or are prepared to offer *sharia*-friendly brands. Muslims the world over look for what is '*halal*' as opposed to what is '*haram*', and there is substantial demand for '*halal*' or *sharia*-compliant products and services. In addition, it is very clear that Western companies are building brands specifically for the Muslim market, and companies from Muslim majority countries are doing the same. There can be no doubt then, that Islamic branding and marketing is a reality and not a myth. From a numerical point of view this conclusion also stands up to scrutiny. The Muslim population represents around 23 per cent of the world's total population, but a cautionary note here is that it is not a homogenous market in terms of behaviour despite being bound by certain values that all Muslims share.

The myth versus reality question raises related questions, such as, 'is it worthwhile or proper to carry out branding based on religion?', or 'is it a good thing to discriminate in branding on the basis of religion?' The most important fact that I believe counts in answering these and similar questions for Muslims and marketers is that Islam is a way of life, and the values and principles of Islam influence the everyday life of Muslims. In other words, we are dealing with a huge number of people who have shared values and beliefs and share similar wants and needs. As branding and marketing are organizational activities focused on addressing consumer shared values, and meeting consumer wants and needs, it is a legitimate way of segmenting the market.

It is because Islam influences all Muslims to a larger or lesser extent on an everyday basis, that brand owners and marketers who wish to gain a strong foothold in a market of nearly 1.6 billion people must cater to their needs, and with Islam this means demonstrating a thorough understanding of Islamic values, principles and practises. This requirement to understand the market raises the issue of what information is available on the Muslim market in terms of demographics and consumer behaviour, and more questions must be answered. Do all Muslims think the same? Do all Muslims behave in the same way? Do all Muslims want the same products and services? Do Muslims want Western brands or Islamic brands? Sadly, for brand and marketing professionals there is a lack of available data to help them answer these questions, although many researchers are increasingly interested in the subject area and more companies are asking for such information.

In the last three years, research carried out at the Saïd Business School, University of Oxford, and other research surveys have provided up to date information about the demographic aspects of global Muslim markets – how many Muslims there are and how they are dispersed. This knowledge has inspired many people in business and in the public sector to realize that the global Muslim market is virtually untapped. This inspiration is not confined to the Western brands, who are constantly looking for growth opportunities, but also to Muslim companies who realize that the 1.57 billion Muslims constitute a market that they can relate to in terms of common values, and work with to grow their brands. Research has also discovered that not all Muslims behave as one homogenous group and that there are both similarities and differences between markets, as I will shortly illustrate. Before doing so it is important to have a closer look at elements that are driving the market.

Interestingly, some businesses, academics, and people living in the West often think of the Islamic population as concentrated in a handful of nations, especially in the Middle East and South East Asia, but the truth is that there are significant Muslim minority populations around the world, from India to China, and France to Japan. Throughout the Middle East, Asia, Africa and Europe in Islamic majority and minority countries there is massive business activity, with Islamic trade currently assessed in trillions of dollars. In terms of global economic power and commercial success, it is becoming clear that Islamic countries are gaining ground on their Western counterparts.

However, the rising prosperity and spreading population of Islam is only part of the story. From a marketing perspective, just as the Western world has done, the Muslim world would dearly like to develop an array of leading global brands of its own, and Muslim consumers are no different to non-Muslims in their love of brands. Muslim countries would also like to see their local brands going global, because they have seen how powerful brands can be in terms of economic contribution and how they shape national images. In particular, they have noticed that the cultivation of intangible assets such as strong brands is seen as an essential feature of mature, stable, and growing national economies. Finally, many Muslim countries want to diversify their business interests and rely less on narrow resource-based industries, such as energy, which have finite supplies.

From the late 1980s, there was a substantial increase in the number and success of Western held brands. During the 1990s, we saw a competitive response from Asia, with brands from countries such as Singapore, South Korea, India and China making considerable progress in regional and global markets. While most Western brands are currently targeting the giant markets of China and India, the 'forgotten' 1.57 billion Muslims in the global market represent the next vast opportunity for growth in international marketing. Muslim countries and companies are also realizing the huge potential that lies waiting for attention.

It is thus perhaps not surprising that early signs of branding success from Islamic countries such as those in the Middle East and Asia are emerging, and I believe that the next wave of brand development and success will come from the Islamic world. At the same time, the vast potential represented by large Muslim populations everywhere has caught the eye of the multinationals rooted in the West.

Principally, the impetus for doing more business in Islamic majority and minority markets has come from three sources:

1. The rapid expansion of Western brands to penetrate these markets in order to gain a truly global presence.
2. The response from Islamic companies and the need to rely less on oil and gas production.
3. The rise of industries that conform to Islamic practice, such as Islamic financial services.

By way of response, Islamic audiences love the Western big brands, but there are three main reasons why they wish to have their own. Firstly, Western brands are often not compliant with Islamic values (or their ethical base), for instance in hospitality, food and beverage, pharmaceutical and medical products and services markets. Secondly, Islamic countries want to create their own global brands which they see as strategic business assets and national brand ambassadors. Thirdly, the growth of the educated middle class in Muslim minority and majority cultures and countries has created an impetus to developing businesses, products and services that are competitive with the long established and accepted brands.

As a consequence of the above, there is now a considerable surge in demand within Islamic countries and companies to master the branding and marketing techniques and skills so ably demonstrated by the West to essentially address international perceptions of Islamic products, services, businesses and the countries and cultures of their origin.

OPPORTUNITIES IN A LARGE AND DISPARATE MARKET

The introduction above tells us that the Muslim market is huge, but one of the interesting findings of the Oxford University research is that despite the large numbers there is no homogenous Islamic or Muslim market, and that within this massive global segment there are many different forms of consumer behaviour dependent on a lot of variables, many of which have not yet been researched properly. Here are some of the similarities and differences across global Muslim markets.

Similarities

- Common faith, values and identity as Muslims
- Similar dietary requirements (*halal*)
- Similar lifestyle requirements (finance, education, entertainment etc.)
- Strong sense of community and welfare

Differences

- Diverse locations
- Multiple languages and dialects

- Various cultural and lifestyle differences
- Varying degrees of Islamic religiosity
- Varying degrees of education, affluence and marketing sophistication.

There is a very clear message here that stands out above all others. This message is that the lack of uniformity across the Muslim market will force brand managers and marketers to adopt multiple marketing strategies in order to build international brands that appeal to Muslims.

It should also be noted that much of the world's Muslim population is relatively poor and situated in developing economies. Marketers should bear this in mind, but they should also consider that as these economies develop and populations gain in spending power then so do the opportunities for branding and marketing. For instance, the most populous Muslim minority country is India, with 161 million Muslim people, and as more of these people enter India's middle class their spending power increases and their desire for buying brands grows in parallel. Other countries such as Bangladesh are not yet at this stage of development. Opportunities at the luxury end of the market are more confined to elite cadres in Muslim majority countries, especially in the Gulf. Marketers thus need to search for markets in stages of development that may suit their products and understand what drives consumer behaviour in those segments. Governments also need to understand different markets so that they can encourage and assist the right industries for the future. Clearly much more research is needed in Muslim markets, especially in the field of consumer behaviour, but despite the challenges posed there are a huge number of opportunities that marketers can pursue, especially in the following categories.

Food and beverages

According to the *Halal Journal* (2009), the global *halal* food market's estimated size in 2004 was US$587.2 billion and this figure increased to US$632.4 billion in 2009. Although this figure is growing it represents only around 16 per cent of the world's total food expenditure as Muslims have lower purchasing power than other populations across all categories, including food products. Out of this figure, Asian countries represent the largest market, which is not surprising given that 62 per cent of Muslims live in this region. The *halal* food and beverage market is thus a major opportunity for Islamic companies to go international and global. Some companies are trying to develop their own brands and some countries are assisting places and destinations to do the same. However, at present many of the branding opportunities are being taken up by global Western brands such as Nestlé, a company that earned US$5.2 billion in *halal* revenues in 2008.

Education

While traditionally Islamic education has been under the purview of the mosques and those in charge of them, over the last two to three decades there has been an explosion of Islamic educational institutions, in primary, secondary and tertiary education. Such institutions often teach conventional as well as Islamic subjects, and there is now considerable competition in this sector. Examples range from Al-Azhar University, considered by some to be the oldest university in the world, to Qids Kindergarten in Malaysia.

Tourism and hospitality

Islamic travel, tourism and leisure form another segment of the Islamic market that offers products and services to both Muslims and non-Muslims. From tourist destinations in the Middle East to *halal* airlines and fully *halal* hotels and resorts, there is something for everyone, and most Muslim majority countries are trying to cash in on the growth of tourism and tourism-related travel. Pure Islamic tourism and hospitality is growing slowly but surely as companies such as Al Jawhara Group of Hotels and Apartments comply with *sharia* rules throughout all their operations.

Medical, pharmaceutical, cosmetics and personal care

This promises to be the next largest growth area in the global Islamic market. For many Muslims who want to comply with *sharia* law and consume only what is *halal* there is a growing industry in generic medical, pharmaceutical and healthcare products that do not contain non-compliant substances such as certain animal-based gelatines. Plant-based products, such as the European skincare brand Saaf Pure Skincare, contain highly concentrated healing botanicals, anti-inflammatory seed oils, shea butter and other ingredients that offer an alternative not just to Muslims but to anyone interested in using plant as opposed to animal ingredients. The growth of this category, spurred on by new standards and *halal* accreditation availability, has meant that some countries such as Malaysia are strategically earmarking companies manufacturing medicines, pharmaceutical and cosmetics products for special assistance. Brunei is another country that has already produced accreditation standards in such categories.

Entertainment

Art, sports and entertainment can be enjoyed by anyone and there are hundreds of television channels throughout the world dedicated to the Muslim consumer, varying in content, usually by country but not always. Even in Muslim minority countries entertainment brands are doing well, for instance Islam Channel in the UK. As all brand and marketing managers know, brands are not confined to companies; personalities and celebrities are often managed as 'brands', and Sami Yusuf, the Muslim pop star, demonstrates the success that can be attained.

Internet and digital products and services

The Internet, media and digital products area provides perhaps the most exciting of the opportunities available to those wishing to serve Islamic markets. The range of products available is plentiful and Muslims can easily find digital libraries, digital art and photography, digital Islamic clock widgets and a whole host of other products. Non-Islamic brands can also see the market potential in digital products. For example, mobile phone manufacturer LG launched handsets in August 2009 with a number of special features, including a *qibla* indicator, and prayer time alarm functions as well as Qur'an software, the *hijri* calendar and a *zakat* calculator.

More interesting is the area of social media, where brands such as Muxlim.com are emerging and growing. Muxlim claims to be the world's largest Muslim lifestyle media company and was highlighted in an earlier chapter. Muxlim.com is the company's flagship social media service, combining interactive video, audio, blogs, polls and images. 'The company is focused on the Muslim lifestyle as part of a diverse, all-inclusive world which recognizes and welcomes people of all faiths and backgrounds, who want to share, learn and have fun' (Muxlim.com, 2010).

Financial products and services
The first sustainable and recognized Islamic bank was Dubai Islamic Bank, which was founded in 1974, followed by the Islamic Development Bank in 1975. Now there are hundreds of banks offering Islamic finance, and countries such as Malaysia, Singapore, Hong Kong, London, and others are competing to capitalize on this trend and become Islamic finance hubs. Following the recent global recession, issues regarding lack of trust in the conventional banking system have added impetus to the growth of Islamic finance and its purportedly more ethical and transparent base. While the breakdown of the conventional global finance between 2007 and 2009 caused havoc in most countries, Islamic finance was not affected to as large an extent at all, although there were some *sukuk* (corporate bond) defaults in places such as Dubai. The resilience of Islamic finance under such trying circumstances has been attributed by many players and observers in the industry to features associated 'ethical banking'. The implication of this is that the success of Islamic finance is based on principles that are accepted widely within non-Muslim as well as Muslim markets. Indeed, the Oxford research shows that many Islamic banks are attracting many more non-Muslim new customers than Muslims.

Lifestyle and fashion products
In addition to the categories of lifestyle media magazines and beauty products, the world of Islamic clothing and fashion has started to blossom globally, offering women a vast array of products that combine fashion with Islamic principles. There are also new products that are more recreational in nature such as Burqini swimwear.

It is interesting to note that many Western companies are already providing brands in most of these categories alongside brands that are indigenous to Muslim majority countries. The opportunities remain substantial across all categories because Islam is a lifestyle that influences the daily lives of all Muslims, but there are challenges for brands from the Muslim world to tackle before they can take advantage of them.

KEY CHALLENGES FOR ASPIRING MUSLIM BRANDS – THE 6 'A'S

It is, and will continue to be, no easy task for Islamic brands to break into and progressively gain a share in their chosen markets, especially where Western brands are already in dominant positions, and they will have to overcome a variety of challenges, the most important of which fall into six main areas:

1. Awareness
2. Accessibility
3. Acceptability
4. Adequacy
5. Affinity
6. Attack

Here is a brief explanation of these challenges.

1. Awareness

One of the most fundamental obstacles to the growth of Islamic brands is simply the difficulty of achieving brand awareness when entering already crowded markets dominated by other, often Western, brands. In particular, there are strategic questions that must be answered such as, how can brand managers move past the obstacles of gaining consumer trial, purchase and preference for their brands when the established brands have strong brand equity and loyalty?

This is no easy task, and even existing players may face growth difficulties if there is a powerful leader of the pack, which is often found in consumer markets. For example, in the sports shoes and apparel market, Nike has around 40 per cent global market share with the others way behind. This is a major issue for any brand that is not well known or is not the number one player.

To gain awareness and entry into such markets sounds a daunting task but it can be done. A good example of how a niche market can be created without directly challenging the global giants is in the mass media. While CNN is probably the worldwide leader in news followed by the BBC, Al-Jazeera is well on the way to becoming a global brand, targeted at Muslim audiences and people who want a different view of news about the Muslim world and world news from a Muslim perspective. Al Jazeera provides a choice not just in Arabic but also in English for anyone in the world who wants an alternative to the market leaders, providing all the news and sports items that a global media company needs to offer to global citizens. The lesson here is that there is always room for an alternative choice, but not many alternative choices.

2. Accessibility

A second challenge to Islamic companies wishing to build their brands is the issue of how to gain access in crowded markets. In order to become successful as an international brand, especially in fast-moving consumer and retail goods, it is important to get critical mass in terms of distribution. In established markets this can be difficult. For example, gaining shelf space in supermarkets located in major cities is tremendously difficult for smaller brands, where large companies dominate consumer 'eyeballs'. For example, in the US, *halal* food products are outnumbered by kosher products in supermarkets by a ratio of 86:1, and 16 per cent of Muslims as a consequence buy kosher food as they cannot gain access to their preferred *halal* food. If a *halal* food brand wanted to gain entry into minority Muslim markets such as the US, United Kingdom and France, it would have difficulty getting the shelf space in the large retailers such as Tesco, Asda, Wal-Mart, and Carrefour.

There are two ways to approach this challenge, the first of which is to create an alliance or strategic partnership with the big retailers, as several companies have done by becoming supply partners to Tesco in countries such as Malaysia, and secondly, to go for a niche target market with carefully planned distribution to avoid competing, and perhaps tempt them in to giving you space once you have made a market impact.

3. Acceptability

That a brand needs acceptability by consumers to gain entry into a market is an obvious but critical factor, and many influences come into play, not the least of which is the brand's country of origin. The country-of-origin effect can be highly influential and is very important when it comes to consumer purchase decisions. In the absence of powerful branding, consumers are very risk-averse, and do not like to buy products from countries about which they have doubts or prejudices. This is typified by the 'made-in-China' quality syndrome, and whether it is based on reality or falsehood the actual quality of Chinese products does not matter as in the world of branding perception is reality. What people believe is true to them.

In branding and marketing, prejudice might also arise if, for example, a brand is perceived as coming from an 'Islamic' country. The issue here is not so much concerned with religion – it is about how the country from which a brand originates is perceived, what mental associations accompany the mention of it, and, in some cases, the geo-political circumstances that underpin these. As a result, the decision a brand owner has to make is whether to play up or play down the country of origin, and market research can be particularly useful in determining what associations might transfer to the image of the brand. But even negative perceptions can be successfully avoided with carefully planned communications strategies. The message is that care should be taken to understand how the market feels about the country of origin of your brand, and whether such associations are likely to have any positive or negative impact for short and long term brand and market development. Only then can a company prioritize, create, and tailor its campaigns accordingly.

Finally, many Islamic companies may want to attract both Muslim and non-Muslim audiences, and so will have to be very selective in the way in which they build their brands (especially with respect to what values they use and how these are communicated) and in what messages they project. This comes down to skilful brand and market communications that can deliver key messages seen as relevant to either Muslim consumers, or non-Muslim consumers or both.

4. Adequacy

The word adequacy in this context means the capability of a company to produce branded products and services that are of top quality and are acceptable to those markets they intend to sell them in. It is well known that it is impossible to build and sustain a strong brand in the absence of top class product and service quality. There is no escape from this rule. And brands that want to do well in *halal* markets have to make sure they have the correct accreditation in place from the relevant authorities. This is not as easy as it sounds, and the issue of *halal* accreditation and quality standards is worth commenting on briefly because, despite much government support, many Muslim companies do not make it to the international stage because they only satisfy the local part of the criteria – the accreditation side. But even this can pose problems as there is no one globally acknowledged accreditation system.

The need for standardization in *halal* accreditation has been debated intensely over many years, but the differing standards between many countries remain and this situation does make it difficult for any player to be a global or multi-national leader in *halal* foods. Moreover, accreditation is often not linked to quality standards, and there are many instances of companies that have achieved local *halal* accreditation standards and recognition in their own country, but have not been able to export their products to the European Union, or indeed other Muslim countries, because they do not meet the necessary quality and *halal* standards respectively.

In addition to achieving the right accreditation logos to go on packaging, if the aim of a brand is to enter Muslim minority markets where there is an opportunity also to attract non-Muslims, then it is also necessary to educate consumers as to what *halal* actually means. One implication for brand communications is to keep the *halal* profile low and the product and brand profile high. Thus the Muslims who are looking for clarity of *halal* accreditation can find a *halal* certification logo in small print on the back of the packaging, and non-Muslims can see the brand's more upfront messaging that highlights various product attributes such as healthy, wellness, organic authenticity and so on.

5. Affinity

One 'must have' for any aspiring international or global brand is affinity, and by this I mean trust. Without trust there is no loyalty, and customers will not stay with your brand. A good example of great affinity between a brand and its customers is that of Apple. Many global brands have this brand strength. People trust them, like them, and are loyal to them.

One of the elements that engender trust is quality, already mentioned above as a requirement for entry into many markets. Once consumers have experienced a brand and the quality of its products or services, then they expect the same again and again. A slip in quality can mean a loss of customers and profits as demonstrated in the 2009 case of Toyota, a company that had to recall over 8 million cars because of defective parts that caused accidents and injury. At the time of writing legal proceedings are still going on, and Toyota are in the midst of spending billions of dollars to replace parts and recapture falling demand for its products in the US and elsewhere.

Service quality is another element that affects trust for brands. In Asian countries, for example, service quality is still variable and only found to be reliably high in more affluent outlets, such as high class hotels and boutiques. There is no consistency and this therefore represents both an opportunity and a challenge. The challenge is that quality of the brand experience must be consistently good for affinity to grow, and the opportunity is that there is plenty of room for brands to make ground here, as consistently great brand experiences are few and far between.

6. Attack

The last of the 6 'A's is a somewhat mighty challenge, and this is the potential or actual attack from established and major brand competitors, especially the global brands. Many major brands have moved quickly and deeply into these markets with powerful positioning, strong brand names and good value propositions that are already known and respected both globally and in the Muslim world. A good example here is Nestlé, a global corporate brand that is gradually ensuring that its product range of 4600 plus brands conforms to *halal* standards and achieves *halal* accreditation. Other global brand names localizing their products to suit the Muslim market include McDonald's and Subway in fast foods, and Standard Chartered and HSBC in Islamic finance. The point about the success of these big brands in Muslim markets is not that they are always technically superior in their products, but that their brand names are so well known and trusted wherever they go that they are almost guaranteed success. Indeed, in technical areas such as Islamic finance, it should be Islamic banks from Islamic countries that lead the way rather than follow behind, but they have not developed their brands enough to be able to do so.

The challenges facing Islamic brands in entering Muslim and non-Muslim markets as described may seem at first daunting, but there are some good strategies that can be used for effective brand-building and marketing.

In addition to the strategic examples mentioned above, the next section discusses how other strategies can be employed to overcome these challenges and achieve international success, and gives examples of Islamic brands that are taking very positive steps to implement them.

STRATEGIES FOR SUCCESS

The main strategies for building Islamic brands are:

1. Understand the market clearly

Market acceptability depends to a large extent upon how well a company understands that market and what consumers really need and want, but it is surprising how many companies do not do their homework well, in the form of market research and gathering consumer insight. They just do not understand the market properly. Understanding a market means understanding not just the demographics among the target population, but also the psychographics of consumers – how they feel, what they want, what makes them buy certain brands, and so on. Research on these kinds of consumer insights is often neglected, but is critical to successful marketing and brand building. In addition to pure market research, brand audits are sometimes used to discover this kind of information to ensure that companies really understand not just what customers, suppliers, employees, and other stakeholders want, but how they perceive competitive brands as well as their own in meeting their expectations.

2. Build your brand on Islamic values with universal emotional appeal

As great brands are always built on emotional values of universal appeal, then to my mind the building of brands on Islamic values represents one of the greatest opportunities there is. Some words translated from Arabic include true, honest, trusted, responsible, intelligent, wise, communicative, pure, honest, fair and kind.

A list that contained the above and more would give aspiring Islamic brands a variety of powerful values that would not only be appreciated by Muslims themselves, but would be attractive to all global audiences, as shown in point 4 below.

3. Position your companies and products on relevance to the market

Some brands fail because they become irrelevant to the market, in other words, they no longer satisfy the changing needs of their consumer base. And the converse is true: a brand can be highly successful by being relevant to what consumers actually want and their changing lifestyles. For example, the Islamic Bank of Britain uses multi-lingual employees in its branches and call centres so that any customer can feel 'at home'. Relevance can also be seen in *halal* food. In the UK and other European countries the trend is towards fusion foods and those that are more 'oriental' and spicy. This applies to both fast food and mainstream restaurant food. Chicken Cottage Ltd. is an example of a company that has built a focused *halal* food brand by understanding market changes and tastes in Britain and combining traditional western fast food products with flavors of the East.

4. Communicate the brand appropriately

Having a great product is important, but communicating the brand to consumers is equally valuable in establishing the relationship and building market share. If you have created a brand that is both relevant and possesses strong Islamic values, then that brand has to be communicated in the most appropriate way for its target audiences. For example, Al Rajhi bank communicates its values of 'Truth', 'Respect', and 'Honour' conservatively, the values coming across strongly but without being ultra-modern; this is appropriate for a financial services company that operates primarily in Muslim majority countries.

5. Gain first mover advantage in new industries and categories

New industries are rapidly emerging that are offering a multitude of opportunities for enterprising new and existing companies. Most of these are a direct result of technological advancements that enhance consumer lifestyles, such as digital and Internet products. Google is now the most valuable brand in the world and one of the largest companies by market capitalization, and Apple has revolutionized mobile communications. Many such opportunities are waiting in the Muslim digital world.

6. Consider mergers, acquisitions and partnerships

If a company wants to fast track its branding and business development efforts it can do so by entering into agreements with other Muslim or non-Muslim brands, or indeed by acquiring them. A good example of an acquisition that lifted a corporate brand's portfolio and added global reach was the takeover of Godiva by ÜLKER Group in 2007 for US$850 million, when Campbell Soup Company decided to divest the brand. ÜLKER Group is a major company in Turkey that had mainly focused on its home market throughout its history and now is learning how to manage a global luxury brand, an experience that will enable the Group to more easily reach out to global markets with some of its other products.

7. Develop new and ethical business models using Islamic values and practices

There are some very interesting new ways of developing businesses in the Islamic world through applying traditional Islamic values and religious practice to corporate life and brand building. For example, most people would probably view Corporate Social

Responsibility (CSR) as a largely Western invention, but CSR is one of the foundation stones of the Islamic way of life, and has been for centuries. One of the most successful, intriguing and innovative developments in this area is the creation of 'corporate *waqf*', driven through 'intrapreneurship' and the development of entrepreneurs. This combination of social responsibility and practical entrepreneurship has benefited many people at the 'bottom of the pyramid'.

8. Build an international brand using Western techniques

There are occasions when some companies do not wish to build brands with an Islamic orientation as they may be competing for global reach and acceptance with giant competitors and feel that although their country of origin is well accepted, the brand must be constructed to compete in global markets using global techniques. They want to be seen as global and not local brands. Petronas from Malaysia is one example.

9. Aim for a niche market

Aiming for a niche market is a good strategy as it tends to play away from the competition, especially from the global brands and in Muslim minority markets, where the target audience is by its nature much smaller. Two good examples here are Ummah Foods, a company that has built a niche chocolate brand range in the UK, where the Muslim population is less than two million, and Bateel, a date producer and retailer producing upmarket gourmet confectionery.

10. Offer a close alternative in a major category

When there are major brand categories that are aimed firmly at one single consumer group, there may be an opportunity for an alternative product, especially if the proposed target audience is similar in terms of what it is looking for in the product, but different enough in terms of another attribute to justify entry. This is the case with Fulla, the alternative to Mattel's Barbie Doll.

Many of the above strategies can be carried out by the smallest of companies, but the encouragement of branding and marketing at all levels in the public and private sectors is in the interests of every government. This leads me to discuss briefly why Islamic countries need to promote branding.

ISLAMIC COUNTRIES NEED TO PROMOTE BRANDING

If Islamic countries clarify what they really stand for and employ brand differentiation strategies they will find that doors will open to the achievement of various national objectives, including:

- Increase in currency stability;
- Restoration of international credibility and investor confidence;
- Reversal of international ratings downgrades;
- Attraction of global capital;
- Increase in international political influence;
- Growth in export of branded products and services;

- Increase in inbound tourism and investment;
- Development of stronger international partnerships;
- Enhancement of nation building (confidence, pride, harmony, ambition, national resolve);
- Reversal of negative thoughts about environmental, human rights and other matters of importance to global audiences;
- Attraction and retention of talent (the human resource and global knowledge)
- Greater access to global markets;
- Improvement in the ability to exceed regional and global business competitors, and defend their own markets; and more.

The above benefits of nation branding are substantial but may not be achieved unless the companies and sectors within the nation are well branded, as there is a link between the brand image of a nation and the brand images of companies and sectors within it – this I call the Nation Brand Effect (NBE) (Temporal, 2004). Strong corporate brands are brand ambassadors for their countries and can have positive effects on the image of their respective countries. Secondly, strong corporate brands increase the values of the respective stock exchanges where they are listed as the brand value contributes to the intangible asset value part of market capitalization. In Western countries, the value of intangible assets, as opposed to tangible ones, on bourses can be as much as 72 per cent and much of the intangible base comes from the value of brands represented on those bourses. Now that it is becoming popular and mandatory in many countries for companies to disclose on an annual basis the value of their brands, this leads to higher market capitalizations. In many Islamic countries this is not yet the case and thus they lag behind, which provides little incentive for boards of directors to build their brands up as they tend to do in the West. Thirdly, strong brands increase foreign direct investment, jobs and wealth creation on their own, despite the national image, although they in turn will do this less effectively if they are perceived to come from a country with a negative image – this is the country-of-origin effect mentioned earlier and is linked to the NBE.

For Islamic countries hoping to diversify into many different industries and encouraging their companies to go regional, international or global, nation branding is a must. But little evidence is seen of activity on this front in the Muslim world. Muslim minority country Singapore and Muslim majority country Malaysia have both been involved in branding activities, having provided branding and promotional grant assistance for all companies wishing to develop their brands overseas. Both have also carried out industry and sector branding but neither has developed a composite, well-defined national brand strategy. Oman has worked on its national brand for some years but is still trying to complete a difficult task, and destinations such as Dubai are presently recovering from what could be called a national brand image crisis. I would encourage these countries not to give up, and ask those countries that have not started to enhance and manage their national images and encourage their companies to proceed with some urgency. Brunei and Sarawak are examples of this trend, both moving towards their own brand objectives in connection with the *halal* industry.

A fundamental lesson from this chapter is that any government has to work on its national image and also encourage both its large companies and its SME sector to build strong corporate brands at the same time.

It is now time to take stock of this chapter and provide some conclusions and thoughts about the future. There are several points to remember that I would like to draw your attention to before moving on to look at the future.

MAJOR POINTS TO REMEMBER

1. Islamic brands are losing market share at home and abroad to Western brands as they fail to move quickly enough into major growth categories such as Islamic finance and food. This is hampering Islamic countries who wish to diversify their economies and move away from dependence on traditional trading and energy reserves.
2. Companies are often a country's best ambassadors, and should be helped in their brand and marketing activities by way of promotional subsidies and consultancy expertise. Large companies can project the national image abroad in a major way, and government assistance for SMEs can generate a great export base. However, more countries need to work not only on this kind of assistance but also on the image of the nation itself if the benefits of the Nation Brand Effect are to be felt in full.
3. The global Muslim market is very large but it is not homogenous, and every Muslim community in every Muslim majority or minority country behaves differently, although they also have certain similarities. Much more research is required, especially in the field of consumer behavior, in order to understand the complexities of Muslim markets. In the absence of generally available research, countries and companies wishing to internationalize or globalize their brands will need to develop multi-brand and marketing strategies that are based on meaningful research of each distinct market, and make the products and marketing mix relevant to that market.
4. When building a brand it is best to establish a number one position in your home market before venturing out into the region and later globally. Most of the world's top brands have adopted this approach. Also, for Islamic brands it may be better to market their products and services in Muslim majority markets first before moving on to minority markets, as they are more likely to understand the different cultures involved.
5. Despite the challenges that exist in building international brands, there are many opportunities in all categories of goods and services for Islamic brands if they adopt the right techniques and focus on the values inherent in the Islamic faith.
6. Niche marketing may bring faster results in the short term and avoid the power of the established global brands. There are always areas of unsatisfied consumer needs in any category that the big brands cannot serve.

CRITICAL SUCCESS FACTORS

The future is always difficult to predict but there are certain critical success factors that Islamic brands should take note of if they are to win in the battle for consumer minds.

These are principally speed, agility, innovation, emotion, and brand as strategy. I will deal with each in turn.

1. Speed
The pace of change grows ever faster, and speed can be a great competitive advantage. Looking at the Western world, the fashion brand Zara, owned by Inditex Group, leads the way. Zara produces around 11 000 products each year, far more than most fashion retailers, and to accomplish this it has developed the ability to drastically shorten the product life cycle. Indeed, from the design stage to in store can take as little as four to five weeks. If the design is just a modification it may only take three weeks. No one design stays in the stores for more than four weeks and if the first week's sales are not up to scratch, the item is withdrawn and production stopped. As a result Zara customers tend to visit stores around seventeen times a year, as opposed to the fashion retailing average of three or four times. Zara wins on profits and customers win on choice and exclusivity. Similar opportunities exist for brands in Muslim markets.

2. Agility
Connected to speed is agility. Consumer lifestyles are changing fast and so must brands and their marketing activities. For example, the advent of social networking has changed the whole way in which brands have to communicate with consumers, and those that do not manage to create ways of engaging consumers in new ways will lose customers to those brands that do. This does not mean having a presence on Facebook or other social networking sites but managing to create conversations with people in new ways. Consumers no longer wish to have advertisements pushed at them, and in the world of social networking, brands are not invited into consumer conversations. Agility in changing marketing activity, channels of distribution and focused spend to provide consumers with real time entertainment is imperative, and more and more this has to be on the Internet. Consumers are now in control – it is they that will build your brand and actually they 'own' it as they have the capability to discard or ignore it if a brand becomes out of touch, reach and relevance. While the Internet continues to change everything on a regular basis, Islamic brands can be just as good as those that are already household names if they brand themselves properly.

3. Innovation
Consumers now demand innovation, and brands that continuously innovate with relevance tend to win. Change means innovation, but innovation without relevance to consumers is worthless. Again, Islamic brands can learn from the Western world, and observe carefully how brands such as Apple continue to provide cutting-edge products that do what people want and are designed with desire in mind. Innovation, design and emotion are a formidable combination and command the best in terms of loyalty and trust.

4. Emotion
Any brand that does not establish emotional connections with consumers will not be sustainable in the long term. This statement is the guiding principle for all brands. Our research reveals that Islamic values are not just of interest to Muslims, but are often

values with universal emotional appeal. This means that Islamic brands can communicate effectively with all global markets on the basis of shared values that support the Islamic shared beliefs. It also means that there need be no difference between the way in which Islamic brands are constructed and marketed and the ways in which Western brands are built.

Given that these important points are positively embraced and implemented, there are no limits to the number and size of brands that can come from the Islamic world, and there will be fewer issues for non-Islamic brands wanting to penetrate and grow their Muslim market base.

5. Brand as strategy

The remaining critical factor that will determine success for brands from the Muslim world will be the use of brand as a strategic vehicle to drive the business. It is a fact now for most global brands that brands drive the businesses and not the other way round, as used to be. Because brands have such a powerful grip on consumer attitudes and purchase behavior, companies use them to move into different categories and industries. Nestlé, HSBC and others are typical examples of the use of brands strategically, and Islamic brand owners would do well to build their brands with these examples in mind.

BRANDING IS A STRATEGIC IMPERATIVE

Today's businesses are subjected to a great deal of turbulent and accelerating change, and Asian companies feel this change to a greater degree than companies elsewhere in the world as they try to catch up and overtake the competition. Since 2007 the tremendous pressures of the global economic roller coaster have intensified the struggle for life experienced by the majority of businesses. Periods of profound and rapid change put a premium on the ability to survive, and unfortunately many companies go under. Take a look at the Fortune 500. A surprising number of corporations that were on the list a decade ago are no longer on it, while the recent economic crises have eliminated others entirely. There are hardly any companies from Islamic countries in the list.

By contrast, the top brands of the 1920s have maintained their industry leadership to this day in many disparate and turbulent markets, and despite changes of management over the years. The key to the success of all these companies is their meticulous attention to the development and management of their brands. Strong brands are amazingly durable, and have the ability to overcome many challenges and stand the test of time.

There are no life cycles for brands as opposed to products (now down to 6–8 weeks in some cases), and so branding is becoming increasingly relevant as the world enters a new era of unprecedented change, upheaval, and uncertainty. This change is strategic, unlike the incremental change of more predictable times, and therefore requires a strategic response. Brand building is exactly such a response. If successful, it can be the strongest weapon in a company's armory and the best guarantee of corporate survival. The reality is that at the basis of all corporate success are solid brand strategies, with clearly defined brand visions, values, positioning and plans for fulfillment. Brand strategies have to be brought to life by people, and the development of a brand culture is vital if companies are to deliver on the messages projected by market communications. As brands are relationships that only exist in people's minds, those relationships have to be built and nurtured with care, and brand successes and failures are linked directly to levels of consumer satisfaction and delight.

CAN ISLAMIC COMPANIES PERFORM IN THE GLOBAL BRANDING ARENA?

Some people say that companies from Islamic countries will find it incredibly difficult to build international and global brands. Their reasoning is that most of the world markets and the product categories in those markets are already dominated by powerful global brands. Furthermore, they claim that companies from the Islamic world have to overcome significant global consumer perceptions of sub-par quality and other concerns relating to the country of origin of the brand. There is a lot of truth in these comments, and it will be no easy task for companies from the Muslim world to develop strong brands of their own, but it is the very nature of the fast-changing business world that can help them. There are no hard and fast rules any more, and innovation no longer belongs to the privileged few. Moreover, there are Muslim corporate leaders with the vision necessary to harness technology and ideas, both of which are freely available, and global niche markets are available to those who can move in quickly. Speed and agility are not strengths possessed by many of the existing global giants. Muslim CEOs must use market dynamics to exploit the weaknesses of the power brand companies and establish new and innovative brands for the future.

For those companies that get it right, the benefits accruing to a strong brand are nothing short of astonishing. Powerful brands provide long-term security and growth, higher sustainable profits, and increased asset value because they achieve

- Competitive differentiation
- Premium prices
- Higher sales volumes
- Economies of scale and reduced costs
- Greater security of demand

So for companies wishing to create sustainable, profitable international and global market positions in Muslim markets, branding is the road to travel. This is the strategy that has been missing from many boardroom discussions over recent years and one that could possibly have saved a number of firms in the last two recessions. A strong brand is essential for survival in the twenty-first century.

SUMMARY: THE FUTURE FOR ISLAMIC BRANDING AND MARKETING

I have said consistently over the last four years that the next wave of branding will come from the Islamic world and I still firmly believe this. As the world becomes one global market and deregulation continues, the pressure for companies and governments to strengthen their brand positioning will become greater. I anticipate that there will be more government activity in this area. We are already witnessing Bahrain, Dubai, Hong Kong, London, Malaysia, Singapore and others competing for 'hub' status on a global or regional basis, and major brands competing in the private sector for both retail and wholesale markets. As Islamic finance continues to expand in double digit figures annually this embryonic market will attract many more players, and although branding and marketing activity is already quite high already I expect this to intensify over the next 5–10 years.

Government to government branding and marketing will also grow, particularly as the more developed Muslim countries begin to see opportunities to help the poorer ones, with the production of *halal* medicines, vaccines and pharmaceutical products. The strides forward now being taken by countries such as Brunei and Malaysia in the testing, accreditation and standards of such product categories will open up the global *halal* market significantly. Business to business marketing will also continue to flourish as Islam has a great, centuries old trading tradition and this is part of the DNA of many countries, especially those in the Gulf.

Arguably the most exciting of all areas for Islamic branding and marketing in the foreseeable future lies in the lifestyle categories. The Western brands have fully realized the potential here already and are progressing with accreditation for many of their food, cosmetics, personal care and other lifestyle product ranges. The challenge for brands from the Islamic world is to move quickly in order to secure a place at the table, and the biggest requirement needed by Islamic brands that I can see is not manufacturing competency or business know-how, but branding and marketing skills and techniques. This is an educational void that needs to be filled. The Islamic business world is now at a similar stage of development to that of Asia in the last decade of the twentieth century. This manifested itself in a desperate pursuit of quality and efficiency, a mindset that thought branding and marketing was tactical advertising and promotion, and a focus on short-term thinking and profitability as opposed to long-term thinking and brand investment. Branding was not seen as a legitimate strategic activity and brands were viewed as intangible marketing speak that did not justify monetary support. All in all, brand and marketing management were not seen as activities important to sustainable profitability and growth.

The scene is changing in developing countries now, and branding and marketing is beginning to lead the way in driving corporate strategy. Chief executives realize that brands are assets that can be worth multiples of the net tangible assets of a company, and treat branding and marketing appropriately, as investments that provides long-term sustainable value. Can Islamic countries and companies take this quantum leap in thinking? If they do not, then they will lose out in playing a significant part in the growth and development of the largest market in the world.

NOTE

*   This chapter is extracted from Paul Temporal's book, *Islamic Branding and Marketing: Creating a Global Islamic Business*, ISBN 978-0-470-82539-6, Copyright 2011. Reproduced with permission of John Wiley & Sons (Asia) Pte Ltd.

REFERENCES

Halal Journal (2009), 'The global halal food industry revisited', May/June, available at: http://www.halaljour nal.com/article/3571/.

Muxlim.com (2010), website homepage, http://www.muxlim.com.

Temporal, Paul (2004), *Public Sector Branding in Asia*, Singapore: Marshall Cavendish International (Asia) Pte Ltd.

24 Islam, consumption and marketing: going beyond the essentialist approaches
Özlem Sandıkcı and Güliz Ger

INTRODUCTION

Islam and marketing are two terms that, until recently, seldom came together. Yet today, there is a burgeoning interest, in both academic and practitioner circles, in understanding Muslim consumers and devising marketing strategies and practices that will enable companies to reach what is now considered to be a highly attractive market segment. One can trace such interest in the increasing number of research articles appearing in scholarly publications; the establishment of a specialist journal, appropriately titled the *Journal of Islamic Marketing*; the organization of academic conferences and executive workshops in various parts of the world, such as the Contemporary Muslim Consumer Cultures Conference at Free University of Berlin (2008), the International Conference on Islamic Marketing and Branding, Kuala Lumpur (2010), the American Muslim Consumers Conference, New Jersey, USA (2009 and 2010), and the Oxford Forum on Islamic Branding (2010); the production of high profile consultancy reports, such as A.T. Kearney's *Addressing the Muslim Market* (2007), JWT's *Understanding the Islamic Consumer* (2009), and Ogilvy and Mather's *Brands, Islam and the New Muslim Consumer* (2010); the circulation of news stories about Muslim consumers and Islamic brands and businesses in the trade press and popular media, such as the *New York Times* (Gooch, 2010), *Time* (Power, 2009), the *Economist* (2007), *Advertising Age* (Hastings-Black, 2008), and *Euromonitor International* (Kasriel, 2008); and the publication of this very Handbook.

Accompanying this rather sudden and strong interest is inevitably the question of why? Why is there an interest in Islam and marketing and why now? After all there has not been a parallel interest in 'Christian marketing' or 'Buddhist marketing'. Certainly, there is some literature on what might loosely be called 'church marketing'; that is, scholarship that seeks to offer insights into promoting church membership and attendance (for example, Barna, 1988; Vokurka and McDaniel, 2004; Webb et al., 1998). And there is certainly a significant body of anthropological and archeological work on religious material culture (for example, Hirschkind, 2008; Starrett, 1995; Zaidman, 2003). Yet neither is comparable to 'Islamic marketing', which now appears to be a standalone and emerging field.

A closer look at the literature suggests that underlying this attention is the identification of Muslims as an untapped and viable market segment. Analogous to the cases of other non-mainstream consumer groups such as blacks, gays and Hispanics in the US, for example, the increasing visibility of Muslims as consumers is intimately linked with their purchasing power. This power is articulated especially through the emergence of a Muslim middle class, which is, although geographically dispersed, united in its interest in consumption and ability to afford branded products (for example, Nasr, 2009; Sandıkcı and Ger, 2010; Wong, 2007). Along with the Muslim middle class, there is increasing visibility of Muslim entrepreneurs, a new breed of businesspeople, located in both Muslim majority and minority societies, who are keenly pursuing Islamic principles as well as capitalist aspirations (for example, Adas, 2006; Osella and Osella, 2009). These entrepreneurs are seen as innovatively blending business and religion and successfully carving out niches for themselves in the global marketplace. Overall, it appears that the changing demographics and purchasing power of Muslim consumers and the success of Muslim entrepreneurs have begun to render Islamic marketing a scholarly and managerially attractive field.

However, there is also a certain unease generated by the term 'Islamic marketing'. The 'Islamic' accent, we believe, carries with it the potential of reifying difference rather than interaction. First, it implies that when addressing Muslim consumers the practice of marketing needs to take on a particular Islamic character. Such marketing is assumed to be different from marketing in general. Second, it implies that Islamic marketing targets Muslim consumers, consumers who are distinctively different from consumers in general, and that it utilizes specific resources, skills, and tools that are relevant and appealing to this particular segment. Finally, it also assumes that there is a preexisting and uniform Muslim consumer segment, which can be targeted, reached and to a certain extent predicted by marketers. As we elaborate later, we believe that such assumptions have the danger of generating an essentialist perspective that produces a rather limited, static, and stereotypical understanding of Muslim consumers and businesses, and related consumption and marketing practices. By essentialism, we refer to viewing identity characteristics, such as being a Muslim, as fixed, universal and context independent traits and overlooking their dynamic, constructed and situated nature. What we argue for instead, is a focus on the interaction and co-constitutive relationship between Islam and marketing. In other words we urge researchers and practitioners to go beyond searching for differences to understanding how Islam and marketing mutually inform each other and how Muslim consumers and entrepreneurs negotiate Islamic values and consumerist and capitalist aspirations in their daily lives and practices.

Hence this chapter is primarily about problematizing the very notion of 'Islamic marketing' and an attempt to shift the academic and managerial attention from a preoccupation with difference to a more critical, situated and dynamic engagement with Muslim consumers and businesses. What follows next is an overview of the interest in Islam and marketing. We then discuss the relationship between morality and marketing. Next we outline a perspective for future research that is more sensitive to the complexities and contextualities of Muslims and their consumption and marketing practices. We conclude the chapter by discussing various managerial and policy implications of our perspective.

SCHOLARSHIP ON ISLAM, CONSUMPTION AND MARKETING

Despite the fact that there have been Muslims for centuries and that they have engaged in consumption and trade, interest in the relationship between Islam and marketing has emerged only recently. A closer look at the marketing and extant social science literatures suggest that the scholarship on Islam and marketing can be discussed in terms of two distinct phases: omission and discovery.

Omission

The phase of omission refers to the dearth of interest in conceptualizing and studying Muslims as consumers. In the consumer behavior and marketing literatures, religion in general is an understudied area. Within this general scarcity, attention on Islam, consumption, and the marketing relationship is even scarcer. The omission was partially related to the marginalization of Muslims as low-income and uneducated people who did not constitute a significant market for branded products. In this respect Muslims were similar to the world's poor, or what Prahalad (2004) labeled the 'bottom-of-the-pyramid'. Although many Kuwaitis or Saudis or other Muslims engaged in extravagant consumption and investment in New York, London or Paris, Muslims did not seem to qualify as proper consumers. As they were not worthy of attention economically, they remained unknown scholarly.

However omission was also due to the stereotyping of Muslims as traditional, uncivilized and even militant people. As Edward Said (1978) lucidly demonstrated in his book *Orientalism*, the prevailing Western view of Islam and Muslims as the inferior Other of the West has been a historical construct, a trope that was based on false and romanticized images of the Middle East and Asia. Said argued that Western writings of the Orient depict it as an irrational, weak, feminized 'Other' in contrast to the rational, strong, masculine West. Underlying this contrast was, according to Said, the need to create 'difference' between West and East that can be attributed to immutable 'essences' in the Oriental make-up (1978, pp. 65–67). In the business context, such Orientalist representations worked to produce and reinforce a view of Islam as incompatible with capitalist consumer ideology and gave way to categorizing Muslims as outside the values and practices of Western consumer culture. This incompatibility view had different justifications.

From the perspective of 'Islamic economics', a body of literature grounded in medieval Islamic thought (Kuran, 2004), the incompatibility has been necessary, deliberate and real. This scholarship has advocated the merits of Islamic economic institutions and values and argued that Islamic principles provide necessary guidance for today's economic practices (for example, Kahn, 1995; Siddiqi, 1992). In regard to consumption, there has been the tendency to treat consumer culture as crass, decadent and corrupting traditional values. Depicting consumer culture as wasteful, harmful, and immoral, fostering individualism and hedonism, the proponents of Islamic economics instructed Muslims to live modest lives and refrain from conspicuous and excessive consumption. Against the evils of a consumer culture associated with Western values, Islam has been offered as an antidote. As Kuran (2004, ix) argues:

> Islamic economics has fueled the illusion that Muslims can solve a wide range of social problems simply by embracing Islam and resisting Mammon – the evils associated with immoral forms of economic gain. It has promoted the spread of antimodern, and in some respects deliberately anti-Western, currents of thought all across the Islamic world. It has also fostered an environment conducive to Islamic militancy.

While Islamic economics deliberately sought to set apart Islamic consumption values and practices from the Western consumer culture by denigrating the latter as wasteful, excessive and the root cause of many societal problems, several prominent sociological analyses carried out in the 1990s propagated a similarly incompatible view of Islam and capitalism but due to a different set of reasons (for example, Barber, 1995; Bocock, 1993; Turner, 1994). Common in these studies was the focus on the rise of Islamic fundamentalism and its ideological repercussions. From this perspective, the problematic relationship between Islam and capitalist consumption, or 'Jihad versus McWorld' in Barber's (1996) famous phrase, has been related to the rise of Islamic fundamentalism as a reactionary response to the conditions of postmodernity, an effect of which has been the pluralization of lifeworlds through the spread of a global system of consumption.

For instance in his book *Orientalism, Postmodernism and Globalism*, Brian Turner argued that 'consumerism offers or promises a range of possible lifestyles which compete with, and in many cases, contradict the uniform lifestyle demanded by Islamic fundamentalism' (1994, p. 90). According to Turner the cultural, aesthetic and stylistic pluralism fostered by postmodernism and the spread of a global system of consumption contradicted the fundamentalist commitment to a unified world organized around incontrovertibly true values and beliefs. While 'the consumer market threatens to break out into a new stage of fragmented postmodernity in late capitalism,' fundamentalism 'acts as a brake on the historical development of world capitalism' (Turner 1994, p. 80). Reminiscent of Huntington's (1997) 'clash of civilizations' thesis, these works reproduced a view of Islam as in clash with capitalist consumerism.

Accordingly for a long time Muslim consumers and businesses remained invisible. While the incompatibility view justified the lack of academic and managerial interest in Islam and marketing, the lack of interest further reinforced the incompatibility view. This cycle came to a halt in the last decade when marketers, rather unexpectedly, discovered the Muslim consumer.

Discovery

There have been several social, political, cultural and economic developments underlying the recent interest in Muslim consumers and businesses. Overall, in the past decades an increased centrality of Islam has become visible across Muslim geographies. In line with this, several studies in the social sciences looking at Islamic movements and examining the changing role of Islam have appeared (for example, Bayat, 2005; Dekmejian, 1995; Esposito, 1998; Wiktorowicz, 2004). These studies discussed political ramifications of these new Islamic movements as well as the effects of the Islamization of everyday life. The events of 9/11 inevitably had an important impact in this emerging interest. Initially, the attacks were read mainly as a reaffirmation of the insurmountable differences between Islam and the Western civilization, and a validation of Huntington's arguments. The attack on the World Trade Center was seen as a symbolic attack against global capitalism. However, the attacks also accelerated the interest in understanding Muslims and their social, political and cultural life worlds.

The emergence of new Islamist social movements (Bayat, 2005; Wiktorowicz, 2004) has been a key development shaping the political landscape in the last decades. In the aftermath of 9/11, understanding the nature and dynamics of Islamic activism has become an important concern. Earlier Islamist movements, such as the Egyptian-based Society of the Muslim Brotherhood, founded in 1928, and the Lebanese Islamic Association, founded in 1948, were rather homogeneous and static collectivities motivated by resistance to Western-style modernization and secular modernity (Dekmejian, 1995; Esposito, 1998). New Islamist movements, on the other hand, (Bayat, 2005; Wiktorowicz, 2004) are not merely reactionary collectivities. Rather than being militant groups seeking a change of regime to *sharia*-based polity, new Islamist social movements are seen as strategic activist structures organized around loosely defined networks and groups that promote particular values through proper observance of Islam. As such they parallel the logic of new social movements and seek to create 'networks of shared meaning' (Melucci, 1996) through mobilization of various resources such as political parties, religious organizations, NGOs, schools, and social networks (Bayat, 2005; Wiktorowicz, 2004). These movements, such as the Turkish-based Gulen community, provide important strategic resources – financial, educational, cultural and social – to their followers (Agai, 2007; Mandaville, 2010).

Studies also indicate that market and consumption play important roles in the growth and spread of these movements (Boubekeur, 2005; Mandaville, 2010; Sandıkcı and Ger, 2010; Yavuz, 2004). In the case of Turkey, for example, Yavuz's (2004) study showed how Islamic groups have benefited from the new 'opportunity spaces' created by economic liberalization. These market-oriented venues to spread ideas and practices, such as the media, financial institutions and businesses, have been instrumental in both propagating the Islamic lifestyles and generating financial resources for the Islamic movements. From a similar perspective, focusing on the change of the meanings and practices of *tesettür*, modest dressing, in Turkey, Sandıkcı and Ger's (2010) study documented how consumption and marketing of fashionable *tesettür* have contributed to the increasing visibility and growth of a new Islamic collectivity. Overall, research on new Islamist movements indicate that in these communities, the feelings of belonging happen less through formal membership in a hierarchical structure but more through engaging in shared patterns of consumption and everyday life (Mandaville, 2010). That is, the location of activism shifts from revolutionary movements to spaces and practices of consumption.

A related and equally important development has been the emergence of Muslim entrepreneurs (for example, Adas, 2006; Demir et al., 2004; Osella and Osella, 2009; Sloane, 1999; Wong, 2007). The term has been used in reference to a new class of business people, located both in Muslim majority and minority societies who successfully blend Islamic ethical principles and values with capitalist business practices. In the case of Muslim-majority countries, the emergence of this business class has been linked to the neoliberal restructuring of economies and the changing dynamics of religion-market interaction (Demir et al., 2004). In the case of Muslim-minority countries, it has arisen from the changing nature of the Muslim diaspora and their increasing confidence and political, economic, and cultural power (Saint-Blancat, 2002). In both cases, these new Muslim entrepreneurs appear to be well connected to the networks of similar-minded business people and benefit from their connections within the new Islamist collectivities and business organizations.

Some scholars liken Muslim entrepreneurs to Calvinists that Weber (1930/1996) discussed in his book *The Protestant Ethic and the Spirit of Capitalism* (Adas, 2006; ESI, 2005). Similar to the Calvinist work ethic, Muslim entrepreneurs 'sanctify hard work, economic success and pursuit of wealth as important religious obligations' and believe that 'a good Muslim should be an entrepreneurial Muslim' (Adas, 2006, p. 129). In pursuing their entrepreneurial goals they seek to combine religious and economic activities through Islamic ethical values and norms. As Osella and Osella (2009) observe, these entrepreneurs 'inscribe their specific business interests and practices into rhetorics of the "common good"' (p. 203) and see combining material success with moral connectedness as the 'exemplary contemporary way of being a modern, moral, Muslim' (p. S204).

From Malaysia to Turkey, India, Syria, the UK, USA and Australia, these entrepreneurs design, manufacture and market products that are crucial to the development of modern Muslim identities as consumer subjects. Some examples that have received media attention include Turkish Tekbir, an Islamic clothing company; Syrian Newboy Design Studio, producer of Fulla dolls; Australian Ahida, marketer of modest swimsuit 'Burqini', a term derived from merging '*burqa*' and 'bikini'; and the UK-based *Emel*, a Muslim lifestyle magazine. In each case, an aspiration to achieve business success and help Muslims live properly Islamic lives underlines the entrepreneurial story: Tekbir's fashionable clothes aim to 'make covering beautiful' and inspire women to adopt the veil (Gokariksel and Secor, 2010; Sandıkcı and Ger, 2007); Fulla dolls act as role models for Muslim girls, offering an alternative to the flirtatious and hedonistic Barbie (Yaqin, 2007); the Burqini acts as a 'modernizing invention that brings Muslim women's fashion and leisure pursuits (nearly) up to speed with those of their non-Muslim female counterparts' (Fitzpatrick, 2009, p. 4); and *Emel* provides lifestyle tips informed by Islamic principles and ethical consumerism to its readers (Lewis, 2010).

Finally, there has been a growing recognition of a Muslim middle class, keen on blending Islamic values and a consumerist ethos (Nasr, 2009; Wong, 2007). As in the case of Muslim entrepreneurs, the emergence of a Muslim middle class is closely linked to the broader socio-economic developments. In many Muslim countries, neoliberal economic restructuring programs have been influential in creating not only new business domains but also opening up countries to foreign brands, shopping malls and various contemporary marketing practices. In countries such as Turkey, Egypt, Malaysia and Indonesia to name a few, accumulation of wealth concomitant with the increasing influence of Islamic movements has resulted in the creation of a new middle class 'conservative in values but avant-garde in consumption practices' (Sandıkcı and Ger, 2002, p. 467; see also Nasr, 2009; Wong, 2007).

Today looking over the marketplaces in Muslim majority and minority contexts as well as the digital space, one can observe a wide variety of products that are positioned as Islamic and *halal* and targeted at Muslim consumers. These offerings range from clothing to holiday resorts, food, gated communities, *hajj* packages, decorative objects, CDs, MP3 recordings of sermons, pop music, toys, lifestyle magazines, and TV and radio stations. Nasr frames the consumption demands of a global Islamic middle class as an economic counterbalance to China's consumer power and asserts that 'this upwardly mobile class consumes Islam as much as practicing it, demanding the same sorts of life-enhancing goods and services as middle classes everywhere' (2009, p. 14). Overall, by harmonizing religion and consumption in everyday practices, the new Muslim middle class contributes to the making of a new and different performative Muslim identity that draws from multiple resources.

The corporate world soon attended to these developments. Since the late 2000s, consultancy reports highlighting the importance of addressing the Muslim market began to appear (for example, A.T. Kearney, 2007; JWT, 2009; Ogilvy and Mather, 2010). Common to these reports is the emphasis on the size of the Muslim market and its purchasing power. Although it is acknowledged that much of the approximately 1.6 billion Muslim population is quite poor, the number of consumers with sufficient purchasing power is deemed as significant enough. Overall the goal of these reports has been to educate and instruct Western multinationals in Islam and Muslim lifestyles.

With the increasing corporate attention on Muslims as consumers, academic research in the area also began to intensify. Although there has been some research on consumption practices of Muslims (for example, Esso and Dibb, 2004; Mokhlis, 2006; Sandıkcı and Ger, 2010; Yavas and Tuncalp, 1984) and the implications of Islamic ethics on marketing practices (for example, Hassan et al., 2008; Rice, 1999; Saeed et al., 2001; Wilson, 2006), scholarly literature on Islam and marketing has been largely missing. In recent years, studies addressing different domains of marketing in the context of the Muslim markets, such as branding (Alserhan, 2010, 2011; Wilson and Liu, 2010), market orientation (Zakaria and Abdul-Talib, 2010), new product development (Rehman and Shabbir, 2010) and sales promotions (Abdullah and Ahmad, 2010; Yusuf, 2010) have begun to appear.

In general terms, the discovery of Muslims as consumers resembles the discovery in the US of non-mainstream communities such as gays, Hispanics, immigrants and blacks as viable market segments (Keating and McLoughlin, 2005). Since the 1980s there has been an increasing academic and managerial interest in these groups. In all these groups there has been a shift in meaning from 'disadvantaged' or 'marginalized' consumers to a lifestyle community embedded in the language of consumption. These marginalized groups gradually came to be seen as having significant purchasing power. For instance, as Halter (2000, p. 25) observes:

> In the aftermath of reports from the 1990 US Census demonstrating that minorities represented the majority of population growth in the 1980s, one toy company executive declared: 'How can you ignore these ethnic streams of revenue? You can't. The color of money is green, and you get it from whatever skin tone has got it.'

Almost three decades later, A.T. Kearney, in a 2007 report titled 'Addressing the Muslim market: can you afford not to?' declares: 'At a time when many other large consumer segments are reaching a saturation point, Muslims are a new outlet from which to build a base for future growth' (p. 1). Clearly reflected in this and similar other reports is the notion that Muslim consumers, who were largely marginalized, can no longer be ignored.

Studies investigating the emergence of Hispanics, gays, blacks and other collectivities as consumer segments report that these 'segments' were not preexisting entities that marketers simply needed to appeal to but constructions (for example, Chasin, 2000; Davila, 2001; Peñaloza, 1996; Sender, 2004). In other words, there was no distinct gay or Hispanic consumer to which marketers could sell their products. Rather it was through marketing practices such as segmentation and targeted product development and advertising that gays or Hispanics came to be gay or Hispanic consumer groups. A closer look at the making of the ethnic and gay markets suggests that similar processes are in operation in the development of the Muslim market. For example, one can observe the emergence of consulting, research and communications companies or units within existing firms specialized in marketing to Muslims. Segmentation surveys aimed at profiling Muslim consumers are now being conducted. There is targeted advertising appearing in specialized media. And there are lifestyle media, in both traditional and digital form, aiming to build a platform through which companies can talk to Muslim consumers and Muslim consumers and businesses can talk with each other. As Lewis also notes 'in non-Muslim majority territories, pioneering titles in the UK and North America seek to create a new niche media and readership just as the Anglo-American lesbian/gay/queer lifestyle press did when it emerged in the 1990s' (2010, p. 58).

Studies on ethnic and gay marketing also show that marketers represent these groups in an assimilationist manner and aim to create the image of a unified market. For example, when marketers refer to the 'gay market' they tend to conceptualize this market mainly as consisting of affluent gay men (Sender, 2004) or when they talk about the 'Hispanic market' they tend to gloss over many different nationalities that are included under this label (Davila, 2001). Clearly there is no single and uniform gay, Hispanic or black consumer collectivity and taste structure. At the very least social class, gender and age dissolve these collectivities into multiple overlapping as well as conflicting consumption tastes and practices.

When approached critically a similarly essentialist and uniform understanding of Islam and Muslim consumers appears to shape much of the contemporary discussions. This understanding becomes especially visible in two key areas: the focus on segmentation and the emphasis on difference.

Both academic and managerial writing on Islamic marketing tend to emphasize segmentation. Religion is regarded as the common descriptor that explains and potentially predicts behavior of Muslim consumers. Although there is a recent acknowledgment of inter-differences, such as those among Muslims living in different countries (for example, Nasr, 2009) or Muslims with different social class positions (for example, Sandıkcı and Ger, 2010), religion continues to be seen as the homogenizing force across Muslims. This perspective has two potential drawbacks. First, it leads to an overemphasis of religion at the expense of other aspects of identity such as gender, social class, age and their interactions. Furthermore, Islam itself is not monolithic and is constituted of many sects. How Islam is experienced and practiced in daily life can vary significantly across different sects.

Second, segmenting the markets by types of consumers may not always be the most productive approach. As Christensen et al. (2005) convincingly argue, segmenting around the job to be done rather than pre-defined consumer groups can prove more successful for companies. At the core of the authors' argument is the idea that when consumers need to get something done, they 'hire' products to do the job for them. For example, if they are looking for something that will ease their boring morning commute, they might hire a milk shake to do the job for them. Hence, as Christensen et al. point out the marketers' task is 'to understand what jobs periodically arise in customers' lives for which they might hire products that the company could make' (2005, p. 76). In the context of Islamic markets, adopting such a frame-of-mind suggests exploring the kind of jobs that Muslim consumers are trying to accomplish (for example, how to dress in a properly Islamic way and enjoy swimming) rather than merely profiling them along demographic, psychographic and behavioral characteristics.

In much of the academic and managerial writing there is also an overt focus on difference. In these writings, Muslims are generally depicted as consumers inherently different from consumers in general. Here, similar to multicultural marketing debates (Burton, 2002), there is an underlying assumption that Muslim consumers have shared characteristics that set them apart from other (read Western) consumers. The emphasis on differences assumes a static model of culture where categories such as Muslim, gay or Hispanic come to be seen as essential and fixed. Such an approach offers only a surface level and stereotypical insight into identity and behavior and helps little towards the understanding of complex empirical realities of people. The focus on difference (re)produces an essentialist understanding of Muslim consumers as really distinct from consumers in general, as if they have no shared characteristics at all.

The emphasis on segmentation and difference is related to a normative view of Islamic ethics, that is, the conceptualization of Islam as a set of rules and norms that are unequivocally and indiscriminately followed by all Muslims. One good example of the limitations of a normative view of ethics and a resultant focus on segmentation and difference is the concept of *halal*. There is an insistence on *halal* in both academic and managerial writings. However, how *halal* unfolds in particular markets and product categories is very complex and dynamic. As religion and consumption intersect with each other, new consumption practices emerge, complicating and transforming the meaning of proper Islamic behavior. For example, in his study of Malay Muslims' consumption practices, Fischer argues that one such transformation is 'halalization', the process of 'the proliferation of the concept of *halal* in a multitude of commodified forms'(2005, p. 281). He further argues that 'this proliferation of halalization has incited a range of elaborate ideas of the boundaries and authenticity of *halal* purity versus *haram* impurity' (ibid). What his analysis documents is that different Muslim groups understand and practice *halal* differently (Fischer, 2005).

A similar complexity in deciding what constitutes the proper Islamic way surfaces in the case of modest dressing. There is a host of studies conducted on veiling and modest Islamic dress in various parts of the world (for example, Brenner, 1996; El Guindi, 1999; Gole, 2003; Mernissi, 1991; Sandıkcı and Ger, 2010). These studies indicate that what is deemed as appropriate religious clothing differs from context to context. Moreover, within one country, the meanings and practices of veiling vary across time and different social classes. For example, Sandıkcı and Ger (2010) show how a new form of veiling, referred to as *tesettür*, emerged in Turkey in the late 1970s/early 1980s and transformed tremendously in the next decades. In the early days *tesettür* had a rather uniform look, consisting of a long loose overcoat and large headscarf. This new veiling style was initially adopted primarily by young, urban, and educated middle class women who were formerly uncovered and whose mothers usually were uncovered. Their adoption of *tesettür* was seen as a symbol of growing Islamist opposition to secular, Westernized lifestyles. Despite the Turkish government's attempts to contain it, *tesettür* spread. Yet by the 1990s, its uniform look fragmented into a plurality of styles and a lucrative and globally connected *tesettür* fashion market developed. Today many different styles and expressions of *tesettür* circulate in the public space.

These examples indicate that although *halal* and modesty are common denominators of the Islamic belief, the ways in which *halal* and modesty are interpreted, negotiated and experienced in the daily lives of Muslims are complex and dynamic. At a deeper level, they also illustrate the multifaceted relationship between morality, consumption and marketing, to which we now turn our attention.

MORALITY, CONSUMPTION AND MARKETING

Obviously Islam is one among other religions; and religion is intimately and essentially linked to morality. Religion can be viewed to be one institution within the three facets of Foucauldian (1990) morality. For Foucault, a moral code is 'a set of values and rules of action that are recommended to individuals through the intermediary of various prescriptive agencies such as the family . . . educational institutions, churches' (Foucault,1990, 25). The parts of such a regulatory compilation interact with each other, may contradict one another, and thus counterbalance and correct each other, allowing room for compromises and loopholes. Foucault identifies the second facet of morality to be the manner in which one deals with these moral codes – how one negotiates such codes and constructs one's own practices. The third facet is the freer mode of evaluating oneself where explicit moral codes are only distantly relevant. Prescriptive institutions include schools, medicine and family in addition to religion. We also have to consider other institutions and structures which transmit persuasive moral codes if not explicitly prescribe them: the pervasive global media including CNN, BBC, the Internet, Google, blogs, and YouTube, as well as international groups such as IMF and the G20. Such structures propagate values, ideologies and ideals – such as free choice, free markets, a consumerist ethos, freedom, democracy, health, and so on, which may or may not be consistent with religious codes. In other words a diverse set of discourses and counter-discourses circulates. Consumers and managers embedded in such a frame, evaluate and conduct themselves by using this multiplicity and negotiating the contradictions inherent in the moral codes and discourses. Thus religion provides yet another discourse, among many others, that frame, shape and legitimize consumption and management practices.

However the role of religion in marketing and consumption has been under-studied. Exceptions include investigations of consumption at religious times – Christmas (Belk, 1989; Hirschman and LaBarbera, 1989; Miller, 1993; Pollay, 1986) – and places such as a religious theme park in the US (O'Guinn and Belk, 1989) and the tension between religiosity and worldliness among nineteenth-century Mormon pioneers (Belk, 1992). Such studies indicate a merger of the sacred with the profane and a sacralization of objects of consumption, so much so that O'Guinn and Belk (1989) argue that 'not only has religion become a consumption object, consumption has become a religion in which wealth and opulence are venerated' (p.237). The alliance of commercialism, consumption and religion has been emphasized further by an éxpose on the similarities among religious missionaries, monetary funds and marketers in the way in which they all promise 'paradise' (Belk, 2000). Other studies examined the differences between Jews, Protestants and Catholics regarding the types of brands or retail outlets they prefer and found that the degree of religiosity, regardless of religion, is a more reliable predictor of consumer behavior than religious affiliation (for example, Delener, 1994; Esso and Dibb, 2004; McDaniel and Burnett, 1990; Wilkes et al., 1986). However Hirschman (1981) found that compared to their cohorts, Jewish consumers displayed more information seeking and consumption innovativeness. Studies also reported differences in shopping and consumption behaviors of more/less or intrinsically/extrinsically religious consumers (for example, Essoo and Dibb, 2004; McDaniel and Burnett, 1990; Sood and Nasu, 1995). More broadly, Belk et.al., (2000) argued that religious systems shape and manifest differences in the nature of consumer desire. Hence the extant literature demonstrates the interplay of the sacred and the profane and the influence of religion and/or religiosity on consumption. Not only the literature but also world history shows that, while all religions commend spirituality and condemn materialism, faith, commerce and consumption have always been intertwined. Yet that interplay has not been investigated empirically at length in the contemporary world.

The literature that pertains to morality beyond religion provides important implications for the interplay between morality and the market. One strand of research has focused on consumerist excesses and materialism versus voluntary simplicity and ethical consumption (for example, Shaw and Newholm, 2002). Another strand of research focuses on moralistic identity projects. For example, Luedicke et al., (2010) explain that Hummer owners use the ideology of American 'foundational myths', such as the 'rugged individual' to construct themselves as pro-American moral protagonists. Studies of brand communities reveal that community members rely on diverse moralistic distinctions, such as portraying consumers of competing brands as less enlightened, more conformist or more status conscious (for example, Muñiz and Schau, 2005). Thus, consumers draw from various morality-forming myths and ideologies as well as marketplace resources in shaping and manifesting their identities.

Such interplay between morality and markets is implicit in some of the current work on Islam and consumption and marketing. Despite the stereotypical perception of Islam as anti-consumerist and anti-capitalist, investigations of consumption in Islamic geographies indicate a consumerist ethos and lifestyle. Muslim consumers, whether they live in Dubai, Istanbul, or London, are just as interested in brands, designer clothes, plasma televisions, five star resorts, luxury homes and fast-foods as any other consumer (Godazgar, 2007; Navaro-Yashin, 2002; Starrett, 1995). Except in rare instances, most Muslims do not oppose consumption – they actively engage in consumption although in an Islamic way: for example, hanging a picture of the *kaaba* rather than a figurative painting on the wall. Likewise, Muslim entrepreneurs and business people, whether they operate in Germany, Kuwait or Malaysia, are as concerned with making profits in beverage, information technology, tourism, media and construction businesses as any other capitalist (Demir et al., 2004). Islam accepts that material things are important in life. However, it requires that acquisitiveness and competition are balanced by fair play, honesty, compassion, generosity, sharing and giving to the poor (Belk et al., 2000). Hence the practices of giving to the poor and discourses of honesty and fairness underwrite the competitive game Muslim firms engage in their markets, given the particular competitive structures and forces of their markets. Muslim companies practice capitalism albeit with some adjustments – real or rhetorical. Far from opposing capitalism, the so-called Muslim companies utilize capitalist tools and compete in domestic and international markets. Empirical research indicates that Islam does not necessarily oppose or offer an alternative to capitalism and consumption. Rather, Islam is deeply embedded in a consumerist and capitalist ethos. Consumption and marketing patterns can be and are appropriated into religiously acceptable styles without undermining consumption and capitalism themselves. The logic of capitalist markets and the ideology of consumerism coexist with the logic and ideology of Islam, constructing market practices that negotiate daily tensions. Privatization and the liberalization of local economies across the world coincide with and perhaps facilitate such alliance between Islam and the capitalism–consumerism twosome.

Historical studies demonstrate that consumption and market cultures have always been shaped by coexistent yet conflicting discourses: Calvinist and humanistic ethics in sixteenth-century and seventeenth-century Netherlands (Schama, 1987), the Protestant and Romantic ethics in eighteenth-century England (Campbell, 1987); and the Orthodox Islamic and Sufi ethics in the sixteenth- and seventeenth-century Ottoman Empire (Karababa and Ger, 2011). The Dutch humanist discourse provided legitimization for expenditure, rather than capital accumulation, as a way to free oneself from the suspicion of greed and promoted expenditure for the benefit of community (Schama, 1987). Similarly the Romantic ethic made room for hedonism in England (Campbell, 1987) and Ottoman Sufism supported leisure consumption (Karababa and Ger, 2011). As Karababa and Ger (2011) argue, 'the formation of market cultures and their consuming subjects is not only a sociocultural but also a political and moral phenomenon located in the broader public sphere.'

Thus, market cultures are co-created through discursive negotiations and practices (Peñaloza, 2000; Thompson, 2004) and a broad network of actors play roles in this co-creation. In addition to the usual marketer–consumer dyad, the network of actors includes the Internet (Giesler, 2008), science/medicine (Thompson, 2004), the state and the religion (Cohen, 2003; Karababa and Ger, 2011; Sandıkcı and Ger, 2010). Since individuals are moral beings who need to justify their acts (Campbell, 1987), discourses serve as justifications and frames as well as motivations for consumer and marketer practices. Moreover, multiple and at times conflicting discourses provide room for very diverse consumer and marketer conduct.

We have seen that diverse ideologies, discourses, ethics and morality in general shape and frame the way marketers and consumers think and act. Furthermore, in the global world, consumers and managers, wherever they may be, are exposed to similarly heterogeneous transnational flows of information, ideas, technologies and images (Appadurai, 1990). Islam, or more accurately, religion, is one among many such global flows and forces that construct consumers' and marketers' moralities, ideals, values and actions. Perhaps the world-wide growth of fundamentalisms across all religions (Almond et al., 2003) further motivates scholars to study the interactions between morality, consumption and marketing.

FUTURE OF RESEARCH ON ISLAM, CONSUMPTION AND MARKETING

It is our contention that understanding Muslim consumers and Islamic markets and marketers requires doing away with essentialist approaches that reify difference. What the examples and discussions presented above indicate is the necessity of adopting a socioculturally embedded approach to Islam and marketing interaction. Instead of focusing on differences and imagining the Muslim market as separate from the market in general, we need to pay attention to how such 'differences' play out in the daily lives of consumers. In other words, we need to examine the religious, political, cultural and economic resources, forces, and tensions that consumers experience and negotiate as they (re)construct and communicate their identities as Muslims. Such an approach requires a focus on practices and discourses and their interrelationships rather than consumers in isolation.

Ethnoconsumerism (Venkatesh, 1995) provides a useful framework to develop a situated understanding of Muslim consumers. As Venkatesh explains, ethnoconsumerism 'is a conceptual framework to study consumer behavior using the theoretical categories originating in a given culture' (p. 26). It calls for studying behavior on the basis of the cultural realities of individuals rather than imposing pre-existing categories to explain that behavior. In order to achieve this one needs to study 'actions, practices, words, thoughts, language, institutions and the interconnections between these categories' (p. 28). Hence, from the perspective of ethnoconsumerism, while studying or addressing the Islamic market, asking the question of 'who is the Muslim consumer?' and trying to answer it only through the lens of religious norms and values produces only a limited understanding. Instead an ethnoconsumerist perspective urges scholars to concentrate on understanding particular Muslims in particular contexts and to examine the practices, discourses, power relationships and dynamics that characterize those contexts.

As we have discussed above, varying Islamic discourses interacting with other discourses and relationships provide different interpretations of religiously appropriate consumption. With multiplicity, tensions at individual and collective levels inevitably arise. Different understandings of Islam enable as well as constrain different consumption practices. As studies increasingly make clear, what constitutes proper Islamic consumption practice is highly contested, dynamic and negotiated. For example, how modest dressing is interpreted and experienced differs greatly across different Muslim communities and over time. Moreover, what came to be known as 'fashionable veiling' generates both praise and criticism, rendering the meaning of 'proper' Islamic dress even more complicated. Given such complexity and multiplicity, understanding the dynamics of 'Islam in local contexts' (Eickelman, 1982) becomes imperative.

A situated understanding of Muslim consumers also calls for attending to the interaction and intersection of religion with other identity variables. The communities of Muslim consumers are linked by faith but, like other consumer groups, they are also marked by gender, class, age, nationality, ethnicity, and so on. For example, consider Muslims in Germany, Turkish Muslims in Germany and Islamists in Turkey. Although Islam is the common description, identities, practices and dynamics are very different in each of these cases. Accordingly, future research needs to address how Muslim religiosity interacts with other ideologies, ethics, values and subjectivities rather than asking questions such as: 'Do all Muslims think the same? Do all Muslims behave in the same way? Do all Muslims want the same products and services? Do Muslims want Western brands or Islamic brands?' As the chapters in this book imply, they don't all think the same, they don't behave in the same way, they don't all want the same products, and they want both Islamic and Western brands. Studies that explicate the social, cultural, economic, political and historical dynamics and actors that have shaped and continue to shape the identities of Muslims as consumers will help render stereotypes redundant and provide novel insights into the religion-marketing intersection. In this regard, there is a general need for studies that examine the formation of consumers and marketers in different religious milieus – be they Muslim, Christian, Buddhist, Jewish, Hindu or any other.

From a critical perspective, future studies should examine how marketing practices help construct Muslims as viable consumer segments. Scholarship on ethnic and gay markets can inform the analysis of the making of Muslim consumer subjectivities.

Questions such as – What are the politics of representation of Muslims in advertising, media and other marketing spaces, and what purposes do they serve? What are the power dynamics involved in such representations, who benefits from them and who is excluded? – remain intriguing and challenging. While there are similarities between Muslim consumers and other non-mainstream consumer groups, the particularities of Muslims also needs to be evaluated. As racism and homophobia have played out differently in the construction of ethnic and gay markets, it is highly likely that Islamophobia will have unique effects in the construction of the Muslim market. On a related domain, the interplay between religion and politics needs to be unpacked. Understanding how Islam and marketing interact in contexts with different political ideologies and experiences of democracy presents interesting research avenues.

Certainly more research is needed on Muslim entrepreneurs, their motives, aspirations, and interpretations and implementations of marketing principles. While ethical and religious principles seem to be articulated loudly by Muslim business owners, to what extent words and deeds correspond needs to be empirically assessed. Furthermore keeping in mind that managers operate within the boundaries of the competitive conditions, how their practices are informed by market forces and structures should also be explained. In examining how MNCs compete in Muslim geographies as well as how Islamic companies compete against MNCs in both Muslim majority and minority contexts, researchers will benefit from adopting a situated and socio-culturally informed approach. Finally, critically informed comparisons of Islamic marketing principles and practices with those of green marketing, fair trade and ethical consumption initiatives constitute interesting research paths. Religion is a key force shaping the contemporary world and is likely to remain as such. Hence unpacking the religion, consumption, and marketing interaction will contribute not only to marketing theory but potentially also to our understanding of the world and its many complexities.

MANAGERIAL AND POLICY IMPLICATIONS

It should be clear by now that marketing managers should not assume Muslims to be a homogeneous segment. Neither should they begin from 'the Muslim segment'. Instead they should focus on the daily practices for which the product may be relevant and generate solutions through the product for everyday problems in that particular context. For example, the emphasis should be on the solutions that will help Muslims be better Muslims and live proper Islamic lives rather than focusing the attention only on achieving the 'halalness' of products. Moreover, such solutions should take into consideration that the interpretations and understandings of 'better Muslims' and 'proper Islamic lives' are multiple, dynamic, contested and negotiated. One-size-fits-all-Muslim products will be unlikely to deliver sustainable success. Instead companies that help consumers solve their daily problems and moral tensions are likely to succeed.

Accordingly managers and market/marketing researchers may have something to learn from the historical trajectory of ethnic and gay marketing and the research on ethnic and gay consumers. While earlier research emphasized the differences of ethnic groups and gays from the mainstream consumers, later studies elucidated the heterogeneity within such groups. Besides, while there are brands specifically catering to, for example, Hispanics or African Americans in the US context, there are also brands providing solutions for consumers regardless of their ethnicity.

To understand Muslim consumers, market researchers need to go beyond a parochial reiteration of the pillars of Islam or demographics of Muslims in different geographies. Managers of Western companies need to develop a situated understanding of Muslim consumers as well as of the Muslim entrepreneurs who compete with them, just as the other way around. That is, they should approach each market considering its specificity – its competitive, moral, sociohistoric and political market context.

Muslim marketing managers will find the underpinnings of Holt's (2004) cultural branding strategy to be very useful in developing their own strategies. If national myths can serve to construct iconic brands, so can religious myths. Muslim marketing managers can potentially employ Holt's cultural strategy to develop more global brands like Al-Jazeera – the influential television news channel and website which broadcasts in English and Arabic and is watched by Muslims and non-Muslims.

In addition to the above managerial implications, there is also one potentially important policy/governance implication. Research makes it clear that Muslim consumers and managers share ideals and ideologies such as the consumerist ethos and capitalism with their cohorts. Moreover, Islamic ethics of compassion, generosity and giving to the poor seem to resonate with the notion of corporate social responsibility. Perhaps Muslim entrepreneurs and managers of MNCs can learn from each other and provide more effective and sustainable benefits to the societies in which they operate. Furthermore, in an era when multiculturalism is no longer embraced (if it ever was), focusing on the moral and ideological commonalities as well as global socioeconomic interdependencies may contribute to more peaceful inter-cultural, inter-religious, and inter-national relations. One might hope that highlighting and working with similarities, rather than differences, especially such shared crucial ideologies and ideals, will enhance a dialogue between 'civilizations,' in this era of growing fundamentalisms.

REFERENCES

Abdullah, K. and M.I. Ahmad (2010), 'Compliance to Islamic marketing practices among businesses in Malaysia', Journal of Islamic Marketing, **1** (3), 286–97.

Adas, A.B. (2006), 'The making of entrepreneurial Islam and the Islamic spirit of capitalism', *Journal for Cultural Research*, **10** (2), 113–25.

Agai, B. (2007), 'Islam and education in secular Turkey: state policies and the emergence of the Fethullah Gülen group', in Robert Hefner and Muhammad Qasim Zaman (eds), *Schooling Islam: The Culture and Politics of Modern Muslim Education*, Princeton, NJ: Princeton University Press.

Almond, G., R.S. Appleby and E. Sivan (2003), *Strong Religion: The Rise of Fundamentalisms around the World*, Chicago: University of Illinois Press.

Alserhan, B.A. (2010) 'On Islamic branding: brands as good deeds',*Journal of Islamic Marketing*, **1** (2), 101–6.

Alserhan, B.A. (2011), 'Islamic branding: a conceptualization of related terms', *Journal of Brand Management* (forthcoming).

Appadurai, Arjun (1990), 'Disjuncture and difference in the global economy', in M. Featherstone (ed.), *Global Culture: Nationalism, Globalization and Modernity*, London: Sage, pp. 295–310.

A.T. Kearney (2007), 'Addressing the Muslim market', available at http://www.atkearney.com/images/global/pdf/AddressingMuslimMarket_S.pdf.

Barber, Benjamin R. (1995), *Jihad vs. McWorld*, New York: Random House.

Barna, George (1988), *Marketing the Church*, Colorado Springs, Co: Navpress.

Bayat, A. (2005), 'Islamism and social movement theory', *Third World Quarterly*, **26** (6), 891–908.

Belk, R.W. (1989), 'Materialism and the modern U.S. Christmas', in Elizabeth C. Hirschman (ed.), *Interpretive Consumer Research*, Provo, UT: Association for Consumer Research, pp. 115–35.

Belk, R.W. (1992), 'Moving possessions: an analysis based on personal documents from the 1847–1869 Mormon migration,' *Journal of Consumer Research*, **19** (3), 339–61.

Belk, R.W. (2000), 'Pimps for paradise: missionaries, monetary funds, and marketers', *Marketing Intelligence & Planning*, **18** (6/7), 337–44.

Belk, R.W., G. Ger and S. Askegaard (2000), 'The missing streetcar named desire', in S. Ratneshwar, David Glen Mick and Cynthia Huffman (eds), *The Why of Consumption*, London: Routledge, pp. 98–119.

Bocock, Robert (1993), *Consumption*, London: Routledge.

Boubekeur, A. (2005), 'Cool and competitive: Muslim culture in the West', *ISIM Review*, **16**, pp. 12–13.

Brenner, S. (1996), 'Reconstructing self and society: Javanese Muslim women and the veil', *American Ethnologist*, **23** (November), 673–97.

Burton, D. (2002), 'Towards a critical multicultural marketing theory', *Marketing Theory*, **2** (2), 207–36.

Campbell, Colin (1987), *The Romantic Ethic and the Spirit of Modern Consumerism*, New York: Blackwell.

Carrette, Jeremy R. and Richard King (2005), *Selling Spirituality: The Silent Takeover of Religion*, Oxfordshire: Routledge.

Chasin, Alexandra (2000), *Selling Out: The Gay and Lesbian Movement Goes to Market*, New York: Palgrave.

Christensen, C.M., S. Cook and T. Hall (2005), 'Marketing malpractice: the cause and the cure', *Harvard Business Review*, December, 74–83.

Cohen, Lizabeth (2003), *A Consumers' Republic: The Politics of Mass Consumption in Postwar America*, New York: Knopf.

Davila, Arlene (2001), *Latinos Inc.: The Marketing and Making of a People*, Berkeley, CA: University of California Press.

Dekmejian, R. Hrair (1995), *Islam in Revolution: Fundamentalism in the Arab World*, Syracuse, NY: Syracuse University Press.

Delener, N. (1994), 'Religious contrasts in consumer decision behaviour patterns: their dimensions and marketing implications', *European Journal of Marketing*, **28** (5), 36–53.

Demir, Ö., M. Acar and M. Toprak (2004), 'Anatolian tigers or Islamic capital: prospects and challenges', *Middle Eastern Studies*, **40** (6), 166–88.

Economist (2007), 'Food, fashion and faith: companies are starting to reach out to Muslim consumers in the West' (2 August), available at:http://www.economist.com/node/9587818.

Eickelman, D. (1982), 'The study of Islam in local contexts', *Contributions to Asian Studies*, **17**, 1–16.

El Guindi, Fadwa (1999), *Veil: Modesty, Privacy and Resistance*, Oxford: Berg.

ESI (2005), 'Islamic Calvinists: change and conservatism in central Anatolia', available at http://www.esiweb.org/pdf/esi_document_id_69.pdf.

Esposito, John L. (1998), *Islam and Politics*, Syracuse, NY: Syracuse University Press.

Esso, N. and Dibb, S. (2004), 'Religious contrasts in consumer decision behavior', *European Journal of Marketing*, **28** (5), 36–53.

Essoo, N. and S. Dibb (2004), 'Religious influences on shopping behaviour: an exploratory study', *Journal of Marketing Management*, **20**, 683–712

Fischer, Johan (2005), 'Feeding secularism: consuming halal among the Malays in London', *Diaspora*, **14** (2/3), 275–97.

Fitzpatrick, S. (2009), 'Covering Muslim women at the beach: media representations of the burkini', *Thinking Gender Papers*, UCLA Center for the Study of Women, UC Los Angeles, available at: http://escholarship.org/uc/item/9d0860x7.

Foucault, Michel (1990), *The Use of Pleasure, The History of Sexuality*, Volume 2, translated by Robert Hurley, New York: Vintage Books.

Giesler, Markus (2008), 'Conflict and compromise: drama in marketplace evolution', *Journal of Consumer Research*, **34** (April), 739–53.

Godazgar, Hossein (2007), 'Islam versus consumerism and postmodernism in the context of Iran', *Social Compass*, **54** (3), 389–418.

Gokariksel, B. and A. Secor (2010), 'Between fashion and tesettür: marketing and consuming women's Islamic dress', *Journal of Middle East Women's Studies*, **6** (3), 118–48.

Göle, N. (2003), 'The voluntary adoption of Islamic stigma symbols', *Social Research*, **70** (Fall), 809–27.

Gooch, Liz (2010), 'Advertisers seek to speak to Muslim consumers,' *New York Times*, http://www.nytimes.com/2010/08/12/business/media/12branding.html, accessed November 2010.

Grewal, Inderpal (2005), *Transnational America: Feminisms, Diasporas, Neoliberalisms*, Durham, NC: Duke University Press.

Halter, Marilyn (2000), *Shopping for Identity: The Marketing of Ethnicity*, New York: Schocken Books.

Hassan, A., A. Chachi and S.A. Latiff (2008), 'Islamic marketing ethics and its impact on customer satisfaction in the Islamic banking industry', *Islamic Economics Journal*, **21** (1), 23–40.

Hastings-Black, Michael (2008), 'Marketers must engage with the Muslim consumer', *Advertising Age*, available at http://adage.com/bigtent/post?article_id=132359.
Hirschkind, C. (2008), 'The ethics of listening: cassette-sermon audition in contemporary Egypt', *American Ethnologist*, **28** (3), 623–49.
Hirschman, E. (1981), 'American Jewish ethnicity: its relationship to some selected aspects of consumer behavior,' *Journal of Marketing*, **45** (Summer), 102–10.
Hirschman, E, and Priscilla A. LaBarbera (1989), 'The meaning of Christmas', in E. Hirschman (ed.), *Interpretive Consumer Research*, Provo, UT: Association of Consumer Research, pp. 136–47.
Holt, Douglas (2004), *How Brands Become Icons: The Principles of Cultural Branding*, Boston, MA: Harvard Business School Press.
Huntington, Samuel P. (1997), *The Clash of Civilizations and the Remaking of World Order*, New York: Simon and Schuster.
JWT (2009), 'Understanding the Islamic consumer', available at http://www.wpp.com/NR/rdonlyres/0EE122EE-C956-431A-BFC9-78BED42011D1/0/marketing_to_muslims.pdf
Kahn, M. Fahim (1995), *Essays in Islamic Economics*, Islamic Foundation UK.
Karababa, E. and G. Ger (2011), 'Early modern Ottoman coffeehouse culture and the formation of the consumer subject', *Journal of Consumer Research* (forthcoming).
Kasriel, D. (2008), 'Spotlighting Europe's Muslim consumers', *Euromonitor International* (10 September) available at http://www.euromonitor.com/Spotlighting_Europes_Muslim_consumers.
Keating, A. and D. McLoughlin (2005), 'Understanding the emergence of markets: a social constructionist perspective on gay economy', *Consumption, Markets and Culture*, **8** (2), 131–52.
Kuran, Timur (2004), *Islam and Mammon: The Economic Predicaments of Islamism*, Princeton, NJ: Princeton University Press.
Lewis, R. (2010), 'Marketing Muslim lifestyle: a new media genre', *Journal of Middle East Women's Studies*, **6** (3), 58–90.
Luedicke, M.K., C.J. Thompson and M. Giesler (2010), 'Consumer identity work as moral protagonism: how myth and ideology animate a brand-mediated moral conflict', *Journal of Consumer Research*, **36** (6), 116–32.
Mandaville, P. (2010), 'Transnational Muslim solidarities and everyday life', paper presented at the 2010 ISA Annual Convention, New Orleans, available at: http://www.allacademic.com/meta/p415795_index.html.
McDaniel, Stephen W. and John J. Burnett (1990), 'Consumer religiosity and retail store evaluation criteria,' *Journal of the Academy of Marketing Science*, **18** (Spring), 101–12.
Melucci, Alberto (1996), *Challenging Codes: Collective Action in the Information Age*, Cambridge: Cambridge University Press.
Mernissi, Fatima (1991), *The Veil and the Male Elite*, Reading, MA: Addison-Wesley.
Miller, Daniel (1993), *Unwrapping Christmas*, Oxford: Oxford University Press.
Mokhlis, Safiek (2006), 'The effect of religiosity on shopping orientation: an exploratory study in Malaysia', *Journal of American Academy of Business*, **9** (1), 64–74.
Muñiz, A.M. and H.J. Schau (2005), 'Religiosity in the abandoned Apple Newton brand community', *Journal of Consumer Research*, **31** (4), 737–47.
Nasr, Vali (2009), *Forces of Fortune*, New York: Simon Schuster.
Navaro-Yashin, Y. (2002), 'The market for identities: secularism, Islamism, Commodities', in Deniz Kandiyoti and Ayşe Saktanber (eds), *Fragments of Culture: The Everyday of Modern Turkey*, London: I.B. Tauris, pp. 221–53.
O'Guinn, T.C. and R.W. Belk (1989), 'Heaven on earth: consumption at Heritage Village, USA', *Journal of Consumer Research*, **16** (2), 227–38.
Ogilvy and Mather (2010), 'Brands, Islam and the new Muslim consumer,' available at http://www.ogilvy.com/News/Press-Releases/May-2010-The-Global-Rise-of-the-New-Muslim-Consumer.aspx.
Osella, F. and C. Osella (2009), 'Muslim entrepreneurs in public life between India and the Gulf: making good and doing good', *Journal of the Royal Anthropological Institute*, S202–S221.
Peñaloza, L. (1996), 'We're here, we're queer, and we're going shopping!', *Journal of Homosexuality*, **31** (1/2), 9–41.
Peñaloza, L. (2000), 'The commodification of the West: marketers' production of culture at a western stock show and rodeo', *Journal of Marketing*, **64** (October), 82–109.
Pollay, R.W. (1986), 'It's the thought that counts: a case study in Xmas excess', in M.Wallendorf, and P.Anderson (eds), *Advances in Consumer Research*, Vol. 14, Urbana, IL: Association of Consumer Research, pp. 140–43.
Power, C. (2009), 'Halal: buying Muslim' (25 May), available at http://www.time.com/time/magazine/article/0,9171,1898247,00.html.
Prahalad, C.K. (2004), *The Fortune at the Bottom-of-the-Pyramid*, Upper Saddle River, NJ: Wharton School Publishing.

Rehman, A. and M.S. Shabbir (2010), 'The relationship between religiosity and new product adoption', *Journal of Islamic Marketing*, **1** (1), 63–9

Rice, G. (1999), 'Islamic ethics and the implications for business', *Journal of Business Ethics*, **18**, 345–58

Saeed, M., Z.U. Ahmed and S.M. Mukhtar (2001), 'International marketing ethics from an Islamic perspective: a value-maximization approach', *Journal of Business Ethics*, **32**, 127–42.

Said, Edward (1978), *Orientalism*, New York: Vintage Books.

Saint-Blancat, C. (2002), 'Islam in diaspora: between reterritorialization and extraterritoriality', *International Journal of Urban and Regional Research*, **26** (1), 138–51.

Sandıkcı, Ö. and G. Ger (2010), 'Veiling in style: how does a stigmatized practice become fashionable?', *Journal of Consumer Research*, **37** (June), 15–36.

Sandıkcı, Ö. and G. Ger (2007) 'Constructing and representing the Islamic consumer in Turkey', *Fashion Theory*, **11** (2/3), 189–210.

Sandıkcı, Ö. and G. Ger (2002), 'In-between modernities and postmodernities: investigating Turkish consumptionscape', in Susan M. Broniarczyk and Kent Nakamoto (eds), *Advances in Consumer Research*, Vol. 29, Valdosta, GA: Association for Consumer Research, pp. 465–70.

Schama, Simon (1987), *The Embarrassment of Riches*, New York: Knopf.

Sender, Katherine (2004), *Business, not Politics: The Making of the Gay Market*, New York: Columbia University Press.

Shaw, D. and T. Newholm (2002), 'Voluntary simplicity and the ethics of consumption', *Psychology and Marketing*, **19** (2), 167–85.

Siddiqi, M.N. (1992), 'Islamic consumer behavior', in S.Tahir A. Ghazaly and S.O.S. Agil (eds), *Readings in Microeconomics in Islamic Perspective*, Kuala Lumpur: Longman Malaysia, pp. 49–60.

Sloane, P. (1999), *Islam, Modernity and Entrepreneurship among the Malays*, New York: St Martin's Press.

Sood, J. and Y. Nasu (1995), 'Religiosity and nationality: an exploratory study of their effect on consumer behavior in Japan and the United States', *Journal of Business Research*, **34** (1), 1–9.

Starrett, Gregory (1995), 'The political economy of religious commodities in Cairo', *American Anthropologist*, **97** (1), 51–68.

Thompson, C.J. (2004), 'Marketplace mythologies and discourses of power', *Journal of Consumer Research*, **31** (June), 162–80.

Turner, Brian (1994), *Orientalism, Postmodernism and Globalism*, London and New York: Routledge.

Venkatesh, Alladi (1995), 'Ethnoconsumerism: a new paradigm', in Janeen A. Costa and Gary J. Bamossy (eds), *Marketing in a Multicultural World. Ethnicity, Nationalism, and Cultural Identity*, London: Sage, pp. 26–67.

Vokurka, R.J. and S.W. McDaniel (2004), 'A taxonomy of church marketing strategy types', *Review of Religious Research*, **46** (2), 132–49.

Webb, M.S., W.B. Joseph, K. Schimmel and C. Mobert (1998), 'Church marketing: strategies for retaining and attracting members', *Journal of Professional Services Marketing*, **17** (2), 1–16.

Weber, Max (1930/1996), *The Protestant Ethic and The Spirit of Capitalism*, Los Angeles: Roxbury.

Wiktorowicz, Quintan (2004), *Islamic Activism: A Social Movement Theory Approach*, Bloomington, IN: Indiana University Press.

Wilkes, R.E., J.J. Burnett and R.D. Howell (1986), 'On the meaning and measurement of religiosity in consumer research', *Journal of the Academy of Marketing Science*, **14** (Spring), 47–56.

Wilson, R. (2006), 'Islam and business', *Thunderbird International Business Review*, **48** (1), 109–23.

Wilson, J.A.J. and J. Liu (2010), 'Shaping the Halal into a brand?', *Journal of Islamic Marketing*, **1** (2), 107–23.

Wong, L. (2007), 'Market cultures, the middle classes and Islam: consuming the market?', *Consumption, Markets and Culture*, **10** (4), 451–80.

Yaqin, A. (2007), 'Islamic Barbie: the politics of gender and performativity', *Fashion Theory*, **11** (2/3), 173–88.

Yavas, U. and S. Tuncalp (1984), 'Perceived risk in grocery outlet selection: a case study in Saudi Arabia', *European Journal of Marketing*, **18**, 13–25.

Yavuz, Hakan (2004), 'Opportunity spaces, identity, and Islamic meaning in Turkey', in Quintan Wiktorowicz (ed.), *Islamic Activism: A Social Movement Theory Approach*, Bloomington, IN: Indiana University Press, pp. 270–88.

Yusuf, J.B. (2010), 'Ethical implications of sales promotion in Ghana: Islamic perspective', *Journal of Islamic Marketing*, **1** (3), 220–30.

Zaidman, N. (2003), 'Commercialization of religious objects: a comparison between traditional and New Age religions', *Social Compass*, **50** (3), 345–60.

Zakaria, N. and A.N. Abdul-Talib (2010), 'Applying Islamic market oriented cultural model to sensitize strategies towards global customers, competitors', *Journal of Islamic Marketing*, **1** (1), 51–62.

Index

Titles of publications are in *italics*.

503